T0281691

Android Recipes

A Problem-Solution Approach

Fifth Edition

Dave Smith
Erik Hellman

Apress®

Android Recipes: A Problem-Solution Approach

Dave Smith
Littleton, Colorado, USA

Erik Hellman
Sundbyberg, Sweden

ISBN-13 (pbk): 978-1-4842-2258-4
DOI 10.1007/978-1-4842-2259-1

ISBN-13 (electronic): 978-1-4842-2259-1

Library of Congress Control Number: 2016961316

Managing Director: Welmoed Spahr
Lead Editor: Steve Anglin
Technical Reviewer: Wallace Jackson
Editorial Board: Steve Anglin, Pramila Balan, Laura Berendson, Aaron Black, Louise Corrigan,
    Jonathan Gennick, Robert Hutchinson, Celestin Suresh John, Nikhil Karkal, James Markham,
    Susan McDermott, Matthew Moodie, Natalie Pao, Gwenan Spearing
Coordinating Editor: Mark Powers
Copy Editor: Mike
Compositor: SPi Global
Indexer: SPi Global
Artist: SPi Global

Distributed to the book trade worldwide by Springer Science+Business Media New York, 233 Spring Street, 6th Floor, New York, NY 10013. Phone 1-800-SPRINGER, fax (201) 348-4505, e-mail orders-ny@springer-sbm.com, or visit www.springeronline.com. Apress Media, LLC is a California LLC and the sole member (owner) is Springer Science + Business Media Finance Inc (SSBM Finance Inc). SSBM Finance Inc is a **Delaware** corporation.

For information on translations, please e-mail rights@apress.com, or visit www.apress.com.

Apress and friends of ED books may be purchased in bulk for academic, corporate, or promotional use. eBook versions and licenses are also available for most titles. For more information, reference our Special Bulk Sales–eBook Licensing web page at www.apress.com/bulk-sales.

Any source code or other supplementary materials referenced by the author in this text are available to readers at www.apress.com/9781484222584. For detailed information about how to locate your book's source code, go to www.apress.com/source-code/. Readers can also access source code at SpringerLink in the Supplementary Material section for each chapter.

Printed on acid-free paper

Contents at a Glance

Contents

About the Authors

 **Dave Smith** is a professional engineer developing hardware and software for mobile and embedded platforms. Dave's engineering efforts are currently focused full-time on Android development. Since 2009, Dave has worked on developing at all levels of the Android platform, from writing user applications using the software development kit to building and customizing the Android source code. Dave regularly communicates via his development blog (http://blog.wiresareobsolete.com) and Twitter stream @devunwired.

Erik Hellman is a professional software engineer who has worked on everything from small embedded systems to large backend systems for telecom and banking. He is currently focused on everything around the Android platform, and has been doing so since 2009. During this time he has been a frequent speaker at conferences and meetup events, teaching new developers how to work with the platform, has been developing a wide variety of apps, and worked for OEMs on integrating Android to new hardware devices. Erik regularly communicates via his development blog (http://www.hellsoft.se) and Twitter stream @ErikHellman.

About the Technical Reviewer

Wallace Jackson has been writing for leading multimedia publications about his work in new media content development since the advent of Multimedia Producer Magazine nearly two decades ago. He has authored a half-dozen Android book titles for Apress, including four titles in the popular Pro Android series. Wallace received his undergraduate degree in business economics from the University of California at Los Angeles and a graduate degree in MIS design and implementation from the University of Southern California. He is currently the CEO of Mind Taffy Design, a new media content production and digital campaign design and development agency.

Acknowledgments

First and foremost, I would like to thank my wife, Lorie, for her eternal patience and support during the long hours I spent compiling and constructing the materials for this book. Second, I send a huge thank you to the editorial team that Apress brought together to work with me and make the book the best it could possibly be; *you guys are the ones who make me look good*. Without your time and effort, this project would not even exist.

—Dave Smith

I want to start with thanking my wife. Without the patience and support from her, my contributions to this book would never have happened. I'd also like to thank Apress and Dave for giving me the opportunity to work on the fifth edition of Android Recipes. Finally, a big thank you to all the people who keep inspiring me to keep writing.

—Erik Hellman

Introduction

Welcome to the fifth edition of *Android Recipes*!

If you are reading this book, you probably don't need to be told of the immense opportunity that mobile devices represent for software developers and users. In recent years, Android has become one of the top mobile platforms for device users. This means that you, as a developer, must know how to harness Android so you can stay connected to this market and the potential that it offers. But any new platform brings with it uncertainty about best practices and solutions to common needs and problems.

What we aim to do with *Android Recipes* is give you the tools to write applications for the Android platform through direct examples targeted at the specific problems you are trying to solve. This book is not a deep dive into the Android SDK, NDK, or any of the other tools. We don't weigh you down with all the details and theory behind the curtain. That's not to say that those details aren't interesting or important. You should take the time to learn them, as they may save you from making future mistakes. However, more often than not, they are simply a distraction when you are just looking for a solution to an immediate problem.

This book is not meant to teach you Java programming or even the building blocks of an Android application. You won't find many basic recipes in this book (such as how to display text with `TextView`, for instance), as we feel these are tasks easily remembered once learned. Instead, we set out to address tasks that developers, once comfortable with Android, need to do often but find too complex to accomplish with a few lines of code.

Treat *Android Recipes* as a reference to consult, a resource-filled cookbook that you can always open to find the pragmatic advice you need to get the job done quickly and well.

What Will You Find in the Book?

We dive into using the Android SDK to solve real problems. You will learn tricks for effectively creating a user interface that runs well across device boundaries. You will become a master at incorporating the collection of hardware (radios, sensors, and cameras) that makes mobile devices unique platforms. We'll even discuss how to make the system work for you by integrating with the services and applications provided by Google and various device manufacturers.

Performance matters if you want your applications to succeed. Most of the time, this isn't a problem, because the Android runtime engines get progressively better at compiling bytecode into the device's native code. However, you might need to leverage the Android NDK to boost performance. Chapter 8 offers you an introduction to the NDK and integrating native code into your application using Java Native Interface (JNI) bindings.

The NDK is a complex technology, which can also reduce your application's portability. Also, while good at increasing performance, the NDK doesn't address multicore processing very well for heavy workloads. Fortunately, Google has eliminated this tedium and simplified the execute-on-multiple-cores task while achieving portability by introducing RenderScript. Chapter 8 introduces you to RenderScript and shows you how to use its compute engine (and automatically leverage CPU cores) to process images.

Keep a Level Eye on the Target

Throughout the book, you will see that we have marked most recipes with the minimum API level that is required to support them. Most of the recipes in this book are marked API Level 9, meaning that the code used can be run in applications targeting any version of Android since 2.3 or later. This is one of the biggest changes in this edition of the book, and the reason is that Google recently deprecated the support for earlier API levels in their Support Library. Where necessary, we use APIs introduced in later versions. Pay close attention to the API level marking of each recipe to ensure that you are not using code that doesn't match up with the version of Android your application is targeted to support.

CHAPTER 1

■ ■ ■

Layouts and Views

The Android platform is designed to operate on a variety of device types, screen sizes, and screen resolutions. To assist developers in meeting this challenge, Android provides a rich toolkit of user interface (UI) components to utilize and customize to the needs of their specific applications. Android also relies heavily on an extensible XML framework and set resource qualifiers to create liquid layouts that can adapt to these environmental changes. In this chapter, we take a look at some practical ways to shape this framework to fit your specific development needs.

1-1. Styling Common Components

Problem

You want to create a consistent look and feel for your application across all the versions of Android your users may be running, while reducing the amount of code required to maintain those customizations.

Solution

(API Level 1)

You can abstract common attributes that define the look and feel of your application views into XML styles. *Styles* are collections of view attribute customizations, such as text size or background color, that should be applied to multiple views throughout the application. Abstracting these attributes into a style allows the common elements to be defined in a single location, making the code easier to update and maintain.

Android also supports grouping multiple styles together in a global element called a *theme*. Themes apply to an entire context (such as an activity or application), and define styles that should apply to all the views within that context. Every activity launch in your application has a theme applied to it, even if you don't define one. In such cases, the default system theme is applied instead.

How It Works

To explore the styles concept, let's create an activity layout that looks like Figure 1-1.

Electronic supplementary material The online version of this chapter (doi:10.1007/978-1-4842-2259-1_1) contains supplementary material, which is available to authorized users.

© Dave Smith and Erik Hellman 2016
D. Smith and E. Hellman, *Android Recipes*, DOI 10.1007/978-1-4842-2259-1_1

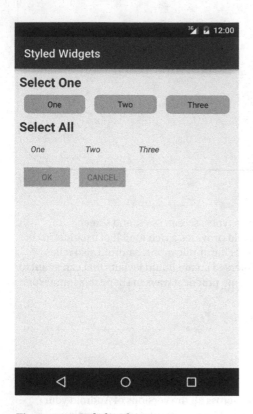

Figure 1-1. *Styled widgets*

As you can see, this view has some elements that we want to customize to look different than they normally do with the styling from the default system theme applied. One option would be to define all the attributes for all the views directly in our activity layout. If we were to do so, it would look like Listing 1-1.

■ **Note**   Although it is possible to apply a style to a standard component to look completely different, one should avoid changing the appearance too much as it could confuse users. Refer to the Material Design specification at http://material.google.com for details on the recommendations for different UI components.

Listing 1-1. res/layout/activity_styled.xml

```xml
<?xml version="1.0" encoding="utf-8"?>
<TableLayout xmlns:android="http://schemas.android.com/apk/res/android"
    android:layout_width="match_parent"
    android:layout_height="match_parent"
    android:padding="8dp">
    <TextView
        android:layout_width="wrap_content"
        android:layout_height="wrap_content"
        android:textSize="22sp"
        android:textStyle="bold"
        android:text="Select One"/>
```

```
<RadioGroup
    android:layout_width="match_parent"
    android:layout_height="wrap_content"
    android:orientation="horizontal">
    <RadioButton
        android:layout_width="0dp"
        android:layout_height="wrap_content"
        android:layout_weight="1"
        android:minHeight="@dimen/buttonHeight"
        android:button="@null"
        android:background="@drawable/background_radio"
        android:gravity="center"
        android:text="One"/>
    <RadioButton
        android:layout_width="0dp"
        android:layout_height="wrap_content"
        android:layout_weight="1"
        android:minHeight="@dimen/buttonHeight"
        android:button="@null"
        android:background="@drawable/background_radio"
        android:gravity="center"
        android:text="Two"/>
    <RadioButton
        android:layout_width="0dp"
        android:layout_height="wrap_content"
        android:layout_weight="1"
        android:minHeight="@dimen/buttonHeight"
        android:button="@null"
        android:background="@drawable/background_radio"
        android:gravity="center"
        android:text="Three"/>
</RadioGroup>

<TextView
    android:layout_width="wrap_content"
    android:layout_height="wrap_content"
    android:textSize="22sp"
    android:textStyle="bold"
    android:text="Select All"/>
<TableRow>
    <CheckBox
        android:layout_width="wrap_content"
        android:layout_height="wrap_content"
        android:minHeight="@dimen/buttonHeight"
        android:minWidth="@dimen/checkboxWidth"
        android:button="@null"
        android:gravity="center"
        android:textStyle="italic"
        android:textColor="@color/text_checkbox"
        android:text="One"/>
```

```xml
    <CheckBox
        android:layout_width="wrap_content"
        android:layout_height="wrap_content"
        android:minHeight="@dimen/buttonHeight"
        android:minWidth="@dimen/checkboxWidth"
        android:button="@null"
        android:gravity="center"
        android:textStyle="italic"
        android:textColor="@color/text_checkbox"
        android:text="Two"/>
    <CheckBox
        android:layout_width="wrap_content"
        android:layout_height="wrap_content"
        android:minHeight="@dimen/buttonHeight"
        android:minWidth="@dimen/checkboxWidth"
        android:button="@null"
        android:gravity="center"
        android:textStyle="italic"
        android:textColor="@color/text_checkbox"
        android:text="Three"/>
    </TableRow>

    <TableRow>
        <Button
            android:layout_width="wrap_content"
            android:layout_height="wrap_content"
            android:minWidth="@dimen/buttonWidth"
            android:background="@drawable/background_button"
            android:textColor="@color/accentPink"
            android:text="@android:string/ok"/>
        <Button
            android:layout_width="wrap_content"
            android:layout_height="wrap_content"
            android:minWidth="@dimen/buttonWidth"
            android:background="@drawable/background_button"
            android:textColor="@color/accentPink"
            android:text="@android:string/cancel"/>
    </TableRow>
</TableLayout>
```

To add emphasis, we've highlighted the attributes in each view that are common to other views of the same type. These are the attributes that make the buttons, text headings, and checkable elements all look the same. There's a lot of duplication to make this happen, and we can clean it up with a style.

First, we need to create a new resource file, and define each attribute group with a <style> tag. Listing 1-2 shows the completed abstractions.

Listing 1-2. res/values/styles.xml

```xml
<resources>
    <!-- Widget Styles -->
    <style name="LabelText" parent="android:TextAppearance.Large">
        <item name="android:textStyle">bold</item>
    </style>
```

```xml
<style name="FormButton" parent="android:Widget.Button">
    <item name="android:minWidth">@dimen/buttonWidth</item>
    <item name="android:background">@drawable/background_button</item>
    <item name="android:textColor">@color/accentPink</item>
</style>

<style name="FormRadioButton" parent="android:Widget.CompoundButton.RadioButton">
    <item name="android:minHeight">@dimen/buttonHeight</item>
    <item name="android:button">@null</item>
    <item name="android:background">@drawable/background_radio</item>
    <item name="android:gravity">center</item>
</style>

<style name="FormCheckBox" parent="android:Widget.CompoundButton.CheckBox">
    <item name="android:minHeight">@dimen/buttonHeight</item>
    <item name="android:minWidth">@dimen/checkboxWidth</item>
    <item name="android:button">@null</item>
    <item name="android:gravity">center</item>
    <item name="android:textStyle">italic</item>
    <item name="android:textColor">@color/text_checkbox</item>
</style>
```

```xml
</resources>
```

A `<style>` groups together the common attributes we need to apply to each view type. Views can accept only a single style definition, so all the attributes for that view must be collected in one group. Styles do support inheritance, however, which allows us to cascade our definitions of each style before they are applied to the view.

Notice how each style also declares a parent. This is the base framework style that we should inherit from. Parent styles are not required, but because of the single style rule on each view, overwriting the default with your custom version replaces the theme's default. If you don't inherit from a base parent, you will be forced to define all the attributes that view needs. Extending a widget's style from the framework's base ensures that we are responsible only for adding the attributes we want to customize beyond the default theme's look and feel.

EXPLICIT VS. IMPLICIT PARENTING

Style inheritance takes one of two forms. A style can explicitly declare its parent, as we've seen before:

```xml
<style name="BaseStyle" />
<style name="NewStyle" parent="BaseStyle" />
```

NewStyle is an extension of BaseStyle, and includes all the attributes defined in the parent. Styles also support an implicit parenting syntax as follows:

```xml
<style name="BaseStyle" />
<style name="BaseStyle.Extended" />
```

In the same way, BaseStyle.Extended inherits its attributes from BaseStyle. The functionality of this version is identical to the explicit example, just in a more compact convention. The two forms should never be mixed, and doing so doesn't allow for multiple parents on a single style. When this is done, the explicit parent always wins anyway, and the readability of the code is reduced.

We can apply the new styles to our original layout file, and the cleaner result is shown in Listing 1-3.

Listing 1-3. res/layout/activity_styled.xml

```xml
<?xml version="1.0" encoding="utf-8"?>
<TableLayout xmlns:android="http://schemas.android.com/apk/res/android"
    android:layout_width="match_parent"
    android:layout_height="match_parent"
    android:padding="8dp">
    <TextView
        android:layout_width="wrap_content"
        android:layout_height="wrap_content"
        android:textAppearance="@style/LabelText"
        android:text="Select One"/>
    <RadioGroup
        android:layout_width="match_parent"
        android:layout_height="wrap_content"
        android:orientation="horizontal">
        <RadioButton
            style="@style/FormRadioButton"
            android:layout_width="0dp"
            android:layout_height="wrap_content"
            android:layout_weight="1"
            android:text="One"/>
        <RadioButton
            style="@style/FormRadioButton"
            android:layout_width="0dp"
            android:layout_height="wrap_content"
            android:layout_weight="1"
            android:text="Two"/>
        <RadioButton
            style="@style/FormRadioButton"
            android:layout_width="0dp"
            android:layout_height="wrap_content"
            android:layout_weight="1"
            android:text="Three"/>
    </RadioGroup>

    <TextView
        android:layout_width="wrap_content"
        android:layout_height="wrap_content"
        android:textAppearance="@style/LabelText"
        android:text="Select All"/>
    <TableRow>
        <CheckBox
            style="@style/FormCheckBox"
```

```
                android:layout_width="wrap_content"
                android:layout_height="wrap_content"
                android:text="One"/>
        <CheckBox
            style="@style/FormCheckBox"
                android:layout_width="wrap_content"
                android:layout_height="wrap_content"
                android:text="Two"/>
        <CheckBox
            style="@style/FormCheckBox"
                android:layout_width="wrap_content"
                android:layout_height="wrap_content"
                android:text="Three"/>
    </TableRow>

    <TableRow>
        <Button
            style="@style/FormButton"
                android:layout_width="wrap_content"
                android:layout_height="wrap_content"
                android:text="@android:string/ok"/>
        <Button
            style="@style/FormButton"
                android:layout_width="wrap_content"
                android:layout_height="wrap_content"
                android:text="@android:string/cancel"/>
    </TableRow>
</TableLayout>
```

By applying a style attribute to each view, we can remove the explicit attribute references that were duplicated in favor of a single reference on each element. The one exception to this behavior is our TextView headings, which accept a special android:textAppearance attribute. This attribute takes a style reference, and applies only to text-formatting attributes (size, style, color, and so forth). When used, a TextView still allows a separate style attribute to be applied concurrently. In this way, it is the one supported instance in the framework of multiple styles on a single view.

Themes

A *theme* in Android is a type of appearance style that is applicable to an entire application or activity. There are two choices when applying a theme: use a system theme or create a custom one. In either case, a theme is applied in the AndroidManifest.xml file, as shown in Listing 1-4.

Listing 1-4. AndroidManifest.xml

```
<?xml version="1.0" encoding="utf-8"?>
<manifest xmlns:android="http://schemas.android.com/apk/res/android"
    ...>
    <!--Apply to the application tag for a global theme -->
    <application android:theme="APPLICATION_THEME_NAME"
        ...>
        <!--Apply to the activity tag for an individual theme -->
```

7

```
        <activity android:name=".Activity"
            android:theme="ACTIVITY_THEME_NAME"
            ...>
            <intent-filter>
                ...
            </intent-filter>
        </activity>
    </application>
</manifest>
```

System Themes

The styles.xml and themes.xml files packaged with the Android framework include a few options for themes with some useful custom properties. Referencing R.style in the SDK documentation will provide the full list, but here are a few useful examples:

- Theme.Light: Variation on the standard theme that uses an inverse color scheme for the background and user elements. This is the default recommended base theme for applications prior to Android 3.0.

- Theme.NoTitleBar.Fullscreen: Removes the title bar and status bar, filling the entire screen (minus any onscreen controls that may be present)

- Theme.Dialog: A useful theme to make an activity look like a dialog box

- Theme.Holo.Light: (API Level 11) Theme that uses an inverse color scheme and that has an action bar by default. This is the default recommended base theme for applications on Android 3.0.

- Theme.Holo.Light.DarkActionBar: (API Level 14) Theme with an inverse color scheme but a dark solid action bar. This is the default recommended base theme for applications on Android 4.0.

- Theme.Material.Light: (API Level 21) Theme with a simplified color scheme governed by a small palette of primary colors. This theme also supports tinting of the standard widgets using the supplied primary colors. This is the default recommended base theme for applications on Android 5.0.

▪ **Note**   When using the AppCompat Library, other versions for each of these themes should be used instead (for example, Theme.AppCompat.Light.DarkActionBar).

Listing 1-5 is an example of a system theme applied to the entire application by setting the android:theme attribute in the AndroidManifest.xml file.

Listing 1-5. Manifest with Theme Set on Application

```
<?xml version="1.0" encoding="utf-8"?>
<manifest xmlns:android="http://schemas.android.com/apk/res/android"
    ...>
    <!--Apply to the application tag for a global theme -->
    <application android:theme="Theme.Material.Light"
```

```
    ...>
    ...
  </application>
</manifest>
```

Custom Themes

Sometimes the provided system choices aren't enough. After all, some of the customizable elements in the window are not even addressed in the system options. Defining a custom theme to do the job is simple.

If there is not one already, create a `styles.xml` file in the `res/values` path of the project. Remember, themes are just styles applied on a wider scale, so they are defined in the same place. Theme aspects related to window customization can be found in the `R.attr` reference of the SDK, but here are the most common items:

- `android:windowNoTitle`: Governs whether to remove the default title bar; set to `true` to remove the title bar

- `android:windowFullscreen`: Governs whether to remove the system status bar; set to `true` to remove the status bar and fill the entire screen.

- `android:windowBackground`: Color or drawable resource to apply as a background

- `android:windowContentOverlay`: Drawable placed over the window content foreground. By default, this is a shadow below the status bar. Set to any resource to use in place of the default status bar shadow, or `null` (`@null` in XML) to remove it.

In addition, the Material themes accept a series of color attributes that are used to tint the application interface widgets:

- `android:colorPrimary`: Used to tint primary interface elements, like the action bar and the scrolling edge glow effects. Also affects the recent tasks title bar color

- `android:colorPrimaryDark`: Tints the system controls, such as the status bar background

- `android:colorAccent`: Default color applied to controls that are focused or activated

- `android:colorControlNormal`: Override color for controls that are not focused or activated

- `android:colorControlActivated`: Override color for focused and activated controls. Takes place of the accent color if both are defined

- `android:colorControlHighlight`: Override color for controls that are being pressed

Listing 1-6 is an example of a `styles.xml` file that creates a custom theme in order to supply brand-specific colors for the application interface.

Listing 1-6. `res/values/styles.xml`

```xml
<?xml version="1.0" encoding="utf-8"?>
<resources>

    <style name="BaseAppTheme" parent="@style/Theme.AppCompat.Light.DarkActionBar">
        <!-- Action bar background color -->
        <item name="colorPrimary">@color/primaryBlue</item>
        <!-- Status bar tint color -->
```

```
        <item name="colorPrimaryDark">@color/primaryDarkBlue</item>
        <!-- Default color applied to all focused/activated controls -->
        <item name="colorAccent">@color/accentPink</item>

        <!-- Unselected controls color -->
        <item name="colorControlNormal">@color/controlNormalGreen</item>
        <!-- Activated control color; overrides accent -->
        <item name="colorControlActivated">@color/controlActivatedGreen</item>
    </style>

</resources>
```

Notice that a theme may also indicate a parent from which to inherit properties, so the entire theme need not be created from scratch. In the example, we inherit from Android's default system theme, customizing only the properties that we needed to differentiate. All platform themes are defined in res/values/themes.xml of the Android package. Refer to the SDK documentation on styles and themes for more details.

Listing 1-7 shows how to apply these themes to individual activity instances in the AndroidManifest.xml.

Listing 1-7. Manifest with Themes Set on Activity

```
<?xml version="1.0" encoding="utf-8"?>
<manifest xmlns:android="http://schemas.android.com/apk/res/android"
    ...>
    <!—Apply to the application tag for a global theme -->
    <application
        ...>
        <!—Apply to the activity tag for an individual theme -->
        <activity android:name=".ThemedActivity"
            android:theme="@style/AppTheme"
            ...>
            <intent-filter>
                <action android:name="android.intent.action.MAIN" />
                <category android:name="android.intent.category.LAUNCHER" />
            </intent-filter>
        </activity>
    </application>
</manifest>
```

1-2. Toggling System UI Elements

Problem

Your application experience requires access to the display, removing any system decorations such as the status bar and software navigation buttons.

Solution

(API Level 11)

Many applications that target a more immersive content experience (such as readers or video players) can benefit from temporarily hiding the system's UI components to provide as much screen real estate as possible to the application when the content is visible. Beginning with Android 3.0, developers are able to adjust many of these properties at runtime without the need to statically request a window feature or declare values inside a theme.

How It Works

Dark Mode

Dark mode is also often called *lights-out mode*. This mode dims the onscreen navigation controls (and the system status bar in later releases) without actually removing them, to prevent any onscreen system elements from distracting the user from the current view in the application.

To enable this mode, we simply have to call setSystemUiVisibility() on any View in our hierarchy with the SYSTEM_UI_FLAG_LOW_PROFILE flag. To set the mode back to the default, call the same method with SYSTEM_UI_FLAG_VISIBLE instead. We can determine which mode we are in by calling getSystemUiVisibility() and checking the current status of the flags (see Listings 1-8 and 1-9).

■ **Note**   These flag names were introduced in API Level 14 (Android 4.0); prior to that they were named STATUS_BAR_HIDDEN and STATUS_BAR_VISIBLE. The values of each are the same, so the new flags will produce the same behavior on Android 3.*x* devices.

Listing 1-8. res/layout/main.xml

```xml
<?xml version="1.0" encoding="utf-8"?>
<RelativeLayout
    xmlns:android="http://schemas.android.com/apk/res/android"
    android:layout_width="match_parent"
    android:layout_height="match_parent" >
    <Button
        android:layout_width="match_parent"
        android:layout_height="wrap_content"
        android:layout_centerVertical="true"
        android:text="Toggle Mode"
        android:onClick="onToggleClick" />
</RelativeLayout>
```

Listing 1-9. Activity Toggling Dark Mode

```java
public class DarkActivity extends Activity {

    @Override
    protected void onCreate(Bundle savedInstanceState) {
        super.onCreate(savedInstanceState);
        setContentView(R.layout.main);
    }
```

```
public void onToggleClick(View v) {
    int currentVis = v.getSystemUiVisibility();
    int newVis;
    if ((currentVis & View.SYSTEM_UI_FLAG_LOW_PROFILE)
            == View.SYSTEM_UI_FLAG_LOW_PROFILE) {
        newVis = View.SYSTEM_UI_FLAG_VISIBLE;
    } else {
        newVis = View.SYSTEM_UI_FLAG_LOW_PROFILE;
    }
    v.setSystemUiVisibility(newVis);
}
}
```

The methods setSystemUiVisibility() and getSystemUiVisibility() can be called on any view currently visible inside the window where you want to adjust these parameters.

Hiding Navigation Controls

(API Level 14)

SYSTEM_UI_FLAG_HIDE_NAVIGATION removes the onscreen HOME and BACK controls for devices that do not have physical buttons. While Android gives developers the ability to do this, it is with caution because these functions are extremely important to the user. If the navigation controls are manually hidden, any tap on the screen will bring them back. Listing 1-10 shows an example of this in practice.

Listing 1-10. Activity Toggling Navigation Controls

```
public class HideActivity extends Activity {

    @Override
    protected void onCreate(Bundle savedInstanceState) {
        super.onCreate(savedInstanceState);
        setContentView(R.layout.main);

    }

    public void onToggleClick(View v) {
        //Here we only need to hide the controls on a tap because
        // Android will make the controls reappear automatically
        // anytime the screen is tapped after they are hidden.
        v.setSystemUiVisibility(
                View.SYSTEM_UI_FLAG_HIDE_NAVIGATION);
    }
}
```

Notice also when running this example that the button will shift up and down to accommodate the changes in content space because of our centering requirement in the root layout. If you plan to use this flag, note that any views being laid out relative to the bottom of the screen will move as the layout changes.

Full-Screen UI Mode

Prior to Android 4.1, there is no method of hiding the system status bar dynamically; it has to be done with a static theme. To hide and show the action bar, however, `ActionBar.show()` and `ActionBar.hide()` will animate the element in and out of view. If `FEATURE_ACTION_BAR_OVERLAY` is requested, this change will not affect the content of the activity; otherwise, the view content will shift up and down to accommodate the change.

(API Level 16)

Listing 1-11 illustrates an example of how to hide all system UI controls temporarily.

Listing 1-11. Activity Toggling All System UI Controls

```
public class FullActivity extends Activity {

    @Override
    protected void onCreate(Bundle savedInstanceState) {
        super.onCreate(savedInstanceState);
        //Request this feature so the ActionBar will hide
        requestWindowFeature(Window.FEATURE_ACTION_BAR_OVERLAY);
        setContentView(R.layout.main);
    }

    public void onToggleClick(View v) {
        //Here we only need to hide the UI on a tap because
        // Android will make the controls reappear automatically
        // anytime the screen is tapped after they are hidden.
        v.setSystemUiVisibility(
                /* This flag tells Android not to shift
                 * our layout when resizing the window to
                 * hide/show the system elements
                 */
                View.SYSTEM_UI_FLAG_LAYOUT_STABLE
                /* This flag hides the system status bar.  If
                 * ACTION_BAR_OVERLAY is requested, it will hide
                 * the ActionBar as well.
                 */
                | View.SYSTEM_UI_FLAG_FULLSCREEN
                /* This flag hides the onscreen controls
                 */
                | View.SYSTEM_UI_FLAG_HIDE_NAVIGATION);
    }
}
```

Similar to the example of hiding only the navigation controls, we do not need to show the controls again because any tap on the screen will bring them back. As a convenience beginning in Android 4.1, when the system clears the `SYSTEM_UI_FLAG_HIDE_NAVIGATION` in this way, it will also clear the `SYSTEM_UI_FLAG_FULLSCREEN`, so the top and bottom elements will become visible together. Android will hide the action bar as part of the full-screen flag only if we request `FEATURE_ACTION_BAR_OVERLAY`; otherwise, only the status bar will be affected.

We have added one other flag of interest in this example: SYSTEM_UI_LAYOUT_STABLE. This flag tells Android not to shift our content view as a result of adding and removing the system UI. Because of this, our button will stay centered as the elements toggle.

1-3. Creating and Displaying Views

Problem

Your application needs view elements in order to display information and interact with the user.

Solution

(API Level 1)

Whether using one of the many views and widgets available in the Android SDK or creating a custom display, all applications need views to interact with the user. The preferred method for creating user interfaces in Android is to define them in XML and inflate them at runtime.

The view structure in Android is a tree, with the root typically being the activity or window's content view. ViewGroups are special views that manage the display of one or more child views, which could be another ViewGroup, and the tree continues to grow. All the standard layout classes descend from ViewGroup, and they are the most common choices for the root node of the XML layout file.

How It Works

Let's define a layout with two Button instances and an EditText to accept user input. We can define a file in res/layout/ called main.xml with the following contents (see Listing 1-12).

Listing 1-12. res/layout/main.xml

```
<LinearLayout
    xmlns:android="http://schemas.android.com/apk/res/android"
    android:layout_width="match_parent"
    android:layout_height="match_parent"
    android:orientation="vertical">
    <EditText
        android:id="@+id/editText"
        android:layout_width="match_parent"
        android:layout_height="wrap_content" />
    <LinearLayout
        android:layout_width="match_parent"
        android:layout_height="wrap_content"
        android:orientation="horizontal">
        <Button
            android:id="@+id/save"
            android:layout_width="wrap_content"
            android:layout_height="wrap_content"
            android:text="Save" />
        <Button
            android:id="@+id/cancel"
            android:layout_width="wrap_content"
```

```
            android:layout_height="wrap_content"
            android:text="Cancel" />
    </LinearLayout>
</LinearLayout>
```

LinearLayout is a ViewGroup that lays out its elements one after the other in either a horizontal or vertical fashion. In main.xml, the EditText and inner LinearLayout are laid out vertically in orientation. The contents of the inner LinearLayout (the buttons) are laid out horizontally. The view elements with an android:id value are elements that will need to be referenced in the Java code for further customization or display.

To make this layout the display contents of an activity, it must be inflated at runtime. The Activity. setContentView() method is overloaded with a convenience method to do this for you, requiring only the layout ID valueqaw. In this case, setting the layout in the activity is as simple as this:

```
public void onCreate(Bundle savedInstanceState) {
    super.onCreate(savedInstanceState);
    setContentView(R.layout.main);
    //Continue Activity initialization
}
```

Nothing beyond supplying the ID value (main.xml automatically has an ID of R.layout.main) is required. If the layout needs a little more customization before it is attached to the window, you can inflate it manually and do some work before adding it as the content view. Listing 1-13 inflates the same layout and adds a third button before displaying it.

Listing 1-13. Layout Modification Prior to Display

```
public void onCreate(Bundle savedInstanceState) {
    super.onCreate(savedInstanceState);
    //Inflate the layout file
    LinearLayout layout = (LinearLayout)getLayoutInflater()
            .inflate(R.layout.main, null);
    //Add a new button
    Button reset = new Button(this);
    reset.setText("Reset Form");
    layout.addView(reset,
        new LinearLayout.LayoutParams(LayoutParams.MATCH_PARENT,
            LayoutParams.WRAP_CONTENT));

    //Attach the view to the window
    setContentView(layout);
}
```

In this instance, the XML layout is inflated in the activity code with a LayoutInflater, whose inflate() method returns a handle to the inflated View. Since LayoutInflater.inflate() returns a View, we must cast it to the specific subclass in the XML in order to do more than just attach it to the window.

■ **Note**   The root element in the XML layout file is the View element returned from LayoutInflater. inflate().

The second parameter to inflate() is the parent ViewGroup, and this is extremely important because it defines how the LayoutParams from the inflated layout are interpreted. Whenever possible, if you know the parent of this inflated hierarchy, it should be passed here; otherwise, the LayoutParams from the root view of the XML will be ignored. When passing a parent, also note that the third parameter of inflate() controls whether the inflated layout is automatically attached to the parent. We will see in future recipes how this can be useful for doing custom views. In this instance, however, we are inflating the top-level view of our activity, so we pass null here.

Completely Custom Views

Sometimes, the widgets available in the SDK just aren't enough to provide the output you need. Or perhaps you want to reduce the number of views you have in your hierarchy by combining multiple display elements into a single view to improve performance. For these cases, you may want to create your own View subclass. In doing so, there are two main interaction points between your class and the framework that need to be observed: measurement and drawing.

Measurement

The first requirement that a custom view must fulfill is to provide a measurement for its content to the framework. Before a view hierarchy is displayed, Android calls onMeasure() for each element (both layouts and view nodes), and passes it two constraints the view should use to govern how it reports the size that it should be. Each constraint is a packed integer known as a MeasureSpec, which includes a mode flag and a size value. The mode will be one of the following values:

- AT_MOST: This mode is typically used when the layout parameters of the view are match_parent, or there is some other upper limit on the size. This tells the view it should report any size it wants, as long as it doesn't exceed the value in the spec.

- EXACTLY: This mode is typically used when the layout parameters of the view are a fixed value. The framework expects the view to set its size to match the spec—no more, no less.

- UNSPECIFIED: This value is often used to figure out how big the view wants to be if unconstrained. This may be a precursor to another measurement with different constraints, or it may simply be because the layout parameters were set to wrap_content and no other constraints exist in the parent. The view may report its size to be whatever it wants in this case. The size in this spec is often zero.

Once you have done your calculations on what size to report, those values *must* be passed in a call to setMeasuredDimension() before onMeasure() returns. If you do not do this, the framework will be quite upset with you.

Measurement is also an opportunity to configure your view's output based on the space available. The measurement constraints essentially tell you how much space has been allocated inside the layout, so if you want to create a view that orients its content differently when it has, say, more or less vertical space, onMeasure() will give you what you need to make that decision.

■ **Note**   During measurement, your view doesn't *actually* have a size yet; it has only a measured dimension. If you want to do some custom work in your view after the size has been assigned, override onSizeChanged() and put your code there.

Drawing

The second, and arguably most important, step for your custom view is drawing content. Once a view has been measured and placed inside the layout hierarchy, the framework will construct a Canvas instance, sized and placed appropriately for your view, and pass it via onDraw() for your view to use. The Canvas is an object that hosts individual drawing calls so it includes methods such as drawLine(), drawBitmap(), and drawText() for you to lay out the view content discretely. Canvas (as the name implies) uses a painter's algorithm, so items drawn last will go on top of items drawn first.

Drawing is clipped to the bounds of the view provided via measurement and layout, so while the Canvas element can be translated, scaled, rotated, and so on, you cannot draw content outside the rectangle where your view has been placed.

Finally, the content supplied in onDraw() does not include the view's background, which can be set with methods such as setBackgroundColor() or setBackgroundResource(). If a background is set on the view, it will be drawn for you, and you do not need to handle that inside onDraw().

Listing 1-14 shows a very simple custom view template that your application can follow. For content, we are drawing a series of concentric circles to represent a bull's-eye target.

Listing 1-14. Custom View Example

```java
public class BullsEyeView extends View {

    private Paint mPaint;

    private Point mCenter;
    private float mRadius;

    /*
     * Java Constructor
     */
    public BullsEyeView(Context context) {
        this(context, null);
    }

    /*
     * XML Constructor
     */
    public BullsEyeView(Context context, AttributeSet attrs) {
        this(context, attrs, 0);
    }

    /*
     * XML Constructor with Style
     */
    public BullsEyeView(Context context, AttributeSet attrs,
            int defStyle) {
        super(context, attrs, defStyle);
        //Do any initialization of your view in this constructor

        //Create a paintbrush to draw with
        mPaint = new Paint(Paint.ANTI_ALIAS_FLAG);
        //We want to draw our circles filled in
        mPaint.setStyle(Style.FILL);
```

```java
        //Create the center point for our circle
        mCenter = new Point();
    }

    @Override
    protected void onMeasure(int widthMeasureSpec,
            int heightMeasureSpec) {
        int width, height;
        //Determine the ideal size of your content, unconstrained
        int contentWidth = 200;
        int contentHeight = 200;

        width = getMeasurement(widthMeasureSpec, contentWidth);
        height = getMeasurement(heightMeasureSpec, contentHeight);
        //MUST call this method with the measured values!
        setMeasuredDimension(width, height);
    }

    /*
     * Helper method to measure width and height
     */
    private int getMeasurement(int measureSpec, int contentSize) {
        int specSize = MeasureSpec.getSize(measureSpec);
        switch (MeasureSpec.getMode(measureSpec)) {
            case MeasureSpec.AT_MOST:
                return Math.min(specSize, contentSize);
            case MeasureSpec.UNSPECIFIED:
                return contentSize;
            case MeasureSpec.EXACTLY:
                return specSize;
            default:
                return 0;
        }
    }

    @Override
    protected void onSizeChanged(int w, int h,
            int oldw, int oldh) {
        if (w != oldw || h != oldh) {
            //If there was a change, reset the parameters
            mCenter.x = w / 2;
            mCenter.y = h / 2;
            mRadius = Math.min(mCenter.x, mCenter.y);
        }
    }

    @Override
    protected void onDraw(Canvas canvas) {
        //Draw a series of concentric circles,
        // smallest to largest, alternating colors
```

```
    mPaint.setColor(Color.RED);
    canvas.drawCircle(mCenter.x, mCenter.y, mRadius, mPaint);

    mPaint.setColor(Color.WHITE);
    canvas.drawCircle(mCenter.x, mCenter.y, mRadius * 0.8f,
        mPaint);

    mPaint.setColor(Color.BLUE);
    canvas.drawCircle(mCenter.x, mCenter.y, mRadius * 0.6f,
        mPaint);

    mPaint.setColor(Color.WHITE);
    canvas.drawCircle(mCenter.x, mCenter.y, mRadius * 0.4f,
        mPaint);

    mPaint.setColor(Color.RED);
    canvas.drawCircle(mCenter.x, mCenter.y, mRadius * 0.2f,
        mPaint);
    }
}
```

The first thing you may notice is that View has three constructors:

- View(Context): This version is used when a view is constructed from within Java code.

- View(Context, AttributeSet): This version is used when a view is inflated from XML. AttributeSet includes all the attributes attached to the XML element for the view.

- View(Context, AttributeSet, int): This version is similar to the previous one, but is called when a style attribute is added to the XML element.

It is a common pattern to chain all three together and implement customizations in only the final constructor, which is what we have done in the example view.

From onMeasure(), we use a simple utility method to return the correct dimension based on the measurement constraints. We basically have a choice between the size we want our content to be (which is arbitrarily selected here, but should represent your view content in a real application) and the size given to us. In the case of AT_MOST, we pick the value that is the lesser of the two; thus saying the view will be the size necessary to fit our content as long as it doesn't exceed the spec. We use onSizeChanged(), called after measurement is finished, to gather some basic data we will need to draw our target circles. We wait until this point to ensure we use the values that exactly match how the view is laid out.

Inside onDraw() is where we construct the display. Five concentric circles are painted onto the Canvas with a steadily decreasing radius and alternating colors. The Paint element controls information about the style of the content being drawn, such as stroke width, text sizes, and colors. When we declared the Paint for this view, we set the style to FILL, which ensures that the circles are filled in with each color. Because of the painter's algorithm, the smaller circles are drawn on top of the larger, giving us the target look we were going for.

Adding this view to an XML layout is simple, but because the view doesn't reside in the android.view or android.widget packages, we need to name the element with the fully qualified package name of the class. So, for example, if our application package were com.androidrecipes.customwidgets, the XML would be as follows:

```
<com.androidrecipes.customwidgets.BullsEyeView
    android:layout_width="match_parent"
    android:layout_height="match_parent" />
```

Figure 1-2 shows the result of adding this view to an activity.

Figure 1-2. *Bull's-eye custom view*

1-4. Animating a View

Problem

Your application needs to animate a view object, either as a transition or for effect.

Solution

(API Level 12)

An ObjectAnimator instance, such as ViewPropertyAnimator, can be used to manipulate the properties of a View, such as its position or rotation. ViewPropertyAnimator is obtained through View.animate() and then modified with the specifics of the animation. Modifications made through this API will alter the actual properties of the View itself.

How It Works

ViewPropertyAnimator is the most convenient method for animating view content. The API works similarly to a builder, where the calls to modify the different properties can be chained together to create a single animation. Any calls made to the same ViewPropertyAnimator during the same iteration of the current thread's Looper will be lumped into a single animation. Listings 1-15 and 1-16 illustrate a simple view transition example activity.

Listing 1-15. res/layout/main.xml

```xml
<?xml version="1.0" encoding="utf-8"?>
<LinearLayout xmlns:android="http://schemas.android.com/apk/res/android"
    android:orientation="vertical"
    android:layout_width="fill_parent"
    android:layout_height="fill_parent">
    <Button
        android:id="@+id/toggleButton"
        android:layout_width="fill_parent"
        android:layout_height="wrap_content"
        android:text="Click to Toggle" />

    <View
        android:id="@+id/theView"
        android:layout_width="fill_parent"
        android:layout_height="wrap_content"
        android:background="#AAA" />
</LinearLayout>
```

Listing 1-16. Activity Using ViewPropertyAnimator

```java
public class AnimateActivity extends Activity implements View.OnClickListener {

    View viewToAnimate;

    @Override
    public void onCreate(Bundle savedInstanceState) {
        super.onCreate(savedInstanceState);
        setContentView(R.layout.main);

        Button button = (Button)findViewById(R.id.toggleButton);
        button.setOnClickListener(this);

        viewToAnimate = findViewById(R.id.theView);
    }

    @Override
    public void onClick(View v) {
        if(viewToAnimate.getAlpha() > 0f) {
            //If the view is visible, slide it out to the right
            viewToAnimate.animate().alpha(0f).translationX(1000f);
        } else {
```

```
            //If the view is hidden, do a fade-in in place
            //Property Animations actually modify the view, so
            // we have to reset the view's location first
            viewToAnimate.setTranslationX(0f);
            viewToAnimate.animate().alpha(1f);
        }
    }
}
```

In this example, the slide and fade-out transition is accomplished by chaining together a modification of the alpha and translationX properties, with a translation value sufficiently large to go offscreen. We do not have to chain these methods together for them to be considered a single animation. If we had called them on two separate lines, they would still execute together because they were both set in the same iteration of the main thread's Looper.

Notice that we have to reset the translation property for our View to fade in without a slide. This is because property animations manipulate the actual View, rather than where it is temporarily drawn (which is the case with the older animation APIs). If we did not reset this property, it would fade in but would still be 1,000 pixels off to the right.

ObjectAnimator

While ViewPropertyAnimator is convenient for animating simple properties quickly, you may find it a bit limiting if you want to do more-complex work such as chaining animations together. For this purpose, we can go to the parent class, ObjectAnimator. With ObjectAnimator, we can set listeners to be notified when the animation begins and ends; also, they can be notified with incremental updates as to what point of the animation we are in.

Listings 1-17 and 1-18 show how we can use this to construct a simple coin-flip animation.

Listing 1-17. res/layout/main.xml

```xml
<?xml version="1.0" encoding="utf-8"?>
<FrameLayout xmlns:android="http://schemas.android.com/apk/res/android"
    android:layout_width="fill_parent"
    android:layout_height="fill_parent">

    <ImageView
        android:id="@+id/flip_image"
        android:layout_width="wrap_content"
        android:layout_height="wrap_content"
        android:layout_gravity="center"/>
</FrameLayout>
```

Listing 1-18. Flipper Animation with ObjectAnimator

```java
public class FlipperActivity extends Activity {

    private boolean mIsHeads;
    private ObjectAnimator mFlipper;
    private Bitmap mHeadsImage, mTailsImage;
    private ImageView mFlipImage;
```

```java
@Override
public void onCreate(Bundle savedInstanceState) {
    super.onCreate(savedInstanceState);
    setContentView(R.layout.main);

    mHeadsImage = BitmapFactory.decodeResource(getResources(), R.drawable.heads);
    mTailsImage = BitmapFactory.decodeResource(getResources(), R.drawable.tails);

    mFlipImage = (ImageView)findViewById(R.id.flip_image);
    mFlipImage.setImageBitmap(mHeadsImage);
    mIsHeads = true;

    mFlipper = ObjectAnimator.ofFloat(mFlipImage, "rotationY", 0f, 360f);
    mFlipper.setDuration(500);
    mFlipper.addUpdateListener(new AnimatorUpdateListener() {
        @Override
        public void onAnimationUpdate(ValueAnimator animation) {
            if (animation.getAnimatedFraction() >= 0.25f && mIsHeads) {
                mFlipImage.setImageBitmap(mTailsImage);
                mIsHeads = false;
            }
            if (animation.getAnimatedFraction() >= 0.75f && !mIsHeads) {
                mFlipImage.setImageBitmap(mHeadsImage);
                mIsHeads = true;
            }
        }
    });
}

@Override
public boolean onTouchEvent(MotionEvent event) {
    if(event.getAction() == MotionEvent.ACTION_DOWN) {
        mFlipper.start();
        return true;
    }
    return super.onTouchEvent(event);
}
}
```

Property animations provide transformations that were not previously available with the older animation system, such as rotations about the x and y axes that create the effect of a three-dimensional transformation. In this example, we don't have to fake the rotation by doing a calculated scale; we can just tell the view to rotate about the y axis. Because of this, we no longer need two animations to flip the coin; we can just animate the rotationY property of the view for one full rotation.

Another powerful addition is the AnimationUpdateListener, which provides regular callbacks while the animation is going on. The getAnimatedFraction() method returns the current percentage to completion of the animation. You can also use getAnimatedValue() to get the exact value of the property at the current point in time.

In the example, we use the first of these methods to swap the heads and tails images when the animation reaches the two points where the coin should change sides (90 degrees and 270 degrees, or 25 percent and 75 percent of the animation duration). Because there is no guarantee that we will get called for every degree, we just change the image as soon as we have crossed the threshold. We also set a Boolean flag to avoid setting the image to the same value on each iteration afterward, which would slow performance unnecessarily.

ObjectAnimator also supports a more traditional AnimationListener for major animation events such as start, end, and repeat, if chaining multiple animations together is still necessary for the application.

■ **Tip**   On Android 4.4+, Animator also supports pause() and resume() methods to suspend a running animation without completely canceling it.

AnimatorSet

When you need to execute multiple animations, they can be collected in an AnimatorSet. Sets of animations can be played together at the same time, or sequenced to play one after the other. Defining collections of animations can get a bit verbose in Java code, so we will turn to the XML animation format for this example. Listing 1-19 defines a set of animations we will apply to our coin flip.

Listing 1-19. res/animator/flip.xml

```xml
<?xml version="1.0" encoding="utf-8"?>
<set xmlns:android="http://schemas.android.com/apk/res/android"
    android:ordering="together">

    <!-- Make a linear repeat for the coin rotations -->
    <objectAnimator
        android:propertyName="rotationX"
        android:duration="400"
        android:valueFrom="0"
        android:valueTo="360"
        android:valueType="floatType"
        android:repeatMode="restart"
        android:repeatCount="3"
        android:interpolator="@android:interpolator/linear"/>

    <!-- Add a lift to show the coin rising in the air -->
    <objectAnimator
        android:propertyName="translationY"
        android:duration="800"
        android:valueTo="-200"
        android:valueType="floatType"
        android:repeatMode="reverse"
        android:repeatCount="1" />
</set>
```

Here we have defined two animations to be played at the same time (via android:ordering="together") inside a <set>. The first animation mirrors what we saw previously, to rotate the coin image once. The animation is set to repeat three times, giving us three full rotations. The default interpolator for this image is an ease-in/ease-out timing curve, which looks off with a coin flip. To provide a consistent speed throughout, we apply the system's linear interpolator to the animation instead.

The second animation causes the coin to slide up in the view during the rotations. This gives more of an effect that the coin is being tossed into the air. Since the coin must also come back down, the animation is set to run once in reverse after it completes.

Listing 1-20 shows this new animation attached to the flipper activity.

Listing 1-20. Flipper Animation with XML AnimatorSet

```java
public class FlipperActivity extends Activity {

    private boolean mIsHeads;
    private AnimatorSet mFlipper;
    private Bitmap mHeadsImage, mTailsImage;
    private ImageView mFlipImage;

    @Override
    public void onCreate(Bundle savedInstanceState) {
        super.onCreate(savedInstanceState);
        setContentView(R.layout.main);

        mHeadsImage = BitmapFactory.decodeResource(getResources(), R.drawable.heads);
        mTailsImage = BitmapFactory.decodeResource(getResources(), R.drawable.tails);

        mFlipImage = (ImageView)findViewById(R.id.flip_image);
        mFlipImage.setImageResource(R.drawable.heads);
        mIsHeads = true;

        mFlipper = (AnimatorSet) AnimatorInflater.loadAnimator(this, R.animator.flip);
        mFlipper.setTarget(mFlipImage);

        ObjectAnimator flipAnimator = (ObjectAnimator) mFlipper.getChildAnimations().get(0);
        flipAnimator.addUpdateListener(new ValueAnimator.AnimatorUpdateListener() {
            @Override
            public void onAnimationUpdate(ValueAnimator animation) {
                if (animation.getAnimatedFraction() >= 0.25f && mIsHeads) {
                    mFlipImage.setImageBitmap(mTailsImage);
                    mIsHeads = false;
                }
                if (animation.getAnimatedFraction() >= 0.75f && !mIsHeads) {
                    mFlipImage.setImageBitmap(mHeadsImage);
                    mIsHeads = true;
                }
            }
        });
    }

    @Override
    public boolean onTouchEvent(MotionEvent event) {
        if(event.getAction() == MotionEvent.ACTION_DOWN) {
            mFlipper.start();
            return true;
        }
```

25

```
        return super.onTouchEvent(event);
    }
}
```

In this case, we've used an `AnimatorInflater` to construct the `AnimatorSet` object from our XML. The resulting animation must be attached to the appropriate target view via `setTarget()`, which is something `ObjectAnimator.ofFloat()` did for us implicitly. We also still need our `AnimatorUpdateListener` to determine when to switch from heads to tails, but that cannot be applied to a set object. Instead, we have to find the rotation animation inside the set using `getChildAnimations()` in order to attach the listener in the appropriate place.

Running this new example will give us a slightly more realistic coin-flip animation.

1-5. Animating Layout Changes

Problem

Your application dynamically adds or removes views from a layout, and you would like those changes to be animated.

Solution

(API Level 11)

Use the `LayoutTransition` object to customize how modifications to the view hierarchy in a given layout should be animated. In Android 3.0 and later, any `ViewGroup` can have changes to its layout animated by simply enabling the `android:animateLayoutChanges` flag in XML or by adding a `LayoutTransition` object in Java code.

There are five states during a layout transition that each `View` in the layout may incur. An application can set a custom animation for each one of the following states:

- `APPEARING`: An item that is appearing in the container

- `DISAPPEARING`: An item that is disappearing from the container

- `CHANGING`: An item that is changing because of a layout change, such as a resize, that doesn't involve views being added or removed

- `CHANGE_APPEARING`: An item changing because of another view appearing

- `CHANGE_DISAPPEARING`: An item changing because of another view disappearing

How It Works

Listings 1-21 and 1-22 illustrate an application that animates changes on a basic `LinearLayout`.

Listing 1-21. `res/layout/main.xml`

```xml
<?xml version="1.0" encoding="utf-8"?>
<LinearLayout
    xmlns:android="http://schemas.android.com/apk/res/android"
    android:layout_width="match_parent"
    android:layout_height="match_parent"
```

```
    android:gravity="center_horizontal"
    android:orientation="vertical"  >

    <Button
        android:id="@+id/button_add"
        android:layout_width="wrap_content"
        android:layout_height="wrap_content"
        android:onClick="onAddClick"
        android:text="Click To Add Item" />

    <LinearLayout
        android:id="@+id/verticalContainer"
        android:layout_width="match_parent"
        android:layout_height="match_parent"
        android:animateLayoutChanges="true"
        android:orientation="vertical" />

</LinearLayout>
```

Listing 1-22. Activity Adding and Removing Views

```java
public class MainActivity extends Activity {

    LinearLayout mContainer;

    @Override
    public void onCreate(Bundle savedInstanceState) {
        super.onCreate(savedInstanceState);
        setContentView(R.layout.main);
        mContainer =
            (LinearLayout) findViewById(R.id.verticalContainer);
    }

    //Add a new button that can remove itself
    public void onAddClick(View v) {
        Button button = new Button(this);
        button.setText("Click To Remove");
        button.setOnClickListener(new View.OnClickListener() {
            @Override
            public void onClick(View v) {
                mContainer.removeView(v);
            }
        });

        mContainer.addView(button, new LinearLayout.LayoutParams(
                LayoutParams.MATCH_PARENT,
                LayoutParams.WRAP_CONTENT));
    }
}
```

This simple example adds `Button` instances to a `LinearLayout` when the Add Item button is tapped. Each new button is outfitted with the ability to remove itself from the layout when it is tapped. In order to animate this process, all we need to do is set `android:animateLayoutChanges="true"` on the `LinearLayout`, and the framework does the rest. By default, a new button will fade in to its new location without disturbing the other views, and a removed button will fade out while the surrounding items slide in to fill the gap.

We can customize the transition animations individually to create custom effects. Take a look at Listing 1-23, where we add some custom transitions to the previous activity.

Listing 1-23. Activity Using Custom `LayoutTransition`

```
public class MainActivity extends Activity {

    LinearLayout mContainer;

    @Override
    public void onCreate(Bundle savedInstanceState) {
        super.onCreate(savedInstanceState);
        setContentView(R.layout.main);

        // Layout Changes Animation
        mContainer = (LinearLayout) findViewById(R.id.verticalContainer);
        LayoutTransition transition = new LayoutTransition();
        mContainer.setLayoutTransition(transition);

        // Override the default appear animation with a flip in
        Animator appearAnim = ObjectAnimator.ofFloat(null,
            "rotationY", 90f, 0f).setDuration(
            transition.getDuration(LayoutTransition.APPEARING));
        transition.setAnimator(LayoutTransition.APPEARING, appearAnim);

        // Override the default disappear animation with a flip out
        Animator disappearAnim = ObjectAnimator.ofFloat(null,
            "rotationX", 0f, 90f).setDuration(
            transition.getDuration(LayoutTransition.DISAPPEARING));
        transition.setAnimator(LayoutTransition.DISAPPEARING,
            disappearAnim);

        // Override the default change with a more animated slide
        // We animate several properties at once, so we create an
        // animation out of multiple PropertyValueHolder objects.
        // This animation slides the views in and temporarily shrinks
        // the view to half size.
        PropertyValuesHolder pvhSlide =
            PropertyValuesHolder.ofFloat("y", 0, 1);
        PropertyValuesHolder pvhScaleY =
            PropertyValuesHolder.ofFloat("scaleY", 1f, 0.5f, 1f);
        PropertyValuesHolder pvhScaleX =
            PropertyValuesHolder.ofFloat("scaleX", 1f, 0.5f, 1f);
        Animator changingAppearingAnim =
            ObjectAnimator.ofPropertyValuesHolder(
                this, pvhSlide, pvhScaleY, pvhScaleX);
```

```
        changingAppearingAnim.setDuration(
            transition.getDuration(LayoutTransition.CHANGE_DISAPPEARING)
        );
        transition.setAnimator(LayoutTransition.CHANGE_DISAPPEARING,
            changingAppearingAnim);
    }

    public void onAddClick(View v) {
        Button button = new Button(this);
        button.setText("Click To Remove");
        button.setOnClickListener(new View.OnClickListener() {
            @Override
            public void onClick(View v) {
                mContainer.removeView(v);
            }
        });

        mContainer.addView(button, new LinearLayout.LayoutParams(
            LayoutParams.MATCH_PARENT, LayoutParams.WRAP_CONTENT));
    }
}
```

In this example, we have modified the APPEARING, DISAPPEARING, and CHANGE_DISAPPEARING transition animations for our Button layout. The first two transitions affect the item being added or removed. When the Add Item button is clicked, the new item horizontally rotates into view. When any of the Remove buttons are clicked, that item will vertically rotate out of view. Both of these transitions are created by making a new ObjectAnimator for the custom rotation property, setting its duration to the default duration for that transition type, and attaching it to our LayoutTransition instance along with a key for the specific transition type. The final transition is a little more complicated; we need to create an animation that slides the surrounding views into their new location, but we also want to apply a scale animation during that time.

■ **Note**   When customizing a change transition, it is important to add a component that moves the location of the view, or you will likely see flickering as the view moves to create or fill the view gap.

In order to do this, we need to create an ObjectAnimator that operates on several properties, in the form of PropertyValuesHolder instances. Each property that will be part of the animation becomes a separate PropertyValuesHolder, and all of them are added to the animator by using the ofPropertyValuesHolder() factory method. This final transition will cause the remaining items below any removed button to slide up and shrink slightly as they move into place.

1-6. Implementing Situation-Specific Layouts

Problem

Your application must be universal, running on different screen sizes and orientations. You need to provide different layout resources for each of these instances.

Solution

(API Level 4)

Build multiple layout files, and use resource qualifiers to let Android pick what's appropriate. We will look at using resources to create layouts specific to different screen orientations and sizes. We will also explore using layout aliases to reduce duplication in cases where multiple configurations share the same layout.

How It Works

Orientation-Specific

In order to create different resources for an activity to use in portrait vs. landscape orientations, use the following qualifiers:

- `resource-land`
- `resource-port`

Using these qualifiers works for all resource types, but they are most commonly found with layouts. Therefore, instead of a `res/layout/` directory in the project, there would be a `res/layout-port/` and a `res/layout-land/` directory.

■ **Note** It is good practice to include a default resource directory without a qualifier. This gives Android something to fall back on if it is running on a device that doesn't match any of the specific criteria you list.

Size-Specific

There are also screen-size qualifiers (physical size, not to be confused with pixel density) that we can use to target large-screen devices such as tablets. In most cases, a single layout will suffice for all physical screen sizes of mobile phones. However, you may want to add more features to a tablet layout to assist in filling the noticeably larger screen real estate the user has to operate.

Prior to Android 3.2 (API Level 13), the following resource qualifiers were acceptable for physical screen sizes:

- `resource-small`: Screen measuring at least 426dp×320dp
- `resource-medium`: Screen measuring at least 470dp×320dp
- `resource-large`: Screen measuring at least 640dp×480dp
- `resource-xlarge`: Screen measuring at least 960dp×720dp

As larger screens became more common on both handset devices and tablets, it was apparent that the four generalized buckets weren't enough to avoid overlap in defining resources. In Android 3.2, a new system based on the screen's actual dimensions (in dp units) was introduced. With the new system, the following resource qualifiers are acceptable for physical screen sizes:

- Smallest Width (`resource-sw___dp`): Screen with at least the noted density-independent pixels in the shortest direction (meaning irrespective of orientation)
  - A 640dp×480dp screen always has a smallest width of 480dp.

- Width (`resource-w___dp`): Screen with at least the noted density-independent pixels in the current horizontal direction

  - A 640dp×480dp screen has a width of 640dp when in landscape and 480dp when in portrait.

- Height (`resource-h___dp`): Screen with at least the noted density-independent pixels in the current vertical direction

  - A 640dp×480dp screen has a height of 640dp when in portrait and 480dp when in landscape.

So, to include a tablet-only layout to a universal application, we could add a res/layout-large/ directory for older tablets and a res/layout-sw720dp/ directory for newer tablets as well.

Layout Aliases

There is one final concept to discuss when creating universal application UIs, and that is layout aliases. Often the same layout should be used for multiple device configurations, but chaining multiple resource qualifiers together (such as a smallest width qualifier and a traditional size qualifier) on the same resource directory can be problematic. This can often lead developers to create multiple copies of the same layout in different directories, which is a maintenance nightmare.

We can solve this problem with aliasing. By creating a single layout file in the default resource directory, we can create multiple aliases to that single file in resource-qualified values directories for each configuration that uses the layout. The following snippet illustrates an alias to the res/layout/main_tablet.xml file:

```
<resources>
    <item name="main" type="layout">@layout/main_tablet</item>
</resources>
```

The name attribute represents the aliased name, which is the resource this alias is meant to represent in the selected configuration. This alias links the main_tablet.xml file to be used when R.layout.main is requested in code. This code could be placed into res/values-xlarge/layout.xml and res/values-sw720dp/layout.xml, and both configurations would link to the same layout.

Tying It Together

Let's look at a quick example that puts this into practice. We'll define a single activity that loads a single layout resource in code. However, this layout will be defined differently in the resources to produce different results in portrait, in landscape, and on tablet devices. First, the activity is shown in Listing 1-24.

Listing 1-24. Simple Activity Loading One Layout

```
public class UniversalActivity extends Activity {

    @Override
    public void onCreate(Bundle savedInstanceState) {
        super.onCreate(savedInstanceState);
        setContentView(R.layout.main);
    }
}
```

We'll now define three separate layouts to use for this activity in different configurations. Listings 1-25 through 1-27 show layouts to be used for the default, landscape, and tablet configurations of the UI.

Listing 1-25. `res/layout/main.xml`

```xml
<?xml version="1.0" encoding="utf-8"?>
<!-- DEFAULT LAYOUT -->
<LinearLayout xmlns:android="http://schemas.android.com/apk/res/android"
    android:layout_width="match_parent"
    android:layout_height="match_parent"
    android:orientation="vertical" >
    <TextView
        android:layout_width="match_parent"
        android:layout_height="wrap_content"
        android:text="This is the default layout" />
    <Button
        android:layout_width="match_parent"
        android:layout_height="wrap_content"
        android:text="Button One" />
    <Button
        android:layout_width="match_parent"
        android:layout_height="wrap_content"
        android:text="Button Two" />
    <Button
        android:layout_width="match_parent"
        android:layout_height="wrap_content"
        android:text="Button Three" />
</LinearLayout>
```

Listing 1-26. `res/layout-land/main.xml`

```xml
<?xml version="1.0" encoding="utf-8"?>
<!-- LANDSCAPE LAYOUT -->
<LinearLayout
    xmlns:android="http://schemas.android.com/apk/res/android"
    android:layout_width="match_parent"
    android:layout_height="match_parent"
    android:orientation="vertical" >
    <TextView
        android:layout_width="wrap_content"
        android:layout_height="wrap_content"
        android:text="This is a horizontal layout for LANDSCAPE"
    />
    <!-- Three buttons to fill screen equally using weight -->
    <LinearLayout
        android:layout_width="match_parent"
        android:layout_height="wrap_content"
        android:orientation="horizontal" >
        <Button
            android:layout_width="0dp"
            android:layout_height="wrap_content"
            android:layout_weight="1"
            android:text="Button One" />
```

```
    <Button
        android:layout_width="0dp"
        android:layout_height="wrap_content"
        android:layout_weight="1"
        android:text="Button Two" />
    <Button
        android:layout_width="0dp"
        android:layout_height="wrap_content"
        android:layout_weight="1"
        android:text="Button Three" />
    </LinearLayout>
</LinearLayout>
```

Listing 1-27. res/layout/main_tablet.xml

```
<?xml version="1.0" encoding="utf-8"?>
<!-- TABLET LAYOUT -->
<LinearLayout xmlns:android="http://schemas.android.com/apk/res/android"
    android:layout_width="match_parent"
    android:layout_height="match_parent"
    android:orientation="horizontal" >
    <!-- Group of user buttons taking 25% of screen width -->
    <LinearLayout
        android:layout_width="0dp"
        android:layout_height="match_parent"
        android:layout_weight="1"
        android:orientation="vertical">
        <TextView
            android:layout_width="match_parent"
            android:layout_height="wrap_content"
            android:text="This is the layout for TABLETS" />
        <Button
            android:layout_width="match_parent"
            android:layout_height="wrap_content"
            android:text="Button One" />
        <Button
            android:layout_width="match_parent"
            android:layout_height="wrap_content"
            android:text="Button Two" />
        <Button
            android:layout_width="match_parent"
            android:layout_height="wrap_content"
            android:text="Button Three" />
        <Button
            android:layout_width="match_parent"
            android:layout_height="wrap_content"
            android:text="Button Four" />
    </LinearLayout>

    <!-- Extra view to show detail content -->
    <TextView
        android:layout_width="0dp"
```

```
        android:layout_height="match_parent"
        android:layout_weight="3"
        android:text="Detail View"
        android:background="#CCC" />
</LinearLayout>
```

One option would have been to create three files with the same name and to place them in qualified directories, such as res/layout-land for landscape and res/layout-large for tablet. That scheme works great if each layout file is used only once, but we will need to reuse each layout in multiple configurations, so in this example we will create qualified aliases to these three layouts. Listings 1-28 through 1-31 reveal how we link each layout to the correct configuration.

Listing 1-28. res/values-large-land/layout.xml

```
<?xml version="1.0" encoding="utf-8"?>
<resources
    xmlns:android="http://schemas.android.com/apk/res/android">
    <item name="main" type="layout">@layout/main_tablet</item>
</resources>
```

Listing 1-29. res/value-sw600dp-land/layout.xml

```
<?xml version="1.0" encoding="utf-8"?>
<resources
    xmlns:android="http://schemas.android.com/apk/res/android">
    <item name="main" type="layout">@layout/main_tablet</item>
</resources>
```

Listing 1-30. res/values-xlarge/layout.xml

```
<?xml version="1.0" encoding="utf-8"?>
<resources
    xmlns:android="http://schemas.android.com/apk/res/android">
    <item name="main" type="layout">@layout/main_tablet</item>
</resources>
```

Listing 1-31. res/values-sw720dp/layout.xml

```
<?xml version="1.0" encoding="utf-8"?>
<resources
    xmlns:android="http://schemas.android.com/apk/res/android">
    <item name="main" type="layout">@layout/main_tablet</item>
</resources>
```

We have defined configuration groups to accommodate three classes of devices: handsets, 7-inch tablet devices, and 10-inch tablet devices. Handset devices will load the default layout when in portrait mode, and the landscape layout when the device is rotated. Because this is the only configuration using these files, they are placed directly into the res/layout and res/layout-land directories, respectively.

The 7-inch tablet devices in the previous size scheme were typically defined as large screens, and in the new scheme they have a smallest width of around 600dp. In portrait mode, we have decided that our application should use the default layout, but in landscape mode we have significantly more real estate, so we load the tablet layout instead. To do this, we create qualified directories for the landscape orientation that match this device size class. Using both smallest-width and bucket-size qualifiers ensures we are compatible with older and newer tablets.

The 10-inch tablet devices in the previous size scheme were considered extra-large screens, and in the new scheme they have a smallest width of around 720dp. For these devices, the screen is large enough to use the tablet layout in both orientations, so we create qualified directories that call out only the screen size. Again, as with the smaller tablets, using both smallest-width and bucket-size qualifiers ensures we are compatible with all tablet versions.

In all cases in which the tablet layout was referenced, we had to create only one layout file to manage, thanks to the power of using aliases. Now when we run the application, you can see how Android selects the appropriate layout to match our configuration. Figure 1-3 shows default and landscape layouts on a handset device.

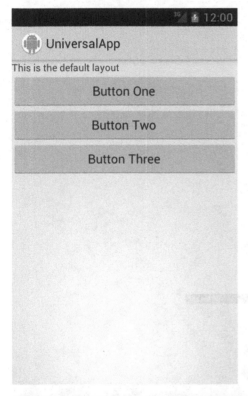

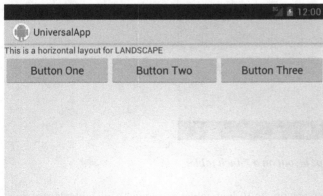

Figure 1-3. *Handset portrait and landscape layouts*

The same application on a 7-inch tablet device displays the default layout in portrait orientation, but we get the full tablet layout in landscape (see Figure 1-4).

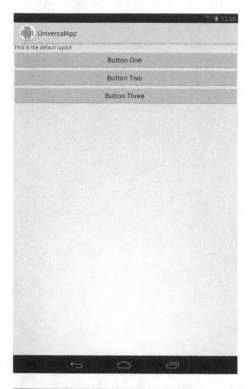

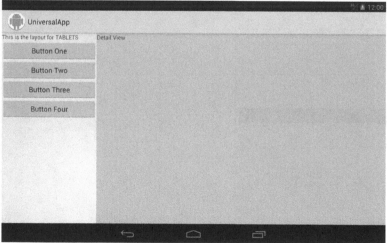

Figure 1-4. *Default portrait and tablet landscape layout on a 7-inch tablet*

Finally, in Figure 1-5 we can see the larger screen on the 10-inch tablet running the full tablet layout in both portrait and landscape orientations.

Figure 1-5. Full tablet layout in both orientations on a 10-inch tablet

With the extensive capabilities of the Android resource selection system, the difficulty of supporting different UI layouts optimized for each device type is greatly reduced.

1-7. Placing Text over Images

Problem

Your application will display a series of photos of different scenes and colors, and you want to display a text overlaid on the ImageView. The color of the text must be changed according to the colors of the photo.

Solution

(API Level 9)

By using the Palette API from the Support Library, you can extract the prominent colors from an image and set the appropriate color on an overlaid TextView. Figure 1-6 shows the result when using the Palette API to modify the TextView color when overlaid on an ImageView.

Figure 1-6. *Text properly colored while overlaid on images*

The code in Listing 1-32 shows how to use the Palette API to perform an asynchronous operation on a `Bitmap` and using the result to set the color on a `TextView`.

Listing 1-32. Method for Setting TextView Color Using the Palette API

```
private void setTextColorForImage(final TextView textView, Bitmap firstPhoto) {
    Palette.from(firstPhoto)
            .generate(new Palette.PaletteAsyncListener() {
                @Override
                public void onGenerated(Palette palette) {
                    Palette.Swatch swatch = palette.getVibrantSwatch();
                    if (swatch == null && palette.getSwatches().size() > 0) {
                        swatch = palette.getSwatches().get(0);
                    }

                    int titleTextColor = Color.WHITE;
                    if (swatch != null) {
                        titleTextColor = swatch.getTitleTextColor();
                        titleTextColor = ColorUtils.setAlphaComponent(titleTextColor, 255);
                    }

                    textView.setTextColor(titleTextColor);
                }
            });
}
```

In the preceding method we perform an asynchronous calculation using the Palette API to get the vibrant color we want to use for the `TextView`. The default behavior is that the color will be translucent, and if we want to disable that we need to use `ColorUtils.setAlphaComponent()` to make the color opaque. Also, the prceding code has two fallbacks; if the vibrant color isn't available we get the first swatch from the ones that are. If we still didn't get a swatch we default to the color white.

1-8. Making Extensible Collection Views

Problem

You have a large collection of data that you would like to present in a unique way, rather than in a vertically scrolling list, or styled in a way that `AdapterView` widgets don't easily support.

Solution

(API Level 9)

Build your solution on top of `RecyclerView` in the Android Support Library. `RecyclerView` is a widget that leverages the same view-recycling capabilities of `AdapterView` components to provide memory-efficient display of large data collections. However, unlike its companions in the core framework, `RecyclerView` is built on a more flexible model in which the placement of child view components is delegated to a `LayoutManager` instance. The library supports two built-in layout managers:

- LinearLayoutManager: Place child views vertically (top to bottom) or horizontally (left to right) in a list. The vertical layout behavior is similar to the framework ListView.

- GridLayoutManager: Place child views vertically (top to bottom) or horizontally (left to right) in a grid. The manager supports adding a row/column span value to stagger the child views within the grid. The vertical layout behavior with single-span items is similar to the framework GridView.

RecyclerView.ItemDecoration instances allow applications to support custom drawing operations above and underneath the child views, in addition to providing direct support for margins to add space between child views. This could be used to draw something as simple as grid lines and connector lines, or a more complex pattern or image within the content area.

RecyclerView.Adapter instances also include new methods for notifying the view of data set changes that better allow the widget to handle animating changes such as adding or removing elements—something that is much more difficult with AdapterView:

- notifyItemInserted(), notifyItemRemoved(), notifyItemChanged(): Indicate a single item in the associated data set that has been added, been removed, or changed position

- notifyItemRangeInserted(), notifyItemRangeRemoved(), notifyItemRangeChanged(): Indicate a position range of items that were modified in the associated data set

Since these methods accept specific item positions, RecyclerView can make intelligent decisions about how to animate the change. The standard notifyDataSetChanged() method is still supported, but it will not animate the changes.

■ **Important**   RecyclerView is available only as part of the Android Support Library; it is not part of the native SDK at any platform level. However, any application targeting API Level 9 or later can make use of the widget with the Support Library included. For more information on including the Support Library in your project, reference http://developer.android.com/tools/support-library/index.html.

How It Works

The following example uses four distinct LayoutManager instances to display the same item data using RecyclerView. Figure 1-7 shows the data displayed in a vertical and horizontal list.

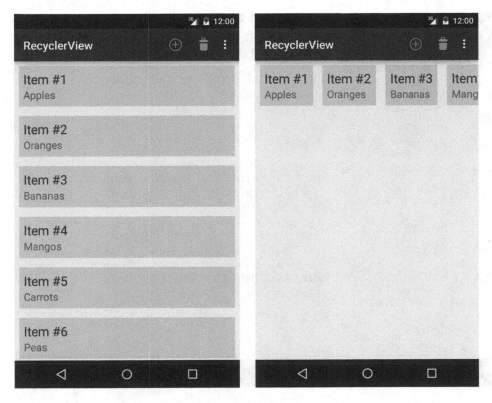

Figure 1-7. *Vertical and horizontal list collections*

Figure 1-8 shows the same data displayed in a staggered vertical and uniform horizontal grid.

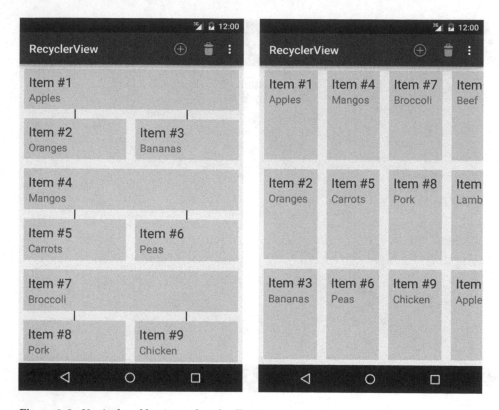

Figure 1-8. *Vertical and horizontal grid collections*

To begin, Listings 1-33 and 1-34 show the activity and options menu used to select the layout.

Listing 1-33. Activity Displaying Data with `RecyclerView`

```
public class SimpleRecyclerActivity extends ActionBarActivity implements
        SimpleItemAdapter.OnItemClickListener {

    private RecyclerView mRecyclerView;
    private SimpleItemAdapter mAdapter;

    /* Layout Managers */
    private LinearLayoutManager mHorizontalManager;
    private LinearLayoutManager mVerticalManager;
    private GridLayoutManager mVerticalGridManager;
    private GridLayoutManager mHorizontalGridManager;

    /* Decorations */
    private ConnectorDecoration mConnectors;

    @Override
    protected void onCreate(Bundle savedInstanceState) {
        super.onCreate(savedInstanceState);
```

```java
        mRecyclerView = new RecyclerView(this);

        mHorizontalManager = new LinearLayoutManager(this,
                LinearLayoutManager.HORIZONTAL, false);
        mVerticalManager = new LinearLayoutManager(this,
                LinearLayoutManager.VERTICAL, false);
        mVerticalGridManager = new GridLayoutManager(this,
                2, /* Number of grid columns */
                LinearLayoutManager.VERTICAL, /* Orient grid vertically */
                false);
        mHorizontalGridManager = new GridLayoutManager(this,
                3, /* Number of grid rows */
                LinearLayoutManager.HORIZONTAL, /* Orient grid horizontally */
                false);

        //Connector line decorations for vertical grid
        mConnectors = new ConnectorDecoration(this);

        //Stagger the vertical grid
        mVerticalGridManager.setSpanSizeLookup(new GridStaggerLookup());

        mAdapter = new SimpleItemAdapter(this);
        mAdapter.setOnItemClickListener(this);
        mRecyclerView.setAdapter(mAdapter);

        //Apply margins decoration to all collections
        mRecyclerView.addItemDecoration(new InsetDecoration(this));

        //Default to vertical layout
        selectLayoutManager(R.id.action_vertical);
        setContentView(mRecyclerView);
    }

    @Override
    public boolean onCreateOptionsMenu(Menu menu) {
        getMenuInflater().inflate(R.menu.layout_options, menu);
        return true;
    }

    @Override
    public boolean onOptionsItemSelected(MenuItem item) {
        return selectLayoutManager(item.getItemId());
    }

    private boolean selectLayoutManager(int id) {
        switch (id) {
            case R.id.action_vertical:
                mRecyclerView.setLayoutManager(mVerticalManager);
                mRecyclerView.removeItemDecoration(mConnectors);
                return true;
            case R.id.action_horizontal:
                mRecyclerView.setLayoutManager(mHorizontalManager);
```

```
                    mRecyclerView.removeItemDecoration(mConnectors);
                    return true;
                case R.id.action_grid_vertical:
                    mRecyclerView.setLayoutManager(mVerticalGridManager);
                    mRecyclerView.addItemDecoration(mConnectors);
                    return true;
                case R.id.action_grid_horizontal:
                    mRecyclerView.setLayoutManager(mHorizontalGridManager);
                    mRecyclerView.removeItemDecoration(mConnectors);
                    return true;
                case R.id.action_add_item:
                    //Insert a new item
                    mAdapter.insertItemAtIndex("Android Recipes", 1);
                    return true;
                case R.id.action_remove_item:
                    //Remove the first item
                    mAdapter.removeItemAtIndex(1);
                    return true;
                default:
                    return false;
            }
        }

    /** OnItemClickListener Methods */

    @Override
    public void onItemClick(SimpleItemAdapter.ItemHolder item, int position) {
        Toast.makeText(this, item.getSummary(), Toast.LENGTH_SHORT).show();
    }
}
```

Listing 1-34. res/menu/layout_options.xml

```xml
<menu xmlns:android="http://schemas.android.com/apk/res/android"
    xmlns:app="http://schemas.android.com/apk/res-auto">
    <item
        android:id="@+id/action_add_item"
        android:title="Add Item"
        android:icon="@android:drawable/ic_menu_add"
        app:showAsAction="ifRoom" />
    <item
        android:id="@+id/action_remove_item"
        android:title="Remove Item"
        android:icon="@android:drawable/ic_menu_delete"
        app:showAsAction="ifRoom" />
    <item
        android:id="@+id/action_vertical"
        android:title="Vertical List"
        app:showAsAction="never"/>
```

```
<item
    android:id="@+id/action_horizontal"
    android:title="Horizontal List"
    app:showAsAction="never"/>
<item
    android:id="@+id/action_grid_vertical"
    android:title="Vertical Grid"
    app:showAsAction="never"/>
<item
    android:id="@+id/action_grid_horizontal"
    android:title="Horizontal Grid"
    app:showAsAction="never"/>
</menu>
```

Our example uses the options menu to select the layout manager we should apply to `RecyclerView`. The `selectLayoutManager()` helper method is triggered on any change to pass the requested manager to `setLayoutManager()`. This will reload the existing data from the existing adapter, so we don't need to maintain multiple `RecyclerView` instances to change the layout on the fly.

As you can see, there isn't much code involved in leveraging the built-in layout managers. The example constructs two `LinearLayoutManager` instances, which take the orientation constant in their constructor (either `VERTICAL` or `HORIZONTAL`). The manager also supports (via the final Boolean parameter) reversing the layout so that the adapter's data is laid out with the last item first.

Similarly, we construct two `GridLayoutManager` instances for horizontal and vertical. This object takes an additional parameter, named `spanCount`, to represent the number of rows (for horizontal grids) or columns (for vertical grids) the layout should use. This parameter does not have anything to do with supporting stagger; we will see that shortly.

As with all collection views, we need to have an adapter to bind our data items to the view. You may have noticed that in the activity listing we have created a `SimpleItemAdapter` class. The implementation can be found in Listings 1-35 and 1-36.

Listing 1-35. `res/layout/collection_item.xml`

```xml
<?xml version="1.0" encoding="utf-8"?>
<LinearLayout xmlns:android="http://schemas.android.com/apk/res/android"
    android:layout_width="match_parent"
    android:layout_height="wrap_content"
    android:orientation="vertical"
    android:padding="8dp"
    android:background="#CCF">
    <TextView
        android:id="@+id/text_title"
        android:layout_width="wrap_content"
        android:layout_height="wrap_content"
        android:textAppearance="?android:textAppearanceLarge"/>
    <TextView
        android:id="@+id/text_summary"
        android:layout_width="wrap_content"
        android:layout_height="wrap_content"
        android:textAppearance="?android:textAppearanceMedium"/>
</LinearLayout>
```

Listing 1-36. Adapter Implementation for RecyclerView

```
public class SimpleItemAdapter extends RecyclerView.Adapter<SimpleItemAdapter.ItemHolder> {

    /*
     * Click handler interface. RecyclerView does not have
     * its own built in like AdapterViews do.
     */
    public interface OnItemClickListener {
        public void onItemClick(ItemHolder item, int position);
    }

    private static final String[] ITEMS = {
            "Apples", "Oranges", "Bananas", "Mangos",
            "Carrots", "Peas", "Broccoli",
            "Pork", "Chicken", "Beef", "Lamb"
    };
    private List<String> mItems;

    private OnItemClickListener mOnItemClickListener;
    private LayoutInflater mLayoutInflater;

    public SimpleItemAdapter(Context context) {
        mLayoutInflater = LayoutInflater.from(context);
        //Create static list of dummy items
        mItems = new ArrayList<String>();
        mItems.addAll(Arrays.asList(ITEMS));
        mItems.addAll(Arrays.asList(ITEMS));
    }

    @Override
    public ItemHolder onCreateViewHolder(ViewGroup parent, int viewType) {
        View itemView = mLayoutInflater.inflate(R.layout.collection_item, parent, false);

        return new ItemHolder(itemView, this);
    }

    @Override
    public void onBindViewHolder(ItemHolder holder, int position) {
        holder.setTitle("Item #"+(position+1));
        holder.setSummary(mItems.get(position));
    }

    @Override
    public int getItemCount() {
        return mItems.size();
    }

    public OnItemClickListener getOnItemClickListener() {
        return mOnItemClickListener;
    }
```

```java
public void setOnItemClickListener(OnItemClickListener listener) {
    mOnItemClickListener = listener;
}

/* Methods to manage modifying the data set */
public void insertItemAtIndex(String item, int position) {
    mItems.add(position, item);
    //Notify the view to trigger a change animation
    notifyItemInserted(position);
}

public void removeItemAtIndex(int position) {
    if (position >= mItems.size()) return;

    mItems.remove(position);
    //Notify the view to trigger a change animation
    notifyItemRemoved(position);
}

/* Required implementation of ViewHolder to wrap item view */
public static class ItemHolder extends RecyclerView.ViewHolder implements
        View.OnClickListener {
    private SimpleItemAdapter mParent;
    private TextView mTitleView, mSummaryView;

    public ItemHolder(View itemView, SimpleItemAdapter parent) {
        super(itemView);
        itemView.setOnClickListener(this);
        mParent = parent;

        mTitleView = (TextView) itemView.findViewById(R.id.text_title);
        mSummaryView = (TextView) itemView.findViewById(R.id.text_summary);
    }

    public void setTitle(CharSequence title) {
        mTitleView.setText(title);
    }

    public void setSummary(CharSequence summary) {
        mSummaryView.setText(summary);
    }

    public CharSequence getSummary() {
        return mSummaryView.getText();
    }

    @Override
    public void onClick(View v) {
        final OnItemClickListener listener = mParent.getOnItemClickListener();
```

```
        if (listener != null) {
            listener.onItemClick(this, getPosition());
        }
    }
  }
}
```

The RecyclerView.Adapter heavily enforces the view holder design pattern, to the point where it requires that the implementation return a subclass of the RecyclerView.ViewHolder type. This class is used internally as a storage location for metadata associated with the child item (such as its current position and stable ID). It is common for your implementation to also provide direct access to the view fields within it, to minimize repeated calls to findViewById(), which can be expensive since it traverses the entire view hierarchy to find the requested child.

RecyclerView.Adapter implements a similar pattern to CursorAdapter, in which the create and bind steps are separated via onCreateViewHolder() and onBindViewHolder(). The former method is called whenever a new view must be created from scratch, so we construct a new ItemHolder to return in this case. The latter method is called anytime the data at a certain position (in our case, just simple strings) needs to be attached to a new view; this view may be newly created or recycled. This is in contrast to an ArrayAdapter, which combines both into the single getView() method.

In our example, we also leverage the adapter to provide one additional feature from AdapterView that is not inherently supported in RecyclerView: item click listeners. In order to handle click events on child views with the least amount of reference swapping, we set each ViewHolder as the OnClickListener for the root item view. These events are then processed by the view holder and sent back to a common listener interface defined on the adapter. This is done so the view holder can add the position metadata into the final listener callback, something we've come to expect from the likes of AdapterView.OnItemClickListener.

Staggered Grid

In the activity example, the vertical grid layout manager was also outfitted with a SpanSizeLookup helper class, which allows us to generate the staggered effect seen in Figure 1-7. Listing 1-37 shows us the implementation.

Listing 1-37. Staggered Grid SpanSizeLookup

```
public class GridStaggerLookup extends GridLayoutManager.SpanSizeLookup {

    @Override
    public int getSpanSize(int position) {
        return (position % 3 == 0 ? 2 : 1);
    }
}
```

The getSpanSize() method lets us provide a lookup that tells the layout manager how many spans (rows or columns, depending on the layout orientation) the given position should take up. This example indicates that every third position should take up two columns, while all others should take only one.

Decorating Items

You may have noticed that we also added two ItemDecoration instances in the activity example. The first decoration, InsetDecoration, is applied to all the example layout managers to provide margins for each child. The second, ConnectorDecoration, is applied to only the vertical staggered grid, and is used to draw connecting lines between the major and minor grid items. These decorations are defined in Listings 1-38 through 1-39.

Listing 1-38. ItemDecoration Providing Inset Margins

```
public class InsetDecoration extends RecyclerView.ItemDecoration {
    private int mInsetMargin;

    public InsetDecoration(Context context) {
        super();
        mInsetMargin = context.getResources()
                .getDimensionPixelOffset(R.dimen.inset_margin);
    }

    @Override
    public void getItemOffsets(Rect outRect, View view, RecyclerView parent,
            RecyclerView.State state) {
        //Apply the calculated margin to all four edges of the child view
        outRect.set(mInsetMargin, mInsetMargin, mInsetMargin, mInsetMargin);
    }
}
```

Listing 1-39. ItemDecoration Providing Connecting Lines

```
public class ConnectorDecoration extends RecyclerView.ItemDecoration {

    private Paint mLinePaint;
    private int mLineLength;

    public ConnectorDecoration(Context context) {
        super();
        mLineLength = context.getResources()
                .getDimensionPixelOffset(R.dimen.inset_margin);
        int connectorStroke = context.getResources()
                .getDimensionPixelSize(R.dimen.connector_stroke);

        mLinePaint = new Paint(Paint.ANTI_ALIAS_FLAG);
        mLinePaint.setColor(Color.BLACK);
        mLinePaint.setStyle(Paint.Style.STROKE);
        mLinePaint.setStrokeWidth(connectorStroke);
    }

    @Override
    public void onDraw(Canvas c, RecyclerView parent, RecyclerView.State state) {
        final RecyclerView.LayoutManager manager = parent.getLayoutManager();

        for (int i=0; i < parent.getChildCount(); i++) {
            final View child = parent.getChildAt(i);
            boolean isLarge = parent.getChildViewHolder(child).getPosition() % 3 == 0;

            if (!isLarge) {
                final int childLeft = manager.getDecoratedLeft(child);
```

```
            final int childRight = manager.getDecoratedRight(child);
            final int childTop = manager.getDecoratedTop(child);
            final int x = childLeft + ((childRight - childLeft) / 2);

            c.drawLine(x, childTop - mLineLength,
                    x, childTop + mLineLength,
                    mLinePaint);
        }
    }
  }
}
```

Listing 1-40. `res/values/dimens.xml`

```
<?xml version="1.0" encoding="utf-8"?>
<resources>
    <dimen name="inset_margin">8dp</dimen>
    <dimen name="connector_stroke">2dp</dimen>
</resources>
```

There are three primary callbacks that an `ItemDecoration` can implement. The first is `getItemOffsets()`, which provides a `Rect` instance that the decorator can use to apply margins to the given child view. In our case we want all child views to have the same margins, so we set the same values in every call.

■ **Tip** Even though you don't get the position as a parameter in `getItemOffsets()`, you can still obtain it from the `RecyclerView` parameter via `getChildViewHolder(view).getPosition()` if you need it to determine how to apply margins.

The remaining callbacks, `onDraw()` and `onDrawOver()`, supply a `Canvas` that the decorator may use to draw additional content. These methods draw underneath and on top of, respectively, the child views. Our `ConnectorDecoration` uses `onDraw()` to render connecting lines between any visible children. To do this we iterate through the child views and draw a centered line above every child that is not taking up two spans (per our staggered lookup described previously).

These drawing callbacks will be invoked anytime the `RecyclerView` needs to redraw, such as while content is scrolling, so we must constantly read where the views are currently positioned in order to know where to draw the lines. Rather than asking the child view directly for its left/top/right/bottom coordinates, requesting this information from the layout manager via the `getDecoratedXxx()` methods is preferred. This is because other decorations (such as our `InsetDecoration`, for example) may modify the bounds of the view after the fact, and our drawing needs to take those into account.

Item Animations

Logic to support change animations for the adapter's data set are built into each layout manager. In order for the manager to appropriately determine how to animate the data set when it changes, we have to use the adapter update methods that are specific to `RecyclerView`, instead of the plain old `notifyDataSetChanged()`.

Modifying the adapter data is a two-step process: the data item must first be added or removed, and then the adapter must notify the view with the exact position where the change occurred. In the example, the add option triggers notifyItemInserted() and the remove option triggers notifyItemRemoved() on the adapter.

1-9. Customizing Empty Lists

Problem

You want to display a custom view when a RecyclerView has an empty data set.

Solution

(API Level 9)

Use the getItemViewType() on the Adapter to determine what type of View to show. Update getItemCount() to return 1 if the data set is empty. Make onCreateViewHolder() and onBindViewHolder() handle the different states using the viewType.

■ **Important**   Be sure to call the notify* methods correctly when the data set for your RecycleView changes.

How It Works

Here is how this would look with a TextView and a Button used as the empty view. First, a layout includes both views, shown in Listing 1-41.

Listing 1-41. res/layout/empty_item.xml

```xml
<?xml version="1.0" encoding="utf-8"?>
<LinearLayout
    xmlns:android="http://schemas.android.com/apk/res/android"
    android:layout_width="match_parent"
    android:layout_height="wrap_content"
    android:layout_margin="8dp"
    android:orientation="vertical">

    <TextView
        android:layout_width="match_parent"
        android:layout_height="wrap_content"
        android:text="No Items to Display"
        android:gravity="center"
        android:textSize="24sp" />

    <Button
        android:id="@+id/refresh_button"
        android:layout_width="match_parent"
        android:layout_height="wrap_content"
        android:text="Tap Here to Refresh" />

</LinearLayout>
```

Then, in the activity, create the Adapter and ViewHolder for the RecyclerView and implement the logic for empty state in the respective methods (see Listing 1-42).

Listing 1-42. Adapter Handling Both Empty and Non-empty Data Set

```
private class EmptyStateAdapter extends RecyclerView.Adapter<MyViewHolder> {
    private static final int SIMPLE_ITEM = 1;
    private static final int EMPTY_ITEM = 2;
    private int itemCount = 0;

    @Override
    public MyViewHolder onCreateViewHolder(ViewGroup parent, int viewType) {
        View itemView;
        switch (viewType) {
            case SIMPLE_ITEM:
                itemView = LayoutInflater.from(EmptyActivity.this)
                        .inflate(R.layout.simple_item, parent, false);
                return new MyViewHolder(itemView);
            case EMPTY_ITEM:
            default:
                itemView = LayoutInflater.from(EmptyActivity.this)
                        .inflate(R.layout.empty_item, parent, false);
                return new MyViewHolder(itemView);
        }
    }

    @Override
    public void onBindViewHolder(final MyViewHolder holder, int position) {
        switch (holder.getItemViewType()) {
            case SIMPLE_ITEM:
                holder.textView.setText("Item nr " + (position + 1) + ". Tap to remove.");
                holder.itemView.setOnClickListener(new View.OnClickListener() {
                    @Override
                    public void onClick(View v) {
                        int itemPosition = holder.getAdapterPosition();
                        itemCount--;
                        notifyItemRemoved(itemPosition);
                        if(itemCount == 0) {
                            notifyItemInserted(0);
                        }
                    }
                });
                break;
            case EMPTY_ITEM:
                holder.refreshButton.setOnClickListener(new View.OnClickListener() {
                    @Override
                    public void onClick(View v) {
                        notifyItemRemoved(0);
                        itemCount = 10;
                        notifyItemRangeInserted(0, 10);
                    }
                });
```

```
                break;
        }
    }

    @Override
    public int getItemViewType(int position) {
        return itemCount == 0 ? EMPTY_ITEM : SIMPLE_ITEM;
    }

    @Override
    public int getItemCount() {
        return itemCount == 0 ? 1 : itemCount;
    }
}
```

1-10. Using CardView in RecyclerView

Problem

Your application needs to use the CardView from the Material Design library when displaying items in a RecyclerView.

Solution

(API Level 7)

Add the CardView and RecyclerView support libraries to the project. In this example we will also use the PercentRelativeLayout from the percent layout support library to make the photo shown inside each card have a 16:9 aspect ratio. Create a custom XML layout for the list items that uses CardView as the root. You can use the custom attributes to configure the look and feel of the cards. Figure 1-9 shows a preview of a RecyclerView with CardView items.

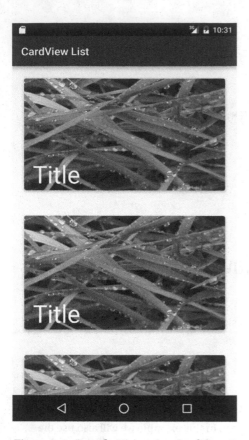

Figure 1-9. *RecyclerView using CardView items*

How It Works

Start with the layout for the cards using the `android.support.v7.widget.CardView` class. Add the XML namespace for the custom attributes (`xmlns:app="http://schemas.android.com/apk/res-auto"`) so you can configure the `CardView` through XML attributes.

The Material Design specification states that large images in these cases should either have a 1:1 or 16:9 aspect ratio. In this example we will go for 16:9, so we need some way of restricting the height of the `ImageView` based on the calculated width. You can either subclass `ImageView` and do the calculations in `onMeasure()` or you can use the `PercentRelativeLayout` as a container within the `CardView`, which already supports this, by setting `app:layout_widthPercent="100%"` and `app:layout_aspectRatio="178%"` (100 * 16/9 = 177,777). Position the other elements inside as you would do with a regular `RelativeLayout` (see Listings 1-43).

Listing 1-43. `res/layout/cardview_item.xml`

```xml
<?xml version="1.0" encoding="utf-8"?>
<android.support.v7.widget.CardView xmlns:android="http://schemas.android.com/apk/res/
android"
                                    xmlns:app="http://schemas.android.com/apk/res-auto"
                                    android:layout_width="match_parent"
                                    android:layout_height="wrap_content"
```

```
                              android:layout_margin="16dp"
                              app:cardBackgroundColor="@color/cardview_light_background"
                              app:cardCornerRadius="4dp"
                              app:cardElevation="4dp"
                              app:cardPreventCornerOverlap="true"
                              app:cardUseCompatPadding="true">

    <android.support.percent.PercentRelativeLayout
        android:layout_width="match_parent"
        android:layout_height="wrap_content">

        <ImageView
            android:id="@+id/image"
            android:layout_alignParentLeft="true"
            android:layout_alignParentStart="true"
            android:layout_alignParentTop="true"
            android:scaleType="centerCrop"
            app:layout_widthPercent="100%"
            app:layout_aspectRatio="178%"/>

        <TextView
            android:id="@+id/title"
            app:layout_widthPercent="100%"
            android:layout_height="wrap_content"
            android:layout_alignBottom="@id/image"
            android:layout_marginLeft="16dp"
            android:layout_marginStart="16dp"
            android:layout_marginRight="16dp"
            android:layout_marginEnd="16dp"
            android:textAppearance="@style/TextAppearance.AppCompat.Display2" />

        <TextView
            android:id="@+id/description"
            app:layout_widthPercent="100%"
            android:layout_height="wrap_content"
            android:layout_below="@id/title"
            android:layout_marginLeft="16dp"
            android:layout_marginStart="16dp"
            android:layout_marginRight="16dp"
            android:layout_marginEnd="16dp"
            android:layout_marginBottom="16dp"
            android:textAppearance="@style/TextAppearance.AppCompat.Medium"/>

    </android.support.percent.PercentRelativeLayout>

</android.support.v7.widget.CardView>
```

This layout will now be used in your adapter class to display items. As the TextView for the title is overlaid on top of the ImageView for the photo, we will use the Palette (see 1-8) to modify the color of the TextView for the title. The relevant onBindViewHolder() method will perform all of this (see Listing 1-44).

Listing 1-44. onBindViewHolder() for Our Adapter

```
@Override
public void onBindViewHolder(final CardViewHolder holder, int position) {
    String title = context.getString(R.string.title_text);
    holder.titleView.setText(title);
    holder.descriptionView.setText(R.string.ipsum_lorem);
    holder.imageView.setImageResource(R.drawable.photo);
    Palette.from(bitmap)
            .generate(new Palette.PaletteAsyncListener() {
                @Override
                public void onGenerated(Palette palette) {
                    Palette.Swatch swatch = palette.getDarkVibrantSwatch();
                    if (swatch == null) {
                        swatch = palette.getSwatches().get(0);
                    }
                    // Default to white color
                    int titleTextColor = Color.WHITE;
                    if (swatch != null) {
                        titleTextColor = swatch.getTitleTextColor();
                        titleTextColor = ColorUtils.setAlphaComponent(titleTextColor, 255);
                    }
                    holder.titleView.setTextColor(titleTextColor);
                }
            });
}
```

Expanding the CardView when clicked

Sometimes we want to hide some details in each list items until the user clicks on them. This saves valuable space on the screen and lets the user more quickly scroll through items and only focus on those that are relevant. In this case, we will keep the TextView for the description text hidden (View.GONE) until the user clicks on the item and then expand that item and display the text. Only one item at a time should be expanded, so we need to collapse (hide) the TextView again when needed. To solve this, we will simply keep a reference to the currently selected position in the adapter and call notifyItemChanged() when a certain item goes from hidden to visible (shown in Listing 1-45), or vice versa.

Listing 1-45. Updated onBindViewHolder() for Our Adapter

```
@Override
public void onBindViewHolder(final CardViewHolder holder, int position) {
    String title = context.getString(R.string.title_text);
    holder.titleView.setText(title);
    holder.descriptionView.setText(R.string.ipsum_lorem);
    if(selectedPosition == position) {
        holder.descriptionView.setVisibility(View.VISIBLE);
    } else {
        holder.descriptionView.setVisibility(View.GONE);
    }
    holder.imageView.setImageResource(R.drawable.photo);
```

```
holder.itemView.setOnClickListener(new View.OnClickListener() {
    @Override
    public void onClick(View v) {
        // Get the position for the item that was clicked
        int position = holder.getAdapterPosition();
        if(selectedPosition == position) {
            // If we clicked the same item a second time
            selectedPosition = -1;
            notifyItemChanged(position);
        } else {
            // If clicking on a different item, remember
            // notify the adapter about a change on the old
            // position as well.
            int oldSelectedPosition = selectedPosition;
            selectedPosition = position;
            if(oldSelectedPosition != -1) {
                notifyItemChanged(oldSelectedPosition);
            }
            notifyItemChanged(selectedPosition);
        }
    }
});

Palette.from(bitmap)
        .generate(new Palette.PaletteAsyncListener() {
            @Override
            public void onGenerated(Palette palette) {
                Palette.Swatch swatch = palette.getDarkVibrantSwatch();
                if (swatch == null) {
                    swatch = palette.getSwatches().get(0);
                }
                int titleTextColor = Color.WHITE;
                if (swatch != null) {
                    titleTextColor = swatch.getTitleTextColor();
                    titleTextColor = ColorUtils.setAlphaComponent(titleTextColor, 255);
                }
                holder.titleView.setTextColor(titleTextColor);
            }
        });
}
```

1-11. Making RecyclerView Section Headers

Problem

You want to create a list with multiple sections, each with a header at the top.

Solution

(API Level 9)

We can achieve this effect by building a custom list adapter that leverages multiple view type support. Adapters rely on getViewTypeCount() and getItemViewType() to determine how many kinds of views will be used as rows in the list. In most cases, when all rows are the same type, these methods are ignored. However, here we can use these callbacks to define a unique type for the header rows vs. the content rows.

How It Works

Figure 1-10 shows a preview of the example list with section headers.

Figure 1-10. *Sectioned list*

We begin by creating a SectionsAdapter that extends RecyclerView.Adapter. We add the method addSection(String section, String[] items) that lets us add the data we want to our list. The implementation for our adapter is shown in Listing 1-46.

Listing 1-46. The Class SectionsAdapter Implementing Our Adapter

```
private class SectionsAdapter extends RecyclerView.Adapter<RecyclerView.ViewHolder> {
    public static final int ITEM = 1;
    public static final int HEADER = 2;
    private List<Pair<String, String[]>> sections = new ArrayList<>();
```

```
public void addSection(String header, String[] items) {
    sections.add(Pair.create(header, items));
}

@Override
public RecyclerView.ViewHolder onCreateViewHolder(ViewGroup parent, int viewType) {
    RecyclerView.ViewHolder viewHolder = null;
    LayoutInflater inflater = LayoutInflater.from(SectionsActivity.this);
    switch (viewType) {
        case ITEM:
            viewHolder = new ItemHolder(inflater.inflate(R.layout.list_item, parent,
            false));
            break;
        case HEADER:
            viewHolder = new HeaderHolder(inflater.inflate(R.layout.list_header, parent,
            false));
            break;
    }
    return viewHolder;
}

@Override
public void onBindViewHolder(RecyclerView.ViewHolder holder, int position) {
    int steps = 0;
    for (int i = 0; i < sections.size(); i++) {
        Pair<String, String[]> section = sections.get(i);
        if(steps == position) {
            ((HeaderHolder) holder).textView.setText(section.first);
            return;
        }
        steps++;

        for (int j = 0; j < section.second.length; j++) {
            if(steps == position) {
                ((ItemHolder) holder).textView.setText(section.second[j]);
                return;
            }
            steps++;
        }
    }
}

@Override
public int getItemViewType(int position) {
    int steps = 0;
    for (int i = 0; i < sections.size(); i++) {
        Pair<String, String[]> section = sections.get(i);
        if(steps == position) {
            return HEADER;
        }
        steps++;
```

```
            for (int j = 0; j < section.second.length; j++) {
                if(steps == position) {
                    return ITEM;
                }
                steps++;
            }
        }
        return 0;
    }

    @Override
    public int getItemCount() {
        int count = 0;
        for (Pair<String, String[]> section : sections) {
            count += section.second.length + 1;
        }
        return count;
    }
}
```

This class uses two different `ViewHolder` classes: `ItemHolder` and `HeaderHolder` (see Listen 1-47). In this example, they are pretty much identical, but you can imagine how these can vary depending on your need.

Listing 1-47. View Holders for the Items and Headers

```
private class ItemHolder extends RecyclerView.ViewHolder {
    private final TextView textView;

    public ItemHolder(View itemView) {
        super(itemView);
        textView = (TextView) itemView.findViewById(android.R.id.text1);
    }
}

private class HeaderHolder extends RecyclerView.ViewHolder {
    private final TextView textView;

    public HeaderHolder(View itemView) {
        super(itemView);
        textView = (TextView) itemView.findViewById(android.R.id.text1);
    }
}
```

1-12. Creating Compound Controls

Problem

You need to create a custom widget that is a collection of existing elements.

Solution

(API Level 1)

Create a custom widget by extending a common ViewGroup and adding functionality. One of the simplest and most powerful ways to create custom or reusable UI elements is to create compound controls, leveraging the existing widgets provided by the Android SDK.

How It Works

ViewGroup (and its subclasses LinearLayout, RelativeLayout, and so on) gives you the tools to make this simple by assisting you with component placement, so you can be more concerned with the added functionality.

TextImageButton

Let's create an example by making a widget that the Android SDK does not have natively: a button containing either an image or text as its content. To do this we are going to create the TextImageButton class, which is an extension of FrameLayout. It will contain a TextView to handle text content as well as an ImageView for image content (see Listing 1-48).

Listing 1-48. Custom TextImageButton Widget

```
public class TextImageButton extends FrameLayout {

    private ImageView imageView;
    private TextView textView;

    /* Constructors */
    public TextImageButton(Context context) {
        this(context, null);
    }

    public TextImageButton(Context context, AttributeSet attrs) {
        this(context, attrs, 0);
    }

    public TextImageButton(Context context, AttributeSet attrs,
            int defaultStyle) {
        //Initialize the parent layout with the system's button style
        // This sets the clickable attributes and button background
        // to match the current theme.
        super(context, attrs, android.R.attr.buttonStyle);
        //Create the child views
        imageView = new ImageView(context, attrs, defaultStyle);
        textView = new TextView(context, attrs, defaultStyle);
        //Create LayoutParams for children to wrap content and center
        FrameLayout.LayoutParams params = new FrameLayout.LayoutParams(
                LayoutParams.WRAP_CONTENT,
                LayoutParams.WRAP_CONTENT,
                Gravity.CENTER);
```

```java
        //Add the views
        this.addView(imageView, params);
        this.addView(textView, params);

        //If an image is present, switch to image mode
        if(imageView.getDrawable() != null) {
            textView.setVisibility(View.GONE);
            imageView.setVisibility(View.VISIBLE);
        } else {
            textView.setVisibility(View.VISIBLE);
            imageView.setVisibility(View.GONE);
        }
    }

    /* Accessors */
    public void setText(CharSequence text) {
        //Switch to text
        textView.setVisibility(View.VISIBLE);
        imageView.setVisibility(View.GONE);
        //Apply text
        textView.setText(text);
    }

    public void setImageResource(int resId) {
        //Switch to image
        textView.setVisibility(View.GONE);
        imageView.setVisibility(View.VISIBLE);
        //Apply image
        imageView.setImageResource(resId);
    }

    public void setImageDrawable(Drawable drawable) {
        //Switch to image
        textView.setVisibility(View.GONE);
        imageView.setVisibility(View.VISIBLE);
        //Apply image
        imageView.setImageDrawable(drawable);
    }
}
```

All of the widgets in the SDK have at least two, and often three, constructors. The first constructor takes only Context as a parameter and is generally used to create a new view in code. The remaining two are used when a view is inflated from XML, where the attributes defined in the XML file are passed in as the AttributeSet parameter. Here we use Java's this() notation to drill the first two constructors down to the one that really does all the work. Building the custom control in this fashion ensures that we can still define this view in XML layouts. Without implementing the attributed constructors, this would not be possible.

In order to make the FrameLayout look like a standard button, we pass the attribute android.R.attr. buttonStyle to the constructor. This defines the style value that should be pulled from the current theme and applied to the view. This sets up the background to match other button instances, but it also makes the view clickable and focusable, as those flags are also part of the system's style. Whenever possible, you should load your custom widget's look and feel from the current theme to allow easy customization and consistency with the rest of your application.

The constructor also creates a TextView and ImageView, and it places them inside the layout. Each child constructor is passed the same set of attributes so that any XML attributes that were set specific to one or the other (such as text or image state) are properly read. The remaining code sets the default display mode (either text or image) based on the data that was passed in as attributes.

The accessor functions are added as a convenience to later switch the button contents. These functions are also tasked with switching between text and image mode if the content change warrants it.

Because this custom control is not in the android.view or android.widget packages, we must use the fully qualified name when it is used in an XML layout. Listings 1-49 and 1-50 show an example activity displaying the custom widget.

Listing 1-49. res/layout/main.xml

```xml
<?xml version="1.0" encoding="utf-8"?>
<LinearLayout
    xmlns:android="http://schemas.android.com/apk/res/android"
    android:layout_width="match_parent"
    android:layout_height="match_parent"
    android:orientation="vertical" >
    <com.examples.customwidgets.TextImageButton
        android:layout_width="match_parent"
        android:layout_height="wrap_content"
        android:text="Click Me!"
        android:textColor="#000" />
    <com.examples.customwidgets.TextImageButton
        android:layout_width="match_parent"
        android:layout_height="wrap_content"
        android:src="@drawable/ic_launcher" />
</LinearLayout>
```

Listing 1-50. Activity Using the New Custom Widget

```java
public class MyActivity extends Activity {


    @Override
    public void onCreate(Bundle savedInstanceState) {
        super.onCreate(savedInstanceState);
        setContentView(R.layout.main);
    }
}
```

Notice that we can still use traditional attributes to define properties such as the text or image to display. This is because we construct each item (the FrameLayout, TextView, and ImageView) with the attributed constructors, so each view sets the parameters it is interested in and ignores the rest.

If we define an activity to use this layout, the result looks like Figure 1-11.

Figure 1-11. `TextImageButton` *displayed in both text and image modes*

1-13. Customizing Transition Animations

Problem

Your application needs to customize the transition animations that happen when moving from one activity to another or between fragments.

Solution

(API Level 9)

To modify an activity transition, use the `overridePendingTransition()` API for a single occurrence, or declare custom animation values in your application's theme to make a more global change. To modify a fragment transition, use the `onCreateAnimation()` or `onCreateAnimator()` API methods.

How It Works

Activity

When customizing the transitions from one activity to another, there are four animations to consider: the enter and exit animation pair when a new activity opens, and the entry and exit animation pair when the current activity closes. Each animation is applied to one of the two activity elements involved in the transition. For example, when starting a new activity, the current activity will run the "open exit" animation and the new activity will run the "open enter" animation. Because these are run simultaneously, they should create somewhat of a complementary pair or they may look visually incorrect. Listings 1-51 through 1-54 illustrate four such animations.

Listing 1-51. `res/anim/activity_open_enter.xml`

```xml
<?xml version="1.0" encoding="utf-8"?>
<set xmlns:android="http://schemas.android.com/apk/res/android">
    <rotate
        android:fromDegrees="90" android:toDegrees="0"
        android:pivotX="0%" android:pivotY="0%"
        android:fillEnabled="true"
        android:fillBefore="true" android:fillAfter="true"
        android:duration="500"  />
    <alpha
        android:fromAlpha="0.0" android:toAlpha="1.0"
        android:fillEnabled="true"
        android:fillBefore="true" android:fillAfter="true"
        android:duration="500" />
</set>
```

Listing 1-52. `res/anim/activity_open_exit.xml`

```xml
<?xml version="1.0" encoding="utf-8"?>
<set xmlns:android="http://schemas.android.com/apk/res/android">
    <rotate
        android:fromDegrees="0" android:toDegrees="-90"
        android:pivotX="0%" android:pivotY="0%"
        android:fillEnabled="true"
        android:fillBefore="true" android:fillAfter="true"
        android:duration="500"  />
    <alpha
        android:fromAlpha="1.0" android:toAlpha="0.0"
        android:fillEnabled="true"
        android:fillBefore="true" android:fillAfter="true"
        android:duration="500" />
</set>
```

Listing 1-53. `res/anim/activity_close_enter.xml`

```xml
<?xml version="1.0" encoding="utf-8"?>
<set xmlns:android="http://schemas.android.com/apk/res/android">
    <rotate
        android:fromDegrees="-90" android:toDegrees="0"
        android:pivotX="0%p" android:pivotY="0%p"
        android:fillEnabled="true"
        android:fillBefore="true" android:fillAfter="true"
        android:duration="500"  />
    <alpha
        android:fromAlpha="0.0" android:toAlpha="1.0"
        android:fillEnabled="true"
```

```
        android:fillBefore="true" android:fillAfter="true"
        android:duration="500" />
</set>
```

Listing 1-54. `res/anim/activity_close_exit.xml`

```
<?xml version="1.0" encoding="utf-8"?>
<set xmlns:android="http://schemas.android.com/apk/res/android" >
    <rotate
        android:fromDegrees="0" android:toDegrees="90"
        android:pivotX="0%p" android:pivotY="0%p"
        android:fillEnabled="true"
        android:fillBefore="true" android:fillAfter="true"
        android:duration="500" />
    <alpha
        android:fromAlpha="1.0" android:toAlpha="0.0"
        android:fillEnabled="true"
        android:fillBefore="true" android:fillAfter="true"
        android:duration="500" />
</set>
```

What we have created are two "open" animations that rotate the old activity out and the new activity in, clockwise. The complementary "close" animations rotate the current activity out and the previous activity in, counterclockwise. Each animation also has with it a fade-out or fade-in effect to make the transition seem more smooth. To apply these custom animations at a specific moment, we can call the method `overridePendingTransition()` immediately after either `startActivity()` or `finish()`, like so:

```
//Start a new Activity with custom transition
Intent intent = new Intent(...);
startActivity(intent);
overridePendingTransition(R.anim.activity_open_enter,
        R.anim.activity_open_exit);

//Close the current Activity with custom transition
finish();
overridePendingTransition(R.anim.activity_close_enter,
        R.anim.activity_close_exit);
```

This is useful if you need to customize transitions in only a few places. But suppose you need to customize every activity transition in your application; calling this method everywhere would be quite a hassle. Instead, it would make more sense to customize the animations in your application's theme. Listing 1-55 illustrates a custom theme that overrides these transitions globally.

Listing 1-55. `res/values/styles.xml`

```
<resources>
    <style name="AppTheme" parent="android:Theme.Holo.Light">
        <item name="android:windowAnimationStyle">
            @style/ActivityAnimation</item>
    </style>
```

```
<style name="ActivityAnimation"
    parent="@android:style/Animation.Activity">
    <item name="android:activityOpenEnterAnimation">
        @anim/activity_open_enter</item>
    <item name="android:activityOpenExitAnimation">
        @anim/activity_open_exit</item>
    <item name="android:activityCloseEnterAnimation">
        @anim/activity_close_enter</item>
    <item name="android:activityCloseExitAnimation">
        @anim/activity_close_exit</item>
</style>

</resources>
```

By supplying a custom attribute for the `android:windowAnimationStyle` value of the theme, we can customize these transition animations. It is important to also refer back to the parent style in the framework because these four animations are not the only ones defined in this style, and you don't want to erase the other existing window animations inadvertently.

Support Fragments

Customizing the animations for fragment transitions is different, depending on whether you are using the Support Library. The variance exists because the native version uses the new `Animator` objects, which are not available in the Support Library version.

When using the Support Library, you can override the transition animations for a single `FragmentTransaction` by calling `setCustomAnimations()`. The version of this method that takes two parameters will set the animation for the add/replace/remove action, but it will not animate on popping the back stack. The version that takes four parameters will add custom animations for popping the back stack as well. Using the same `Animation` objects from our previous example, the following snippet shows how to add these animations to a `FragmentTransaction`:

```
FragmentTransaction ft = getSupportFragmentManager().beginTransaction();
    //Must be called first!
    ft.setCustomAnimations(R.anim.activity_open_enter,
            R.anim.activity_open_exit,
            R.anim.activity_close_enter,
            R.anim.activity_close_exit);
    ft.replace(R.id.container_fragment, fragment);
    ft.addToBackStack(null);
ft.commit();
```

■ **Important** `setCustomAnimations()` *must* be called before `add()`, `replace()`, or any other action method, or the animation will not run. It is good practice to simply call this method first in the transaction block.

If you would like the same animations to run for a certain fragment all the time, you may want to override the `onCreateAnimation()` method inside the fragment instead. Listing 1-56 reveals a fragment with its animations defined in this way.

Listing 1-56. Fragment with Custom Animations

```java
public class SupportFragment extends Fragment {

    @Override
    public View onCreateView(LayoutInflater inflater,
            ViewGroup container, Bundle savedInstanceState) {
        TextView tv = new TextView(getActivity());
        tv.setText("Fragment");
        tv.setBackgroundColor(Color.RED);
        return tv;
    }

    @Override
    public Animation onCreateAnimation(int transit, boolean enter,
            int nextAnim) {
        switch (transit) {
        case FragmentTransaction.TRANSIT_FRAGMENT_FADE:
            if (enter) {
                return AnimationUtils.loadAnimation(getActivity(),
                        android.R.anim.fade_in);
            } else {
                return AnimationUtils.loadAnimation(getActivity(),
                        android.R.anim.fade_out);
            }
        case FragmentTransaction.TRANSIT_FRAGMENT_CLOSE:
            if (enter) {
                return AnimationUtils.loadAnimation(getActivity(),
                        R.anim.activity_close_enter);
            } else {
                return AnimationUtils.loadAnimation(getActivity(),
                        R.anim.activity_close_exit);
            }
        case FragmentTransaction.TRANSIT_FRAGMENT_OPEN:
        default:
            if (enter) {
                return AnimationUtils.loadAnimation(getActivity(),
                        R.anim.activity_open_enter);
            } else {
                return AnimationUtils.loadAnimation(getActivity(),
                        R.anim.activity_open_exit);
            }
        }
    }
}
```

How the fragment animations behave has a lot to do with how the FragmentTransaction is set up. Various transition values can be attached to the transaction with setTransition(). If no call to setTransition() is made, the fragment cannot determine the difference between an open or close animation set, and the only data we have to determine which animation to run is whether this is an entry or exit.

To obtain the same behavior as we implemented previously with setCustomAnimations(), the transaction should be run with the transition set to TRANSIT_FRAGMENT_OPEN. This will call the initial transaction with this transition value, but it will call the action to pop the back stack with TRANSIT_FRAGMENT_CLOSE, allowing the fragment to provide a different animation in this case. The following snippet illustrates constructing a transaction in this way:

```
FragmentTransaction ft = getSupportFragmentManager().beginTransaction();
    //Set the transition value to trigger the correct animations
    ft.setTransition(FragmentTransaction.TRANSIT_FRAGMENT_OPEN);
    ft.replace(R.id.container_fragment, fragment);
    ft.addToBackStack(null);
ft.commit();
```

Fragments also have a third state that you won't find with activities, and it is defined by the TRANSIT_FRAGMENT_FADE transition value. This animation should occur when the transition is not part of a change, such as add or replace, but rather the fragment is just being hidden or shown. In our example we use the standard system-fade animations for this case.

Native Fragments

If your application is targeting API Level 11 or later, you do not need to use fragments from the Support Library, and in this case the custom animation code works slightly differently. The native fragment implementation uses the newer Animator object to create the transitions rather than the older Animation object.

This requires a few modifications to the code; first of all, we need to define all our XML animations with Animator instead. Listings 1-57 through 1-60 show this.

Listing 1-57. res/animator/fragment_exit.xml

```
<?xml version="1.0" encoding="utf-8"?>
<set xmlns:android="http://schemas.android.com/apk/res/android" >
    <objectAnimator
        android:valueFrom="0" android:valueTo="-90"
        android:valueType="floatType"
        android:propertyName="rotation"
        android:duration="500"/>
    <objectAnimator
        android:valueFrom="1.0" android:valueTo="0.0"
        android:valueType="floatType"
        android:propertyName="alpha"
        android:duration="500"/>
</set>
```

Listing 1-58. res/animator/fragment_enter.xml

```
<?xml version="1.0" encoding="utf-8"?>
<set xmlns:android="http://schemas.android.com/apk/res/android" >
    <objectAnimator
        android:valueFrom="90" android:valueTo="0"
        android:valueType="floatType"
        android:propertyName="rotation"
        android:duration="500"/>
```

```
    <objectAnimator
        android:valueFrom="0.0" android:valueTo="1.0"
        android:valueType="floatType"
        android:propertyName="alpha"
        android:duration="500"/>
</set>
```

Listing 1-59. `res/animator/fragment_pop_exit.xml`

```
<?xml version="1.0" encoding="utf-8"?>
<set xmlns:android="http://schemas.android.com/apk/res/android" >
    <objectAnimator
        android:valueFrom="0" android:valueTo="90"
        android:valueType="floatType"
        android:propertyName="rotation"
        android:duration="500"/>
    <objectAnimator
        android:valueFrom="1.0" android:valueTo="0.0"
        android:valueType="floatType"
        android:propertyName="alpha"
        android:duration="500"/>
</set>
```

Listing 1-60. `res/animator/fragment_pop_enter.xml`

```
<?xml version="1.0" encoding="utf-8"?>
<set xmlns:android="http://schemas.android.com/apk/res/android" >
    <objectAnimator
        android:valueFrom="-90" android:valueTo="0"
        android:valueType="floatType"
        android:propertyName="rotation"
        android:duration="500"/>
    <objectAnimator
        android:valueFrom="0.0" android:valueTo="1.0"
        android:valueType="floatType"
        android:propertyName="alpha"
        android:duration="500"/>
</set>
```

Apart from the slightly different syntax, these animations are almost identical to the versions we created previously. The only other difference is that these animations are set to pivot around the center of the view (the default behavior) rather than the top-left corner.

As before, we can customize a single transition directly on a `FragmentTransaction` with `setCustomAnimations()`; however, the newer version takes our `Animator` instances. The following snippet shows this with the newer API:

```
FragmentTransaction ft = getFragmentManager().beginTransaction();
    //Must be called first!
    ft.setCustomAnimations(R.animator.fragment_enter,
            R.animator.fragment_exit,
            R.animator.fragment_pop_enter,
```

```
                R.animator.fragment_pop_exit);
        ft.replace(R.id.container_fragment, fragment);
        ft.addToBackStack(null);
ft.commit();
```

If you prefer to set the same transitions to always run for a given subclass, we can customize the fragment as before. However, a native fragment will not have onCreateAnimation(), but rather an onCreateAnimator() method instead. Have a look at Listing 1-61, which redefines the fragment we created using the newer API.

Listing 1-61. Native Fragment with Custom Transitions

```
public class NativeFragment extends Fragment {

@Override
    public View onCreateView(LayoutInflater inflater,
            ViewGroup container, Bundle savedInstanceState) {
        TextView tv = new TextView(getActivity());
        tv.setText("Fragment");
        tv.setBackgroundColor(Color.BLUE);
        return tv;
    }

    @Override
    public Animator onCreateAnimator(int transit, boolean enter,
            int nextAnim) {
        switch (transit) {
        case FragmentTransaction.TRANSIT_FRAGMENT_FADE:
            if (enter) {
                return AnimatorInflater.loadAnimator(
                        getActivity(),
                        android.R.animator.fade_in);
            } else {
                return AnimatorInflater.loadAnimator(
                        getActivity(),
                        android.R.animator.fade_out);
            }
        case FragmentTransaction.TRANSIT_FRAGMENT_CLOSE:
            if (enter) {
                return AnimatorInflater.loadAnimator(
                        getActivity(),
                        R.animator.fragment_pop_enter);
            } else {
                return AnimatorInflater.loadAnimator(
                        getActivity(),
                        R.animator.fragment_pop_exit);
            }
```

```
        case FragmentTransaction.TRANSIT_FRAGMENT_OPEN:
        default:
            if (enter) {
                return AnimatorInflater.loadAnimator(
                        getActivity(),
                        R.animator.fragment_enter);
            } else {
                return AnimatorInflater.loadAnimator(
                        getActivity(),
                        R.animator.fragment_exit);
            }
        }
    }
}
```

Again, we are checking for the same transition values as in the support example; we are just returning Animator instances instead. Here is the same snippet of code to properly begin a transaction with the transition value set:

```
FragmentTransaction ft = getFragmentManager().beginTransaction();
    //Set the transition value to trigger the correct animations
    ft.setTransition(FragmentTransaction.TRANSIT_FRAGMENT_OPEN);
    ft.replace(R.id.container_fragment, fragment);
    ft.addToBackStack(null);
ft.commit();
```

The final method you can use to set these custom transitions globally for the entire application is to attach them to your application's theme. Listing 1-62 shows a custom theme with our fragment animations applied.

Listing 1-62. res/values/styles.xml

```xml
<resources>
    <style name="AppTheme" parent="android:Theme.Holo.Light">
        <item name="android:windowAnimationStyle">
            @style/FragmentAnimation</item>
    </style>

    <style name="FragmentAnimation"
        parent="@android:style/Animation.Activity">
        <item name="android:fragmentOpenEnterAnimation">
            @animator/fragment_enter</item>
        <item name="android:fragmentOpenExitAnimation">
            @animator/fragment_exit</item>
        <item name="android:fragmentCloseEnterAnimation">
            @animator/fragment_pop_enter</item>
        <item name="android:fragmentCloseExitAnimation">
            @animator/fragment_pop_exit</item>
        <item name="android:fragmentFadeEnterAnimation">
            @android:animator/fade_in</item>
```

```
        <item name="android:fragmentFadeExitAnimation">
            @android:animator/fade_out</item>
    </style>
</resources>
```

As you can see, the attributes for a theme's default fragment animations are part of the same windowAnimationStyle attribute. Therefore, when we customize them, we make sure to inherit from the same parent so as not to erase the other system defaults, such as activity transitions. You must still properly request the correct transition type in your FragmentTransaction to trigger the animation.

If you wanted to customize both the activity and fragment transitions in the theme, you could do so by putting them all together in the same custom style (see Listing 1-63).

Listing 1-63. res/values/styles.xml

```
<resources>
    <style name="AppTheme" parent="android:Theme.Holo.Light">
        <item name="android:windowAnimationStyle">
            @style/TransitionAnimation</item>
    </style>

    <style name="TransitionAnimation"
        parent="@android:style/Animation.Activity">
        <item name="android:activityOpenEnterAnimation">
            @anim/activity_open_enter</item>
        <item name="android:activityOpenExitAnimation">
            @anim/activity_open_exit</item>
        <item name="android:activityCloseEnterAnimation">
            @anim/activity_close_enter</item>
        <item name="android:activityCloseExitAnimation">
            @anim/activity_close_exit</item>
        <item name="android:fragmentOpenEnterAnimation">
            @animator/fragment_enter</item>
        <item name="android:fragmentOpenExitAnimation">
            @animator/fragment_exit</item>
        <item name="android:fragmentCloseEnterAnimation">
            @animator/fragment_pop_enter</item>
        <item name="android:fragmentCloseExitAnimation">
            @animator/fragment_pop_exit</item>
        <item name="android:fragmentFadeEnterAnimation">
            @android:animator/fade_in</item>
        <item name="android:fragmentFadeExitAnimation">
            @android:animator/fade_out</item>
    </style>
</resources>
```

■ **Caution**   Adding fragment transitions to the theme will work only for the native implementation. The Support Library cannot look for these attributes in a theme because they did not exist in earlier platform versions.

1-14. Creating View Transformations

Problem

Your application needs to dynamically transform how views look in order to add visual effects such as perspective.

Solution

(API Level 1)

The API for static transformations that is available on ViewGroup provides a simple method of applying visual effects such as rotation, scale, or alpha changes without resorting to animations. It can also be a convenient place to apply transforms that are easier to apply from the context of a parent view, such as a scale that varies with position.

Static transformations can be enabled on any ViewGroup by calling setStaticTranforma tionsEnabled(true) during initialization. With this enabled, the framework will regularly call getChildStaticTransformation for each child view to allow your application to apply the transform.

How It Works

Let's first take a look at an example in which the transformations are applied once and don't change (see Listing 1-64).

Listing 1-64. Custom Layout with Static Transformations

```
public class PerspectiveLayout extends LinearLayout {

    public PerspectiveLayout(Context context) {
        super(context);
        init();
    }

    public PerspectiveLayout(Context context, AttributeSet attrs) {
        super(context, attrs);
        init();
    }

    public PerspectiveLayout(Context context, AttributeSet attrs,
            int defStyle) {
        super(context, attrs, defStyle);
        init();
    }

    private void init() {
        // Enable static transformations so each child will
        // have getChildStaticTransformation() called.
        setStaticTransformationsEnabled(true);
    }
```

```
@Override
protected boolean getChildStaticTransformation(View child,
        Transformation t) {
    // Clear any existing transformation
    t.clear();

    if (getOrientation() == HORIZONTAL) {
        // Scale children based on distance from left edge
        float delta = 1.0f - ((float) child.getLeft() / getWidth());

        t.getMatrix().setScale(delta, delta, child.getWidth() / 2,
                child.getHeight() / 2);
    } else {
        // Scale children based on distance from top edge
        float delta = 1.0f - ((float) child.getTop() / getHeight());

        t.getMatrix().setScale(delta, delta, child.getWidth() / 2,
                child.getHeight() / 2);
        //Also apply a fade effect based on its location
        t.setAlpha(delta);
    }
    return true;
}
}
```

This example illustrates a custom LinearLayout that applies a scale transformation to each of its children, based on that child's location from the beginning edge of the view. The code in getChildStaticTransformation() calculates the scale factor to apply by figuring out the distance from the left or top edge as a percentage of the full parent size. The return value from this method notifies the framework when a transformation has been set. In any case where your application sets a custom transform, you must also return true to ensure that it gets attached to the view.

Most of the visual effects such as rotation or scale are actually applied to the Matrix of the Transformation. In our example, we adjust the scale of each child by calling getMatrix().setScale() and passing in the scale factor and the pivot point. The *pivot point* is the location about which the scale will take place; we set this to the midpoint of the view so that the scaled result is centered.

If the layout orientation is vertical, we also apply an alpha fade to the child view based on the same distance value, which is set directly on the Transformation with setAlpha(). See Listing 1-65 for an example layout that uses this view.

Listing 1-65. res/layout/main.xml

```
<?xml version="1.0" encoding="utf-8"?>
<LinearLayout
    xmlns:android="http://schemas.android.com/apk/res/android"
    android:layout_width="match_parent"
    android:layout_height="match_parent"
    android:orientation="vertical">
    <!-- Horizontal Custom Layout -->
    <com.examples.statictransforms.PerspectiveLayout
        android:layout_width="match_parent"
        android:layout_height="wrap_content"
        android:orientation="horizontal" >
```

```xml
        <ImageView
            android:layout_width="wrap_content"
            android:layout_height="wrap_content"
            android:src="@drawable/ic_launcher" />
        <ImageView
            android:layout_width="wrap_content"
            android:layout_height="wrap_content"
            android:src="@drawable/ic_launcher" />
        <ImageView
            android:layout_width="wrap_content"
            android:layout_height="wrap_content"
            android:src="@drawable/ic_launcher" />
        <ImageView
            android:layout_width="wrap_content"
            android:layout_height="wrap_content"
            android:src="@drawable/ic_launcher" />
    </com.examples.statictransforms.PerspectiveLayout>
    <!-- Vertical Custom Layout -->
    <com.examples.statictransforms.PerspectiveLayout
        android:layout_width="wrap_content"
        android:layout_height="match_parent"
        android:orientation="vertical" >
        <ImageView
            android:layout_width="wrap_content"
            android:layout_height="wrap_content"
            android:src="@drawable/ic_launcher" />
        <ImageView
            android:layout_width="wrap_content"
            android:layout_height="wrap_content"
            android:src="@drawable/ic_launcher" />
        <ImageView
            android:layout_width="wrap_content"
            android:layout_height="wrap_content"
            android:src="@drawable/ic_launcher" />
        <ImageView
            android:layout_width="wrap_content"
            android:layout_height="wrap_content"
            android:src="@drawable/ic_launcher" />
    </com.examples.statictransforms.PerspectiveLayout>
</LinearLayout>
```

Figure 1-12 shows the results of the example transformation.

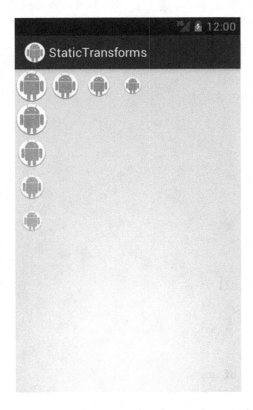

Figure 1-12. *Horizontal and vertical perspective layouts*

In the horizontal layout, as the views move to the right, they have a smaller scale factor applied to them. Similarly, the vertical views reduce in scale as they move down. Additionally, the vertical views begin to fade out because of the alpha change.

Now let's look at an example that provides a more dynamic change. Listing 1-66 shows a custom layout that is meant to be housed within a HorizontalScrollView. This layout uses static transformations to scale the child views as they scroll. The view in the center of the screen is always normal size, and each view scales down as it approaches the edge. This provides the effect that the views are coming closer as they move to the center and then moving away as they scroll to the edges.

Listing 1-66. Custom Perspective Scroll Content

```java
public class PerspectiveScrollContentView extends LinearLayout {

    /* Adjustable scale factor for child views */
    private static final float SCALE_FACTOR = 0.7f;
    /* Anchor point for transformation.  (0,0) is top left,
     * (1,1) is bottom right.  This is currently set for
     * the bottom middle (0.5, 1)
     */
    private static final float ANCHOR_X = 0.5f;
    private static final float ANCHOR_Y = 1.0f;
```

```java
public PerspectiveScrollContentView(Context context) {
    super(context);
    init();
}

public PerspectiveScrollContentView(Context context,
        AttributeSet attrs) {
    super(context, attrs);
    init();
}

public PerspectiveScrollContentView(Context context,
        AttributeSet attrs, int defStyle) {
    super(context, attrs, defStyle);
    init();
}

private void init() {
    // Enable static transformations so each child will
    // have getChildStaticTransformation() called.
    setStaticTransformationsEnabled(true);
}

/*
 * Utility method to calculate the current position of any
 * View in the screen's coordinates
 */
private int getViewCenter(View view) {
    int[] childCoords = new int[2];
    view.getLocationOnScreen(childCoords);
    int childCenter = childCoords[0] + (view.getWidth() / 2);

    return childCenter;
}

@Override
protected boolean getChildStaticTransformation(View child,
        Transformation t) {
    HorizontalScrollView scrollView = null;
    if (getParent() instanceof HorizontalScrollView) {
        scrollView = (HorizontalScrollView) getParent();
    }
    if (scrollView == null) {
        return false;
    }

    int childCenter = getViewCenter(child);
    int viewCenter = getViewCenter(scrollView);

    // Calculate the delta between this and our parent's center.
    // That will determine the scale factor applied.
```

```
        float delta = Math.min(1.0f, Math.abs(childCenter - viewCenter)
                / (float) viewCenter);
        //Set the minimum scale factor to 0.4
        float scale = Math.max(0.4f, 1.0f - (SCALE_FACTOR * delta));
        float xTrans = child.getWidth() * ANCHOR_X;
        float yTrans = child.getHeight() * ANCHOR_Y;

        //Clear any existing transformation
        t.clear();
        //Set the transformation for the child view
        t.getMatrix().setScale(scale, scale, xTrans, yTrans);

        return true;
    }
}
```

In this example, the custom layout calculates the transformation for each child based on its location with respect to the center of the parent HorizontalScrollView. As the user scrolls, each child's transformation will be recalculated so the views will grow and shrink dynamically as they move. The example sets the anchor point of the transformation at the bottom center of each child, which will create the effect of each view growing vertically by remaining centered horizontally. Listing 1-67 shows an example activity that puts this custom layout into practice.

Listing 1-67. Activity Using PerspectiveScrollContentView

```
public class ScrollActivity extends Activity {

    @Override
    protected void onCreate(Bundle savedInstanceState) {
        super.onCreate(savedInstanceState);

        HorizontalScrollView parentView = new HorizontalScrollView(this);
        PerspectiveScrollContentView contentView =
                new PerspectiveScrollContentView(this);

        //Disable hardware acceleration for this view, dynamic adjustment
        // of child transformations does not currently work in hardware.
        //You can also disable for the entire Activity or Application
        // with android:hardwareAccelerated="false" in the manifest,
        // but it is better to disable acceleration in as few places
        // as possible for best performance.
        if (Build.VERSION.SDK_INT >= Build.VERSION_CODES.HONEYCOMB) {
            contentView.setLayerType(View.LAYER_TYPE_SOFTWARE, null);
        }

        //Add a handful of images to scroll through
        for (int i = 0; i < 20; i++) {
            ImageView iv = new ImageView(this);
            iv.setImageResource(R.drawable.ic_launcher);
            contentView.addView(iv);
        }
```

```
        //Add the views to the display
        parentView.addView(contentView);
        setContentView(parentView);
    }
}
```

This example creates a scrolling view and attaches a custom `PerspectiveScrollContentView` with several images to scroll through. The code here isn't much to look at, but there is one very important piece worth mentioning. While static transformations in general are supported, dynamically updating the transform when the view is invalidated does not work with hardware acceleration in the current versions of the SDK. As a result, if your application has a target SDK of 11 or higher, or has enabled hardware acceleration in some other way, it will need to be disabled for this view.

This is done globally in the manifest via `android:hardwareAccelerated="false"` on any `<activity>` or the entire `<application>`, but we can also set it discretely in Java code for just this custom view by calling `setLayerType()` and setting it to `LAYER_TYPE_SOFTWARE`. If your application is targeting an SDK lower than this, hardware acceleration is disabled by default for compatibility reasons, even on newer devices, so this code may not be necessary.

1-15. Using Android Data Bindings

Problem

You want to use a data binding pattern to declaratively populate views from a custom class.

Solution

(API Level 9)

The Data Binding Library provides a simple way of using a declarative way of binding data to views. This is an addition to the Android SDK that compiles a variation of regular XML layouts and provides a way to bind data inside the XML elements.

How It Works

Using Data Bindings require a minor change in your `build.gradle` script for your application module, as shown in Listing 1-68.

Listing 1-68. Build.gradle with Data Binding Enabled

```
android {
    compileSdkVersion 24
    buildToolsVersion "24.0.2"

    dataBinding {
        enabled = true
    }

    defaultConfig {
        applicationId "com.androidrecipes.databinding"
        minSdkVersion 9
```

```
        targetSdkVersion 24
        versionCode 1
        versionName "1.0"
    }
}
```

All that is needed is to add the section dataBinding with the single property enable with the value true. By adding this code, the Android SDK will be able to interpret our special XML layout files and generate the appropriate Java code needed for data binding.

In this example, we will bind a simple data class representing an event to our XML layout. The code for our data class can be seen in Listing 1-69.

Listing 1-69. Event.java Used as the Data Class for Our Data Binding

```java
public class Event {
    private String title;
    private String description;
    private Date startTime;
    private Long duration;

    public Event(String title, String description, Date startTime, long duration) {
        this.description = description;
        this.duration = duration;
        this.startTime = startTime;
        this.title = title;
    }

    public String getDescription() {
        return description;
    }

    public void setDescription(String description) {
        this.description = description;
    }

    public Long getDuration() {
        return duration;
    }

    public void setDuration(Long duration) {
        this.duration = duration;
    }

    public Date getStartTime() {
        return startTime;
    }

    public void setStartTime(Date startTime) {
        this.startTime = startTime;
    }
```

```java
    public String getTitle() {
        return title;
    }

    public void setTitle(String title) {
        this.title = title;
    }
}
```

As you can see, this is a very simple Java class with four different fields. Two of the fields are regular Strings, but the other two are Date and Long. We will now create our XML layout where we bind an Event object to the view. The code for this can be seen in Listing 1-70.

Listing 1-70. layout/android_data_binding.xml

```xml
<layout xmlns:android="http://schemas.android.com/apk/res/android">

    <data>
        <variable
            name="event"
            type="com.androidrecipes.databinding.Event"/>
    </data>

    <LinearLayout
        android:id="@+id/activity_data_binding"
        android:layout_width="match_parent"
        android:layout_height="match_parent"
        android:orientation="vertical"
        android:paddingBottom="@dimen/activity_vertical_margin"
        android:paddingLeft="@dimen/activity_horizontal_margin"
        android:paddingRight="@dimen/activity_horizontal_margin"
        android:paddingTop="@dimen/activity_vertical_margin">

        <TextView
            android:layout_width="wrap_content"
            android:layout_height="wrap_content"
            android:layout_margin="@dimen/activity_vertical_margin"
            android:text="@{event.title}"
            android:textAppearance="@style/TextAppearance.AppCompat.Medium"/>

        <TextView
            android:layout_width="wrap_content"
            android:layout_height="wrap_content"
            android:layout_margin="@dimen/activity_vertical_margin"
            android:text="@{event.description}"
            android:textAppearance="@style/TextAppearance.AppCompat.Medium"/>

        <TextView
            android:layout_width="wrap_content"
            android:layout_height="wrap_content"
            android:layout_margin="@dimen/activity_vertical_margin"
            android:text="@{event.startTime}"
            android:textAppearance="@style/TextAppearance.AppCompat.Medium"/>
```

```
    <TextView
        android:layout_width="wrap_content"
        android:layout_height="wrap_content"
        android:layout_margin="@dimen/activity_vertical_margin"
        android:text="@{@string/duration_minutes(event.duration)}"
        android:textAppearance="@style/TextAppearance.AppCompat.Medium"/>

    </LinearLayout>
</layout>
```

The magic from Data Binding comes from using the @{} syntax in the appropriate attribute. In this case we only use the android:text attributes, but most of the view attributes support data binding and you can also create custom binding adapters for your own attributes.

An XML layout always starts with the element layout. The first child in the hierarchy is the data element, and this is where we specify the variables we want to use in our view. Each variable is defined with a variable element where you specify the name and the type (class name). As the data binding syntax has a limited support for Java code, you can also import additional classes here using an import element.

The first to TextViews will contain simple String objects, so all we need to do here is specify the variable (event) and the field (title and description). Note that this code supports the Java Beans syntax, so we don't need to write the method name of the getter but rather the Java Beans property name.

The third field (startTime) is of type Date, but we will still specify it in the same way as we do for the String fields. We will get back to this in a moment and show how a custom type can be set to a regular attribute that would otherwise be impossible.

The fourth field is a Long that represents the duration, in minutes, of the event. Here we see an example of referring to a parameterized string resource. This works for all other string and integer resources as well.

The final part is to tie it all together inside our Activity. The code for this can be seen in Listing 1-71.

Listing 1-71. DataBindingActivity.java

```java
public class DataBindingActivity extends AppCompatActivity {

    private ActivityDataBindingBinding mBinding;

    @Override
    protected void onCreate(Bundle savedInstanceState) {
        super.onCreate(savedInstanceState);

        mBinding = DataBindingUtil.setContentView(this, R.layout.activity_data_binding);

        Calendar calendar = Calendar.getInstance();
        calendar.set(2016, 9, 10, 11, 0);
        Date eventTime = calendar.getTime();
        Event event = new Event("First event", "This is the first event", eventTime, 120);

        mBinding.setEvent(event);
    }

    @BindingAdapter("android:text")
    public static void setTextFromDate(TextView textView, Date date) {
        DateFormat dateFormat = DateFormat.getDateInstance(DateFormat.MEDIUM);
        textView.setText(dateFormat.format(date));
    }
}
```

In our onCreate() method, where we usually call setContentView() with the ID of our XML layout, we now use the utility method DataBindingUtils.setContentView(). This method will return a data binding object. This class is generated by the data binding library and gets a name based on the filename for the XML layout, but with proper camel-case naming and the suffix Binding added (activity_data_binding -> ActivityDataBindingBinding). This class will contain all the methods you need to bind data to the View. As soon as you call setEvent() on this object, the Data Binding library will automatically bind all the data according to your declarative specification in the XML layout.

An example of a custom binding method is shown in the static method setTextFromDate() which is annotated with @BindingAdapter("android:text"). The Data Binding library will inspect all methods with this annotation and use those when appropriate. If you specify an adapter with the correct type (in this case a TextView where we want to set the content from a Date object), it will call this one instead. This makes it possible to bind complex object where you do custom formatting.

The Data binding library is a very convenient way of binding data to views in a declarative fashion. For a more complex object, you may want to extend your data object from the BaseObservable class, which makes it easier to update the view automatically when the data changes.

Summary

In this chapter, you saw many of the tools that the Android framework provides to display content to the user. We explored techniques for creating, customizing, and animating views. You were exposed to the many customizations available in the application window, including custom transition animations from one screen to another. Next, we looked at how you can leverage the resource qualifier system to create optimized view layouts for different screen configurations. Finally, we looked at a simple example of using the Data Binding library in Android to bind data objects to views in a declarative fashion.

In the next chapter, we will examine some more of the elements in the UI toolkit that are focused on interacting with the user and implementing common patterns for app navigation.

CHAPTER 2

■ ■ ■

User Interaction Recipes

Afz great-looking application design means nothing if users do not find the application easy to use and its features easy to discover. The user interaction patterns found in most Android applications are designed to engineer experiences that are consistent for users from one application to another. By maintaining consistency with the platform, users will feel familiar with your application's functionality even if they have never used it before. In this chapter, you'll investigate some of the common implementation patterns for presenting information to users and retrieving their input.

2-1. Leveraging the Action Bar

Problem

You want to use the latest action bar patterns in your application, while staying backward compatible with older devices, and you want to customize the look and feel to match your application's theme.

Solution

(API Level 9)

The action bar was introduced to the SDK in Android 3.0 (API Level 11), but was back-ported to earlier versions via AppCompatActivity within the AppCompat component of the Android Support Library. Using AppCompatActivity, along with the included styles and resources from AppCompat, we can put an action bar into any application targeting Android 2.3 and later.

■ **Important** AppCompatActivity is available only in the AppCompat Library, found as part of the Android Support Library; it is not part of the native SDK at any platform level. However, any application targeting API Level 9 or later can make use of the widget with the Support Library included. For more information on including the Support Library in your project, reference http://developer.android.com/tools/support-library/index.html.

The action bar is part of the top-level window décor, which means that application content will always be rendered below it. This makes tasks such as drawing content over the bar or animating the bar's location difficult. When this is necessary, use Toolbar in place of the traditional action bar. A toolbar is placed inside your layout, giving you control over where it sits. When given a toolbar reference, an activity will treat that view as its décor action bar instead.

© Dave Smith and Erik Hellman 2016
D. Smith and E. Hellman, *Android Recipes*, DOI 10.1007/978-1-4842-2259-1_2

■ **Note**   `Toolbar` was introduced in API Level 21, but is also available in AppCompat.

How It Works

Figure 2-1 shows an activity with a standard action bar in place.

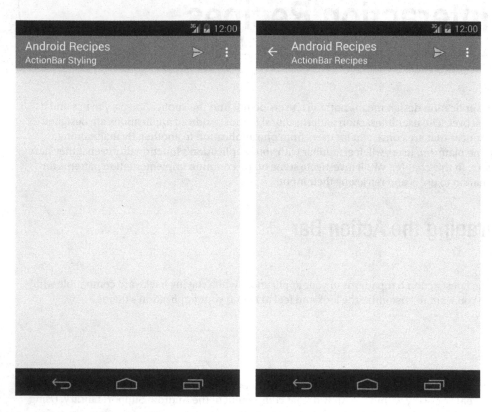

Figure 2-1. *Standard action bar (left) with Up button (right)*

To have an action bar added to our window décor, we simply need to apply a theme to the activity that enables it. All the default Holo and Material native themes include the action bar. This is true of AppCompat as well. Notice that the action bar supports a title and subtitle on the left, and a series of action buttons on the right. There is also an optional Up navigation button that we can enable to provide navigation similar to the Back button. We'll discuss that more in a later chapter.

You can see in Listings 2-1 through 2-3 how we attach an AppCompat theme to our activity to achieve the look from Figure 2-1.

Listing 2-1. Manifest with Action Bar Theme

```xml
<?xml version="1.0" encoding="utf-8"?>
<manifest xmlns:android="http://schemas.android.com/apk/res/android"
    package="com.androidrecipes.actionbar">
```

```
<application
    android:allowBackup="true"
    android:icon="@drawable/ic_launcher"
    android:label="@string/app_name">
    <activity
        android:name=".SupportActionActivity"
        android:label="@string/label_actionbar"
        android:theme="@style/AppTheme">
        <intent-filter>
            <action android:name="android.intent.action.MAIN" />
            <category android:name="android.intent.category.LAUNCHER" />
        </intent-filter>
    </activity>
</manifest>
```

Listing 2-2. res/values/styles.xml

```
<?xml version="1.0" encoding="utf-8"?>
<resources
    >
    <!-- Defines a "theme" that will apply to the entire application,
        or at least a handful of its activities -->
    <style name="AppTheme" parent="@style/Theme.AppCompat.Light.DarkActionBar">
        <!-- Provide decor theme colors -->
        <item name="colorPrimary">@color/primaryGreen</item>
        <item name="colorPrimaryDark">@color/darkGreen</item>
        <item name="colorAccent">@color/accentGreen</item>

    </style>
</resources>
```

Listing 2-3. res/values/colors.xml

```
<?xml version="1.0" encoding="utf-8"?>
<resources>
    <color name="primaryGreen">#259b24</color>
    <color name="darkGreen">#0a7e07</color>
    <color name="accentGreen">#d0f8ce</color>
</resources>
```

By applying Theme.AppCompat.Light.DarkActionBar to the activity, we enable the action bar to show up. We also use the standard color theming attributes to apply the green shade to the activity.

The icons on the right side are generated by the activity's options menu, which we see defined in Listing 2-4. We will talk about using options menus later in this chapter; this menu is simply added here for completeness. In Listing 2-5, we can see how the basic attributes of the action bar are set up in code.

Listing 2-4. res/menu/support.xml

```
<?xml version="1.0" encoding="utf-8"?>
<menu xmlns:android="http://schemas.android.com/apk/res/android"
    xmlns:app="http://schemas.android.com/apk/res-auto">
    <item android:id="@+id/action_send"
```

```
        android:title="@string/action_send"
        android:icon="@android:drawable/ic_menu_send"
        app:showAsAction="ifRoom" />
    <item android:id="@+id/action_settings"
        android:title="@string/action_settings"
        android:orderInCategory="100"
        app:showAsAction="never"/>
</menu>
```

Listing 2-5. Action Bar Setup

```java
public class SupportActionActivity extends AppCompatActivity {

    @Override
    protected void onCreate(Bundle savedInstanceState) {
        super.onCreate(savedInstanceState);

        ActionBar actionBar = getSupportActionBar();

        //Display home with the "up" arrow indicator
        actionBar.setDisplayHomeAsUpEnabled(true);
        //Set the title text
        actionBar.setTitle("Android Recipes");
        //Set the subtitle text
        actionBar.setSubtitle("ActionBar Recipes");
    }

    @Override
    public boolean onCreateOptionsMenu(Menu menu) {
        getMenuInflater().inflate(R.menu.support, menu);
        return true;
    }

    @Override
    public boolean onOptionsItemSelected(MenuItem item) {
        switch (item.getItemId()) {
            case android.R.id.home:
                Toast.makeText(this, "Home", Toast.LENGTH_SHORT).show();
            default:
                return super.onOptionsItemSelected(item);
        }
    }
}
```

We obtain a reference to the action bar in onCreate() via getSupportActionBar(), and commence setting its title attributes. The subtitle is optional, but if a title is not provided, the action bar will display the android:label string present in the manifest for the activity.

Using the setDisplayHomeAsUpEnabled() method, we can activate the optional Up arrow if we need it. This is used to provide navigation back to a parent activity, and is generally not enabled on top-level activities. The behavior of the Up button is defined by the application. User clicks on the button will trigger in the activity's onOptionsItemSelected() method with the android.R.id.home value.

Custom Views

Action bars also support a custom view. When set, this view is displayed between the title and the action buttons. If the view layout fills width, it will hide the title text. A custom view cannot overlap the Up button if it is enabled. Listing 2-6 shows us an activity enabling a custom view in the action bar.

Listing 2-6. Action Bar Custom View

```
public class SupportActionActivity extends AppCompatActivity {

    @Override
    protected void onCreate(Bundle savedInstanceState) {
        super.onCreate(savedInstanceState);

        ActionBar actionBar = getSupportActionBar();

        actionBar.setDisplayShowCustomEnabled(true);

        //Show an image in place of the titles
        ImageView imageView = new ImageView(this);
        imageView.setImageResource(R.drawable.ic_launcher);
        imageView.setScaleType(ImageView.ScaleType.CENTER);

        ActionBar.LayoutParams lp = new ActionBar.LayoutParams(
                ActionBar.LayoutParams.MATCH_PARENT,
                ActionBar.LayoutParams.MATCH_PARENT);

        actionBar.setCustomView(imageView, lp);
    }
}
```

This will place an image of the application's launcher icon into the action bar, where the title text was before—producing the result we see in Figure 2-2.

Figure 2-2. *Action bar custom view*

Toolbar

When your application design calls for more control over the placement and ordering of the action bar, Toolbar can step in to replace it. A toolbar replaces the standard action bar, so we have to apply a theme to the activity that removes the action bar from the window décor. Listings 2-7 and 2-8 start us off with the modified theme applied.

Listing 2-7. Toolbar Activity Manifest

```
<?xml version="1.0" encoding="utf-8"?>
<manifest xmlns:android="http://schemas.android.com/apk/res/android"
    package="com.androidrecipes.actionbar">

    <application
        android:allowBackup="true"
        android:icon="@drawable/ic_launcher"
        android:label="@string/app_name">
        <activity
            android:name=".SupportToolbarActivity"
            android:label="@string/label_toolbar"
            android:theme="@style/AppToolbarTheme">
            <intent-filter>
                <action android:name="android.intent.action.MAIN" />
```

```
            <category android:name="android.intent.category.LAUNCHER" />
        </intent-filter>
    </activity>
</application>

</manifest>
```

Listing 2-8. res/values/styles.xml

```
<?xml version="1.0" encoding="utf-8"?>
<resources>
    <!-- The toolbar will replace the standard action bar, so we
        need a theme that removes the action bar from the window decor -->
    <style name="AppToolbarTheme" parent="@style/Theme.AppCompat.Light.NoActionBar">
        <!-- Provide decor theme colors -->
        <item name="colorPrimary">@color/primaryGreen</item>
        <item name="colorPrimaryDark">@color/darkGreen</item>
        <item name="colorAccent">@color/accentGreen</item>

    </style>
</resources>
```

In this case, our styles theme inherits from Theme.AppCompat.Light.NoActionBar, which removes the default action bar in the window; we will be replacing it with our own instead. Listing 2-9 shows the layout for our toolbar activity.

Listing 2-9. res/layout/activity_toolbar.xml

```
<?xml version="1.0" encoding="utf-8"?>
<LinearLayout xmlns:android="http://schemas.android.com/apk/res/android"
    xmlns:app="http://schemas.android.com/apk/res-auto"
    android:orientation="vertical"
    android:layout_width="match_parent"
    android:layout_height="match_parent">
    <!-- Toolbar widget -->
    <android.support.v7.widget.Toolbar
        android:id="@+id/toolbar"
        android:layout_height="wrap_content"
        android:layout_width="match_parent"
        android:minHeight="?attr/actionBarSize"
        android:background="?attr/colorPrimary"
        app:theme="@style/ThemeOverlay.AppCompat.Dark.ActionBar"/>

    <!-- Remaining application view contents here -->

</LinearLayout>
```

The Toolbar widget must be somewhere in our view hierarchy, typically at the top of the view. Toolbars don't receive theme styling automatically, so we need to set the background color as the colorPrimary attribute from the current active theme. We must also pass a theme attribute to the toolbar. This attribute will be used by the toolbar to style the inflated resources it creates, such as the action buttons and pop-up list menus. ThemeOverlay.AppCompat.Dark.ActionBar is part of a special "overlay" class of themes that AppCompat supplies to apply only the elements necessary for an action bar or toolbar to style its internal components. Listing 2-10 shows the activity code to wire everything together.

Listing 2-10. Toolbar Activity

```java
public class SupportToolbarActivity extends AppCompatActivity {

    private Toolbar mToolbar;

    @Override
    protected void onCreate(Bundle savedInstanceState) {
        super.onCreate(savedInstanceState);
        setContentView(R.layout.activity_toolbar);

        //We have to tell the activity where the toolbar is
        mToolbar = (Toolbar) findViewById(R.id.toolbar);
        setSupportActionBar(mToolbar);
    }

    @Override
    protected void onPostCreate(Bundle savedInstanceState) {
        super.onPostCreate(savedInstanceState);

        /*
         * With a toolbar, we have to set the title text after
         * onCreate(), or the default label will overwrite our
         * settings.
         */

        //Set the title text
        mToolbar.setTitle("Android Recipes");
        //Set the subtitle text
        mToolbar.setSubtitle("Toolbar Recipes");
    }

    @Override
    public boolean onCreateOptionsMenu(Menu menu) {
        getMenuInflater().inflate(R.menu.support, menu);
        return true;
    }
}
```

Inside onCreate(), we are responsible for passing the activity a reference to Toolbar inside the layout via setSupportActionBar(). Despite the ambiguous naming, this method does require Toolbar as a parameter. This allows the activity to apply the options menu and other specific items to that view.

There is one modification we have to make to our previous example when using a toolbar. The activity implementation sets the title values of a toolbar instance after onCreate() is complete. This means that any title we set in onCreate() would get reset back to the manifest's android:label value. To counteract this behavior, we must make our changes in onPostCreate() for our changes to stick.

If you run this activity, it ought to look exactly like Figure 2-1. Later in this chapter, we'll see examples of how different UI paradigms favor the use of toolbars instead of top-level action bars.

2-2. Locking Activity Orientation

Problem

A certain activity in your application should not be allowed to rotate, or rotation requires more direct intervention from the application code.

Solution

(API Level 1)

Using static declarations in the `AndroidManifest.xml` file, you can modify each individual activity to lock into either portrait or landscape orientation. This can be applied only to the `<activity>` tag, so it cannot be done once for the entire application scope.

Simply add the `android:screenOrientation` attribute to the `<activity>` element, and the activity will always display in the specified orientation, regardless of how the device is positioned. The following attributes are the most commonly used:

- `portrait`: Screen oriented with the top of the device pointing up

- `landscape`: Screen oriented with the right side of the device pointing up

- `sensorPortrait`: Screen oriented in portrait mode (smallest width horizontal) with either short side of the device pointing up

- `sensorLandscape`: Screen oriented in landscape mode (smallest width vertical) with either long side of the device pointing up

- `behind`: Screen oriented to match the previous activity in the stack

For a complete list of available options, consult the SDK documentation for the `<activity>` manifest element.

How It Works

The example `AndroidManifest.xml` depicted in Listing 2-11 has three activities, each locked in a different orientation.

Listing 2-11. Manifest with one Activities Locked in portrait

```xml
<?xml version="1.0" encoding="utf-8"?>
<manifest
    xmlns:android="http://schemas.android.com/apk/res/android"
    package="com.examples.rotation"
    android:versionCode="1"
    android:versionName="1.0">
    <application android:icon="@drawable/icon"
        android:label="@string/app_name">
        <activity android:name=".MainActivity"
            android:label="@string/app_name"
            android:screenOrientation="portrait">
            <intent-filter>
                <action
                    android:name="android.intent.action.MAIN" />
```

```
            <category
                android:name="android.intent.category.LAUNCHER" />
        </intent-filter>
    </activity>

    <activity android:name=".ResultActivity"
        android:screenOrientation="landscape"/>

    <activity android:name=".UserEntryActivity"
        android:screenOrientation="sensorLandscape"/>
    </application>
</manifest>
```

2-3. Performing Dynamic Orientation Locking

Problem

Conditions exist during which the screen should not rotate, but the condition is temporary or dependent on user wishes.

Solution

(API Level 1)

Using the requested orientation mechanism in Android, an application can adjust the screen orientation used to display the activity, fixing it to a specific orientation or releasing it to the device to decide. This is accomplished through the use of the Activity.setRequestedOrientation() method, which takes an integer constant from the ActivityInfo.screenOrientation attribute grouping.

By default, the requested orientation is set to SCREEN_ORIENTATION_UNSPECIFIED, which allows the device to decide for itself which orientation should be used. This is a decision typically based on the physical orientation of the device. The current requested orientation can be retrieved at any time as well by using Activity.getRequestedOrientation().

How It Works

As an example, let's create a ToggleButton instance that controls whether to lock the current orientation, allowing the user to control at any point whether the activity should change orientation. Listing 2-12 depicts a simple layout in which a ToggleButton instance is defined.

Listing 2-12. res/layout/activity_lock.xml

```
<?xml version="1.0" encoding="utf-8"?>
<FrameLayout xmlns:android="http://schemas.android.com/apk/res/android"
    android:layout_width="match_parent"
    android:layout_height="match_parent">

    <ToggleButton
        android:id="@+id/toggleButton"
        android:layout_width="match_parent"
        android:layout_height="wrap_content"
```

```
        android:layout_gravity="center"
        android:textOff="Lock"
        android:textOn="LOCKED"
        />
</FrameLayout>
```

In the activity code, we will create a listener to the button's state that locks and releases the screen orientation based on its current value (see Listing 2-13).

Listing 2-13. Activity to Dynamically Lock/Unlock Screen Orientation

```
public class LockActivity extends Activity {

    protected void onCreate(Bundle savedInstanceState) {
        super.onCreate(savedInstanceState);
        setContentView(R.layout.activity_lock);

        //Get handle to the button resource
        ToggleButton toggle = (ToggleButton)findViewById(R.id.toggleButton);
        //Set the default state before adding the listener
        if( getRequestedOrientation() != ActivityInfo.SCREEN_ORIENTATION_UNSPECIFIED ) {
            toggle.setChecked(true);
        } else {
            toggle.setChecked(false);
        }
        //Attach the listener to the button
        toggle.setOnCheckedChangeListener(new OrientationLockListener());
    }

    private class OrientationLockListener implements CompoundButton.OnCheckedChangeListener {

        public void onCheckedChanged(CompoundButton buttonView, boolean isChecked) {
            int current = getResources().getConfiguration().orientation;
            if(isChecked) {
                switch(current) {
                case Configuration.ORIENTATION_LANDSCAPE:
                    setRequestedOrientation(ActivityInfo.SCREEN_ORIENTATION_LANDSCAPE);
                    break;
                case Configuration.ORIENTATION_PORTRAIT:
                    setRequestedOrientation(ActivityInfo.SCREEN_ORIENTATION_PORTRAIT);
                    break;
                default:
                    setRequestedOrientation(ActivityInfo.SCREEN_ORIENTATION_UNSPECIFIED);
                }
            } else {
                setRequestedOrientation(ActivityInfo.SCREEN_ORIENTATION_UNSPECIFIED);
            }
        }
    };

}
```

The code in the listener is the key ingredient to this recipe. If the user presses the button and it toggles to the ON state, the current orientation is read by storing the orientation parameter from Resources.getCo nfiguration(). The Configuration object and the requested orientation use different constants to map the states, so we switch on the current orientation and call setRequestedOrientation() with the appropriate constant.

■ **Note**   If an orientation is requested that is different from the current state, and your activity is in the foreground, the activity will change immediately to accommodate the request.

If the user presses the button and it toggles to the OFF state, we no longer want to lock the orientation, so setRequestedOrientation() is called with the SCREEN_ORIENTATION_UNSPECIFIED constant again to return control back to the device. This may also cause an immediate change to occur if the device's physical orientation differs from the activity orientation when the lock is removed.

■ **Note**   Setting a requested orientation does not keep the default activity life cycle from occurring. If a device configuration change occurs (the keyboard slides out or the device orientation changes), the activity will still be destroyed and re-created, so all rules about persisting activity state still apply.

2-4. Manually Handling Rotation

Problem

The default behavior destroying and re-creating an activity during rotation causes an unacceptable performance penalty in the application.

Without customization, Android will respond to configuration changes by finishing the current activity instance and creating a new one in its place, appropriate for the new configuration. This can cause undue performance penalties because the UI state must be saved and then completely rebuilt.

Solution

(API Level 1)

Utilize the android:configChanges manifest parameter to instruct Android that a certain activity will handle rotation events without assistance from the runtime. This reduces the amount of work required not only from Android, destroying and re-creating the activity instance, but also from your application. With the activity instance intact, the application does not have to necessarily spend time to save and restore the current state in order to maintain consistency for the user.

An activity that registers for one or more configuration changes will be notified via the Activity. onConfigurationChanged() callback method, where it can perform any necessary manual handling associated with the change.

There are three configuration change parameters the activity should register for in order to handle rotation completely: orientation, keyboardHidden, and screenSize.

- orientation: Registers the activity for any event when the device orientation changes

- screenSize: Registers the activity for events when the device screen aspect ratio changes. This also occurs on every orientation change.

- keyboardHidden: Registers the activity for the event when the user slides a physical keyboard in or out

While the latter may not be directly of interest, if you do not register for these events, Android will re-create your activity when they occur, which may subvert your efforts in handling rotation in the first place.

How It Works

These parameters are added to any <activity> element in AndroidManifest.xml, like so:

```
<activity android:name=".ManualRotationActivity"
    android:configChanges="orientation|keyboardHidden|screenSize" />
```

Multiple changes can be registered in the same assignment statement, using a pipe (|) character between them. Because these parameters cannot be applied to an <application> element, each individual activity must register in the manifest file.

Upon a configuration change, the registered activities receive a call to their onConfigurationChanged() method. Listings 2-14 through 2-16 define a simple activity definition that can be used to handle the callback received when the changes occur.

Listing 2-14. res/layout/activity_manual.xml

```
<?xml version="1.0" encoding="utf-8"?>
<LinearLayout xmlns:android="http://schemas.android.com/apk/res/android"
    android:orientation="vertical"
    android:layout_width="match_parent"
    android:layout_height="match_parent">
    <TextView
        android:layout_width="match_parent"
        android:layout_height="wrap_content"
        android:gravity="center_horizontal"
        android:text="Rotate the device, Activity will remain"/>
    <CheckBox
        android:id="@+id/override"
        android:layout_width="wrap_content"
        android:layout_height="wrap_content"
        android:text="Check to Force Reload View"/>
    <EditText
        android:id="@+id/text"
        android:layout_width="match_parent"
        android:layout_height="wrap_content"/>
</LinearLayout>
```

Listing 2-15. res/layout-land/activity_manual.xml

```xml
<?xml version="1.0" encoding="utf-8"?>
<LinearLayout xmlns:android="http://schemas.android.com/apk/res/android"
    android:orientation="horizontal"
    android:layout_width="match_parent"
    android:layout_height="match_parent">
    <CheckBox
        android:id="@+id/override"
        android:layout_width="wrap_content"
        android:layout_height="wrap_content"
        android:text="Check to Force Reload View"/>
    <EditText
        android:id="@+id/text"
        android:layout_width="match_parent"
        android:layout_height="wrap_content"/>
</LinearLayout>
```

Listing 2-16. Activity to Manage Rotation Manually

```java
public class ManualRotationActivity extends Activity {

    //References to view elements
    private EditText mEditText;
    private CheckBox mCheckBox;

    @Override
    protected void onCreate(Bundle savedInstanceState) {
        //Calling super is required
        super.onCreate(savedInstanceState);
        //Load view resources
        loadView();
    }

    @Override
    public void onConfigurationChanged(Configuration newConfig) {
        //Calling super is required
        super.onConfigurationChanged(newConfig);

        //Only reload the view under the new configuration
        // if the box is checked.
        if (mCheckBox.isChecked()) {
            final Bundle uiState = new Bundle();
            //Store important UI state
            saveState(uiState);
            //Reload the view
            loadView();
            //Restore UI state
            restoreState(uiState);
        }
    }
```

```
//Implement any code to persist the UI state
private void saveState(Bundle state) {
    state.putBoolean("checkbox", mCheckBox.isChecked());
    state.putString("text", mEditText.getText().toString());
}

//Restore any elements you saved before reloading
private void restoreState(Bundle state) {
    mCheckBox.setChecked(state.getBoolean("checkbox"));
    mEditText.setText(state.getString("text"));
}

//Set the content view and obtain view references
private void loadView() {
    setContentView(R.layout.activity_manual);

    //We have to reset our view references anytime a new layout is set
    mCheckBox = (CheckBox) findViewById(R.id.override);
    mEditText = (EditText) findViewById(R.id.text);
}
}
```

■ **Note**   Google does not recommend handling rotation in this fashion unless it is necessary for the application's performance. All configuration-specific resources must be loaded manually in response to each change event.

Google recommends allowing the default re-creation behavior on activity rotation unless the performance of your application requires circumventing it. Primarily, this is because you lose all assistance Android provides for loading alternative resources if you have them stored in resource-qualified directories (such as res/layout-land/ for landscape layouts).

In the example activity, all code dealing with the view layout is abstracted to a private method, loadView(), called from both onCreate() and onConfigurationChanged(). In this method, code such as setContentView() is placed to ensure that the appropriate layout is loaded to match the configuration.

Calling setContentView() will completely reload the view, so any UI state that is important still needs to be saved, without the assistance of life-cycle callbacks such as onSaveInstanceState() and onRestoreInstanceState(). We implement our own saveState() and restoreState() methods for this purpose.

To demonstrate the behavior of the activity without any view reloading code, we have wired up the check box in the layout to determine whether the view loads again on a configuration change. With this check box selected, the activity will still rotate and redraw its contents in the new orientation. However, the opposite configuration layout (landscape or portrait) will not be reloaded.

2-5. Creating Contextual Actions

Problem

You want to provide the user with multiple actions to take as a result of that user selecting a certain part of the UI.

Solution

(API Level 11)

For contextual actions related to a single item, use a PopupMenu to display them anchored to the related view. In the case where multiple items should be affected, enable an ActionMode in response to the user action.

■ **Note**   This example uses the AppCompat support library to achieve the best version compatibility. If your application is purely supporting later platforms versions, you can use the native APIs to achieve the same result. For more information on including the Support Library in your project, reference http://developer.android. com/tools/support-library/index.html.

How It Works

For this example, we will construct an activity that looks like Figure 2-3.

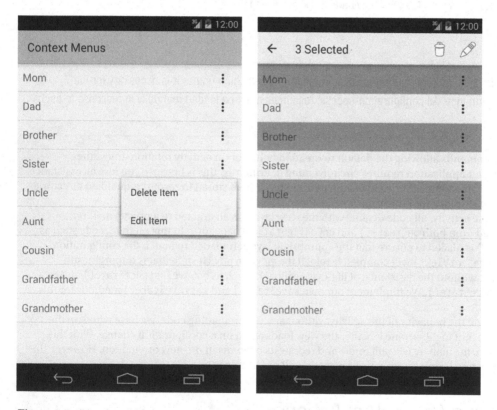

Figure 2-3. *List view with contextual actions (left) and action mode (right)*

The items in each list provide contextual actions via a pop-up list when the overflow button on the right side of the item view is tapped. When any of the items are long-pressed, the activity will activate an action mode that can apply the same action to multiple selected items.

Contextual Pop-ups

PopupMenu allows you to take an options menu resource and easily attach it as a small pop-up window to any view. First, we need to create an XML file in res/menu/ to define the menu itself; we'll call this one contextmenu.xml (see Listing 2-17).

Listing 2-17. res/menu/contextmenu.xml

```xml
<?xml version="1.0" encoding="utf-8"?>
<menu xmlns:android="http://schemas.android.com/apk/res/android">
    <item
        android:id="@+id/menu_delete"
        android:icon="@android:drawable/ic_menu_delete"
        android:title="Delete Item"
    />
    <item
        android:id="@+id/menu_edit"
        android:icon="@android:drawable/ic_menu_edit"
        android:title="Edit Item"
    />
</menu>
```

We will inflate this resource into a PopupMenu instance for each item housed inside the list. To better encapsulate the logic, Listings 2-18 and 2-19 define a custom ContextListItem class for the list row layouts.

Listing 2-18. Custom Row Item View

```java
public class ContextListItem extends LinearLayout implements
        PopupMenu.OnMenuItemClickListener,
        View.OnClickListener {

    private PopupMenu mPopupMenu;
    private TextView mTextView;

    public ContextListItem(Context context) {
        super(context);
    }

    public ContextListItem(Context context, AttributeSet attrs) {
        super(context, attrs);
    }

    public ContextListItem(Context context, AttributeSet attrs, int defStyleAttr) {
        super(context, attrs, defStyleAttr);
    }

    @Override
    protected void onFinishInflate() {
        super.onFinishInflate();
        mTextView = (TextView) findViewById(R.id.text);
```

```java
        //Attach click handlers
        View contextButton = findViewById(R.id.context);
        contextButton.setOnClickListener(this);

        //Create the context menu
        mPopupMenu = new PopupMenu(getContext(), contextButton);
        mPopupMenu.setOnMenuItemClickListener(this);
        mPopupMenu.inflate(R.menu.contextmenu);
    }

    @Override
    public void onClick(View v) {
        //Handle context button click to show the menu
        mPopupMenu.show();
    }

    @Override
    public boolean onMenuItemClick(MenuItem item) {
        String itemText = mTextView.getText().toString();

        switch (item.getItemId()) {
            case R.id.menu_edit:
                Toast.makeText(getContext(), "Edit "+itemText, Toast.LENGTH_SHORT).show();
                break;
            case R.id.menu_delete:
                Toast.makeText(getContext(), "Delete "+itemText, Toast.LENGTH_SHORT).show();
                break;
        }
        return true;
    }
}
```

Listing 2-19. res/layout/list_item.xml

```xml
<com.examples.popupmenus.ContextListItem
    xmlns:android="http://schemas.android.com/apk/res/android"
    android:orientation="horizontal"
    android:layout_width="match_parent"
    android:layout_height="?android:attr/listPreferredItemHeightSmall"
    android:paddingLeft="?android:attr/listPreferredItemPaddingLeft"
    android:paddingRight="?android:attr/listPreferredItemPaddingRight"
    android:background="?android:attr/activatedBackgroundIndicator" >
    <TextView
        android:id="@+id/text"
        android:layout_width="0dp"
        android:layout_height="wrap_content"
        android:layout_weight="1"
        android:textAppearance="?android:attr/textAppearanceListItemSmall"
        android:layout_gravity="center_vertical" />
```

```
<ImageView
    android:id="@+id/context"
    style="@style/Widget.AppCompat.Light.ActionButton.Overflow"
    android:layout_width="?android:attr/listPreferredItemHeightSmall"
    android:layout_height="match_parent"
    android:clickable="true"
    android:focusable="false"/>
</com.examples.popupmenus.ContextListItem>
```

ContextListItem is a LinearLayout containing a text item and image button for the context menu. For platform consistency, we apply the Widget.AppCompat.Light.ActionButton.Overflow style to the button so that it looks and behaves like a standard overflow menu button. When the view is created, we build a PopupMenu to display R.menu.contextmenu, and wire it up to show any time the overflow button is pressed. The row view is also set as the OnMenuItemClickLIstener in order to handle the selection of the appropriate option from the pop-up.

■ **Note**   Clickable items inside ListView need to have android:focusable set to false, or the ability to also click the top-level list item will be disabled.

To bind this view to the data in our list, we need to create a basic adapter that references our list item layout:

```
ArrayAdapter<String> adapter = new ArrayAdapter<String>(this,
        R.layout.list_item, R.id.text, ITEMS);
```

We'll see the full activity code that ties this in with the other features soon, but first let's look at implementing the multiple selection logic.

ActionMode

The ActionMode API solves a similar problem of allowing the user to take actions on specific items in your user interface; however, it does so in a slightly different way. Activating ActionMode overtakes the window's action bar with an overlay that includes menu options you provide and an extra option to exit ActionMode. It also allows you to select multiple items at once on which to apply a single action. Listing 2-20 illustrates this feature.

Listing 2-20. Activity Utilizing Contextual Actions

```
public class ActionActivity extends AppCompatActivity implements AbsListView.
MultiChoiceModeListener {


    private static final String[] ITEMS = {
            "Mom", "Dad", "Brother", "Sister", "Uncle", "Aunt",
            "Cousin", "Grandfather", "Grandmother"};

    private ListView mList;
```

```
protected void onCreate(Bundle savedInstanceState) {
    super.onCreate(savedInstanceState);
    //Register a button for context events
    mList = new ListView(this);
    ArrayAdapter<String> adapter = new ArrayAdapter<String>(this,
            R.layout.list_item, R.id.text, ITEMS);
    mList.setAdapter(adapter);
    mList.setChoiceMode(ListView.CHOICE_MODE_MULTIPLE_MODAL);
    mList.setMultiChoiceModeListener(this);

    setContentView(mList, new ViewGroup.LayoutParams(
            ViewGroup.LayoutParams.MATCH_PARENT,
            ViewGroup.LayoutParams.MATCH_PARENT));
}

@Override
public boolean onPrepareActionMode(ActionMode mode, Menu menu) {
    //You can do extra work here to update the menu if the
    // ActionMode is ever invalidated
    return true;
}

@Override
public void onDestroyActionMode(ActionMode mode) {
    //This is called when the action mode has ben exited
}

@Override
public boolean onCreateActionMode(ActionMode mode, Menu menu) {
    MenuInflater inflater = mode.getMenuInflater();
    inflater.inflate(R.menu.contextmenu, menu);
    return true;
}

@Override
public boolean onActionItemClicked(ActionMode mode, MenuItem item) {
    SparseBooleanArray items = mList.getCheckedItemPositions();
    //Switch on the item's ID to find the action the user selected
    switch(item.getItemId()) {
    case R.id.menu_delete:
        //Perform delete actions
        break;
    case R.id.menu_edit:
        //Perform edit actions
        break;
    default:
        return false;
    }
    return true;
}

@Override
```

```
    public void onItemCheckedStateChanged(ActionMode mode, int position,
            long id, boolean checked) {
        int count = mList.getCheckedItemCount();
        mode.setTitle(String.format("%d Selected", count));
    }
}
```

To use our ListView to activate a multiple selection ActionMode, we set its choiceMode attribute to CHOICE_MODE_MULTIPLE_MODAL. This is different from the traditional CHOICE_MODE_MULTIPLE, which will provide selection widgets on each list item to make the selection. The modal flag applies this selection mode only while an ActionMode is active.

A series of callbacks are required to implement an ActionMode that are not built directly into an activity like the ContextMenu. We need to implement the ActionMode.Callback interface to respond to the events of creating the menu and selecting options. ListView has a special interface called MultiChoiceModeListener, a subinterface of ActionMode.Callback, which we implement in the example.

In onCreateActionMode(), we respond similarly to onCreateContextMenu(), just inflating our menu options for the overlay to display. Your menu does not need to contain icons; ActionMode can display the item names instead. The onItemCheckedStateChanged() method is where we will get feedback for each item selection. Here, we use that change to update the title of ActionMode to display the number of items that are currently selected.

The onActionItemClicked() method will be called when the user has finished making selections and taps an option item. Because there are multiple items to work on, we go back to the list to get all the items selected with getCheckedItemPositions() so we can apply the selected operation.

2-6. Displaying a User Dialog Box

Problem

You need to display a simple pop-up dialog box to the user to either notify of an event or present a list of selections.

Solution

(API Level 1)

AlertDialog is the most efficient method of displaying important modal information to your user quickly. The content it displays is easy to customize, and the framework provides a convenient AlertDialog. Builder class to construct a pop-up quickly.

How It Works

When you use AlertDialog.Builder, you can construct a similar alert dialog box but with some additional options. AlertDialog is a versatile class for creating simple pop-ups to get feedback from the user. With AlertDialog.Builder, a single or multichoice list, buttons, and a message string can all be easily added into one compact widget.

To illustrate this, let's create the same pop-up selection as before by using AlertDialog. This time, we will add a Cancel button to the bottom of the options list (see Listing 2-21).

Listing 2-21. Action Menu Using AlertDialog

```java
public class DialogActivity extends Activity implements
        DialogInterface.OnClickListener,
        View.OnClickListener {

    private static final String[] ZONES = {
            "Pacific Time", "Mountain Time",
            "Central Time", "Eastern Time",
            "Atlantic Time"};

    Button mButton;
    AlertDialog mActions;

    @Override
    protected void onCreate(Bundle savedInstanceState) {
        super.onCreate(savedInstanceState);

        mButton = new Button(this);
        mButton.setText("Click for Time Zones");
        mButton.setOnClickListener(this);

        AlertDialog.Builder builder =
                new AlertDialog.Builder(this);
        builder.setTitle("Select Time Zone");
        builder.setItems(ZONES, this);
        //Cancel action does nothing but dismiss, we could
        // add another listener here to do something extra
        // when the user hits the Cancel button
        builder.setNegativeButton("Cancel", null);
        mActions = builder.create();

        setContentView(mButton);
    }

    //List selection action handled here
    @Override
    public void onClick(DialogInterface dialog, int which) {
        String selected = ZONES[which];
        mButton.setText(selected);
    }

    //Button action handled here (pop up the dialog)
    @Override
    public void onClick(View v) {
        mActions.show();
    }
}
```

In this example, we create a new AlertDialog.Builder instance and use its convenience methods to add the following items:

- A title, using `setTitle()`

- The selectable list of options, using `setItems()` with an array of strings (also works with array resources)

- A Cancel button, using `setNegativeButton()`

The listener that we attach to the list items returns which list item was selected as a zero-based index into the array we supplied, so we use that information to update the text of the button with the user's selection. We pass in `null` for the Cancel button's listener, because in this instance we just want Cancel to dismiss the dialog. If there is some important work to be done upon pressing Cancel, another listener could be passed in to the `setNegativeButton()` method.

The builder provides several other options for you to set the content of the dialog to something other than a selectable list:

- `setMessage()` applies a simple text message as the body content.

- `setSingleChoiceItems()` and `setMultiChoiceItems()` create a list similar to this example but with selection modes applied so that the items will appear as being selected.

- `setView()` applies any arbitrary custom view as the dialog's content.

The resulting application looks like Figure 2-4 when the button is pressed.

Figure 2-4. *Alert dialog box with items list*

Custom List Items

AlertDialog.Builder allows for a custom ListAdapter to be passed in as the source of the list items the dialog box should display. This means we can create custom row layouts to display more-detailed information to the user. In Listings 2-22 and 2-23, we enhance the previous example by using a custom row layout to display extra data for each item.

Listing 2-22. res/layout/list_item.xml

```xml
<?xml version="1.0" encoding="utf-8"?>
<RelativeLayout
    xmlns:android="http://schemas.android.com/apk/res/android"
    android:layout_width="match_parent"
    android:layout_height="wrap_content"
    android:paddingLeft="10dp"
    android:paddingRight="10dp"
    android:minHeight="?android:attr/listPreferredItemHeight">
    <TextView
        android:id="@+id/text_name"
        android:layout_width="wrap_content"
        android:layout_height="wrap_content"
        android:layout_centerVertical="true"
        android:textAppearance="?android:attr/textAppearanceMedium"
    />
    <TextView
        android:id="@+id/text_detail"
        android:layout_width="wrap_content"
        android:layout_height="wrap_content"
        android:layout_alignParentRight="true"
        android:layout_centerVertical="true"
        android:textAppearance="?android:attr/textAppearanceSmall"
    />
</RelativeLayout>
```

Listing 2-23. AlertDialog with Custom Layout

```java
public class CustomItemActivity extends Activity implements
        DialogInterface.OnClickListener,
        View.OnClickListener {

    private static final String[] ZONES = {
            "Pacific Time", "Mountain Time",
            "Central Time", "Eastern Time",
            "Atlantic Time"};

    private static final String[] OFFSETS = {
            "GMT-08:00", "GMT-07:00", "GMT-06:00",
            "GMT-05:00", "GMT-04:00"};

    Button mButton;
    AlertDialog mActions;
```

```java
@Override
protected void onCreate(Bundle savedInstanceState) {
    super.onCreate(savedInstanceState);

    mButton = new Button(this);
    mButton.setText("Click for Time Zones");
    mButton.setOnClickListener(this);

    ArrayAdapter<String> adapter = new ArrayAdapter<String>(
            this,
            R.layout.list_item) {
        @Override
        public View getView(int position, View convertView,
                ViewGroup parent) {
            View row = convertView;
            if (row == null) {
                row = getLayoutInflater().inflate(R.layout.list_item,
                        parent, false);
            }

            TextView name =
                    (TextView) row.findViewById(R.id.text_name);
            TextView detail =
                    (TextView) row.findViewById(R.id.text_detail);

            name.setText(ZONES[position]);
            detail.setText(OFFSETS[position]);

            return row;
        }

        @Override
        public int getCount() {
            return ZONES.length;
        }
    };

    AlertDialog.Builder builder = new AlertDialog.Builder(this);
    builder.setTitle("Select Time Zone");
    builder.setAdapter(adapter, this);
    //Cancel action does nothing but dismiss, we could add
    // another listener here to do something extra when the
    // user hits the Cancel button
    builder.setNegativeButton("Cancel", null);
    mActions = builder.create();

    setContentView(mButton);
}
```

```
//List selection action handled here
@Override
public void onClick(DialogInterface dialog, int which) {
    String selected = ZONES[which];
    mButton.setText(selected);
}

//Button action handled here (pop up the dialog)
@Override
public void onClick(View v) {
    mActions.show();
}
}
```

Here we have provided an ArrayAdapter to the builder instead of simply passing the array of items. This adapter has a custom implementation of getView() that returns a custom layout we've defined in XML to display two text labels: one aligned left and the other aligned right. With this custom layout, we can now display the Greenwich Mean Time (GMT) offset value alongside the time-zone name. We'll talk more about the specifics of custom adapters later in this chapter. Figure 2-5 displays our new, more useful pop-up dialog box.

Figure 2-5. AlertDialog *with custom items*

2-7. Customizing Menus and Actions

Problem

Your application needs to provide a set of actions to the user that you don't want to have taking up screen real estate in your view hierarchy.

Solution

(API Level 7)

Use the options menu functionality in the framework to provide commonly used actions inside the action bar, and additional options in an overflow pop-up menu. Additionally, menus can be attached to any existing view and shown as a floating drop-down by using PopupMenu. This feature allows you to place menus anywhere in your application besides just the action bar, but still keep them out of view until the user requires them.

The menu functionality in Android varies, depending on the device. In early releases, all Android devices had a physical MENU key that would trigger this functionality. Starting with Android 3.0, devices without physical buttons started to emerge, and the menu functionality became part of the action bar.

Action items resident in the action bar can also expand to reveal a custom widget known as an *action view*. This is helpful for providing features such as a search field that requires additional user input, but that you want to hide behind a single action item until the user taps to reveal it.

■ **Note**   This example uses several compatibility classes from the Android Support Library to foster compatibility back to devices running Android 2.1 (API Level 7). For more information on including the Support Library in your project, reference http://developer.android.com/tools/support-library/index.html.

How It Works

Listing 2-24 defines the options menu we will use in XML.

Listing 2-24. res/menu/options.xml

```xml
<menu xmlns:android="http://schemas.android.com/apk/res/android"
    xmlns:appcompat="http://schemas.android.com/apk/res-auto">
    <item android:id="@+id/menu_add"
        android:title="Add Item"
        android:icon="@android:drawable/ic_menu_add"
        appcompat:showAsAction="always|collapseActionView"
        appcompat:actionLayout="@layout/view_action" />
    <item android:id="@+id/menu_remove"
        android:title="Remove Item"
        android:icon="@android:drawable/ic_menu_delete"
        appcompat:showAsAction="ifRoom" />
    <item android:id="@+id/menu_edit"
        android:title="Edit Item"
        android:icon="@android:drawable/ic_menu_edit"
        appcompat:showAsAction="ifRoom" />
```

```
<item android:id="@+id/menu_settings"
    android:title="Settings"
    android:icon="@android:drawable/ic_menu_preferences"
    appcompat:showAsAction="never" />
</menu>
```

The title and icon attributes define how each item will be displayed; older platforms will show both values, while newer versions will show one or the other based on placement. Only Android 3.0 and later devices will recognize the showAsAction attribute, which defines whether the item should be promoted to an action on the action bar or placed into the overflow menu. The most common values for this attribute are as follows:

- always: Always display as an action by its icon.

- never: Always display in the overflow menu by its name.

- ifRoom: Display as an action if there is room on the action bar; otherwise, place in overflow.

The first item in our menu also defines an android:actionLayout resource that points to the widget we want to expand into when this item is tapped, and an additional display flag, collapseActionView, to tell the framework this item has a collapsible action view to display. Listing 2-25 shows the action view layout, which is just a simple layout with two CheckBox instances.

Listing 2-25. `res/layout/view_action.xml`

```
<?xml version="1.0" encoding="utf-8"?>
<LinearLayout
    xmlns:android="http://schemas.android.com/apk/res/android"
    android:layout_width="match_parent"
    android:layout_height="wrap_content"
    android:orientation="horizontal">
    <CheckBox
        android:id="@+id/option_first"
        android:layout_width="0dp"
        android:layout_height="wrap_content"
        android:layout_weight="1"
        android:text="First"/>
    <CheckBox
        android:id="@+id/option_second"
        android:layout_width="0dp"
        android:layout_height="wrap_content"
        android:layout_weight="1"
        android:text="Second"/>
</LinearLayout>
```

Listing 2-26 shows the full activity in which we are inflating our options menu into the action bar and housing an expandable action view inside one of our action items.

Listing 2-26. Activity Overriding Menu Action

```
public class OptionsActivity extends AppCompatActivity implements
        PopupMenu.OnMenuItemClickListener,
        CompoundButton.OnCheckedChangeListener {
```

```
private MenuItem mOptionsItem;
private CheckBox mFirstOption, mSecondOption;

@Override
public void onCreate(Bundle savedInstanceState) {
    super.onCreate(savedInstanceState);

    //No additional work in this example
}

@Override
public boolean onCreateOptionsMenu(Menu menu) {
    //Use this callback to create the menu and do any
    // initial setup necessary
    getMenuInflater().inflate(R.menu.options, menu);

    //Find and initialize our action item
    mOptionsItem = menu.findItem(R.id.menu_add);
    MenuItemCompat.setOnActionExpandListener(mOptionsItem,
            new MenuItemCompat.OnActionExpandListener() {

        @Override
        public boolean onMenuItemActionExpand(MenuItem item) {
            //Must return true to have item expand
            return true;
        }

        @Override
        public boolean onMenuItemActionCollapse(MenuItem item) {
            mFirstOption.setChecked(false);
            mSecondOption.setChecked(false);
            //Must return true to have item collapse
            return true;
        }
    });

    mFirstOption = (CheckBox) MenuItemCompat.getActionView(mOptionsItem)
            .findViewById(R.id.option_first);
    mFirstOption.setOnCheckedChangeListener(this);
    mSecondOption = (CheckBox) MenuItemCompat.getActionView(mOptionsItem)
            .findViewById(R.id.option_second);
    mSecondOption.setOnCheckedChangeListener(this);

    return true;
}

/* CheckBox Callback Methods */

@Override
public void onCheckedChanged(CompoundButton buttonView, boolean isChecked) {
    if (mFirstOption.isChecked() && mSecondOption.isChecked()) {
```

```
        MenuItemCompat.collapseActionView(mOptionsItem);
    }
}

@Override
public boolean onPrepareOptionsMenu(Menu menu) {
    //Use this callback to do setup that needs to happen
    // each time the menu opens
    return super.onPrepareOptionsMenu(menu);
}

//Callback from the PopupMenu click
public boolean onMenuItemClick(MenuItem item) {
    menuItemSelected(item);
    return true;
}

//Callback from a standard options menu click
@Override
public boolean onOptionsItemSelected(MenuItem item) {
    menuItemSelected(item);
    return true;
}

//Private helper so each unique callback can trigger the same actions
private void menuItemSelected(MenuItem item) {
    //Get the selected option by id
    switch (item.getItemId()) {
    case R.id.menu_add:
        //Do add action
        break;
    case R.id.menu_remove:
        //Do remove action
        break;
    case R.id.menu_edit:
        //Do edit action
        break;
    case R.id.menu_settings:
        //Do settings action
        break;
    default:
        break;
    }
}
}
```

When the user presses the MENU key on the device, or an activity loads with an action bar present, the onCreateOptionsMenu() method is called to set up the menu. There is a special LayoutInflater object called MenuInflater that is used to create menus from XML. We use the instance already available to the activity with getMenuInflater() to return our XML menu.

If there are any actions you need to take each time the user opens the menu, you can do so in onPrepareOptionsMenu(). Be advised that any actions promoted to the action bar will not trigger this callback when the user selects them; actions in the overflow menu, however, will still trigger it.

When the user makes a selection, the onOptionsItemSelected() callback will be triggered with the selected menu item. Since we defined a unique ID for each item in our XML menu, we can use a switch statement to check which item the user selected and take the appropriate action.

Finally, we find some additional setup for our expandable action view inside onCreateOptionsMenu(). Here we obtain a reference to the menu item that includes the action view layout and attach an OnActionExpandListener callback. The callback is used here simply to clear both selected elements in the action view whenever the item collapses.

■ **Important**   If you provide an OnActionExpandListener, you will need to return true inside onMenuItemActionExpand(), or the expansion will never occur!

We can use the getActionView() method from MenuItem to get a reference to the inflated action layout set in the menu XML. In our example, we use this to set a selected listener on each CheckBox inside the layout. Whenever both items are selected inside the action view, we call collapseActionView() to turn the view back into a single action item icon.

Figure 2-6 shows how this menu is displayed across different device versions and configurations. Devices that have physical keys will display the promoted actions in the action bar, but the overflow menu is still triggered by the MENU key. Devices with soft keys will display the overflow menu as a button next to the action bar actions.

Figure 2-6. *Android with physical keys (left) and with soft keys (right)*

Figure 2-7 shows the expandable action view that is displayed when the Add action is tapped in the action bar.

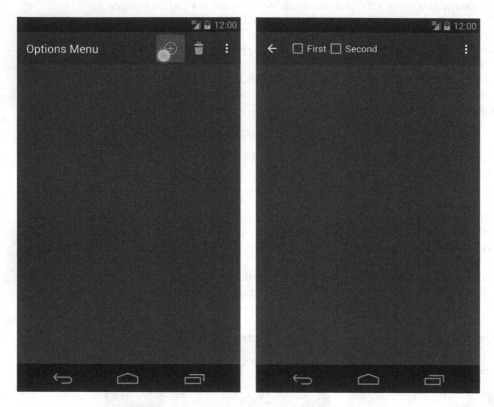

Figure 2-7. Custom action view

2-8. Customizing BACK Behavior

Problem

Your application needs to handle the user pressing the hardware BACK button in a custom manner.

Solution

(API Level 5)

Use the onBackPressed() callback inside an activity, or manipulate the back stack inside a fragment.

How It Works

If you need to be notified when the user presses BACK on your activity, you can override onBackPressed() as follows:

```
@Override
public void onBackPressed() {
    //Custom back button processing

    //Call super to do normal processing (like finishing Activity)
    super.onBackPressed();
}
```

The default implementation of this method will pop any fragments currently on the back stack and then finish the activity. If you are not intending to interrupt this workflow, you will want to make sure to call the super class implementation when you are done to ensure this processing still happens normally.

■ **Caution**   Overriding hardware button events should be done with care. All hardware buttons have consistent functionality across the Android system, and adjusting the functionality to work outside these bounds will be confusing and upsetting to users.

BACK Behavior and Fragments

When working with fragments in your UI, you have further opportunities to customize the behavior of the devices' BACK button. By default, the action of adding or replacing fragments in your UI is not something added to the task's back stack, so when the user presses the BACK button, that user won't be able to step backward through those actions. However, any FragmentTransaction can be added as an entry in the back stack by simply calling addToBackStack() before the transaction is committed.

By default, the activity will call FragmentManager.popBackStackImmediate() when the user presses BACK, so each FragmentTransaction added in this way will unravel with each tap until there are none left; then the activity will finish. Variations on this method, however, allow you to jump directly to places in the stack as well. Let's take a look at Listings 2-27 and 2-28.

Listing 2-27. res/layout/main.xml

```xml
<?xml version="1.0" encoding="utf-8"?>
<LinearLayout xmlns:android="http://schemas.android.com/apk/res/android"
    android:layout_width="match_parent"
    android:layout_height="match_parent"
    android:orientation="vertical">
    <Button
        android:layout_width="match_parent"
        android:layout_height="wrap_content"
        android:text="Go Home"
        android:onClick="onHomeClick" />
    <FrameLayout
        android:id="@+id/container_fragment"
        android:layout_width="match_parent"
        android:layout_height="match_parent"/>
</LinearLayout>
```

Listing 2-28. Activity Customizing Fragment Back Stack

```java
public class MyActivity extends FragmentActivity {

    @Override
    protected void onCreate(Bundle savedInstanceState) {
        super.onCreate(savedInstanceState);
        setContentView(R.layout.main);
        //Build a stack of UI fragments
        FragmentTransaction ft =
                getSupportFragmentManager().beginTransaction();
        ft.add(R.id.container_fragment,
                MyFragment.newInstance("First Fragment"));
        ft.commit();

        ft = getSupportFragmentManager().beginTransaction();
        ft.add(R.id.container_fragment,
                MyFragment.newInstance("Second Fragment"));
        ft.addToBackStack("second");
        ft.commit();

        ft = getSupportFragmentManager().beginTransaction();
        ft.add(R.id.container_fragment,
                MyFragment.newInstance("Third Fragment"));
        ft.addToBackStack("third");
        ft.commit();

        ft = getSupportFragmentManager().beginTransaction();
        ft.add(R.id.container_fragment,
                MyFragment.newInstance("Fourth Fragment"));
        ft.addToBackStack("fourth");
        ft.commit();
    }

    public void onHomeClick(View v) {
        getSupportFragmentManager().popBackStack("second",
                FragmentManager.POP_BACK_STACK_INCLUSIVE);
    }

    public static class MyFragment extends Fragment {
        private CharSequence mTitle;

        public static MyFragment newInstance(String title) {
            MyFragment fragment = new MyFragment();
            fragment.setTitle(title);

            return fragment;
        }
```

```
    @Override
    public View onCreateView(LayoutInflater inflater,
            ViewGroup container, Bundle savedInstanceState) {
        TextView text = new TextView(getActivity());
        text.setText(mTitle);
        text.setBackgroundColor(Color.WHITE);

        return text;
    }

    public void setTitle(CharSequence title) {
        mTitle = title;
    }
  }
}
```

■ **Note**   We are using the Support Library in this example to allow the use of fragments prior to Android 3.0. If your application is targeting API Level 11 or higher, you can replace FragmentActivity with Activity, and getSupportFragmentManager() with getFragmentManager().

This example loads four custom fragment instances into a stack, so the last one added is displayed when the application runs. With each transaction, we call addToBackStack() with a tag name to identify this transaction. This is not required, and if you do not wish to jump to places in the stack, it is easier to just pass null here. With each press of the BACK button, a single fragment is removed until only the first remains, at which point the activity will finish normally.

Notice the first transaction was not added to the stack; this is because here we want the first fragment to act as the root view. Adding it to the back stack as well would cause it to pop off the stack before finishing the activity, leaving the UI in a blank state.

This application also has a button marked Go Home, which immediately takes users back to the root fragment no matter where they currently are. It does this by calling popBackStack() on FragmentManager, taking the tag of the transaction we want to jump back to. We also pass the flag POP_BACK_STACK_INCLUSIVE to instruct the manager to also remove the transaction we've indicated from the stack. Without this flag, the example would jump to the "second" fragment, rather than the root.

■ **Note**   Android pops back to the first transaction that matches the given tag. If the same tag is used multiple times, it will pop to the first transaction added, not the most recent.

We cannot go directly to the root with this method because we do not have a back stack tag associated with that transaction to reference. There is another version of this method that takes a unique transaction ID (the return value from commit() on FragmentTransaction). Using this method, we could jump directly to the root without requiring the inclusive flag.

2-9. Emulating the HOME Button

Problem

Your application needs to take the same action as if the user pressed the hardware HOME button.

Solution

(API Level 5)

When the user hits the HOME button, this sends an Intent to the system telling it to load the Home activity. This is no different from starting any other activity in your application; you just have to construct the proper Intent to get the effect.

How It Works

Add the following lines wherever you want this action to occur in your activity:

```
Intent intent = new Intent(Intent.ACTION_MAIN);
intent.addCategory(Intent.CATEGORY_HOME);
startActivity(intent);
```

A common use of this function is to override the BACK button to go home instead of to the previous activity. This is useful when everything underneath the foreground activity may be protected (by a login screen, for instance), and letting the default BACK button behavior occur could allow unsecured access to the system.

■ **Important**   Whenever you are modifying the behavior of a system button, be extremely sure you are not disrupting what the user's expectation of that action should be.

Here is an example of using the two in concert to make a certain activity bring up the home screen when BACK is pressed:

```
@Override
public void onBackPressed() {
    Intent intent = new Intent(Intent.ACTION_MAIN);
    intent.addCategory(Intent.CATEGORY_HOME);
    startActivity(intent);
}
```

2-10. Monitoring TextView Changes

Problem

Your application needs to continuously monitor for text changes in a TextView widget (for example, EditText).

Solution

(API Level 1)

Implement the `android.text.TextWatcher` interface. `TextWatcher` provides three callback methods during the process of updating text:

```
public void beforeTextChanged(CharSequence s, int start, int count, int after);
public void onTextChanged(CharSequence s, int start, int before, int count);
public void afterTextChanged(Editable s);
```

The `beforeTextChanged()` and `onTextChanged()` methods are provided mainly as notifications, as you cannot actually make changes to the `CharSequence` in either of these methods. If you are attempting to intercept the text entered into the view, changes may be made when `afterTextChanged()` is called.

How It Works

To register a `TextWatcher` instance with a `TextView`, call the `TextView.addTextChangedListener()` method. Notice from the syntax that more than one `TextWatcher` can be registered with a `TextView`.

Character Counter Example

A simple use of `TextWatcher` is to create a live character counter that follows an `EditText` as the user types or deletes information. Listing 2-29 is an example activity that implements `TextWatcher` for this purpose, registers with an `EditText` widget, and prints the character count in the activity title.

Listing 2-29. Character Counter Activity

```
public class MyActivity extends Activity implements TextWatcher {


    EditText text;
    int textCount;

    @Override
    protected void onCreate(Bundle savedInstanceState) {
        super.onCreate(savedInstanceState);
        //Create an EditText widget and add the watcher
        text = new EditText(this);
        text.addTextChangedListener(this);

        setContentView(text);
    }

    /* TextWatcher Implementation Methods */
    @Override
    public void beforeTextChanged(CharSequence s, int start, int count,
            int after) { }

    @Override
    public void onTextChanged(CharSequence s, int start, int before,
```

```
            int count) {
        textCount = text.getText().length();
        setTitle(String.valueOf(textCount));
    }

    @Override
    public void afterTextChanged(Editable s) { }

}
```

Because our needs do not include modifying the text being inserted, we can read the count from onTextChanged(), which happens as soon as the text change occurs. The other methods are unused and left empty.

Currency Formatter Example

The SDK has a handful of predefined TextWatcher instances to format text input; PhoneNumberFormattingTextWatcher is one of these. Their job is to apply standard formatting for users while they type, reducing the number of keystrokes required to enter legible data.

In Listing 2-30, we create a CurrencyTextWatcher to insert the currency symbol and separator point into a TextView.

Listing 2-30. Currency Formatter

```
public class CurrencyTextWatcher implements TextWatcher {

    boolean mEditing;

    public CurrencyTextWatcher() {
        mEditing = false;
    }

    @Override
    public synchronized void afterTextChanged(Editable s) {
        if(!mEditing) {
            mEditing = true;

            //Strip symbols
            String digits = s.toString().replaceAll("\\D", "");
            NumberFormat nf = NumberFormat.getCurrencyInstance();
            try{
                String formatted =
                        nf.format(Double.parseDouble(digits)/100);
                s.replace(0, s.length(), formatted);
            } catch (NumberFormatException nfe) {
                s.clear();
            }

            mEditing = false;
        }
    }
```

```
    @Override
    public void beforeTextChanged(CharSequence s, int start, int count,
            int after) { }

    @Override
    public void onTextChanged(CharSequence s, int start, int before,
            int count) { }

}
```

■ **Note**   Making changes to the `Editable` value in `afterTextChanged()` will cause the `TextWatcher` methods to be called again (after all, you just changed the text). For this reason, custom `TextWatcher` implementations that edit should use a Boolean or some other tracking mechanism to track where the editing is coming from, or you may create an infinite loop.

We can apply this custom text formatter to `EditText` in an activity (see Listing 2-31).

Listing 2-31. Activity Using Currency Formatter

```
public class MyActivity extends Activity {

    EditText text;

    @Override
    protected void onCreate(Bundle savedInstanceState) {
        super.onCreate(savedInstanceState);
        text = new EditText(this);
        text.addTextChangedListener(new CurrencyTextWatcher());

        setContentView(text);
    }

}
```

If you are formatting user input with this formatter, it is handy to define `EditText` in XML so you can apply the `android:inputType` and `android:digits` constraints to easily protect the field against entry errors. In particular, adding `android:digits="0123456789."` (notice the period at the end for a decimal point) to `EditText` will protect this formatter as well as the user.

2-11. Customizing Keyboard Actions

Problem

You want to customize the appearance of the soft keyboard's Enter key, the action that occurs when a user taps it, or both.

Solution

(API Level 3)

Customize the input method (IME) options for the widget in which the keyboard is entering data.

How It Works

Custom Enter Key

When the keyboard is visible onscreen, the text on the Enter key typically indicates its action based on the order of focusable items in the view. While unspecified, the keyboard will display a "next" action if there are more focusables in the view to move to, or a "done" action if the last item is currently focused on. In the case of a multiline field, this action is a line return. This value is customizable, however, for each input view by setting the android:imeOptions value in the view's XML. The values you may set to customize the Enter key are listed here:

- actionUnspecified: Default. Displays action of the device's choice
  - Action event is IME_NULL
- actionGo: Displays Go as the Enter key
  - Action event is IME_ACTION_GO
- actionSearch: Displays a search glass as the Enter key
  - Action event is IME_ACTION_SEARCH
- actionSend: Displays Send as the Enter key
  - Action event is IME_ACTION_SEND
- actionNext: Displays Next as the Enter key
  - Action event is IME_ACTION_NEXT
- actionDone: Displays Done as the Enter key
  - Action event is IME_ACTION_DONE

Let's look at an example layout with two editable text fields, shown in Listing 2-32. The first will display the search magnifying glass on the Enter key, and the second will display Go.

Listing 2-32. `res/layout/main.xml`

```
<LinearLayout
    xmlns:android="http://schemas.android.com/apk/res/android"
    android:layout_width="match_parent"
    android:layout_height="match_parent"
    android:orientation="vertical">
    <EditText
        android:id="@+id/text1"
        android:layout_width="match_parent"
        android:layout_height="wrap_content"
        android:singleLine="true"
        android:imeOptions="actionSearch" />
    <EditText
```

```
            android:id="@+id/text2"
            android:layout_width="match_parent"
            android:layout_height="wrap_content"
            android:singleLine="true"
            android:imeOptions="actionGo" />
</LinearLayout>
```

The resulting display of the keyboard will vary somewhat, as some manufacturer-specific UI kits include different keyboards, but the results on a pure Google UI will show up as in Figure 2-8.

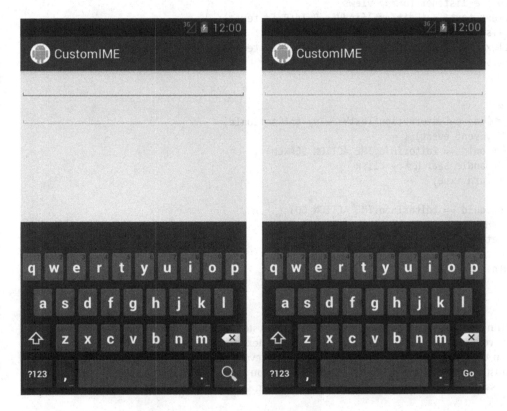

Figure 2-8. Result of custom input options on the Enter key

■ **Note** Custom editor options apply only to the soft input methods. Changing this value will not affect the events that are generated when the user presses Enter on a physical hardware keyboard.

Custom Action

Customizing what happens when the user presses the Enter key can be just as important as adjusting its display. Overriding the default behavior of any action simply requires that TextView. OnEditorActionListener be attached to the view of interest. Let's continue with the preceding example layout, and this time we'll add a custom action to both views (see Listing 2-33).

Listing 2-33. Activity Implementing a Custom Keyboard Action

```java
public class MyActivity extends Activity implements
        OnEditorActionListener {

    @Override
    public void onCreate(Bundle savedInstanceState) {
        super.onCreate(savedInstanceState);
        setContentView(R.layout.main);

        //Add the listener to the views
        EditText text1 = (EditText)findViewById(R.id.text1);
        text1.setOnEditorActionListener(this);
        EditText text2 = (EditText)findViewById(R.id.text2);
        text2.setOnEditorActionListener(this);
    }

    @Override
    public boolean onEditorAction(TextView v, int actionId,
            KeyEvent event) {
        if(actionId == EditorInfo.IME_ACTION_SEARCH) {
            //Handle search key click
            return true;
        }
        if(actionId == EditorInfo.IME_ACTION_GO) {
            //Handle go key click
            return true;
        }
        return false;
    }
}
```

The Boolean return value of onEditorAction() tells the system whether your implementation has consumed the event or whether it should be passed on to the next possible responder, if any. It is important for you to return true when your implementation handles the event, so no other processing occurs. However, it is just as important for you to return false when you are not handling the event, so your application does not steal key events from the rest of the system.

■ **Note**   If your application customizes the actionId value returned for a certain keyboard, be aware that this will happen only on soft keyboard IMEs. If the device has a physical keyboard attached, the Enter key on that keyboard will always return an actionId of 0 or IME_NULL.

2-12. Dismissing the Soft Keyboard

Problem

You need an event on the UI to hide or dismiss the soft keyboard from the screen.

Solution

(API Level 3)

Tell the Input Method Manager explicitly to hide any visible input methods by using the `InputMethodManager.hideSoftInputFromWindow()` method.

How It Works

Here is an example of how to call this method inside `View.OnClickListener`:

```
public void onClick(View view) {
    InputMethodManager imm = (InputMethodManager)getSystemService(
            Context.INPUT_METHOD_SERVICE);
    imm.hideSoftInputFromWindow(view.getWindowToken(), 0);
}
```

The `hideSoftInputFromWindow()` takes an `IBinder` window token as a parameter. This can be retrieved from any `View` object currently attached to the window via `View.getWindowToken()`. In most cases, the callback method for the specific event will either have a reference to the `TextView` where the editing is taking place or the view that was tapped to generate the event (for example, a button). These views are the most convenient objects to call on to get the window token and pass it to the `InputMethodManager`.

2-13. Handling Complex Touch Events

Problem

Your application needs to implement customized single or multitouch interactions with the UI.

Solution

(API Level 3)

Use the `GestureDetector` and `ScaleGestureDetector` in the framework, or just manually handle all touch events passed to your views by overriding `onTouchEvent()` and `onInterceptTouchEvent()`. Working with the former is a very simple way to add complex gesture control to your application. The latter option is extremely powerful, but it has some pitfalls to be aware of.

Android handles touch events on the UI by using a top-down dispatch system, which is a common pattern in the framework for sending messages through a hierarchy. Touch events originate at the top-level window and are delivered to the activity first. From there, they are dispatched to the root view of the loaded hierarchy and subsequently passed down from parent to child view until something consumes the event or the entire chain has been traversed.

It is the job of each parent view to validate which children a touch event should be sent to (usually by checking the view's bounds) and to dispatch the event in the correct order. If multiple children are valid candidates (such as when they overlap), the parent will deliver the event to each child in the reverse order that they were added, so as to guarantee that the child view with the highest z-order (visibly layered on top) gets a chance first. If no children consume the event, the parent itself will get a chance to consume it before the event is passed back up the hierarchy.

Any view can declare interest in a particular touch event by returning `true` from its `onTouchEvent()` method, which consumes the event and stops it from being delivered elsewhere. Any `ViewGroup` has the additional ability to intercept or steal touch events being delivered to its children via the onInterceptTouchEvent() callback. This is helpful in cases where the parent view needs to take over control for a particular use case, for example, a ScrollView taking control of touches after it detects that the user is dragging a finger.

Touch events will have several action identifiers during the course of a gesture:

- ACTION_DOWN: Initial event when the first finger hits the screen. This event is always the beginning of a new gesture.

- ACTION_MOVE: Event that occurs when one of the fingers on the screen has changed location

- ACTION_UP: Final event, when the last finger leaves the screen. This event is always the end of a gesture.

- ACTION_CANCEL: Received by child views when their parent has intercepted the gesture they were currently receiving. Like ACTION_UP, this should signal the view that the gesture is over from their perspective.

- ACTION_POINTER_DOWN: Event that occurs when an additional finger hits the screen. Useful for switching into a multitouch gesture

- ACTION_POINTER_UP: Event that occurs when an additional finger leaves the screen. Useful for switching out of a multitouch gesture

For efficiency, Android will not deliver subsequent events to any view that did not consume ACTION_DOWN. Therefore, if you are doing custom touch handling and want to do something interesting with later events, you must return true for ACTION_DOWN.

If you are implementing a custom touch handler inside a parent ViewGroup, you will probably also need to have some code in onInterceptTouchEvent(). This method works in a similar fashion to onTouchEvent() in that, if you return true, your custom view will take over receiving all touch events for the remainder of that gesture (that is, until ACTION_UP). This operation cannot be undone, so do not intercept these events until you are sure you want to take them all!

Finally, Android provides a number of useful threshold constants that are scaled for device screen density and should be used to build custom touch interaction. These constants are all housed in the ViewConfiguration class. In this example, we will use the minimum and maximum fling velocity values and the touch slop constant, which denotes how far ACTION_MOVE events should be allowed to vary before considering them as an actual move of the user's finger.

How It Works

Listing 2-34 illustrates a custom ViewGroup that implements pan-style scrolling, meaning it allows the user to scroll in both horizontal and vertical directions, assuming the content is large enough to do so. This implementation uses GestureDetector to handle the touch events.

Listing 2-34. Custom ViewGroup with GestureDetector

```
public class PanGestureScrollView extends FrameLayout {

    private GestureDetector mDetector;
    private Scroller mScroller;

    /* Positions of the last motion event */
    private float mInitialX, mInitialY;
    /* Drag threshold */
    private int mTouchSlop;
```

```
public PanGestureScrollView(Context context) {
    super(context);
    init(context);
}

public PanGestureScrollView(Context context, AttributeSet attrs) {
    super(context, attrs);
    init(context);
}

public PanGestureScrollView(Context context, AttributeSet attrs,
        int defStyle) {
    super(context, attrs, defStyle);
    init(context);
}

private void init(Context context) {
    mDetector = new GestureDetector(context, mListener);
    mScroller = new Scroller(context);
    // Get system constants for touch thresholds
    mTouchSlop = ViewConfiguration.get(context).getScaledTouchSlop();
}

/*
 * Override measureChild... implementations to guarantee the child
 * view gets measured to be as large as it wants to be. The default
 * implementation will force some children to be only as large as
 * this view.
 */
@Override
protected void measureChild(View child, int parentWidthMeasureSpec,
        int parentHeightMeasureSpec) {
    int childWidthMeasureSpec;
    int childHeightMeasureSpec;

    childWidthMeasureSpec = MeasureSpec.makeMeasureSpec(0,
            MeasureSpec.UNSPECIFIED);
    childHeightMeasureSpec = MeasureSpec.makeMeasureSpec(0,
            MeasureSpec.UNSPECIFIED);

    child.measure(childWidthMeasureSpec, childHeightMeasureSpec);
}

@Override
protected void measureChildWithMargins(View child,
        int parentWidthMeasureSpec, int widthUsed,
        int parentHeightMeasureSpec, int heightUsed) {
    final MarginLayoutParams lp =
            (MarginLayoutParams) child.getLayoutParams();

    final int childWidthMeasureSpec = MeasureSpec.makeMeasureSpec(
            lp.leftMargin + lp.rightMargin, MeasureSpec.UNSPECIFIED);
```

```
        final int childHeightMeasureSpec = MeasureSpec.makeMeasureSpec(
                lp.topMargin + lp.bottomMargin, MeasureSpec.UNSPECIFIED);

        child.measure(childWidthMeasureSpec, childHeightMeasureSpec);
    }


    // Listener to handle all the touch events
    private SimpleOnGestureListener mListener =
            new SimpleOnGestureListener() {
        public boolean onDown(MotionEvent e) {
            // Cancel any current fling
            if (!mScroller.isFinished()) {
                mScroller.abortAnimation();
            }
            return true;
        }

        public boolean onFling(MotionEvent e1, MotionEvent e2,
                float velocityX, float velocityY) {
            // Call a helper method to start the scroller animation
            fling((int) -velocityX / 3, (int) -velocityY / 3);
            return true;
        }

        public boolean onScroll(MotionEvent e1, MotionEvent e2,
                float distanceX, float distanceY) {
            // Any view can be scrolled by simply calling scrollBy()
            scrollBy((int) distanceX, (int) distanceY);
            return true;
        }
    };


    @Override
    public void computeScroll() {
        if (mScroller.computeScrollOffset()) {
            // This is called at drawing time by ViewGroup. We use
            // this method to keep the fling animation going through
            // to completion.
            int oldX = getScrollX();
            int oldY = getScrollY();
            int x = mScroller.getCurrX();
            int y = mScroller.getCurrY();

            if (getChildCount() > 0) {
                View child = getChildAt(0);
                x = clamp(x,
                        getWidth() - getPaddingRight() - getPaddingLeft(),
                        child.getWidth());
                y = clamp(y,
                        getHeight() - getPaddingBottom() - getPaddingTop(),
                        child.getHeight());
```

```
            if (x != oldX || y != oldY) {
                scrollTo(x, y);
            }
        }

        // Keep on drawing until the animation has finished.
        postInvalidate();
    }
}


// Override scrollTo to do bounds checks on any scrolling request
@Override
public void scrollTo(int x, int y) {
    // we rely on the fact the View.scrollBy calls scrollTo.
    if (getChildCount() > 0) {
        View child = getChildAt(0);
        x = clamp(x,
                getWidth() - getPaddingRight() - getPaddingLeft(),
                child.getWidth());
        y = clamp(y,
                getHeight() - getPaddingBottom() - getPaddingTop(),
                child.getHeight());
        if (x != getScrollX() || y != getScrollY()) {
            super.scrollTo(x, y);
        }
    }
}


/*
 * Monitor touch events passed down to the children and intercept
 * as soon as it is determined we are dragging
 */
@Override
public boolean onInterceptTouchEvent(MotionEvent event) {
    switch (event.getAction()) {
    case MotionEvent.ACTION_DOWN:
        mInitialX = event.getX();
        mInitialY = event.getY();
        // Feed the down event to the detector so it has
        // context when/if dragging begins
        mDetector.onTouchEvent(event);
        break;
    case MotionEvent.ACTION_MOVE:
        final float x = event.getX();
        final float y = event.getY();
        final int yDiff = (int) Math.abs(y - mInitialY);
        final int xDiff = (int) Math.abs(x - mInitialX);
        // Verify that either difference is enough to be a drag
        if (yDiff > mTouchSlop || xDiff > mTouchSlop) {
            // Start capturing events
            return true;
        }
```

```java
            break;
        }

        return super.onInterceptTouchEvent(event);
    }

    /*
     * Feed all touch events we receive to the detector for processing.
     */
    @Override
    public boolean onTouchEvent(MotionEvent event) {
        return mDetector.onTouchEvent(event);
    }

    /*
     * Utility method to initialize the Scroller and start redrawing
     */
    public void fling(int velocityX, int velocityY) {
        if (getChildCount() > 0) {
            int height =
                    getHeight() - getPaddingBottom() - getPaddingTop();
            int width =
                    getWidth() - getPaddingLeft() - getPaddingRight();
            int bottom = getChildAt(0).getHeight();
            int right = getChildAt(0).getWidth();

            mScroller.fling(getScrollX(), getScrollY(),
                    velocityX, velocityY,
                    0, Math.max(0, right - width),
                    0, Math.max(0, bottom - height));

            invalidate();
        }
    }

    /*
     * Utility method to assist in doing bounds checking
     */
    private int clamp(int n, int my, int child) {
        if (my >= child || n < 0) {
            // The child is beyond one of the parent bounds
            // or is smaller than the parent and can't scroll
            return 0;
        }
        if ((my + n) > child) {
            // Requested scroll is beyond right bound of child
            return child - my;
        }
        return n;
    }
}
```

Similar to `ScrollView` or `HorizontalScrollView`, this example takes a single child and scrolls its contents based on user input. Much of the code in this example is not directly related to touch handling; instead it scrolls and keeps the scroll position from going beyond the bounds of the child.

As a `ViewGroup`, the first place where we will see any touch event will be `onInterceptTouchEvent()`. This method is where we must analyze the user touches and see whether they are actually dragging. The interaction between `ACTION_DOWN` and `ACTION_MOVE` in this method is designed to determine how far the user has moved their finger, and if it's greater than the system's touch slop constant, we call it a *drag event* and intercept subsequent touches. This implementation allows simple tap events to go on to the children, so buttons and other widgets can safely be children of this view and still get click events. If no interactive widgets were children of this view, the events would pass directly to our `onTouchEvent()` method, but since we want to allow that possibility, we have to do this initial checking here.

The `onTouchEvent()` method here is straightforward, because all events simply get forwarded to our `GestureDetector`, which does all the tracking and calculations to know when the user is doing specific actions. We then react to those events through the `SimpleOnGestureListener`, specifically the `onScroll()` and `onFling()` events. To ensure that the `GestureDetector` has the initial point of the gesture correctly set, we also forward the `ACTION_DOWN` event from `onInterceptTouchEvent()` to it.

The `onScroll()` method is called repeatedly with the incremental distance traveled by the user's finger. Conveniently, we can pass these values directly to the view's `scrollBy()` method to move the content while the finger is dragging.

The `onFling()` method requires slightly more work. For those unaware, in a *fling* operation, the user rapidly moves a finger on the screen and lifts it. The resulting expected behavior of this is an animated inertial scroll. Again, the work of calculating the velocity of the user's finger when it is lifted is done for us, but we must still do the scrolling animation. This is where `Scroller` comes in. `Scroller` is a component of the framework designed to take the user input values and provide the time-interpolated animation slices necessary to animate the view's scrolling. The animation is started by calling `fling()` on the `Scroller` and invalidating the view.

■ **Note** If you are targeting API Level 9 and higher, you can drop `OverScroller` in place of `Scroller`, and it will provide more-consistent performance on newer devices. It will also allow you to include the overscroll glow animations. You can spice up the fling animation by passing a custom `Interpolator` to either one.

This starts a looping process in which the framework will call `computeScroll()` regularly as it draws the view. We use this opportunity to check the current state of the `Scroller` and to nudge the view forward if the animation is not complete. This is something many developers can find confusing about `Scroller`. It is a component designed to animate the view, but it doesn't actually do any animation. It simply provides the timing and calculations for how far the view should move on each draw frame. The application must both call `computeScrollOffset()` to get the new locations and then actually call a method to incrementally change the view, which in our example is `scrollTo()`.

The final callback we use in the `GestureDetector` is `onDown()`, which gets called with any `ACTION_DOWN` the detector receives. We use this callback to abort any currently running fling animation if the user presses a finger back onto the screen. Listing 2-35 shows how we can use this custom view inside an activity.

Listing 2-35. Activity Using `PanGestureScrollView`

```
public class PanScrollActivity extends Activity {

    @Override
    protected void onCreate(Bundle savedInstanceState) {
        super.onCreate(savedInstanceState);
```

133

```
        PanGestureScrollView scrollView =
                new PanGestureScrollView(this);

        LinearLayout layout = new LinearLayout(this);
        layout.setOrientation(LinearLayout.VERTICAL);
        for(int i=0; i < 5; i++) {
            ImageView iv = new ImageButton(this);
            iv.setImageResource(R.drawable.ic_launcher);
            //Make each view large enough to require scrolling
            layout.addView(iv,
                    new LinearLayout.LayoutParams(1000, 500) );
        }

        scrollView.addView(layout);
        setContentView(scrollView);
    }
}
```

We use a handful of ImageButton instances to fill up the custom scroller view on purpose to illustrate that you can click any one of these buttons and the event will still go through, but as soon as you drag or fling your finger, the scrolling will take over. To illustrate just how much work GestureDetector does for us, take a look at Listing 2-36, which implements the same functionality but by manually handling all touches in onTouchEvent().

Listing 2-36. PanScrollView Using Custom Touch Handling

```
public class PanScrollView extends FrameLayout {

    // Fling components
    private Scroller mScroller;
    private VelocityTracker mVelocityTracker;

    /* Positions of the last motion event */
    private float mLastTouchX, mLastTouchY;
    /* Drag threshold */
    private int mTouchSlop;
    /* Fling Velocity */
    private int mMaximumVelocity, mMinimumVelocity;
    /* Drag Lock */
    private boolean mDragging = false;

    public PanScrollView(Context context) {
        super(context);
        init(context);
    }

    public PanScrollView(Context context, AttributeSet attrs) {
        super(context, attrs);
        init(context);
    }
```

```
public PanScrollView(Context context, AttributeSet attrs,
        int defStyle) {
    super(context, attrs, defStyle);
    init(context);
}

private void init(Context context) {
    mScroller = new Scroller(context);
    mVelocityTracker = VelocityTracker.obtain();
    // Get system constants for touch thresholds
    mTouchSlop = ViewConfiguration.get(context).getScaledTouchSlop();
    mMaximumVelocity = ViewConfiguration.get(context)
            .getScaledMaximumFlingVelocity();
    mMinimumVelocity = ViewConfiguration.get(context)
            .getScaledMinimumFlingVelocity();
}

/*
 * Override measureChild... implementations to guarantee the child
 * view gets measured to be as large as it wants to be. The default
 * implementation will force some children to be only as large as
 * this view.
 */
@Override
protected void measureChild(View child, int parentWidthMeasureSpec,
        int parentHeightMeasureSpec) {
    int childWidthMeasureSpec;
    int childHeightMeasureSpec;

    childWidthMeasureSpec = MeasureSpec.makeMeasureSpec(0,
            MeasureSpec.UNSPECIFIED);
    childHeightMeasureSpec = MeasureSpec.makeMeasureSpec(0,
            MeasureSpec.UNSPECIFIED);

    child.measure(childWidthMeasureSpec, childHeightMeasureSpec);
}

@Override
protected void measureChildWithMargins(View child,
        int parentWidthMeasureSpec, int widthUsed,
        int parentHeightMeasureSpec, int heightUsed) {
    final MarginLayoutParams lp =
            (MarginLayoutParams) child.getLayoutParams();

    final int childWidthMeasureSpec = MeasureSpec.makeMeasureSpec(
            lp.leftMargin + lp.rightMargin, MeasureSpec.UNSPECIFIED);
    final int childHeightMeasureSpec = MeasureSpec.makeMeasureSpec(
            lp.topMargin + lp.bottomMargin, MeasureSpec.UNSPECIFIED);

    child.measure(childWidthMeasureSpec, childHeightMeasureSpec);
}
```

```java
    @Override
    public void computeScroll() {
        if (mScroller.computeScrollOffset()) {
            // This is called at drawing time by ViewGroup. We use
            // this method to keep the fling animation going through
            // to completion.
            int oldX = getScrollX();
            int oldY = getScrollY();
            int x = mScroller.getCurrX();
            int y = mScroller.getCurrY();

            if (getChildCount() > 0) {
                View child = getChildAt(0);
                x = clamp(x,
                        getWidth() - getPaddingRight() - getPaddingLeft(),
                        child.getWidth());
                y = clamp(y,
                        getHeight() - getPaddingBottom() - getPaddingTop(),
                        child.getHeight());
                if (x != oldX || y != oldY) {
                    scrollTo(x, y);
                }
            }

            // Keep on drawing until the animation has finished.
            postInvalidate();
        }
    }

    // Override scrollTo to do bounds checks on any scrolling request
    @Override
    public void scrollTo(int x, int y) {
        // we rely on the fact the View.scrollBy calls scrollTo.
        if (getChildCount() > 0) {
            View child = getChildAt(0);
            x = clamp(x,
                getWidth() - getPaddingRight() - getPaddingLeft(),
                child.getWidth());
            y = clamp(y,
                getHeight() - getPaddingBottom() - getPaddingTop(),
                child.getHeight());
            if (x != getScrollX() || y != getScrollY()) {
                super.scrollTo(x, y);
            }
        }
    }

    /*
     * Monitor touch events passed down to the children and
     * intercept as soon as it is determined we are dragging.
     * This allows child views to still receive touch events
```

```
 * if they are interactive (i.e., Buttons)
 */
@Override
public boolean onInterceptTouchEvent(MotionEvent event) {
    switch (event.getAction()) {
    case MotionEvent.ACTION_DOWN:
        // Stop any flinging in progress
        if (!mScroller.isFinished()) {
            mScroller.abortAnimation();
        }
        // Reset the velocity tracker
        mVelocityTracker.clear();
        mVelocityTracker.addMovement(event);
        // Save the initial touch point
        mLastTouchX = event.getX();
        mLastTouchY = event.getY();
        break;
    case MotionEvent.ACTION_MOVE:
        final float x = event.getX();
        final float y = event.getY();
        final int yDiff = (int) Math.abs(y - mLastTouchY);
        final int xDiff = (int) Math.abs(x - mLastTouchX);
        // Verify that either difference is enough for a drag
        if (yDiff > mTouchSlop || xDiff > mTouchSlop) {
            mDragging = true;
            mVelocityTracker.addMovement(event);
            // Start capturing events ourselves
            return true;
        }
        break;
    case MotionEvent.ACTION_CANCEL:
    case MotionEvent.ACTION_UP:
        mDragging = false;
        mVelocityTracker.clear();
        break;
    }

    return super.onInterceptTouchEvent(event);
}

/*
 * Feed all touch events we receive to the detector
 */
@Override
public boolean onTouchEvent(MotionEvent event) {
    mVelocityTracker.addMovement(event);

    switch (event.getAction()) {
    case MotionEvent.ACTION_DOWN:
        // We've already stored the initial point,
        // but if we got here, a child view didn't capture
```

```
            // the event, so we need to.
            return true;
        case MotionEvent.ACTION_MOVE:
            final float x = event.getX();
            final float y = event.getY();
            float deltaY = mLastTouchY - y;
            float deltaX = mLastTouchX - x;
            // Check for slop on direct events
            if ( (Math.abs(deltaY) > mTouchSlop
                    || Math.abs(deltaX) > mTouchSlop)
                    && !mDragging) {
                mDragging = true;
            }
            if (mDragging) {
                // Scroll the view
                scrollBy((int) deltaX, (int) deltaY);
                // Update the last touch event
                mLastTouchX = x;
                mLastTouchY = y;
            }
            break;
        case MotionEvent.ACTION_CANCEL:
            mDragging = false;
            // Stop any flinging in progress
            if (!mScroller.isFinished()) {
                mScroller.abortAnimation();
            }
            break;
        case MotionEvent.ACTION_UP:
            mDragging = false;
            // Compute the current velocity and start a fling if
            // it is above the minimum threshold.
            mVelocityTracker.computeCurrentVelocity(1000,
                    mMaximumVelocity);
            int velocityX = (int) mVelocityTracker.getXVelocity();
            int velocityY = (int) mVelocityTracker.getYVelocity();
            if (Math.abs(velocityX) > mMinimumVelocity
                    || Math.abs(velocityY) > mMinimumVelocity) {
                fling(-velocityX, -velocityY);
            }
            break;
    }
    return super.onTouchEvent(event);
}

/*
 * Utility method to initialize the Scroller and
 * start redrawing
 */
public void fling(int velocityX, int velocityY) {
```

```
        if (getChildCount() > 0) {
            int height =
                getHeight() - getPaddingBottom() - getPaddingTop();
            int width =
                getWidth() - getPaddingLeft() - getPaddingRight();
            int bottom = getChildAt(0).getHeight();
            int right = getChildAt(0).getWidth();

            mScroller.fling(getScrollX(), getScrollY(),
                    velocityX, velocityY,
                    0, Math.max(0, right - width),
                    0, Math.max(0, bottom - height) );

            invalidate();
        }
    }

    /*
     * Utility method to assist in doing bounds checking
     */
    private int clamp(int n, int my, int child) {
        if (my >= child || n < 0) {
            // The child is beyond one of the parent bounds
            // or is smaller than the parent and can't scroll
            return 0;
        }
        if ((my + n) > child) {
            // Requested scroll is beyond right bound of child
            return child - my;
        }
        return n;
    }
}
```

In this example, both onInterceptTouchEvent() and onTouchEvent() have a bit more going on. If a child view is currently handling initial touches, ACTION_DOWN and the first few move events will be delivered through onInterceptTouchEvent() before we take control; however, if no interactive child exists, all those initial events will go directly to onTouchEvent(). Therefore, we must do the slop checking for the initial drag in both places and set a flag to indicate when a scroll event has truly started. Once we have flagged the user dragging, the code to scroll the view is the same as before, with a call to scrollBy().

■ **Tip**   As soon as a ViewGroup returns true from onTouchEvent(), no more events will be delivered to onInterceptTouchEvent(), even if an intercept was not explicitly requested.

To implement the fling behavior, we must manually track the user's scroll velocity by using a VelocityTracker object. This object collects touch events as they occur with the addMovement() method, and it then calculates the average velocity on demand with computeCurrentVelocity(). Our custom view calculates this value each time the user's finger is lifted and determines, based on the ViewConfiguration minimum velocity, whether to start a fling animation.

■ **Tip**   In cases where you don't need to explicitly return `true` to consume an event, return the super implementation rather than `false`. Often there is a lot of hidden processing for `View` and `ViewGroup` that you don't want to override.

Listing 2-37 shows our example activity again, this time with the new custom view in place.

Listing 2-37. Activity Using `PanScrollView`

```
public class PanScrollActivity extends Activity {

    @Override
    protected void onCreate(Bundle savedInstanceState) {
        super.onCreate(savedInstanceState);

        PanScrollView scrollView = new PanScrollView(this);

        LinearLayout layout = new LinearLayout(this);
        layout.setOrientation(LinearLayout.VERTICAL);
        for(int i=0; i < 5; i++) {
            ImageView iv = new ImageView(this);
            iv.setImageResource(R.drawable.ic_launcher);
            layout.addView(iv,
                    new LinearLayout.LayoutParams(1000, 500));
        }

        scrollView.addView(layout);
        setContentView(scrollView);
    }
}
```

We have also changed the content to be `ImageView` instead of `ImageButton`, to illustrate the contrast when the child views are not interactive.

Multitouch Handling

(API Level 8)

Now let's take a look at an example of handling multitouch events. Listing 2-38 contains a customized `ImageView` with some multitouch interactions added in.

Listing 2-38. `ImageView` with Multitouch Handling

```
public class RotateZoomImageView extends ImageView {

    private ScaleGestureDetector mScaleDetector;
    private Matrix mImageMatrix;
    /* Last Rotation Angle */
    private int mLastAngle = 0;
    /* Pivot Point for Transforms */
    private int mPivotX, mPivotY;
```

```java
public RotateZoomImageView(Context context) {
    super(context);
    init(context);
}

public RotateZoomImageView(Context context, AttributeSet attrs) {
    super(context, attrs);
    init(context);
}

public RotateZoomImageView(Context context, AttributeSet attrs,
        int defStyle) {
    super(context, attrs, defStyle);
    init(context);
}

private void init(Context context) {
    mScaleDetector = new ScaleGestureDetector(context,
            mScaleListener);

    setScaleType(ScaleType.MATRIX);
    mImageMatrix = new Matrix();
}

/*
 * Use onSizeChanged() to calculate values based on the view's size.
 * The view has no size during init(), so we must wait for this
 * callback.
 */
@Override
protected void onSizeChanged(int w, int h, int oldw, int oldh) {
    if (w != oldw || h != oldh) {
        //Shift the image to the center of the view
        int translateX =
                Math.abs(w - getDrawable().getIntrinsicWidth()) / 2;
        int translateY =
                Math.abs(h - getDrawable().getIntrinsicHeight()) / 2;
        mImageMatrix.setTranslate(translateX, translateY);
        setImageMatrix(mImageMatrix);
        //Get the center point for future scale and rotate transforms
        mPivotX = w / 2;
        mPivotY = h / 2;
    }
}

private SimpleOnScaleGestureListener mScaleListener =
        new SimpleOnScaleGestureListener() {
    @Override
    public boolean onScale(ScaleGestureDetector detector) {
        // ScaleGestureDetector calculates a scale factor based on
        // whether the fingers are moving apart or together
```

141

```
        float scaleFactor = detector.getScaleFactor();
        //Pass that factor to a scale for the image
        mImageMatrix.postScale(scaleFactor, scaleFactor,
                mPivotX, mPivotY);
        setImageMatrix(mImageMatrix);

        return true;
    }
};


/*
 * Operate on two-finger events to rotate the image.
 * This method calculates the change in angle between the
 * pointers and rotates the image accordingly.  As the user
 * rotates their fingers, the image will follow.
 */
private boolean doRotationEvent(MotionEvent event) {
    //Calculate the angle between the two fingers
    float deltaX = event.getX(0) - event.getX(1);
    float deltaY = event.getY(0) - event.getY(1);
    double radians = Math.atan(deltaY / deltaX);
    //Convert to degrees
    int degrees = (int)(radians * 180 / Math.PI);

    switch (event.getAction()) {
    case MotionEvent.ACTION_DOWN:
        //Mark the initial angle
        mLastAngle = degrees;
        break;
    case MotionEvent.ACTION_MOVE:
        // ATAN returns a converted value between +/-90deg
        // which creates a point when two fingers are vertical
        // where the angle flips sign.  We handle this case by
        // rotating a small amount (5 degrees) in the
        // direction we were traveling

        if ((degrees - mLastAngle) > 45) {
            //Going CCW across the boundary
            mImageMatrix.postRotate(-5, mPivotX, mPivotY);
        } else if ((degrees - mLastAngle) < -45) {
            //Going CW across the boundary
            mImageMatrix.postRotate(5, mPivotX, mPivotY);
        } else {
            //Normal rotation, rotate the difference
            mImageMatrix.postRotate(degrees - mLastAngle,
                    mPivotX, mPivotY);
        }
        //Post the rotation to the image
        setImageMatrix(mImageMatrix);
        //Save the current angle
        mLastAngle = degrees;
```

```
            break;
        }

        return true;
    }

    @Override
    public boolean onTouchEvent(MotionEvent event) {
        if (event.getAction() == MotionEvent.ACTION_DOWN) {
            // We don't care about this event directly, but we
            // declare interest to get later multitouch events.
            return true;
        }

        switch (event.getPointerCount()) {
        case 3:
            // With three fingers down, zoom the image
            // using the ScaleGestureDetector
            return mScaleDetector.onTouchEvent(event);
        case 2:
            // With two fingers down, rotate the image
            // following the fingers
            return doRotationEvent(event);
        default:
            //Ignore this event
            return super.onTouchEvent(event);
        }
    }
}
```

This example creates a custom ImageView that listens for multitouch events and transforms the image content in response. The two events this view will detect are a two-finger rotate and a three-finger pinch. The rotate event is handled manually by processing each MotionEvent, while ScaleGestureDetector handles the pinch events. The ScaleType of the view is set to MATRIX, which will allow us to modify the image's appearance by applying different Matrix transformations.

Once the view is measured and laid out, the onSizeChanged() callback will trigger. This method can get called more than once, so we make changes only if the values from one instance to the next have changed. We take this opportunity to set up some values based around the view's size; we will need these values to center the image content inside the view and later perform the correct transformations. We also perform the first transformation here, which centers the image inside the view.

We decide which event to process by analyzing the events we receive in onTouchEvent(). By checking the getPointerCount() method of each MotionEvent, we can determine how many fingers are down and can deliver the event to the appropriate handler. As we've said before, we must also consume the initial ACTION_DOWN event here; otherwise, the subsequent event for the user's other fingers will never get delivered to this view. While we don't have anything interesting to do in this case, it is still necessary to explicitly return true.

ScaleGestureDetector operates by analyzing each touch event the application feeds to it and calling a series of OnScaleGestureListener callback methods when scale events occur. The most important callback is onScale(), which gets called regularly as the user's fingers move, but developers can also use onScaleBegin() and onScaleEnd() to do processing before and after the gesture.

ScaleGestureDetector provides a number of useful calculated values that the application can use in modifying the UI:

- getCurrentSpan(): Gets the distance between the two pointers being used in this gesture

- getFocusX()/getFocusY(): Gets the coordinates of the focal point for the current gesture. This is the average location about which the pointers are expanding and contracting.

- getScaleFactor(): Gets the ratio of span changes between this event and the previous event. As fingers move apart, this value will be slightly larger than 1, and as they move together, it will be slightly less than 1.

This example takes the scale factor from the detector and uses it to scale up or down the image content of the view by using postScale() on the image's Matrix.

Our two-finger rotate event is handled manually. For each event that is passed in, we calculate the x and y distance between the two fingers with getX() and getY(). The parameter these methods take is the pointer index, where 0 would be the initial pointer, and 1 would be the secondary pointer.

With these distances, we can do a little trigonometry to figure out the angle of the invisible line that would be formed between the two fingers. This angle is the control value we will use for our transformation. During ACTION_DOWN, we take whatever that angle is to be the initial value and simply store it. On subsequent ACTION_MOVE events, we post a rotation to the image based on the difference in angle between each touch event.

There is one edge case this example has to handle, and it has to do with the Math.atan() trig function. This method will return an angle in the range of –90 degrees to +90 degrees, and this rollover happens when the two fingers are vertically one above the other. The issue this creates is that the touch angle is no longer a gradual change: it jumps from +90 to –90 immediately as the fingers rotate, making the image jump. To solve this issue, we check for the case where the previous and current angle values cross this boundary, and then apply a small 5-degree rotation in the same direction of travel to keep the animation moving smoothly.

Notice that in all cases we are transforming the image with postScale() and postRotate(), rather than the setXXX versions of these methods as we did with setTranslation(). This is because each transformation is meant to be additive, meaning it should augment the current state rather than replace it. Calling setScale() or setRotate() would erase the existing state and leave that as the only transformation in the Matrix.

We also do each of these transformations around the pivot point that we calculated in onSizeChanged() as the midpoint of the view. We do this because, by default, the transformations would occur with a target point of (0,0), which is the top-left corner of the view. Because we have centered the image, we need to make sure all transformations also occur at the same center.

2-14. Forwarding Touch Events

Problem

You have views or other touch targets in your application that are too small for the average finger to reliably activate.

Solution

(API Level 1)

Use TouchDelegate to designate an arbitrary rectangle to forward touch events to your small views. TouchDelegate is designed to attach to a parent ViewGroup for the purpose of forwarding touch events it detects within a specific space to one of its children. TouchDelegate modifies each event to look to the target view as if it had happened within its own bounds.

How It Works

Listings 2-39 and 2-40 illustrate the use of TouchDelegate within a custom parent ViewGroup.

Listing 2-39. Custom Parent Implementing TouchDelegate

```
public class TouchDelegateLayout extends FrameLayout {

    public TouchDelegateLayout(Context context) {
        super(context);
        init(context);
    }

    public TouchDelegateLayout(Context context, AttributeSet attrs) {
        super(context, attrs);
        init(context);
    }

    public TouchDelegateLayout(Context context, AttributeSet attrs,
            int defStyle) {
        super(context, attrs, defStyle);
        init(context);
    }

    private CheckBox mButton;
    private void init(Context context) {
        //Create a small child view we want to forward touches to.
        mButton = new CheckBox(context);
        mButton.setText("Tap Anywhere");

        LayoutParams lp = new FrameLayout.LayoutParams(
                LayoutParams.WRAP_CONTENT,
                LayoutParams.WRAP_CONTENT,
                Gravity.CENTER);
        addView(mButton, lp);
    }

    /*
     * TouchDelegate is applied to this view (parent) to delegate all
     * touches within the specified rectangle to the CheckBox (child).
     * Here, the rectangle is the entire size of this parent view.
     *
     * This must be done after the view has a size so we know how big
     * to make the Rect, thus we've chosen to add the delegate in
     * onSizeChanged()
     */
```

```
@Override
protected void onSizeChanged(int w, int h, int oldw, int oldh) {
    if (w != oldw || h != oldh) {
        //Apply the whole area of this view as the delegate area
        Rect bounds = new Rect(0, 0, w, h);
        TouchDelegate delegate = new TouchDelegate(bounds, mButton);
        setTouchDelegate(delegate);
    }
}
}
```

Listing 2-40. Example Activity

```
public class DelegateActivity extends Activity {

    @Override
    protected void onCreate(Bundle savedInstanceState) {
        super.onCreate(savedInstanceState);
        TouchDelegateLayout layout =
                new TouchDelegateLayout(this);

        setContentView(layout);
    }
}
```

In this example, we create a parent view that contains a centered check box. This view also contains a TouchDelegate that will forward touches received anywhere inside the bounds of the parent to the check box. Because we want to pass the full size of the parent layout as the rectangle to forward events, we wait until onSizeChanged() is called on the view to construct and attach the TouchDelegate instance. Doing so in the constructor would not work, because at that point, the view has not been measured and will not have a size we can read.

The framework automatically dispatches unhandled touch events from the parent through TouchDelegate to its delegate view, so no additional code is needed to forward these events. You can see in Figure 2-9 that this application is receiving touch events far away from the check box, and the check box reacts as if it has been touched directly.

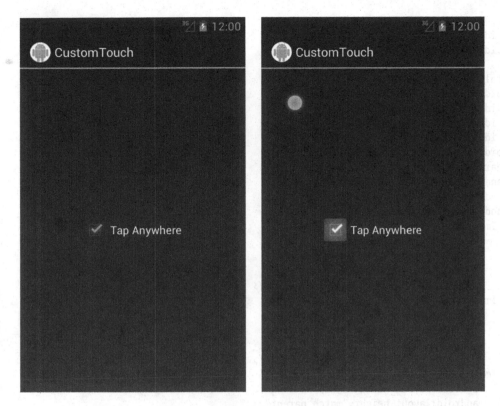

Figure 2-9. *Sample application with check box (left), and check box receiving a forwarded touch event (right). Note that the touch event received in the left image is when the finger is still on the screen.*

Custom Touch Forwarding (Remote Scroller)

TouchDelegate is great for forwarding tap events, but it has one drawback: each event forwarded to the delegate first has its location reset to the exact midpoint of the delegate view. This means that if you attempt to forward a series of ACTION_MOVE events through TouchDelegate, the results won't be what you expect, because they will look to the delegate view as if the finger isn't really moving at all.

If you need to reroute touch events in a more pure form, you can do so by manually calling the dispatchTouchEvent() method of the target view. Have a look at Listings 2-41 and 2-42 to see how this works.

Listing 2-41. `res/layout/main.xml`

```xml
<LinearLayout
    xmlns:android="http://schemas.android.com/apk/res/android"
    android:layout_width="match_parent"
    android:layout_height="match_parent"
    android:orientation="vertical" >

    <TextView
        android:id="@+id/text_touch"
        android:layout_width="match_parent"
        android:layout_height="0dp"
```

```
        android:layout_weight="1"
        android:gravity="center"
        android:text="Scroll Anywhere Here" />

    <HorizontalScrollView
        android:id="@+id/scroll_view"
        android:layout_width="match_parent"
        android:layout_height="0dp"
        android:layout_weight="1"
        android:background="#CCC">
        <LinearLayout
            android:layout_width="wrap_content"
            android:layout_height="match_parent"
            android:orientation="horizontal" >
            <ImageView
                android:layout_width="250dp"
                android:layout_height="match_parent"
                android:scaleType="fitXY"
                android:src="@drawable/ic_launcher" />
            <ImageView
                android:layout_width="250dp"
                android:layout_height="match_parent"
                android:scaleType="fitXY"
                android:src="@drawable/ic_launcher" />
            <ImageView
                android:layout_width="250dp"
                android:layout_height="match_parent"
                android:scaleType="fitXY"
                android:src="@drawable/ic_launcher" />
            <ImageView
                android:layout_width="250dp"
                android:layout_height="match_parent"
                android:scaleType="fitXY"
                android:src="@drawable/ic_launcher" />
        </LinearLayout>
    </HorizontalScrollView>
</LinearLayout>
```

Listing 2-42. Activity Forwarding Touches

```
public class RemoteScrollActivity extends Activity implements
        View.OnTouchListener {

    private TextView mTouchText;
    private HorizontalScrollView mScrollView;

    @Override
    protected void onCreate(Bundle savedInstanceState) {
        super.onCreate(savedInstanceState);
        setContentView(R.layout.main);
```

```
        mTouchText = (TextView) findViewById(R.id.text_touch);
        mScrollView =
            (HorizontalScrollView) findViewById(R.id.scroll_view);
        //Attach a listener for touch events to the top view
        mTouchText.setOnTouchListener(this);
    }

    @Override
    public boolean onTouch(View v, MotionEvent event) {
        // You can massage the event location if necessary.
        // Here we set the vertical location for each event to
        // the middle of the HorizontalScrollView.

        // Views expect events to be relative to their
        // local coordinates.
        event.setLocation(event.getX(),
                mScrollView.getHeight() / 2);

        // Forward each event from the TextView to the
        // HorizontalScrollView
        mScrollView.dispatchTouchEvent(event);
        return true;
    }
}
```

This example displays an activity that is divided in half. The top half is a TextView that prompts you to touch and scroll around, and the bottom half is a HorizontalScrollView with a series of images contained inside. The activity is set as the OnTouchListener for the TextView, so that we can forward all touches it receives to the HorizontalScrollView.

We want the events that the HorizontalScrollView sees to look, from its perspective, as if they were originally inside the view bounds. So before we forward the event, we call setLocation() to change the x/y coordinates. In this case, the x coordinate is fine as is, but we adjust the y coordinate to be in the center of the HorizontalScrollView. Now the events look as if the user's finger is moving back and forth along the middle of the view. We then call dispatchTouchEvent() with the modified event to have the HorizontalScrollView process it.

■ **Note** Avoid calling onTouchEvent() directly to forward touches. Calling dispatchTouchEvent() allows the event processing of the target view to take place the same way it does for normal touch events, including any intercepts that may be necessary.

2-15. Blocking Touch Thieves

Problem

You have designed nested touch interactions in your application views that don't work well with the standard flow of touch hierarchy, in which higher-level container views handle touch events directly by stealing them back from child views.

Solution

(API Level 1)

ViewGroup, which is the base class for all layouts and containers in the framework, provides the descriptively named method requestDisallowTouchIntercept() for just this purpose. Setting this flag on any container view indicates to the framework that, for the duration of the current gesture, we would prefer the container not intercept the events coming into its child views.

How It Works

To showcase this in action, we have created an example in which two competing touchable views live in the same space. The outer containing view is a ListView, which responds to touch events that indicate a vertical drag by scrolling the content. Inside the ListView, added as a header, is a ViewPager, which responds to horizontal drag touch events for swiping between pages. In and of itself, this creates a problem in that any attempts to horizontally swipe the ViewPager that even remotely vary in the vertical direction will be cancelled in favor of the ListView scrolling, because ListView is monitoring and intercepting those events. Since humans are not very capable of dragging in an exactly horizontal or vertical motion, this creates a usability problem.

To set up this example, we first have to declare a dimension resource (see Listing 2-43), and then the full activity is found in Listing 2-44.

Listing 2-43. res/values/dimens.xml

```
<?xml version="1.0" encoding="utf-8"?>
<resources>
    <dimen name="header_height">150dp</dimen>
</resources>
```

Listing 2-44. Activity Managing Touch Intercept

```
public class DisallowActivity extends Activity implements
        ViewPager.OnPageChangeListener {
    private static final String[] ITEMS = {
            "Row One", "Row Two", "Row Three", "Row Four",
            "Row Five", "Row Six", "Row Seven", "Row Eight",
            "Row Nine", "Row Ten"
    };

    private ViewPager mViewPager;

    private ListView mListView;

    @Override
    protected void onCreate(Bundle savedInstanceState) {
        super.onCreate(savedInstanceState);

        //Create a header view of horizontal swiping items
        mViewPager = new ViewPager(this);
        //As a ListView header, ViewPager must have a fixed height
        mViewPager.setLayoutParams(new ListView.LayoutParams(
                ListView.LayoutParams.MATCH_PARENT,
```

```
                getResources().getDimensionPixelSize(
                        R.dimen.header_height)) );
        // Listen for paging state changes to disable
        // parent touches
        mViewPager.setOnPageChangeListener(this);
        mViewPager.setAdapter(new HeaderAdapter(this));

        // Create a vertical scrolling list
        mListView = new ListView(this);
        // Add the pager as the list header
        mListView.addHeaderView(mViewPager);
        // Add list items
        mListView.setAdapter(new ArrayAdapter<String>(this,
                android.R.layout.simple_list_item_1, ITEMS));

        setContentView(mListView);
    }

    /* OnPageChangeListener Methods */

    @Override
    public void onPageScrolled(int position,
            float positionOffset, int positionOffsetPixels) { }

    @Override
    public void onPageSelected(int position) { }

    @Override
    public void onPageScrollStateChanged(int state) {
        //While the ViewPager is scrolling, disable the
        // ScrollView touch intercept so it cannot take over and
        // try to vertical scroll. This flag must be set for each
        // gesture you want to override.
        boolean isScrolling =
                state != ViewPager.SCROLL_STATE_IDLE;
        mListView.requestDisallowInterceptTouchEvent(isScrolling);
    }

    private static class HeaderAdapter extends PagerAdapter {
        private Context mContext;

        public HeaderAdapter(Context context) {
            mContext = context;
        }

        @Override
        public int getCount() {
            return 5;
        }
```

```
@Override
public Object instantiateItem(ViewGroup container,
        int position) {
    // Create a new page view
    TextView tv = new TextView(mContext);
    tv.setText(String.format("Page %d", position + 1));
    tv.setBackgroundColor((position % 2 == 0) ? Color.RED
            : Color.GREEN);
    tv.setGravity(Gravity.CENTER);
    tv.setTextColor(Color.BLACK);

    // Add as the view for this position, and return as
    // the object for this position
    container.addView(tv);
    return tv;
}

@Override
public void destroyItem(ViewGroup container,
        int position, Object object) {
    View page = (View) object;
    container.removeView(page);
}

@Override
public boolean isViewFromObject(View view,
        Object object) {
    return (view == object);
}
    }
  }
}
```

In this activity, we have a ListView that is the root view with a basic adapter included to display a static list of string items. Also in onCreate(), a ViewPager instance is created and added to the list as its header view. We will talk in more detail about how ViewPager works later in this chapter, but suffice it to say here that we are creating a simple ViewPager instance with a custom PagerAdapter that displays a handful of colored views as its pages for the user to swipe between.

When the ViewPager is created, we construct and apply a set of ListView.LayoutParams to govern how it should be displayed as the header. We must do this because the ViewPager itself has no inherent content size and list headers don't work well with a view that isn't explicit about its height. The fixed height is applied from our dimension's resource so we can easily get a properly scaled dp value that is device independent. This is simpler than attempting to fully construct a dp value completely in Java code.

The key to this example is in the OnPageChangeListener the activity implements (which is then applied to the ViewPager). This callback is triggered as the user interacts with ViewPager and swipes left and right. Inside the onPageScrollStateChanged() method, we are passed a value that indicates whether the ViewPager is idle, actively scrolling, or settling to a page after being scrolled. This is a perfect place to control the touch intercept behavior of the parent ListView. Whenever the scrolling state of the ViewPager is not idle, we don't want the ListView to steal the touch events ViewPager is using, so we set the flag in requestDisallowTouchIntercept().

There is another reason we continuously trigger this value. We mentioned in the original solution that this flag is valid *for the current gesture*. This means that each time a new ACTION_DOWN event occurs, we need to set the flag again. Rather than adding touch listeners just to look for specific events, we continuously set the flag based on the scrolling behavior of the child view and we get the same effect.

2-16. Making Drag-and-Drop Views

Problem

Your application's UI needs to allow the user to drag views around on the screen and to possibly drop them on top of other views.

Solution

(API Level 11)

Use the drag-and-drop APIs available in the Android 3.0 framework. The View class includes all the enhancements necessary to manage a drag event on the screen, and the OnDragListener interface can be attached to any View that needs to be notified of drag events as they occur. To begin a drag event, simply call startDrag() on the view you would like the user to begin dragging. This method takes a DragShadowBuilder instance, which will be used to construct what the dragging portion of the view should look like, and two additional parameters that will be passed forward to the drop targets and listeners.

The first of these is a ClipData object to pass forward a set of text or a Uri instance. This can be useful for passing a file location or a query to be made on a ContentProvider. The second is an Object referred to as the *local state* of the drag event. This can be any object and is designed to be a lightweight instance describing something application specific about the drag. The ClipData will be available only to the listener where the dragged view is dropped, but the local state will be accessible to any listener at any time by calling getLocalState() on the DragEvent.

The OnDragListener.onDrag() method will get called for each specific event that occurs during the drag-and-drop process, passing in a DragEvent to describe the specifics of each event. Each DragEvent will have one of the following actions:

- ACTION_DRAG_STARTED: Sent to all views when a new drag event begins with a call to startDrag()

  - The location can be obtained with getX() and getY().

- ACTION_DRAG_ENTERED: Sent to a view when the drag event enters its bounding box

- ACTION_DRAG_EXITED: Sent to a view when the drag event leaves its bounding box

- ACTION_DRAG_LOCATION: Sent to a view between ACTION_DRAG_ENTERED and ACTION_DRAG_EXITED with the current location of the drag inside that view

  - The location can be obtained with getX() and getY().

- ACTION_DROP: Sent to a view when the drag terminates and is still currently inside the bounds of that view

  - The location can be obtained with getX() and getY().

  - ClipData passed with the event can be obtained with getClipData() for this action only.

- ACTION_DRAG_ENDED: Sent to all views when the current drag event is complete

  - The result of the drag operation can be obtained here with getResult().

  - This return value is based on whether the target view of the drop had an active OnDragListener that returned true for the ACTION_DROP event.

This method works in a similar way to custom touch handling, in that the value you return from the listener will govern how future events are delivered. If a particular OnDragListener does not return true for ACTION_DRAG_STARTED, it will not receive any further events for the remainder of the drag except for ACTION_DRAG_ENDED.

How It Works

Let's look at an example of the drag-and-drop functionality, starting with Listing 2-45. Here we have created a custom ImageView that implements the OnDragListener interface.

Listing 2-45. Custom View Implementing OnDragListener

```
public class DropTargetView extends ImageView implements OnDragListener {

    private boolean mDropped;

    public DropTargetView(Context context) {
        super(context);
        init();
    }

    public DropTargetView(Context context, AttributeSet attrs) {
        super(context, attrs);
        init();
    }

    public DropTargetView(Context context, AttributeSet attrs,
            int defaultStyle) {
        super(context, attrs, defaultStyle);
        init();
    }

    private void init() {
        //We must set a valid listener to receive DragEvents
        setOnDragListener(this);
    }

    @Override
    public boolean onDrag(View v, DragEvent event) {
        PropertyValuesHolder pvhX, pvhY;
        switch (event.getAction()) {
        case DragEvent.ACTION_DRAG_STARTED:
            //React to a new drag by shrinking the view
            pvhX = PropertyValuesHolder.ofFloat("scaleX", 0.5f);
            pvhY = PropertyValuesHolder.ofFloat("scaleY", 0.5f);
```

```
        ObjectAnimator.ofPropertyValuesHolder(this,
                pvhX, pvhY).start();
        //Clear the current drop image on a new event
        setImageDrawable(null);
        mDropped = false;
        break;
    case DragEvent.ACTION_DRAG_ENDED:
        // React to a drag ending by resetting the view size
        // if we weren't the drop target.
        if (!mDropped) {
            pvhX = PropertyValuesHolder.ofFloat("scaleX", 1f);
            pvhY = PropertyValuesHolder.ofFloat("scaleY", 1f);
            ObjectAnimator.ofPropertyValuesHolder(this,
                    pvhX, pvhY).start();
            mDropped = false;
        }
        break;
    case DragEvent.ACTION_DRAG_ENTERED:
        //React to a drag entering this view by growing slightly
        pvhX = PropertyValuesHolder.ofFloat("scaleX", 0.75f);
        pvhY = PropertyValuesHolder.ofFloat("scaleY", 0.75f);
        ObjectAnimator.ofPropertyValuesHolder(this,
                pvhX, pvhY).start();
        break;
    case DragEvent.ACTION_DRAG_EXITED:
        //React to a drag leaving by returning to previous size
        pvhX = PropertyValuesHolder.ofFloat("scaleX", 0.5f);
        pvhY = PropertyValuesHolder.ofFloat("scaleY", 0.5f);
        ObjectAnimator.ofPropertyValuesHolder(this,
                pvhX, pvhY).start();
        break;
    case DragEvent.ACTION_DROP:
        // React to a drop event with a short keyframe animation
        // and setting this view's image to the drawable passed along
        // with the drag event

        // This animation shrinks the view briefly down to nothing
        // and then back.
        Keyframe frame0 = Keyframe.ofFloat(0f, 0.75f);
        Keyframe frame1 = Keyframe.ofFloat(0.5f, 0f);
        Keyframe frame2 = Keyframe.ofFloat(1f, 0.75f);
        pvhX = PropertyValuesHolder.ofKeyframe("scaleX",
                frame0, frame1, frame2);
        pvhY = PropertyValuesHolder.ofKeyframe("scaleY",
                frame0, frame1, frame2);
        ObjectAnimator.ofPropertyValuesHolder(this,
                pvhX, pvhY).start();
        //Set our image from the Object passed with the DragEvent
        setImageDrawable((Drawable) event.getLocalState());
```

```
            //We set the dropped flag so the ENDED animation will
            // not also run
            mDropped = true;
            break;
        default:
            //Ignore events we aren't interested in
            return false;
    }
    //Declare interest in all events we have noted
    return true;
    }

}
```

This ImageView is set up to monitor incoming drag events and animate itself accordingly. Whenever a new drag begins, the ACTION_DRAG_STARTED event will be sent here, and this view will scale itself down to 50 percent size. This is a good indication to the user where they can drag this view they've just picked up. We also make sure that this listener is structured to return true from this event so that it receives other events during the drag.

If the user drags their view onto this one, ACTION_DRAG_ENTERED will trigger the view to scale up slightly, indicating it as the active recipient if the view were to be dropped. ACTION_DRAG_EXITED will be received if the view is dragged away, and this view will respond by scaling back down to the same size as when we entered "drag mode." If the user releases the drag over the top of this view, ACTION_DROP will be triggered, and a special animation is run to indicate the drop was received. We also read the local state variable of the event at this point, assume it is a Drawable, and set it as the image content for this view.

ACTION_DRAG_ENDED will notify this view to return to its original size because we are no longer in drag mode. However, if this view was also the target of the drop, we want it to keep its size, so we ignore this event in that case.

Listings 2-46 and 2-47 show an example activity that allows the user to long-press an image and then drag that image to our custom drop target.

Listing 2-46. res/layout/main.xml

```xml
<?xml version="1.0" encoding="utf-8"?>
<RelativeLayout
    xmlns:android="http://schemas.android.com/apk/res/android"
    android:layout_width="match_parent"
    android:layout_height="match_parent" >

    <!-- Top Row of Draggable Items -->
    <LinearLayout
        android:layout_width="match_parent"
        android:layout_height="wrap_content"
        android:orientation="horizontal" >
        <ImageView
            android:id="@+id/image1"
            android:layout_width="0dp"
            android:layout_height="wrap_content"
            android:layout_weight="1"
            android:src="@drawable/ic_send" />
        <ImageView
            android:id="@+id/image2"
            android:layout_width="0dp"
```

```
                android:layout_height="wrap_content"
                android:layout_weight="1"
                android:src="@drawable/ic_share" />
        <ImageView
                android:id="@+id/image3"
                android:layout_width="0dp"
                android:layout_height="wrap_content"
                android:layout_weight="1"
                android:src="@drawable/ic_favorite" />
    </LinearLayout>

    <!-- Bottom Row of Drop Targets -->
    <LinearLayout
            android:layout_width="match_parent"
            android:layout_height="wrap_content"
            android:layout_alignParentBottom="true"
            android:orientation="horizontal" >
        <com.examples.dragtouch.DropTargetView
                android:id="@+id/drag_target1"
                android:layout_width="0dp"
                android:layout_height="100dp"
                android:layout_weight="1"
                android:background="#A00" />
        <com.examples.dragtouch.DropTargetView
                android:id="@+id/drag_target2"
                android:layout_width="0dp"
                android:layout_height="100dp"
                android:layout_weight="1"
                android:background="#0A0" />
        <com.examples.dragtouch.DropTargetView
                android:id="@+id/drag_target3"
                android:layout_width="0dp"
                android:layout_height="100dp"
                android:layout_weight="1"
                android:background="#00A" />
    </LinearLayout>

</RelativeLayout>
```

Listing 2-47. Activity Forwarding Touches

```
public class DragTouchActivity extends Activity implements
        OnLongClickListener {

    @Override
    public void onCreate(Bundle savedInstanceState) {
        super.onCreate(savedInstanceState);
        setContentView(R.layout.main);
```

```
        //Attach long-press listener to each ImageView
        findViewById(R.id.image1).setOnLongClickListener(this);
        findViewById(R.id.image2).setOnLongClickListener(this);
        findViewById(R.id.image3).setOnLongClickListener(this);
    }

    @Override
    public boolean onLongClick(View v) {
        DragShadowBuilder shadowBuilder =
                new DragShadowBuilder(v);
        // Start a drag, and pass the View's image along as
        // the local state
        v.startDrag(null, shadowBuilder,
                ((ImageView) v).getDrawable(), 0);

        return true;
    }

}
```

This example displays a row of three images at the top of the screen, along with three of our custom drop target views at the bottom of the screen. Each image is set up with a listener for long-press events, and the long-press triggers a new drag via startDrag(). The DragShadowBuilder passed to the drag initializer is the default implementation provided by the framework. In the next section, we'll look at how this can be customized, but this version just creates a slightly transparent copy of the view being dragged and places it centered underneath the touch point.

We also capture the image content of the view the user selected with getDrawable() and pass that along as the local state of the drag, which the custom drop target will use to set as its image. This will create the appearance that the view was dropped on the target. Figure 2-10 shows how this example looks when it loads, during a drag operation, and after the image has been dropped on a target.

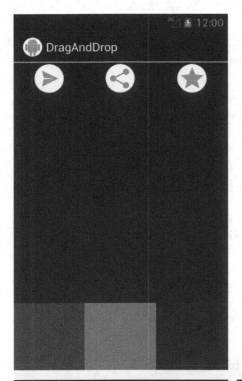

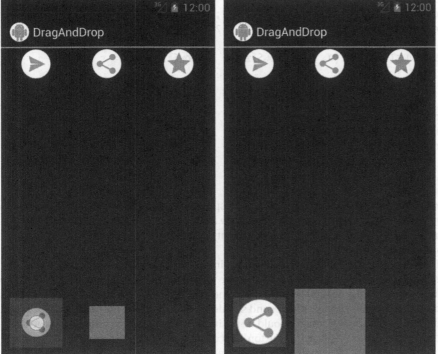

Figure 2-10. *Drag example before the drag (top), while the user is dragging and hovering over a target (bottom left), and after the view has been dropped (bottom right)*

Customizing DragShadowBuilder

The default implementation of DragShadowBuilder is extremely convenient, but it may not be what your application needs. Let's take a look at Listing 2-48, which is a customized builder implementation.

Listing 2-48. Custom DragShadowBuilder

```java
public class DrawableDragShadowBuilder extends DragShadowBuilder {
    private Drawable mDrawable;

    public DrawableDragShadowBuilder(View view, Drawable drawable) {
        super(view);
        // Set the Drawable and apply a green filter to it
        mDrawable = drawable;
        mDrawable.setColorFilter( new PorterDuffColorFilter(
                Color.GREEN, PorterDuff.Mode.MULTIPLY) );
    }

    @Override
    public void onProvideShadowMetrics(Point shadowSize,
            Point touchPoint) {
        // Fill in the size
        shadowSize.x = mDrawable.getIntrinsicWidth();
        shadowSize.y = mDrawable.getIntrinsicHeight();
        // Fill in the location of the shadow relative to the touch.
        // Here we center the shadow under the finger.
        touchPoint.x = mDrawable.getIntrinsicWidth() / 2;
        touchPoint.y = mDrawable.getIntrinsicHeight() / 2;

        mDrawable.setBounds(new Rect(0, 0, shadowSize.x, shadowSize.y));
    }

    @Override
    public void onDrawShadow(Canvas canvas) {
        //Draw the shadow view onto the provided canvas
        mDrawable.draw(canvas);
    }
}
```

This custom implementation takes in the image that it will display as the shadow as a separate Drawable parameter rather than making a visual copy of the source view. We also apply a green ColorFilter to it for added effect. It turns out that DragShadowBuilder is a fairly straightforward class to extend. Two primary methods are required to effectively override it.

The first is onProvideShadowMetrics(), which is called once initially with two Point objects for the builder to fill in. The first should be filled with the size of the image to be used for the shadow, where the desired width is set as the x value and the desired height is set as the y value. In our example, we have set this to be the intrinsic width and height of the image. The second should be filled with the desired touch location for the shadow. This defines how the shadow image should be positioned in relation to the user's finger; for example, setting both x and y to zero would place it at the top-left corner of the image. In our example, we have set it to the image's midpoint so the image will be centered under the user's finger.

The second method is onDrawShadow(), which is called repeatedly to render the shadow image. The Canvas passed into this method is created by the framework based on the information contained in onProvideShadowMetrics(). Here you can do all sorts of custom drawing as you might with any other custom view. Our example simply tells Drawable to draw itself on the Canvas.

2-17. Using the Material Design Navigation Drawer

Problem

Your application needs a top-level navigation menu, and you want to implement one that animates in and out from the side of the screen in compliance with the latest Google design guidelines.

Solution

(API Level 9)

Integrate the DrawerLayout widget to manage menu views that slide in from the left or right of the screen, available in the Android Support Library. DrawerLayout is a container widget that manages each of the first child views in its hierarchy with a specified Gravity value of LEFT or RIGHT (or START/END if supporting right-to-left layouts) as an animated content drawer. By default, each view is hidden, but will be animated in from its respective side when either the openDrawer() method is called or a finger swipe occurs inward from the appropriate side bezel. To help indicate the presence of a drawer, DrawerLayout will also show a peek of the appropriate view if a finger is held down on the appropriate side of the screen.

DrawerLayout supports multiple drawers, one for each gravity setting, and they can be placed anywhere in the layout hierarchy. The only soft rule is that they should be added after the main content view in the layout (that is, placed after that view element in the layout XML). Otherwise, the z-ordering of the views will keep the drawer(s) from being visible.

Integration with the action bar is also supported by way of the ActionBarDrawerToggle element. This is a widget that monitors taps on the Home button area of the action bar and toggles the visibility of the "main" drawer (the drawer with Gravity.LEFT or Gravity.START set).

Finally, integration with the NavigationView from the Android Design Support library provides a way to easily add a customizable navigation drawer to your application. This widget allows you to use regular menu XML for specifying menu options and specify an XML layout to be used for the header. It is also possible to fully customize the content of a navigation drawer inside the NavigationView widget.

■ **Important** DrawerLayout and the other widgets used in this example are available only in the Android Support Library; it is not part of the native SDK at any platform level. However, any application targeting API Level 9 or later can use the widget with the Support Library included. For more information on including the Support Library in your project, reference http://developer.android.com/tools/support-library/index.html.

How It Works

While it is not required for you to use an action bar at all with DrawerLayout, it is the most common use case. The following examples show how to create navigation drawers with DrawerLayout as well as integrate the action bar.

The following example creates an application with two navigation drawers: a main drawer on the left with a list of options to select from, and a secondary drawer on the right with some additional interactive content. Selecting an item from the list in the main drawer will modify the background color of the primary content view.

In Listing 2-49, we have a layout that includes a DrawerLayout. Notice that because this widget is not a core element, we must use its fully qualified class name in the XML.

Listing 2-49. res/layout/activity_main.xml

```xml
<?xml version="1.0" encoding="utf-8"?>
<android.support.v4.widget.DrawerLayout
    xmlns:android="http://schemas.android.com/apk/res/android"
    xmlns:app="http://schemas.android.com/apk/res-auto"
    android:id="@+id/drawer_layout"
    android:layout_width="match_parent"
    android:layout_height="match_parent"
    android:fitsSystemWindows="true"

    <android.support.design.widget.CoordinatorLayout
        android:layout_width="match_parent"
        android:layout_height="match_parent"
        android:fitsSystemWindows="true"

        <android.support.design.widget.AppBarLayout
            android:layout_width="match_parent"
            android:layout_height="wrap_content"
            android:theme="@style/AppTheme.AppBarOverlay">

            <android.support.v7.widget.Toolbar
                android:id="@+id/toolbar"
                android:layout_width="match_parent"
                android:layout_height="?attr/actionBarSize"
                android:background="?attr/colorPrimary"
                app:popupTheme="@style/AppTheme.PopupOverlay"/>

        </android.support.design.widget.AppBarLayout>

        <FrameLayout
            android:id="@+id/content_main"
            android:layout_width="match_parent"
            android:layout_height="match_parent"
            app:layout_behavior="@string/appbar_scrolling_view_behavior"/>

    </android.support.design.widget.CoordinatorLayout>

    <android.support.design.widget.NavigationView
        android:id="@+id/nav_view"
        android:layout_width="wrap_content"
        android:layout_height="match_parent"
        android:layout_gravity="start"
        android:fitsSystemWindows="true"
        app:headerLayout="@layout/nav_header_main"
        app:menu="@menu/activity_main_drawer"/>

    <android.support.design.widget.NavigationView
        android:id="@+id/second_nav_view"
```

```
    android:layout_width="wrap_content"
    android:layout_height="match_parent"
    android:layout_gravity="end"
    android:fitsSystemWindows="true">
    <ImageView
        android:layout_width="match_parent"
        android:layout_height="wrap_content"
        android:layout_gravity="center"
        android:scaleType="fitCenter"
        android:src="@mipmap/ic_launcher"
        android:onClick="onSecondDrawerImageClick"/>
</android.support.design.widget.NavigationView>

</android.support.v4.widget.DrawerLayout>
```

We have included two NavigationView views that will be drawers in our application, one on the left and another on the right; we control the alignment by setting their android:layout_gravity attributes. DrawerLayout does the rest, mapping each view by inspecting the gravity, so we do not need to link them in any other way. Before we get to the activity, our project has one more resource in it; we have created an options menu to display an action inside the action bar (see Listing 2-50).

Listing 2-50. res/menu/main.xml

```
<menu xmlns:android="http://schemas.android.com/apk/res/android"
      xmlns:app="http://schemas.android.com/apk/res-auto">
    <item android:id="@+id/action_second_drawer"
          android:orderInCategory="100"
          android:title="@string/action_second_drawer"
          app:showAsAction="never"/>
</menu>
```

Finally, we have the activity in Listing 2-51. In addition to the DrawerLayout, this example includes an ActionBarDrawerToggle to provide integration with the action bar Home button.

Listing 2-51. Activity with DrawerLayout Integrated

```
public class NavigationDrawerActivity extends AppCompatActivity
        implements NavigationView.OnNavigationItemSelectedListener {

    @Override
    protected void onCreate(Bundle savedInstanceState) {
        super.onCreate(savedInstanceState);
        setContentView(R.layout.activity_main);
        Toolbar toolbar = (Toolbar) findViewById(R.id.toolbar);
        setSupportActionBar(toolbar);

        DrawerLayout drawer = (DrawerLayout) findViewById(R.id.drawer_layout);
        ActionBarDrawerToggle toggle = new ActionBarDrawerToggle(
                this, drawer, toolbar, R.string.navigation_drawer_open,
                R.string.navigation_drawer_close);
        drawer.addDrawerListener(toggle);
        toggle.syncState();
```

```java
        NavigationView navigationView = (NavigationView) findViewById(R.id.nav_view);
        navigationView.setNavigationItemSelectedListener(this);
        if (savedInstanceState == null) {
            ExampleFragment fragment = ExampleFragment.newInstance("Camera");
            getSupportFragmentManager().beginTransaction()
                    .replace(R.id.content_main,fragment)
                    .commit();
        }
    }

    @Override
    public void onBackPressed() {
        DrawerLayout drawer = (DrawerLayout) findViewById(R.id.drawer_layout);
        if (drawer.isDrawerOpen(GravityCompat.START)) {
            drawer.closeDrawer(GravityCompat.START);
        } else if (drawer.isDrawerOpen(GravityCompat.END)) {
            drawer.closeDrawer(GravityCompat.END);
        } else {
            super.onBackPressed();
        }
    }

    @Override
    public boolean onCreateOptionsMenu(Menu menu) {
        getMenuInflater().inflate(R.menu.main, menu);
        return true;
    }

    @Override
    public boolean onOptionsItemSelected(MenuItem item) {
        int id = item.getItemId();

        if (id == R.id.action_second_drawer) {
            DrawerLayout drawer = (DrawerLayout) findViewById(R.id.drawer_layout);
            drawer.openDrawer(GravityCompat.END);
            return true;
        }

        return super.onOptionsItemSelected(item);
    }

    @SuppressWarnings("StatementWithEmptyBody")
    @Override
    public boolean onNavigationItemSelected(MenuItem item) {
        Fragment fragment;
        String text = null;

        switch (item.getItemId()) {
            case R.id.nav_camera:
                text = "Camera";
                break;
```

```
                case R.id.nav_gallery:
                    text = "Gallery";
                    break;
                case R.id.nav_slideshow:
                    text = "Slideshow";
                    break;
                case R.id.nav_manage:
                    text = "Tools";
                    break;
            }

            fragment = ExampleFragment.newInstance(text);
            getSupportFragmentManager()
                    .beginTransaction()
                    .replace(R.id.content_main, fragment)
                    .addToBackStack(text)
                    .commit();

            DrawerLayout drawer = (DrawerLayout) findViewById(R.id.drawer_layout);
            drawer.closeDrawer(GravityCompat.START);
            return true;
        }

        public void onSecondDrawerImageClick(View view) {
            DrawerLayout drawer = (DrawerLayout) findViewById(R.id.drawer_layout);
            drawer.closeDrawer(GravityCompat.END);
        }
    }
```

When the activity is initialized, we create an `ActionBarDrawerToggle` instance and set it as the `DrawerListener` of the `DrawerLayout`. This is required so the toggle can listen for events, but it also means we cannot listen for those events in our application unless we extend `ActionBarDrawerToggle` to override the listener method, which we've done here. The toggle is linked to the hosting activity and the `DrawerLayout` it should control.

`DrawerLayout` is designed to close an open drawer when the main content view receives touch events (that is, the user touches outside the drawer). Touch events inside the layout (such as tapping an item in our main list or the button in our secondary drawer) require us to close the drawer manually when necessary. Inside the `OnItemClickListener` registered to our list, after changing the background color of the content view, we call `closeDrawer()` to do just that.

Notice how methods such as `openDrawer()` and `closeDrawer()` take a view as an argument. Since `DrawerLayout` can manage more than one drawer, we have to tell it which drawer widget to act on. These methods can also be triggered using the `Gravity` parameter associated with the drawer if your application doesn't have a reference to the drawer view itself.

The NavigationView is basically a convenience class that extends FrameLayout with functions useful for a navigation drawer. One of the most appreciated features is the possibility to populate the navigation menu using regular menu XML, the same we use for the options menu. In this example, we define four different menu options as show in Listing 2-52.

Listing 2-52. Menu XML for a NavigationView

```xml
<?xml version="1.0" encoding="utf-8"?>
<menu xmlns:android="http://schemas.android.com/apk/res/android">

    <group android:checkableBehavior="single"
        android:id="@+id/first_section">
        <item
            android:id="@+id/nav_camera"
            android:icon="@drawable/ic_menu_camera"
            android:checked="true"
            android:title="Import"/>
        <item
            android:id="@+id/nav_gallery"
            android:icon="@drawable/ic_menu_gallery"
            android:title="Gallery"/>
        <item
            android:id="@+id/nav_slideshow"
            android:icon="@drawable/ic_menu_slideshow"
            android:title="Slideshow"/>
    </group>

    <group android:checkableBehavior="single"
            android:id="@+id/second_section">
        <item
            android:id="@+id/nav_manage"
            android:icon="@drawable/ic_menu_manage"
            android:title="Tools"/>
    </group>

</menu>
```

This XML is interpreted by the NavigationView when it gets inflated and it will use the value from app:menu="@menu/activity_main_drawer" to decide which menu file to use. The NavigationView will keep track on which item you selected and highlight that and all you need to provide is a unique id for each item, a title and an icon (title and icon are optional, but highly recommended). You can create dividers between groups of items by wrapping the menu items in a group element. The important thing here is to add a unique id to each group, or the divider won't appear. Also, in order for highlighting of the selected item to work, you must set android:checkableBehavior="single" on the group.

You can also specify a header for the NavigationView using the attribute app:headerLayout, which will point to an XML layout. In this example, you can see the layout for our first navigation drawer in Listing 2-53.

Listing 2-53. Menu XML for a NavigationView

```xml
<?xml version="1.0" encoding="utf-8"?>
<LinearLayout
    xmlns:android="http://schemas.android.com/apk/res/android"
    xmlns:app="http://schemas.android.com/apk/res-auto"
    android:layout_width="match_parent"
    android:layout_height="@dimen/nav_header_height"
    android:background="@drawable/side_nav_bar"
    android:gravity="bottom"
```

```
    android:orientation="vertical"
    android:paddingBottom="@dimen/activity_vertical_margin"
    android:paddingLeft="@dimen/activity_horizontal_margin"
    android:paddingRight="@dimen/activity_horizontal_margin"
    android:paddingTop="@dimen/activity_vertical_margin"
    android:theme="@style/ThemeOverlay.AppCompat.Light">

    <ImageView
        android:id="@+id/imageView"
        android:layout_width="wrap_content"
        android:layout_height="wrap_content"
        android:paddingTop="@dimen/nav_header_vertical_spacing"
        app:srcCompat="@android:drawable/sym_def_app_icon"/>

    <TextView
        android:layout_width="match_parent"
        android:layout_height="wrap_content"
        android:paddingTop="@dimen/nav_header_vertical_spacing"
        android:text="Android Recipes"
        android:textAppearance="@style/TextAppearance.AppCompat.Body1"/>

    <TextView
        android:id="@+id/textView"
        android:layout_width="wrap_content"
        android:layout_height="wrap_content"
        android:text="developer@androidrecipes.com"/>

</LinearLayout>
```

This header is optional, but it is also a great place to put information about the current user or a bigger logo of your company. The layout works as any regular XML layout and you can add click listeners and such to the elements within. This is useful for such use cases where your application supports multiple user accounts (see most Google applications).

The second drawer we created in this example is triggered through the options menu. In this case we're not using any menu XML or a header layout, but instead let the NavigationView wrap an ImageView. We could basically have used something other than NavigationView for this drawer, but as this widget provides much of the functionality needed for a drawer, it is recommended to use it even if your navigation drawer won't contain the regular menu items.

Figure 2-11 shows how tapping the Home button in the action bar expands the main drawer to expose the options list; notice also that the actions are gone when the drawer is open. Figure 2-12 illustrates the secondary drawer peeking in from a bezel swipe on the right side of the screen, and then fully open.

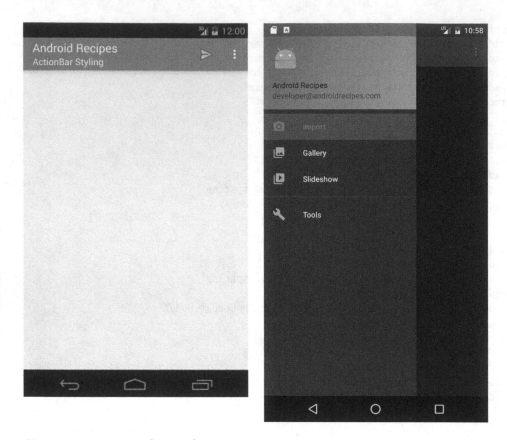

Figure 2-11. *Activity with main drawer*

Figure 2-12. *Activity with secondary drawer*

The DrawerLayout, ActionBarToggle and NavigationView are powerful and easy to use components for building UI navigation on Android. It is highly recommended that you start with these before trying to implement your widgets, even if you need something with a more custom look and feel. The Android Studio Activity templates will automatically create most of the code needed, so we recommend using that at first. However, make sure you understand how the widgts work and how to configure them as well.

2-18. Swiping Between Views

Problem

You need to implement paging with a swipe gesture in your application's UI in order to move between views or fragments.

Solution

(API Level 9)

Implement the ViewPager widget to provide paging with swipe scroll gestures. ViewPager is a modified implementation of the AdapterView pattern that the framework uses for widgets such as ListView and GridView. It requires its own adapter implementation as a subclass of PagerAdapter, but it is conceptually very similar to the patterns used in BaseAdapter and ListAdapter. It does not inherently implement recycling of the components being paged, but it does provide callbacks to create and destroy the items on the fly so that only a fixed number of content views are in memory at a given time.

■ **Important** ViewPager is available only in the Android Support Library; it is not part of the native SDK at any platform level. However, any application targeting API Level 9 or later can use the widget with the Support Library included. For more information on including the Support Library in your project, reference http:// developer.android.com/tools/support-library/index.html.

How It Works

Most of the heavy lifting in working with ViewPager is in the PagerAdapter implementation you provide. Let's start with a simple example, shown in Listing 2-54, that pages between a series of images.

Listing 2-54. Custom PagerAdapter for Images

```
public class ImagePagerAdapter extends PagerAdapter {
    private Context mContext;

    private static final int[] IMAGES = {
        android.R.drawable.ic_menu_camera,
        android.R.drawable.ic_menu_add,
        android.R.drawable.ic_menu_delete,
        android.R.drawable.ic_menu_share,
        android.R.drawable.ic_menu_edit
    };

    private static final int[] COLORS = {
        Color.RED,
        Color.BLUE,
        Color.GREEN,
        Color.GRAY,
        Color.MAGENTA
    };

    public ImagePagerAdapter(Context context) {
        super();
        mContext = context;
    }

    /*
     * Provide the total number of pages
     */
    @Override
    public int getCount() {
        return IMAGES.length;
    }
```

```
/*
 * Override this method if you want to show more than one page
 * at a time inside the ViewPager's content bounds.
 */
@Override
public float getPageWidth(int position) {
    return 1f;
}

@Override
public Object instantiateItem(ViewGroup container, int position) {
    // Create a new ImageView and add it to the supplied container
    ImageView iv = new ImageView(mContext);
    // Set the content for this position
    iv.setImageResource(IMAGES[position]);
    iv.setBackgroundColor(COLORS[position]);

    // You MUST add the view here, the framework will not
    container.addView(iv);
    //Return this view also as the key object for this position
    return iv;
}

@Override
public void destroyItem(ViewGroup container, int position,
        Object object) {
    //Remove the view from the container here
    container.removeView((View) object);
}

@Override
public boolean isViewFromObject(View view, Object object) {
    // Validate that the object returned from instantiateItem()
    // is associated with the view added to the container in
    // that location.  Our example uses the same object in
    // both places.
    return (view == object);
}

}
```

In this example, we have an implementation of PagerAdapter that serves up a series of ImageView instances for the user to page through. The first required override in the adapter is getCount(), which, just like its AdapterView counterpart, should return the total number of items available.

ViewPager works by keeping track of a *key* object for each item alongside a view to display for that object; this keeps the separation between the adapter items and their views that developers are used to with AdapterView. However, the implementation is a bit different. With AdapterView, the adapter's getView() method is called to construct and return the view to display for that item. With ViewPager, the callback's instantiateItem() and destroyItem() will be called when a new view needs to be created, or when one has scrolled outside the bounds of the pager's limit and should be removed; the number of items that any ViewPager will keep hold of is set by the setOffscreenPageLimit() method.

■ **Note**   The default value for the offscreen page limit is 3. This means ViewPager will track the currently visible page, one to the left, and one to the right. The number of tracked pages is always centered around the currently visible page.

In our example, we use instantiateItem() to create a new ImageView and then apply the properties for that particular position. Unlike AdapterView, the PagerAdapter must attach the View to display to the supplied ViewGroup in addition to returning the unique key object to represent this item. These two things don't have to be the same, but they can be in a simple example like this. The callback isViewFromObject() is a required override on PagerAdapter so the application can provide the link between which key object goes with which view. In our example, we attach the ImageView to the supplied parent and then also return the same instance as the key from instantiateItem(). The code for isViewFromObject() becomes simple, then, as we return true if both parameters are the same instance.

Complementary to instantiate, PagerAdapter must also remove the specified view from the parent container in destroyItem(). If the views displayed in the pager are heavyweight and you wanted to implement some basic view recycling in your adapter, you could hold on to the view after it was removed so it could be handed back to instantiateItem() to attach to another key object. See Listing 2-55, which shows an example activity using our custom adapter with a ViewPager. The resulting application is shown in Figure 2-13.

Listing 2-55. Activity Using ViewPager and ImagePagerAdapter

```
public class PagerActivity extends Activity {

    @Override
    protected void onCreate(Bundle savedInstanceState) {
        super.onCreate(savedInstanceState);
        ViewPager pager = new ViewPager(this);
        pager.setAdapter(new ImagePagerAdapter(this));

        setContentView(pager);
    }
}
```

Figure 2-13. `ViewPager` *dragging between two pages*

Running this application, the user can horizontally swipe a finger to page between all the images provided by the custom adapter, and each page displays full-screen. There is one method defined in the example we did not mention: getPageWidth(). This method allows you to define for each position how large the page should be as a percentage of the ViewPager size. By default it is set to 1, and the previous example didn't change this. But let's say we wanted to display multiple pages at once; we can adjust the value this method returns.

If we modify getPageWidth() as in the following snippet, we can display three pages at once:

```
/*
 * Override this method if you want to show more than one page
 * at a time inside the ViewPager's content bounds.
 */
@Override
public float getPageWidth(int position) {
    //Page width should be 1/3 of the view
    return 0.333f;
}
```

You can see in Figure 2-14 how this modifies the resulting application.

Figure 2-14. ViewPager *showing three pages at once*

Adding and Removing Pages

Listing 2-56 illustrates a slightly more complex adapter for use with ViewPager. This example uses
FragmentPagerAdapter as a base, which is another class in the framework where each page item is a
fragment instead of a simple view.

This example is designed to take a long list of data and break it into smaller sections that display on each
page. The Fragment this adapter displays is a custom inner implementation that receives a List of items and
displays them in a ListView.

Listing 2-56. ListPagerAdapter *for displaying a list of fragments*

```
public class ListPagerAdapter extends FragmentPagerAdapter {

    private static final int ITEMS_PER_PAGE = 3;

    private List<String> mItems;

    public ListPagerAdapter(FragmentManager manager,
            List<String> items) {
        super(manager);
        mItems = items;
    }
```

```java
/*
 * This method will get called only the first time a
 * fragment is needed for this position.
 */
@Override
public Fragment getItem(int position) {
    int start = position * ITEMS_PER_PAGE;
    return ArrayListFragment.newInstance(
            getPageList(position), start);
}

@Override
public int getCount() {
    // Get whole number
    int pages = mItems.size() / ITEMS_PER_PAGE;
    // Add one more page for any remaining values if list size
    // is not divisible by page size
    int excess = mItems.size() % ITEMS_PER_PAGE;
    if (excess > 0) {
        pages++;
    }

    return pages;
}

/*
 * This will get called after getItem() for new Fragments, but
 * also when Fragments beyond the offscreen page limit are added
 * back; we need to make sure to update the list for these elements.
 */
@Override
public Object instantiateItem(ViewGroup container, int position) {
    ArrayListFragment fragment =
            (ArrayListFragment) super.instantiateItem(container,
                    position);
    fragment.updateListItems(getPageList(position));
    return fragment;
}

/*
 * Called by the framework when notifyDataSetChanged() is called,
 * we must decide how each Fragment has changed for the new data set.
 * We also return POSITION_NONE if a Fragment at a particular
 * position is no longer needed so the adapter can remove it.
 */
@Override
public int getItemPosition(Object object) {
    ArrayListFragment fragment = (ArrayListFragment)object;
    int position = fragment.getBaseIndex() / ITEMS_PER_PAGE;
    if(position >= getCount()) {
        //This page no longer needed
```

```
            return POSITION_NONE;
        } else {
            //Refresh fragment data display
            fragment.updateListItems(getPageList(position));

            return position;
        }
    }

    /*
     * Helper method to obtain the piece of the overall list that
     * should be applied to a given Fragment
     */
    private List<String> getPageList(int position) {
        int start = position * ITEMS_PER_PAGE;
        int end = Math.min(start + ITEMS_PER_PAGE, mItems.size());
        List<String> itemPage = mItems.subList(start, end);

        return itemPage;
    }

    /*
     * Internal custom Fragment that displays a list section inside
     * of a ListView, and provides external methods for updating the list
     */
    public static class ArrayListFragment extends Fragment {
        private ArrayList<String> mItems;
        private ArrayAdapter<String> mAdapter;
        private int mBaseIndex;

        //Fragments are created by convention using a Factory
        static ArrayListFragment newInstance(List<String> page,
                int baseIndex) {
            ArrayListFragment fragment = new ArrayListFragment();
            fragment.updateListItems(page);
            fragment.setBaseIndex(baseIndex);
            return fragment;
        }

        public ArrayListFragment() {
            super();
            mItems = new ArrayList<String>();
        }

        @Override
        public void onCreate(Bundle savedInstanceState) {
            super.onCreate(savedInstanceState);
            //Make a new adapter for the list items
            mAdapter = new ArrayAdapter<String>(getActivity(),
                    android.R.layout.simple_list_item_1, mItems);
        }
```

```
    @Override
    public View onCreateView(LayoutInflater inflater,
            ViewGroup container, Bundle savedInstanceState) {
        //Construct and return a ListView with our adapter
        ListView list = new ListView(getActivity());
        list.setAdapter(mAdapter);
        return list;
    }

    //Save the index in the global list where this page starts
    public void setBaseIndex(int index) {
        mBaseIndex = index;
    }

    //Retrieve the index where this page starts
    public int getBaseIndex() {
        return mBaseIndex;
    }
    public void updateListItems(List<String> items) {
        mItems.clear();
        for (String piece : items) {
            mItems.add(piece);
        }

        if (mAdapter != null) {
            mAdapter.notifyDataSetChanged();
        }
    }
}
}
```

FragmentPagerAdapter implements some of the underlying requirements of PagerAdapter for us. Instead of implementing instantiateItem(), destroyItem(), and isViewFromObject(), we only need to override getItem() to provide the Fragment for each page position. This example defines a constant for the number of list items that should display on each page. When we create the Fragment in getItem(), we pass in a subsection of the list based on the index offset and this constant. The number of pages required, returned by getCount(), is determined by the total size of the items list divided by the constant number of items per page.

■ **Tip** FragmentPagerAdapter retains all fragment instances as active whether or not they are actively within the offscreen page limit. If your pager needs to hold a larger number of fragments, or some are more heavyweight, look at using FragmentStatePagerAdapter instead. The latter destroys fragments outside the offscreen page limit while maintaining their saved state—similar to a rotation operation.

This adapter also overrides one more method we did not see in the simple example, which is getItemPosition(). This method will get called when notifyDataSetChanged() gets called externally by the application. Its primary function is to sort out whether page items should be moved or removed as a result of the change. If the item's position has changed, the implementation should return the new position

value. If the item should not be moved, the implementation should return the constant value `PagerAdapter.`
`POSITION_UNCHANGED`. If the page should be removed, the application should return `PagerAdapter.`
`POSITION_NONE`.

The example checks the current page position (which we have to re-create from the initial index data) against the current page count. If this page is greater than the count, we have removed enough items from the list so that this page is no longer needed, and we return `POSITION_NONE`. In any other case, we update the list of items that should now be displayed for the current fragment and return the new calculated position.

The method `getItemPosition()` will get called for every page currently being tracked by `ViewPager`, which will be the number of pages returned by `getOffscreenPageLimit()`. However, even though `ViewPager` doesn't track a fragment that scrolls outside the limit, `FragmentManager` still does. So when a previous fragment is scrolled back in, `getItem()` will not be called again because the fragment exists. But, because of this, if a data set change occurs during this time, the fragment list data will not update. This is why we have overridden `instantiateItem()`. While it is not required to override `instantiateItem()` for this adapter, we do need to update fragments that are outside the offscreen page limit when modifications to the list take place. Because `instantiateItem()` will get called each time a fragment scrolls back inside the page limit, it is an opportune place to reset the display list.

Let's look at an example application that uses this adapter. See Listings 2-57 and 2-58.

Listing 2-57. `res/layout/main.xml`

```xml
<?xml version="1.0" encoding="utf-8"?>
<LinearLayout xmlns:android="http://schemas.android.com/apk/res/android"
    android:layout_width="match_parent"
    android:layout_height="match_parent"
    android:orientation="vertical" >
    <Button
        android:layout_width="match_parent"
        android:layout_height="wrap_content"
        android:text="Add Item"
        android:onClick="onAddClick" />
    <Button
        android:layout_width="match_parent"
        android:layout_height="wrap_content"
        android:text="Remove Item"
        android:onClick="onRemoveClick" />

    <!-- ViewPager is a support widget, it needs the full name -->
    <android.support.v4.view.ViewPager
        android:id="@+id/view_pager"
        android:layout_width="match_parent"
        android:layout_height="match_parent" />
</LinearLayout>
```

Listing 2-58. Activity with `ListPagerAdapter`

```java
public class FragmentPagerActivity extends FragmentActivity {

    private ArrayList<String> mListItems;
    private ListPagerAdapter mAdapter;
```

```
@Override
protected void onCreate(Bundle savedInstanceState) {
    super.onCreate(savedInstanceState);
    setContentView(R.layout.main);
    //Create the initial data set
    mListItems = new ArrayList<String>();
    mListItems.add("Mom");
    mListItems.add("Dad");
    mListItems.add("Sister");
    mListItems.add("Brother");
    mListItems.add("Cousin");
    mListItems.add("Niece");
    mListItems.add("Nephew");
    //Attach the data to the pager
    ViewPager pager =
            (ViewPager) findViewById(R.id.view_pager);
    mAdapter = new ListPagerAdapter(
            getSupportFragmentManager(),
            mListItems);

    pager.setAdapter(mAdapter);
}

public void onAddClick(View v) {
    //Add a new unique item to the end of the list
    mListItems.add("Crazy Uncle "
            + System.currentTimeMillis());
    mAdapter.notifyDataSetChanged();
}

public void onRemoveClick(View v) {
    //Remove an item from the head of the list
    if (!mListItems.isEmpty()) {
        mListItems.remove(0);
    }
    mAdapter.notifyDataSetChanged();
}
}
```

This example consists of two buttons to add and remove items from the data set as well as a ViewPager. Notice that the ViewPager must be defined in XML using its fully qualified package name because it is only part of the Support Library and does not exist in the android.widget or android.view packages. The activity constructs a default list of items, and it passes it to our custom adapter, which is then attached to the ViewPager.

Each Add button click appends a new item to the end of the list and triggers ListPagerAdapter to update by calling notifyDataSetChanged(). Each Remove button click removes an item from the front of the list and again notifies the adapter. With each change, the adapter adjusts the number of pages available and updates the ViewPager. If all the items are removed from the currently visible page, that page is removed and the previous page will be displayed.

Using Other Helpful Methods

There are a few other methods on ViewPager that can be useful in your applications:

- setPageMargin() and setPageMarginDrawable() allow you to set some extra space between pages and optionally supply a Drawable that will be used to fill the margin spaces.

- setCurrentItem() allows you to programmatically set the page that should be shown, with an option to disable the scrolling animation while it switches pages.

- OnPageChangeListener can be used to notify the application of scroll and change actions.

  - onPageSelected() will be called when a new page is displayed.

  - onPageScrolled() will be called continuously while a scroll operation is taking place.

  - onPageScrollStateChanged() will be called when the ViewPager toggles from being idle, to being actively scrolled by the user, to automatically scrolling to snap to the closest page.

2-19. Navigating with Tabs

Problem

You need to provide selectable tabs in your application for lateral screen navigation.

Solution

(API Level 9)

The Design Support Library from Google provides the TabLayout that wc can use to implement tab navigation. Google has fully deprecated previous incarnations of Android tabs, such as TabWidget and ActionBar.Tab, but TabLayout from is consistent with the current design patterns for tabs.

TabLayout is designed to work tightly with ViewPager, because part of the tabs design pattern is to allow swiping between each view. Therefore, there is no API to manually add tab items. Instead the tabs are derived from the page titles returned by the attached PagerAdapter. If the tab contents extend beyond the display width, the user can scroll the tabs left or right. As the pager is swiping, the current tab will automatically scroll to be visible at the same time.

How It Works

The new TabLayout in the design support library provides a simple integration and can be done completely using the XML layout.

When the example is complete, we should have something like Figure 2-15.

Figure 2-15. *Sliding tabs activity*

Notice that the tabs sit below the action bar, and match the action bar background to provide the appearance that they are a single element. Listings 2-59 and 2-60 define an activity and layout to construct the tabs.

Listing 2-59. res/layout/activity_tabs.xml

```
<?xml version="1.0" encoding="utf-8"?>
<LinearLayout xmlns:android="http://schemas.android.com/apk/res/android"
              xmlns:app="http://schemas.android.com/apk/res-auto"
              android:orientation="vertical"
              android:layout_width="match_parent"
              android:layout_height="match_parent">
    <android.support.v4.view.ViewPager
        android:id="@+id/pager"
        android:layout_width="match_parent"
        android:layout_height="match_parent">
        <android.support.design.widget.TabLayout
            android:layout_width="match_parent"
            android:layout_height="wrap_content"
            app:tabMode="scrollable"/>
    </android.support.v4.view.ViewPager>
</LinearLayout>
```

Listing 2-60. Sliding tabs activity

```java
public class ActionTabsActivity extends AppCompatActivity {

    @Override
    protected void onCreate(Bundle savedInstanceState) {
        super.onCreate(savedInstanceState);
        setContentView(R.layout.activity_tabs);

        ViewPager viewPager = (ViewPager) findViewById(R.id.pager);
        viewPager.setAdapter(new TabsPagerAdapter(this));
    }

    @Override
    public boolean onCreateOptionsMenu(Menu menu) {
        getMenuInflater().inflate(R.menu.tabs, menu);
        return true;
    }

    /*
     * Simple PagerAdapter to display page views with static images
     */
    private static class TabsPagerAdapter extends PagerAdapter {
        private Context mContext;

        public TabsPagerAdapter(Context context) {
            mContext = context;
        }

        /*
         * SlidingTabLayout requires this method to define the
         * text that each tab will display.
         */
        @Override
        public CharSequence getPageTitle(int position) {
            switch (position) {
                case 0:
                    return "Primary";
                case 1:
                    return "Secondary";
                case 2:
                    return "Tertiary";
                case 3:
                    return "Quaternary";
                case 4:
                    return "Quinary";
                default:
                    return "";
            }
        }
```

```
    @Override
    public int getCount() {
        return 5;
    }

    @Override
    public Object instantiateItem(ViewGroup container, int position) {
        ImageView pageView = new ImageView(mContext);
        pageView.setScaleType(ImageView.ScaleType.CENTER);
        pageView.setImageResource(R.drawable.ic_launcher);

        container.addView(pageView);

        return pageView;
    }

    @Override
    public void destroyItem(ViewGroup container, int position, Object object) {
        container.removeView((View) object);
    }

    @Override
    public boolean isViewFromObject(View view, Object object) {
        return (view == object);
    }
    }
}
```

Inside onCreate(), we only need to set the PagerAdapter for ViewPager in order for everything to work. The reason for this is that we place the TabLayout element inside the ViewPager element in our XML layout. The ViewPager will then treat the TabLayout as part of its décor and populate the tabs from its own PagerAdapter.

If you want to place the tabs outside the ViewPager décor (for instance, inside the app bar), you need to call the method setupWithViewPager() on the TabLayout instance in order to connect it to the ViewPager and PagerAdapter.

2-20. Actionable User Feedback Using Snackbar

Problem

The user performs an action where you want to confirm the result (success or failure) as well as giving the option to undo. You cannot use the Toast widget, as it doesn't allow user feedback.

Solution

(API Level 9)

The Snackbar is a widget that is part of the material design and included in the Design Support Library from Google. It brings an implementation of the Snackbar to API Level 9 and later that is fully compliant with the material design specification.

A Snackbar can be as simple as just showing a message to the user and disappearing after a short period, or it can be more complex and react to user interaction or trigger a background operation once dismissed.

How It Works

To display a Snackbar, simply construct a new instance using the Snackbar.make() method and construct it with the options you need. The minimal Snackbar requires a View in your current layout to attacht to (usually your content view), a message and delay. The delay can be either Snackbar.LENGTH_SHORT, Snackbar.LENGTH_LONG or Snackbar.LENGTH_INDEFINITE. LENGTH_INDEFINITIE means that the Snackbar will be displayed until the user will dismiss it manually by swiping it away. Once you have constructed your Snackbar, simply call Snackbar.show() to display it. See Figure 2-16 for how the Snackbar looks in our example.

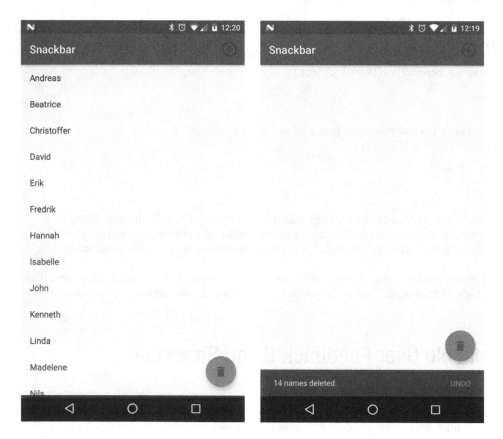

Figure 2-16. *Example of using Snackbar for user feedback with an undo action*

In this example we will provide a Snackbar when the user presses the FloatingActionButton which will clear the list of names. Once cleared, the Snackbar will display a message and also provide an action to the user to undo the operation and put the old content back into the list. The source code for this can be seen in Listing 2-60 and 2-61.

Listing 2-61. SnackbarActivity.java

```java
public class SnackbarActivity extends AppCompatActivity {
    private static String[] NAMES = {"Andreas", "Beatrice", "Christoffer",
            "David", "Erik", "Fredrik", "Hannah", "Isabelle", "John",
            "Kenneth", "Linda", "Madelene", "Nils", "Olof"};

    private NameAdapter mAdapter;
    @Nullable
    private ArrayList<String> mClearedNames;

    @Override
    protected void onCreate(Bundle savedInstanceState) {
        super.onCreate(savedInstanceState);
        setContentView(R.layout.activity_main);
        RecyclerView listOfNames = (RecyclerView) findViewById(R.id.list_of_names);
        listOfNames.setHasFixedSize(true);
        mAdapter = new NameAdapter();
        listOfNames.setAdapter(mAdapter);
        if (savedInstanceState == null) {
            mAdapter.addNames(Arrays.asList(NAMES));
        } else {
            ArrayList<String> names = savedInstanceState.getStringArrayList("names");
            mAdapter.addNames(names);
            if (savedInstanceState.containsKey("clearedNames")) {
                ArrayList<String> clearedNames = savedInstanceState
                        .getStringArrayList("clearedNames");
                showClearSnackbar(clearedNames);
            }
        }

        findViewById(R.id.fab).setOnClickListener(new View.OnClickListener() {
            @Override
            public void onClick(View v) {
                mAdapter.clearList();
            }
        });
    }

    @Override
    protected void onSaveInstanceState(Bundle outState) {
        super.onSaveInstanceState(outState);
        outState.putStringArrayList("names", mAdapter.mNames);
        if (mClearedNames != null) {
            outState.putStringArrayList("clearedNames", mClearedNames);
        }
    }

    @Override
    public boolean onCreateOptionsMenu(Menu menu) {
        MenuInflater menuInflater = getMenuInflater();
        menuInflater.inflate(R.menu.main, menu);
```

```java
        return true;
    }

    @Override
    public boolean onOptionsItemSelected(MenuItem item) {
        switch (item.getItemId()) {
            case R.id.add_items:
                mAdapter.addNames(Arrays.asList(NAMES));
                return true;
            default:
                return false;
        }
    }

    private void showClearSnackbar(final ArrayList<String> names) {
        Snackbar.make(findViewById(R.id.activity_main),
                getString(R.string.names_deleted, names.size()),
                Snackbar.LENGTH_INDEFINITE)
                .setCallback(new Snackbar.Callback() {
                    @Override
                    public void onDismissed(Snackbar snackbar, int event) {
                        super.onDismissed(snackbar, event);
                        mClearedNames = null;
                    }

                    @Override
                    public void onShown(Snackbar snackbar) {
                        super.onShown(snackbar);
                        mClearedNames = names;
                    }
                })
                .setAction(R.string.undo_label, new View.OnClickListener() {
                    @Override
                    public void onClick(View v) {
                        // Undo click - revert delete action
                        mAdapter.addNames(names);
                    }
                })
                .show();
    }

    private static class NameViewHolder extends RecyclerView.ViewHolder {
        TextView nameView;

        NameViewHolder(View itemView) {
            super(itemView);
            nameView = (TextView) itemView.findViewById(android.R.id.text1);
        }
    }
```

```java
    private class NameAdapter extends RecyclerView.Adapter<NameViewHolder> {
        private final ArrayList<String> mNames = new ArrayList<>();

        @Override
        public NameViewHolder onCreateViewHolder(ViewGroup parent, int viewType) {
            View itemView = LayoutInflater.from(SnackbarActivity.this)
                    .inflate(android.R.layout.simple_list_item_1, parent, false);
            return new NameViewHolder(itemView);
        }

        @Override
        public void onBindViewHolder(NameViewHolder holder, int position) {
            holder.nameView.setText(mNames.get(position));
        }

        @Override
        public int getItemCount() {
            return mNames.size();
        }

        void clearList() {
            int oldSize = mNames.size();
            ArrayList<String> oldNames = new ArrayList<>(mNames);
            mNames.clear();
            if (oldSize > 0) {
                notifyItemRangeRemoved(0, oldSize);
                showClearSnackbar(oldNames);
            }
        }

        void addNames(List<String> names) {
            int oldSize = mNames.size();
            mNames.addAll(names);
            notifyItemRangeInserted(oldSize, names.size());
        }
    }
}
```

Listing 2-62. layout/activity_main.xml

```xml
<android.support.design.widget.CoordinatorLayout
    xmlns:android="http://schemas.android.com/apk/res/android"
    xmlns:app="http://schemas.android.com/apk/res-auto"
    xmlns:tools="http://schemas.android.com/tools"
    android:id="@+id/activity_main"
    android:layout_width="match_parent"
    android:layout_height="match_parent"
    android:fitsSystemWindows="true"
    tools:context="com.androidrecipes.snackbar.SnackbarActivity">
```

```xml
<android.support.v7.widget.RecyclerView
    android:id="@+id/list_of_names"
    app:layoutManager="android.support.v7.widget.LinearLayoutManager"
    android:layout_width="match_parent"
    android:layout_height="match_parent"/>

<android.support.design.widget.FloatingActionButton
    android:id="@+id/fab"
    android:layout_width="wrap_content"
    android:layout_height="wrap_content"
    android:layout_gravity="bottom|end"
    android:layout_margin="16dp"
    android:onClick="doClearList"
    android:src="@drawable/ic_action_clear"
    app:fabSize="normal"
    app:layout_anchor="@id/list_of_names"
    app:layout_anchorGravity="bottom|right|end" />

</android.support.design.widget.CoordinatorLayout>
```

In the code above we start by creating the adapter for our RecyclerView. We also connect the options menu action to add items to our list. The FloatingActionButton has a click listener that will clear the list of all items and display the Snackbar.

The magic with our Snackbar comes with the use of the callback we add to it through Snackbar.setCallback(). This callback is called when the Snackbar is shown and when it's dismissed, making it suitable for keeping track of the data until the user either dismisses the Snackbar or presses the undo action we added with Snackbar.setAction().

Note that snackbars are not automatically handled during configuration changes, so we also need to implement this in the onCreate() and onSaveInstanceState().

Summary

In this chapter, we explored techniques that we can use to build a compelling user interface that conforms to the design guidelines that Google has set forth for the Android platform. We started out looking at how to effectively use the action bar interface elements in applications. We explored managing configuration changes such as device orientation in creative ways. You saw techniques for managing user input through text and touch handling. Next, you were exposed to implementing common navigation patterns such as the drawer layout, swipe-paging views, and tabs. Finally, we looked at how to use the new Snackbar to provide user feedback that also allows a user to perform an action.

In the next chapter, we will look at using the SDK to communicate with the outside world by accessing network resources and talking to other devices by using technologies such as USB and Bluetooth.

CHAPTER 3

■ ■ ■

Communications and Networking

The key to many successful mobile applications is their ability to connect and interact with remote data sources. Web services and APIs are abundant in today's world, allowing an application to interact with just about any service, from weather forecasts to personal financial information. Bringing this data into the palm of a user's hand and making it accessible from anywhere is one of the greatest powers of the mobile platform. Android builds on the web foundations that Google is known for and provides a rich toolset for communicating with the outside world.

3-1. Displaying Web Information

Problem

HTML or image data from the Web needs to be presented in the application without any modification or processing.

Solution

(API Level 3)

Display the information in a WebView. WebView is a view widget that can be embedded in any layout to display web content, both local and remote, in your application. WebView is based on the same open source engine that powers the Android Browser application, affording applications the same level of power and capability.

How It Works

WebView has some very desirable properties when displaying assets downloaded from the Web, not the least of which are two-dimensional scrolling (horizontal and vertical at the same time) and zoom controls. A WebView can be the perfect place to house a large image, such as a stadium map, in which the user may want to pan and zoom around. Here we will discuss how to do this with both local and remote assets.

© Dave Smith and Erik Hellman 2016
D. Smith and E. Hellman, *Android Recipes*, DOI 10.1007/978-1-4842-2259-1_3

Display a URL

The simplest case is displaying an HTML page or image by supplying the URL of the resource to the WebView. The following are a handful of practical uses for this technique in your applications:

- Provide access to your corporate site without leaving the application.

- Display a page of live content from a web server, such as an FAQ section, that can be changed without requiring an upgrade to the application.

- Display a large image resource that the user would want to interact with using pan/zoom.

Let's take a look at a simple example that loads a popular web page inside the content view of an activity instead of within the browser (see Listings 3-1 and 3-2).

Listing 3-1. Activity Containing a WebView

```
public class MyActivity extends Activity {
    @Override
    public void onCreate(Bundle savedInstanceState) {
        super.onCreate(savedInstanceState);

        WebView webview = new WebView(this);
        //Enable JavaScript support
        webview.getSettings().setJavaScriptEnabled(true);
        webview.loadUrl("http://www.android.com/");

        setContentView(webview);
    }
}
```

■ **Note**   By default, WebView has JavaScript support disabled. Be sure to enable JavaScript in the WebView. WebSettings object if the content you are displaying requires it.

Listing 3-2. AndroidManifest.xml Setting the Required Permissions

```
<?xml version="1.0" encoding="utf-8"?>
<manifest
    xmlns:android="http://schemas.android.com/apk/res/android"
    package="com.examples.webview">

    <uses-permission android:name="android.permission.INTERNET" />

    <application android:icon="@drawable/icon"
        android:label="@string/app_name">
        <activity android:name=".MyActivity">
            <intent-filter>
                <action
                    android:name="android.intent.action.MAIN" />
                <category
```

```
              android:name="android.intent.category.LAUNCHER" />
        </intent-filter>
      </activity>
    </application>
</manifest>
```

___

■ **Important**   If the content you are loading into WebView is remote, AndroidManifest.xml must declare that it uses the android.permission.INTERNET permission.

___

The result displays the HTML page in your activity (see Figure 3-1).

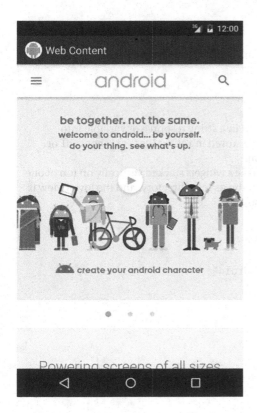

Figure 3-1. *HTML page in a* WebView

Note that if you click on any links inside the view, the device's browser application will launch. This is because all web URL loads are handled by the system as intents by default. If you want to handle links internally, you have to intercept those events. We will discuss how to do that later in this chapter.

Display Local Assets

WebView is also quite useful in displaying local content to take advantage of either HTML/CSS formatting or the pan/zoom behavior it provides to its contents. You may use the assets directory of your Android project to store resources you would like to display in a WebView, such as large images or HTML files. To better organize the assets, you may also create subdirectories under assets to store files in.

■ **Note**   By default, Android Studio will not create the assets directory for you, so you'll have to do this manually. This directory should be placed next to the java and res folders and should always be named assets.

WebView.loadUrl() can display files stored under assets by using the file:///android_ asset/<resource path> URL schema. For example, if the file android.jpg was placed into the assets directory, it could be loaded into a WebView using the following URL:

file:///android_asset/android.jpg

If that same file were placed in a directory named images under assets, WebView could load it with the following URL:

file:///android_asset/images/android.jpg

In addition, WebView.loadData() will load raw HTML stored in a string resource or variable into the view. Using this technique, preformatted HTML text could be stored in res/values/strings.xml or downloaded from a remote API and displayed in the application.

Listings 3-3 and 3-4 show an example activity with two WebView widgets stacked vertically on top of one another. The upper view is displaying a large image file stored in the assets directory, and the lower view is displaying an HTML string stored in the application's string resources.

Listing 3-3. res/layout/main.xml

```
<LinearLayout
  xmlns:android="http://schemas.android.com/apk/res/android"
  android:layout_width="match_parent"
  android:layout_height="match_parent"
  android:orientation="vertical">
  <WebView
    android:id="@+id/upperview"
    android:layout_width="match_parent"
    android:layout_height="0dp"
    android:layout_weight="1"/>

  <WebView
    android:id="@+id/lowerview"
    android:layout_width="match_parent"
    android:layout_height="0dp"
    android:layout_weight="1"/>
</LinearLayout>
```

Listing 3-4. Activity to Display Local Web Content

```java
public class MyActivity extends Activity {
    @Override
    public void onCreate(Bundle savedInstanceState) {
        super.onCreate(savedInstanceState);
        setContentView(R.layout.main);

        WebView upperView = (WebView)findViewById(R.id.upperview);
        //Zoom feature must be enabled
        upperView.getSettings().setBuiltInZoomControls(true);
        if (Build.VERSION.SDK_INT >= Build.VERSION_CODES.HONEYCOMB) {
            //Android 3.0+ has pinch-zoom, don't need buttons
            upperView.getSettings().setDisplayZoomControls(false);
        }
        upperView.loadUrl("file:///android_asset/android.jpg");

        WebView lowerView = (WebView)findViewById(R.id.lowerview);
        String htmlString =
                "<h1>Header</h1><p>This is HTML text<br />"
                + "<i>Formatted in italics</i></p>";
        lowerView.loadData(htmlString, "text/html", "utf-8");
    }
}
```

When the activity is displayed, each WebView occupies half of the screen's vertical space. The HTML string is formatted as expected, while the large image can be scrolled both horizontally and vertically; the user may even zoom in or out (see Figure 3-2).

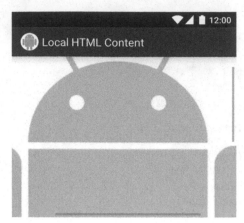

Header

This is HTML text
Formatted in italics

Figure 3-2. *Two WebViews displaying local resources*

We enable the user to zoom in and out of the content via setBuiltInZoomControls(true). By default this will also display a button overlay with tappable zoom controls. On Android 3.0 and later, you might additionally consider including WebView.getSettings().setDisplayZoomControls(false). These platforms natively support zooming with a pinch gesture, so showing the overlay buttons is unnecessary. This does not replace setBuiltInZoomControls(), which must also be enabled for pinch to work.

3-2. Intercepting WebView Events

Problem

Your application is using a WebView to display content, but it also needs to listen and respond to users clicking links on the page.

Solution

(API Level 1)

Implement a WebViewClient and attach it to the WebView. WebViewClient and WebChromeClient are two WebKit classes that allow an application to get event callbacks and customize the behavior of the WebView. By default, WebView will pass a URL to the ActivityManager to be handled if no WebViewClient is present, which usually results in any clicked link loading in the Browser application instead of the current WebView.

How It Works

In Listing 3-5, we create an activity with a WebView that will handle its own URL loading.

Listing 3-5. Activity with a WebView That Handles URLs

```
public class MyActivity extends Activity {
    @Override
    public void onCreate(Bundle savedInstanceState) {
        super.onCreate(savedInstanceState);

        WebView webview = new WebView(this);
        webview.getSettings().setJavaScriptEnabled(true);
        //Add a client to the view
        webview.setWebViewClient(new WebViewClient());
        webview.loadUrl("http://www.android.com");
        setContentView(webview);
    }
}
```

In this example, simply providing a plain vanilla WebViewClient to WebView allows it to handle any URL requests itself, instead of passing them up to the ActivityManager, so clicking a link will load the requested page inside the same view. This is because the default implementation simply returns false for shouldOverrideUrlLoading(), which tells the client to pass the URL to the WebView and not to the application.

In this next case, we will take advantage of the WebViewClient.shouldOverrideUrlLoading() callback to intercept and monitor user activity (see Listing 3-6).

Listing 3-6. Activity That Intercepts WebView URLs

```
public class MyActivity extends Activity {
    @Override
    public void onCreate(Bundle savedInstanceState) {
        super.onCreate(savedInstanceState);

        WebView webview = new WebView(this);
        webview.getSettings().setJavaScriptEnabled(true);
        //Add a client to the view
        webview.setWebViewClient(mClient);
        webview.loadUrl("http://www.google.com");
        setContentView(webview);
    }

    private WebViewClient mClient = new WebViewClient() {
        @Override
        public boolean shouldOverrideUrlLoading(WebView view,
                String url) {
            Uri request = Uri.parse(url);

            if(TextUtils.equals(request.getAuthority(),
                    "www.google.com")) {
```

```
        //Allow the load
        return false;
    }

    Toast.makeText(MyActivity.this,
        "Sorry, buddy",
        Toast.LENGTH_SHORT).show();
    return true;
    }
  };
}
```

In this example, shouldOverrideUrlLoading() determines whether to load the content back in this WebView based on the URL it was passed, keeping the user from leaving Google's site. Uri.getAuthority() returns the hostname portion of a URL, and we use that to check whether the link the user clicked is on Google's domain (www.google.com). If we can verify that the link is to another Google page, returning false allows the WebView to load the content. If not, we notify the user and, returning true, tell the WebViewClient that the application has taken care of this URL and not to allow the WebView to load it.

This technique can be more sophisticated, enabling the application to actually handle the URL by doing something interesting. A custom schema could even be developed to create a full interface between your application and the WebView content.

3-3. Accessing WebView with JavaScript

Problem

Your application needs access to the raw HTML of the current contents displayed in a WebView, either to read or modify specific values.

Solution

(API Level 1)

Create a JavaScript interface to bridge between the WebView and application code.

How It Works

WebView.addJavascriptInterface() binds a Java object to JavaScript so that its methods can then be called within the WebView. Using this interface, JavaScript can be used to marshal data between your application code and the WebView's HTML.

■ **Caution**   Allowing JavaScript to control your application can inherently present a security threat, allowing remote execution of application code. This interface should be utilized with that possibility in mind.

Let's look at an example of this in action. Listing 3-7 presents a simple HTML form to be loaded into the WebView from the local assets directory. Listing 3-8 is an activity that uses two JavaScript functions to exchange data between the activity preferences and content in the WebView.

Listing 3-7. assets/form.html

```
<!DOCTYPE HTML PUBLIC "-//W3C//DTD HTML 4.01//EN"
    "http://www.w3.org/TR/html4/strict.dtd">
<html>

<form name="input" action="form.html" method="get">
Enter Email: <input type="text" id="emailAddress" />
<input type="submit" value="Submit" />
</form>

</html>
```

Listing 3-8. Activity with JavaScript Bridge Interface

```
public class MyActivity extends Activity {
    @Override
    public void onCreate(Bundle savedInstanceState) {
        super.onCreate(savedInstanceState);

        WebView webview = new WebView(this);
        //JavaScript is not enabled by default
        webview.getSettings().setJavaScriptEnabled(true);
        webview.setWebViewClient(mClient);
        //Attach the custom interface to the view
        webview.addJavascriptInterface(new MyJavaScriptInterface(), "BRIDGE");

        setContentView(webview);

        webview.loadUrl("file:///android_asset/form.html");
    }

    private static final String JS_SETELEMENT =
            "javascript:document.getElementById('%s').value='%s'";
    private static final String JS_GETELEMENT =
            "javascript:window.BRIDGE"
            + ".storeElement('%s',document.getElementById('%s').value)";
    private static final String ELEMENTID = "emailAddress";

    private WebViewClient mClient = new WebViewClient() {
        @Override
        public boolean shouldOverrideUrlLoading(WebView view, String url) {
            //Before leaving the page, attempt to retrieve the email
            // using JavaScript
            executeJavascript(view,
                    String.format(JS_GETELEMENT, ELEMENTID, ELEMENTID) );
            return false;
        }
```

```
    @Override
    public void onPageFinished(WebView view, String url) {
        //When page loads, inject address into page using JavaScript
        SharedPreferences prefs = getPreferences(Activity.MODE_PRIVATE);
        executeJavascript(view, String.format(JS_SETELEMENT, ELEMENTID,
                prefs.getString(ELEMENTID, "")) );
    }
};

private void executeJavascript(WebView view, String script) {
    if (Build.VERSION.SDK_INT >= Build.VERSION_CODES.KITKAT) {
        view.evaluateJavascript(script, null);
    } else {
        view.loadUrl(script);
    }
}

private class MyJavaScriptInterface {
    //Store an element in preferences
    @JavascriptInterface
    public void storeElement(String id, String element) {
        SharedPreferences.Editor edit =
                getPreferences(Activity.MODE_PRIVATE).edit();
        edit.putString(id, element);
        edit.commit();
        //If element is valid, raise a Toast
        if(!TextUtils.isEmpty(element)) {
            Toast.makeText(MyActivity.this, element, Toast.LENGTH_SHORT)
                    .show();
        }
    }
}
}
```

In this somewhat contrived example, a single element form is created in HTML and displayed in a WebView. In the activity code, we look for a form value in the WebView with the ID of emailAddress, and its value is saved to SharedPreferences every time a link is clicked on the page (in this case, the Submit button of the form) through the shouldOverrideUrlLoading() callback. Whenever the page finishes loading (that is, onPageFinished() is called), we attempt to inject the current value from SharedPreferences back into the web form.

■ **Note**   JavaScript is not enabled by default in WebView. In order to inject or even simply render JavaScript, we must call WebSettings.setJavaScriptEnabled(true) when initializing the view.

A Java class is created called MyJavaScriptInterface, which defines the method storeElement(). When the view is created, we call the WebView.addJavascriptInterface() method to attach this object to the view and give it the name BRIDGE. When calling this method, the string parameter is a name used to reference the interface inside JavaScript code.

We have defined two JavaScript methods as constant strings here: JS_GETELEMENT and JS_SETELEMENT. Prior to Android 4.4, we executed these methods on the WebView by calling the same loadUrl() method we've seen before. However, in API Level 19 and beyond, we have a new method on WebView named evaluateJavascript() for this purpose. The example code verifies the API level currently in use and calls the appropriate method.

Notice that JS_GETELEMENT is a reference to calling our custom interface function (referenced as BRIDGE.storeElement), which will call that method on MyJavaScriptInterface and store the form element's value in preferences. If the value retrieved from the form is not blank, a Toast will also be raised.

Any JavaScript may be executed on the WebView in this manner, and it does not need to be a method included as part of the custom interface. JS_SETELEMENT, for example, uses pure JavaScript to set the value of the form element on the page.

One popular application of this technique is to remember form data that a user may need to enter in the application, but the form must be web based, such as a reservation form or payment form for a web application that doesn't have a lower-level API to access.

3-4. Displaying Online Images

Problem

Your application needs to download and display images from the Web or another remote server.

Solution

(API Level 10) Depending on the library used.

While it is possible to download an image using the standard Android framework API, like AsyncTask, it tends to be very complicated using such a solution when you have to display many different images.

A better solution in these cases is to use one of the available image downloading libraries instead. In this case we will use the library Glide from Bump Technologies which you can find on GitHub at https://github.com/bumptech/glide. Other libraries, such as Picasso from Square or Universal Image Loader by developer Sergey Tarasevich, can also be used and work in a similar way as described in this section.

The advantages of using a library for this is that it handles all of the challenges that comes with displaying online images, such as background networking, cross fading the result, caching or cancelling an ongoing request when the view is no longer visible. Glide, and most other image loading libraries, takes care of this for us and also provides options for setting placeholder images while loading, and gives us a better option for handling any errors that might occur.

How It Works

Before you can use a third-party library, you need to include it in your project dependencies. This is done by adding a line to the dependencies section of the file build.gradle in the project module that will need the library. The code for the example shown in this section is shown in Listing 3-9.

Listing 3-9. OnlineImagesActivity

```
dependencies {
    // Check the latest version on https://github.com/bumptech/glide
    compile "com.github.bumptech.glide:glide:3.7.0"
}
```

Once you've added this, Android Studio will ask you to sync the project settings so that the new library is downloaded and you can start using its API.

Online images are usually accessed through some sort of web API or online service. In this example we will use an image placeholder service called Unsplash It (https://unsplash.it/), which gives us a way to download and display unique online photos. We will display 1000 images in a list using a RecyclerView. The code for this is implemented in our OnlineImagesActivity (see Listing 3-10).

Listing 3-10. OnlineImagesActivity

```java
public class OnlineImageActivity extends AppCompatActivity {
    private static final String BASE_IMAGE_URL = "https://unsplash.it/200/300?image=";

    @Override
    protected void onCreate(Bundle savedInstanceState) {
        super.onCreate(savedInstanceState);
        setContentView(R.layout.activity_main);
        RecyclerView recyclerView
                        = (RecyclerView) findViewById(R.id.image_grid);
        recyclerView.setLayoutManager(new GridLayoutManager(this, 2));
        recyclerView.setHasFixedSize(true);
        recyclerView.setAdapter(new ImagesAdapter());
    }

    private class ImagesAdapter extends RecyclerView.Adapter<ImageViewHolder> {
        @Override
        public ImageViewHolder onCreateViewHolder(ViewGroup parent,
                                                  int viewType) {
            View view = LayoutInflater.from(OnlineImageActivity.this)
                    .inflate(R.layout.image_item, parent, false);
            return new ImageViewHolder(view);
        }

        @Override
        public void onBindViewHolder(ImageViewHolder holder, int position) {
            Glide.with(OnlineImageActivity.this)
                    .load(BASE_IMAGE_URL + position)
                    .diskCacheStrategy(DiskCacheStrategy.RESULT)
                    .centerCrop()
                    .placeholder(R.drawable.ic_cloud_download_black_24dp)
                    .error(R.drawable.ic_warning_black_24dp)
                    .crossFade()
                    .into(holder.image);
        }

        @Override
        public void onViewRecycled(ImageViewHolder holder) {
            super.onViewRecycled(holder);
            Glide.clear(holder.image);
        }

        @Override
        public int getItemCount() {
```

```
        return 1000;
    }
}

private class ImageViewHolder extends RecyclerView.ViewHolder{
    ImageView image;

    public ImageViewHolder(View itemView) {
        super(itemView);
        image = (ImageView) itemView.findViewById(R.id.image);
    }
}
}
```

As you can see, the API for using Glide is quite simple and straightforward. You call the static method load() and give it the URL for each image. In this case, the URL is determined using the BASE_IMAGE_URL constant and the integer position of that image from the adapter. We then tell Glide what caching strategy to use, how to fit the image once it is downloaded (in this case, crop from center if necessary). We also give a placeholder drawable to use while we're loading as well as an error drawable in case the network request failed. Finally, we tell Glide to cross fade between the placeholder and the final image (or the error drawable) and which ImageView to use for displaying.

Also notice that we override the method onViewRecycled() of the adapter. This lets us know when a view is recycled by the adapter so that we can safely cancel any network request that was ongoing in that case. This reduces the number of concurrent network calls and makes sure we won't get too many requests in case the users scroll through the list really fast.

In this example, we learned how to use a third party library for downloading and displaying online images. These libraries greatly reduce the complexity of handling images and can also be used for loading images that are local on the device. Always consider using an image loading library when the source for the images is not from your application resources.

3-5. Downloading Completely in the Background

Problem

The application must download a large resource to the device, such as a movie file, that must not require the user to keep the application active.

Solution

(API Level 9)

Use the DownloadManager API. The DownloadManager is a service added to the SDK with API Level 9 that allows a long-running download to be handed off and managed completely by the system. The primary advantage of using this service is that DownloadManager will continue attempting to download the resource despite failures, connection changes, and even device reboots.

How It Works

Listing 3-11 is a sample activity that uses DownloadManager to handle the download of a large image file. When complete, the image is displayed in an ImageView. Whenever you utilize DownloadManager to access content from the Web, be sure to declare you are using android.permission.INTERNET in the application's manifest.

Listing 3-11. DownloadManager Sample Activity

```java
public class DownloadActivity extends Activity {

    private static final String DL_ID = "downloadId";
    private SharedPreferences prefs;

    private DownloadManager dm;
    private ImageView imageView;

    @Override
    public void onCreate(Bundle savedInstanceState) {
        super.onCreate(savedInstanceState);
        imageView = new ImageView(this);
        setContentView(imageView);

        prefs =
            PreferenceManager.getDefaultSharedPreferences(this);
        dm = (DownloadManager)getSystemService(DOWNLOAD_SERVICE);
    }

    @Override
    public void onResume() {
        super.onResume();

        if(!prefs.contains(DL_ID)) {
            //Start the download
            Uri resource = Uri.parse(
                    "http://www.bigfoto.com/dog-animal.jpg");
            DownloadManager.Request request =
                    new DownloadManager.Request(resource);
            //Set allowed connections to process download
            request.setAllowedNetworkTypes(
                    DownloadManager.Request.NETWORK_MOBILE
                    | DownloadManager.Request.NETWORK_WIFI);
            request.setAllowedOverRoaming(false);

            //Display in the notification bar
            request.setTitle("Download Sample");
            long id = dm.enqueue(request);
            //Save the unique id
            prefs.edit().putLong(DL_ID, id).commit();
        } else {
            //Download already started, check status
            queryDownloadStatus();
        }

        registerReceiver(receiver, new IntentFilter(
                DownloadManager.ACTION_DOWNLOAD_COMPLETE));
    }
```

```java
    @Override
    public void onPause() {
        super.onPause();
        unregisterReceiver(receiver);
    }

    private BroadcastReceiver receiver = new BroadcastReceiver() {
        @Override
        public void onReceive(Context context, Intent intent) {
            queryDownloadStatus();
        }
    };

    private void queryDownloadStatus() {
        DownloadManager.Query query = new DownloadManager.Query();
        query.setFilterById(prefs.getLong(DL_ID, 0));
        Cursor c = dm.query(query);

        if(c.moveToFirst()) {
            int status = c.getInt(
                c.getColumnIndex(DownloadManager.COLUMN_STATUS));

            switch(status) {
            case DownloadManager.STATUS_PAUSED:
            case DownloadManager.STATUS_PENDING:
            case DownloadManager.STATUS_RUNNING:
                //Do nothing, still in progress
                break;
            case DownloadManager.STATUS_SUCCESSFUL:
                //Done, display the image
                try {
                    ParcelFileDescriptor file =
                        dm.openDownloadedFile(
                            prefs.getLong(DL_ID, 0) );
                    FileInputStream fis = new ParcelFileDescriptor
                        .AutoCloseInputStream(file);
                    imageView.setImageBitmap(
                        BitmapFactory.decodeStream(fis));
                } catch (Exception e) {
                    e.printStackTrace();
                }
                break;
            case DownloadManager.STATUS_FAILED:
                //Clear the download and try again later
                dm.remove(prefs.getLong(DL_ID, 0));
                prefs.edit().clear().commit();
                break;
            }
        }
    }
}
```

■ **Important**   As of this book's publishing date, a bug in the SDK throws an `Exception` claiming that `android.permission.ACCESS_ALL_DOWNLOADS` is required to use `DownloadManager`. This `Exception` is actually thrown when `android.permission.INTERNET` is not in your manifest.

This example does all of its useful work in the `Activity.onResume()` method so the application can determine the status of the download each time the user returns to the activity. Downloads within the manager can be referenced using a long ID value that is returned when `DownloadManager.enqueue()` is called. In the example, we persist that value in the application's preferences in order to monitor and retrieve the downloaded content at any time.

Upon the first launch of the example application, a `DownloadManager.Request` object is created to represent the content to download. At a minimum, this request needs the `Uri` of the remote resource. However, there are many useful properties to set on the request, as well to control its behavior. Some of the useful properties include the following:

- `Request.setAllowedNetworkTypes()`: Set specific network types over which the download may be retrieved.

- `Request.setAllowedOverRoaming()`: Set if the download is allowed to occur while the device is on a roaming connection.

- `Request.setDescription()`: Set a description to be displayed in the system notification for the download.

- `Request.setTitle()`: Set a title to be displayed in the system notification for the download.

Once an ID has been obtained, the application uses that value to check the status of the download. By registering a `BroadcastReceiver` to listen for the `ACTION_DOWNLOAD_COMPLETE` broadcast, the application will react to the download finishing by setting the image file on the activity's `ImageView`. If the activity is paused while the download completes, upon the next resume the status will be checked and the `ImageView` content will be set.

It is important to note that `ACTION_DOWNLOAD_COMPLETE` is a broadcast sent by the `DownloadManager` for every download it may be managing. Because of this, we still must check that the download ID we are interested in is really ready.

Destinations

In Listing 3-11, we never told the `DownloadManager` where to place the file. Instead, when we wanted to access the file, we used the `DownloadManager.openDownloadedFile()` method with the ID value stored in preferences to get a `ParcelFileDescriptor`, which can be turned into a stream the application can read from. This is a simple and straightforward way to gain access to the downloaded content, but it has some caveats to be aware of.

Without a specific destination, files are downloaded to the shared download cache, where the system retains the right to delete them at any time to reclaim space. Downloading in this fashion is a convenient way to get data quickly, but if your needs for the download are more long-term, a permanent destination should be specified on external storage by using one of the `DownloadManager.Request` methods:

- `Request.setDestinationInExternalFilesDir()`: Set the destination to a hidden directory on external storage.

- `Request.setDestinationInExternalPublicDir()`: Set the destination to a public directory on external storage.

- `Request.setDestinationUri()`: Set the destination to a file `Uri` located on external storage.

■ **Note** All destination methods writing to external storage will require your application to declare use of `android.permission.WRITE_EXTERNAL_STORAGE` in the manifest.

Files without an explicit destination also often get removed when `DownloadManager.remove()` gets called to clear the entry from the manager list or the user clears the downloads list; files downloaded to external storage will not be removed by the system under these conditions.

3-6. Accessing a REST API

Problem

Your application needs to access a RESTful API over HTTP to interact with the web services of a remote host.

■ **Note** *REST* stands for *Representational State Transfer*. It is a common architectural style for web services today. RESTful APIs are typically built using standard HTTP verbs to create requests of the remote resource, and the responses are typically returned in a structured document format, such as XML, JSON, or comma-separated values (CSV).

Solution

(API Level 9)

The Android framework APIs comes with two HTTP clients, `HttpURLConnection` and Apache `HttpComponents` (which is now deprecated). While `HttpURLConnection` can work fine for simple use cases, it quickly becomes very complicated to use it in more real-life scenarios, such as accessing REST services. This is why it is recommended to use a library such as Retrofit from Square when accessing a REST service. In this example we will use the library Retrofit together with the JSON parsing library Moshi in order to access and consume an online REST service.

How It Works

Just as we did in Section 3-4, where we downloaded and displayed online images, we will need to add the dependency to the necessary third-party libraries before we can implement the code. Usually when using Retrofit you will need two libraries: Retrofit itself and the converter, depending on the format of the responses from the REST service. In this case we will access a simple REST service that returns JSON data, so we need a converter that can handle JSON. One such converter is using the Moshi library (which will be covered in detail in Section 3-7), and the code for adding these dependencies can be seen in Listen 3-12.

Listing 3-12. Library Dependencies for Retrofit and Moshi

```
dependencies {
    // Remember to check for the latest versions of these!
    compile 'com.squareup.retrofit2:retrofit:2.1.0'
    compile 'com.squareup.retrofit2:converter-moshi:2.1.0'
}
```

The base URL for this service is http://jsonplaceholder.typicode.com. If you look at this URL in your web browser, you will see documentation for how to use the REST service. We will use the service found at the / posts endpoint, which will give us an array of JSON objects. You can see a small sample of this in Listing 3-13.

Listing 3-13. Sample JSON Response from the /Posts Service

```
[
  {
    "userId": 1,
    "id": 1,
    "title": "sunt aut facere repellat provident occaecati excepturi optio reprehenderit",
    "body": "quia et suscipit\nsuscipit recusandae consequuntur expedita et cum\
nreprehenderit molestiae ut ut quas totam\nnostrum rerum est autem sunt rem eveniet
architecto"
  },
  {
    "userId": 1,
    "id": 2,
    "title": "qui est esse",
    "body": "est rerum tempore vitae\nsequi sint nihil reprehenderit dolor beatae ea dolores
neque\nfugiat blanditiis voluptate porro vel nihil molestiae ut reiciendis\nqui aperiam
non debitis possimus qui neque nisi nulla"
  },
  {
    "userId": 1,
    "id": 3,
    "title": "ea molestias quasi exercitationem repellat qui ipsa sit aut",
    "body": "et iusto sed quo iure\nvoluptatem occaecati omnis eligendi aut ad\nvoluptatem
doloribus vel accusantium quis pariatur\nmolestiae porro eius odio et labore et velit aut"
  }
]
```

In order to work with the JSON data, we want to convert the JSON objects into regular Java objects. To do so, we implement a very simple Java class where we can map the keys in the JSON object to individual Java member fields. In this case we only need one such class, which we will call Post (see Listen 3-14).

Listing 3-14. Code for Post.java

```
public class Post implements Parcelable {
    public Long id;
    public Long userId;
    public String title;
    public String body;
```

```java
    protected Post(Parcel in) {
        id = in.readLong();
        userId = in.readLong();
        title = in.readString();
        body = in.readString();
    }

    @Override
    public int describeContents() {
        return 0;
    }

    @Override
    public void writeToParcel(@NonNull Parcel dest, int flags) {
        dest.writeLong(id);
        dest.writeLong(userId);
        dest.writeString(title);
        dest.writeString(body);
    }

    public static final Parcelable.Creator<Post> CREATOR
                            = new Parcelable.Creator<Post>() {
        @Override
        public Post createFromParcel(Parcel in) {
            return new Post(in);
        }

        @Override
        public Post[] newArray(int size) {
            return new Post[size];
        }
    };

    @Override
    public boolean equals(Object o) {
        if (this == o) return true;
        if (o == null || getClass() != o.getClass()) return false;

        Post post = (Post) o;

        return id != null ? id.equals(post.id) : post.id == null;

    }

    @Override
    public int hashCode() {
        return id != null ? id.hashCode() : 0;
    }
}
```

The class Post will basically only contain a number of public member fields that can be mapped to the data in our JSON response. We also implement the equals and hashCode methods so that we can effectively use objects of these classes when comparing or adding them to collections. Finally, we also implement the Parcelable interface so that we can keep these objects during configuration changes of the activity where they will be shown. That way, we don't have to reload the data from the server when the device rotates.

The Moshi converter we included will automatically map JSON to Java for us as long as the Java fields are primitive types, String, or collections of these. In Section 3-7 we will look at more advanced examples of using Moshi as well.

Next, we will need to define a Java equivalent of the REST service for use in Retrofit. This is done using a simple Java interface where each method is mapped to a HTTP call using annotations. In this case, we call this interface PostsService (see Listen 3-15).

Listing 3-15. Code for PostsService.java

```java
public interface PostsService {
    @GET("posts")
    Call<List<Post>> getPosts();

    @GET("posts")
    Call<List<Post>> getPosts(@Query("userId") Long userId);

    @POST("posts")
    Call<Post> createPost(@Body Post post);

    @PUT("posts/{id}")
    Call<Post> updatePost(@Path("id") Long id, @Body Post post);

    @DELETE("posts/{id}")
    Call<Void> deletePost(@Path("id") Long id);
}
```

Each method in our interface is annotated with @GET, @POST, @PUT or @DELETE, depending on the HTTP method used in that case. Each annotation contains the path (without a / prefix) that maps to the request path. When a certain HTTP method and path requires query parameters, we can add arguments in the method definition that is annotated with @Query, as shown in the second method called getPosts(). When the method require a body, such as the createPost() and updatePost(), we simply specify a Java object that can be mapped to the JSON data, and annotate that with @Body. When the request path is dynamic, such as the preceding example when the id for a post is contained in the path, we can add that as a parameter in the @GET, @POST, @PUT or @DELETE annotation using curly braces and then add a method parameter with the same id.

The return value from the methods in our interface is always of type Call, with the generic type representing the response, such as Call<Post> when a single object is returned. If the request will return a JSON array with objects, the return value would be Call<List<Post>>.

Our final step is to set up Retrofit, create an instance of our interface, and access the REST service using that. This is done using Retrofit.Builder, which lets you specify and configure all aspects of the final Retrofit instance and then using that to create an instance of the interface (See Listing 3-16).

Listing 3-16. Code for Creating a Service Instance

```
String REST_API_BASEURL = "http://jsonplaceholder.typicode.com/";

Retrofit retrofit = new Retrofit.Builder()
        .baseUrl(REST_API_BASEURL)
        .addConverterFactory(MoshiConverterFactory.create())
        .build();
PostsService postsService = retrofit.create(PostsService.class);
```

This is the simplest case of using Retrofit for a JSON service. Note how we don't have to implement the interface PostService ourself, but simply give it to the create() method of our Retrofit instance, which will use reflection internally to create it for us.

We're now ready to put this all together and implement it in a real application. When we call the methods on our interface, we receive a Call object. This object allows us to perform either a synchronous execution of the actual network call, or an asynchronous call where we provide a callback. In most cases you will want to use the asynchronous version so that you don't have to worry about executing the network calls on a background thread. Our callback contains two methods, onResponse() and onFailure(), allowing us to react to successful and failed requests respectively. When onResponse() is called, we simply extract the Java representation of the JSON response and give it to the adapter of our RecyclerView (See Listing 3-17).

Listing 3-17. Full Code for our RetrofitActivity

```
public class RetrofitActivity extends AppCompatActivity implements Callback<List<Post>> {
    private static final String KEY_POSTS = "posts";
    private static final String REST_API_BASEURL = "http://jsonplaceholder.typicode.com/";
    private PostsService postsService;
    private Call<List<Post>> listCall;
    private List<Post> posts;
    private PostAdapter postAdapter;

    @Override
    protected void onCreate(Bundle savedInstanceState) {
        super.onCreate(savedInstanceState);
        setContentView(R.layout.activity_retrofit);
        Toolbar toolbar = (Toolbar) findViewById(R.id.toolbar);
        setSupportActionBar(toolbar);

        postAdapter = new PostAdapter();
        ((RecyclerView) findViewById(R.id.content_retrofit))
                .setAdapter(postAdapter);
        ((RecyclerView) findViewById(R.id.content_retrofit))
                .setLayoutManager(new LinearLayoutManager(this,
                            LinearLayoutManager.VERTICAL, false));

        Retrofit retrofit = new Retrofit.Builder()
                .baseUrl(REST_API_BASEURL)
                .addConverterFactory(MoshiConverterFactory.create())
                .build();
        PostsService postsService = retrofit.create(PostsService.class);
```

```java
        // Make sure we can handle rotation change without having
        // to reload from the REST API
        if(savedInstanceState != null) {
            // Restore the data from a previous state
            posts = savedInstanceState.getParcelableArrayList(KEY_POSTS);
            postAdapter.notifyDataSetChanged();
        }
    }

    @Override
    protected void onSaveInstanceState(Bundle outState) {
        super.onSaveInstanceState(outState);
        if(posts != null) {
            // Save the data between configuration changes
            outState.putParcelableArrayList(KEY_POSTS,
                                    new ArrayList<Parcelable>(posts));
        }
    }

    @Override
    protected void onDestroy() {
        super.onDestroy();
        if (listCall != null) {
            listCall.cancel();
        }
    }

    @Override
    public boolean onCreateOptionsMenu(Menu menu) {
        // Inflate the menu; this adds items to the action bar if it is present.
        getMenuInflater().inflate(R.menu.menu, menu);
        return super.onCreateOptionsMenu(menu);
    }

    public void doRefresh(MenuItem item) {
        if (listCall == null) {
            listCall = postsService.getPosts();
            listCall.enqueue(this);
        } else {
            listCall.cancel();
            listCall = null;
        }
    }

    @Override
    public void onResponse(Call<List<Post>> call,
                            Response<List<Post>> response) {
        if (response.isSuccessful()) {
            posts = response.body();
            postAdapter.notifyDataSetChanged();
        }
```

```
            listCall = null;
    }

    @Override
    public void onFailure(Call<List<Post>> call, Throwable t) {
        Toast.makeText(this, "Failed to fetch posts!",
                        Toast.LENGTH_SHORT).show();
        listCall = null;
    }

    private class PostAdapter extends RecyclerView.Adapter<PostViewHolder> {
        @Override
        public PostViewHolder onCreateViewHolder(ViewGroup parent,
                                                int viewType) {
            View view = LayoutInflater.from(RetrofitActivity.this)
                    .inflate(R.layout.post_item, parent, false);
            return new PostViewHolder(view);
        }

        @Override
        public void onBindViewHolder(PostViewHolder holder, int position) {
            Post post = posts.get(position);
            holder.bindData(post);
        }

        @Override
        public int getItemCount() {
            return posts != null ? posts.size() : 0;
        }
    }

    private class PostViewHolder extends RecyclerView.ViewHolder {
        private final TextView title;
        private final TextView body;

        public PostViewHolder(View itemView) {
            super(itemView);
            title = (TextView) itemView.findViewById(R.id.title);
            body = (TextView) itemView.findViewById(R.id.body);
        }

        public void bindData(Post post) {
            title.setText(post.title);
            body.setText(post.body);
        }
    }
}
```

Accessing REST service using the default HTTP client in Android can be a complex and frustrating task. By using a library such as Retrofit that is well tested and provides an easy-to-use API, you can spend more time focusing on the overall user experience of your application. While Retrofit is currently the state-of-the-art library for consuming REST services, you should also look at the alternatives because your requirements might be different from the ones in this example.

3-7. Parsing JSON

Problem

Your application needs to parse responses from an API or other source that is formatted in JavaScript Object Notation (JSON).

Solution

(API Level 1)

Android has a built-in JSON library called org.json. This provides a simple API for working with JSON objects and arrays, as well as the primitive type contained in the objects. However, in the same way as the built-in HTTP clients in Android are very basic, the org.json API can be cumbersome to use when working with large and complex JSON data.

To handle this, it is recommended that you use a serialization library that can map between JSON and Java objects. One such library is Moshi from Square. There are also two other alternatives, Gson and Jackson, which are more generic Java libraries. However, Moshi is better adapted to Android so we will use it in this example.

How It Works

Moshi, as well as most other serialization libraries, use annotations and reflection to determine how to map between Java and JSON. In this example we will use a rather complex JSON document, and show how to configure Moshi to map it to our Java classes. Consider the JSON in Listing 3-18.

Listing 3-18. Example JSON

```
{
  "purchase_id": "ab07c952-4207-46c3-b1f1-1b55a4cfb1b1",
  "timestamp": "2016-06-25 13:45:25",
  "product_name": "Nexus 5X",
  "product_id": "N5X",
  "delivery_address": {
    "name": "Anders Johnson",
    "street": "Homestreet 10",
    "zip": "123456",
    "city": "Hometown",
    "state": "CA",
    "country": "USA"
  },
  "units": 1,
  "purchase_amount": 15045,
  "currency": "$"
}
```

This defines an object that is supposed to map a purchase of a specific product. The root object contains a child object that defines the delivery address. While all the fields could be mapped to either an integer or a String, we want to use more specific types when possible. The purchase_id field contains a UUID, so we want to use that class instead. Meanwhile, the timestamp could be mapped to a Date object, and we want to create a Java enum for the different type of currencies we support. The Java classes that we will map the JSON to can be seen in Listen 3-19.

Listing 3-19. Java Class That Maps to our JSON Data

```java
public class Purchase {
    @Json(name = "purchase_id")
    public UUID id;
    public Date timestamp;
    @Json(name = "product_name")
    public String productName;
    @Json(name = "product_id")
    public String productId;
    @Json(name = "delivery_address")
    public Address deliveryAddress;
    public Integer units;
    @Json(name = "purchase_amount")
    public Long amount;
    public Currency currency;

    @SuppressWarnings("WeakerAccess")
    public static class Address {
        public String name;
        public String street;
        public String zip;
        public String city;
        public String state;
        public String country;

        @Override
        public String toString() {
            return String.format("%s\n%s\n%s %s\n%s\n%s", name,
                                  street, city, zip, street, country);
        }
    }

    @SuppressWarnings("WeakerAccess")
    public enum Currency {
        Euro("€", true), Dollars("$", true),
        BritishPounds("£", true), SwedishKrona("SEK", false);

        private final String sign;
        private final boolean prefix;

        Currency(String sign, boolean prefix) {
            this.sign = sign;
            this.prefix = prefix;
        }

        @Nullable
        public static Currency fromSign(String sign) {
            for (Currency currency : values()) {
                if (currency.sign.equals(sign)) {
                    return currency;
                }
```

```
        }
        return null;
    }

    public String getSign() {
        return sign;
    }

    @SuppressLint("DefaultLocale")
    public String toString(Long amount) {
        long characteristicPart = amount / 100;
        long fractionalPart = amount % 100;

        if (prefix) {
            return String.format("%s %d,%d", sign,
                                characteristicPart, fractionalPart);
        } else {
            return String.format("%d,%d %s",
                                characteristicPart, fractionalPart, sign);
        }
    }
    }
}
}
```

This defines one class for the purchase and an inner class for the delivery address. We use the annotation @Json to define what the key in the JSON object will be, which lets us handle cases where the JSON key name would be an illegal Java identifier.

However, as powerful as Moshi and other serialization libraries can be, they are not able to automatically map from a JSON value to a custom Java class. To do this, we need to provide an adapter for each of the custom classes in our Java class. The code the adapers can be seen in Listing 3-20.

Listing 3-20. Moshi Adapters for Our Custom Classes

```
private class UuidAdapter {

    @ToJson
    String toJson(UUID uuid) {
        return uuid.toString();
    }

    @FromJson
    UUID fromJson(String json) {
        return UUID.fromString(json);
    }

}
```

```java
private class DateAdapter {

    @ToJson
    String toJson(Date date) {
        return DATE_FORMAT.format(date);
    }

    @FromJson
    Date fromJson(String json) {
        try {
            return DATE_FORMAT.parse(json);
        } catch (ParseException e) {
            return null;
        }
    }
}

private class CurrencyAdapter {
    @ToJson
    String toJson(Purchase.Currency currency) {
        return currency.getSign();
    }

    @FromJson
    Purchase.Currency fromJson(String json) {
        return Purchase.Currency.fromSign(json);
    }
}
```

These show how to create adapters for Moshi that convert from a JSON string to a Java class. Note that these are regular objects and the names of their methods are not important (although, these method names are recommended for readability). The "magic" happens using the annotations @FromJson and @ToJson, which in turn will be used by Moshi to determine which method to use in each case.

Now all we need to do is to create our Moshi instance and convert to and from a JSON document (see Listing 3-21).

Listing 3-21. Using Moshi to Covert from and to JSON

```java
moshi = new Moshi.Builder()
        .add(new UuidAdapter())
        .add(new CurrencyAdapter())
        .add(new DateAdapter())
        .build();

JsonAdapter<Purchase> jsonAdapter = moshi.adapter(Purchase.class);

try {
    // Convert from a JSON document stored in the raw resources
    InputStream inputStream = getResources().openRawResource(R.raw.purchase);
    Source source = Okio.source(inputStream);
    Purchase purchase = jsonAdapter.fromJson(Okio.buffer(source));
```

```
    // Convert back to JSON
    String json = jsonAdapter.toJson(purchase);
} catch (IOException e) {
    e.printStackTrace();
}
```

This shows how you can use Moshi to serialize between JSON and Java objects. This becomes especially useful when used together with Retrofit, as shown in Section 3-6. JSON has become the de facto standard for many online cloud services, which makes libraries such as Moshi especially powerful for Android applications.

3-8. Parsing XML

Problem

Your application needs to parse responses, from an API or other source, that are formatted as XML.

Solution

(API Level 1)

As with JSON, Android already has APIs for reading and writing XML. However, these APIs are very low level, and for most Android applications we want to serialize between XML and Java objects, rather than manually parsing an XML document. To do that, we use an XML serialization library called Simple XML. It is very similar to how Moshi works for JSON, but has a slightly different syntax and API.

How It Works

In this example, we will use an XML document that describes a purchase, similar to what we had in Section 3-7. The XML document we will deserialize is shown in Listing 3-22.

Listing 3-22. XML Document

```
<?xml version="1.0" encoding="utf-8"?>
<purchase id="ab07c952-4207-46c3-b1f1-1b55a4cfb1b1">
    <timestamp>2016-06-25 13:45:25</timestamp>
    <productName>Nexus 5X</productName>
    <productId>N5X</productId>
    <deliveryAddress>
        <name>Anders Johnson</name>
        <street>Homestreet 10</street>
        <zip>123456</zip>
        <city>Hometown</city>
        <state>CA</state>
        <country>USA</country>
    </deliveryAddress>
    <units>1</units>
    <amount>15045</amount>
    <currency>$</currency>
</purchase>
```

First, we need to add the dependencies to the Simple XML library so we can use the API, as shown in Listing 3-23.

Listing 3-23. Dependencies for Simple XML

```
dependencies {
    compile('org.simpleframework:simple-xml:2.7.1') {
        exclude module: 'stax'
        exclude module: 'stax-api'
        exclude module: 'xpp3'
    }
}
```

Not that this dependency looks a bit different to the ones from earlier examples. This is because we need to exclude certain transitive dependencies, which the Android framework already contains.

Next, we use the same Java classes as in the previous example (see Section 3-7) but with different annotations (see Listing 3-24).

Listing 3-24. Java Object for Our XML Serialization

```
@Root(name = "purchase")
public class Purchase {
    @Attribute
    public UUID id;
    @Element()
    public Date timestamp;
    @Element
    public String productName;
    @Element
    public String productId;
    @Element
    public Address deliveryAddress;
    @Element
    public Integer units;
    @Element
    public Long amount;
    @Element
    public Currency currency;

    @SuppressWarnings("WeakerAccess")
    public static class Address {
        @Element
        public String name;
        @Element
        public String street;
        @Element
        public String zip;
        @Element
        public String city;
        @Element
        public String state;
        @Element
```

```java
        public String country;

        @Override
        public String toString() {
            return String.format("%s\n%s\n%s %s\n%s\n%s",
                                  name, street, city, zip, street, country);
        }
    }

    @SuppressWarnings("WeakerAccess")
    public enum Currency {
        Euro("€", true), Dollars("$", true),
        BritishPounds("£", true), SwedishKrona("SEK", false);

        private final String sign;
        private final boolean prefix;

        Currency(String sign, boolean prefix) {
            this.sign = sign;
            this.prefix = prefix;
        }

        @Nullable
        public static Currency fromSign(String sign) {
            for (Currency currency : values()) {
                if (currency.sign.equals(sign)) {
                    return currency;
                }
            }
            return null;
        }

        public String getSign() {
            return sign;
        }

        @SuppressLint("DefaultLocale")
        public String toString(Long amount) {
            long characteristicPart = amount / 100;
            long fractionalPart = amount % 100;

            if (prefix) {
                return String.format("%s %d,%d", sign,
                                      characteristicPart, fractionalPart);
            } else {
                return String.format("%d,%d %s",
                                      characteristicPart, fractionalPart, sign);
            }
        }
    }
}
```

Note that this time we need to annotate the top-level class with @Root. The fields are annotated with @Element or @Attribute, depending on where in the XML document the appear.

As with the JSON example in Section 3-7, we need to define a class that handles the conversion between XML and our Java classes when they are not of primitive types or String. To do this we use the Transform interface from Simple XML (see Listen 3-25).

Listing 3-25. Transform Classes for Simple XML

```
public static class UuidConverter implements Transform<UUID> {
    @Override
    public UUID read(String value) throws Exception {
        return UUID.fromString(value);
    }

    @Override
    public String write(UUID value) throws Exception {
        return value.toString();
    }

}

public static class DateConverter implements Transform<Date> {
    @Override
    public Date read(String value) throws Exception {
        return DATE_FORMAT.parse(value);
    }

    @Override
    public String write(Date value) throws Exception {
        return DATE_FORMAT.format(value);
    }
}

public static class CurrencyConverter implements Transform<Purchase.Currency> {
    @Override
    public Purchase.Currency read(String value) throws Exception {
        return Purchase.Currency.fromSign(value);
    }

    @Override
    public String write(Purchase.Currency value) throws Exception {
        return value.getSign();
    }
}
```

These classes use generics instead of annotations to define what type of class they convert to and from. Note that it doesn't matter if the value is in an XML attribute or an element, the Transformer works on both. Now that we have everything defined, we can create our Simple XML Persister instance and use it (see Listing 3-26).

Listing 3-26. Transform Classes for Simple XML

```
RegistryMatcher registryMatcher = new RegistryMatcher();
registryMatcher.bind(UUID.class, new UuidConverter());
registryMatcher.bind(Date.class, new DateConverter());
registryMatcher.bind(Purchase.Currency.class, new CurrencyConverter());

Serializer serializer = new Persister(registryMatcher);

try {
    // Deserialize XML document from our raw resources
    InputStream inputStream = getResources().openRawResource(R.raw.purchase);
    Purchase purchase = serializer.read(Purchase.class, inputStream);

    // Serialize a Purchase instance to XML
    StringWriter stringWriter = new StringWriter();
    serializer.write(purchase, stringWriter);
} catch (Exception e) {
    e.printStackTrace();
}
```

We now have an efficient way to represent XML data as Java objects. While XML is becoming less popular for online services, there are still a lot of cases where you need to read and write XML. Simple XML helps with this, has good performance, and is easy to use.

3-9. Receiving SMS

Problem

Your application must react to incoming SMS messages, commonly called *text messages*.

Solution

(API Level 4)

Register a `BroadcastReceiver` to listen for incoming messages, and process them in `onReceive()`. The operating system will fire a broadcast intent with the `android.provider.Telephony.SMS_RECEIVED` action whenever there is an incoming SMS message. Your application can register a `BroadcastReceiver` to filter for this intent and process the incoming data.

■ **Note**   Receiving this broadcast does not prevent the rest of the system's applications from receiving it as well. The default messaging application will still receive and display any incoming SMS.

How It Works

In previous recipes, we defined `BroadcastReceivers` as private internal members to an activity. In this case, it is probably best to define the receiver separately and register it in `AndroidManifest.xml` by using the `<receiver>` tag. This will allow your receiver to process the incoming events even when your application is not active. Listings 3-27 and 3-28 show an example of a receiver that monitors all incoming SMS and raises a Toast when one arrives from the party of interest.

Listing 3-27. Incoming SMS BroadcastReceiver

```
public class SmsReceiver extends BroadcastReceiver {
    //Device address we would like to listen for (phone number, shortcode, etc.)
    private static final String SENDER_ADDRESS = "<ENTER YOUR NUMBER HERE>";

    @Override
    public void onReceive(Context context, Intent intent) {
        Bundle bundle = intent.getExtras();

        Object[] messages = (Object[])bundle.get("pdus");
        SmsMessage[] sms = new SmsMessage[messages.length];
        //Create messages for each incoming PDU
        for(int n=0; n < messages.length; n++) {
            sms[n] =
                SmsMessage.createFromPdu((byte[]) messages[n]);
        }

        for(SmsMessage msg : sms) {
            //Verify if the message came from our known sender
            if(TextUtils.equals(
                    msg.getOriginatingAddress(), SENDER_ADDRESS)) {
                //Keep other apps from processing this message
                abortBroadcast();

                //Display our own notification
                Toast.makeText(context,
                        "Received message from the mothership: "
                        + msg.getMessageBody(),
                        Toast.LENGTH_SHORT).show();
            }
        }
    }
}
```

Listing 3-28. Partial AndroidManifest.xml

```
<?xml version="1.0" encoding="utf-8"?>
<manifest ...>

    <uses-permission
        android:name="android.permission.RECEIVE_SMS" />

  <application ...>
    <receiver android:name=".SmsReceiver">
      <!-- Add a priority to catch the ordered broadcast -->
      <intent-filter android:priority="5">
        <action
          android:name="android.provider.Telephony.SMS_RECEIVED"
```

```
        />
      </intent-filter>
    </receiver>
  </application>

</manifest>
```

■ **Important**   Receiving SMS messages requires that the android.permission.RECEIVE_SMS permission be declared in the manifest!

Incoming SMS messages are passed via the extras of the broadcast intent as an Object array of byte arrays, each byte array representing an SMS protocol data unit (PDU). SmsMessage.createFromPdu() is a convenience method allowing us to create SmsMessage objects from the raw PDU data. With the setup work complete, we can inspect each message to determine whether there is something interesting to handle or process. In the example, we compare the originating address of each message against a known short code, and the user is notified when one arrives.

The broadcast triggered by the framework is an ordered broadcast message, which means that each registered receiver will receive the message in order and will have an opportunity to modify the broadcast before it is handed to the next receiver or to cancel it and stop any lower priority receivers from receiving it at all.

In the AndroidManifest.xml entry for the <intent-filter>, we had added an arbitrary priority value to insert our receiver above the core system Messages application (which uses the default priority of zero). This allows our application to process the SMS message first.

■ **Note**   With an ordered broadcast, receivers that are registered at the same priority will receive the intent at the "same time," such that the order between them is not determined. Additionally, one receiver cannot cancel the broadcast from being delivered to the other(s) of the same priority.

Then, once we verify that the message we are looking at came from the sender we are tracking, a call to abortBroadcast() terminates the responder chain. This keeps the SMS messages we are processing from displaying to the user and cluttering up the user's SMS inbox.

■ **Important**   There is no external method of verifying that other apps on the system may also be registered to handle this broadcast and have a very high priority (or at least, higher than your app). Your application is at the mercy of a higher-priority application not aborting the broadcast for the message you want to process.

At the point in the example where the Toast is raised, you may wish to provide something more useful to the user. Perhaps the SMS message includes an offer code for your application, and you could launch the appropriate activity to display this information to the user within the application.

```
DEFAULT SMS APPLICATIONS
```

Starting with Android 4.4, the behavior of applications using SMS has changed. The device's Settings application now provides the user with a Default SMS App option that selects the application the user would prefer to use for SMS. At the framework level, this augments some of the behaviors around sending and receiving messages.

Applications that are not selected as the default may still send outgoing SMS and monitor incoming messages by using the same ordered broadcast described in this recipe. However, two new broadcast actions have been added for the default SMS app to receive messages:

- android.provider.telephony.SMS_DELIVER

- android.provider.telephony.WAP_PUSH_DELIVER

The framework will broadcast incoming SMS/MMS message data to the default SMS app separately from other applications using these two actions. Although the original SMS_RECEIVED action is still an ordered broadcast, aborting that broadcast can no longer be used as a technique to intercept certain messages from being delivered to that application. However, aborting the broadcast will still interrupt the chain from going to any other third-party app that is monitoring incoming SMS.

Additionally, an SMS application marked as the default is responsible for writing all SMS data received on the device to the device's internal content provider exposed publicly in API Level 19 via android. provider.Telephony. This application is the only one on the system with privileges to write data to the SMS provider, regardless of an application's request to obtain the android.permission.WRITE_SMS permission.

Other applications may still read the SMS provider data if they have obtained the android.permission. READ_SMS permission. We will look in more detail at reading the SMS provider in Chapter 7.

3-10. Sending an SMS Message

Problem

Your application must issue outgoing SMS messages.

Solution

(API Level 4)

Use the SMSManager to send text and data SMS messages. SMSManager is a system service that handles sending SMS and providing feedback to the application about the status of the operation. SMSManager provides methods to send text messages by using SmsManager.sendTextMessage() and SmsManager. sendMultipartTextMessage(), or data messages by using SmsManager.sendDataMessage(). Each of these methods takes PendingIntent parameters to deliver status for the send operation and the message delivery back to a requested destination.

How It Works

Let's take a look at a simple example activity that sends an SMS message and monitors its status (see Listing 3-29).

Listing 3-29. Activity to Send SMS Messages

```
public class SmsActivity extends Activity {
    //Device address where we would like to send (phone number, shortcode, etc.)
    private static final String RECIPIENT_ADDRESS = "<ENTER YOUR NUMBER HERE>";

    private static final String ACTION_SENT =
            "com.examples.sms.SENT";
    private static final String ACTION_DELIVERED =
            "com.examples.sms.DELIVERED";

    @Override
    public void onCreate(Bundle savedInstanceState) {
        super.onCreate(savedInstanceState);

        Button sendButton = new Button(this);
        sendButton.setText("Hail the Mothership");
        sendButton.setOnClickListener(new View.OnClickListener() {
            @Override
            public void onClick(View v) {
                sendSMS("Beam us up!");
            }
        });

        setContentView(sendButton);
    }

    @Override
    protected void onResume() {
        super.onResume();
        //Monitor status of the operations
        registerReceiver(sent, new IntentFilter(ACTION_SENT));
        registerReceiver(delivered, new IntentFilter(ACTION_DELIVERED));
    }

    @Override
    protected void onPause() {
        super.onPause();
        //Make sure receivers aren't active while we are in the background
        unregisterReceiver(sent);
        unregisterReceiver(delivered);
    }

    private void sendSMS(String message) {
        PendingIntent sIntent = PendingIntent.getBroadcast(
            this, 0, new Intent(ACTION_SENT), 0);
```

```
        PendingIntent dIntent = PendingIntent.getBroadcast(
            this, 0, new Intent(ACTION_DELIVERED), 0);

        //Send the message
        SmsManager manager = SmsManager.getDefault();
        manager.sendTextMessage(RECIPIENT_ADDRESS, null, message,
                sIntent, dIntent);
    }

    private BroadcastReceiver sent = new BroadcastReceiver(){
        @Override
        public void onReceive(Context context, Intent intent) {
            switch (getResultCode()) {
            case Activity.RESULT_OK:
                //Handle sent success
                break;
            case SmsManager.RESULT_ERROR_GENERIC_FAILURE:
            case SmsManager.RESULT_ERROR_NO_SERVICE:
            case SmsManager.RESULT_ERROR_NULL_PDU:
            case SmsManager.RESULT_ERROR_RADIO_OFF:
                //Handle sent error
                break;
            }
        }
    };

    private BroadcastReceiver delivered = new BroadcastReceiver(){
        @Override
        public void onReceive(Context context, Intent intent) {
            switch (getResultCode()) {
            case Activity.RESULT_OK:
                //Handle delivery success
                break;
            case Activity.RESULT_CANCELED:
                //Handle delivery failure
                break;
            }
        }
    };
}
```

■ **Important**   Sending SMS messages requires that the `android.permission.SEND_SMS` permission be declared in the manifest!

In the example, an SMS message is sent out via the SMSManager whenever the user taps the button. Because SMSManager is a system service, the static SMSManager.getDefault() method must be called to get a reference to it. sendTextMessage() takes the destination address (number), service center address, and message as parameters. The service center address should be null to allow SMSManager to use the system default.

Two BroadcastReceivers are registered to receive the callback intents that will be sent: one for status of the send operation and the other for status of the delivery. The receivers are registered only while the operations are pending, and they unregister themselves as soon as the intent is processed.

3-11. Communicating over Bluetooth

Problem

You want to leverage Bluetooth communication to transmit data between devices in your application.

Solution

(API Level 5)

Use the Bluetooth APIs introduced in API Level 5 to create a peer-to-peer connection over the radio frequency communications (RFCOMM) protocol interface. Bluetooth is a popular wireless radio technology that is in almost all mobile devices today. Many users think of Bluetooth as a way for their mobile devices to connect with a wireless headset or integrate with a vehicle's stereo system. However, Bluetooth can also be a simple and effective way for developers to create peer-to-peer connections in their applications.

How It Works

■ **Important**   Bluetooth is not currently supported in the Android emulator. To execute the code in this example, Bluetooth must be run on an Android device. Furthermore, to appropriately test the functionality, you need two devices running the application simultaneously.

Bluetooth Peer-to-Peer

Listings 3-30 through 3-32 illustrate an example that uses Bluetooth to find other users nearby and quickly exchange contact information (in this case, just an e-mail address). Connections are made over Bluetooth by discovering available "services" and connecting to them by referencing their 128-bit universally unique identifier (UUID) value. The UUID of the service you want to use must either be discovered or known ahead of time.

In this example, the same application is running on both devices on each end of the connection, so we have the freedom to define the UUID in code as a constant because both devices will have a reference to it.

■ **Note**   To ensure that the UUID you choose is unique, use one of the many free UUID generators available on the Web or tools such as uuidgen on Mac/Linux.

Listing 3-30. AndroidManifest.xml

```xml
<?xml version="1.0" encoding="utf-8"?>
<manifest
    xmlns:android="http://schemas.android.com/apk/res/android"
    package="com.examples.bluetooth">
```

```
<uses-permission android:name="android.permission.BLUETOOTH"/>
<uses-permission
    android:name="android.permission.BLUETOOTH_ADMIN"/>

<application android:icon="@drawable/icon"
    android:label="@string/app_name">
    <activity android:name=".ExchangeActivity"
        android:label="@string/app_name">
        <intent-filter>
            <action
                android:name="android.intent.action.MAIN" />
            <category
                android:name="android.intent.category.LAUNCHER" />
        </intent-filter>
    </activity>
</application>
</manifest>
```

■ **Important**   Remember that android.permission.BLUETOOTH must be declared in the manifest to use these APIs. In addition, android.permission.BLUETOOTH_ADMIN must be declared to make changes to preferences such as discoverability and to enable/disable the adapter.

Listing 3-31. res/layout/main.xml

```
<?xml version="1.0" encoding="utf-8"?>
<RelativeLayout
    xmlns:android="http://schemas.android.com/apk/res/android"
    android:layout_width="match_parent"
    android:layout_height="match_parent">
    <TextView
        android:id="@+id/label"
        android:layout_width="wrap_content"
        android:layout_height="wrap_content"
        android:textAppearance="?android:attr/textAppearanceLarge"
        android:text="Enter Your Email:" />
    <EditText
        android:id="@+id/emailField"
        android:layout_width="match_parent"
        android:layout_height="wrap_content"
        android:layout_below="@id/label"
        android:singleLine="true"
        android:inputType="textEmailAddress" />
    <Button
        android:id="@+id/scanButton"
        android:layout_width="match_parent"
        android:layout_height="wrap_content"
        android:layout_alignParentBottom="true"
        android:text="Connect and Share" />
```

```
    <Button
        android:id="@+id/listenButton"
        android:layout_width="match_parent"
        android:layout_height="wrap_content"
        android:layout_above="@id/scanButton"
        android:text="Listen for Sharers" />
</RelativeLayout>
```

The user interface for this example consists of an EditText for users to enter an e-mail address, and two buttons to initiate communication. The Listen for Sharers button puts the device into listen mode. In this mode, the device will accept and communicate with any device that attempts to connect with it. The Connect and Share button puts the device into search mode. In this mode, the device searches for any device that is currently listening and makes a connection (see Listing 3-32).

Listing 3-32. Bluetooth Exchange Activity

```java
public class ExchangeActivity extends Activity {

    // Unique UUID for this application
    private static final UUID MY_UUID =
        UUID.fromString("321cb8fa-9066-4f58-935e-ef55d1ae06ec");
    //Friendly name to match while discovering
    private static final String SEARCH_NAME = "bluetooth.recipe";

    BluetoothAdapter mBtAdapter;
    BluetoothSocket mBtSocket;
    Button listenButton, scanButton;
    EditText emailField;

    @Override
    public void onCreate(Bundle savedInstanceState) {
        super.onCreate(savedInstanceState);
        requestWindowFeature(
                Window.FEATURE_INDETERMINATE_PROGRESS);
        setContentView(R.layout.main);

        //Check the system status
        mBtAdapter = BluetoothAdapter.getDefaultAdapter();
        if(mBtAdapter == null) {
            Toast.makeText(this, "Bluetooth is not supported.",
                Toast.LENGTH_SHORT).show();
            finish();
            return;
        }
        if (!mBtAdapter.isEnabled()) {
            Intent enableIntent = new Intent(
                    BluetoothAdapter.ACTION_REQUEST_ENABLE);
            startActivityForResult(enableIntent, REQUEST_ENABLE);
        }
```

```java
        emailField = (EditText)findViewById(R.id.emailField);
        listenButton = (Button)findViewById(R.id.listenButton);
        listenButton.setOnClickListener(
                new View.OnClickListener() {
            @Override
            public void onClick(View v) {
                //Make sure the device is discoverable first
                if (mBtAdapter.getScanMode() != BluetoothAdapter
                        .SCAN_MODE_CONNECTABLE_DISCOVERABLE) {
                    Intent discoverableIntent = new Intent(
                            BluetoothAdapter
                                .ACTION_REQUEST_DISCOVERABLE);
                    discoverableIntent.putExtra(BluetoothAdapter.
                            EXTRA_DISCOVERABLE_DURATION, 300);
                    startActivityForResult(discoverableIntent,
                            REQUEST_DISCOVERABLE);
                    return;
                }
                startListening();
            }
        });
        scanButton = (Button)findViewById(R.id.scanButton);
        scanButton.setOnClickListener(new View.OnClickListener() {
            @Override
            public void onClick(View v) {
                mBtAdapter.startDiscovery();
                setProgressBarIndeterminateVisibility(true);
            }
        });
    }

    @Override
    public void onResume() {
        super.onResume();
        //Register the activity for broadcast intents
        IntentFilter filter = new IntentFilter(
                BluetoothDevice.ACTION_FOUND);
        registerReceiver(mReceiver, filter);
        filter = new IntentFilter(
                BluetoothAdapter.ACTION_DISCOVERY_FINISHED);
        registerReceiver(mReceiver, filter);
    }

    @Override
    public void onPause() {
        super.onPause();
        unregisterReceiver(mReceiver);
    }

    @Override
    public void onDestroy() {
        super.onDestroy();
```

```java
    try {
        if(mBtSocket != null) {
            mBtSocket.close();
        }
    } catch (IOException e) {
        e.printStackTrace();
    }
}

private static final int REQUEST_ENABLE = 1;
private static final int REQUEST_DISCOVERABLE = 2;

@Override
protected void onActivityResult(int requestCode,
        int resultCode, Intent data) {
    switch(requestCode) {
    case REQUEST_ENABLE:
        if(resultCode != Activity.RESULT_OK) {
            Toast.makeText(this, "Bluetooth Not Enabled.",
                Toast.LENGTH_SHORT).show();
            finish();
        }
        break;
    case REQUEST_DISCOVERABLE:
        if(resultCode == Activity.RESULT_CANCELED) {
            Toast.makeText(this, "Must be discoverable.",
                Toast.LENGTH_SHORT).show();
        } else {
            startListening();
        }
        break;
    default:
        break;
    }
}

//Start a server socket and listen
private void startListening() {
    AcceptTask task = new AcceptTask();
    task.execute(MY_UUID);
    setProgressBarIndeterminateVisibility(true);
}

//AsyncTask to accept incoming connections
private class AcceptTask extends
        AsyncTask<UUID, Void, BluetoothSocket> {

    @Override
    protected BluetoothSocket doInBackground(UUID... params) {
        String name = mBtAdapter.getName();
        try {
            //While listening, set the discovery name to
```

```
                // a specific value
                mBtAdapter.setName(SEARCH_NAME);
                BluetoothServerSocket socket = mBtAdapter
                        .listenUsingRfcommWithServiceRecord(
                            "BluetoothRecipe", params[0]);
                BluetoothSocket connected = socket.accept();
                //Reset the BT adapter name
                mBtAdapter.setName(name);
                return connected;
            } catch (IOException e) {
                e.printStackTrace();
                mBtAdapter.setName(name);
                return null;
            }
        }

        @Override
        protected void onPostExecute(BluetoothSocket socket) {
            if(socket == null) {
                return;
            }
            mBtSocket = socket;
            ConnectedTask task = new ConnectedTask();
            task.execute(mBtSocket);
        }

    }

    //AsyncTask to receive a single line of data and post
    private class ConnectedTask extends
            AsyncTask<BluetoothSocket,Void,String> {

        @Override
        protected String doInBackground(
                BluetoothSocket... params) {
            InputStream in = null;
            OutputStream out = null;
            try {
                //Send your data
                out = params[0].getOutputStream();
                String email = emailField.getText().toString();
                out.write(email.getBytes());
                //Receive the other's data
                in = params[0].getInputStream();
                byte[] buffer = new byte[1024];
                in.read(buffer);
                //Create a clean string from results
                String result = new String(buffer);
                //Close the connection
                mBtSocket.close();
                return result.trim();
```

```java
        } catch (Exception exc) {
            return null;
        }
    }

    @Override
    protected void onPostExecute(String result) {
        Toast.makeText(ExchangeActivity.this, result,
                Toast.LENGTH_SHORT).show();
        setProgressBarIndeterminateVisibility(false);
    }
}

// The BroadcastReceiver that listens for discovered devices
private BroadcastReceiver mReceiver =
        new BroadcastReceiver() {
    @Override
    public void onReceive(Context context, Intent intent) {
        String action = intent.getAction();

        // When discovery finds a device
        if (BluetoothDevice.ACTION_FOUND.equals(action)) {
            // Get the BluetoothDevice object from the Intent
            BluetoothDevice device =
                intent.getParcelableExtra(
                    BluetoothDevice.EXTRA_DEVICE);
            if(TextUtils.equals(device.getName(),
                    SEARCH_NAME)) {
                //Matching device found, connect
                mBtAdapter.cancelDiscovery();
                try {
                    mBtSocket = device
                        .createRfcommSocketToServiceRecord(
                            MY_UUID);
                    mBtSocket.connect();
                    ConnectedTask task = new ConnectedTask();
                    task.execute(mBtSocket);
                } catch (IOException e) {
                    e.printStackTrace();
                }
            }
        //When discovery is complete
        } else if (BluetoothAdapter.ACTION_DISCOVERY_FINISHED
                .equals(action)) {
            setProgressBarIndeterminateVisibility(false);
        }

    }
};
}
```

When the application first starts up, it runs some basic checks on the Bluetooth status of the device. If BluetoothAdapter.getDefaultAdapter() returns null, it is an indication that the device does not have Bluetooth support, and the application will go no further. Even with Bluetooth on the device, it must be enabled for the application to use it. If Bluetooth is disabled, the preferred method for enabling the adapter is to send an intent to the system with BluetoothAdapter.ACTION_REQUEST_ENABLE as the action. This notifies the user of the issue, and that user can then enable Bluetooth. A BluetoothAdapter can be manually enabled with the enable() method, but we strongly discourage you from doing this unless you have requested the user's permission another way.

With Bluetooth validated, the application waits for user input. As mentioned previously, the example can be put into one of two modes on each device: listen mode or search mode. Let's look at the path each mode takes.

Listen Mode

Tapping the Listen for Sharers button starts the application listening for incoming connections. In order for a device to accept incoming connections from devices it may not know, it must be set as discoverable. The application verifies this by checking whether the adapter's scan mode is equal to SCAN_MODE_CONNECTABLE_ DISCOVERABLE. If the adapter does not meet this requirement, another intent is sent to the system to notify the user to allow the device to be discoverable, similar to the method used to request that Bluetooth be enabled. If the user accepts this request, the activity will return a result equal to the length of time that user allowed the device to be discoverable; if the user cancels the request, the activity will return Activity. RESULT_CANCELED. Our example monitors for a user canceling in onActivityResult(), and finishes under those conditions.

If the user allows discovery, or if the device was already discoverable, an AcceptTask is created and executed. This task creates a listener socket for the specified UUID of the service we defined, and it blocks the calling thread while waiting for an incoming connection request. Once a valid request is received, it is accepted, and the application moves into connected mode.

During the period of time while the device is listening, its Bluetooth name is set to a known unique value (SEARCH_NAME) to speed up the discovery process (you'll see more about why in the "Search Mode" section). Once the connection is established, the default name given to the adapter is restored.

Search Mode

Tapping the Connect and Share button tells the application to begin searching for another device to connect with. It does this by starting a Bluetooth discovery process and handling the results in a BroadcastReceiver. When a discovery is started via BluetoothAdapter.startDiscovery(), Android will asynchronously call back with broadcasts under two conditions: when another device is found, and when the process is complete.

The private receiver mReceiver is registered at all times when the activity is visible to the user, and it will receive a broadcast with each new discovered device. Recall from the discussion on listen mode that the device name of a listening device was set to a unique value. Upon each discovery made, the receiver checks that the device name matches our known value, and it attempts to connect when one is found. This is important to the speed of the discovery process, because otherwise the only way to validate each device is to attempt a connection to the specific service UUID and see whether the operation is successful. The Bluetooth connection process is heavyweight and slow and should be done only when necessary to keep things performing well.

This method of matching devices also relieves the user of the need to select manually which device to connect to. The application is smart enough to find another device that is running the same application and in a listening mode to complete the transfer. Removing the user also means that this value should be unique and obscure so as to avoid finding other devices that may accidentally have the same name.

With a matching device found, we cancel the discovery process (as it is also heavyweight and will slow down the connection) and then make a connection to the service's UUID. With a successful connection made, the application moves into connected mode.

■ **Tip** There are many places where you can generate your own unique ID (UUID) value. Sites on the Web, such as https://www.uuidgenerator.net/, will create one on the fly. Users of Mac OS X and Linux can also run uuidgen from the command line.

Connected Mode

Once connected, the application on both devices will create a ConnectedTask to send and receive the user contact information. The connected BluetoothSocket has an InputStream and an OutputStream available to do data transfer. First, the current value of the e-mail text field is packaged up and written to the OutputStream. Then, the InputStream is read to receive the remote device's information. Finally, each device takes the raw data it received and packages this into a clean string to display for the user.

The ConnectedTask.onPostExecute() method is tasked with displaying the results of the exchange to the user; currently, this is done by raising a Toast with the received contents. After the transaction, the connection is closed, and both devices are in the same mode and ready to execute another exchange.

For more information on this topic, take a look at the BluetoothChat sample application provided with the Android SDK. This application provides a great demonstration of making a long-lived connection for users to send chat messages between devices.

BLUETOOTH BEYOND ANDROID

As we mentioned in the beginning of this section, Bluetooth is found in many wireless devices besides mobile phones and tablets. RFCOMM interfaces also exist in devices such as Bluetooth modems and serial adapters. The same APIs that were used to create the peer-to-peer connection between Android devices can also be used to connect to other embedded Bluetooth devices for the purposes of monitoring and control.

The key to establishing a connection with these embedded devices is obtaining the UUID of the RFCOMM services they support. Bluetooth services that are part of a profile standard, and their identifiers, are defined by the Bluetooth Special Interest Group (SIG); so you may be able to obtain the UUID you require for a given device from the documentation provided on www.bluetooth.org. However, if your device manufacturer has defined a device-specific UUID for a custom service type and it is not readily documented, we must have a way to discover it. As with the previous example, with the proper UUID we can create a BluetoothSocket and transmit data.

The capability to do this exists in the SDK, although prior to Android 4.0.3 (API Level 15) it was not part of the public SDK. Two methods on BluetoothDevice will provide this information: fetchUuidsWithSdp() and getUuids(). The latter simply returns the cached instances for the device found during discovery, while the former asynchronously connects to the device and does a fresh query. Because of this, when using fetchUuidsWithSdp(), you must register a BroadcastReceiver that will receive intents set with the BluetoothDevice.ACTION_UUID action string to discover the UUID values.

3-12. Querying Network Reachability

Problem

Your application needs to be aware of changes in network connectivity.

Solution

(API Level 1)

Keep tabs on the device's connectivity with ConnectivityManager. One of the paramount issues to consider in mobile application design is that the network is not always available for use. As people move about, the speeds and capabilities of networks are subject to change. An application that uses network resources should always be able to detect whether those resources are reachable and then notify the user when they are not.

In addition to reachability, ConnectivityManager can provide the application with information about the connection type. This allows you to make decisions such as whether to download a large file because the user is currently roaming and it may cost the user a fortune.

How It Works

Listing 3-33 creates a wrapper method you can place in your code to check for network connectivity.

Listing 3-33. ConnectivityManager Wrapper

```
public static boolean isNetworkReachable(Context context) {
    final ConnectivityManager mManager =
            (ConnectivityManager)context.getSystemService(
                    Context.CONNECTIVITY_SERVICE);
    NetworkInfo current = mManager.getActiveNetworkInfo();
    if(current == null) {
        return false;
    }
    return (current.getState() == NetworkInfo.State.CONNECTED);
}
```

ConnectivityManager does the work of evaluating which network data interface is considered active (Wi-Fi or cellular). In the simplest case, we check only if the given interface is connected. Note that ConnectivityManager.getActiveNetworkInfo() will return null if there is no active data connection available, so we must check for that case first. If there is an active network, we can inspect its state, which will return one of the following:

- DISCONNECTED

- CONNECTING

- CONNECTED

- DISCONNECTING

When the state returns as CONNECTED, the network is considered stable and we can utilize it to access remote resources.

Verifying a Route

Mobile devices have multiple connectivity routes (Wi-Fi, 3G/4G, and so forth), and it is common for a device to be connected to a network that doesn't have a route to the external Web; this is especially common with Wi-Fi networks. ConnectivityManager alone simply notifies you of whether or not your device has associated with a particular network, but says nothing of that network's ability to access an outside IP address. Add to this the fact that when a device attempts to connect through a network that is "connected" but has no valid route, the time the network stack can take to time out and fail properly can be minutes.

You may find yourself in a situation where it is smarter to check for a valid Internet connection rather than just an association with a network. Listing 3-34 builds on the previous reachability check to do just that.

Listing 3-34. Smarter ConnectivityManager Wrapper

```
public static boolean hasNetworkConnection(Context context) {
        final ConnectivityManager connectivityManager =
                (ConnectivityManager) context.getSystemService(
                        Context.CONNECTIVITY_SERVICE);
        final NetworkInfo activeNetworkInfo =
                connectivityManager.getActiveNetworkInfo();

        //If we aren't even associated with a network, we're done
        boolean connected = (null != activeNetworkInfo)
                && activeNetworkInfo.isConnected();
        if (!connected) return false;

        //Check if we can access a remote server
        boolean routeExists;
        try {
            //Check Google Public DNS
            InetAddress host = InetAddress.getByName("8.8.8.8");

            Socket s = new Socket();
            s.connect(new InetSocketAddress(host, 53), 5000);
            //It exists if no exception is thrown
            routeExists = true;
            s.close();
        } catch (IOException e) {
            routeExists = false;
        }

        return (connected && routeExists);
    }
```

After verifying the same reachability condition as before, Listing 3-35 goes a step further and attempts to open a socket to the well-known standard IPv4 address for the Google Public DNS (8.8.8.8) with a 5-second time-out. If a connection to this host succeeds, we can have a relatively high level of confidence that the device can access any active Internet resource. The advantage to this approach over attempting to fully connect directly to your remote server is that this code will fail faster, forcing up to only a 5-second delay before telling the user they really don't have the Internet connection they think they do.

It is considered good practice to call a reachability check whenever a network request fails and to notify the user that the request failed because of a lack of connectivity. Listing 3-35 is an example of doing this when a network access fails.

Listing 3-35. Notify User of Connectivity Failure

```
try {
    //Attempt to access network resource. May throw
    // HttpResponseException or some other IOException on failure
} catch (Exception e) {
    if( !isNetworkReachable() ) {
        AlertDialog.Builder builder =
                new AlertDialog.Builder(context);
        builder.setTitle("No Network Connection");
        builder.setMessage("The Network is unavailable."
                + " Please try your request again later.");
        builder.setPositiveButton("OK",null);
        builder.create().show();
    }
}
```

Determining Connection Type

When it is also essential to know whether the user is connected to a network that charges for bandwidth, we can call NetworkInfo.getType() on the active network connection (see Listing 3-36).

Listing 3-36. ConnectivityManager Bandwidth Checking

```
public boolean isWifiReachable(Context context) {
    ConnectivityManager mManager =
            (ConnectivityManager)context.getSystemService(
                    Context.CONNECTIVITY_SERVICE);
    NetworkInfo current = mManager.getActiveNetworkInfo();
    if(current == null) {
        return false;
    }
    return (current.getType() == ConnectivityManager.TYPE_WIFI);
}
```

This modified version of the reachability check determines whether the user is attached to a Wi-Fi connection, typically indicating that the user has a faster connection where bandwidth isn't tariffed.

3-13. Transferring Data with NFC

Problem

You have an application that must quickly transfer small data packets between two Android devices with minimal setup.

Solution

(API Level 16)

Use the near field communication (NFC) Beam APIs. NFC communication was originally added to the SDK in Android 2.3 and was expanded in 4.0 to make short-message transfer between devices painless through a process called *Android Beam*. In Android 4.1, even more was added to make the Beam APIs fully mature for transferring data between two devices.

One of the major additions in 4.1 was the ability to transfer large data over alternate connections. NFC is a great method of discovering devices and setting up an initial connection, but it is low bandwidth and inefficient for sending large data packets such as full-color images. Previously, developers could use NFC to connect two devices but would need to manually negotiate a second connection over Wi-Fi Direct or Bluetooth to transfer the file data. In Android 4.1, the framework now handles that entire process, and any application can share large files over any available connection with a single API call.

How It Works

Depending on the size of the content you wish to push, two mechanisms are available to transfer data from one device to another.

Beaming with Foreground Push

If you want to send simple content between devices over NFC, you can use the foreground push mechanism to create an NfcMessage containing one or more NfcRecord instances. Listings 3-37 and 3-38 illustrate creating a simple NfcMessage to push to another device.

Listing 3-37. AndroidManifest.xml

```xml
<manifest
    xmlns:android="http://schemas.android.com/apk/res/android"
    package="com.examples.nfcbeam">

    <uses-permission android:name="android.permission.NFC" />
    <application
        android:icon="@drawable/ic_launcher"
        android:label="NfcBeam">
        <activity
            android:name=".NfcActivity"
            android:label="NfcActivity"
            android:launchMode="singleTop">
            <intent-filter>
                <action android:name="android.intent.action.MAIN" />
                <category android:name="android.intent.category.LAUNCHER" />
            </intent-filter>
            <intent-filter>
                <action android:name="android.nfc.action.NDEF_DISCOVERED" />
                <category android:name="android.intent.category.DEFAULT" />
                <data android:mimeType=
                    "application/com.example.androidrecipes.beamtext"/>
            </intent-filter>
```

```
        </activity>
    </application>
</manifest>
```

First notice that `android.permission.NFC` is required to work with the NFC service. Second, note the custom `<intent-filter>` placed on our activity. This is how Android will know which application to launch in response to the content it receives.

Listing 3-38. Activity Generating an NFC Foreground Push

```java
public class NfcActivity extends Activity implements
        CreateNdefMessageCallback, OnNdefPushCompleteCallback {
    private static final String TAG = "NfcBeam";
    private NfcAdapter mNfcAdapter;
    private TextView mDisplay;

    @Override
    public void onCreate(Bundle savedInstanceState) {
        super.onCreate(savedInstanceState);
        mDisplay = new TextView(this);
        setContentView(mDisplay);

        // Check for available NFC Adapter
        mNfcAdapter = NfcAdapter.getDefaultAdapter(this);
        if (mNfcAdapter == null) {
          mDisplay.setText("NFC not available on this device.");
        } else {
            // Register callback to set NDEF message. Setting
            // this makes NFC data push active while the Activity
            // is in the foreground.
            mNfcAdapter.setNdefPushMessageCallback(this, this);
            // Register callback for message-sent success
            mNfcAdapter.setOnNdefPushCompleteCallback(this, this);
        }
    }

    @Override
    public void onResume() {
        super.onResume();
        // Check to see if a Beam launched this Activity
        if (NfcAdapter.ACTION_NDEF_DISCOVERED
                .equals(getIntent().getAction())) {
            processIntent(getIntent());
        }
    }

    @Override
    public void onNewIntent(Intent intent) {
        // onResume gets called after this to handle the intent
        setIntent(intent);
    }
```

```java
void processIntent(Intent intent) {
    Parcelable[] rawMsgs = intent.getParcelableArrayExtra(
            NfcAdapter.EXTRA_NDEF_MESSAGES);
    // only one message sent during the beam
    NdefMessage msg = (NdefMessage) rawMsgs[0];
    // record O contains the MIME type
    mDisplay.setText(new String(
            msg.getRecords()[0].getPayload()) );
}

@Override
public NdefMessage createNdefMessage(NfcEvent event) {
    String text = String.format(
            "Sending A Message From Android Recipes at %s",
            DateFormat.getTimeFormat(this)
                    .format(new Date()) );
    NdefMessage msg = new NdefMessage(NdefRecord.createMime(
            "application/com.example.androidrecipes.beamtext",
            text.getBytes()) );
    return msg;
}

@Override
public void onNdefPushComplete(NfcEvent event) {
    //This callback happens on a binder thread, don't update
    // the UI directly from this method.
    Log.i(TAG, "Message Sent!");
}
}
```

This example application encompasses both the sending and receiving of an NFC push, so the same application should be installed on both devices: the one that is sending and the one that is receiving the data. The activity registers itself for foreground push by using the setNdefPushMessageCallback() method on the NfcAdapter. This call does two things simultaneously. It tells the NFC service to call this activity at the moment a transfer is initiated to receive the message it needs to send, and it also activates an NFC push whenever this activity is in the foreground. There is also an alternate version of this called setNdefPushMessage() that takes the message directly rather than implementing a callback.

The callback method constructs an NdefMessage containing a single NFC Data Exchange Format (NDEF) MIME record (created with the NdefRecord.createMime() method). MIME records are simple ways of passing application-specific data. The createMime() method takes both a string for the MIME type and a byte array for the raw data. The information can be anything from a text string to a small image; your application is responsible for packing and unpacking it. Notice that the MIME type here matches the type defined in the manifest's <intent-filter>.

In order for the push to work, the sending device must have this activity active in the foreground, and the receiving device must not be locked. When the user touches the two devices together, the sending screen shows Android's Touch to Beam UI, and a tap of the screen sends the message to the other device. As soon as the message is received, the application launches on the receiving device, and the sending device's onNdefPushComplete() callback is triggered.

On the receiving device, the activity is launched with the ACTION_NDEF_DISCOVERED intent, so our example will inspect the intent for the NdefMessage and unpack the payload, turning it back from bytes into a string. This method of using intent matching to send NFC data is the most flexible, but sometimes you want your application to be explicitly called. This is where Android Application Records come in.

Android Application Records

Your application can provide an additional NdefRecord inside an NdefMessage that directs Android to call a specific package name on the receiving device. To include this in our previous example, we would simply modify the CreateNdefMessageCallback, like so:

```
@Override
public NdefMessage createNdefMessage(NfcEvent event) {
    String text = String.format(
            "Sending A Message From Android Recipes at %s",
            DateFormat.getTimeFormat(this)
                    .format(new Date()) );
    NdefMessage msg = new NdefMessage(NdefRecord.createMime(
            "application/com.example.androidrecipes.beamtext",
            text.getBytes()),
            NdefRecord
                .createApplicationRecord("com.examples.nfcbeam"));
    return msg;
}
```

With the addition of NdefRecord.createApplicationRecord(), this push message is now guaranteed to launch only our com.examples.nfcbeam package. The text information is still the first record in the message, so our unpacking of the received message remains unchanged.

Beaming Larger Content

We mentioned at the beginning of this recipe that sending large content blobs over NFC is not a great idea. However, Android Beam has the capability to handle that as well. Have a look at Listings 3-39 through 3-41 for examples of sending large image files over Beam.

Listing 3-39. AndroidManifest.xml

```
<manifest
    xmlns:android="http://schemas.android.com/apk/res/android"
    package="com.examples.nfcbeam">

    <uses-permission android:name="android.permission.NFC" />
    <application
        android:icon="@drawable/ic_launcher"
        android:label="NfcBeam">
        <activity
            android:name=".BeamActivity"
            android:label="BeamActivity"
            android:launchMode="singleTop">
            <intent-filter>
                <action android:name="android.intent.action.MAIN" />
                <category
                    android:name="android.intent.category.LAUNCHER" />
            </intent-filter>
            <intent-filter>
                <action android:name="android.intent.action.VIEW" />
```

```
            <data android:mimeType="image/*" />
        </intent-filter>
    </activity>
</application>

</manifest>
```

Listing 3-40. res/layout/main.xml

```
<LinearLayout xmlns:android="http://schemas.android.com/apk/res/android"
    android:layout_width="match_parent"
    android:layout_height="match_parent"
    android:orientation="vertical" >
    <Button
        android:layout_width="match_parent"
        android:layout_height="wrap_content"
        android:text="Select Image"
        android:onClick="onSelectClick" />
    <TextView
        android:id="@+id/text_uri"
        android:layout_width="match_parent"
        android:layout_height="wrap_content" />
    <ImageView
        android:id="@+id/image_preview"
        android:layout_width="match_parent"
        android:layout_height="match_parent"
        android:scaleType="center" />
</LinearLayout>
```

Listing 3-41. Activity to Transfer an Image File

```
public class BeamActivity extends Activity implements
        CreateBeamUrisCallback, OnNdefPushCompleteCallback {
    private static final String TAG = "NfcBeam";
    private static final int PICK_IMAGE = 100;

    private NfcAdapter mNfcAdapter;
    private Uri mSelectedImage;

    private TextView mUriName;
    private ImageView mPreviewImage;

    @Override
    protected void onCreate(Bundle savedInstanceState) {
        super.onCreate(savedInstanceState);
        setContentView(R.layout.main);

        mUriName = (TextView) findViewById(R.id.text_uri);
        mPreviewImage =
                (ImageView) findViewById(R.id.image_preview);
```

```java
    // Check for available NFC Adapter
    mNfcAdapter = NfcAdapter.getDefaultAdapter(this);
    if (mNfcAdapter == null) {
        mUriName.setText("NFC not available on this device.");
    } else {
        // Register callback to set NDEF message
        mNfcAdapter.setBeamPushUrisCallback(this, this);
        // Register callback for message-sent success
        mNfcAdapter.setOnNdefPushCompleteCallback(this, this);
    }
}

@Override
protected void onActivityResult(int requestCode,
        int resultCode, Intent data) {
    if (requestCode == PICK_IMAGE && resultCode == RESULT_OK
            && data != null) {
        mUriName.setText( data.getData().toString() );
        mSelectedImage = data.getData();
    }
}

@Override
public void onResume() {
    super.onResume();
    //Check to see that the Activity started due to
    // an Android Beam
    if (Intent.ACTION_VIEW.equals(getIntent().getAction())) {
        processIntent(getIntent());
    }
}

@Override
public void onNewIntent(Intent intent) {
    // onResume gets called after this to handle the intent
    setIntent(intent);
}

void processIntent(Intent intent) {
    Uri data = intent.getData();
    if(data != null) {
        mPreviewImage.setImageURI(data);
    } else {
        mUriName.setText("Received Invalid Image Uri");
    }
}

public void onSelectClick(View v) {
    Intent intent = new Intent(Intent.ACTION_GET_CONTENT);
    intent.setType("image/*");
    startActivityForResult(intent, PICK_IMAGE);
}
```

```
    @Override
    public Uri[] createBeamUris(NfcEvent event) {
        if (mSelectedImage == null) {
            return null;
        }
        return new Uri[] {mSelectedImage};
    }

    @Override
    public void onNdefPushComplete(NfcEvent event) {
        //This callback happens on a binder thread, don't update
        // the UI directly from this method. This is a good time
        // to tell your user they don't need to hold
        // their phones together anymore!
        Log.i(TAG, "Push Complete!");
    }
}
```

This example uses CreateBeamUrisCallback, which allows an application to construct an array of Uri instances pointing to content you would like to transmit. Android will do the work of negotiating the initial connection over NFC but will then drop to a more suitable connection such as Bluetooth or Wi-Fi Direct to finish the larger transfers.

In this case, the data on the receiving device is launched using the system's standard Intent.ACTION_ VIEW action, so it is not necessary to load the application on both devices. However, our application does filter for ACTION_VIEW so the receiving device could use it to view the received image content if the user prefers.

Here, the user is asked to select an image from the device to transfer, and then the Uri of that content is displayed once selected. As soon as the user touches that device to another, the same Touch to Beam UI (see Figure 3-3) displays, and the transfer begins when the screen is tapped.

Figure 3-3. Activity with Touch to Beam activated

Once the NFC portion of the transfer is complete, the onNdefPushComplete() method is called on the sending device. At this point, the transfer has moved to another connection, so the users don't need to hold their phones together anymore.

The receiving device will display a progress notification in the system's window shade while the file is transferring. When the transfer is complete, the user can tap on the notification to view the content. If this application is chosen as the content viewer, the image will be shown in our application's ImageView. One possible disadvantage to registering your application with such a generic intent is that every application on the device can then ask your application to view images, so choose your filters wisely!

3-14. Connecting over USB

Problem

Your application needs to communicate with a USB device for the purposes of control or transferring data.

Solution

(API Level 12)

Android has built-in support for devices that contain USB Host circuitry to allow them to enumerate and communicate with connected USB devices. USBManager is the system service that provides applications access to any external devices connected via USB, and we are going to see how you can use that service to establish a connection from your application.

USB Host circuitry is becoming more common on devices, but it is still rare. Initially, only tablet devices had this capability, but it is growing rapidly and may soon become a commonplace interface on commercial Android handsets as well. However, because of this you will certainly want to include the following element in your application manifest:

```
<uses-feature android:name="android.hardware.usb.host" />
```

This will limit your application to devices that have the available hardware to do the communications.

The APIs provided by Android are pretty much direct mirrors of the USB specification, without much in the way of higher-level abstraction. This means that if you would like to use them, you will need at least a basic knowledge of USB and how devices communicate.

USB Overview

Before looking at an example of how Android interacts with USB devices, let's take a moment to define some USB terms:

- *Endpoint*: The smallest building block of a USB device. These are what your application eventually connects to for the purpose of sending and receiving data. They can take the form of four main types:

  - *Control*: Used for configuration and status commands. Every device has at least one control endpoint, called *endpoint 0*, that is not attached to any interface.

  - *Interrupt*: Used for small, high-priority control commands

  - *Bulk*: Large data transfer. Commonly found in bidirectional pair (1 IN and 1 OUT)

  - *Isochronous*: Used for real-time data transfer such as audio. Not supported by the latest Android SDK as of this writing

- *Interface*: A collection of endpoints to represent a "logical" device

  - Physical USB devices can manifest themselves to the host as multiple logical devices, and they do this by exposing multiple interfaces.

- *Configuration*: Collection of one or more interfaces. The USB protocol enforces that only one configuration can be active at any one time on a device. In fact, most devices have only one configuration at all. Think of this as the device's operating mode.

How It Works

Listings 3-42 and 3-43 show examples that use UsbManager to inspect devices connected over USB and then use control transfers to further query the configuration.

Listing 3-42. `res/layout/main.xml`

```xml
<LinearLayout
    xmlns:android="http://schemas.android.com/apk/res/android"
    android:layout_width="match_parent"
    android:layout_height="match_parent"
    android:orientation="vertical" >
    <Button
        android:id="@+id/button_connect"
        android:layout_width="match_parent"
        android:layout_height="wrap_content"
        android:text="Connect"
        android:onClick="onConnectClick" />
    <TextView
        android:id="@+id/text_status"
        android:layout_width="match_parent"
        android:layout_height="wrap_content" />
    <TextView
        android:id="@+id/text_data"
        android:layout_width="match_parent"
        android:layout_height="wrap_content" />

</LinearLayout>
```

Listing 3-43. Activity on USB Host Querying Devices

```java
public class USBActivity extends Activity {
    private static final String TAG = "UsbHost";

    TextView mDeviceText, mDisplayText;
    Button mConnectButton;

    UsbManager mUsbManager;
    UsbDevice mDevice;
    PendingIntent mPermissionIntent;

    @Override
    public void onCreate(Bundle savedInstanceState) {
        super.onCreate(savedInstanceState);
        setContentView(R.layout.main);

        mDeviceText = (TextView) findViewById(R.id.text_status);
        mDisplayText = (TextView) findViewById(R.id.text_data);
        mConnectButton =
            (Button) findViewById(R.id.button_connect);

        mUsbManager =
            (UsbManager) getSystemService(Context.USB_SERVICE);
    }
```

```java
    @Override
    protected void onResume() {
        super.onResume();
        mPermissionIntent =
            PendingIntent.getBroadcast(this, 0,
                new Intent(ACTION_USB_PERMISSION), 0);
        IntentFilter filter =
            new IntentFilter(ACTION_USB_PERMISSION);
        registerReceiver(mUsbReceiver, filter);

        //Check currently connected devices
        updateDeviceList();
    }

    @Override
    protected void onPause() {
        super.onPause();
        unregisterReceiver(mUsbReceiver);
    }

    public void onConnectClick(View v) {
        if (mDevice == null) {
            return;
        }
        mDisplayText.setText("---");

        //This will either prompt the user with a grant permission
        // dialog, or immediately fire the ACTION_USB_PERMISSION
        // broadcast if the user has already granted it to us.
        mUsbManager.requestPermission(mDevice, mPermissionIntent);
    }

    /*
     * Receiver to catch user permission responses, which are
     * required in order to actually interact with a connected
     * device.
     */
    private static final String ACTION_USB_PERMISSION =
            "com.android.recipes.USB_PERMISSION";
    private final BroadcastReceiver mUsbReceiver =
            new BroadcastReceiver() {
        public void onReceive(Context context, Intent intent) {
            String action = intent.getAction();
            if (ACTION_USB_PERMISSION.equals(action)) {
                UsbDevice device =
                    (UsbDevice) intent.getParcelableExtra(
                        UsbManager.EXTRA_DEVICE);

                if (intent.getBooleanExtra(
                    UsbManager.EXTRA_PERMISSION_GRANTED, false)
                    && device != null) {
```

```
                //Query the device's descriptor
                getDeviceStatus(device);
            } else {
                Log.d(TAG, "permission denied for " + device);
            }
        }
    }
};

//Type: Indicates whether this is a read or write
// Matches USB_ENDPOINT_DIR_MASK for either IN or OUT
private static final int REQUEST_TYPE = 0x80;
//Request: GET_CONFIGURATION_DESCRIPTOR = 0x06
private static final int REQUEST = 0x06;
//Value: Descriptor Type (High) and Index (Low)
// Configuration Descriptor = 0x2
// Index = 0x0 (First configuration)
private static final int REQ_VALUE = 0x200;
private static final int REQ_INDEX = 0x00;
private static final int LENGTH = 64;

/*
 * Initiate a control transfer to request the first
 * configuration descriptor of the device.
 */
private void getDeviceStatus(UsbDevice device) {
    UsbDeviceConnection connection =
            mUsbManager.openDevice(device);
    //Create a sufficiently large buffer for incoming data
    byte[] buffer = new byte[LENGTH];
    connection.controlTransfer(REQUEST_TYPE, REQUEST,
            REQ_VALUE, REQ_INDEX, buffer, LENGTH, 2000);
    //Parse received data into a description
    String description = parseConfigDescriptor(buffer);

    mDisplayText.setText(description);
    connection.close();
}

/*
 * Parse the USB configuration descriptor response per the
 * USB Specification.  Return a printable description of
 * the connected device.
 */
private static final int DESC_SIZE_CONFIG = 9;
private String parseConfigDescriptor(byte[] buffer) {
    StringBuilder sb = new StringBuilder();
    //Parse configuration descriptor header
    int totalLength = (buffer[3] &0xFF) << 8;
    totalLength += (buffer[2] & 0xFF);
    //Interface count
```

```
int numInterfaces = (buffer[5] & 0xFF);
//Configuration attributes
int attributes = (buffer[7] & 0xFF);
//Power is given in 2mA increments
int maxPower = (buffer[8] & 0xFF) * 2;

sb.append("Configuration Descriptor:\n");
sb.append("Length: " + totalLength + " bytes\n");
sb.append(numInterfaces + " Interfaces\n");
sb.append(String.format("Attributes:%s%s%s\n",
    (attributes & 0x80) == 0x80 ? " BusPowered" : "",
    (attributes & 0x40) == 0x40 ? " SelfPowered" : "",
    (attributes & 0x20) == 0x20 ? " RemoteWakeup" : ""));
sb.append("Max Power: " + maxPower + "mA\n");

//The rest of the descriptor is interfaces and endpoints
int index = DESC_SIZE_CONFIG;
while (index < totalLength) {
    //Read length and type
    int len = (buffer[index] & 0xFF);
    int type = (buffer[index+1] & 0xFF);
    switch (type) {
    case 0x04: //Interface Descriptor
        int intfNumber = (buffer[index+2] & 0xFF);
        int numEndpoints = (buffer[index+4] & 0xFF);
        int intfClass = (buffer[index+5] & 0xFF);

        sb.append( String.format(
                "- Interface %d, %s, %d Endpoints\n",
                intfNumber,
                nameForClass(intfClass),
                numEndpoints) );
        break;
    case 0x05: //Endpoint Descriptor
        int endpointAddr = ((buffer[index+2] & 0xFF));
        //Number is lower 4 bits
        int endpointNum = (endpointAddr & 0x0F);
        //Direction is high bit
        int direction = (endpointAddr & 0x80);

        int endpointAttrs = (buffer[index+3] & 0xFF);
        //Type is the lower two bits
        int endpointType = (endpointAttrs & 0x3);

        sb.append(String.format("-- Endpoint %d, %s %s\n",
                endpointNum,
                nameForEndpointType(endpointType),
                nameForDirection(direction) ));
        break;
    }
```

```java
            //Advance to next descriptor
            index += len;
        }

        return sb.toString();
    }

    private void updateDeviceList() {
        HashMap<String, UsbDevice> connectedDevices =
                mUsbManager.getDeviceList();
        if (connectedDevices.isEmpty()) {
            mDevice = null;
            mDeviceText.setText("No Devices Currently Connected");
            mConnectButton.setEnabled(false);
        } else {
            StringBuilder builder = new StringBuilder();
            for (UsbDevice device : connectedDevices.values()) {
                //Use the last device detected (if multiple)
                // to open
                mDevice = device;
                builder.append(readDevice(device));
                builder.append("\n\n");
            }
            mDeviceText.setText(builder.toString());
            mConnectButton.setEnabled(true);
        }
    }

    /*
     * Enumerate the endpoints and interfaces on the connected
     * device. We do not need permission to do anything here, it
     * is all "publicly available" until we try to connect to
     * an actual device.
     */
    private String readDevice(UsbDevice device) {
        StringBuilder sb = new StringBuilder();
        sb.append("Device Name: " + device.getDeviceName()
                + "\n");
        sb.append( String.format(
                "Device Class: %s -> Subclass: 0x%02x -> "
                    + "Protocol: 0x%02x\n",
                nameForClass(device.getDeviceClass()),
                device.getDeviceSubclass(),
                device.getDeviceProtocol())
        );

        for (int i = 0; i < device.getInterfaceCount(); i++) {
            UsbInterface intf = device.getInterface(i);
            sb.append( String.format(
                    "+--Interface %d Class: %s -> "
                        + "Subclass: 0x%02x -> Protocol: 0x%02x\n",
```

```
                intf.getId(),
                nameForClass(intf.getInterfaceClass()),
                intf.getInterfaceSubclass(),
                intf.getInterfaceProtocol())
        );

        for (int j = 0; j < intf.getEndpointCount(); j++) {
            UsbEndpoint endpoint = intf.getEndpoint(j);
            sb.append( String.format(
                    "   +---Endpoint %d: %s %s\n",
                    endpoint.getEndpointNumber(),
                    nameForEndpointType(endpoint.getType()),
                    nameForDirection(endpoint.getDirection()))
            );
        }
    }

    return sb.toString();
}


/* Helper Methods to Provide Readable Names for USB Constants
 */

private String nameForClass(int classType) {
    switch (classType) {
    case UsbConstants.USB_CLASS_APP_SPEC:
        return String.format(
                "Application Specific 0x%02x", classType);
    case UsbConstants.USB_CLASS_AUDIO:
        return "Audio";
    case UsbConstants.USB_CLASS_CDC_DATA:
        return "CDC Control";
    case UsbConstants.USB_CLASS_COMM:
        return "Communications";
    case UsbConstants.USB_CLASS_CONTENT_SEC:
        return "Content Security";
    case UsbConstants.USB_CLASS_CSCID:
        return "Content Smart Card";
    case UsbConstants.USB_CLASS_HID:
        return "Human Interface Device";
    case UsbConstants.USB_CLASS_HUB:
        return "Hub";
    case UsbConstants.USB_CLASS_MASS_STORAGE:
        return "Mass Storage";
    case UsbConstants.USB_CLASS_MISC:
        return "Wireless Miscellaneous";
    case UsbConstants.USB_CLASS_PER_INTERFACE:
        return "(Defined Per Interface)";
    case UsbConstants.USB_CLASS_PHYSICA:
        return "Physical";
    case UsbConstants.USB_CLASS_PRINTER:
        return "Printer";
```

```
        case UsbConstants.USB_CLASS_STILL_IMAGE:
            return "Still Image";
        case UsbConstants.USB_CLASS_VENDOR_SPEC:
            return String.format(
                    "Vendor Specific 0x%02x", classType);
        case UsbConstants.USB_CLASS_VIDEO:
            return "Video";
        case UsbConstants.USB_CLASS_WIRELESS_CONTROLLER:
            return "Wireless Controller";
        default:
            return String.format("0x%02x", classType);
        }
    }

    private String nameForEndpointType(int type) {
        switch (type) {
        case UsbConstants.USB_ENDPOINT_XFER_BULK:
            return "Bulk";
        case UsbConstants.USB_ENDPOINT_XFER_CONTROL:
            return "Control";
        case UsbConstants.USB_ENDPOINT_XFER_INT:
            return "Interrupt";
        case UsbConstants.USB_ENDPOINT_XFER_ISOC:
            return "Isochronous";
        default:
            return "Unknown Type";
        }
    }

    private String nameForDirection(int direction) {
        switch (direction) {
        case UsbConstants.USB_DIR_IN:
            return "IN";
        case UsbConstants.USB_DIR_OUT:
            return "OUT";
        default:
            return "Unknown Direction";
        }
    }
}
```

When the activity first comes into the foreground, it registers a BroadcastReceiver with a custom action (which we'll discuss in more detail shortly), and it queries the list of currently connected devices by using UsbManager.getDeviceList(), which returns a HashMap of UsbDevice items that we can iterate over and interrogate. For each device connected, we query each interface and endpoint, building a description string to print to the user about what this device is. We then print all that data to the user interface.

■ **Note**   This application, as it stands, does not require any manifest permissions. We do not need to declare a permission simply to query information about devices connected to the host.

You can see that `UsbManager` provides APIs to inspect just about every piece of information you would need to discover if a connected device is the one you are interested in communicating with. All standard definitions for device classes, endpoint types, and transfer directions are also defined in `UsbConstants`, so you can match the types you want without defining all of this yourself.

So, what about that `BroadcastReceiver` we registered? The remainder of this example code takes action when the user presses the Connect button on the screen. At this point, we would like to talk to the connected device, which is an operation that does require user permission. Here, when the user clicks the button, we call `UsbManager.requestPermission()` to ask the user if we can connect. If permission has not yet been granted, the user will see a dialog box asking him or her to grant permission to connect.

Upon saying yes, the `PendingIntent` passed along to the method will get fired. In our example, that intent was a broadcast with a custom action string we defined, so this will trigger `onReceive()` in that `BroadcastReceiver`; any subsequent calls to `requestPermission()` will immediately trigger the receiver as well. Inside the receiver, we check to make sure that the result was a permission-granted response, and we attempt to open a connection to the device with `UsbManager.openDevice()`, which returns a `UsbDeviceConnection` instance when successful.

With a valid connection made, we request some more detailed information about the device by requesting its configuration descriptor via a control transfer. Control transfers are requests always made on endpoint 0 of the device. A configuration descriptor contains information about the configuration as well as each interface and endpoint, so its length is variable. We allocate a decent-sized buffer to ensure we capture everything.

Upon returning from `controlTransfer()`, the buffer is filled with the response data. Our application then processes the bytes, determining some more information about the device, including its maximum power draw and whether the device is configured to be powered from the USB post (bus-powered) or by an external source (self-powered). This example parses out only a fraction of the useful information that can be found inside these descriptors. Once again, all the parsed data is put into a string report and displayed to the user interface.

Much of the data read in the first section from the framework APIs and in the second section directly from the device is the same. Therefore the content displayed in the user interface should match in each section. One thing to note is that this application works only if the device is already connected when the application runs: it will not be notified if a connection happens while it is in the foreground. We will look at how to handle that scenario in the next section.

Getting Notified of Device Connections

In order for Android to notify your application when a particular device is connected, you need to register the device types you are interested in with an `<intent-filter>` in the manifest. Take a look at Listings 3-44 and 3-45 to see how this is done.

Listing 3-44. Partial `AndroidManifest.xml`

```
<activity
    android:name=".USBActivity"
    android:label="@string/title_activity_usb" >
    <intent-filter>
      <action android:name="android.intent.action.MAIN" />
      <category android:name="android.intent.category.LAUNCHER" />
    </intent-filter>
    <intent-filter>
      <action android:name=
          "android.hardware.usb.action.USB_DEVICE_ATTACHED" />
    </intent-filter>
```

```
<meta-data android:name=
    "android.hardware.usb.action.USB_DEVICE_ATTACHED"
    android:resource="@xml/device_filter" />
</activity>
```

Listing 3-45. `res/xml/device_filter.xml`

```xml
<?xml version="1.0" encoding="utf-8"?>
<resources>
    <usb-device vendor-id="5432" product-id="9876" />
</resources>
```

The activity you want to launch with a connection has a filter added to it with the USB_DEVICE_ATTACHED action string and with some XML metadata describing the devices you are interested in. There are several device attribute fields you can place into <usb-device> to filter which connection events notify your application:

- vendor-id

- product-id

- class

- subclass

- protocol

You can define as many of these as necessary to fit your application. For example, if you want to communicate with only one specific device, you might define both vendor-id and product-id as the example code did. If you are more interested in all devices of a given type (say, all mass-storage devices), you might define only the class attribute. It is even allowable to define *no* attributes, and have your application match on *any* device connected!

3-15. Scanning for Bluetooth Low Energy beacons

Problem

You have an application that needs to scan for Bluetooth Low Energy (also known as Bluetooth Smart) beacons and read their broadcasted information.

Solution

(API Level 18)

Support for Bluetooth Low Energy (or Bluetooth Smart, which is the marketing name for the technology) was introduced in Android 4.3. It was updated in Android 5.0 with an improved API for scanning, as well as some additional APIs for advanced communication.

How It Works

Bluetooth Low Energy, or BLE, on Android uses a different API for communication than Bluetooth Classic (see Section 3-11). BLE uses the GATT protocol where you work with services, characteristics and descriptors. Explaining the entire BLE stack is beyond the scope of this book. In this section we will instead focus on the use of the API for scanning and interpreting Bluetooth Low Energy Beacons.

The BLE Scanning API is different depening on API level. For API level 18 and 19 there is a basic API for initating scanning, while API level 21 and later have a more advanced API with more features.

In this example we will scan for three different types of devices: heart rate monitors, blood pressure monitors, and indoor positioning monitors. These are all defined by the Bluetooth SIG (Special Interest Group) and each have a unique id. We define these IDs as three UUID constants in our code (see Listing 3-46).

Listing 3-46. Defining Service UUIDs for Scanning

```
private static final UUID HEART_RATE_MONITOR
        = UUID.fromString("0000180D-0000-1000-8000-00805F9B34FB");
private static final UUID BLOOD_PRESSURE_MONITOR
        = UUID.fromString("00001810-0000-1000-8000-00805F9B34FB");
private static final UUID INDOOR_POSITIONING_MONITOR
        = UUID.fromString("00001821-0000-1000-8000-00805F9B34FB");
```

These IDs will now be used when scanning for specific devices. If we don't specify a filter, all nearby BLE devices will be returned. While it is possible to filter out discovered devices in our application code, it is usually more efficient to let the API do it for us. It is therefore recommended to use a service UUID filter when scanning if possible.

Scanning for Beacons (API Level 18)

In order to start scanning for BLE devices on API level 18 or 19, you start by getting a reference to the BluetoothAdapter. Next, you call the method startLeScan() with an array of the service UUIDs you want to filter on and the callback where you want to receive the result (See Listing 3-47).

Listing 3-47. Start BLE Scanning on API Level 18 or 19

```
public void bleScanningLegacy() {
    BluetoothManager bluetoothManager =
            (BluetoothManager) getSystemService(BLUETOOTH_SERVICE);
    BluetoothAdapter adapter = bluetoothManager.getAdapter();
    legacyScanCallback = new LegacyScanCallback();
    // Just scan for heart rate monitors
    UUID[] filters = new UUID[] {HEART_RATE_MONITOR};
    adapter.startLeScan(filters, legacyScanCallback);
}
```

The LegacyScanCallback is our implementation of BluetoothAdapter.LeScanCallback and defines a single method, onLeScan(). This method will be called for each device that the BLE scanning process discovers (see Listing 3-48).

Listing 3-48. LeScanCallback implementation

```
private class LegacyScanCallback implements BluetoothAdapter.LeScanCallback {
    @Override
    public void onLeScan(BluetoothDevice device, int rssi, byte[] scanRecord) {
        // Add discovered device to our list of known devices
        discoveredDevices.add(device);
    }
}
```

Since BLE scanning is a hardware process that can consume a lot of battery if left enabled for too long, we also need to stop the scanning at some point. For API level 18 and 19, this is done using the method stopLeScan() on the BluetoothAdapter (see Listing 3-49).

Listing 3-49. Stop BLE Scanning on API Level 18 and 19

```
public void stopScanningLegacy() {
    BluetoothManager bluetoothManager =
            (BluetoothManager) getSystemService(BLUETOOTH_SERVICE);
    BluetoothAdapter adapter = bluetoothManager.getAdapter();
    adapter.stopLeScan(legacyScanCallback);
}
```

Scanning for Beacons (API Level 21)

On API level 21 and later, the BLE scanning works a little bit differently. We start by getting a BluetoothLeScanner from the BluetoothAdapter. Next, we create the necessary ScanSettings and ScanFilter instances and call the method startScan() (See Listing 3-50).

Listing 3-50. Starting BLE Scanning on API Level 21 and Later

```
public void bleScanningLollipop() {
    BluetoothManager bluetoothManager =
            (BluetoothManager) getSystemService(BLUETOOTH_SERVICE);
    BluetoothAdapter adapter = bluetoothManager.getAdapter();
    BluetoothLeScanner bluetoothLeScanner = adapter.getBluetoothLeScanner();
    List<ScanFilter> filters = new ArrayList<>();
    ScanFilter filter = new ScanFilter.Builder()
            .setServiceUuid(new ParcelUuid(HEART_RATE_MONITOR))
            .build();
    filters.add(filter);
    ScanSettings scanSettings = new ScanSettings.Builder()
            .setScanMode(ScanSettings.SCAN_MODE_LOW_LATENCY)
            .build();
    lollipopScanCallback = new LollipopScanCallback();
    bluetoothLeScanner.startScan(filters, scanSettings, lollipopScanCallback);
}
```

This method allows us to control the scanning process in more detail. In this case we only filter on the service UUID for heart rate monitors, but we also tell the Bluetooth chip to scan more aggressively so we can get more results. This process uses more battery, but can be useful if low latency in the scanning process is important.

Our callback is implemented in LollipopScanCallback, which extends the base class ScanCallback (see Listing 3-51). The callback method onScanResult() will give us the same amount of result as the legacy callback implementation, but wrapped in objects that are easier to use (i.e., you don't have to parse the data yourself if you want additional details).

Listing 3-51. Scanning Callback for API Level 21 and Later

```
private class LollipopScanCallback extends ScanCallback {

    @Override
    public void onScanResult(int callbackType, ScanResult result) {
        super.onScanResult(callbackType, result);
        discoveredDevices.add(result.getDevice());
    }

    @Override
    public void onScanFailed(int errorCode) {
        super.onScanFailed(errorCode);
    }
}
```

Finally, we need to be able to stop the scanning once we're done. We do this by simply calling stopScanning() on the BluetoothLeScanner (see Listing 3-52).

Listing 3-52. Stopping BLE Scanning on API Level 21 and Later

```
public void stopScanningLollipop() {
    BluetoothManager bluetoothManager =
            (BluetoothManager) getSystemService(BLUETOOTH_SERVICE);
    BluetoothAdapter adapter = bluetoothManager.getAdapter();
    adapter.getBluetoothLeScanner().stopScan(lollipopScanCallback);
}
```

Summary

Connecting an Android application to the Web and web services is a great way to add user value in today's connected world. Android's framework for connecting to the Web and other remote hosts makes adding this functionality straightforward. We've explored how to bring the standards of the Web into your application, using HTML and JavaScript to interact with the user, but within a native context. You also saw how to use Android to download content from remote servers and consume it in your application, and how to efficiently convert the data to Java, making it much easier to use in your code. We also showed that a web server is not the only host worth connecting to, by using Bluetooth (Classic and Low Energy), NFC, USB, and SMS to communicate directly from one device to another. In the next chapter, we will look at using the tools that Android provides to interact with a device's hardware resources.

CHAPTER 4

■ ■ ■

Interacting with Device Hardware and Media

Integrating application software with device hardware presents opportunities to create unique user experiences that only the mobile platform can provide. Capturing media by using the microphone and camera allows applications to incorporate a personal touch through a photo or recorded greeting. Integration of sensor and location data can help you develop applications to answer relevant questions such as "Where am I?" and "What am I looking at?"

In this chapter, we investigate how to leverage the location, media, and sensor APIs provided by Android to add that unique value the mobile device brings to your applications.

4-1. Integrating Device Location

Problem

You want to leverage the device's ability to report its current physical location in an application.

Solution

(API Level 9)

Utilize Google's fused location provider, available inside the Google Play Services library. One of the most powerful benefits that a mobile application can often provide to the user is the ability to add context by including information based on where that user is currently located. Applications may ask the location services to provide updates of a device's location based on the following criteria:

- *Frequency*: Minimum amount of time (in milliseconds) before another update is delivered to the application.

- *Distance*: Minimum distance device must move before another update is delivered.

- *Count*: Maximum number of updates to deliver before shutting down the provider.

- *Expiration time*: Maximum amount of time after the request is initialized before the provider is shut down.

© Dave Smith and Erik Hellman 2016

D. Smith and E. Hellman, *Android Recipes*, DOI 10.1007/978-1-4842-2259-1_4

■ **Note** Android has non-Google location services directly available in the `LocationManager` as well. This API is less assistive, and developers have to manage requests from discrete location sources separately.

Android allows applications to obtain location data from multiple sources. High-accuracy (and also high-power-drain) fixes come from on on-board GPS. Lower-accuracy data is obtained from network sources, such as cellular towers and Wi-Fi hotspots. Google's fused location provider gets its name from "fusing" these multiple sources together to provide developers with the best result at all times. Location requests are made with higher-level criteria, and the device does the work of determining which hardware interfaces should be involved:

- PRIORITY_BALANCED_POWER_ACCURACY: Provides a mix of GPS and network sources to get good accuracy with lower power and quicker fixes

- PRIORITY_HIGH_ACCURACY: Requires a final fix to come from GPS (most accurate), though initial fixes may come from elsewhere. This option also requires the most power as the GPS is typically on all the time.

- PRIORITY_LOW_POWER: Provides the quickest fixes—but without GPS assistance, the accuracy is generally not better than "city" level.

- PRIORITY_NO_POWER: Enables your application to be a passive observer. Updates will be delivered only when another application triggers them.

■ **Important** The location services in this example are distributed as part of the Google Play Services library; they are not part of the native SDK at any platform level. However, any application targeting API Level 9 or later and devices inside the Google Play ecosystem can use the mapping library. For more information on including Google Play Services in your project, reference `https://developer.android.com/google/play-services/setup.html`.

How It Works

In Listing 4-1, we register an activity to listen for location updates while it is visible to the user and to display that location onscreen.

■ **Note** This example uses `ActionBarActivity` from the AppCompat Library to allow the use of fragments prior to API Level 11.

Listing 4-1. Activity Monitoring Location Updates

```
public class MainActivity extends AppCompatActivity implements
        LocationListener, GoogleApiClient.ConnectionCallbacks {
    private static final String TAG = "AndroidRecipes";
```

```
private static final int UPDATE_INTERVAL = 15 * 1000;
private static final int FASTEST_UPDATE_INTERVAL = 2 * 1000;
private static final int REQUEST_CODE_PERMISSIONS = 101;

private GoogleApiClient mApiClient;
/* Metadata about updates we want to receive */
private LocationRequest mLocationRequest;
/* Last-known device location */
private Location mCurrentLocation;

private TextView mLocationView;

@Override
public void onCreate(Bundle savedInstanceState) {
    super.onCreate(savedInstanceState);
    mLocationView = new TextView(this);
    setContentView(mLocationView);

    //Verify play services is active and up to date
    int resultCode = GoogleApiAvailability.getInstance()
            .isGooglePlayServicesAvailable(this);
    switch (resultCode) {
        case ConnectionResult.SUCCESS:
            Log.d(TAG, "Google Play Services is ready to go!");
            break;
        default:
            showPlayServicesError(resultCode);
            return;
    }

    mApiClient = new GoogleApiClient.Builder(this)
            .addApi(LocationServices.API)
            .addConnectionCallbacks(this)
            .build();

    mLocationRequest = LocationRequest.create()
            //Set the required accuracy level
            .setPriority(LocationRequest.PRIORITY_HIGH_ACCURACY)
            //Set the desired (inexact) frequency of location updates
            .setInterval(UPDATE_INTERVAL)
            //Throttle the max rate of update requests
            .setFastestInterval(FASTEST_UPDATE_INTERVAL);
}

@Override
public void onResume() {
    super.onResume();
    //When we move into the foreground, attach to Play Services
    mApiClient.connect();
}
```

```java
@Override
public void onPause() {
    super.onPause();
    //Disable updates when we are not in the foreground
    if (mApiClient.isConnected()) {
        LocationServices.FusedLocationApi
                .removeLocationUpdates(mApiClient, this);
    }
    //Detach from Play Services
    mApiClient.disconnect();
}

private void updateDisplay() {
    if (mCurrentLocation == null) {
        mLocationView.setText("Determining Your Location...");
    } else {
        mLocationView.setText(
                String.format("Your Location:\n%.2f, %.2f",
                mCurrentLocation.getLatitude(),
                mCurrentLocation.getLongitude()));
    }
}
/*
 * When Play Services is missing or at the wrong version, the client
 * library will assist with a dialog to help the user update.
 */
private void showPlayServicesError(int errorCode) {
    GoogleApiAvailability.getInstance()
            .showErrorDialogFragment(this, errorCode, 10,
                    new DialogInterface.OnCancelListener() {
                        @Override
                        public void onCancel(DialogInterface dialogInterface) {
                            finish();
                        }
                    });
}

@Override
public void onConnected(Bundle bundle) {
    Log.d(TAG, "Connected to Play Services");

    //Get last known location immediately
    if (ActivityCompat.checkSelfPermission(this,
            android.Manifest.permission.ACCESS_FINE_LOCATION)
            != PackageManager.PERMISSION_GRANTED
            && ActivityCompat.checkSelfPermission(this,
            android.Manifest.permission.ACCESS_COARSE_LOCATION)
            != PackageManager.PERMISSION_GRANTED) {
        ActivityCompat.requestPermissions(this,
                new String[]{Manifest.permission.ACCESS_FINE_LOCATION,
                        Manifest.permission.ACCESS_COARSE_LOCATION},
```

```java
                REQUEST_CODE_PERMISSIONS);
        return;
    }
    fetchAndListenForLocation();
}

@SuppressWarnings("MissingPermission")
private void fetchAndListenForLocation() {
    mCurrentLocation = LocationServices.FusedLocationApi
            .getLastLocation(mApiClient);
    //Register for updates
    LocationServices.FusedLocationApi.requestLocationUpdates(mApiClient,
            mLocationRequest, this);
}

@Override
public void onConnectionSuspended(int i) {

}

/**
 * LocationListener Callbacks
 */

@Override
public void onLocationChanged(Location location) {
    Log.d(TAG, "Received location update");
    mCurrentLocation = location;
    updateDisplay();
}

@Override
public void onRequestPermissionsResult(int requestCode,
                                @NonNull String[] permissions,
                                @NonNull int[] grantResults) {
    super.onRequestPermissionsResult(requestCode, permissions,
            grantResults);

    if (requestCode == REQUEST_CODE_PERMISSIONS) {
        for (int i = 0; i < grantResults.length; i++) {
            int grantResult = grantResults[i];
            String permission = permissions[i];
            if (grantResult != PackageManager.PERMISSION_GRANTED) {
                Log.d(TAG, "Permission " + permission
                        + " is required for this application to work.");
                finish();
                return;
            }
        }
    }
}
}
```

■ **Important**   When using location services in an application, keep in mind that android.permission. ACCESS_COARSE_LOCATION or android.permission.ACCESS_FINE_LOCATION must be declared in the application manifest. If you declare android.permission.ACCESS_FINE_LOCATION, you do not need both because it includes coarse permissions as well.

In this example we start by setting up the GoogleApiClient we need for the LocationServices API. Google Play Services APIs are *asynchronous* API, which means that when mApiClient.connect() is called, we have to wait until the callback onConnected() is called before we can access the location APIs.

Next, we construct a LocationRequest containing all the criteria we want applied to the updates received. We instruct the service to return only high-accuracy results, at an interval of 15 seconds. This interval is inexact, meaning Android will deliver the updates *roughly* every 15 seconds—maybe more, maybe less. The only guarantee is that you will receive at most one update in that interval. In order to set an upper bound on this interval, we also set the fastest interval to 2 seconds. This throttles the updates to ensure that we never receive any two updates faster than 2 seconds apart.

Gathering location data is a resource-intensive operation, so we want to make sure it happens only while our activity is in the foreground. Our example waits until onResume() to connect to the location services, and disconnects immediately in onPause().

Once we're connected to the Play Services APIs, we can use the LocationServices.FusedLocationApi to request location updates. The updates will be delivered through the callback onLocationChanged().

EMULATING LOCATION CHANGES

If you are testing your application inside the Android emulator, your application will not be able to receive real location data from any of the system providers. Using the Monitor tool in the SDK, however, you are able to inject location change events manually.

With the DDMS perspective active, select the Emulator Control tab and find the Location Controls section. A tabbed interface allows you to enter a latitude/longitude pair directly, or have series of them read from common file formats.

When entering a single value manually, a valid latitude and longitude must be entered in the text boxes. You may then click the Send button to inject that location as an event inside the selected emulator. Any applications registered to listen to location changes will also receive an update with this location value.

When location updates arrive, the onLocationChanged() method of the registered listener is called. The example keeps a running reference to the latest location it received, and with each incoming update, the location value is reset and the user interface display is updated to reflect the new change.

■ **Note**   If you are receiving updates in a service or other background operation, Google recommends that the minimum time interval should be no less than 60,000 (60 seconds).

For this application to build and function properly, we need to set up some additional hooks. Listings 4-2 and 4-3 describe these requirements.

Listing 4-2. Partial build.gradle

```
apply plugin: 'com.android.application'

android {
    compileSdkVersion 24
    buildToolsVersion "24.0.1"

    defaultConfig {
        applicationId "com.androidrecipes.mylocation"
        ...
    }

    ...
}

dependencies {
    compile 'com.google.android.gms:play-services:9.2.1'
    compile 'com.android.support:appcompat-v7:24.1.1'
}
```

Listing 4-3. Partial AndroidManifest.xml

```
<?xml version="1.0" encoding="utf-8"?>
<manifest xmlns:android="http://schemas.android.com/apk/res/android"
    package="com.examples.mylocation">

    <uses-permission
        android:name="android.permission.ACCESS_FINE_LOCATION"/>
    <uses-permission
        android:name="android.permission.ACCESS_COARSE_LOCATION"/>

    <application ...>

        <!-- Required boilerplate to launch Play Services -->
        <meta-data
            android:name="com.google.android.gms.version"
            android:value="@integer/google_play_services_version" />

        <activity ...>
            <intent-filter>
                <action android:name="android.intent.action.MAIN" />
                <category android:name="android.intent.category.LAUNCHER" />
            </intent-filter>
        </activity>

    </application>
</manifest>
```

Inside the project's `build.gradle` file, Google Play Services must be added as a dependency. Here we are using the plus notation to ensure that we always build with the latest client library. Play Services also requires adding a `<meta-data>` element to the application with the client library version. This is what the library uses to determine whether the Play Services version on the device is current enough. The version number resource is built into the library, so don't worry about defining it.

Since we are accessing location services of the device, we need to request the `ACCESS_FINE_LOCATION` permission as well. This permission is required to access GPS location services. If your application uses a lower accuracy value, you may be able to get away with requesting the `ACCESS_COARSE_LOCATION` permission instead.

WHEN GOOGLE PLAY SERVICES IS UNAVAILABLE

At the top of this example (in Listing 4-1), there is some boilerplate code for checking whether Google Play Services is running and up-to-date on the device with `isGooglePlayServicesAvailable()` from `GoogleApiAvailability`. This method will verify that Play Services is running on the device with at least the version specified in your client application.

If this check is not successful, Play Services also provides the UI, using the method `showErrorDialogFragment()` from `GoogleApiAvailability`, to display to users for getting them up-to-date. The dialog box will trigger the proper settings UI to automatically update Play Services to the latest version. In our example, the `showPlayServicesError()` method handles this. We will see this same pattern in all the recipes this book uses that include Play Services access.

4-2. Mapping Locations

Problem

You would like to display one or more locations on a map for the user. Additionally, you would like to display the user's own location on that same map.

Solution

(API Level 9)

The simplest way to show the user a map is to create an intent with the location data and pass it to the Android system to launch in a mapping application. We'll look more in depth at this method for doing various tasks in Chapter 6. You can embed maps within your application by using `MapView` and `MapFragment`, provided by the Google Maps v2 library component of the Google Play Services library.

■ **Important** Google Maps v2 is distributed as part of the Google Play Services library; it is not part of the native SDK at any platform level. However, any application targeting API Level 9 or later and devices inside the Google Play ecosystem can use the mapping library. For more information on including Google Play Services in your project, reference `https://developer.android.com/google/play-services/setup.html`.

Obtaining an API Key

To get started with Maps v2, you will need to create an API project, enable the Maps v2 service inside that project, and generate an API key to include in your application code. Without an API key, the mapping classes may be utilized, but no map tiles will be returned to the application. Follow these steps:

Visit https://code.google.com/apis/console/ and log in with your Google account to access the Google API console.

1. Select Create Project to make a new project for your maps. If you already have an existing project, you can add the Maps v2 service and keys to that if you prefer. In that case, select the project where you would like to add Maps v2.

2. In the navigation panel, select Services, scroll down to Google Maps Android API v2, and enable the service.

3. Select API Access in the navigation panel, and select Create New Android Key.

4. Follow the onscreen instructions to add keystore signature/application package pairs to your key for the apps you want to use. In our case, the package name for the sample application is com.androidrecipes.mapper, and the signature comes from the debug key on your development machine, usually located at <USERHOME>/.android/debug.keystore.

■ **Note** For more information on the SDK, and the most up-to-date instructions on getting an API key, visit https://developers.google.com/maps/documentation/android/start.

If you are running code in an emulator to test, that emulator must be built using an SDK target of Android 4.3 or later that includes the Google APIs for mapping to operate properly. Previous versions of the SDK are bundled in the Maps v1 library rather than Google Play Services, so they will not work for testing.

If you create emulators from the command line, these targets are named Google Inc.:Google APIs:*X*, where *X* is the API version indicator. If you create emulators from inside an IDE (such as Eclipse), the target has a similar naming convention of Google APIs (Google Inc.) – *X*, where *X* is the API version indicator.

Meeting Manifest Requirements

Once you have obtained a valid API key, you need to include it in your AndroidManifest.xml file. The following code block must be inside the <application> element:

```
<meta-data
    android:name="com.google.android.maps.v2.API_KEY"
    android:value="YOUR_KEY_HERE" />
```

Additionally, Maps v2 has a device requirement of at least OpenGL ES 2.0. We can require this as a device feature by adding the following block inside your <manifest> element, placed just above the <application> element:

```
<!-- Maps v2 requires OpenGL ES 2.0 -->
<uses-feature
    android:glEsVersion="0x00020000"
    android:required="true" />
```

Finally, Maps v2 requires a set of permissions to talk to Google Play Services and render the map tiles. So we must add one more block inside the <manifest> element, typically placed just above the <application> element:

```
<!-- Permissions Required to Display a Map -->
<uses-permission android:name="android.permission.INTERNET" />
<uses-permission
    android:name="android.permission.ACCESS_NETWORK_STATE" />
<uses-permission
    android:name="android.permission.WRITE_EXTERNAL_STORAGE"
/>
<uses-permission android:name=
    "com.google.android.providers.gsf.permission.READ_GSERVICES"
/>
```

Altogether, your manifest should look something like Listing 4-4.

Listing 4-4. Partial AndroidManifest.xml

```
<manifest xmlns:android="http://schemas.android.com/apk/res/android"
    package="com.androidrecipes.mapper">

    <!-- Required to display the user's location on the map -->
    <uses-permission android:name="android.permission.ACCESS_FINE_LOCATION" />

    <!-- Permissions Required to Display a Map -->
    <uses-permission android:name="android.permission.INTERNET" />
    <uses-permission
      android:name="android.permission.ACCESS_NETWORK_STATE" />
    <uses-permission
      android:name="android.permission.WRITE_EXTERNAL_STORAGE"
    />
    <uses-permission android:name=
      "com.google.android.providers.gsf.permission.READ_GSERVICES"
    />

    <!-- Maps v2 requires OpenGL ES 2.0 -->
    <uses-feature
        android:glEsVersion="0x00020000"
        android:required="true" />

    <application
        android:icon="@drawable/ic_launcher"
        android:label="@string/app_name"
        android:theme="@style/AppTheme" >

        <!-- Activities, Services, Providers, and such -->

        <meta-data
            android:name="com.google.android.maps.v2.API_KEY"
            android:value="YOUR_KEY_HERE" />
```

```
    <meta-data
        android:name="com.google.android.gms.version"
        android:value="@integer/google_play_services_version"/>
</application>

</manifest>
```

With the API key in hand and a suitable test platform in place, you are ready to begin.

How It Works

To display a map, simply create an instance of `MapView` or `MapFragment`. The API key is global to your application, so any instance of these elements will use this value. You do not need to add the key to each instance, as was the case with Maps v1.

■ **Note**   In addition to the permissions described previously, we must also add `android.permission.ACCESS_FINE_LOCATION` for this example. This is required only because this example is hooking back up to the `LocationManager` to get the cached location value.

We are going to create a simple application that shows the user's last-known location on a Google map, as seen in Figure 4-1.

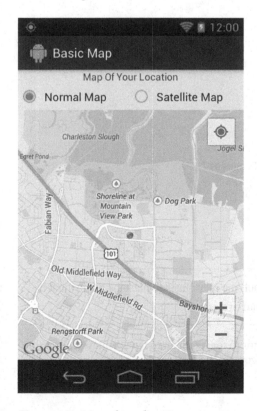

Figure 4-1. *Map of user location*

Now, let's begin by looking at the layout we need to construct this view. See Listing 4-5.

Listing 4-5. `res/layout/main.xml`

```xml
<?xml version="1.0" encoding="utf-8"?>
<LinearLayout
    xmlns:android="http://schemas.android.com/apk/res/android"
    android:layout_width="match_parent"
    android:layout_height="match_parent"
    android:orientation="vertical" >
    <TextView
        android:layout_width="match_parent"
        android:layout_height="wrap_content"
        android:gravity="center_horizontal"
        android:text="Map Of Your Location" />
    <RadioGroup
        android:id="@+id/group_maptype"
        android:layout_width="match_parent"
        android:layout_height="wrap_content"
        android:orientation="horizontal" >
        <RadioButton
            android:id="@+id/type_normal"
            android:layout_width="0dp"
            android:layout_height="wrap_content"
            android:layout_weight="1"
            android:text="Normal Map" />
        <RadioButton
            android:id="@+id/type_satellite"
            android:layout_width="0dp"
            android:layout_height="wrap_content"
            android:layout_weight="1"
            android:text="Satellite Map" />
    </RadioGroup>

    <fragment
        class="com.google.android.gms.maps.SupportMapFragment"
        android:id="@+id/map"
        android:layout_width="match_parent"
        android:layout_height="match_parent"/>
</LinearLayout>
```

■ **Note**   When adding `MapView` or `MapFragment` to an XML layout, the fully qualified package name must be included, because the class does not exist in `android.view` or `android.widget`.

Here we have created a simple layout that includes a selector to toggle the map type displayed alongside a `MapFragment` instance. Listing 4-6 reveals the activity code to control the map.

Listing 4-6. Activity Displaying Cached Location

```
public class BasicMapActivity extends FragmentActivity implements
        RadioGroup.OnCheckedChangeListener, OnMapReadyCallback {
    private static final String TAG = "AndroidRecipes";
    private static final int REQUEST_CODE_PERMISSIONS = 10;

    private SupportMapFragment mMapFragment;
    private GoogleMap mMap;

    @Override
    public void onCreate(Bundle savedInstanceState) {
        super.onCreate(savedInstanceState);
        setContentView(R.layout.main);

        //Verify play services is active and up to date
        int resultCode = GoogleApiAvailability.getInstance()
                .isGooglePlayServicesAvailable(this);
        switch (resultCode) {
            case ConnectionResult.SUCCESS:
                Log.d(TAG, "Google Play Services is ready to go!");
                break;
            default:
                showPlayServicesError(resultCode);
                return;
        }

        mMapFragment = (SupportMapFragment)
                getSupportFragmentManager().findFragmentById(R.id.map);

        // Wire up the map type selector UI
        // Disable until we get a reference to GoogleMap
        RadioGroup typeSelect
                = (RadioGroup) findViewById(R.id.group_maptype);
        typeSelect.setEnabled(false);
        typeSelect.setOnCheckedChangeListener(this);
        typeSelect.check(R.id.type_normal);
    }

    @Override
    public void onResume() {
        super.onResume();

        if (ActivityCompat.checkSelfPermission(this,
                    android.Manifest.permission.ACCESS_FINE_LOCATION)
                != PackageManager.PERMISSION_GRANTED &&
                ActivityCompat.checkSelfPermission(this,
                    android.Manifest.permission.ACCESS_COARSE_LOCATION)
                    != PackageManager.PERMISSION_GRANTED) {
```

```java
        ActivityCompat.requestPermissions(this,
            new String[]{android.Manifest.permission.ACCESS_FINE_LOCATION,
            android.Manifest.permission.ACCESS_COARSE_LOCATION},
            REQUEST_CODE_PERMISSIONS);
        return;
    }

    RadioGroup typeSelect
        = (RadioGroup) findViewById(R.id.group_maptype);
    typeSelect.setEnabled(true);
    mMapFragment.getMapAsync(this);
}

@Override
public void onPause() {
    super.onResume();
    if (mMap != null) {
        //Disable user location when not visible
        //noinspection MissingPermission
        mMap.setMyLocationEnabled(false);
    }
}

/*
 * When Play Services is missing or at the wrong version, the client
 * library will assist with a dialog to help the user update.
 */
private void showPlayServicesError(int errorCode) {
    // Get the error dialog from Google Play services
    GoogleApiAvailability.getInstance()
            .showErrorDialogFragment(this, errorCode, 1,
                    new DialogInterface.OnCancelListener() {
                        @Override
                        public void onCancel(DialogInterface dialogInterface) {
                            finish();
                        }
                    });
}

/**
 * OnCheckedChangeListener Methods
 */
@Override
public void onCheckedChanged(RadioGroup group, int checkedId) {
    switch (checkedId) {
        case R.id.type_satellite:
            //Show the satellite map view
            mMap.setMapType(GoogleMap.MAP_TYPE_SATELLITE);
            break;
        case R.id.type_normal:
```

```
        default:
            //Show the normal map view
            mMap.setMapType(GoogleMap.MAP_TYPE_NORMAL);
            break;
    }
}

@SuppressWarnings("MissingPermission")
@Override
public void onMapReady(GoogleMap googleMap) {
    mMap = googleMap;
    mMap.setMyLocationEnabled(true);

    //Quickly see if our last known user location is valid, and center
    // the map around that point.  If not, use a default location.
    LocationManager manager
            = (LocationManager) getSystemService(Context.LOCATION_SERVICE);
    Location location =
            manager.getLastKnownLocation(LocationManager.GPS_PROVIDER);

    LatLng mapCenter;
    if (location != null) {
        mapCenter = new LatLng(location.getLatitude(),
                                    location.getLongitude());
    } else {
        //Use a default location
        mapCenter = new LatLng(37.4218, -122.0840);
    }

    //Center and zoom the map simultaneously
    CameraUpdate newCamera
            = CameraUpdateFactory.newLatLngZoom(mapCenter, 13);
    mMap.moveCamera(newCamera);
}

@Override
public void onRequestPermissionsResult(int requestCode,
                                    @NonNull String[] permissions,
                                    @NonNull int[] grantResults) {
    super.onRequestPermissionsResult(requestCode, permissions,
            grantResults);

    if (requestCode == REQUEST_CODE_PERMISSIONS) {
        for (int i = 0; i < grantResults.length; i++) {
            int grantResult = grantResults[i];
            String permission = permissions[i];
```

```
            if (grantResult != PackageManager.PERMISSION_GRANTED) {
                Log.d(TAG, "Permission " + permission
                        + " is required for this application to work.");
                finish();
                return;
            }
        }
    }
}

}
```

Our first order of business is to verify that the correct version of Google Play Services is installed on this device. Google manages the Google Play Services library automatically as the user of the device interacts with Google applications such as Google Play. Play Services is automatically updated in the background, so we need to verify at runtime that the user has what we need by using methods from GooglePlayServicesUtil. The result we receive from isGooglePlayServicesAvailable() will tell us whether the services are the correct version, need an update, or are even installed at all.

This activity takes the latest user location and centers the map on that point. All control of the map is done through a GoogleMap instance, which we obtain by calling MapFragment.getMap(). In this example, we use the map's moveCamera() method to adjust the map display with a CameraUpdate object.

A CameraUpdate allows you to make adjustments to one or more components of the map display at once, such as modifying the zoom as well as the center point. The map's zoom level is a discrete value between 2.0 and 21.0, with the lowest value making the entire world approximately 1,024dp wide, and each increasing level doubling the width of the world on the display.

When the user selects a different radio button, the map type is toggled between satellite view and the traditional map view. In addition to the values used in the example, other allowable map types are as follows:

- MAP_TYPE_HYBRID: Displays map data (for example, streets and points of interest) over the top of the satellite view

- MAP_TYPE_TERRAIN: Displays a map with terrain elevation contour lines

Finally, to enable the user location display and controls, we simply need to call setMyLocationEnabled() on the map. Because this method will enable location tracking and likely turn on elements such as the GPS, it should also be disabled when no longer needed (when the view is not visible).

To properly build this application, Listing 4-7 shows us what dependencies we need in the build. gradle file.

Listing 4-7. Partial build.gradle

```
apply plugin: 'com.android.application'

android {
    compileSdkVersion 24
    buildToolsVersion "24.0.1"

    defaultConfig {
        applicationId "com.androidrecipes.mapper"
        ...
    }

    ...
}
```

```
dependencies {
    compile 'com.android.support:support-v4:24.1.1'
    compile 'com.google.android.gms:play-services:9.2.1'
}
```

This is a great start, but perhaps a little boring. To bring in some more interactivity, Recipe 4-3 will create markers and other annotations for the map, and show you how to customize them.

4-3. Annotating Maps

Problem

In addition to displaying a map centered on a specific location, your application needs to mark a location more explicitly with an annotation.

Solution

(API Level 9)

Add Marker objects and shape elements such as Circle and Polygon to the map. Marker objects are interactive objects defined by an icon that displays over a given location. That location can be fixed, or you can set the Marker to be dragged by the user to any point. Each Marker can respond to touch events such as taps and long-presses. Additionally, a Marker can be given metadata including a title and text snippet that should be displayed in a pop-up info window when the marker is tapped. You also can customize the display of these windows.

Maps v2 also supports drawing discrete shape elements. These elements are not inherently interactive, though you will see it is not difficult to add the capability to interact with a shape. We can also use the Polyline shape to draw routes onto a map; Polyline does not attempt to draw as a closed, filled shape like the other options.

■ **Important**   Google Maps v2 is distributed as part of the Google Play Services library; it is not part of the native SDK at any platform level. However, any application targeting API Level 9 or later and devices inside the Google Play ecosystem can use the mapping library. For more information on including Google Play Services in your project, reference https://developer.android.com/google/play-services/setup.html.

How It Works

c2 shows our previous map application with some points of interest added using markers.

Figure 4-2. *Map with custom markers*

Listings 4-8 and 4-9 show a new activity example with some markers added to the map. The XML layout is the same as we used in the previous recipe, so we won't spend time dissecting its components again, but it is added here for completeness.

Listing 4-8. res/layout/main.xml

```
<?xml version="1.0" encoding="utf-8"?>
<LinearLayout
    xmlns:android="http://schemas.android.com/apk/res/android"
    android:layout_width="match_parent"
    android:layout_height="match_parent"
    android:orientation="vertical" >
    <TextView
        android:layout_width="match_parent"
        android:layout_height="wrap_content"
        android:gravity="center_horizontal"
        android:text="Map Of Your Location" />
    <RadioGroup
        android:id="@+id/group_maptype"
        android:layout_width="match_parent"
        android:layout_height="wrap_content"
        android:orientation="horizontal" >
```

```xml
        <RadioButton
            android:id="@+id/type_normal"
            android:layout_width="0dp"
            android:layout_height="wrap_content"
            android:layout_weight="1"
            android:text="Normal Map" />
        <RadioButton
            android:id="@+id/type_satellite"
            android:layout_width="0dp"
            android:layout_height="wrap_content"
            android:layout_weight="1"
            android:text="Satellite Map" />
    </RadioGroup>

    <fragment
        class="com.google.android.gms.maps.SupportMapFragment"
        android:id="@+id/map"
        android:layout_width="match_parent"
        android:layout_height="match_parent"/>
</LinearLayout>
```

Listing 4-9. Activity Showing Map with Markers

```java
public class MarkerMapActivity extends FragmentActivity implements
        RadioGroup.OnCheckedChangeListener,
        GoogleMap.OnMarkerClickListener,
        GoogleMap.OnMarkerDragListener,
        GoogleMap.OnInfoWindowClickListener,
        GoogleMap.InfoWindowAdapter, OnMapReadyCallback {
    private static final String TAG = "AndroidRecipes";
    private static final int REQUEST_CODE_PERMISSIONS = 10;

    private SupportMapFragment mMapFragment;
    private GoogleMap mMap;

    @Override
    protected void onCreate(Bundle savedInstanceState) {
        super.onCreate(savedInstanceState);
        setContentView(R.layout.main);

        //Verify play services is active and up to date
        int resultCode = GoogleApiAvailability.getInstance()
                .isGooglePlayServicesAvailable(this);
        switch (resultCode) {
            case ConnectionResult.SUCCESS:
                Log.d(TAG, "Google Play Services is ready to go!");
                break;
            default:
                showPlayServicesError(resultCode);
                return;
        }
```

```java
    mMapFragment = (SupportMapFragment) getSupportFragmentManager()
            .findFragmentById(R.id.map);

    // Wire up the map type selector UI
    RadioGroup typeSelect
            = (RadioGroup) findViewById(R.id.group_maptype);
    typeSelect.setEnabled(false);
    typeSelect.setOnCheckedChangeListener(this);
    typeSelect.check(R.id.type_normal);
}

@Override
protected void onResume() {
    super.onResume();
    mMapFragment.getMapAsync(this);
}

@Override
protected void onPause() {
    super.onPause();
    mMap = null;
}

/**
 * OnCheckedChangeListener Methods
 */
@Override
public void onCheckedChanged(RadioGroup group, int checkedId) {
    switch (checkedId) {
        case R.id.type_satellite:
            mMap.setMapType(GoogleMap.MAP_TYPE_SATELLITE);
            break;
        case R.id.type_normal:
        default:
            mMap.setMapType(GoogleMap.MAP_TYPE_NORMAL);
            break;
    }
}

/**
 * OnMarkerClickListener Methods
 */

@Override
public boolean onMarkerClick(Marker marker) {
    // Return true to disable auto-center and info pop-up
    return false;
}
```

```java
/**
 * OnMarkerDragListener Methods
 */

@Override
public void onMarkerDrag(Marker marker) {
    // Do something while the marker is moving
}

@Override
public void onMarkerDragEnd(Marker marker) {
    Log.i("MarkerTest", "Drag " + marker.getTitle()
            + " to " + marker.getPosition());
}

@Override
public void onMarkerDragStart(Marker marker) {
    Log.d("MarkerTest", "Drag " + marker.getTitle()
            + " from " + marker.getPosition());
}

/**
 * OnInfoWindowClickListener Methods
 */

@Override
public void onInfoWindowClick(Marker marker) {
    // Act upon the selection event, here we just close the window
    marker.hideInfoWindow();
}

/**
 * InfoWindowAdapter Methods
 */

/*
 * Return a content view to be placed inside a standard info window. Only
 * called if getInfoWindow() returns null.
 */
@Override
public View getInfoContents(Marker marker) {
    //Try returning createInfoView() here instead
    return null;
}

/*
 * Return the entire info window to be displayed.
 */
```

```java
    @Override
    public View getInfoWindow(Marker marker) {
        View content = createInfoView(marker);
        content.setBackgroundResource(R.drawable.background);
        return content;
    }

    /*
     * Private helper method to construct the content view
     */
    private View createInfoView(Marker marker) {
        // We have no parent for layout, so pass null
        View content = getLayoutInflater().inflate(
                R.layout.info_window, null);
        ImageView image = (ImageView) content
                .findViewById(R.id.image);
        TextView text = (TextView) content
                .findViewById(R.id.text);

        image.setImageResource(R.drawable.ic_launcher);
        text.setText(marker.getTitle());

        return content;
    }

    /*
     * When Play Services is missing or at the wrong version, the client
     * library will assist with a dialog to help the user update.
     */
    private void showPlayServicesError(int errorCode) {
        // Get the error dialog from Google Play services
        GoogleApiAvailability.getInstance()
                .showErrorDialogFragment(this, errorCode, 1,
                        new DialogInterface.OnCancelListener() {
                            @Override
                            public void onCancel(DialogInterface dialogInterface) {
                                finish();
                            }
                        });
    }

    @Override
    public void onMapReady(GoogleMap googleMap) {
        mMap = googleMap;

        // Monitor interaction with marker elements
        mMap.setOnMarkerClickListener(this);
        mMap.setOnMarkerDragListener(this);
        // Set our application to serve views for the info windows
        mMap.setInfoWindowAdapter(this);
        // Monitor click events on info windows
        mMap.setOnInfoWindowClickListener(this);
```

```
// Google HQ 37.427,-122.099
Marker marker = mMap.addMarker(new MarkerOptions()
        .position(new LatLng(37.4218, -122.0840))
        .title("Google HQ")
        // Show an image resource from our app as the marker
        .icon(BitmapDescriptorFactory
                .fromResource(R.drawable.logo))
        //Reduce the opacity
        .alpha(0.6f));
//Make this marker draggable on the map
marker.setDraggable(true);

// Subtract 0.01 degrees
mMap.addMarker(new MarkerOptions()
        .position(new LatLng(37.4118, -122.0740))
        .title("Neighbor #1")
        .snippet("Best Restaurant in Town")
        // Show a default marker, in the default color
        .icon(BitmapDescriptorFactory.defaultMarker()));

// Add 0.01 degrees
mMap.addMarker(new MarkerOptions()
        .position(new LatLng(37.4318, -122.0940))
        .title("Neighbor #2")
        .snippet("Worst Restaurant in Town")
        // Show a default marker, with a blue tint
        .icon(BitmapDescriptorFactory
                .defaultMarker(BitmapDescriptorFactory.HUE_AZURE)));

// Center and zoom the map simultaneously
LatLng mapCenter = new LatLng(37.4218, -122.0840);
CameraUpdate newCamera = CameraUpdateFactory
        .newLatLngZoom(mapCenter, 13);
mMap.moveCamera(newCamera);

RadioGroup typeSelect
        = (RadioGroup) findViewById(R.id.group_maptype);
typeSelect.setEnabled(true);
    }
}
```

■ **Disclaimer** We have not visited the locations on this map to know if they are actually restaurants, or if their customer ratings qualify them for the subtitles we've placed here!

We've added some new listener interfaces to our activity, which is now set up to monitor for click-and-drag events on each Marker, as well as click events on the pop-up info window shown from a Marker tap. Additionally, we have implemented InfoWindowAdapter, which will allow us to customize the pop-up windows eventually, but let's table that for now.

281

Markers are added to the map by passing a MarkerOptions instance into GoogleMap.addMarker(). MarkerOptions works like a builder, in that you can simply chain all the information you want to apply right off the constructor (which is what we have done). Basic information such as the marker location, display icon, and title are set here. You will also find additional options available for modifying the marker display, such as alpha, rotation, and anchor point. We've chosen to add a marker at Google HQ in Mountain View, and two other markers nearby.

There are a host of supported methods for creating a Marker icon. These are applied using a BitmapDescriptor object and BitmapDescriptorFactory, two classes that provide methods for creating all of them. For two of our elements, we have chosen defaultMarker(), which creates a standard Google pin to display. We can also pass in one of several constants to control the display color of the pin.

The marker at Google HQ has been customized to display as an icon we have in our application resources using fromResource(). You may also apply images that may be in our assets directory with a separate factory method. Additionally, we have set this marker to be draggable by the user. This means if the user were to long-press on this icon, it would be picked up from its current location and the user could drag and drop the pin anywhere desired, somewhere else on the map. The OnMarkerDragListener we implemented provides callbacks as to where the marker is being placed.

If the user taps one of the markers, the standard info window will show above the icon. That window will show the title and snippet applied to that marker. We have implemented an OnInfoWindowClickListener that closes this window when it is tapped, which is not the default behavior.

Note we do not need to implement OnMarkerClickListener in order to get this described behavior; but if we want to override it, we will. By default, the info window will display and the map will center on a selected marker. If we return true from onMarkerClick(), we can disable this and provide our own behavior.

Customizing the Info Window

To see how we can customize the info window that pops up on a marker tap, let's add a custom UI for the window (see Listings 4-10 and 4-11) and modify the InfoWindowAdapter methods implemented in our activity to look like Listing 4-12.

Listing 4-10. res/layout/info_window.xml

```xml
<?xml version="1.0" encoding="utf-8"?>
<LinearLayout
    xmlns:android="http://schemas.android.com/apk/res/android"
    android:layout_width="wrap_content"
    android:layout_height="wrap_content"
    android:orientation="vertical" >
    <ImageView
        android:id="@+id/image"
        android:layout_width="35dp"
        android:layout_height="35dp"
        android:layout_gravity="center_horizontal"
        android:scaleType="fitCenter" />
    <TextView
        android:id="@+id/text"
        android:layout_width="wrap_content"
        android:layout_height="wrap_content" />
</LinearLayout>
```

Listing 4-11. res/drawable/background.xml

```xml
<?xml version="1.0" encoding="utf-8"?>
<shape xmlns:android="http://schemas.android.com/apk/res/android"
    android:shape="rectangle">
    <corners
        android:radius="10dp"/>
    <solid
        android:color="#CCC"/>
    <padding
        android:left="10dp"
        android:right="10dp"
        android:top="10dp"
        android:bottom="10dp"/>
</shape>
```

Listing 4-12. InfoWindowAdapter Methods

```java
/*
 * Return a content view to be placed inside a standard info
 * window. Only called if getInfoWindow() returns null.
 */
@Override
public View getInfoContents(Marker marker) {
    //Try returning createInfoView() here instead
    return null;
}

/*
 * Return the entire info window to be displayed.
 */
@Override
public View getInfoWindow(Marker marker) {
    View content = createInfoView(marker);
    content.setBackgroundResource(R.drawable.background);
    return content;
}

/*
 * Private helper method to construct the content view
 */
private View createInfoView(Marker marker) {
    // We have no parent for layout, so pass null
    View content = getLayoutInflater().inflate(
            R.layout.info_window, null);
    ImageView image = (ImageView) content
            .findViewById(R.id.image);
    TextView text = (TextView) content
            .findViewById(R.id.text);
```

```
image.setImageResource(R.drawable.ic_launcher);
text.setText(marker.getTitle());

return content;
}
```

By returning a valid View from getInfoContents(), the view will be used as the content inside the standard window background display. Returning the same View from getInfoWindow() will display it as a fully custom window with no standard components. We have abstracted the creation of our pop-up into a helper method so you can easily try it both ways.

Working with Shapes

Let's talk about adding shape elements to a map. In the next example, we've created a custom class called ShapeAdapter that creates and adds circular or rectangular shapes on the map to describe map regions. The result will look like Figure 4-3.

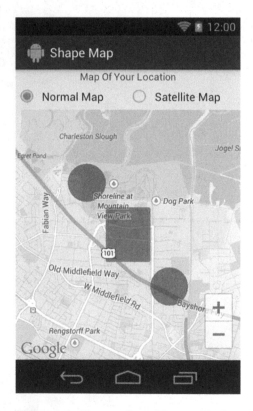

Figure 4-3. *Map overlay with tappable shape regions*

This example also uses the OnMapClickListener of GoogleMap to validate when a user has tapped a certain region to select it. Listing 4-13 shows the adapter code.

Listing 4-13. ShapeAdapter to Map Shapes

```java
public class ShapeAdapter implements OnMapClickListener {

    private static final float STROKE_SELECTED = 6.0f;
    private static final float STROKE_NORMAL = 2.0f;
    /* Colors for the drawn regions */
    private static final int COLOR_STROKE = Color.RED;
    private static final int COLOR_FILL =
            Color.argb(127, 0, 0, 255);

    /*
     * External interface to notify listeners of a change in
     * the selected region based on user taps
     */
    public interface OnRegionSelectedListener {
        //User selected one of our tracked regions
        public void onRegionSelected(Region selectedRegion);
        //User selected an area where we have no regions
        public void onNoRegionSelected();
    }

    /*
     * Base definition of an interactive region on the map.
     * Defines methods to change display and check user taps
     */
    public static abstract class Region {
        private String mRegionName;
        public Region(String regionName) {
            mRegionName = regionName;
        }

        public String getName() {
            return mRegionName;
        }
        //Check if a location is inside this region
        public abstract boolean hitTest(LatLng point);
        //Change display of the region based on selection
        public abstract void setSelected(boolean isSelected);
    }

    /*
     * Implementation of a region drawn as a circle
     */
    private static class CircleRegion extends Region {
        private Circle mCircle;

        public CircleRegion(String name, Circle circle) {
            super(name);
            mCircle = circle;
        }
```

```java
    @Override
    public boolean hitTest(LatLng point) {
        final LatLng center = mCircle.getCenter();
        float[] result = new float[1];
        Location.distanceBetween(center.latitude,
                center.longitude,
                point.latitude,
                point.longitude,
                result);

        return (result[0] < mCircle.getRadius());
    }

    @Override
    public void setSelected(boolean isSelected) {
        mCircle.setStrokeWidth(isSelected ?
                STROKE_SELECTED : STROKE_NORMAL);
    }

}

/*
 * Implementation of a region drawn as a rectangle
 */
private static class RectRegion extends Region {
    private Polygon mRect;
    private LatLngBounds mRectBounds;

    public RectRegion(String name, Polygon rect,
            LatLng southwest, LatLng northeast) {
        super(name);
        mRect = rect;
        mRectBounds = new LatLngBounds(southwest, northeast);
    }

    @Override
    public boolean hitTest(LatLng point) {
        return mRectBounds.contains(point);
    }

    @Override
    public void setSelected(boolean isSelected) {
        mRect.setStrokeWidth(isSelected ?
                STROKE_SELECTED : STROKE_NORMAL);
    }
}

private GoogleMap mMap;

private OnRegionSelectedListener mRegionSelectedListener;
private ArrayList<Region> mRegions;
private Region mCurrentRegion;
```

```java
public ShapeAdapter(GoogleMap map) {
    //Internally track regions for selection validation
    mRegions = new ArrayList<Region>();

    mMap = map;
    mMap.setOnMapClickListener(this);
}

public void setOnRegionSelectedListener(
        OnRegionSelectedListener listener) {
    mRegionSelectedListener = listener;
}

/*
 * Construct and add a new circular region around the
 * given point.
 */
public void addCircularRegion(String name, LatLng center,
        double radius) {
    CircleOptions options = new CircleOptions()
            .center(center)
            .radius(radius);
    //Set display properties of the shape
    options
        .strokeWidth(STROKE_NORMAL)
        .strokeColor(COLOR_STROKE)
        .fillColor(COLOR_FILL);

    Circle c = mMap.addCircle(options);
    mRegions.add(new CircleRegion(name, c));
}

/*
 * Construct and add a new rectangular region with the
 * given boundaries.
 */
public void addRectangularRegion(String name,
        LatLng southwest, LatLng northeast) {
    PolygonOptions options = new PolygonOptions().add(
            new LatLng(southwest.latitude,
                    southwest.longitude),
            new LatLng(southwest.latitude,
                    northeast.longitude),
            new LatLng(northeast.latitude,
                    northeast.longitude),
            new LatLng(northeast.latitude,
                    southwest.longitude));
```

287

```
        //Set display properties of the shape
        options
            .strokeWidth(STROKE_NORMAL)
            .strokeColor(COLOR_STROKE)
            .fillColor(COLOR_FILL);

        Polygon p = mMap.addPolygon(options);
        mRegions.add(new RectRegion(name, p,
                southwest, northeast));
    }

    /*
     * Handle incoming tap events from the map object.
     * Determine which region element may have been selected.
     * If regions overlap at this point, the first added will
     * be selected.
     */
    @Override
    public void onMapClick(LatLng point) {
        Region newSelection = null;
        //Find and select the tapped region
        for (Region region : mRegions) {
            if (region.hitTest(point) && newSelection == null) {
                region.setSelected(true);
                newSelection = region;
            } else {
                region.setSelected(false);
            }
        }

        if (mCurrentRegion != newSelection) {
            //Notify and update the change
            if (newSelection != null
                    && mRegionSelectedListener != null) {
                mRegionSelectedListener
                        .onRegionSelected(newSelection);
            } else if (mRegionSelectedListener != null) {
                mRegionSelectedListener.onNoRegionSelected();
            }

            mCurrentRegion = newSelection;
        }
    }
}
```

This class defines an abstract type called Region that we can use to define common patterns between our shape types. Primarily, each region must define the logic for whether a map location is inside the given region, and what to do when that region is selected. We then define implementations of this for a Circle shape and a Polygon, which we will use to draw a rectangle. A center point and a radius define the circular region, while the rectangular region is defined by its southwest and northeast point. We construct the rectangle as a Polygon defined by the four corner coordinates that make up the shape.

Tap events will come in through the onMapClick() method of the listener interface, and the Maps library gives us the tap location as a LatLng location. We can validate that these events are inside a circular region simply enough by checking whether the distance between the center and the tap is larger than the radius. Location has a convenience method for calculating direct distance between two map points. For a rectangular region, we use the LatLngBounds class that is part of the Maps library because it can directly validate whether a given point is inside or outside our shape.

For each tap event, we iterate over our list of regions to find the first one that considers this location a hit. If we find no regions, the selected region is set to null. We then determine whether the selection has changed, and call back one of the methods on our custom OnRegionSelectedListener interface that higher-level objects can use to be notified of these events.

Listing 4-14 shows how we can use this adapter inside an activity.

Listing 4-14. Activity Integrating ShapeAdapter

```
public class ShapeMapActivity extends FragmentActivity implements
        RadioGroup.OnCheckedChangeListener,
        ShapeAdapter.OnRegionSelectedListener, OnMapReadyCallback {
    private static final String TAG = "AndroidRecipes";

    private SupportMapFragment mMapFragment;
    private GoogleMap mMap;

    @Override
    protected void onCreate(Bundle savedInstanceState) {
        super.onCreate(savedInstanceState);
        setContentView(R.layout.main);

        //Verify play services is active and up to date
        int resultCode = GoogleApiAvailability.getInstance()
                .isGooglePlayServicesAvailable(this);
        switch (resultCode) {
            case ConnectionResult.SUCCESS:
                Log.d(TAG, "Google Play Services is ready to go!");
                break;
            default:
                showPlayServicesError(resultCode);
                return;
        }

        mMapFragment = (SupportMapFragment) getSupportFragmentManager()
                .findFragmentById(R.id.map);

        //Wire up the map type selector UI
        RadioGroup typeSelect
                = (RadioGroup) findViewById(R.id.group_maptype);
        typeSelect.setEnabled(false);
        typeSelect.setOnCheckedChangeListener(this);
        typeSelect.check(R.id.type_normal);
    }
```

```java
@Override
protected void onResume() {
    super.onResume();
    mMapFragment.getMapAsync(this);
}

@Override
protected void onPause() {
    super.onPause();
}

/**
 * OnCheckedChangeListener Methods
 */
@Override
public void onCheckedChanged(RadioGroup group, int checkedId) {
    switch (checkedId) {
        case R.id.type_satellite:
            mMap.setMapType(GoogleMap.MAP_TYPE_SATELLITE);
            break;
        case R.id.type_normal:
        default:
            mMap.setMapType(GoogleMap.MAP_TYPE_NORMAL);
            break;
    }
}

/**
 * OnRegionSelectedListener Methods
 */
@Override
public void onRegionSelected(Region selectedRegion) {
    Toast.makeText(this, selectedRegion.getName(),
            Toast.LENGTH_SHORT).show();
}

@Override
public void onNoRegionSelected() {
    Toast.makeText(this, "No Region", Toast.LENGTH_SHORT).show();
}

/*
 * When Play Services is missing or at the wrong version, the client
 * library will assist with a dialog to help the user update.
 */
private void showPlayServicesError(int errorCode) {
    // Get the error dialog from Google Play services
    GoogleApiAvailability.getInstance()
            .showErrorDialogFragment(this, errorCode, 1,
```

```
                    new DialogInterface.OnCancelListener() {
                        @Override
                        public void onCancel(DialogInterface dialogInterface) {
                            finish();
                        }
                    });
    }

    @Override
    public void onMapReady(GoogleMap googleMap) {
        mMap = googleMap;

        ShapeAdapter adapter = new ShapeAdapter(mMap);
        adapter.setOnRegionSelectedListener(this);

        adapter.addRectangularRegion("Google HQ",
                new LatLng(37.4168, -122.0890),
                new LatLng(37.4268, -122.0790));
        adapter.addCircularRegion("Neighbor #1",
                new LatLng(37.4118, -122.0740), 400);
        adapter.addCircularRegion("Neighbor #2",
                new LatLng(37.4318, -122.0940), 400);

        //Center and zoom map simultaneously
        LatLng mapCenter = new LatLng(37.4218, -122.0840);
        CameraUpdate newCamera
                = CameraUpdateFactory.newLatLngZoom(mapCenter, 13);
        mMap.moveCamera(newCamera);

        RadioGroup typeSelect
                = (RadioGroup) findViewById(R.id.group_maptype);
        typeSelect.setEnabled(true);
    }
}
```

Here we have added the same locations from our previous example, but this time as shape regions using our new ShapeAdapter. Google HQ is added as a rectangular region, and the other two as circles. When the user makes a selection change affecting any of these regions, either of the methods onRegionSelected() or onNoRegionSelected() will be called and a message displayed.

4-4. Monitoring Location Regions

Problem

You need your application to provide contextual information to your users when they enter or exit specific location areas.

Solution

(API Level 9)

Use the geofencing features available as part of Google Play Services. With these features, your application can define circular areas around a particular point for which you want to receive callbacks when the user moves into or out of that region. Your application can create multiple Geofence instances that are either tracked indefinitely, or automatically removed for you after an expiration time.

Using region-based monitoring of a user's location can be a significantly more power-efficient method of tracking that user's arrival at a location that you find important. Allowing the services framework to track location and call you back in this manner will often result in much better battery life than your application continuously tracking user location to find out when that user reaches a given destination.

■ **Important**   The geofencing features described here are part of the Google Play Services library; they are not part of the native SDK at any platform level. However, any application targeting API Level 9 or later and devices inside the Google Play ecosystem can use the mapping library. For more information on including Google Play Services in your project, reference `https://developer.android.com/google/play-services/setup.html`.

How It Works

We are going to create an application that consists of a simple activity to allow users to set a geofence around their current location (see Figure 4-4), and then explicitly start or stop monitoring.

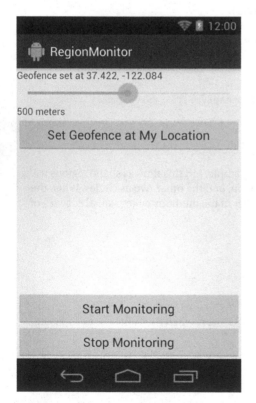

Figure 4-4. *RegionMonitor's control activity*

Once monitoring is enabled, a background service will be activated to respond to events related to the user's location transitioning into or out of the geofence area. The service component allows us to respond to these events without the need for our application's UI to be in the foreground.

■ **Important**   Because we are accessing the user's location in this example, we need to request the `android.permission.ACCESS_FINE_LOCATION` permission in our `AndroidManifest.xml`.

Let's start with Listing 4-15, which describes the layout of the activity.

Listing 4-15. `res/layout/activity_main.xml`

```xml
<?xml version="1.0" encoding="utf-8"?>
<LinearLayout
    xmlns:android="http://schemas.android.com/apk/res/android"
    android:layout_width="match_parent"
    android:layout_height="match_parent"
    android:orientation="vertical">

    <TextView
        android:id="@+id/status"
        android:layout_width="match_parent"
        android:layout_height="wrap_content" />
    <SeekBar
        android:id="@+id/radius"
        android:layout_width="match_parent"
        android:layout_height="wrap_content"
        android:max="1000"/>
    <TextView
        android:id="@+id/radius_text"
        android:layout_width="match_parent"
        android:layout_height="wrap_content" />
    <Button
        android:layout_width="match_parent"
        android:layout_height="wrap_content"
        android:text="Set Geofence at My Location"
        android:onClick="onSetGeofenceClick" />

    <!-- Spacer -->
    <View
        android:layout_width="match_parent"
        android:layout_height="0dp"
        android:layout_weight="1" />

    <Button
        android:layout_width="match_parent"
        android:layout_height="wrap_content"
        android:text="Start Monitoring"
        android:onClick="onStartMonitorClick" />
```

```
    <Button
        android:layout_width="match_parent"
        android:layout_height="wrap_content"
        android:text="Stop Monitoring"
        android:onClick="onStopMonitorClick" />
</LinearLayout>
```

The layout contains a SeekBar that enables the user to slide a finger to select the desired radius value. The user can lock in the new geofence by tapping the uppermost button, and start or stop monitoring by using the buttons at the bottom. Listing 4-16 shows the activity code to manage the geofence monitoring.

Listing 4-16. Activity to Set a Geofence

```
public class MainActivity extends Activity implements
        OnSeekBarChangeListener, GoogleApiClient.ConnectionCallbacks,
        GoogleApiClient.OnConnectionFailedListener, ResultCallback<Status> {
    private static final String TAG = "RegionMonitorActivity";
    //Unique identifier for our single geofence
    private static final String FENCE_ID = "com.androidrecipes.FENCE";
    private static final int REQUEST_CODE_PERMISSIONS = 10;

    private SeekBar mRadiusSlider;
    private TextView mStatusText, mRadiusText;

    private Geofence mCurrentFence;
    private PendingIntent mCallbackIntent;
    private GoogleApiClient mGoogleApiClient;

    @Override
    protected void onCreate(Bundle savedInstanceState) {
        super.onCreate(savedInstanceState);
        setContentView(R.layout.activity_main);

        //Wire up the UI connections
        mStatusText = (TextView) findViewById(R.id.status);
        mRadiusText = (TextView) findViewById(R.id.radius_text);
        mRadiusSlider = (SeekBar) findViewById(R.id.radius);
        mRadiusSlider.setOnSeekBarChangeListener(this);
        mRadiusText.setText(mRadiusSlider.getProgress() + " meters");

        //Check if Google Play Services is up to date.
        int errorCode = GoogleApiAvailability.getInstance()
                .isGooglePlayServicesAvailable(this);
        switch (errorCode) {
            case ConnectionResult.SUCCESS:
                //Do nothing, move on
                break;
            default:
                DialogInterface.OnCancelListener onCancelListener
                        = new DialogInterface.OnCancelListener() {
```

```java
            @Override
            public void onCancel(DialogInterface dialogInterface) {
                finish();
            }
        };
        GoogleApiAvailability.getInstance()
                .showErrorDialogFragment(this, errorCode, 10,
                        onCancelListener);
        return;
    }

    //Create an Intent to trigger our service
    Intent serviceIntent = new Intent(this, RegionMonitorService.class);
    //Create a PendingIntent for Google Services to use with callbacks
    mCallbackIntent = PendingIntent.getService(this, 0, serviceIntent,
            PendingIntent.FLAG_UPDATE_CURRENT);

    //Create a client for Google Services
    mGoogleApiClient = new GoogleApiClient.Builder(this)
            .addApi(LocationServices.API)
            .addConnectionCallbacks(this)
            .addOnConnectionFailedListener(this)
            .build();
}

@Override
protected void onResume() {
    super.onResume();
    if (ActivityCompat.checkSelfPermission(this,
            android.Manifest.permission.ACCESS_FINE_LOCATION)
            != PackageManager.PERMISSION_GRANTED &&
            ActivityCompat.checkSelfPermission(this,
                    android.Manifest.permission.ACCESS_COARSE_LOCATION)
                    != PackageManager.PERMISSION_GRANTED) {
        ActivityCompat.requestPermissions(this,
          new String[]{android.Manifest.permission.ACCESS_FINE_LOCATION,
          android.Manifest.permission.ACCESS_COARSE_LOCATION},
          REQUEST_CODE_PERMISSIONS);
        return;
    }

    //Connect to all services
    mGoogleApiClient.connect();
}

@Override
protected void onPause() {
    super.onPause();
    //Disconnect when not in the foreground
}
```

```
@SuppressWarnings("MissingPermission")
public void onSetGeofenceClick(View v) {
    //Obtain the last location from services and radius
    // from the UI
    Location current = LocationServices.FusedLocationApi
            .getLastLocation(mGoogleApiClient);

    int radius = mRadiusSlider.getProgress();

    //Create a new Geofence using the Builder
    Geofence.Builder builder = new Geofence.Builder();
    mCurrentFence = builder
            //Unique to this geofence
            .setRequestId(FENCE_ID)
            //Size and location
            .setCircularRegion(
                    current.getLatitude(),
                    current.getLongitude(),
                    radius)
            //Events both in and out of the fence
            .setTransitionTypes(Geofence.GEOFENCE_TRANSITION_ENTER
                    | Geofence.GEOFENCE_TRANSITION_EXIT
                    | Geofence.GEOFENCE_TRANSITION_DWELL)
            .setLoiteringDelay(30)
            //Keep alive
            .setExpirationDuration(Geofence.NEVER_EXPIRE)
            .build();

    String text = String.format(Locale.getDefault(),
            "Geofence set at %.3f, %.3f",
            current.getLatitude(), current.getLongitude());
    mStatusText.setText(text);
}

@SuppressWarnings("MissingPermission")
public void onStartMonitorClick(View v) {
    if (mCurrentFence == null) {
        Toast.makeText(this, "Geofence Not Yet Set",
                Toast.LENGTH_SHORT).show();
        return;
    }

    //Add the fence to start tracking, the PendingIntent will
    // be triggered with new updates
    ArrayList<Geofence> geofences = new ArrayList<>();
    geofences.add(mCurrentFence);
    GeofencingRequest geofencingRequest
            = new GeofencingRequest.Builder()
            .addGeofences(geofences)
            .setInitialTrigger(GeofencingRequest.INITIAL_TRIGGER_DWELL)
            .build();
```

```java
        LocationServices.GeofencingApi
                .addGeofences(mGoogleApiClient, geofencingRequest,
                        mCallbackIntent)
        .setResultCallback(this);
}

public void onStopMonitorClick(View v) {
    //Remove to stop tracking
    LocationServices.GeofencingApi
            .removeGeofences(mGoogleApiClient, mCallbackIntent);
}

/**
 * SeekBar Callbacks
 */

@Override
public void onProgressChanged(SeekBar seekBar, int progress,
                              boolean fromUser) {
    mRadiusText.setText(seekBar.getProgress() + " meters");
}

@Override
public void onStartTrackingTouch(SeekBar seekBar) {
}

@Override
public void onStopTrackingTouch(SeekBar seekBar) {
}

@Override
public void onConnected(Bundle connectionHint) {
    Log.v(TAG, "Google Services Connected");
}

@Override
public void onConnectionSuspended(int i) {
}

@Override
public void onConnectionFailed(ConnectionResult result) {
    Log.w(TAG, "Google Services Connection Failure");
}

@Override
public void onRequestPermissionsResult(int requestCode,
                                       @NonNull String[] permissions,
                                       @NonNull int[] grantResults) {
    super.onRequestPermissionsResult(requestCode, permissions,
            grantResults);
```

```java
        if (requestCode == REQUEST_CODE_PERMISSIONS) {
            for (int i = 0; i < grantResults.length; i++) {
                int grantResult = grantResults[i];
                String permission = permissions[i];
                if (grantResult != PackageManager.PERMISSION_GRANTED) {
                    Log.d(TAG, "Permission " + permission
                            + " is required for this application to work.");
                    finish();
                    return;
                }
            }
        }
    }

    @Override
    public void onResult(@NonNull Status status) {
        if (status.isSuccess()) {
            Log.d(TAG, "Geofence operation successful");
        } else {
            Log.d(TAG, "Geofence operation failed: " +
                    status.getStatusMessage());
        }
    }
}
```

Our first order of business after the activity has been created is to verify that Google Play Services exists and is up-to-date. If not, we need to encourage the user to visit Google Play to trigger the latest automatic update.

With that out of the way, we make a connection to the Play Services API. We want to stay connected to this only while in the foreground, so the connection calls are balanced between onResume() and onPause(). This connection is asynchronous, so we must wait for the onConnected() method before doing anything further. In our case, we need to access the LocationServices.GeofencingApi only when the user presses a button, so there is nothing of specific interest to do in this method.

■ **Tip** *Asynchronous* doesn't have to mean *slow*. Just because a method call is asynchronous doesn't mean we should expect it to take a long time. It simply means we cannot access the object immediately after the function returns. In most cases, these callbacks are still triggered long before the activity is fully visible.

Once the user has selected the desired radius and taps the Set Geofence button, we obtain the last-known location from the LocationServices.FusedLocationApi and the selected radius to build our geofence. Geofence instances are created using the Geofence.Builder, which allows us to set the location of the geofence, a unique identifier, and any additional properties we may need.

With setTransitionTypes(), we control which transitions generate notifications. There are two possible values for transitions: GEOFENCE_TRANSITION_ENTER and GEOFENCE_TRANSITION_EXIT. You may request callbacks on one or both events; we've chosen both.

The expiration time, when positive, represents a time in the future from when the Geofence is added that it should be automatically removed. Setting the value to NEVER_EXPIRE allows us to track this region indefinitely until we remove it manually.

At any point in the future when the user taps the Start Monitoring button, we will request updates for this region by calling `LocationServices.FusedLocationApi.addGeofences()` with both the `Geofence` and a `PendingIntent` that the framework will fire for each new monitoring event. Notice in our case that `PendingIntent` points to a service. This request will register the `Geofence` in Play Services, which will make sure that the `PendingIntent` is triggered at the right location. At this point, a start command is sent to our background service, which we will discuss in more detail shortly.

Finally, when the user taps the Stop Monitoring button, the geofence will be removed and new updates will cease. We reference which element(s) to remove by using the same `PendingIntent` that was passed to the original request. Geofences can also be removed by using the unique identifier they were originally built with. Once the asynchronous remove is complete, a stop command is sent to our background service.

In both the start and stop cases, we are sending an intent to the service with a unique action string so the service can differentiate between these requests and the updates it will receive from location services. Listing 4-17 reveals this background service that we've been hearing so much about.

Listing 4-17. Region Monitor Service

```
public class RegionMonitorService extends Service {
    //Unique action to identify start requests vs. events
    public static final String ACTION_INIT =
            "com.androidrecipes.regionmonitor.ACTION_INIT";
    private static final String TAG = "RegionMonitorService";
    private static final int NOTE_ID = 100;
    private NotificationManager mNoteManager;

    @Override
    public void onCreate() {
        super.onCreate();
        mNoteManager
            = (NotificationManager) getSystemService(NOTIFICATION_SERVICE);
        //Post a system notification when the service starts
        NotificationCompat.Builder builder =
                new NotificationCompat.Builder(this);
        builder.setSmallIcon(R.drawable.ic_launcher);
        builder.setContentTitle("Geofence Service");
        builder.setContentText("Waiting for transition...");
        builder.setOngoing(true);

        Notification note = builder.build();
        mNoteManager.notify(NOTE_ID, note);
    }

    @Override
    public int onStartCommand(Intent intent, int flags, int startId) {
        //Nothing to do yet, just starting the service
        if (ACTION_INIT.equals(intent.getAction())) {
            //We don't care if this service dies unexpectedly
            return START_NOT_STICKY;
        }
```

```
        GeofencingEvent geofencingEvent
                        = GeofencingEvent.fromIntent(intent);
        if (geofencingEvent.hasError()) {
            //Log any errors
            Log.w(TAG, "Error monitoring region: "
                    + geofencingEvent.getErrorCode());
        } else {
            //Update the ongoing notification from the new event
            NotificationCompat.Builder builder =
                    new NotificationCompat.Builder(this);
            builder.setSmallIcon(R.drawable.ic_launcher);
            builder.setDefaults(Notification.DEFAULT_SOUND
                    | Notification.DEFAULT_LIGHTS);
            builder.setOngoing(true);

            int transitionType = geofencingEvent.getGeofenceTransition();

            //Check whether we entered or exited the region
            if (transitionType == Geofence.GEOFENCE_TRANSITION_ENTER) {
                builder.setContentTitle("Geofence Transition");
                builder.setContentText("Entered your Geofence");
            } else if (transitionType == Geofence.GEOFENCE_TRANSITION_EXIT) {
                builder.setContentTitle("Geofence Transition");
                builder.setContentText("Exited your Geofence");
            }

            Notification note = builder.build();
            mNoteManager.notify(NOTE_ID, note);
        }

        //We don't care if this service dies unexpectedly
        return START_NOT_STICKY;
    }

    @Override
    public void onDestroy() {
        super.onDestroy();
        //When the service dies, cancel our ongoing notification
        mNoteManager.cancel(NOTE_ID);
    }

    /* We are not binding to this service */
    @Override
    public IBinder onBind(Intent intent) {
        return null;
    }
}
```

The primary role of this service is to receive updates from the location services about our monitored region and post them to a notification in the status bar so the user can see the change. We will talk in more detail about how notifications work and how to create them in Chapter 6.

When the service is first created (which will happen when the start command is sent after our button press), an initial notification is created and posted to the status bar. This will be followed by the first onStartCommand(), where we find our unique action string and do nothing further.

Relatively immediately after this occurs, the first region-monitoring event will come into this service, calling onStartCommand() again. This first event is a transition that indicates the initial state of the device location with respect to the Geofence. In this case, we check to see whether the Intent contains an error message, and if it is a successful tracking event, we construct an updated notification based on the transition information contained within and post the update to the status bar.

This process will repeat for each new event we receive while the region monitoring is active. When the user finally returns to our activity and presses Stop Monitoring, that stop command will cause onDestroy() to be called in the service. It is here that we remove the notification from the status bar to signify to the user that monitoring is no longer active.

4-5. Capturing Images and Video

Problem

Your application needs to use the device's camera in order to capture media, whether it be still images or short video clips.

Solution

(API Level 3)

Send an intent to Android to transfer control to the Camera application and to return the image the user captured. Android does contain APIs for directly accessing the camera hardware, previewing, and taking snapshots or videos. However, if your only goal is to simply get the media content by using the camera with an interface the user is familiar with, there is no better solution than a handoff.

How It Works

Let's take a look at how to use the Camera application to take both still images and video clips.

Image Capture

Let's take a look at an example activity that will activate the Camera application when the Take a Picture button is pressed; you will receive the result of this operation as a Bitmap. See Listings 4-18 and 4-19.

Listing 4-18. res/layout/main.xml

```
<?xml version="1.0" encoding="utf-8"?>
<LinearLayout
    xmlns:android="http://schemas.android.com/apk/res/android"
    android:orientation="vertical"
    android:layout_width="match_parent"
    android:layout_height="match_parent">
    <Button
        android:id="@+id/capture"
        android:layout_width="match_parent"
        android:layout_height="wrap_content"
        android:text="Take a Picture" />
```

```
    <ImageView
        android:id="@+id/image"
        android:layout_width="match_parent"
        android:layout_height="match_parent"
        android:scaleType="centerInside" />
</LinearLayout>
```

Listing 4-19. Activity to Capture an Image

```
public class MyActivity extends Activity {

    private static final int REQUEST_IMAGE = 100;

    Button captureButton;
    ImageView imageView;

    @Override
    public void onCreate(Bundle savedInstanceState) {
        super.onCreate(savedInstanceState);
        setContentView(R.layout.main);

        captureButton = (Button)findViewById(R.id.capture);
        captureButton.setOnClickListener(listener);

        imageView = (ImageView)findViewById(R.id.image);
    }

    @Override
    protected void onActivityResult(int requestCode,
            int resultCode, Intent data) {
        if(requestCode == REQUEST_IMAGE
                && resultCode == Activity.RESULT_OK) {
            //Process and display the image
            Bitmap userImage =
                    (Bitmap)data.getExtras().get("data");
            imageView.setImageBitmap(userImage);
        }
    }

    private View.OnClickListener listener =
            new View.OnClickListener() {
        @Override
        public void onClick(View v) {
            try {
                Intent intent =
                        new Intent(MediaStore.ACTION_IMAGE_CAPTURE);
                startActivityForResult(intent, REQUEST_IMAGE);
            } catch (ActivityNotFoundException e) {
                //Handle if no application exists
            }
        }
    };
}
```

In this example, we construct an intent to activate the Camera application and capture an image. While it is unlikely, we want to be prepared for the case that a Camera application does not exist on the device. In this case, the call to startActivity() will throw an ActivityNotFoundException, so we have wrapped the call in a try block in order to handle this case gracefully.

■ **Tip**   You can also query whether camera hardware is present with the PackageManager.
hasSystemFeature() method, passing in PackageManager.FEATURE_CAMERA as the parameter.

This method captures the image and returns a scaled-down Bitmap as an extra in the data field. If you need to capture the full-sized image, insert a Uri for the image destination into the MediaStore.EXTRA_OUTPUT field of the intent before starting the capture, and the image will be saved at that location. See Listing 4-20.

Listing 4-20. Full-Size Image Capture to File

```java
public class MyActivity extends Activity {

    private static final int REQUEST_IMAGE = 100;

    Button captureButton;
    ImageView imageView;
    File destination;

    @Override
    public void onCreate(Bundle savedInstanceState) {
        super.onCreate(savedInstanceState);
        setContentView(R.layout.main);

        captureButton = (Button)findViewById(R.id.capture);
        captureButton.setOnClickListener(listener);

        imageView = (ImageView)findViewById(R.id.image);

        destination = new File(Environment
                .getExternalStorageDirectory(), "image.jpg");
    }

    @Override
    protected void onActivityResult(int requestCode,
            int resultCode, Intent data) {
        if(requestCode == REQUEST_IMAGE
                && resultCode == Activity.RESULT_OK) {
            try {
                FileInputStream in =
                        new FileInputStream(destination);
                BitmapFactory.Options options =
                        new BitmapFactory.Options();
                options.inSampleSize = 10; //Downsample by 10x
```

```
                Bitmap userImage = BitmapFactory
                        .decodeStream(in, null, options);
                imageView.setImageBitmap(userImage);
            } catch (Exception e) {
                e.printStackTrace();
            }
        }
    }

    private View.OnClickListener listener =
            new View.OnClickListener() {
        @Override
        public void onClick(View v) {
            try {
                Intent intent =
                        new Intent(MediaStore.ACTION_IMAGE_CAPTURE);
                //Add extra to save full-image somewhere
                intent.putExtra(MediaStore.EXTRA_OUTPUT,
                        Uri.fromFile(destination));
                startActivityForResult(intent, REQUEST_IMAGE);
            } catch (ActivityNotFoundException e) {
                //Handle if no application exists
            }
        }
    };
}
```

This method will instruct the Camera application to store the image elsewhere (in this case, on the device's SD card as image.jpg), and the result will not be scaled down. When retrieving the image after the operation returns, we now go directly to the file location where we told the camera to store the image.

■ **Tip** The documentation states that only one image output should be expected. If no Uri exists, a small image is returned as data. Otherwise, the image is saved to the Uri location. You should not expect to receive both, even if some devices in the market behave this way.

Using BitmapFactory.Options, however, we do still scale the image down prior to displaying to the screen to avoid loading the full-size Bitmap into memory at once. Also note that this example chose a file location that was on the device's external storage, which requires the android.permission.WRITE_EXTERNAL_STORAGE permission to be declared in API Levels 4 and above. If your final solution writes the file elsewhere, this may not be necessary.

Video Capture

Capturing video clips by using this method is just as straightforward, although the results produced are slightly different. There is no case under which the actual video-clip data is returned directly in the intent extras, and it is always saved to a destination file location. The following two parameters may be passed along as extras:

- MediaStore.EXTRA_VIDEO_QUALITY: Integer value to describe the quality level used to capture the video. Allowed values are 0 for low quality and 1 for high quality.

- MediaStore.EXTRA_OUTPUT: Uri destination of where to save the video content. If this
  is not present, the video will be saved in a standard location for the device.

When the video recording is complete, the actual location where the data was saved is returned as a Uri in the data field of the result Intent. Let's take a look at a similar example that allows the user to record and save videos and then display the saved location back to the screen. See Listings 4-21 and 4-22.

Listing 4-21. res/layout/main.xml

```xml
<?xml version="1.0" encoding="utf-8"?>
<LinearLayout
    xmlns:android="http://schemas.android.com/apk/res/android"
    android:orientation="vertical"
    android:layout_width="match_parent"
    android:layout_height="match_parent">
    <Button
        android:id="@+id/capture"
        android:layout_width="match_parent"
        android:layout_height="wrap_content"
        android:text="Take a Video" />
    <TextView
        android:id="@+id/file"
        android:layout_width="match_parent"
        android:layout_height="match_parent" />
</LinearLayout>
```

Listing 4-22. Activity to Capture a Video Clip

```java
public class MyActivity extends Activity {

    private static final int REQUEST_VIDEO = 100;

    Button captureButton;
    TextView text;
    File destination;

    @Override
    public void onCreate(Bundle savedInstanceState) {
        super.onCreate(savedInstanceState);
        setContentView(R.layout.main);

        captureButton = (Button)findViewById(R.id.capture);
        captureButton.setOnClickListener(listener);

        text = (TextView)findViewById(R.id.file);

        destination = new File(Environment
                .getExternalStorageDirectory(), "myVideo");
    }
```

305

```
    @Override
    protected void onActivityResult(int requestCode,
            int resultCode, Intent data) {
        if(requestCode == REQUEST_VIDEO
                && resultCode == Activity.RESULT_OK) {
            String location = data.getData().toString();
            text.setText(location);
        }
    }

    private View.OnClickListener listener =
            new View.OnClickListener() {
        @Override
        public void onClick(View v) {
            try {
                Intent intent =
                        new Intent(MediaStore.ACTION_VIDEO_CAPTURE);
                //Add (optional) extra to save video to our file
                intent.putExtra(MediaStore.EXTRA_OUTPUT,
                        Uri.fromFile(destination));
                //Optional extra to set video quality
                intent.putExtra(MediaStore.EXTRA_VIDEO_QUALITY, 0);
                startActivityForResult(intent, REQUEST_VIDEO);

            } catch (ActivityNotFoundException e) {
                //Handle if no application exists
            }
        }
    };
}
```

This example, like the previous example saving an image, puts the recorded video on the device's SD card (which requires the android.permission.WRITE_EXTERNAL_STORAGE permission for API Levels 4+). To initiate the process, we send an intent with the MediaStore.ACTION_VIDEO_CAPTURE action string to the system. Android will launch the default Camera application to handle recording the video and return with an OK result when recording is complete. We retrieve the location where the data was stored as a Uri by calling Intent.getData() in the onActivityResult() callback method, and then display that location to the user.

This example requests explicitly that the video be shot using the low-quality setting, but this parameter is optional. If MediaStore.EXTRA_VIDEO_QUALITY is not present in the request intent, the device will usually choose to shoot using high quality.

In cases where MediaStore.EXTRA_OUTPUT is provided, the Uri returned should match the location you requested, unless an error occurs that keeps the application from writing to that location. If this parameter is not provided, the returned value will be a content:// Uri to retrieve the media from the system's MediaStore Content Provider.

Later, in Recipe 4-10, we will look at practical ways to play this media back in your application.

4-6. Making a Custom Camera Overlay

Problem

Many applications need more direct access to the camera, either for the purposes of overlaying a custom UI for controls or displaying metadata about what is visible through information based on location and direction sensors (augmented reality).

Solution

(API Level 5)

Render preview frames directly from the camera hardware in an activity's view hierarchy. Android provides APIs to directly access the device's camera for the purposes of obtaining the preview feed and taking photos. We can access these when the needs of the application grow beyond simply snapping and returning a photo for display.

■ **Note**   Because we are taking a more direct approach to the camera here, the `android.permission.CAMERA` permission must be declared in the manifest.

How It Works

We start by creating a `SurfaceView`, a dedicated view for live drawing where we will attach the camera's preview stream. This provides us with a live preview inside a view that we can lay out any way we choose inside an activity. From there, it's simply a matter of adding other views and controls that suit the context of the application. Let's take a look at the code (see Listings 4-23 and 4-24).

■ **Note**   The `Camera` class used here is `android.hardware.Camera`, not to be confused with `android.graphics.Camera`. Ensure that you have imported the correct reference within your application.

Listing 4-23. `res/layout/main.xml`

```xml
<?xml version="1.0" encoding="utf-8"?>
<RelativeLayout
    xmlns:android="http://schemas.android.com/apk/res/android"
    android:layout_width="match_parent"
    android:layout_height="match_parent">
    <SurfaceView
        android:id="@+id/preview"
        android:layout_width="match_parent"
        android:layout_height="match_parent" />
</RelativeLayout>
```

Listing 4-24. Activity Displaying Live Camera Preview

```
import android.hardware.Camera;

public class PreviewActivity extends Activity implements
        SurfaceHolder.Callback {

    Camera mCamera;
    SurfaceView mPreview;

    @Override
    public void onCreate(Bundle savedInstanceState) {
        super.onCreate(savedInstanceState);
        setContentView(R.layout.main);

        mPreview = (SurfaceView)findViewById(R.id.preview);
        mPreview.getHolder().addCallback(this);
        //Needed for support prior to Android 3.0
        mPreview.getHolder()
                .setType(SurfaceHolder.SURFACE_TYPE_PUSH_BUFFERS);

        mCamera = Camera.open();
    }

    @Override
    public void onPause() {
        super.onPause();
        mCamera.stopPreview();
    }

    @Override
    public void onDestroy() {
        super.onDestroy();
        mCamera.release();
    }

    //Surface Callback Methods
    @Override
    public void surfaceChanged(SurfaceHolder holder, int format,
            int width, int height) {
        Camera.Parameters params = mCamera.getParameters();
        //Get the device's supported sizes and pick the first,
        // which is the largest
        List<Camera.Size> sizes =
                params.getSupportedPreviewSizes();
        Camera.Size selected = sizes.get(0);
        params.setPreviewSize(selected.width,selected.height);
        mCamera.setParameters(params);

        mCamera.startPreview();
    }
```

```
@Override
public void surfaceCreated(SurfaceHolder holder) {
    try {
        mCamera.setPreviewDisplay(mPreview.getHolder());
    } catch (Exception e) {
        e.printStackTrace();
    }
}

@Override
public void surfaceDestroyed(SurfaceHolder holder) { }
}
```

■ **Note** If you are testing on an emulator, there may not be a camera to preview. Newer versions of the SDK have started to use cameras built into some host machines, but this is not universal. If a camera is unavailable, the emulator displays a fake preview that looks slightly different depending on the version you are running. To verify that this code is working properly, open the Camera application on your specific emulator and take note of what the preview looks like. The same display should appear in this sample. It is always best to test code that integrates with device hardware on an actual device.

In the example, we create a SurfaceView that fills the window and tells it that our activity is to be notified of all the SurfaceHolder callbacks. The camera cannot begin displaying preview information on the surface until it is fully initialized, so we wait until surfaceCreated() gets called to attach the SurfaceHolder of our view to the Camera instance. Similarly, we wait to size the preview and start drawing until the surface has been given its size, which occurs when surfaceChanged() is called.

The camera hardware resources are opened and claimed for this application by calling Camera.open(). An alternate version of this method, introduced in Android 2.3 (API Level 9), takes an integer parameter (valid values being from 0 to getNumberOfCameras() - 1) to determine which camera you would like to access for devices that have more than one. On these devices, the version that takes no parameters will always default to the rear-facing camera.

■ **Important** Some devices, such as Google's Nexus 7 2012 tablet, do not have a rear-facing camera, and so the old implementation of Camera.open() will return null. If you have a Camera application that supports older versions of Android, you will want to branch your code and use the newer API where available to get whatever camera the device has to offer.

Calling Parameters.getSupportedPreviewSizes() returns a list of all the sizes the device will accept, and they are typically ordered largest to smallest. In the example, we pick the first (and, thus, largest) preview resolution and use it to set the size.

■ **Note** In versions earlier than 2.0 (API Level 5), it was acceptable to directly pass the height and width parameters from this method as to Parameters.setPreviewSize(); but in 2.0 and later, the camera will set its preview to only one of the supported resolutions of the device. Attempts otherwise will result in an exception.

Camera.startPreview()begins the live drawing of camera data on the surface. Notice that the preview always displays in a landscape orientation. Prior to Android 2.2 (API Level 8), there was no official way to adjust the rotation of the preview display. For that reason, it is recommended that an activity using the camera preview have its orientation fixed with android:screenOrientation="landscape" in the manifest to match if you must support devices running older versions.

The Camera service can be accessed by only one application at a time. For this reason, it is important that you call Camera.release()as soon as the camera is no longer needed. In the example, we no longer need the camera when the activity is finished, so this call takes place in onDestroy().

Changing Capture Orientation

(API Level 8)

Starting with Android 2.2, the ability to rotate the actual camera preview was added. Applications can now call Camera.setDisplayOrientation()to rotate the incoming data to match the orientation of their activity. Valid values are degrees of 0, 90, 180, and 270; 0 will map to the default landscape orientation. This method affects primarily how the preview data is drawn on the surface before the capture.

To rotate the output data from the camera, use the method setRotation()on Camera.Parameters. This method's implementation depends on the device; it will either rotate the actual image output, update the EXIF data with a rotation parameter, or both.

Overlaying the Preview

We can now add on to the previous example any controls or views that are appropriate to display on top of the camera preview. Let's modify the preview to include a Cancel button and a Snap Photo button. See Listings 4-25 and 4-26.

Listing 4-25. res/layout/main.xml

```xml
<?xml version="1.0" encoding="utf-8"?>
<RelativeLayout
    xmlns:android-"http://schemas.android.com/apk/res/android"
    android:layout_width="match_parent"
    android:layout_height="match_parent">
    <SurfaceView
        android:id="@+id/preview"
        android:layout_width="match_parent"
        android:layout_height="match_parent" />
    <RelativeLayout
        android:layout_width="match_parent"
        android:layout_height="100dip"
        android:layout_alignParentBottom="true"
        android:gravity="center_vertical"
        android:background="#A000">
        <Button
            android:layout_width="100dip"
            android:layout_height="wrap_content"
            android:text="Cancel"
            android:onClick="onCancelClick" />
```

```
        <Button
            android:layout_width="100dip"
            android:layout_height="wrap_content"
            android:layout_alignParentRight="true"
            android:text="Snap Photo"
            android:onClick="onSnapClick" />
    </RelativeLayout>
</RelativeLayout>
```

Listing 4-26. Activity with Photo Controls Added

```java
public class PreviewActivity extends Activity implements
        SurfaceHolder.Callback, Camera.ShutterCallback, Camera.PictureCallback {

    Camera mCamera;
    SurfaceView mPreview;

    @Override
    public void onCreate(Bundle savedInstanceState) {
        super.onCreate(savedInstanceState);
        setContentView(R.layout.main);

        mPreview = (SurfaceView)findViewById(R.id.preview);
        mPreview.getHolder().addCallback(this);
        //Needed for support prior to Android 3.0
        mPreview.getHolder()
                .setType(SurfaceHolder.SURFACE_TYPE_PUSH_BUFFERS);

        mCamera = Camera.open();
    }

    @Override
    public void onPause() {
        super.onPause();
        mCamera.stopPreview();
    }

    @Override
    public void onDestroy() {
        super.onDestroy();
        mCamera.release();
        Log.d("CAMERA","Destroy");
    }

    public void onCancelClick(View v) {
        finish();
    }

    public void onSnapClick(View v) {
        //Snap a photo
        mCamera.takePicture(this, null, null, this);
    }
```

```java
    //Camera Callback Methods
    @Override
    public void onShutter() {
        Toast.makeText(this, "Click!", Toast.LENGTH_SHORT).show();
    }

    @Override
    public void onPictureTaken(byte[] data, Camera camera) {

        //Store the picture off somewhere
        //Here, we chose to save to external storage
        try {
            File directory = Environment.getExternalStoragePublicDirectory(
                    Environment.DIRECTORY_PICTURES);
            FileOutputStream out =
                    new FileOutputStream(new File(directory, "picture.jpg"));
            out.write(data);
            out.flush();
            out.close();
        } catch (FileNotFoundException e) {
            e.printStackTrace();
        } catch (IOException e) {
            e.printStackTrace();
        }

        //Must restart preview
        camera.startPreview();
    }

    //Surface Callback Methods
    @Override
    public void surfaceChanged(SurfaceHolder holder, int format,
            int width, int height) {
        Camera.Parameters params = mCamera.getParameters();
        List<Camera.Size> sizes = params.getSupportedPreviewSizes();
        Camera.Size selected = sizes.get(0);
        params.setPreviewSize(selected.width,selected.height);
        mCamera.setParameters(params);

        mCamera.setDisplayOrientation(90);
        mCamera.startPreview();
    }

    @Override
    public void surfaceCreated(SurfaceHolder holder) {
        try {
            mCamera.setPreviewDisplay(mPreview.getHolder());
        } catch (Exception e) {
            e.printStackTrace();
        }
    }
```

```
@Override
public void surfaceDestroyed(SurfaceHolder holder) { }
}
```

Here we have added a simple, partially transparent overlay to include a pair of controls for camera operation. The action taken by Cancel is nothing to speak of; we simply finish the activity. However, Snap Photo introduces more of the Camera API in manually taking and returning a photo to the application. A user action will initiate the Camera.takePicture() method, which takes a series of callback pointers.

Notice that the activity in this example implements two more interfaces: Camera.ShutterCallback and Camera.PictureCallback. The former is called as near as possible to the moment when the image is captured (when the "shutter" closes), while the latter can be called at multiple instances when different forms of the image are available.

The parameters of takePicture() are a single ShutterCallback and up to three PictureCallback instances. The PictureCallbacks will be called at the following times (in the order they appear as parameters):

- After the image is captured with RAW image data. This may return null on devices with limited memory.

- After the image is processed with scaled image data (known as the POSTVIEW image). This may return null on devices with limited memory.

- After the image is compressed with JPEG image data

This example cares to be notified only when the JPEG is ready. Consequently, that is also the last callback made and the point in time when the preview must be started back up again. If startPreview() is not called again after a picture is taken, then the preview on the surface will remain frozen at the captured image.

■ **Tip** If you would like to guarantee that your application is downloaded only on devices that have the appropriate hardware, you can use the market filter for the camera in your manifest with the following line: <uses-feature android:name="android.hardware.camera" />.

4-7. Recording Audio

Problem

You have an application that needs to use the device microphone to record audio input.

Solution

(API Level 1)

Use MediaRecorder to capture the audio and store it in a file.

How It Works

MediaRecorder is quite simple to use. All you need to provide is some basic information about the file format to use for encoding and where to store the data. Listings 4-27 and 4-28 provide examples of how to record an audio file to the device's SD card, monitoring user actions for when to start and stop.

■ **Important**   In order to use MediaRecorder to record audio input, you must also declare the android.permission.RECORD_AUDIO permission in the application manifest.

Listing 4-27. res/layout/main.xml

```xml
<?xml version="1.0" encoding="utf-8"?>
<LinearLayout
    xmlns:android="http://schemas.android.com/apk/res/android"
    android:orientation="vertical"
    android:layout_width="match_parent"
    android:layout_height="match_parent">
    <Button
        android:id="@+id/startButton"
        android:layout_width="match_parent"
        android:layout_height="wrap_content"
        android:text="Start Recording" />
    <Button
        android:id="@+id/stopButton"
        android:layout_width="match_parent"
        android:layout_height="wrap_content"
        android:text="Stop Recording"
        android:enabled="false" />
</LinearLayout>
```

Listing 4-28. Activity for Recording Audio

```java
public class RecordActivity extends Activity {

    private MediaRecorder recorder;
    private Button start, stop;
    File path;

    @Override
    public void onCreate(Bundle savedInstanceState) {
        super.onCreate(savedInstanceState);
        setContentView(R.layout.main);

        start = (Button)findViewById(R.id.startButton);
        start.setOnClickListener(startListener);
        stop = (Button)findViewById(R.id.stopButton);
        stop.setOnClickListener(stopListener);

        recorder = new MediaRecorder();
        path = new File(Environment.getExternalStorageDirectory(),
                "myRecording.3gp");
```

```java
        resetRecorder();
    }

    @Override
    public void onDestroy() {
        super.onDestroy();
        recorder.release();
    }

    private void resetRecorder() {
        recorder.setAudioSource(MediaRecorder.AudioSource.MIC);
        recorder.setOutputFormat(
                MediaRecorder.OutputFormat.THREE_GPP);
        recorder.setAudioEncoder(
                MediaRecorder.AudioEncoder.DEFAULT);
        recorder.setOutputFile(path.getAbsolutePath());
        try {
            recorder.prepare();
        } catch (Exception e) {
            e.printStackTrace();
        }
    }

    private View.OnClickListener startListener =
            new View.OnClickListener() {
        @Override
        public void onClick(View v) {
            try {
                recorder.start();

                start.setEnabled(false);
                stop.setEnabled(true);
            } catch (Exception e) {
                e.printStackTrace();
            }
        }
    };

    private View.OnClickListener stopListener =
            new View.OnClickListener() {
        @Override
        public void onClick(View v) {
            recorder.stop();
            resetRecorder();

            start.setEnabled(true);
            stop.setEnabled(false);
        }
    };
}
```

The UI for this example is very basic. There are two buttons, and their uses alternate based on the recording state. When the user presses Start, we enable the Stop button and begin recording. When the user presses Stop, we re-enable the Start button and reset the recorder to run again.

MediaRecorder setup is just as straightforward. We create a file on the SD card entitled myRecording.3gp and pass the path in setOutputFile(). The remaining setup methods tell the recorder to use the device microphone as input (AudioSource.MIC), and it will create a 3GP file format for the output using the default encoder.

For now, you could play this audio file by using any of the device's file browser or media player applications. Later, in Recipe 4-10, we will point out how to play audio back through the application as well.

4-8. Capturing Custom Video

Problems

Your application requires video capture, but you need more control over the video recording process than Recipe 4-5 provides.

Solution

(API Level 8)

Use MediaRecorder and Camera directly in concert with each other to create your own video capture activity. This is slightly more complex than working with MediaRecorder in an audio-only context as we did with the previous recipe. We want the user to be able to see the camera preview even during the times that we aren't recording video, and to do this, we must manage the access to the camera between the two objects.

How It Works

Listings 4-29 through 4-31 illustrate an example of recording video to the device's external storage.

Listing 4-29. Partial AndroidManifest.xml

```xml
<uses-permission android:name="android.permission.RECORD_AUDIO" />
<uses-permission android:name="android.permission.CAMERA" />
<uses-permission
    android:name="android.permission.WRITE_EXTERNAL_STORAGE" />

...

<activity
    android:name=".VideoCaptureActivity"
    android:screenOrientation="portrait" >
    <intent-filter>
        <action android:name="android.intent.action.MAIN" />
        <category
            android:name="android.intent.category.LAUNCHER" />
    </intent-filter>
</activity>
```

The key element to point out in the manifest is that we have set our activity orientation to be fixed in portrait. There is also a small host of permissions required to access the camera and to make a recording that includes the audio track.

Listing 4-30. res/layout/main.xml

```xml
<RelativeLayout
    xmlns:android="http://schemas.android.com/apk/res/android"
    android:layout_width="match_parent"
    android:layout_height="match_parent" >

    <Button
        android:id="@+id/button_record"
        android:layout_width="match_parent"
        android:layout_height="wrap_content"
        android:layout_alignParentBottom="true"
        android:onClick="onRecordClick" />

    <SurfaceView
        android:id="@+id/surface_video"
        android:layout_width="match_parent"
        android:layout_height="match_parent"
        android:layout_above="@id/button_record" />
</RelativeLayout>
```

Listing 4-31. Activity Capturing Video

```java
public class VideoCaptureActivity extends Activity implements
        SurfaceHolder.Callback {

    private Camera mCamera;
    private MediaRecorder mRecorder;

    private SurfaceView mPreview;
    private Button mRecordButton;

    private boolean mRecording = false;

    @Override
    public void onCreate(Bundle savedInstanceState) {
        super.onCreate(savedInstanceState);
        setContentView(R.layout.main);

        mRecordButton = (Button) findViewById(R.id.button_record);
        mRecordButton.setText("Start Recording");

        mPreview = (SurfaceView) findViewById(R.id.surface_video);
        mPreview.getHolder().addCallback(this);
        mPreview.getHolder()
                .setType(SurfaceHolder.SURFACE_TYPE_PUSH_BUFFERS);
```

```java
    mCamera = Camera.open();
    //Rotate the preview display to match portrait
    mCamera.setDisplayOrientation(90);
    mRecorder = new MediaRecorder();
}

@Override
protected void onDestroy() {
    mCamera.release();
    mCamera = null;
    super.onDestroy();
}

public void onRecordClick(View v) {
    updateRecordingState();
}

/*
 * Initialize the camera and recorder.
 * The order of these methods is important because MediaRecorder is
 * a strict state machine that moves through states as each method
 * is called.
 */
private void initializeRecorder() throws
        IllegalStateException, IOException {
    //Unlock the camera to let MediaRecorder use it
    mCamera.unlock();
    mRecorder.setCamera(mCamera);
    //Update the source settings
    mRecorder.setAudioSource(
            MediaRecorder.AudioSource.CAMCORDER);
    mRecorder.setVideoSource(
            MediaRecorder.VideoSource.CAMERA);
    //Update the output settings
    File recordOutput = new File(
            Environment.getExternalStorageDirectory(),
            "recorded_video.mp4");
    if (recordOutput.exists()) {
        recordOutput.delete();
    }
    CamcorderProfile cpHigh = CamcorderProfile.get(
            CamcorderProfile.QUALITY_HIGH);
    mRecorder.setProfile(cpHigh);
    mRecorder.setOutputFile(recordOutput.getAbsolutePath());
    //Attach the surface to the recorder to allow
    // preview while recording
    mRecorder.setPreviewDisplay(
            mPreview.getHolder().getSurface());
```

```java
        //Optionally, set limit values on recording
        mRecorder.setMaxDuration(50000); // 50 seconds
        mRecorder.setMaxFileSize(5000000); // Approximately 5MB

        mRecorder.prepare();
    }

    private void updateRecordingState() {
        if (mRecording) {
            mRecording = false;
            //Reset the recorder state for the next recording
            mRecorder.stop();
            mRecorder.reset();
            //Take the camera back to let preview continue
            mCamera.lock();
            mRecordButton.setText("Start Recording");
        } else {
            try {
                //Reset the recorder for the next session
                initializeRecorder();
                //Start recording
                mRecording = true;
                mRecorder.start();
                mRecordButton.setText("Stop Recording");
            } catch (Exception e) {
                //Error occurred initializing recorder
                e.printStackTrace();
            }
        }
    }

    @Override
    public void surfaceCreated(SurfaceHolder holder) {
        //When we get a surface, immediately start camera preview
        try {
            mCamera.setPreviewDisplay(holder);
            mCamera.startPreview();
        } catch (IOException e) {
            e.printStackTrace();
        }
    }

    @Override
    public void surfaceChanged(SurfaceHolder holder, int format,
            int width, int height) { }

    @Override
    public void surfaceDestroyed(SurfaceHolder holder) { }
}
```

When this activity is first created, it obtains an instance of the device's camera and sets its display orientation to match the portrait orientation we defined in the manifest. This call will affect how only the preview content is displayed, not the recorded output; we will talk more about this later in the section. When the activity becomes visible, we will receive the `surfaceCreated()` callback, at which point the `Camera` begins sending preview data.

When the user decides to press the button and start recording, the `Camera` is unlocked and handed over to `MediaRecorder` for use. The recorder is then set up with the proper sources and formats that it should use to capture video, including both a time and file-size limit to keep users from overloading their storage.

■ **Note** It is possible to record video with `MediaRecorder` without having to manage the `Camera` directly, but you will be unable to modify the display orientation and the application will display only preview frames while recording is taking place.

Once recording is finished, the file is automatically saved to external storage and we reset the recorder instance to be ready if the user wants to record again. We also regain control of the `Camera` so that preview frames will continue to draw.

Output Format Orientation

(API Level 9)

In our example, we used `Camera.setDisplayOrientation()` to match the preview display orientation to our portrait activity. However, in some cases, if you play this video back on your computer, the playback will still be in landscape. To fix this problem, we can use the `setOrientationHint()` method on `MediaRecorder`. This method takes a value in degrees that would match up with our display orientation and applies that value to the metadata of the video container file (that is, the 3GP or MP4 file) to notify other video player applications that the video should be oriented a certain way.

This may not be necessary because some video players determine orientation based on which dimension of the video size is smaller. It is for this reason, and to keep compatibility with API Level 8, that we have not added it to the example here.

4-9. Adding Speech Recognition

Problem

Your application needs speech-recognition technology in order to interpret voice input.

Solution

(API Level 3)

Use the classes of the `android.speech` package to leverage the built-in speech-recognition technology of every Android device. Every Android device that is equipped with voice search (available since Android 1.5) provides applications with the ability to use the built-in `SpeechRecognizer` to process voice input.

To activate this process, the application needs only to send a `RecognizerIntent` to the system, where the recognition service will handle recording the voice input and processing it; then it returns to you a list of strings indicating what the recognizer thought it heard.

How It Works

Let's examine this technology in action. See Listing 4-32.

Listing 4-32. Activity Launching and Processing Speech Recognition

```
public class RecognizeActivity extends Activity {

    private static final int REQUEST_RECOGNIZE = 100;

    TextView tv;

    @Override
    public void onCreate(Bundle savedInstanceState) {
        super.onCreate(savedInstanceState);
        tv = new TextView(this);
        setContentView(tv);

        Intent intent = new Intent(
                RecognizerIntent.ACTION_RECOGNIZE_SPEECH);
        intent.putExtra(RecognizerIntent.EXTRA_LANGUAGE_MODEL,
                RecognizerIntent.LANGUAGE_MODEL_FREE_FORM);
        intent.putExtra(RecognizerIntent.EXTRA_PROMPT,
                "Tell Me Your Name");
        try {
            startActivityForResult(intent, REQUEST_RECOGNIZE);
        } catch (ActivityNotFoundException e) {
            //If no recognizer exists, download from Google Play
            showDownloadDialog();
        }
    }

    private void showDownloadDialog() {
        AlertDialog.Builder builder =
                new AlertDialog.Builder(this);
        builder.setTitle("Not Available");
        builder.setMessage(
            "There is no recognition application installed."
            + "  Would you like to download one?");
        builder.setPositiveButton("Yes",
                new DialogInterface.OnClickListener() {
            @Override
            public void onClick(DialogInterface dialog,
                    int which) {
                //Download, for example, Google Voice Search
                Intent marketIntent =
                        new Intent(Intent.ACTION_VIEW);
                marketIntent.setData(
                    Uri.parse("market://details?"
                        + "id=com.google.android.voicesearch") );
            }
        });
```

```
        builder.setNegativeButton("No", null);
        builder.create().show();
    }

    @Override
    protected void onActivityResult(int requestCode,
            int resultCode, Intent data) {
        if(requestCode == REQUEST_RECOGNIZE &&
                resultCode == Activity.RESULT_OK) {
            ArrayList<String> matches =
                    data.getStringArrayListExtra(RecognizerIntent.EXTRA_RESULTS);
            StringBuilder sb = new StringBuilder();
            for(String piece : matches) {
                sb.append(piece);
                sb.append('\n');
            }
            tv.setText(sb.toString());
        } else {
            Toast.makeText(this, "Operation Canceled",
                    Toast.LENGTH_SHORT).show();
        }
    }
}
```

■ **Note**   If you are testing your application in the emulator, beware that neither Google Play nor any voice recognizers will likely be installed. It is best to test the operation of this example on a device.

This example automatically starts the speech-recognition activity upon launch of the application and asks the user, "Tell Me Your Name." Upon receiving speech from the user and processing the result, the activity returns with a list of possible items the user could have said. This list is in order of probability, and so in many cases, it would be prudent to simply call matches.get(0) as the best possible choice and move on. However, this activity takes all the returned values and displays them on the screen for entertainment purposes.

When starting up the SpeechRecognizer, a number of extras can be passed in the intent to customize the behavior. This example uses the two that are most common:

- EXTRA_LANGUAGE_MODEL: A value to help fine-tune the results from the speech processor

    - Typical speech-to-text queries should use the LANGUAGE_MODEL_FREE_FORM option.

    - If shorter request-type queries are being made, LANGUAGE_MODEL_WEB_SEARCH may produce better results.

- EXTRA_PROMPT: This string value displays as the prompt for user speech.

In addition to these, a handful of other parameters may be useful to pass along:

- EXTRA_MAX_RESULTS: This integer sets the maximum number of returned results.

- EXTRA_LANGUAGE: This requests that results be returned in a language other than the current system default. The string value is a valid IETF language tag, such as en-US or es.

4-10. Playing Back Audio/Video

Problem

An application needs to play audio or video content, either local or remote, on the device.

Solution

(API Level 1)

Use the MediaPlayer to play local or streamed media. Whether the content is audio or video, local or remote, MediaPlayer will connect, prepare, and play the associated media efficiently. In this recipe, we will also explore using MediaController and VideoView as simple ways to include interaction and video play in an activity layout.

How It Works

■ **Note**   Before expecting a specific media clip or stream to play, please read the "Android Supported Media Formats" section of the developer documentation to verify support.

Audio Playback

Let's look at a simple example of just using MediaPlayer to play a sound. See Listing 4-33.

Listing 4-33. Activity Playing Local Sound

```
public class PlayActivity extends Activity implements
        MediaPlayer.OnCompletionListener {

    private Button mPlay;
    private MediaPlayer mPlayer;

    @Override
    public void onCreate(Bundle savedInstanceState) {
        super.onCreate(savedInstanceState);

        mPlay = new Button(this);
        mPlay.setText("Play Sound");
        mPlay.setOnClickListener(playListener);

        setContentView(mPlay);
    }
```

```java
@Override
public void onDestroy() {
    super.onDestroy();
    if(mPlayer != null) {
        mPlayer.release();
    }
}

private View.OnClickListener playListener =
        new View.OnClickListener() {
    @Override
    public void onClick(View v) {
        if(mPlayer == null) {
            try {
                mPlayer = MediaPlayer.create(PlayActivity.this,
                        R.raw.sound);
                mPlayer.start();
            } catch (Exception e) {
                e.printStackTrace();
            }
        } else {
            mPlayer.stop();
            mPlayer.release();
            mPlayer = null;
        }
    }
};

//OnCompletionListener Methods
@Override
public void onCompletion(MediaPlayer mp) {
    mPlayer.release();
    mPlayer = null;
}

}
```

This example uses a button to start and stop playback of a local sound file that is stored in the res/raw directory of a project. MediaPlayer.create() is a convenience method with several forms, intended to construct and prepare a player object in one step. The form used in this example takes a reference to a local resource ID, but create() can also be used to access and play a remote resource using MediaPlayer.create(Context context, Uri uri).

Once created, the example starts playing the sound immediately. While the sound is playing, the user may press the button again to stop play. The activity also implements the MediaPlayer.OnCompletionListener interface, so it receives a callback when the playing operation completes normally.

In either case, after play is stopped, the MediaPlayer instance is released. This method allows the resources to be retained only as long as they are in use, and the sound may be played multiple times. To be sure resources are not unnecessarily retained, the player is also released when the activity is destroyed if it still exists.

If your application needs to play many different sounds, you may consider calling reset() instead of release() when playback is over. Remember, though, to still call release() when the player is no longer needed (or the activity goes away).

Audio Player

Beyond just simple playback, what if the application needs to create an interactive experience for the user to be able to play, pause, and seek through the media? Methods are available on MediaPlayer to implement all these functions with custom UI elements, but Android also provides the MediaController view so you don't have to.

Let's construct a simple audio playback activity, as seen in Figure 4-5.

Figure 4-5. *Activity using MediaController*

Listings 4-34 and 4-35 describe the layout and activity source code for this example.

Listing 4-34. res/layout/main.xml

```xml
<?xml version="1.0" encoding="utf-8"?>
<LinearLayout
    xmlns:android="http://schemas.android.com/apk/res/android"
    android:id="@+id/root"
    android:orientation="vertical"
    android:layout_width="match_parent"
    android:layout_height="match_parent">
```

```
    <TextView
        android:layout_width="wrap_content"
        android:layout_height="wrap_content"
        android:layout_gravity="center_horizontal"
        android:text="Now Playing..." />
    <ImageView
        android:id="@+id/coverImage"
        android:layout_width="match_parent"
        android:layout_height="match_parent"
        android:scaleType="centerInside" />
</LinearLayout>
```

Listing 4-35. Activity Playing Audio with `MediaController`

```java
public class PlayerActivity extends Activity implements
        MediaController.MediaPlayerControl,
        MediaPlayer.OnBufferingUpdateListener {

    MediaController mController;
    MediaPlayer mPlayer;
    ImageView coverImage;

    int bufferPercent = 0;

    @Override
    public void onCreate(Bundle savedInstanceState) {
        super.onCreate(savedInstanceState);
        setContentView(R.layout.main);

        coverImage = (ImageView)findViewById(R.id.coverImage);

        mController = new MediaController(this);
        mController.setAnchorView(findViewById(R.id.root));
    }

    @Override
    public void onResume() {
        super.onResume();
        mPlayer = new MediaPlayer();
        //Set the audio data source
        try {
            mPlayer.setDataSource(this,
                    Uri.parse("<URI_TO_REMOTE_AUDIO>"));
            mPlayer.prepare();
        } catch (Exception e) {
            e.printStackTrace();
        }
        //Set an image for the album cover
        coverImage.setImageResource(R.drawable.icon);

        mController.setMediaPlayer(this);
        mController.setEnabled(true);
    }
```

```java
@Override
public void onPause() {
    super.onPause();
    mPlayer.release();
    mPlayer = null;
}

@Override
public boolean onTouchEvent(MotionEvent event) {
    mController.show();
    return super.onTouchEvent(event);
}

//MediaPlayerControl Methods
@Override
public int getBufferPercentage() {
    return bufferPercent;
}

@Override
public int getCurrentPosition() {
    return mPlayer.getCurrentPosition();
}

@Override
public int getDuration() {
    return mPlayer.getDuration();
}

@Override
public boolean isPlaying() {
    return mPlayer.isPlaying();
}

@Override
public void pause() {
    mPlayer.pause();
}

@Override
public void seekTo(int pos) {
    mPlayer.seekTo(pos);
}

@Override
public void start() {
    mPlayer.start();
}
```

```
    //BufferUpdateListener Methods
    @Override
    public void onBufferingUpdate(MediaPlayer mp, int percent) {
        bufferPercent = percent;
    }

    //Android 2.0+ Target Callbacks
    @Override
    public boolean canPause() {
        return true;
    }

    @Override
    public boolean canSeekBackward() {
        return true;
    }

    @Override
    public boolean canSeekForward() {
        return true;
    }

    //Android 4.3+ Target Callbacks
    @Override
    public int getAudioSessionId() {
        return mPlayer.getAudioSessionId();
    }
}
```

This example creates a simple audio player that displays an image for the artist or cover art associated with the audio being played (we just set it to the application icon here). The example still uses a MediaPlayer instance, but this time we are not creating it by using the create() convenience method. Instead we use setDataSource() after the instance is created to set the content. When attaching the content in this manner, the player is not automatically prepared, so we must also call prepare() to ready the player for use.

At this point, the audio is ready to start. We would like MediaController to handle all playback controls, but MediaController can attach to only objects that implement the MediaController.MediaPlayerControl interface. Strangely, MediaPlayer alone does not implement this interface, so we appoint the activity to do that job instead. Seven of the eleven methods included in the interface are actually implemented by MediaPlayer, so we just call down to those directly.

LATE ADDITIONS

If your application is targeting API Level 18 or later, there is one additional method to implement in the MediaController.MediaPlayerControl interface:

getAudioSessionId()

This method is another wrapper around the method already implemented by MediaPlayer. This method is not required if you target a lower API level, but you may implement it for best results when running on later versions.

The final method required to use MediaController is getBufferPercentage(). To obtain this data, the activity is also tasked with implementing MediaPlayer.OnBufferingUpdateListener, which updates the buffer percentage as it changes.

MediaController has one trick to its implementation. It is designed as a widget that floats above an active view in its own window and it is visible for only a few seconds at a time. As a result, we do not instantiate the widget in the XML layout of the content view, but rather in code. The link is made between MediaController and the content view by calling setAnchorView(), which also determines where the controller will show up onscreen. In this example, we anchor it to the root layout object, so it will display at the bottom of the screen when visible. If MediaController is anchored to a child view in the hierarchy, it will display next to that child instead.

Also, because of the controller's separate window, MediaController.show() must not be called from within onCreate(), and doing so will cause a fatal exception. MediaController is designed to be hidden by default and activated by the user. In this example, we override the onTouchEvent() method of the activity to show the controller whenever the user taps the screen. Unless show() is called with a parameter of 0, it will fade out after the amount of time noted by the parameter. Calling show() without any parameter tells it to fade out after the default timeout, which is around 3 seconds.

Now all features of the audio playback are handled by the standard controller widget. The version of setDataSource() used in this example takes a Uri, making it suitable for loading audio from a ContentProvider or a remote location. Keep in mind that all of this works just as well with local audio files and resources using the alternate forms of setDataSource().

Video Player

When playing video, typically a full set of playback controls is required to play, pause, and seek through the content. In addition, MediaPlayer must have a reference to a SurfaceHolder onto which it can draw the frames of the video. As we mentioned in the previous example, Android provides APIs to do all of this and create a custom video-playing experience. However, in many cases the most efficient path forward is to let the classes provided with the SDK, namely MediaController and VideoView, do all the heavy lifting.

Let's take a look at an example of creating a video player in an activity. See Listing 4-36.

Listing 4-36. Activity to Play Video Content

```
public class VideoActivity extends Activity {

    VideoView videoView;
    MediaController controller;

    @Override
    public void onCreate(Bundle savedInstanceState) {
        super.onCreate(savedInstanceState);
        videoView = new VideoView(this);

        videoView.setVideoURI( Uri.parse("URI_TO_REMOTE_VIDEO") );
        controller = new MediaController(this);
        videoView.setMediaController(controller);
        videoView.start();

        setContentView(videoView);
    }
```

```
    @Override
    public void onDestroy() {
        super.onDestroy();
        videoView.stopPlayback();
    }
}
```

■ **Note**   If you are pulling video content from a remote URI, don't forget the INTERNET permission in your manifest!

This example passes the URI of a remote video location to VideoView and tells it to handle the rest. VideoView can be embedded in larger XML layout hierarchies as well, although often it is the only view and is displayed as full screen, so setting it in code as the only view in the layout tree is not uncommon.

With VideoView, interaction with MediaController is much simpler. VideoView implements the MediaController.MediaPlayerControl interface, so no additional glue logic is required to make the controls functional. VideoView also internally handles the anchoring of the controller to itself, so it displays onscreen in the proper location.

Handling Redirects

We have one final note about using the MediaPlayer classes to handle remote content. Many media content servers on the Web today do not publicly expose a direct URL to the video container. Either for the purposes of tracking or security, public media URLs can often redirect one or more times before ending up at the true media content. MediaPlayer does not handle this redirect process, and it will return an error when presented with a redirected URL.

If you are unable to directly retrieve locations of the content you want to display in an application, that application must trace the redirect path before handing the URL to MediaPlayer. Listing 4-37 is an example of a simple AsyncTask tracer that will do the job.

Listing 4-37. RedirectTracerTask

```
public class RedirectTracerTask extends AsyncTask<Uri, Void, Uri> {

    private VideoView mVideo;
    private Uri initialUri;

    public RedirectTracerTask(VideoView video) {
        super();
        mVideo = video;
    }

    @Override
    protected Uri doInBackground(Uri... params) {
        initialUri = params[0];
        String redirected = null;
        try {
            URL url = new URL(initialUri.toString());
            HttpURLConnection connection =
                    (HttpURLConnection)url.openConnection();
```

```
        //Once connected, see where you ended up
        redirected = connection.getHeaderField("Location");

        return Uri.parse(redirected);
    } catch (Exception e) {
        e.printStackTrace();
        return null;
    }
}

@Override
protected void onPostExecute(Uri result) {
    if(result != null) {
        mVideo.setVideoURI(result);
    } else {
        mVideo.setVideoURI(initialUri);
    }
    mVideo.start();
}

}
```

This helper class tracks down the final location by retrieving it out of the HTTP headers. If there were no redirects in the supplied Uri, the background operation would end up returning null, in which case the original Uri would be passed to VideoView.

Making use of this helper class, passing a Uri to the view would now look like the following snippet:

```
VideoView videoView = new VideoView(this);
RedirectTracerTask task = new RedirectTracerTask(videoView);
Uri location = Uri.parse("URI_TO_REMOTE_VIDEO");

task.execute(location);
```

4-11. Playing Sound Effects

Problem

Your application requires short sound effects that need to be played in response to user interaction with very low latency.

Solution

(API Level 1)

Use SoundPool to buffer-load your sound files into memory and play them back quickly in response to the user's actions. The Android framework provides SoundPool as a way to decode small sound files and hold them in memory for rapid and repeated playback. It also has some added features enabling the volume and pitch of each sound to be controlled at runtime. The sounds themselves can be housed in assets, resources, or just in the device's filesystem.

How It Works

Let's take a look at how to use SoundPool to load up some sounds and attach them to Button clicks. See Listings 4-38 and 4-39.

Listing 4-38. `res/layout/main.xml`

```xml
<?xml version="1.0" encoding="utf-8"?>
<LinearLayout
    xmlns:android="http://schemas.android.com/apk/res/android"
    android:layout_width="match_parent"
    android:layout_height="match_parent"
    android:orientation="vertical" >
    <Button
        android:id="@+id/button_beep1"
        android:layout_width="match_parent"
        android:layout_height="wrap_content"
        android:text="Play Beep 1" />
    <Button
        android:id="@+id/button_beep2"
        android:layout_width="match_parent"
        android:layout_height="wrap_content"
        android:text="Play Beep 2" />
        <Button
        android:id="@+id/button_beep3"
        android:layout_width="match_parent"
        android:layout_height="wrap_content"
        android:text="Play Beep 3" />
</LinearLayout>
```

Listing 4-39. Activity with SoundPool

```java
public class SoundPoolActivity extends Activity implements
        View.OnClickListener {

    private AudioManager mAudioManager;
    private SoundPool mSoundPool;
    private SparseIntArray mSoundMap;

    @Override
    protected void onCreate(Bundle savedInstanceState) {
        super.onCreate(savedInstanceState);
        setContentView(R.layout.main);

        //Get the AudioManager system service
        mAudioManager =
                (AudioManager) getSystemService(AUDIO_SERVICE);
        //Set up pool to play only one sound at a time over the
        // standard speaker output.
        mSoundPool =
                new SoundPool(1, AudioManager.STREAM_MUSIC, 0);
```

```java
        findViewById(R.id.button_beep1).setOnClickListener(this);
        findViewById(R.id.button_beep2).setOnClickListener(this);
        findViewById(R.id.button_beep3).setOnClickListener(this);

        //Load each sound and save their streamId into a map
        mSoundMap = new SparseIntArray();
        AssetManager manager = getAssets();
        try {
            int streamId;
            streamId = mSoundPool.load(
                    manager.openFd("Beep1.ogg"), 1);
            mSoundMap.put(R.id.button_beep1, streamId);

            streamId = mSoundPool.load(
                    manager.openFd("Beep2.ogg"), 1);
            mSoundMap.put(R.id.button_beep2, streamId);

            streamId = mSoundPool.load(
                    manager.openFd("Beep3.ogg"), 1);
            mSoundMap.put(R.id.button_beep3, streamId);
        } catch (IOException e) {
            Toast.makeText(this, "Error Loading Sound Effects",
                    Toast.LENGTH_SHORT).show();
        }
    }

    @Override
    public void onDestroy() {
        super.onDestroy();
        mSoundPool.release();
        mSoundPool = null;
    }

    @Override
    public void onClick(View v) {
        //Retrieve the appropriate sound ID
        int streamId = mSoundMap.get(v.getId());
        if (streamId > 0) {
            float streamVolumeCurrent = mAudioManager
                    .getStreamVolume(AudioManager.STREAM_MUSIC);
            float streamVolumeMax = mAudioManager
                    .getStreamMaxVolume(AudioManager.STREAM_MUSIC);
            float volume = streamVolumeCurrent / streamVolumeMax;

            //Play the sound at the specified volume, with no loop
            // and at the standard playback rate
            mSoundPool.play(streamId, volume, volume, 1, 0, 1.0f);
        }
    }
}
```

This example is fairly straightforward. The activity initially loads three sound files from the application's assets directory into the SoundPool. This step decodes them into raw PCM audio and buffers them in memory. Each time a sound is loaded into the pool with load(), a stream identifier is returned that will be used to play the sound later. We attach each sound to play with a particular button by storing them together as a key/value pair inside SparseIntArray.

■ **Note** SparseIntArray (and its sibling SparseBooleanArray) is a key/value store similar to a Map. However, it is significantly more efficient at storing primitive data such as integers because it avoids unnecessary object creation caused by auto-boxing. Whenever possible, these classes should be chosen over Map for best performance.

When the user presses one of the buttons, the stream identifier to play and call SoundPool again to play the audio is retrieved. Because the maxStreams property of the SoundPool constructor was set to 1, if the user taps multiple buttons in quick succession, new sounds will cause older ones to stop. If this value is increased, multiple sounds can be played together.

The parameters of the play() method allow the sound to be configured with each access. Features such as looping the sound or playing it back slower or faster than the original source can be controlled from here:

- Looping supports any finite number of loops, or the value can be set to –1 to loop infinitely.

- Rate control supports any value between 0.5 and 2.0 (half-speed to double-speed).

If you want to use SoundPool to dynamically change which sounds are loaded into memory at a given time, without re-creating the pool, you can use the unload() method to remove items from the pool in order to load() more in. When you are completely done with a SoundPool, call release() to relinquish its native resources.

4-12. Creating a Tilt Monitor

Problem

Your application requires feedback from the device's accelerometer that goes beyond just understanding whether the device is oriented in portrait or landscape.

Solution

(API Level 3)

Use SensorManager to receive constant feedback from the accelerometer sensor. SensorManager provides a generic abstracted interface for working with sensor hardware on Android devices. The accelerometer is just one of many sensors that an application can register to receive regular updates from.

How It Works

■ **Important** Device sensors such as the accelerometer do not exist in the emulator. It is best to test SensorManager code on an Android device.

This example activity registers with SensorManager for accelerometer updates and displays the data onscreen. The raw X/Y/Z data is displayed in a TextView at the bottom of the screen, but in addition the device's "tilt" is visualized through a simple graph of four views in a TableLayout. See Listings 4-40 and 4-41.

■ **Note** It is also recommended that you add android:screenOrientation="portrait" or android:scree nOrientation="landscape" to the application's manifest to keep the activity from trying to rotate as you move and tilt the device.

Listing 4-40. res/layout/main.xml

```xml
<?xml version="1.0" encoding="utf-8"?>
<RelativeLayout
    xmlns:android="http://schemas.android.com/apk/res/android"
    android:layout_width="match_parent"
    android:layout_height="match_parent">
    <TableLayout
        android:layout_width="match_parent"
        android:layout_height="match_parent"
        android:stretchColumns="0,1,2">
        <TableRow
            android:layout_weight="1">
            <View
                android:id="@+id/top"
                android:layout_column="1" />
        </TableRow>
        <TableRow
            android:layout_weight="1">
            <View
                android:id="@+id/left"
                android:layout_column="0" />
            <View
                android:id="@+id/right"
                android:layout_column="2" />
        </TableRow>
        <TableRow
            android:layout_weight="1">
            <View
                android:id="@+id/bottom"
                android:layout_column="1" />
        </TableRow>
    </TableLayout>
    <TextView
        android:id="@+id/values"
        android:layout_width="match_parent"
        android:layout_height="wrap_content"
        android:layout_alignParentBottom="true" />
</RelativeLayout>
```

Listing 4-41. Tilt Monitoring Activity

```java
public class TiltActivity extends Activity implements
        SensorEventListener {

    private SensorManager mSensorManager;
    private Sensor mAccelerometer;
    private TextView valueView;
    private View mTop, mBottom, mLeft, mRight;

    public void onCreate(Bundle savedInstanceState) {
        super.onCreate(savedInstanceState);
        setContentView(R.layout.main);

        mSensorManager =
                (SensorManager)getSystemService(SENSOR_SERVICE);
        mAccelerometer = mSensorManager.getDefaultSensor(
                Sensor.TYPE_ACCELEROMETER);

        valueView = (TextView)findViewById(R.id.values);
        mTop = findViewById(R.id.top);
        mBottom = findViewById(R.id.bottom);
        mLeft = findViewById(R.id.left);
        mRight = findViewById(R.id.right);
    }

    protected void onResume() {
        super.onResume();
        mSensorManager.registerListener(this, mAccelerometer,
            SensorManager.SENSOR_DELAY_UI);
    }

    protected void onPause() {
        super.onPause();
        mSensorManager.unregisterListener(this);
    }

    public void onAccuracyChanged(Sensor sensor, int accuracy) { }

    public void onSensorChanged(SensorEvent event) {
        final float[] values = event.values;
        float x = values[0] / 10;
        float y = values[1] / 10;
        int scaleFactor;

        if(x > 0) {
            scaleFactor = (int)Math.min(x * 255, 255);
            mRight.setBackgroundColor(Color.TRANSPARENT);
            mLeft.setBackgroundColor(
                    Color.argb(scaleFactor, 255, 0, 0));
        } else {
```

```
            scaleFactor = (int)Math.min(Math.abs(x) * 255, 255);
            mRight.setBackgroundColor(
                    Color.argb(scaleFactor, 255, 0, 0));
            mLeft.setBackgroundColor(Color.TRANSPARENT);
        }

        if(y > 0) {
            scaleFactor = (int)Math.min(y * 255, 255);
            mTop.setBackgroundColor(Color.TRANSPARENT);
            mBottom.setBackgroundColor(
                    Color.argb(scaleFactor, 255, 0, 0));
        } else {
            scaleFactor = (int)Math.min(Math.abs(y) * 255, 255);
            mTop.setBackgroundColor(
                    Color.argb(scaleFactor, 255, 0, 0));
            mBottom.setBackgroundColor(Color.TRANSPARENT);
        }
        //Display the raw values
        valueView.setText(String.format(
                "X: %1$1.2f, Y: %2$1.2f, Z: %3$1.2f",
                values[0], values[1], values[2]));
    }
}
```

The orientation of the three axes on the device accelerometer is as follows, from the perspective of looking at the device screen, upright in portrait:

- *X*: Horizontal axis with positive pointing to the right

- *Y*: Vertical axis with positive pointing up

- *Z*: Perpendicular axis with positive pointing back at you

When the activity is visible to the user (between onResume() and onPause()), it registers with SensorManager to receive updates about the accelerometer. When registering, the last parameter to registerListener() defines the update rate. The chosen value, SENSOR_DELAY_UI, is the fastest recommended rate to receive updates and still directly modify the UI with each update.

With each new sensor value, the onSensorChanged() method of our registered listener is called with a SensorEvent value; this event contains the X/Y/Z acceleration values.

■ **Quick science note** An *accelerometer* measures the acceleration due to forces applied. When a device is at rest, the only force operating on it is the force of gravity (~9.8 m/s^2). The output value on each axis is the product of this force (pointing down to the ground) and each orientation vector. When the two are parallel, the value will be at its maximum (~9.8–10). When the two are perpendicular, the value will be at its minimum (~0.0). Therefore, a device lying flat on a table will read ~0.0 for both X and Y, and ~9.8 for Z.

The example application displays the raw acceleration values for each axis in the TextView at the bottom of the screen. In addition, four Views are arranged in a grid (top/bottom/left/right pattern), and we proportionally adjust the background color of this grid based on the orientation. When the device is perfectly flat, both X and Y should be close to zero and the entire screen will be black. As the device tilts, the squares on the low side of the tilt will start to glow red until they are completely red once the device orientation reaches upright in either position.

■ **Tip** Try modifying this example with some of the other rate values, such as SENSOR_DELAY_NORMAL. Notice how the change affects the update rate in the example.

In addition, you can shake the device and see alternating grid boxes highlight as the device accelerates in each direction.

SENSOR BATCHING

In Android 4.4 and later, applications can request that the sensors they interact with run in *batch mode* to reduce overall power consumption when you need to monitor the sensor for an extended period of time. In this mode, sensor events may be queued up in hardware buffers for a period without waking up the application processor each time.

To enable batch mode for a sensor, simply utilize a version of SensorManager.registerListener() that takes a maxBatchReportLatencyUs parameter. This parameter tells the hardware how long events can be queued before the batch is sent to the application.

Additionally, if the application needs to get the current batch prior to the next interval, a flush() can be called on SensorManager to force the sensor to deliver what it has to the listener.

Not all sensors will support batching on all devices, and in these cases the implementation will fall back to the default continuous operation mode.

4-13. Monitoring Compass Orientation

Problem

Your application wants to know which major direction the user is facing by monitoring the device's compass sensor.

Solution

(API Level 3)

SensorManager comes to the rescue once again. Android doesn't provide a "compass" sensor exactly; instead it includes the necessary methods to infer where the device is pointing based on other sensor data. In this case, the device's magnetic field sensor will be used with the accelerometer to ascertain in which direction the user is facing.

We can then ask SensorManager for the user's orientation with respect to the Earth by using getOrientation().

How It Works

■ **Important**   Device sensors such as the accelerometer do not exist in the emulator. It is best to test SensorManager code on an Android device.

As with the previous accelerometer example, we use SensorManager to register for updates on all sensors of interest (in this case, there are two) and to then process the results in onSensorChanged(). This example calculates and displays the user orientation from the device camera's point of view, as it would be required for an application such as augmented reality. See Listings 4-42 and 4-43.

Listing 4-42. res/layout/main.xml

```xml
<?xml version="1.0" encoding="utf-8"?>
<RelativeLayout
    xmlns:android="http://schemas.android.com/apk/res/android"
    android:layout_width="match_parent"
    android:layout_height="match_parent">
    <TextView
        android:id="@+id/direction"
        android:layout_width="wrap_content"
        android:layout_height="wrap_content"
        android:layout_centerInParent="true"
        android:textSize="64sp"
        android:textStyle="bold" />
    <TextView
        android:id="@+id/values"
        android:layout_width="wrap_content"
        android:layout_height="wrap_content"
        android:layout_alignParentBottom="true" />
</RelativeLayout>
```

Listing 4-43. Activity Monitoring User Orientation

```java
public class CompassActivity extends Activity implements SensorEventListener {

    private SensorManager mSensorManager;
    private Sensor mAccelerometer, mField;
    private TextView valueView, directionView;

    private float[] mGravity = new float[3];
    private float[] mMagnetic = new float[3];

    public void onCreate(Bundle savedInstanceState) {
        super.onCreate(savedInstanceState);
        setContentView(R.layout.main);

        mSensorManager = (SensorManager)getSystemService(SENSOR_SERVICE);
        mAccelerometer =
                mSensorManager.getDefaultSensor(Sensor.TYPE_ACCELEROMETER);
        mField =
                mSensorManager.getDefaultSensor(Sensor.TYPE_MAGNETIC_FIELD);
```

```
        valueView = (TextView)findViewById(R.id.values);
        directionView = (TextView)findViewById(R.id.direction);
    }

    protected void onResume() {
        super.onResume();
        mSensorManager.registerListener(this, mAccelerometer,
                SensorManager.SENSOR_DELAY_UI);
        mSensorManager.registerListener(this, mField,
                SensorManager.SENSOR_DELAY_UI);
    }

    protected void onPause() {
        super.onPause();
        mSensorManager.unregisterListener(this);
    }

    //Allocate data arrays once and reuse
    float[] temp = new float[9];
    float[] rotation = new float[9];
    float[] values = new float[3];

    private void updateDirection() {
        //Load rotation matrix into R
        SensorManager.getRotationMatrix(temp, null, mGravity, mMagnetic);
        //Remap to camera's point of view
        SensorManager.remapCoordinateSystem(temp,
                SensorManager.AXIS_X, SensorManager.AXIS_Z, rotation);
        //Return the orientation values
        SensorManager.getOrientation(rotation, values);
        //Convert to degrees
        for (int i=0; i < values.length; i++) {
            Double degrees = (values[i] * 180) / Math.PI;
            values[i] = degrees.floatValue();
        }
        //Display the compass direction
        directionView.setText( getDirectionFromDegrees(values[0]) );
        //Display the raw values
        valueView.setText(
                String.format("Azimuth: %1$1.2f, Pitch: %2$1.2f, Roll: %3$1.2f",
                values[0], values[1], values[2]));
    }

    private String getDirectionFromDegrees(float degrees) {
        if(degrees >= -22.5 && degrees < 22.5) { return "N"; }
        if(degrees >= 22.5 && degrees < 67.5) { return "NE"; }
        if(degrees >= 67.5 && degrees < 112.5) { return "E"; }
        if(degrees >= 112.5 && degrees < 157.5) { return "SE"; }
        if(degrees >= 157.5 || degrees < -157.5) { return "S"; }
```

```
        if(degrees >= -157.5 && degrees < -112.5) { return "SW"; }
        if(degrees >= -112.5 && degrees < -67.5) { return "W"; }
        if(degrees >= -67.5 && degrees < -22.5) { return "NW"; }

        return null;
    }

    public void onAccuracyChanged(Sensor sensor, int accuracy) { }

    public void onSensorChanged(SensorEvent event) {
        //Copy the latest values into the correct array
        switch(event.sensor.getType()) {
        case Sensor.TYPE_ACCELEROMETER:
            System.arraycopy(event.values, 0,
                    mGravity, 0,
                    event.values.length);
            break;
        case Sensor.TYPE_MAGNETIC_FIELD:
            System.arraycopy(event.values, 0,
                    mMagnetic, 0,
                    event.values.length);
            break;
        default:
            return;
        }

        if(mGravity != null && mMagnetic != null) {
            updateDirection();
        }
    }
}
```

This example activity displays the three raw values returned by the sensor calculation at the bottom of the screen in real time. In addition, the compass direction associated with where the user is currently facing is converted and displayed center-stage. As updates are received from the sensors, local copies of the latest values from each are maintained. As soon as we have received at least one reading from both sensors of interest, we allow the UI to begin updating.

updateDirection()is where all the heavy lifting takes place. SensorManager.getOrientation() provides the output information we require to display direction. The method returns no data, and instead an empty float array is passed in for the method to fill in three angle values, and they represent (in order):

- *Azimuth*: Angle of rotation about an axis pointing directly into the Earth. This is the value of interest in the example.

- *Pitch*: Angle of rotation about an axis pointing west

- *Roll*: Angle of rotation about an axis pointing at magnetic north

One of the parameters passed to getOrientation() is a float array representing a rotation matrix. A *rotation matrix* is a representation of how the current coordinate system of the devices is oriented, so the method may provide appropriate rotation angles based on its reference coordinates. The rotation matrix for the device orientation is obtained by using getRotationMatrix(), which takes the latest values from the accelerometer and magnetic-field sensor as input. Like getOrientation(), it also returns void; an empty float array of length 9 or 16 (to represent a 3×3 or 4×4 matrix) must be passed in as the first parameter for the method to fill in.

Finally, we want the output of the orientation calculation to be specific to the camera's point of view. To further transform the obtained rotation, we use the remapCoordinateSystem() method. This method takes four parameters (in order):

1. Input array representing the matrix to transform

2. Which axis of the world (globe) is aligned with the device's x axis

3. Which axis of the world (globe) is aligned with the device's y axis

4. Empty array to fill in the result

In our example, we want to leave the x axis untouched, so we map X to X. However, we would like to align the device's y axis (vertical axis) to the world's z axis (the one pointing into the Earth). This orients the rotation matrix we receive to match up with the device being held vertically upright, as if the user is using the camera and looking at the preview on the screen.

With the angular data calculated, we do some data conversion and display the result on the screen. The unit output of getOrientation() is radians, so we first have to convert each result to degrees before displaying it. In addition, we need to convert the azimuth value to a compass direction; getDirectionFromDegrees() is a helper method to return the proper direction based on the range the current reading falls within. Going in a full clockwise circle, the azimuth will read from 0 to 180 degrees from north to south. Continuing around the circle, the azimuth will read –180 to 0 degrees rotating from south to north.

4-14. Retrieving Metadata from Media Content

Problem

Your application needs to gather thumbnail screenshots or other metadata from media content on the device.

Solution

(API Level 10)

Use MediaMetadataRetriever to read media files and return useful information. This class can read and track information such as album and artist data or data about the content itself, such as the size of a video. In addition, you can use it to grab a screenshot of any frame within a video file, either at a specific time or just any frame that Android considers representative.

MediaMetadataRetriever is a great option for applications that work with lots of media content from the device and that need to display extra data about the media to enrich the user interface.

How It Works

Listings 4-44 and 4-45 show how to access this extra metadata on the device.

Listing 4-44. `res/layout/main.xml`

```xml
<RelativeLayout
    xmlns:android="http://schemas.android.com/apk/res/android"
    android:layout_width="match_parent"
    android:layout_height="match_parent" >
    <Button
        android:id="@+id/button_select"
        android:layout_width="match_parent"
        android:layout_height="wrap_content"
        android:text="Pick Video"
        android:onClick="onSelectClick" />
    <TextView
        android:id="@+id/text_metadata"
        android:layout_width="wrap_content"
        android:layout_height="wrap_content"
        android:layout_below="@id/button_select"
        android:layout_margin="15dp" />
    <ImageView
        android:id="@+id/image_frame"
        android:layout_width="wrap_content"
        android:layout_height="wrap_content"
        android:layout_alignParentBottom="true"
        android:layout_centerHorizontal="true"
        android:layout_margin="10dp" />
</RelativeLayout>
```

Listing 4-45. Activity with MediaMetadataRetriever

```java
public class MetadataActivity extends Activity {
    private static final int PICK_VIDEO = 100;

    private ImageView mFrameView;
    private TextView mMetadataView;

    @Override
    public void onCreate(Bundle savedInstanceState) {
        super.onCreate(savedInstanceState);
        setContentView(R.layout.main);

        mFrameView = (ImageView) findViewById(R.id.image_frame);
        mMetadataView =
                (TextView) findViewById(R.id.text_metadata);
    }

    @Override
    protected void onActivityResult(int requestCode,
            int resultCode, Intent data) {
        if (requestCode == PICK_VIDEO
                && resultCode == RESULT_OK
                && data != null) {
```

```java
            Uri video = data.getData();
            MetadataTask task = new MetadataTask(this, mFrameView,
                    mMetadataView);
            task.execute(video);
        }
    }

    public void onSelectClick(View v) {
        Intent intent = new Intent(Intent.ACTION_GET_CONTENT);
        intent.setType("video/*");
        startActivityForResult(intent, PICK_VIDEO);
    }

    public static class MetadataTask
            extends AsyncTask<Uri, Void, Bundle> {
        private Context mContext;
        private ImageView mFrame;
        private TextView mMetadata;
        private ProgressDialog mProgress;

        public MetadataTask(Context context, ImageView frame,
                TextView metadata) {
            mContext = context;
            mFrame = frame;
            mMetadata = metadata;
        }

        @Override
        protected void onPreExecute() {
            mProgress = ProgressDialog.show(mContext, "",
                    "Analyzing Video File...", true);
        }

        @Override
        protected Bundle doInBackground(Uri... params) {
            Uri video = params[0];
            MediaMetadataRetriever retriever =
                    new MediaMetadataRetriever();
            retriever.setDataSource(mContext, video);

            Bitmap frame = retriever.getFrameAtTime();

            String date = retriever.extractMetadata(
                MediaMetadataRetriever.METADATA_KEY_DATE);
            String duration = retriever.extractMetadata(
                MediaMetadataRetriever.METADATA_KEY_DURATION);
            String width = retriever.extractMetadata(
                MediaMetadataRetriever.METADATA_KEY_VIDEO_WIDTH);
            String height = retriever.extractMetadata(
                MediaMetadataRetriever.METADATA_KEY_VIDEO_HEIGHT);
```

```java
        Bundle result = new Bundle();
        result.putParcelable("frame", frame);
        result.putString("date", date);
        result.putString("duration", duration);
        result.putString("width", width);
        result.putString("height", height);

        return result;
    }

    @Override
    protected void onPostExecute(Bundle result) {
        if (mProgress != null) {
            mProgress.dismiss();
            mProgress = null;
        }

        Bitmap frame = result.getParcelable("frame");
        mFrame.setImageBitmap(frame);
        String metadata = String.format("Video Date: %s\n"
                + "Video Duration: %s\nVideo Size: %s x %s",
                result.getString("date"),
                result.getString("duration"),
                result.getString("width"),
                result.getString("height") );
        mMetadata.setText(metadata);
    }
}

}
```

In this example, the user can select a video file from the device to process. Upon receipt of a valid video Uri, the activity starts an AsyncTask to parse some metadata out of the video. We create an AsyncTask for this purpose because the process can take a few seconds or more to complete, and we don't want to block the UI thread while this is going on.

The background task creates a new MediaMetadataRetriever and sets the selected video as its data source. We then call the method getFrameAtTime() to return a Bitmap image of a frame in the video. This method is useful for creating thumbnails for a video in your UI. The version we call takes no parameters, and the frame it returns is semirandom. If you are more interested in a specific frame, an alternate version of the method can take the presentation time (in microseconds) of the video where you would like a frame. In this case, it will return a key frame in the video that is closest to the requested time.

In addition to the frame image, we also gather some basic information about the video, including when it was created, how long it is, and how big it is. All the resulting data is packaged into a bundle and passed back from the background thread. The onPostExecute() method of the task is called on the main thread, so we use it to update the UI with the data we retrieved.

4-15. Detecting User Motion

Problem

You would like your application to respond to changes in user behavior, such as whether the device is sitting still, or if the user is currently active and in motion.

Solution

(API Level 9)

Google Play Services includes features to monitor user activity via the `ActivityRecognitionClient`. The user activity tracking service is a low-power method of receiving regular updates about what a user is doing. The service periodically monitors local sensor data on the device in short bursts rather than relying on high-power means like web services or GPS.

Using this API, applications will receive updates for one of the following events:

- `IN_VEHICLE`: The user is likely driving or riding in a vehicle, such as a car, bus, or train.

- `ON_BICYCLE`: The user is likely on a bicycle.

- `ON_FOOT`: The user is likely walking or running.

- `STILL`: The user, or at least the device, is currently sitting still.

- `TILTING`: The device has recently been tilted. This can happen when the device is picked up from rest or an orientation change occurs.

- `UNKNOWN`: There is not enough data to determine with significant confidence what the user is currently doing.

When working with `ActivityRecognitionClient`, an application initiates periodic updates by calling `requestActivityUpdates()`. The parameters this method takes define the frequency of updates to the application and a `PendingIntent` that will be used to trigger each event.

An application can pass any frequency interval, in milliseconds; passing a value of zero will send updates as fast as possible to the application. This rate is not guaranteed by Google Play Services; samples can be delayed if the service requires more sensor samples to make.a particular determination. In addition, if multiple applications are requesting activity updates, Google Play Services will deliver updates to all applications at the fastest rate requested.

Each event includes a list of `DetectedActivity` instances, which wrap the activity type (one of the options described previously) and the level of confidence the service has in its prediction. The list is sorted by confidence, so the most probable user activity is first.

■ **Important**   User-activity tracking is part of the Google Play Services library; it is not part of the native SDK at any platform level. However, any application targeting API Level 9 or later on devices inside the Google Play ecosystem can use the tracking library. For more information on including Google Play Services in your project, reference `https://developer.android.com/google/play-services/setup.html`.

How It Works

Let's take a look at a basic example application that monitors user activity changes, logs them to the display, and includes a safety precaution that locks the user out from the application if the user attempts to access it while in a car or on a bicycle. We'll start with Listing 4-46, which is a snippet of the `AndroidManfest.xml` that reveals the permissions we need to work with this service.

■ **Note**   This example uses `ActionBarActivity` from the AppCompat Library to allow the use of fragments prior to API Level 11.

Listing 4-46. `AndroidManifest.xml`

```xml
<?xml version="1.0" encoding="utf-8"?>
<manifest xmlns:android="http://schemas.android.com/apk/res/android"
    package="com.androidrecipes.usermotionactivity">

    <!-- Required permission to User Activity Recognition -->
    <uses-permission
        android:name="com.google.android.gms.permission.ACTIVITY_RECOGNITION" />

    <application
        android:allowBackup="true"
        android:icon="@drawable/ic_launcher"
        android:label="@string/app_name"
        android:theme="@style/AppTheme" >

        <!-- Required boilerplate for Google Play Services -->
        <meta-data
            android:name="com.google.android.gms.version"
            android:value="@integer/google_play_services_version" />

        <activity
            android:name=".MainActivity"
            android:label="User Activity"
            android:screenOrientation="portrait" >
            <intent-filter>
                <action android:name="android.intent.action.MAIN" />
                <category android:name="android.intent.category.LAUNCHER" />
            </intent-filter>
        </activity>

        <service android:name=".UserMotionService" />
    </application>

</manifest>
```

You can see that we must declare a custom permission in the manifest specifically to read activity recognition data from Google Play Services. We also need to be sure to have the `<meta-data>` element defining the required version. This allows the client library to determine whether the device is running the proper Play Services or requires an update. Listings 4-47 and 4-48 describe the activity we will use.

Listing 4-47. `res/layout/activity_main.xml`

```xml
<FrameLayout
    xmlns:android="http://schemas.android.com/apk/res/android"
    android:layout_width="match_parent"
    android:layout_height="match_parent">
    <!-- List with transcript enabled to autoscroll content -->
    <ListView
        android:id="@+id/list"
        android:layout_width="match_parent"
        android:layout_height="match_parent"
        android:stackFromBottom="true"
        android:transcriptMode="normal" />

    <!-- Safety Blocking View -->
    <!-- Clickable to consume touch events when visible -->
    <TextView
        android:id="@+id/blocker"
        android:layout_width="match_parent"
        android:layout_height="match_parent"
        android:gravity="center"
        android:clickable="true"
        android:textSize="32sp"
        android:textColor="#F55"
        android:text="Do not operate your device in a vehicle!"
        android:background="#C333"
        android:visibility="gone" />
</FrameLayout>
```

Listing 4-48. Activity Displaying User Motion

```java
public class MainActivity extends ActionBarActivity implements
        ServiceConnection,
        UserMotionService.OnActivityChangedListener,
        GooglePlayServicesClient.ConnectionCallbacks,
        GooglePlayServicesClient.OnConnectionFailedListener {
    private static final String TAG = "UserActivity";

    private Intent mServiceIntent;
    private PendingIntent mCallbackIntent;
    private UserMotionService mService;

    private ActivityRecognitionClient mRecognitionClient;
    //Custom list adapter to display our results
    private ActivityAdapter mListAdapter;

    private View mBlockingView;
```

```
@Override
protected void onCreate(Bundle savedInstanceState) {
    super.onCreate(savedInstanceState);
    setContentView(R.layout.activity_main);

    mBlockingView = findViewById(R.id.blocker);

    //Construct a simple list adapter that will display all the
    // incoming activity change events from the service.
    ListView list = (ListView) findViewById(R.id.list);
    mListAdapter = new ActivityAdapter(this);
    list.setAdapter(mListAdapter);

    //When the list is clicked, display all the probable activities
    list.setOnItemClickListener(new AdapterView.OnItemClickListener() {
        @Override
        public void onItemClick(AdapterView<?> parent, View v,
                int position, long id) {
            showDetails(mListAdapter.getItem(position));
        }
    });

    //Verify Play Services is active and up-to-date
    int resultCode =
            GooglePlayServicesUtil.isGooglePlayServicesAvailable(this);
    switch (resultCode) {
        case ConnectionResult.SUCCESS:
            Log.d(TAG, "Google Play Services is ready to go!");
            break;
        default:
            showPlayServicesError(resultCode);
            return;
    }

    //Create a client instance for talking to Google Services
    mRecognitionClient = new ActivityRecognitionClient(this, this, this);
    //Create an Intent to bind to the service
    mServiceIntent = new Intent(this, UserMotionService.class);
    //Create a PendingIntent that Google Services will use for callbacks
    mCallbackIntent = PendingIntent.getService(this, 0,
            mServiceIntent, PendingIntent.FLAG_UPDATE_CURRENT);
}

@Override
protected void onResume() {
    super.onResume();
    //Connect to Google Services and our Service
    mRecognitionClient.connect();
    bindService(mServiceIntent, this, BIND_AUTO_CREATE);
}
```

```java
@Override
protected void onPause() {
    super.onPause();
    //Disconnect from all services
    mRecognitionClient.removeActivityUpdates(mCallbackIntent);
    mRecognitionClient.disconnect();

    disconnectService();
    unbindService(this);
}

/** ServiceConnection Methods */

public void onServiceConnected(ComponentName name, IBinder service) {
    //Attach ourselves to our Service as a callback for events
    mService = ((LocalBinder) service).getService();
    mService.setOnActivityChangedListener(this);
}

@Override
public void onServiceDisconnected(ComponentName name) {
    disconnectService();
}

private void disconnectService() {
    if (mService != null) {
        mService.setOnActivityChangedListener(null);
    }
    mService = null;
}

/** Google Services Connection Callbacks */

@Override
public void onConnected(Bundle connectionHint) {
    //We must wait until the services are connected
    // to request any updates.
    mRecognitionClient.requestActivityUpdates(5000, mCallbackIntent);
}

@Override
public void onDisconnected() {
    Log.w(TAG, "Google Services Disconnected");
}

@Override
public void onConnectionFailed(ConnectionResult result) {
    Log.w(TAG, "Google Services Connection Failure");
}
```

```java
/** OnActivityChangedListener Methods */

@Override
public void onUserActivityChanged(int bestChoice, int bestConfidence,
        ActivityRecognitionResult newActivity) {
    //Add latest event to the list
    mListAdapter.add(newActivity);
    mListAdapter.notifyDataSetChanged();

    //Determine user action based on our custom algorithm
    switch (bestChoice) {
        case DetectedActivity.IN_VEHICLE:
        case DetectedActivity.ON_BICYCLE:
            mBlockingView.setVisibility(View.VISIBLE);
            break;
        case DetectedActivity.ON_FOOT:
        case DetectedActivity.STILL:
            mBlockingView.setVisibility(View.GONE);
            break;
        default:
            //Ignore other states
            break;
    }
}

/*
 * Utility that builds a simple Toast with all the probable
 * activity choices with their confidence values
 */
private void showDetails(ActivityRecognitionResult activity) {
    StringBuilder sb = new StringBuilder();
    sb.append("Details:");
    for(DetectedActivity element : activity.getProbableActivities()) {
        sb.append("\n"+UserMotionService.getActivityName(element)
                + ", " + element.getConfidence() + "% sure");
    }

    Toast.makeText(this, sb.toString(), Toast.LENGTH_SHORT).show();
}

/*
 * ListAdapter to display each activity result we receive from the service
 */
private static class ActivityAdapter extends
        ArrayAdapter<ActivityRecognitionResult> {

    public ActivityAdapter(Context context) {
        super(context, android.R.layout.simple_list_item_1);
    }
```

```
    @Override
    public View getView(int position, View convertView, ViewGroup parent) {
        if (convertView == null) {
            convertView = LayoutInflater.from(getContext())
                .inflate(android.R.layout.simple_list_item_1, parent, false);
        }
        //Display the most probable activity with its confidence in the list
        TextView tv = (TextView) convertView;
        ActivityRecognitionResult result = getItem(position);
        DetectedActivity newActivity = result.getMostProbableActivity();
        String entry = DateFormat.format("hh:mm:ss", result.getTime())
                + ": " + UserMotionService.getActivityName(newActivity)
                + ", " + newActivity.getConfidence() + "% confidence";
        tv.setText(entry);

        return convertView;
    }
}

/*
 * When Play Services is missing or at the wrong version, the client
 * library will assist with a dialog to help the user update.
 */
private void showPlayServicesError(int errorCode) {
    // Get the error dialog from Google Play Services
    Dialog errorDialog = GooglePlayServicesUtil.getErrorDialog(
            errorCode,
            this,
            1000 /* RequestCode */);
    // If Google Play Services can provide an error dialog
    if (errorDialog != null) {
        // Create a new DialogFragment for the error dialog
        SupportErrorDialogFragment errorFragment =
                SupportErrorDialogFragment.newInstance(errorDialog);
        // Show the error dialog in the DialogFragment
        errorFragment.show(
                getSupportFragmentManager(),
                "Activity Tracker");
    }
}
}
```

In this example, our first order of business is to check whether Google Play Services is available on the device and is up-to-date. With that verified, we can create our ActivityRecognitionClient, an intent we will need to connect to our service (which we haven't seen yet), and the PendingIntent that we will give the recognition services to use in calling us back.

■ **Note** Do not confuse Activity, the application component that displays UI, with *activity* as it is used in this context to describe a user's physical activity. The word is thrown around a lot in this API, so keep in mind the difference.

When the application is brought to the foreground, we make a connection request to the recognition service. This process is asynchronous, and we will later receive a call in onConnected() when the connection is complete. To ensure that we don't drain unnecessary power, we remove these updates when going into the background.

During those same events, we bind and unbind with our own service so that binding is active only while we are in the foreground. We will see shortly the significance this service will have in the overall application.

■ **Tip** With bound services, onServiceDisconnected() is called only if the service crashes or disconnects unexpectedly. Any cleanup you wish to do when disconnecting explicitly must also be done alongside unbindService().

Once the recognition service is connected to us, we initiate updates using requestActivityUpdates() with an interval of 5 seconds and our PendingIntent, which describes where the updates will go. In our case, the PendingIntent is set to trigger the UserMotionService, and the code for this service is in Listing 4-49.

Listing 4-49. Service Receiving Motion Updates

```java
public class UserMotionService extends IntentService {
    private static final String TAG = "UserMotionService";

    /*
     *                      .
     * Callback interface for detected activity type changes
     */
    public interface OnActivityChangedListener{
        public void onUserActivityChanged(int bestChoice,
                int bestConfidence,
                ActivityRecognitionResult newActivity);
    }

    /* Last detected activity type */
    private DetectedActivity mLastKnownActivity;

    /*
     * Marshals requests from the background thread so the
     * callbacks can be made on the main (UI) thread.
     */
    private CallbackHandler mHandler;
    private static class CallbackHandler extends Handler {
        /* Callback for activity changes */
        private OnActivityChangedListener mCallback;

        public void setCallback(
                OnActivityChangedListener callback) {
            mCallback = callback;
        }

        @Override
        public void handleMessage(Message msg) {
            if (mCallback != null) {
```

```
                //Read payload data out of the message and
                // fire callback
                ActivityRecognitionResult newActivity =
                        (ActivityRecognitionResult) msg.obj;
                mCallback.onUserActivityChanged(
                        msg.arg1,
                        msg.arg2,
                        newActivity);
            }
        }
    }

    public UserMotionService() {
        //String is used to name the background thread created
        super("UserMotionService");
        mHandler = new CallbackHandler();
    }

    public void setOnActivityChangedListener(
            OnActivityChangedListener listener) {
        mHandler.setCallback(listener);
    }

    @Override
    public void onDestroy() {
        super.onDestroy();
        Log.w(TAG, "Service is stopping...");
    }

    /*
     * Incoming action events from the framework will come
     * in here.  This is called on a background thread, so
     * we can do long processing here if we wish.
     */
    @Override
    protected void onHandleIntent(Intent intent) {
        if (ActivityRecognitionResult.hasResult(intent)) {
            //Extract the result from the Intent
            ActivityRecognitionResult result =
                    ActivityRecognitionResult.extractResult(intent);
            DetectedActivity activity =
                    result.getMostProbableActivity();
            Log.v(TAG, "New User Activity Event");

            //If the highest probability is UNKNOWN, but the
            // confidence is low, check if another exists and
            // select it instead.
            if (activity.getType() == DetectedActivity.UNKNOWN
                    && activity.getConfidence() < 60
                    && result.getProbableActivities().size() > 1){
```

```java
            //Select the next probable element
            activity = result.getProbableActivities().get(1);
        }

        //On a change in activity, alert the callback
        if (mLastKnownActivity == null
                || mLastKnownActivity.getType()
                        != activity.getType()
                || mLastKnownActivity.getConfidence()
                        != activity.getConfidence()) {
            //Pass the results to the main thread in a Message
            Message msg = Message.obtain(null,
                    0,                          //what
                    activity.getType(),         //arg1
                    activity.getConfidence(),   //arg2
                    result);                    //obj
            mHandler.sendMessage(msg);
        }
        mLastKnownActivity = activity;
    }
}

/*
 * This is called when the Activity wants to bind to the
 * service.  We have to provide a wrapper around this instance
 * to pass it back.
 */
@Override
public IBinder onBind(Intent intent) {
    return mBinder;
}

/*
 * This is a simple wrapper that we can pass to the Activity
 * to allow it direct access to this service.
 */
private LocalBinder mBinder = new LocalBinder();
public class LocalBinder extends Binder {
    public UserMotionService getService() {
        return UserMotionService.this;
    }
}

/*
 * Utility to get a good display name for each state
 */
public static String getActivityName(
        DetectedActivity activity) {
    switch(activity.getType()) {
        case DetectedActivity.IN_VEHICLE:
            return "Driving";
```

```
            case DetectedActivity.ON_BICYCLE:
                return "Biking";
            case DetectedActivity.ON_FOOT:
                return "Walking";
            case DetectedActivity.STILL:
                return "Not Moving";
            case DetectedActivity.TILTING:
                return "Tilting";
            case DetectedActivity.UNKNOWN:
            default:
                return "No Clue";
        }
    }
}
```

UserMotionService is an IntentService, which is a service that forwards all intent commands to a background thread it creates and processes them in the onHandleIntent() method. Its primary advantage is a built-in mechanism to queue up intent requests and process them in order, in the background, via this method.

When the activity binds to this service, it will be automatically started and returned via onBind() to the caller. The activity will receive the service instance in onServiceConnected(), where we will register the activity as a callback for user activity change events determined in the service. Once the activity unbinds from the service, it will automatically stop itself as well.

Once the point is reached where the activity has registered for update events from Google Play Services, the framework will start triggering the PendingIntent on a regular basis, which results in onHandleIntent() in our service.

For each event, we use the utility methods on ActivityRecognitionResult to unpack the data from the incoming intent. We then determine what the most probable user activity was. We have customized the algorithm a little bit, in that if the most probable activity is UNKNOWN, but the confidence in that decision is low, we will pick the next best option to return instead. This pattern will work well for any additional custom decision logic you would like to put into your application as well.

Once we have selected the user activity to compare, we check whether this is the same activity type or a change in activity has occurred. In the case of a change, we want to post a callback to the activity that registered itself when we were bound. We use a Handler instead of calling the method directly because onHandleIntent() is running on a background thread, and we want to post our callback on the main thread in case the activity (or other listeners) want to do any work that involves updating the UI.

Finally, Listing 4-50 reminds us of the requirements we need; primarily, we must be sure that the Play Services library is included as a dependency in our module build.

Listing 4-50. Partial build.gradle

```
apply plugin: 'com.android.application'

android {
    compileSdkVersion 18
    buildToolsVersion "20.0.0"

    defaultConfig {
        applicationId "com.androidrecipes.usermotionactivity"
        ...
    }

    ...
}
```

356

```
dependencies {
    compile 'com.android.support:support-v4:18.0.0'
    compile 'com.google.android.gms:play-services:+'
}
```

4-16. Making Applications Context Aware

Problem

You would like your application to react to the context of the user in order to provide a better user experience. For instance, your application should give the user a notification if they start walking or have the application perform a certain action when the headphones are plugged in.

Solution

(API Level 9)

Google Play Services contain an Awareness API that lets a developer query for a number of context signals, enabling context aware applications. An example of the signals that one can register for is state of headphones (plugged in or not), location, user activity (walking, running etc.) and time. These can be combined to form a virtual fence that is triggered when all the parameters are true.

In this example, we will simply demonstrate how the API works by providng a simply user interface for selecting a trigger, activating the fence and receiving a callback once triggered.

Since this is part of the Google Play Services APIs, we start by connecting to the Google API Client after constructing it with the Awareness API.

Listing 4-51. Setting up the Google API Client with Awareness API

```
mApiClient = new GoogleApiClient.Builder(this)
        .addApi(Awareness.API)
        .addConnectionCallbacks(this)
        .build();
mApiClient.connect();
```

Once we receive the onConnected() callback, we can start registering an AwarenesFence. In this example, we provide a simple set of RadioButtons where the user can select the type of fence they want.

Listing 4-52. XML Layout for Radio Button

```
<?xml version="1.0" encoding="utf-8"?>
<LinearLayout
    xmlns:android="http://schemas.android.com/apk/res/android"
    xmlns:tools="http://schemas.android.com/tools"
    android:id="@+id/activity_main"
    android:layout_width="match_parent"
    android:layout_height="match_parent"
    android:gravity="center"
    android:orientation="vertical"
    tools:context="com.androidrecipes.awareness.AwarnessActivity">
```

```
<TextView
    android:layout_width="wrap_content"
    android:layout_height="wrap_content"
    android:text="Select awareness fence type."
    android:textAppearance="@style/TextAppearance.AppCompat.Title"/>

<RadioGroup
    android:id="@+id/fenceSelection"
    android:layout_width="match_parent"
    android:layout_height="wrap_content">

    <RadioButton
        android:id="@+id/beaconFence"
        android:layout_width="wrap_content"
        android:layout_height="wrap_content"
        android:layout_weight="1"
        android:text="Beacon"/>

    <RadioButton
        android:id="@+id/walkingFence"
        android:layout_width="wrap_content"
        android:layout_height="wrap_content"
        android:layout_weight="1"
        android:text="Walking"/>

    <RadioButton
        android:id="@+id/headphoneFence"
        android:layout_width="wrap_content"
        android:layout_height="wrap_content"
        android:layout_weight="1"
        android:text="Headphone (plugged in)"/>

    <RadioButton
        android:id="@+id/locationFence"
        android:layout_width="wrap_content"
        android:layout_height="wrap_content"
        android:layout_weight="1"
        android:text="Location (Google HQ)"/>

    <RadioButton
        android:id="@+id/lunchtimeFence"
        android:layout_width="wrap_content"
        android:layout_height="wrap_content"
        android:layout_weight="1"
        android:text="Lunchtime (daily)"/>
</RadioGroup>
```

```
    <Button
        android:id="@+id/fenceActivateBtn"
        android:layout_width="wrap_content"
        android:layout_height="wrap_content"
        android:text="Activate"
        android:onClick="doActivateFence"/>

</LinearLayout>
```

The button fenceActiveBtn will be used to enable the fence once the user has selected. The onClick method doActivateFence() will implement the code for creating and registering the AwarenessFence.

Listing 4-53. The Click Callback for Registering an AwarenessFence

```
public void doActivateFence(View view) {
    Intent intent = new Intent(getApplicationContext(),
                                AwarenessTriggeredService.class);
    intent.setAction(AwarenessTriggeredService.ACTION_AWARENESS_TRIGGERED);
    AwarenessFence awarenessFence;
    String fenceKey;
    RadioGroup fenceSelection
                    = (RadioGroup) findViewById(R.id.fenceSelection);
    int checkedRadioButtonId = fenceSelection.getCheckedRadioButtonId();
    switch (checkedRadioButtonId) {
        case R.id.beaconFence:
            awarenessFence = BeaconFence.found(BeaconState
                        .TypeFilter.with(BEACON_NAMESPACE, BEACON_TYPE));
            fenceKey = KEY_BEACON;
            break;
        case R.id.walkingFence:
            awarenessFence = DetectedActivityFence
                        .starting(DetectedActivityFence.WALKING);
            fenceKey = KEY_WALKING;
            break;
        case R.id.headphoneFence:
            awarenessFence = HeadphoneFence.pluggingIn();
            fenceKey = KEY_HEADPHONE;
            break;
        case R.id.locationFence:
            awarenessFence
                = LocationFence.entering(37.4218, -122.0840, 500);
            fenceKey = KEY_LOCATION;
            break;
        case R.id.lunchtimeFence:
            awarenessFence
                = TimeFence.inDailyInterval(TimeZone.getDefault(),
                                            START_TIME, END_TIME);
            fenceKey = KEY_LUNCHTIME;
            break;
        default:
            return;
    }
```

```
    PendingIntent pendingIntent = PendingIntent
            .getService(getApplicationContext(), 0,
                        intent, PendingIntent.FLAG_CANCEL_CURRENT);
    FenceUpdateRequest fenceUpdateRequest = new FenceUpdateRequest.Builder()
            .addFence(fenceKey, awarenessFence, pendingIntent)
            .build();
    Awareness.FenceApi.updateFences(mApiClient, fenceUpdateRequest);
}
```

In the previous code we see how we construct an AwarenessFence based on the user's selection from the radio buttons. Once we have the fence, we create a PendingIntent that will be sent to the AwarenessTriggeredService when the fence has been triggered.

Listing 4-54. The IntentService Triggered by an AwarenessFence

```
public class AwarenessTriggeredService extends IntentService {
    static final String ACTION_AWARENESS_TRIGGERED
                    = "com.androidrecipes.awareness.AWARENESS_TRIGGERED";

    public AwarenessTriggeredService() {
        super("AwarenessTriggeredService");
    }

    @Override
    protected void onHandleIntent(Intent intent) {
        if (intent != null
                && ACTION_AWARENESS_TRIGGERED.equals(intent.getAction())) {
            FenceState fenceState = FenceState.extract(intent);
            if (fenceState.getCurrentState() != FenceState.TRUE) {
                return;
            }

            String fenceKey = fenceState.getFenceKey();
            GoogleApiClient googleApiClient
                = new GoogleApiClient.Builder(this)
                    .addApi(Awareness.API)
                    .build();
            ConnectionResult connectionResult
                        = googleApiClient.blockingConnect();
            if (connectionResult.isSuccess()) {
                switch (fenceKey) {
                    case AwarnessActivity.KEY_BEACON:
                        showBeaconState(googleApiClient);
                        break;
                    case AwarnessActivity.KEY_WALKING:
                        showIsWalkingInfo(googleApiClient);
                        break;
                    case AwarnessActivity.KEY_LOCATION:
                        showLocationInfo(googleApiClient);
                        break;
```

```
                case AwarnessActivity.KEY_HEADPHONE:
                    showHeadphoneInfo(googleApiClient);
                    break;
                case AwarnessActivity.KEY_LUNCHTIME:
                    showLunchtimeInfo();
                    break;
            }
        }
    }
}

private void showLunchtimeInfo() {
    showNotification("Lunchtime!", "It is now.");
}

private void showHeadphoneInfo(GoogleApiClient googleApiClient) {
    HeadphoneState headphoneState = Awareness.SnapshotApi
            .getHeadphoneState(googleApiClient)
            .await(5, TimeUnit.SECONDS).getHeadphoneState();

    String stateDescription;
    if (headphoneState.getState() == HeadphoneState.PLUGGED_IN) {
        stateDescription = "Headphones are plugged in.";
    } else {
        stateDescription = "Headphones are NOT plugged in.";
    }
    showNotification("Headphone state changed", stateDescription);
}

private void showLocationInfo(GoogleApiClient googleApiClient) {
    Location location = Awareness.SnapshotApi
            .getLocation(googleApiClient)
            .await(5, TimeUnit.SECONDS).getLocation();
    showNotification("Location changed!",
                    "New location: " + location.toString());
}

private void showIsWalkingInfo(GoogleApiClient googleApiClient) {
    ActivityRecognitionResult activityRecognitionResult = Awareness
            .SnapshotApi.getDetectedActivity(googleApiClient)
            .await(5, TimeUnit.SECONDS).getActivityRecognitionResult();

    if (activityRecognitionResult.getMostProbableActivity().getType()
            == DetectedActivity.WALKING) {
        showNotification("Activity detected!",
                        "You are currently walking!");
    }
}
```

```
private void showBeaconState(GoogleApiClient googleApiClient) {
    BeaconState.TypeFilter typeFilter = BeaconState.TypeFilter
            .with(AwarnessActivity.BEACON_NAMESPACE,
                    AwarnessActivity.BEACON_TYPE);
    PendingResult<BeaconStateResult> pendingResult
        = Awareness.SnapshotApi
                    .getBeaconState(googleApiClient, typeFilter);
    BeaconState beaconState
        = pendingResult.await(5, TimeUnit.SECONDS)
                        .getBeaconState();
    BeaconState.BeaconInfo beaconInfo
        = beaconState.getBeaconInfo().get(0);
    showNotification("Beacon found!", "Content: " + Base64
            .encodeToString(beaconInfo.getContent(), Base64.DEFAULT));
}

private void showNotification(String title, String content) {
    Notification notification = new NotificationCompat.Builder(this)
            .setContentTitle(title)
            .setContentText(content)
            .setSmallIcon(R.drawable.ic_mood_black_24dp)
            .build();
    NotificationManagerCompat.from(this).notify(101, notification);
}
}
```

When a fence is triggered that matches the user's selection, our AwarenessTriggeredService will be started and receive an Intent. We can now use the static method FenceState.extract() to extract information about the fence that was triggered. In order to retrieve detailed information about the signal triggered, we use the snapshot version of the Awareness API. Finally, we create a notification based on the snapshot data we just retrieved.

The Awareness API can be seen as a simplified replacement for many other, more advanced APIs. If the features in your applications can be fulfilled by the more limited set of signals and data provided by the Awareness API, it will save a lot of work and testing, as Google has implemented a lot of the boilerplate that is otherwise necessary.

4-17. Authenticating Users Using Fingerprint Reader

Problem

You want to add a level of security to your application using the built-in fingerprint reader in order to protect unauthorized access to app-specific data or features.

Solution

(API Level 23)

Starting in Marshmallow (API level 23), Android has native support for fingerprint readers. An application developer can use these through an API that makes it easy to add additional authentication and protcection within Android applications.

The first thing we need to do is to retrieve the FingerprintManager service from the system services. Next, we check that we ask for permission for using the fingerprint reader before we continue setting up the reader.

Once we know we have permission from the user, we check call hasEnrolledFingerprints() on the FingerprintManager to ensure that the user has set up the fingerprint reader with their fingerprints. If the user hasn't yet enrolled their fingerprint with the reader, this is a good time to provide instruction and direct them to the system settings application to do so first.

The final step for setting up the fingerprint reader is to to call authenticate() on the FingerprintManager. In this example we leave the CryptoObject parameter null, but this can be used if we want to combine the FingerprintManager with the Android KeyStore for signing, encrypting, and decrypting data. The second parameter is our cancellation signal that we use to abort any ongoing authentication if necessary. The flags parameter is always null in this version. We finally pass an AuthenticationCallback and a Handler that will be used for performing the authentication process. In this example, we create a Handler with dedicated HandlerThread, in case we want to do some additional processing off the main thread in the authentication callback.

Listing 4-55. The IntentService Triggered by an AwarenessFence

```
mCancellationSignal = new CancellationSignal();
HandlerThread handlerThread = new HandlerThread("AuthThread");
handlerThread.start();
mAuthHandler = new Handler(handlerThread.getLooper());
mFingerprintManager.authenticate(null, mCancellationSignal, 0,
    new FingerprintManager.AuthenticationCallback() {
        @Override
        public void onAuthenticationError(int errorCode, CharSequence errString) {
            super.onAuthenticationError(errorCode, errString);
            Log.d(TAG, "onAuthenticationError: " + errString);
        }

        @Override
        public void onAuthenticationHelp(int helpCode, CharSequence helpString) {
            super.onAuthenticationHelp(helpCode, helpString);
            Log.d(TAG, "onAuthenticationHelp: " + helpString);
        }

        @Override
        public void onAuthenticationSucceeded(FingerprintManager.AuthenticationResult
        result) {
            super.onAuthenticationSucceeded(result);
            Log.d(TAG, "onAuthenticationSucceeded");
            showResult("Authentication succeeded!");
        }

        @Override
        public void onAuthenticationFailed() {
            super.onAuthenticationFailed();
            Log.d(TAG, "onAuthenticationFailed");
            showResult("Authentication failed!");
        }
    },
    mAuthHandler);
```

As can be seen in the previous example, there are several callback methods. In this case, we are only interested in success or failure. In a real-life application, these callbacks can be used as additional authentication or confirmation to more sensitive features inside the app.

4-18. Scanning QR Codes Using Vision API

Problem

You need to integrate scanning of QR codes using the camera in your application.

Solution

(API Level 9)

Google Play Services contains a number of useful APIs. One of the latest additions is the Vision API, which provides a simplified method for detecting faces, barcodes, or text in images. The images can be either regular bitmaps or frames captured from the smartphone camera.

In this example we will use the Vision API in Google Play Services to scan for QR codes using the smartphone camera. Although the Vision API is part of Google Play Services, we don't need to set up and connect to the Play Services client to access this API. Instead, we must first create a BarcodeDetector and give it a Processor that will receive the detection result. Finally, we must create a CameraSource, which we connect to a SurfaceView for displaying the preview frames.

Listing 4-56. Setting up the Vision API for QR Code Scanning

```
private void setupQrCodeScanning() {
    // Check for Camera permission!
    if (ActivityCompat.checkSelfPermission(this, Manifest.permission.CAMERA)
            != PackageManager.PERMISSION_GRANTED) {
        ActivityCompat.requestPermissions(this,
                new String[]{Manifest.permission.CAMERA},
                REQUEST_CODE_PERMISSIONS);
        return;
    }

    mQrCodeDetector = new BarcodeDetector.Builder(this)
            .setBarcodeFormats(Barcode.QR_CODE)
            .build();
    Detector.Processor<Barcode> barcodeProcessor = new MyQRCodeProcessor();
    mQrCodeDetector.setProcessor(barcodeProcessor);

    mCameraSource = new CameraSource.Builder(this, mQrCodeDetector)
            .setAutoFocusEnabled(true)
            .setFacing(CameraSource.CAMERA_FACING_BACK)
            .build();

    SurfaceView surfaceView
                = (SurfaceView) findViewById(R.id.camera_preview);
    surfaceView.getHolder().addCallback(new SurfaceHolder.Callback() {
        @SuppressWarnings("MissingPermission")
```

```
    @Override
    public void surfaceCreated(SurfaceHolder surfaceHolder) {
        try {
            mCameraSource.start(surfaceHolder);
        } catch (IOException e) {
            Log.e(TAG, "Failed to start camera preview.", e);
        }
    }

    @Override
    public void surfaceChanged(SurfaceHolder surfaceHolder, int i,
                               int i1, int i2) {

    }

    @Override
    public void surfaceDestroyed(SurfaceHolder surfaceHolder) {
        mCameraSource.stop();
        mQrCodeDetector.release();
    }
});
}
```

We need to tell the BarcodeDetector what type of barcodes we want to scan for. In this case we are interested in QR codes, but many other types of barcodes are also supported.

The CameraSource needs to be configured as well. In this case we tell the API to use the back facing camera and to enable auto focus.

Note that we add a SurfaceHolder.Callback to our SurfaceView. This lets us know when the SurfaceView is ready to display the preview frames from the camera. Once that happens, we can start the process of scanning for QR codes.

We provide our own simple implementation of the Processor interface, MyQRCodeProcessor, which iterates over the result in the receiveDetections() method and displays the result in a regular TextView.

Listing 4-57. Postprocessing of the Scanning Result

```
private class MyQRCodeProcessor implements Detector.Processor<Barcode> {
    @Override
    public void release() {

    }

    @Override
    public void receiveDetections(Detector.Detections<Barcode> detections) {
        SparseArray<Barcode> detectedItems = detections.getDetectedItems();
        int size = detectedItems.size();
        for (int i = 0; i < size; i++) {
            final Barcode barcode = detectedItems.get(i);
            if (barcode != null) {
                Log.d(TAG, "Found QR code: " + barcode.rawValue);
                if (barcode.format == Barcode.URL) {
                    Log.d(TAG, "Found URL: " + barcode.url.url);
```

```
                    Runnable runnable = new Runnable() {
                        public void run() {
                            ((TextView) findViewById(R.id.qr_code_result))
                                            .setText(barcode.url.url);
                        }
                    };
                    runOnUiThread(runnable);
                }
            }
        }
    }
}
```

In this example we are not doing much more than scanning and displaying results of QR codes that contain URLs. The other supported detection types in the Vision API are faces and text. For faces, you might want to draw an overlay on the SurfaceView to indicate which face was dected and for text you might want to do some processing. Both of these cases are outside the scope of this example, but using the content from earlier sections you should be able to construct fairly advanced image detection and processing features.

Summary

This collection of recipes exposed how to integrate maps, user location, and device sensor data about the user's surroundings into your Android applications. You learned about the many additional APIs that Google provides to Android devices that exist within the Google Play ecosystem. We also discussed how to utilize the device's camera and microphone, allowing users to capture, and sometimes interpret, what's around them. We also showed, using the media APIs, how to take media content, either captured locally by the user or downloaded remotely from the Web, and play it back from within your applications. We showed how to use the Awareness API to capture context-relevant information to better adapt an application to the users need. Using a built-in fingerprint reader on an Android smartphone, you can secure data and authenticate a user from within an application. Finally, we covered how to use the Vision API to scan for QR codes. In the next chapter, we will discuss how to use Android's many persistence techniques to store nonvolatile data on the device.

■ ■ ■

CHAPTER 5

Persisting Data

Even in the midst of grand architectures designed to shift as much user data into the cloud as possible, the transient nature of mobile applications will always require that at least some user data be persisted locally on the device. This data may range from cached responses from a web service guaranteeing offline access to preferences that the user has set for specific application behaviors. Android provides a series of helpful frameworks to take the pain out of using files and databases to persist data.

5-1. Making a Preference Screen

Problem

You need to create a simple way to store, change, and display user preferences and settings within your application.

Solution

(API Level 9)

Use `PreferenceActivity` and an XML `Preference` hierarchy to provide the user interface, key/value combinations, and persistence all at once. Using this method will create a user interface that is consistent with the Settings application on Android devices, and it will keep users' experiences consistent with their expectations.

Within the XML, an entire set of one or more screens can be defined with the associated settings displayed and grouped into categories by using the `PreferenceScreen`, `PreferenceCategory`, and associated `Preference` elements. The activity can then load this hierarchy for the user by using very little code.

How It Works

Figure 5-1 illustrates the interface this example will have. We will be building a preferences interface that consists of two screens, a primary and a secondary.

© Dave Smith and Erik Hellman 2016

D. Smith and E. Hellman, *Android Recipes*, DOI 10.1007/978-1-4842-2259-1_5

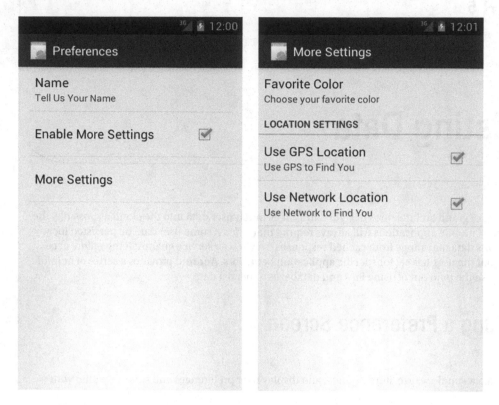

Figure 5-1. *The root* PreferenceScreen *(left) displays first. If the user checks Enable More Settings and taps More Settings, the secondary screen (right) displays.*

Listings 5-1 and 5-2 show the basic settings for an Android application. The XML defines two screens with a variety of all the common preference types that this framework supports. Notice that one screen is nested inside the other; the internal screen will be displayed when the user clicks on its associated list item from the root screen.

Listing 5-1. res/xml/settings.xml

```xml
<?xml version="1.0" encoding="utf-8"?>
<PreferenceScreen xmlns:android="http://schemas.android.com/apk/res/android">
    <EditTextPreference
        android:key="namePref"
        android:title="Name"
        android:summary="Tell Us Your Name"
        android:defaultValue="Apress" />
    <CheckBoxPreference
        android:key="morePref"
        android:title="Enable More Settings"
        android:defaultValue="false" />
    <PreferenceScreen
        android:key="moreScreen"
        android:title="More Settings"
        android:dependency="morePref">
```

```xml
        <ListPreference
            android:key="colorPref"
            android:title="Favorite Color"
            android:summary="Choose your favorite color"
            android:entries="@array/color_names"
            android:entryValues="@array/color_values"
            android:defaultValue="GRN" />
        <PreferenceCategory
            android:title="Location Settings">
            <CheckBoxPreference
                android:key="gpsPref"
                android:title="Use GPS Location"
                android:summary="Use GPS to Find You"
                android:defaultValue="true" />
            <CheckBoxPreference
                android:key="networkPref"
                android:title="Use Network Location"
                android:summary="Use Network to Find You"
                android:defaultValue="true" />
        </PreferenceCategory>
    </PreferenceScreen>
</PreferenceScreen>
```

Listing 5-2. res/values/arrays.xml

```xml
<?xml version="1.0" encoding="utf-8"?>
<resources>
    <string-array name="color_names">
        <item>Black</item>
        <item>Red</item>
        <item>Green</item>
    </string-array>
    <string-array name="color_values">
        <item>BLK</item>
        <item>RED</item>
        <item>GRN</item>
    </string-array>
</resources>
```

Notice first the convention used to create the XML file. Although this resource could be inflated from any directory (such as res/layout), the convention is to put it into a generic directory for the project titled simply xml.

Also, notice that we provide an android:key attribute for each Preference object instead of android:id. When each stored value is referenced elsewhere in the application through a SharedPreferences object, it will be accessed using the key. In addition, PreferenceActivity includes the findPreference() method for obtaining a reference to an inflated Preference in Java code, which is more efficient than using findViewById(); findPreference() also takes the key as a parameter.

When inflated, the root PreferenceScreen presents a list with the following three options (in order):

1. *Name*: This is an instance of EditTextPreference, which stores a string value. Tapping this item will present a text box so that the user can type a new preference value.

2. *Enable More Settings*: This is an instance of CheckBoxPreference, which stores a Boolean value. Tapping this item will toggle the checked status of the check box.

3. *More Settings*: Tapping this item will load another PreferenceScreen with more items.

When the user taps the More Settings item, a second screen is displayed with three more items: a ListPreference item and two more CheckBoxPreferences grouped together by a PreferenceCategory. PreferenceCategory is simply a way to create section breaks and headers in the list for grouping actual preference items.

ListPreference is the final preference type used in the example. This item requires two array parameters (although they can both be set to the same array) that represent a set of choices the user may pick from. The android:entries array is the list of human-readable items to display, while the android:entryValues array represents the actual value to be stored.

All the preference items may optionally have a default value set for them as well. This value is not automatically loaded, however. It will load the first time this XML file is inflated when the PreferenceActivity is displayed *or* when a call to PreferenceManager.setDefaultValues() is made.

Now let's take a look at how a PreferenceActivity would load and manage this. See Listing 5-3.

Listing 5-3. PreferenceActivity in Action

```java
public class SettingsActivity extends PreferenceActivity {

    @Override
    public void onCreate(Bundle savedInstanceState) {
        super.onCreate(savedInstanceState);
        //Load preference data from XML
        addPreferencesFromResource(R.xml.settings);
    }
}
```

All that is required to display the preferences and allow the user to make changes is a call to addPreferencesFromResource(). There is no need to call setContentView() when we extend PreferenceActivity; addPreferencesFromResource() inflates the XML and manages displaying the content in a list. However, a custom layout may be provided as long as it contains a ListView with the android:id="@android:id/list" attribute set, which is where PreferenceActivity will load the preference items.

Preference items can also be placed in the list for the sole purpose of controlling access. In the example, we put the Enable More Settings item in the list just to allow the user to enable or disable access to the second PreferenceScreen. To accomplish this, our nested PreferenceScreen includes the android:dependency attribute, which links its enabled state to the state of another preference. Whenever the referenced preference is either not set or false, this preference will be disabled.

Loading Defaults and Accessing Preferences

Typically, a PreferenceActivity such as this one is not the root of an application. Often, if default values are set, they may need to be accessed by the rest of the application before the user ever visits Settings (the first case under which the defaults will load). Therefore, it can be helpful to put a call to the following method elsewhere in your application to ensure that the defaults are loaded prior to being used:

```
PreferenceManager.setDefaultValues(Context context, int resId, boolean readAgain);
```

This method may be called multiple times, and the defaults will not get loaded over again. It may be placed in the main activity so it is called on first launch, or perhaps it could be in a common place where the application can call it before any access to shared preferences.

Preferences that are stored by using this mechanism are put into the default shared preferences object, which can be accessed with any Context pointer by using the following:

```
PreferenceManager.getDefaultSharedPreferences(Context context);
```

An example activity that would load the defaults set in our previous example and access some of the current values stored would look like Listing 5-4.

Listing 5-4. Activity Loading Preference Defaults

```java
public class HomeActivity extends Activity {

    @Override
    public void onCreate(Bundle savedInstanceState) {
        super.onCreate(savedInstanceState);
        setContentView(R.layout.main);

        //Load the preference defaults
        PreferenceManager.setDefaultValues(this, R.xml.settings, false);
    }

    @Override
    public void onResume() {
        super.onResume();
        //Access the current settings
        SharedPreferences settings =
                PreferenceManager.getDefaultSharedPreferences(this);

        String name = settings.getString("namePref", "");
        boolean isMoreEnabled = settings.getBoolean("morePref", false);
    }
}
```

Calling setDefaultValues() will create a value in the preference store for any item in the XML file that includes an android:defaultValue attribute. This will make those defaults accessible to the application, even if the user has not yet visited the settings screen.

These values can then be accessed using a set of typed accessor functions on the SharedPreferences object. Each of these accessor methods requires both the name of the preference key and a default value to be returned if a value for the preference key does not yet exist.

Using PreferenceFragment

(API Level 11)

Starting with Android 3.0, a new method of creating preference screens was introduced in the form of PreferenceFragment. This class is not in the Support Library, so it can be used as a replacement for PreferenceActivity only if your application targets a minimum of API Level 11. Listings 5-5 and 5-6 modify the previous example to use PreferenceFragment instead.

Listing 5-5. Activity Containing Fragments

```
public class MainActivity extends Activity {

    @Override
    protected void onCreate(Bundle savedInstanceState) {
        super.onCreate(savedInstanceState);

        FragmentTransaction ft = getFragmentManager().beginTransaction();
        ft.add(android.R.id.content, new SettingsFragment());
        ft.commit();
    }
}
```

Listing 5-6. New PreferenceFragment

```
public class SettingsFragment extends PreferenceFragment {

    @Override
    public void onCreate(Bundle savedInstanceState) {
        super.onCreate(savedInstanceState);
        //Load preference data from XML
        addPreferencesFromResource(R.xml.settings);
    }
}
```

Now the preferences themselves are housed inside a PreferenceFragment, which manages them in the same way as before. The other required change is that a fragment cannot live on its own; it must be contained inside an activity, so we have created a new root activity where the fragment is attached.

The Android framework has moved to fragments for preferences in order to more easily allow multiple preference hierarchies (perhaps representing different top-level categories of settings) to be easily displayed inside a single activity rather than forcing the user to jump in and out of each category with multiple activity instances.

KITKAT SECURITY

As of Android 4.4, a PreferenceActivity must override the isValidFragment() method in applications targeting SDK Level 19 or higher. This method prevents external applications from performing fragment injection by supplying an incorrect class name in the Intent extras directed at an exported PreferenceActivity that hosts PreferenceFragment instances.

In applications with a lower SDK target, this method will always return true for compatibility, which also leaves the security hole open. It is prudent for developers to update their target to 19+ and implement this method to validate that only fragments you expect can be instantiated. If isValidFragment() is not overridden on an app with an updated target SDK, an exception will be thrown.

5-2. Displaying Custom Preferences

Problem

The Preference elements provided by the framework are not flexible enough, and you need to add a more specific UI for modifying the value.

Solution

(API Level 9)

Extend Preference, or one of its subclasses, to integrate a new type into a PreferenceActivity or PreferenceFragment. When creating a new preference type, you need to keep in mind two major objectives: how to provide an interface to the user for modifying the preference, and how to persist the user's selection back into SharedPreferences.

With regard to the user interface, there are several callback methods you may want to override. Notice that they use a similar pattern to the adapters we see in ListView:

- onCreateView(): Construct a new layout to be used for this preference element in the list. This is called the first time an instance of this preference is needed. If multiple elements of the same type exist, these views will be recycled when possible. If you don't override this, the default view with a title and summary will be displayed.

- onBindView(): Attach the data for this current preference to the view constructed in onCreateView(), which is passed into this method as a parameter. This will be called every time the preference is about to be displayed.

- getSummary(): Override the summary value displayed in the standard UI layout. This is useful only if you don't override onCreateView()/onBindView().

- onClick(): Handle an event when the user taps this item in the list.

Basic preferences in the framework, such as CheckBoxPreference, simply toggle the persisted state on each click. Other preferences, such as EditTextPreference or ListPreference, are subclasses of DialogPreference, which use the click event to display a dialog box to provide a more complex UI for updating the given setting.

The second set of overrides you may have in a custom Preference deal with retrieving and persisting data:

- onGetDefaultValue(): This method will be called to allow you to read the android:defaultValue attribute from the preference's XML definition. You will receive the TypedArray where the attributes live and the index necessary to obtain the value, using whichever typed method makes sense for the preference value.

- onSetInitialValue(): Locally set the value of this preference instance. The restorePersistedValue flag indicates whether the value should come from SharedPreferences or from the default value. The default value parameter is the instance returned from onGetDefaultValue().

Anytime that your preference needs to read the current value saved in SharedPreferences, you can invoke one of the typed getPersistedXxx() methods to return the value type your preference is persisting (integer, boolean, string, and so forth). Conversely, when the preference needs to save a new value, you can use the typed persistXxx() methods to update SharedPreferences.

How It Works

In the following example, we create a ColorPreference: a simple extension of DialogPreference that provides the user interface to select a color as three sliders that provide the RGB values discretely. When we're done, the results should look like Figure 5-2.

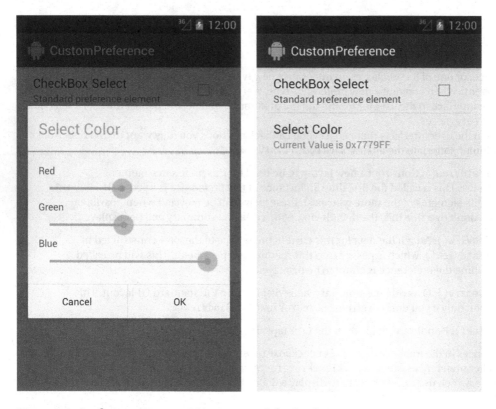

Figure 5-2. *PreferenceScreen with our custom ColorPreference*

Similar to ListPreference, an AlertDialog will display when the preference is selected from the list. This is where the user will make a selection and save or cancel the change, rather than in the list UI directly (as with CheckBoxPreference, for example). Listing 5-7 shows the layout for our custom dialog box, followed by Listing 5-8, which reveals our ColorPreference implementation.

Listing 5-7. res/layout/preference_color.xml

```xml
<?xml version="1.0" encoding="utf-8"?>
<LinearLayout xmlns:android="http://schemas.android.com/apk/res/android"
    android:layout_width="wrap_content"
    android:layout_height="wrap_content"
    android:padding="16dp"
    android:minWidth="300dp"
    android:orientation="vertical" >
    <TextView
        android:layout_width="wrap_content"
        android:layout_height="wrap_content"
        android:text="Red" />
    <SeekBar
        android:id="@+id/selector_red"
        android:layout_width="match_parent"
        android:layout_height="wrap_content"
        android:max="255" />

    <TextView
        android:layout_width="wrap_content"
        android:layout_height="wrap_content"
        android:text="Green" />
    <SeekBar
        android:id="@+id/selector_green"
        android:layout_width="match_parent"
        android:layout_height="wrap_content"
        android:max="255" />

    <TextView
        android:layout_width="wrap_content"
        android:layout_height="wrap_content"
        android:text="Blue" />
    <SeekBar
        android:id="@+id/selector_blue"
        android:layout_width="match_parent"
        android:layout_height="wrap_content"
        android:max="255" />
</LinearLayout>
```

Listing 5-8. Custom Preference Definition

```
public class ColorPreference extends DialogPreference {

    private static final int DEFAULT_COLOR = Color.WHITE;
    /* Local copy of the current color setting */
    private int mCurrentColor;
    /* Sliders to set color components */
    private SeekBar mRedLevel, mGreenLevel, mBlueLevel;

    public ColorPreference(Context context, AttributeSet attrs) {
        super(context, attrs);
    }

    /*
     * Called to construct a new dialog to show when the preference
     * is clicked.  We create and set up a new content view for
     * each instance.
     */
    @Override
    protected void onPrepareDialogBuilder(Builder builder) {
        //Create the dialog's content view
        View rootView =
                LayoutInflater.from(getContext()).inflate(R.layout.preference_color, null);
        mRedLevel = (SeekBar) rootView.findViewById(R.id.selector_red);
        mGreenLevel = (SeekBar) rootView.findViewById(R.id.selector_green);
        mBlueLevel = (SeekBar) rootView.findViewById(R.id.selector_blue);

        mRedLevel.setProgress(Color.red(mCurrentColor));
        mGreenLevel.setProgress(Color.green(mCurrentColor));
        mBlueLevel.setProgress(Color.blue(mCurrentColor));

        //Attach the content view
        builder.setView(rootView);
        super.onPrepareDialogBuilder(builder);
    }

    /*
     * Called when the dialog is closed with the result of
     * the button tapped by the user.
     */
    @Override
    protected void onDialogClosed(boolean positiveResult) {
        if (positiveResult) {
            //When OK is pressed, obtain and save the color value
            int color = Color.rgb(
                    mRedLevel.getProgress(),
                    mGreenLevel.getProgress(),
                    mBlueLevel.getProgress());
            setCurrentValue(color);
        }
    }
```

```
/*
 * Called by the framework to obtain the default value
 * passed in the preference XML definition
 */
@Override
protected Object onGetDefaultValue(TypedArray a, int index) {
    //Return the default value from XML as a color int
    ColorStateList value = a.getColorStateList(index);
    if (value == null) {
        return DEFAULT_COLOR;
    }
    return value.getDefaultColor();
}

/*
 * Called by the framework to set the initial value of the
 * preference, either from its default or the last persisted
 * value.
 */
@Override
protected void onSetInitialValue(boolean restorePersistedValue, Object defaultValue) {
    setCurrentValue( restorePersistedValue ?
            getPersistedInt(DEFAULT_COLOR) : (Integer)defaultValue );
}

/*
 * Return a custom summary based on the current setting
 */
@Override
public CharSequence getSummary() {
    //Construct the summary with the color value in hex
    int color = getPersistedInt(DEFAULT_COLOR);
    String content = String.format("Current Value is 0x%02X%02X%02X",
            Color.red(color), Color.green(color), Color.blue(color));
    //Return the summary text as a Spannable, colored by the selection
    Spannable summary = new SpannableString (content);
    summary.setSpan(new ForegroundColorSpan(color), 0, summary.length(), 0);
    return summary;
}

private void setCurrentValue(int value) {
    //Update latest value
    mCurrentColor = value;

    //Save new value
    persistInt(value);
    //Notify preference listeners
    notifyDependencyChange(shouldDisableDependents());
    notifyChanged();
}

}
```

When the ColorPreference is first created from XML, onGetDefaultValue() will be called with the android:defaultValue attribute (if one was added) so we can parse it. We want to allow any color attribute to be used, so we read the attribute's value using getColorStateList(), which supports reading color strings and references to color resources, and return the result (which will be an integer).

Later, when the preference is attached to the activity, onSetInitialValue() will tell us whether we should read that default value in or use a value already saved in SharedPreferences. On the first run, we will choose the default, while each attempt after that will read the saved value using getPersistedInt(). The parameter to getPersistedInt() is the default value we should use if the persisted value doesn't exist or can't be read as an integer.

For the user interface, rather than monitoring onClick(), we have two new callbacks provided by DialogPreference: onPrepareDialogBuilder() and onDialogClosed(). The former is triggered with an AlertDialog.Builder instance so we can customize the dialog box to be shown when a user clicks the preference; this will happen on each new click. We are using this method to inflate and attach our dialog box layout containing the three sliders—one each for the red, green, and blue components.

When we receive onDialogClosed(), we are told whether the user selected OK to save the preference or Cancel to revert the change. In the positive case, we want to create the new color from the UI sliders and persist the value using persistInt(). In the negative case, we take no action to change the current setting.

Finally, whenever a new change is persisted, we call notifyDependencyChange() and notifyChanged() to alert any preference listeners of the update. This also alerts the PreferenceActivity to update the list display.

We have made one final customization using getSummary(). In this example, we didn't provide a completely new layout, but rather we are customizing the summary display to include the current color selection (as a hex string), and that text will be colored with the selection. We can do this because getSummary() returns a CharSequence (instead of a pure String), allowing styled Spannable types to be returned.

With our new preference constructed, we can simply add it to an XML definition of a <PreferenceScreen> alongside other standard preferences, just as we saw in the previous recipe (see Listings 5-9 and 5-10).

Listing 5-9. res/xml/settings.xml

```xml
<?xml version="1.0" encoding="utf-8"?>
<PreferenceScreen xmlns:android="http://schemas.android.com/apk/res/android">
    <CheckBoxPreference
        android:key="dummyPref"
        android:title="CheckBox Select"
        android:summary="Standard preference element"
        android:defaultValue="false" />
    <com.androidrecipes.custompreference.ColorPreference
        android:key="customColorPref"
        android:title="Select Color"
        android:defaultValue="@android:color/black" />
</PreferenceScreen>
```

Listing 5-10. PreferenceActivity with New Settings

```java
public class CustomPreferenceActivity extends PreferenceActivity {

    @Override
    protected void onCreate(Bundle savedInstanceState) {
        super.onCreate(savedInstanceState);
        addPreferencesFromResource(R.xml.settings);
    }
}
```

We have set the default value of our color preference to a framework resource for black, which will be read by our onGetDefaultValue() override. You can see in Listing 5-10 that inflating this new preference hierarchy requires no modifications to the existing PreferenceActivity code we saw in the previous recipe.

5-3. Persisting Simple Data

Problem

Your application needs a simple, low-overhead method of storing basic data such as numbers and strings in persistent storage.

Solution

(API Level 1)

Using SharedPreferences objects, applications can quickly create one or more persistent stores where data can be saved and retrieved at a later time. Underneath the hood, these objects are actually stored as XML files in the application's user data area. However, unlike directly reading and writing data from files, SharedPreferences provide an efficient framework for persisting basic data types.

Creating multiple SharedPreferences as opposed to dumping all your data in the default object can be a good habit to get into, especially if the data you are storing will have a shelf life. Keeping in mind that all preferences stored using the XML and PreferenceActivity framework are also stored in the default location, what if you wanted to store a group of items related to, say, a logged-in user? When that user logs out, you will need to remove all the persisted data that goes along with that. If you store all that data in default preferences, you will most likely need to remove each item individually. However, if you create a preference object just for those settings, logging out can be as simple as calling SharedPreferences.Editor. clear().

How It Works

Let's look at a practical example of using SharedPreferences to persist simple data. Listings 5-11 and 5-12 create a data entry form for the user to send a simple message to a remote server. To aid the user, we will remember all the data he or she enters for each field until a successful request is made. This will allow the user to leave the screen (or be interrupted by a text message or phone call) without having to enter all the information again.

Listing 5-11. res/layout/form.xml

```xml
<?xml version="1.0" encoding="utf-8"?>
<LinearLayout xmlns:android="http://schemas.android.com/apk/res/android"
    android:orientation="vertical"
    android:layout_width="match_parent"
    android:layout_height="match_parent">
    <TextView
        android:layout_width="match_parent"
        android:layout_height="wrap_content"
        android:text="Email:"
        android:padding="5dip" />
```

```xml
    <EditText
        android:id="@+id/email"
        android:layout_width="match_parent"
        android:layout_height="wrap_content"
        android:singleLine="true" />
    <CheckBox
        android:id="@+id/age"
        android:layout_width="match_parent"
        android:layout_height="wrap_content"
        android:text="Are You Over 18?" />
    <TextView
        android:layout_width="match_parent"
        android:layout_height="wrap_content"
        android:text="Message:"
        android:padding="5dip" />
    <EditText
        android:id="@+id/message"
        android:layout_width="match_parent"
        android:layout_height="wrap_content"
        android:minLines="3"
        android:maxLines="3" />
    <Button
        android:id="@+id/submit"
        android:layout_width="match_parent"
        android:layout_height="wrap_content"
        android:text="Submit" />
</LinearLayout>
```

Listing 5-12. Entry Form with Persistence

```java
public class FormActivity extends Activity implements View.OnClickListener {

    FditText email, message;
    CheckBox age;
    Button submit;

    SharedPreferences formStore;

    boolean submitSuccess = false;

    @Override
    public void onCreate(Bundle savedInstanceState) {
        super.onCreate(savedInstanceState);
        setContentView(R.layout.form);

        email = (EditText)findViewById(R.id.email);
        message = (EditText)findViewById(R.id.message);
        age = (CheckBox)findViewById(R.id.age);

        submit = (Button)findViewById(R.id.submit);
        submit.setOnClickListener(this);
```

```
        //Retrieve or create the preferences object
        formStore = getPreferences(Activity.MODE_PRIVATE);
    }

    @Override
    public void onResume() {
        super.onResume();
        //Restore the form data
        email.setText(formStore.getString("email", ""));
        message.setText(formStore.getString("message", ""));
        age.setChecked(formStore.getBoolean("age", false));
    }

    @Override
    public void onPause() {
        super.onPause();
        if(submitSuccess) {
            //Editor calls can be chained together
            formStore.edit().clear().commit();
        } else {
            //Store the form data
            SharedPreferences.Editor editor = formStore.edit();
            editor.putString("email", email.getText().toString());
            editor.putString("message", message.getText().toString());
            editor.putBoolean("age", age.isChecked());
            editor.commit();
        }
    }

    @Override
    public void onClick(View v) {

        //DO SOME WORK SUBMITTING A MESSAGE

        //Mark the operation successful
        submitSuccess = true;
        //Close
        finish();
    }
}
```

We start with a typical user form containing two simple EditText entry fields and a check box. When the activity is created, we gather a SharedPreferences object using Activity.getPreferences(), and this is where all the persisted data will be stored. If at any time the activity is paused for a reason other than a successful submission (controlled by the Boolean member), the current state of the form will be quickly loaded into the preferences and persisted.

■ **Note** When saving data into SharedPreferences using an Editor, always remember to call commit() or apply() after the changes are made. Otherwise, your changes will not be saved.

Conversely, whenever the activity becomes visible, onResume() loads the user interface with the latest information stored in the preferences object. If no preferences exist, either because they were cleared or never created (first launch), then the form is set to blank.

When a user presses Submit and the fake form submits successfully, the subsequent call to onPause() will clear any stored form data in preferences. Because all these operations were done on a private preferences object, clearing the data does not affect any user settings that may have been stored using other means.

■ **Note**　Methods called from an Editor always return the same Editor object, allowing them to be chained together in places where doing so makes your code more readable.

Creating Common SharedPreferences

The previous example illustrated how to use a single SharedPreferences object within the context of a single activity with an object obtained from Activity.getPreferences(). Truth be told, this method is really just a convenience wrapper for Context.getSharedPreferences(), in which it passes the activity name as the preference store name. If the data you are storing is best shared between two or more activity instances, it might make sense to call getSharedPreferences() instead and pass a more common name so the data can be accessed easily from different places in code. See Listing 5-13.

Listing 5-13. Two Activities Using the Same Preferences

```
public class ActivityOne extends Activity {
    public static final String PREF_NAME = "myPreferences";
    private SharedPreferences mPreferences;

    @Override
    public void onCreate(Bundle savedInstanceState) {
        super.onCreate(savedInstanceState);
        mPreferences = getSharedPreferences(PREF_NAME, Activity.MODE_PRIVATE);
    }
}

public class ActivityTwo extends Activity {

    private SharedPreferences mPreferences;

    @Override
    public void onCreate(Bundle savedInstanceState) {
        super.onCreate(savedInstanceState);
        mPreferences = getSharedPreferences(ActivityOne.PREF_NAME,
            Activity.MODE_PRIVATE);
    }

}
```

In this example, both activity classes retrieve the SharedPreferences object using the same name (defined as a constant string): thus they will be accessing the same set of preference data. Furthermore, both references are even pointing at the same *instance* of preferences, as the framework creates a singleton object for each set of SharedPreferences (a set being defined by its name). This means that changes made on one side will immediately be reflected on the other.

A NOTE ABOUT MODE

Context.getSharedPreferences() also takes a mode parameter. Passing 0 or MODE_PRIVATE provides the default behavior of allowing only the application that created the preferences (or another application with the same user ID) to gain read/write access. This method supports two more mode parameters: MODE_WORLD_READABLE and MODE_WORLD_WRITEABLE. These modes allow other applications to gain access to these preferences by setting the user permissions on the file it creates appropriately. However, the external application still requires a valid Context pointing back to the package where the preference file was created.

For example, let's say you created SharedPreferences with world-readable permission in an application with the package com.examples.myfirstapplication. In order to access those preferences from a second application, the second application would obtain them using the following code:

```
Context otherContext = createPackageContext("com.examples.myfirstapplication", 0);
SharedPreferences externalPreferences = otherContext.getSharedPreferences(PREF_NAME, 0);
```

■ **Caution**   If you choose to use the mode parameter to allow external access, be sure that you are consistent in the mode you provide everywhere that getSharedPreferences() is called. This mode is used only the first time the preference file gets created, so calling up SharedPreferences with different mode parameters at different times will only lead to confusion on your part.

5-4. Reading and Writing Files

Problem

Your application needs to read data in from an external file or write more-complex data out for persistence.

Solution

(API Level 1)

Sometimes, there is no substitute for working with a filesystem. Working with files allows your application to read and write data that does not lend itself well to other persistence options such as key/value preferences and databases. Android also provides a number of cache locations for files you can use to place data that you need to persist on a temporary basis.

Android supports all the standard Java file I/O APIs for create, read, update, and delete (CRUD) operations, along with some additional helpers to make accessing those files in specific locations a little more convenient. There are three main locations in which an application can work with files:

- *Internal storage*: Protected directory space to read and write file data.

- *External storage*: Externally mountable space to read and write file data. Requires the WRITE_EXTERNAL_STORAGE permission in API Level 4+. Often, this is a physical SD card in the device.

- *Assets*: Protected read-only space inside the APK bundle. Good for local resources that can't or shouldn't be compiled.

While the underlying mechanism to work with file data remains the same, we will look at the details that make working with each destination slightly different.

How It Works

As we stated earlier, the traditional Java FileInputStream and FileOutputStream classes constitute the primary method of accessing file data. In fact, you can create a File instance at any time with an absolute path location and use one of these streams to read and write data. However, with root paths varying on different devices and certain directories being protected from your application, we recommend some slightly more efficient ways to work with files.

Internal Storage

In order to create or modify a file's location on internal storage, utilize the Context.openFileInput() and Context.openFileOutput() methods. These methods require only the name of the file as a parameter, instead of the entire path, and will reference the file in relation to the application's protected directory space, regardless of the exact path on the specific device. See Listing 5-14.

Listing 5-14. CRUD a File on Internal Storage

```
public class InternalActivity extends Activity {

    private static final String FILENAME = "data.txt";

    @Override
    public void onCreate(Bundle savedInstanceState) {
        super.onCreate(savedInstanceState);
        TextView tv = new TextView(this);
        setContentView(tv);

        //Create a new file and write some data
        try {
            FileOutputStream mOutput = openFileOutput(FILENAME, Activity.MODE_PRIVATE);
            String data = "THIS DATA WRITTEN TO A FILE";
            mOutput.write(data.getBytes());
            mOutput.flush();
            mOutput.close();
```

```
    } catch (FileNotFoundException e) {
        e.printStackTrace();
    } catch (IOException e) {
        e.printStackTrace();
    }

    //Read the created file and display to the screen
    try {
        FileInputStream mInput = openFileInput(FILENAME);
        byte[] data = new byte[128];
        mInput.read(data);
        mInput.close();

        String display = new String(data);
        tv.setText(display.trim());
    } catch (FileNotFoundException e) {
        e.printStackTrace();
    } catch (IOException e) {
        e.printStackTrace();
    }

    //Delete the created file
    deleteFile(FILENAME);
    }
}
```

This example uses `Context.openFileOutput()` to write some simple string data out to a file. When using this method, the file will be created if it does not already exist. It takes two parameters: a file name and an operating mode. In this case, we use the default operation by defining the mode as `MODE_PRIVATE`. This mode will overwrite the file with each new write operation; use `MODE_APPEND` if you prefer that each write append to the end of the existing file.

After the write is complete, the example uses `Context.openFileInput()`, which requires only the file name again as a parameter to open an `InputStream` and read the file data. The data will be read into a byte array and displayed to the user interface through a `TextView`. Upon completing the operation, `Context.deleteFile()` is used to remove the file from storage.

■ **Note**   Data is written to the file streams as bytes, so higher-level data (even strings) must be converted into and out of this format.

This example leaves no traces of the file behind, but we encourage you to try the same example without running `deleteFile()` at the end in order to keep the file in storage. Using the SDK's DDMS tool with an emulator or unlocked device, you may view the filesystem and can find the file this application creates in its respective application data folder.

Because these methods are a part of `Context`, and not bound to an activity, this type of file access can occur anywhere in an application that you require, such as a `BroadcastReceiver` or even a custom class. Many system constructs either are a subclass of `Context` or will pass a reference to one in their callbacks. This allows the same open/close/delete operations to take place anywhere.

External Storage

The key differentiator between internal and external storage is that external storage is mountable. This means that the user can connect his or her device to a computer and have the option of mounting that external storage as a removable disk on the PC. Often, the storage itself is physically removable (such as an SD card), but this is not a requirement of the platform.

■ **Important**   Writing to the external storage of the device will require that you add a declaration for `android.permission.WRITE_EXTERNAL_STORAGE` to the application manifest. Reading from external storage requires `android.permission.READ_EXTERNAL_STORAGE` as well on API Level 19+.

During periods when the device's external storage is either mounted externally or physically removed, it is not accessible to an application. Because of this, it is always prudent to check whether external storage is ready by checking `Environment.getExternalStorageState()`.

Let's modify the file example to do the same operation with the device's external storage. See Listing 5-15.

Listing 5-15.   CRUD a File on External Storage

```java
public class ExternalActivity extends Activity {

    private static final String FILENAME = "data.txt";

    @Override
    public void onCreate(Bundle savedInstanceState) {
        super.onCreate(savedInstanceState);
        TextView tv = new TextView(this);
        setContentView(tv);

        //Create the file reference
        File dataFile = new File(Environment.getExternalStorageDirectory(), FILENAME);

        //Check if external storage is usable
        if(!Environment.getExternalStorageState().equals(Environment.MEDIA_MOUNTED)) {
            Toast.makeText(this, "Cannot use storage.", Toast.LENGTH_SHORT).show();
            finish();
            return;
        }

        //Create a new file and write some data
        try {
            FileOutputStream mOutput = new FileOutputStream(dataFile, false);
            String data = "THIS DATA WRITTEN TO A FILE";
            mOutput.write(data.getBytes());
            mOutput.flush();
            //With external files, it is often good to sync the file
            mOutput.getFD().sync();
            mOutput.close();
        } catch (FileNotFoundException e) {
            e.printStackTrace();
```

```
    } catch (IOException e) {
        e.printStackTrace();
    }

    //Read the created file and display to the screen
    try {
        FileInputStream mInput = new FileInputStream(dataFile);
        byte[] data = new byte[128];
        mInput.read(data);
        mInput.close();

        String display = new String(data);
        tv.setText(display.trim());
    } catch (FileNotFoundException e) {
        e.printStackTrace();
    } catch (IOException e) {
        e.printStackTrace();
    }

    //Delete the created file
    dataFile.delete();
    }
}
```

With external storage, we utilize a little more of the traditional Java file I/O. The key to working with external storage is calling `Environment.getExternalStorageDirectory()` to retrieve the root path to the device's external storage location.

Before any operations can take place, the status of the device's external storage is first checked with `Environment.getExternalStorageState()`. If the value returned is anything other than `Environment.MEDIA_MOUNTED`, we do not proceed because the storage cannot be written to, so the activity is closed. Otherwise, a new file can be created and the operations may commence.

The input and output streams must now use default Java constructors, as opposed to the `Context` convenience methods. The default behavior of the output stream will be to overwrite the current file or to create it if it does not exist. If your application must append to the end of the existing file with each write, change the Boolean parameter in the `FileOutputStream` constructor to true.

Often, it makes sense to create a special directory on external storage for your application's files. We can accomplish this simply by using more of Java's file API. See Listing 5-16.

Listing 5-16. CRUD a File Inside a New Directory

```
public class ExternalActivity extends Activity {

    private static final String FILENAME = "data.txt";
    private static final String DNAME = "myfiles";

    @Override
    public void onCreate(Bundle savedInstanceState) {
        super.onCreate(savedInstanceState);
        TextView tv = new TextView(this);
        setContentView(tv);
```

```java
        //Create a new directory on external storage
        File rootPath = new File(Environment.getExternalStorageDirectory(), DNAME);
        if(!rootPath.exists()) {
            rootPath.mkdirs();
        }
        //Create the file reference
        File dataFile = new File(rootPath, FILENAME);

        //Create a new file and write some data
        try {
            FileOutputStream mOutput = new FileOutputStream(dataFile, false);
            String data = "THIS DATA WRITTEN TO A FILE";
            mOutput.write(data.getBytes());
            mOutput.flush();
            //With external files, it is often good to wait for the write
            mOutput.getFD().sync();

            mOutput.close();
        } catch (FileNotFoundException e) {
            e.printStackTrace();
        } catch (IOException e) {
            e.printStackTrace();
        }

        //Read the created file and display to the screen
        try {
            FileInputStream mInput = new FileInputStream(dataFile);
            byte[] data = new byte[128];
            mInput.read(data);
            mInput.close();

            String display = new String(data);
            lv.setText(display.trim());
        } catch (FileNotFoundException e) {
            e.printStackTrace();
        } catch (IOException e) {
            e.printStackTrace();
        }

        //Delete the created file
        dataFile.delete();
    }
}
```

In this example, we created a new directory path within the external storage directory and used that new location as the root location for the data file. Once the file reference is created using the new directory location, the remainder of the example is the same.

```
┌─────────────────────────────────────────────────────────────────────┐
│                    A NOTE ABOUT WRITING FILES                         │
└─────────────────────────────────────────────────────────────────────┘
```

A NOTE ABOUT WRITING FILES

Android applications run inside a virtual machine environment. This has some effects to be aware of when working with certain aspects of the system, such as the filesystem. Java APIs like `FileOutputStream` do not share a 1:1 relationship with the native file descriptor inside the kernel. Typically, when data is written to the stream by using the `write()` method, that data is written directly into a memory buffer for the file and asynchronously written out to disk. In most cases, as long as your file access is strictly within the VM, you will never see this implementation detail. A file you just wrote could be opened and immediately read without issue, for example.

However, when dealing with removable storage such as an SD card on a mobile handset or tablet, we may often need to guarantee that the file data has made it all the way to the filesystem before returning an operation to the user, since the user has the ability to physically remove the storage medium. The following is a good standard code block to use when writing external files:

```
//Write the data
out.write();
//Clear the stream buffers
out.flush();
//Sync all data to the filesystem
out.getFD().sync();
//Close the stream
out.close();
```

The `flush()` method on an `OutputStream` is designed to ensure that all the data resident in the stream is written out of the VM's memory buffer. In the direct case of `FileOutputStream`, this method actually does nothing. However, in cases where that stream may be wrapped inside another (such as a `BufferedOutputStream`), this method can be essential in clearing out internal buffers, so it is a good habit to get into by calling it on every file write before closing the stream.

Additionally, with external files, we can issue a `sync()` to the underlying `FileDescriptor`. This method will block until all the data has been successfully written to the underlying filesystem, so it is the best indicator of when a user could safely remove physical storage media without file corruption.

External System Directories

There are additional methods in `Environment` and `Context` that provide standard locations on external storage where specific files can be written. Some of these locations have additional properties as well.

- `Environment.getExternalStoragePublicDirectory(String type)`

  - API Level 8

  - Returns a common directory where all applications store media files. The contents of these directories are visible to users and other applications. In particular, the media placed here will likely be scanned and inserted into the device's `MediaStore` for applications such as the Gallery.

  - Valid type values include DIRECTORY_PICTURES, DIRECTORY_MUSIC, DIRECTORY_MOVIES, and DIRECTORY_RINGTONES.

- `Context.getExternalFilesDir(String type)`

  - API Level 8

  - Returns a directory on external storage for media files that are specific to the application. Media placed here will not be considered public, however, and won't show up in `MediaStore`.

  - This is external storage, however, so it is still possible for users and other applications to see and edit the files directly: there is no security enforced.

  - Files placed here will be removed when the application is uninstalled, so it can be a good location in which to place large content files the application needs that one may not want on internal storage.

  - Valid type values include `DIRECTORY_PICTURES`, `DIRECTORY_MUSIC`, `DIRECTORY_MOVIES`, and `DIRECTORY_RINGTONES`.

- `Context.getExternalCacheDir()`

  - API Level 8

  - Returns a directory on internal storage for app-specific temporary files. The contents of this directory are visible to users and other applications.

  - Files placed here will be removed when the application is uninstalled, so it can be a good location in which to place large content files the application needs that one may not want on internal storage.

- `Context.getExternalFilesDirs()` and `Context.getExternalCacheDirs()`

  - API Level 19

  - Identical features as their counterparts described previously, but returns a list of paths for each storage volume on the device (primary and any secondary volumes)

  - For example, a single device may have a block of internal flash for primary external storage, and a removable SD card for secondary external storage.

- `Context.getExternalMediaDirs()`

  - API Level 21

  - Files placed in these volumes will be automatically scanned and added to the device's media store to expose them to other applications. These will generally also be visible to the user through core applications like the Gallery.

■ **Note** As of KitKat (API Level 19), permissions are no longer required to read and write the directory paths returned by `getExternalFilesDir()` and `getExternalCacheDir()` for your application. Primary volumes are still writable outside these directories with the aforementioned permissions. Secondary volumes (also new to the KitKat APIs) are fully write-protected outside these directories, even if the `WRITE_EXTERNAL_STORAGE` permission is granted.

5-5. Using Files as Resources

Problem

Your application must utilize resource files that are in a format Android cannot compile into a resource ID.

Solution

(API Level 1)

Use the `assets` directory to house files your application needs to read from, such as local HTML, comma-separated values (CSV), or proprietary data. The `assets` directory is a protected resource location for files in an Android application. The files placed in this directory will be bundled with the final APK but will not be processed or compiled. Like all other application resources, the files in `assets` are read-only.

How It Works

There are a few specific instances that we've seen already in this book, where `assets` can be used to load content directly into widgets, such as `WebView` and `MediaPlayer`. However, in most cases, `assets` is best accessed through a traditional `InputStream`. Listings 5-17 and 5-18 provide an example in which a private CSV file is read from `assets` and displayed onscreen.

Listing 5-17. `assets/data.csv`

```
John,38,Red
Sally,42,Blue
Rudy,31,Yellow
```

Listing 5-18. Reading from an Asset File

```java
public class AssetActivity extends Activity {

    @Override
    public void onCreate(Bundle savedInstanceState) {
        super.onCreate(savedInstanceState);
        TextView tv = new TextView(this);
        setContentView(tv);

        try {
            //Access application assets
            AssetManager manager = getAssets();
            //Open our data file
            InputStream in = manager.open("data.csv");

            //Parse the CSV data and display
            ArrayList<Person> cooked = parse(in);
            StringBuilder builder = new StringBuilder();
            for(Person piece : cooked) {
                builder.append(String.format("%s is %s years old, and likes the color %s",
                        piece.name, piece.age, piece.color));
                builder.append('\n');
            }
```

```java
                tv.setText(builder.toString());
        } catch (FileNotFoundException e) {
            e.printStackTrace();
        } catch (IOException e) {
            e.printStackTrace();
        }

    }

    /* Simple CSV Parser */
    private static final int COL_NAME = 0;
    private static final int COL_AGE = 1;
    private static final int COL_COLOR = 2;

    private ArrayList<Person> parse(InputStream in) throws IOException {
        ArrayList<Person> results = new ArrayList<Person>();

        BufferedReader reader = new BufferedReader(new InputStreamReader(in));
        String nextLine = null;
        while ((nextLine = reader.readLine()) != null) {
            String[] tokens = nextLine.split(",");
            if (tokens.length != 3) {
                Log.w("CSVParser", "Skipping Bad CSV Row");
                continue;
            }

            //Add new parsed result
            Person current = new Person();
            current.name = tokens[COL_NAME];
            current.color = tokens[COL_COLOR];
            current.age = tokens[COL_AGE];

            results.add(current);
        }

        in.close();

        return results;
    }

    private class Person {
        public String name;
        public String age;
        public String color;

        public Person() { }
    }
}
```

The key to accessing files in assets lies in using AssetManager, which will allow the application to open any resource currently residing in the assets directory. Passing the name of the file we are interested in to AssetManager.open() returns an InputStream for us to read the file data. Once the stream is read into memory, the example passes the raw data off to a parsing routine and displays the results to the user interface.

Parsing the CSV

This example also illustrates a simple method of taking data from a CSV file and parsing it into a model object (called Person in this case). The method used here takes the entire file and reads it into a byte array for processing as a single string. This method is not the most memory efficient when the amount of data to be read is quite large, but for small files like this one it works just fine.

The raw string is passed into a StringTokenizer instance, along with the required characters to use as breakpoints for the tokens: comma and new line. At this point, each individual chunk of the file can be processed in order. Using a basic state machine approach, the data from each line is inserted into new Person instances and loaded into the resulting list.

5-6. Managing a Database

Problem

Your application needs to persist data that can later be queried or modified as subsets or individual records.

Solution

(API Level 1)

Create a SQLiteDatabase with the assistance of an SQLiteOpenHelper to manage your data store. SQLite is a fast and lightweight database technology that utilizes SQL syntax to build queries and manage data. Support for SQLite is baked into the Android SDK, making it very easy to set up and use in your applications.

How It Works

Customizing SQLiteOpenHelper allows you to manage the creation and modification of the database schema itself. It is also an excellent place to insert any initial or default values you may want in the database when it is created. Listing 5-19 is an example of how to customize the helper in order to create a database with a single table that stores basic information about people.

Listing 5-19. Custom SQLiteOpenHelper

```
public class MyDbHelper extends SQLiteOpenHelper {

    private static final String DB_NAME = "mydb";
    private static final int DB_VERSION = 1;

    public static final String TABLE_NAME = "people";
    public static final String COL_NAME = "pName";
    public static final String COL_DATE = "pDate";
```

```
private static final String STRING_CREATE =
    "CREATE TABLE "+TABLE_NAME+" (_id INTEGER PRIMARY KEY AUTOINCREMENT, "
    + COL_NAME + " TEXT, " + COL_DATE + " DATE);";

public MyDbHelper(Context context) {
    super(context, DB_NAME, null, DB_VERSION);
}

@Override
public void onCreate(SQLiteDatabase db) {
    //Create the database table
    db.execSQL(STRING_CREATE);

    //You may also load initial values into the database here
    ContentValues cv = new ContentValues(2);
    cv.put(COL_NAME, "John Doe");
    //Create a formatter for SQL date format
    SimpleDateFormat dateFormat = new SimpleDateFormat("yyyy-MM-dd HH:mm:ss");
    cv.put(COL_DATE, dateFormat.format(new Date())); //Insert 'now' as the date
    db.insert(TABLE_NAME, null, cv);
}

@Override
public void onUpgrade(SQLiteDatabase db, int oldVersion, int newVersion) {
    //For now, clear the database and re-create
    db.execSQL("DROP TABLE IF EXISTS "+TABLE_NAME);
    onCreate(db);
}
}
```

The key pieces of information you will need for your database are a name and version number. Creating and upgrading a SQLiteDatabase does require some light knowledge of SQL, so we recommend glancing at an SQL reference briefly if you are unfamiliar with some of the syntax. The helper will call onCreate() anytime this particular database is accessed, using either SQLiteOpenHelper.getReadableDatabase() or SQLiteOpenHelper.getWritableDatabase(), if it does not already exist.

The example abstracts the table and column names as constants for external use (a good practice to get into). Here is the actual SQL create string that is used in onCreate() to make our table:

```
CREATE TABLE people (_id INTEGER PRIMARY KEY AUTOINCREMENT, pName TEXT, pAge INTEGER,
pDate DATE);
```

When using SQLite in Android, the database must have a small amount of formatting in order to work properly with the framework. Most of this formatting is created for you, but one piece that the tables you create must have is a column for _id. The remainder of this string creates two more columns for each record in the table:

- A text field for the person's name

- A date field for the date this record was entered

Data is inserted into the database by using ContentValues objects. The example illustrates how to use ContentValues to insert some default data into the database when it is created. SQLiteDatabase.insert() takes a table name, null column hack, and ContentValues representing the record to insert as parameters.

The null column hack is not used here but serves a purpose that may be vital to your application. SQL cannot insert an entirely empty value into the database, and attempting to do so will cause an error. If there is a chance that your implementation may pass an empty ContentValues to insert(), the null column hack is used to instead insert a record where the value of the referenced column is NULL.

A Note About Upgrading

SQLiteOpenHelper also does a great job of assisting you with migrating your database schema in future versions of the application. Whenever the database is accessed, but the version on disk does not match the current version (meaning the version passed in the constructor), onUpgrade() will be called.

In our example, we took the lazy way out and simply dropped the existing database and re-created it. In practice, this may not be a suitable method if the database contains user-entered data; a user probably won't be too happy to see it disappear. So let's digress for a moment and look at an example of onUpgrade() that may be more useful. Take, for example, the following three databases used throughout the lifetime of an application:

- *Version 1*: First release of the application

- *Version 2*: Application upgrade to include phone-number field

- *Version 3*: Application upgrade to include the date that the entry was inserted

We can leverage onUpgrade() to alter the existing database instead of erasing all the current information in place. See Listing 5-20.

Listing 5-20. Sample of onUpgrade()

```
@Override
public void onUpgrade(SQLiteDatabase db, int oldVersion, int newVersion) {
    //Upgrade from v1. Adding phone number
    if(oldVersion <= 1) {
        db.execSQL("ALTER TABLE "+TABLE_NAME+" ADD COLUMN phone_number INTEGER;");
    }
    //Upgrade from v2. Add entry date
    if(oldVersion <= 2) {
        db.execSQL("ALTER TABLE "+TABLE_NAME+" ADD COLUMN entry_date DATE;");
    }
}
```

In this example, if the user's existing database version is 1, both statements will be called to add columns to the database. If a user already has version 2, just the latter statement is called to add the entry date column. In both cases, any existing data in the application database is preserved.

■ **Tip** SQLiteOpenHelper also supports onDowngrade() for API Level 11+. This method will be called if the database version on disk is higher than the current version requested by the application code.

Using the Database

Looking back to our original sample, let's see how an activity would utilize the database we've created. See Listings 5-21 and 5-22.

Listing 5-21. `res/layout/main.xml`

```xml
<?xml version="1.0" encoding="utf-8"?>
<LinearLayout xmlns:android="http://schemas.android.com/apk/res/android"
    android:orientation="vertical"
    android:layout_width="match_parent"
    android:layout_height="match_parent">
    <EditText
        android:id="@+id/name"
        android:layout_width="match_parent"
        android:layout_height="wrap_content" />
    <Button
        android:id="@+id/add"
        android:layout_width="match_parent"
        android:layout_height="wrap_content"
        android:text="Add New Person" />
    <ListView
        android:id="@+id/list"
        android:layout_width="match_parent"
        android:layout_height="match_parent" />
</LinearLayout>
```

Listing 5-22. Activity to View and Manage Database

```java
public class DbActivity extends Activity implements View.OnClickListener,
        AdapterView.OnItemClickListener {

    EditText mText;
    Button mAdd;
    ListView mList;

    MyDbHelper mHelper;
    SQLiteDatabase mDb;
    Cursor mCursor;
    SimpleCursorAdapter mAdapter;

    @Override
    public void onCreate(Bundle savedInstanceState) {
        super.onCreate(savedInstanceState);
        setContentView(R.layout.main);

        mText = (EditText)findViewById(R.id.name);
        mAdd = (Button)findViewById(R.id.add);
        mAdd.setOnClickListener(this);
        mList = (ListView)findViewById(R.id.list);
        mList.setOnItemClickListener(this);

        mHelper = new MyDbHelper(this);
    }
```

```java
    @Override
    public void onResume() {
        super.onResume();
        //Open connections to the database
        mDb = mHelper.getWritableDatabase();
        String[] columns = new String[] {"_id", MyDbHelper.COL_NAME, MyDbHelper.COL_DATE};
        mCursor = mDb.query(MyDbHelper.TABLE_NAME, columns, null, null, null, null,
                null);
        //Refresh the list
        String[] headers = new String[] {MyDbHelper.COL_NAME, MyDbHelper.COL_DATE};
        mAdapter = new SimpleCursorAdapter(this, android.R.layout.two_line_list_item,
                mCursor, headers, new int[]{android.R.id.text1, android.R.id.text2});
        mList.setAdapter(mAdapter);
    }

    @Override
    public void onPause() {
        super.onPause();
        //Close all connections
        mDb.close();
        mCursor.close();
    }

    @Override
    public void onClick(View v) {
        //Add a new value to the database
        ContentValues cv = new ContentValues(2);
        cv.put(MyDbHelper.COL_NAME, mText.getText().toString());
        //Create a formatter for SQL date format
        SimpleDateFormat dateFormat = new SimpleDateFormat("yyyy-MM-dd HH:mm:ss");
        //Insert 'now' as the date
        cv.put(MyDbHelper.COL_DATE, dateFormat.format(new Date()));
        mDb.insert(MyDbHelper.TABLE_NAME, null, cv);
        //Refresh the list
        mCursor.requery();
        mAdapter.notifyDataSetChanged();
        //Clear the edit field
        mText.setText(null);
    }

    @Override
    public void onItemClick(AdapterView<?> parent, View v, int position, long id) {
        //Delete the item from the database
        mCursor.moveToPosition(position);
         //Get the id value of this row
        String rowId = mCursor.getString(0); //Column 0 of the cursor is the id
        mDb.delete(MyDbHelper.TABLE_NAME, "_id = ?", new String[]{rowId});
        //Refresh the list
        mCursor.requery();
        mAdapter.notifyDataSetChanged();
    }
}
```

In this example, we utilize our custom `SQLiteOpenHelper` to give us access to a database instance, and it displays each record in that database as a list to the user interface. Information from the database is returned in the form of a `Cursor`, an interface designed to read, write, and traverse the results of a query.

When the activity becomes visible, a database query is made to return all records in the `people` table. An array of column names must be passed to the query to tell the database which values to return. The remaining parameters of `query()` are designed to narrow the selection data set, and we will investigate this further in the next recipe. It is important to close all database and cursor connections when they are no longer needed. In the example, we do this in `onPause()`, when the activity is no longer in the foreground.

`SimpleCursorAdapter` is used to map the data from the database to the standard Android two-line list item view. The string and int array parameters constitute the mapping; the data from each item in the string array will be inserted into the view with the corresponding ID value in the int array. The list of column names passed here is slightly different from the array passed to the query. This is because we will need to know the record ID for other operations, but it is not necessary in mapping the data to the user interface.

The user may enter a name in the text field and then press the Add New Person button to create a new `ContentValues` instance and insert it into the database. At that point, in order for the UI to display the change, we call `Cursor.requery()` and `ListAdapter.notifyDataSetChanged()`.

Conversely, tapping an item in the list will remove that specified item from the database. To accomplish this, we must construct a simple SQL statement telling the database to remove only records where the `_id` value matches this selection. At that point, the cursor and list adapter are refreshed again.

The `_id` value of the selection is obtained by moving the cursor to the selected position and calling `getString(0)` to get the value of column index zero. This request returns the `_id` because the first parameter (`index 0`) passed in the columns list to the query was `_id`. The `delete` statement is composed of two parameters: the statement string and the arguments. An argument from the passed array will be inserted in the statement for each question mark that appears in the string.

5-7. Querying a Database

Problem

Your application uses a `SQLiteDatabase`, and you need to return specific subsets of the data contained therein.

Solution

(API Level 1)

Using fully structured SQL queries, it is very simple to create filters for specific data and return those subsets from the database. There are several overloaded forms of `SQLiteDatabase.query()` used to gather information from the database. We'll examine the most verbose of them here:

```
public Cursor query(String table, String[] columns,
        String selection,
        String[] selectionArgs,
        String groupBy,
        String having,
        String orderBy,
        String limit)
```

The first two parameters simply define the table in which to query data, as well as the columns for each record that we would like to have access to. The remaining parameters define how we will narrow the scope of the results.

- selection: SQL WHERE clause for the given query

- selectionArgs: If question marks are in the selection, these items fill in those fields.

- groupBy: SQL GROUP BY clause for the given query

- having: SQL ORDER BY clause for the given query

- orderBy: SQL ORDER BY clause for the given query

- limit: Maximum number of results returned from the query

As you can see, all of these parameters are designed to provide the full power of SQL to the database queries.

How It Works

Let's construct some example queries to address common practical use cases:

- Return all rows with a value that matches a given parameter.

```
String[] COLUMNS = new String[] {COL_NAME, COL_DATE};
String selection = COL_NAME+" = ?";
String[] args = new String[] {"NAME_TO_MATCH"};
Cursor result = db.query(TABLE_NAME, COLUMNS, selection, args, null, null, null, null);
```

This query is fairly straightforward. The selection statement just tells the database to match any data in the name column with the argument supplied (which is inserted in place of ? in the selection string).

- Return the last 10 rows inserted into the database.

```
String orderBy = "_id DESC";
String limit = "10";
Cursor result = db.query(TABLE_NAME, COLUMNS, null, null, null, null, orderBy, limit);
```

This query has no special selection criteria but instead tells the database to order the results by the auto-incrementing _id value, with the newest (highest _id) records first. The limit clause sets the maximum number of returned results to 10.

- Return rows with a date field that is within a specified range (within the year 2000, in this example).

```
String[] COLUMNS = new String[] {COL_NAME, COL_DATE};
String selection = "datetime("+COL_DATE+") > datetime(?)"+
        " AND datetime("+COL_DATE+") < datetime(?)";
String[] args = new String[] {"2000-1-1 00:00:00","2000-12-31 23:59:59"};
Cursor result = db.query(TABLE_NAME, COLUMNS, selection, args, null, null, null, null);
```

SQLite does not reserve a specific data type for dates, although it allows DATE as a declaration type when creating a table. However, the standard SQL date and time functions can be used to create representations of the data as TEXT, INTEGER, or REAL. Here, we compare the return values of datetime() for both the value in the database and a formatted string for the start and end dates of the range.

- Return rows with an integer field that is within a specified range (between 7 and 10 in the example).

```
String[] COLUMNS = new String[] {COL_NAME, COL_AGE};
String selection = COL_AGE+" > ? AND "+COL_AGE+" < ?";
String[] args = new String[] {"7","10"};
Cursor result = db.query(TABLE_NAME, COLUMNS, selection, args, null, null, null, null);
```

This is similar to the previous example but is much less verbose. Here, we simply have to create the selection statement to return values greater than the low limit, but less than the high limit. Both limits are provided as arguments to be inserted so they can be dynamically set in the application.

5-8. Backing Up Data

Problem

Your application persists data on the device, and you need to provide users with a way to back up and restore this data in cases where they change devices or are forced to reinstall the application.

Solution

(API Level 3)

Use the device's external storage as a safe location to copy databases and other files. External storage is often physically removable, allowing the user to place it in another device and do a restore. Even in cases where this is not possible, external storage can always be mounted when the user connects a device to the computer, allowing data transfer to take place.

How It Works

Listing 5-23 shows an implementation of AsyncTask that copies a database file back and forth between the device's external storage and its location in the application's data directory. It also defines an interface for an activity to implement to get notified when the operation is complete. File operations such as copy can take some time to complete, so you can implement this by using an AsyncTask so it can happen in the background and not block the main thread.

Listing 5-23. AsyncTask for Backup and Restore

```
public class BackupTask extends AsyncTask<String,Void,Integer> {

    public interface CompletionListener {
        void onBackupComplete();
        void onRestoreComplete();
        void onError(int errorCode);
    }
```

```
public static final int BACKUP_SUCCESS = 1;
public static final int RESTORE_SUCCESS = 2;
public static final int BACKUP_ERROR = 3;
public static final int RESTORE_NOFILEERROR = 4;

public static final String COMMAND_BACKUP = "backupDatabase";
public static final String COMMAND_RESTORE = "restoreDatabase";

private Context mContext;
private CompletionListener listener;

public BackupTask(Context context) {
    super();
    mContext = context;
}

public void setCompletionListener(CompletionListener aListener) {
    listener = aListener;
}

@Override
protected Integer doInBackground(String... params) {

    //Get a reference to the database
    File dbFile = mContext.getDatabasePath("mydb");
    //Get a reference to the directory location for the backup
    File exportDir =
            new File(Environment.getExternalStorageDirectory(), "myAppBackups");
    if (!exportDir.exists()) {
        exportDir.mkdirs();
    }
    File backup = new File(exportDir, dbFile.getName());

    //Check the required operation
    String command = params[0];
    if(command.equals(COMMAND_BACKUP)) {
        //Attempt file copy
        try {
            backup.createNewFile();
            fileCopy(dbFile, backup);

            return BACKUP_SUCCESS;
        } catch (IOException e) {
            return BACKUP_ERROR;
        }
    } else if(command.equals(COMMAND_RESTORE)) {
        //Attempt file copy
        try {
            if(!backup.exists()) {
                return RESTORE_NOFILEERROR;
            }
```

```
                dbFile.createNewFile();
                fileCopy(backup, dbFile);
                return RESTORE_SUCCESS;
            } catch (IOException e) {
                return BACKUP_ERROR;
            }
        } else {
            return BACKUP_ERROR;
        }
    }

    @Override
    protected void onPostExecute(Integer result) {

        switch(result) {
        case BACKUP_SUCCESS:
            if(listener != null) {
                listener.onBackupComplete();
            }
            break;
        case RESTORE_SUCCESS:
            if(listener != null) {
                listener.onRestoreComplete();
            }
            break;
        case RESTORE_NOFILEERROR:
            if(listener != null) {
                listener.onError(RESTORE_NOFILEERROR);
            }
            break;
        default:
            if(listener != null) {
                listener.onError(BACKUP_ERROR);
            }
        }
    }

    private void fileCopy(File source, File dest) throws IOException {
        FileChannel inChannel = new FileInputStream(source).getChannel();
        FileChannel outChannel = new FileOutputStream(dest).getChannel();
        try {
            inChannel.transferTo(0, inChannel.size(), outChannel);
        } finally {
            if (inChannel != null)
                inChannel.close();
            if (outChannel != null)
                outChannel.close();
        }
    }
}
```

As you can see, BackupTask operates by copying the current version of a named database to a specific directory in external storage when COMMAND_BACKUP is passed to execute(), and it copies the file back when COMMAND_RESTORE is passed.

Once executed, the task uses Context.getDatabasePath() to retrieve a reference to the database file we need to back up. This line could easily be replaced with a call to Context.getFilesDir(), accessing a file on the system's internal storage to back up instead. A reference to a backup directory we've created on external storage is also obtained.

The files are copied using traditional Java file I/O, and if all is successful, the registered listener is notified. During the process, any exceptions thrown are caught and an error is returned to the listener instead. Now let's take a look at an activity that utilizes this task to back up a database (see Listing 5-24).

Listing 5-24. Activity Using BackupTask

```
public class BackupActivity extends Activity implements BackupTask.CompletionListener {

    @Override
    public void onCreate(Bundle savedInstanceState) {
        super.onCreate(savedInstanceState);
        setContentView(R.layout.main);
        //Dummy example database
        SQLiteDatabase db = openOrCreateDatabase("mydb", Activity.MODE_PRIVATE, null);
        db.close();
    }

    @Override
    public void onResume() {
        super.onResume();
        if( Environment.getExternalStorageState().equals(Environment.MEDIA_MOUNTED) ) {
            BackupTask task = new BackupTask(this);
            task.setCompletionListener(this);
            task.execute(BackupTask.COMMAND_RESTORE);
        }
    }

    @Override
    public void onPause() {
        super.onPause();
        if( Environment.getExternalStorageState().equals(Environment.MEDIA_MOUNTED) ) {
            BackupTask task = new BackupTask(this);
            task.execute(BackupTask.COMMAND_BACKUP);
        }
    }

    @Override
    public void onBackupComplete() {
        Toast.makeText(this, "Backup Successful", Toast.LENGTH_SHORT).show();
    }
```

```
    @Override
    public void onError(int errorCode) {
        if(errorCode == BackupTask.RESTORE_NOFILEERROR) {
            Toast.makeText(this, "No Backup Found to Restore",
                Toast.LENGTH_SHORT).show();
        } else {
            Toast.makeText(this, "Error During Operation: "+errorCode,
                Toast.LENGTH_SHORT).show();
        }
    }

    @Override
    public void onRestoreComplete() {
        Toast.makeText(this, "Restore Successful", Toast.LENGTH_SHORT).show();
    }
}
```

The activity implements the CompletionListener defined by BackupTask, so it may be notified when operations are finished or an error occurs. For the purposes of the example, a dummy database is created in the application's database directory. We call openOrCreateDatabase() only to allow a file to be created, so the connection is immediately closed afterward. Under normal circumstances, this database would already exist and these lines would not be necessary.

The example does a restore operation each time the activity is resumed, registering itself with the task so it can be notified and raise a Toast to the user of the status result. Notice that the task of checking whether external storage is usable falls to the activity as well, and no tasks are executed if external storage is not accessible. When the activity is paused, a backup operation is executed, this time without registering for callbacks. This is because the activity is no longer interesting to the user, so we won't need to raise a toast to point out the operation results.

Extra Credit

This background task could be extended to save the data to a cloud-based service for maximum safety and data portability. Many options are available to accomplish this, including Google's own set of web APIs, and we recommend you give this a try.

Android, as of API Level 8, also includes an API for backing up data to a cloud-based service. This API may suit your purposes; however, we will not discuss it here. The Android framework cannot guarantee that this service will be available on all Android devices, and there is no API as of this writing to determine whether the device the user has will support the Android backup, so it is not recommended for critical data.

5-9. Sharing Your Database

Problem

Your application would like to provide the database content it maintains to other applications on the device.

Solution

(API Level 4)

Create a `ContentProvider` to act as an external interface for your application's data. `ContentProvider` exposes an arbitrary set of data to external requests through a database-like interface of `query()`, `insert()`, `update()`, and `delete()`, though the implementer is free to design how the interface maps to the actual data model. Creating a `ContentProvider` to expose the data from a `SQLiteDatabase` is straightforward and simple. With some minor exceptions, the developer needs only to pass calls from the provider down to the database.

Arguments about which data set to operate on are typically encoded in the `Uri` passed to the `ContentProvider`. For example, sending a query `Uri` such as

```
content://com.examples.myprovider/friends
```

would tell the provider to return information from the `friends` table within its data set, while

```
content://com.examples.myprovider/friends/15
```

would instruct just the record ID 15 to return from the query. It should be noted that these are only the conventions used by the rest of the system, and that you are responsible for making the `ContentProvider` you create behave in this manner. There is nothing inherent about `ContentProvider` that provides this functionality for you.

How It Works

First of all, to create a `ContentProvider` that interacts with a database, we must have a database in place to interact with. Listing 5-25 is a sample `SQLiteOpenHelper` implementation that we will use to create and access the database itself.

Listing 5-25. Sample `SQLiteOpenHelper`

```java
public class ShareDbHelper extends SQLiteOpenHelper {

    private static final String DB_NAME = "frienddb";
    private static final int DB_VERSION = 1;

    public static final String TABLE_NAME = "friends";
    public static final String COL_FIRST = "firstName";
    public static final String COL_LAST = "lastName";
    public static final String COL_PHONE = "phoneNumber";

    private static final String STRING_CREATE =
        "CREATE TABLE "+TABLE_NAME+" (_id INTEGER PRIMARY KEY AUTOINCREMENT, "
        +COL_FIRST+" TEXT, "+COL_LAST+" TEXT, "+COL_PHONE+" TEXT);";

    public ShareDbHelper(Context context) {
        super(context, DB_NAME, null, DB_VERSION);
    }
```

```
@Override
public void onCreate(SQLiteDatabase db) {
    //Create the database table
    db.execSQL(STRING_CREATE);

    //Inserting example values into database
    ContentValues cv = new ContentValues(3);
    cv.put(COL_FIRST, "John");
    cv.put(COL_LAST, "Doe");
    cv.put(COL_PHONE, "8885551234");
    db.insert(TABLE_NAME, null, cv);
    cv = new ContentValues(3);
    cv.put(COL_FIRST, "Jane");
    cv.put(COL_LAST, "Doe");
    cv.put(COL_PHONE, "8885552345");
    db.insert(TABLE_NAME, null, cv);
    cv = new ContentValues(3);
    cv.put(COL_FIRST, "Jill");
    cv.put(COL_LAST, "Doe");
    cv.put(COL_PHONE, "8885553456");
    db.insert(TABLE_NAME, null, cv);
}

@Override
public void onUpgrade(SQLiteDatabase db, int oldVersion, int newVersion) {
    //For now, clear the database and re-create
    db.execSQL("DROP TABLE IF EXISTS "+TABLE_NAME);
    onCreate(db);
}
}
```

Overall, this helper is fairly simple, creating a single table to keep a list of our friends with just three columns for housing text data. For the purposes of this example, three row values are inserted. Now let's take a look at a ContentProvider that will expose this database to other applications: see Listings 5-26 and 5-27.

Listing 5-26. Manifest Declaration for ContentProvider

```
<manifest xmlns:android="http://schemas.android.com/apk/res/android" ...>
    <application ...>
        <provider android:name=".FriendProvider"
            android:authorities="com.examples.sharedb.friendprovider">
        </provider>
    </application>
</manifest>
```

Listing 5-27. ContentProvider for a Database

```java
public class FriendProvider extends ContentProvider {

    public static final Uri CONTENT_URI =
            Uri.parse("content://com.examples.sharedb.friendprovider/friends");

    public static final class Columns {
        public static final String _ID = "_id";
        public static final String FIRST = "firstName";
        public static final String LAST = "lastName";
        public static final String PHONE = "phoneNumber";
    }

    /* Uri Matching */
    private static final int FRIEND = 1;
    private static final int FRIEND_ID = 2;

    private static final UriMatcher matcher = new UriMatcher(UriMatcher.NO_MATCH);
    static {
        matcher.addURI(CONTENT_URI.getAuthority(), "friends", FRIEND);
        matcher.addURI(CONTENT_URI.getAuthority(), "friends/#", FRIEND_ID);
    }

    SQLiteDatabase db;

    @Override
    public int delete(Uri uri, String selection, String[] selectionArgs) {
        int result = matcher.match(uri);
        switch(result) {
        case FRIEND:
            return db.delete(ShareDbHelper.TABLE_NAME, selection, selectionArgs);
        case FRIEND_ID:
            return db.delete(ShareDbHelper.TABLE_NAME, "_ID = ?",
                    new String[]{uri.getLastPathSegment()});
        default:
            return 0;
        }
    }

    @Override
    public String getType(Uri uri) {
        return null;
    }

    @Override
    public Uri insert(Uri uri, ContentValues values) {
        long id = db.insert(ShareDbHelper.TABLE_NAME, null, values);
        if(id >= 0) {
            return Uri.withAppendedPath(uri, String.valueOf(id));
        } else {
            return null;
        }
    }
```

```java
@Override
public boolean onCreate() {
    ShareDbHelper helper = new ShareDbHelper(getContext());
    db = helper.getWritableDatabase();
    return true;
}

@Override
public Cursor query(Uri uri, String[] projection, String selection,
    String[] selectionArgs, String sortOrder) {
    int result = matcher.match(uri);
    switch(result) {
    case FRIEND:
        return db.query(ShareDbHelper.TABLE_NAME, projection, selection,
            selectionArgs, null, null, sortOrder);
    case FRIEND_ID:
        return db.query(ShareDbHelper.TABLE_NAME, projection, "_ID = ?",
                new String[]{uri.getLastPathSegment()}, null, null, sortOrder);
    default:
        return null;
    }
}

@Override
public int update(Uri uri, ContentValues values, String selection,
    String[] selectionArgs) {
    int result = matcher.match(uri);
    switch(result) {
    case FRIEND:
        return db.update(ShareDbHelper.TABLE_NAME, values, selection,
            selectionArgs);
    case FRIEND_ID:
        return db.update(ShareDbHelper.TABLE_NAME, values, "_ID = ?",
                new String[]{uri.getLastPathSegment()});
    default:
        return 0;
    }
}

}
```

A ContentProvider must be declared in the application's manifest with the authority string that it represents. This allows the provider to be accessed from external applications, but the declaration is still required even if you use the provider only internally within your application. The authority is what Android uses to match Uri requests to the provider, so it should match the authority portion of the public CONTENT_URI.

The six required methods to override when extending ContentProvider are query(), insert(), update(), delete(), getType(), and onCreate(). The first four of these methods have direct counterparts in SQLiteDatabase, so the database method is simply called with the appropriate parameters. The primary difference between the two is that the ContentProvider method passes in a Uri, which the provider should inspect to determine which portion of the database to operate on.

These four primary CRUD methods are called on the provider when an activity or other system component calls the corresponding method on its internal ContentResolver (you see this in action in Listing 5-27).

To adhere to the Uri convention mentioned in the first part of this recipe, insert() returns a Uri object created by appending the newly created record ID onto the end of the path. This Uri should be considered by its requester to be a direct reference back to the record that was just created.

The remaining methods (query(), update(), and delete()) adhere to the convention by inspecting the incoming Uri to see whether it refers to a specific record or to the whole table. This task is accomplished with the help of the UriMatcher convenience class. The UriMatcher.match() method compares a Uri to a set of supplied patterns and returns the matching pattern as an int, or UriMatcher.NO_MATCH if one is not found. If a Uri is supplied with a record ID appended, the call to the database is modified to affect only that specific row.

A UriMatcher should be initialized by supplying a set of patterns with UriMatcher.addURI(); Google recommends that this all be done in a static context within the ContentProvider, so it will be initialized the first time the class is loaded into memory. Each pattern added is also given a constant identifier that will be the return value when matches are made. Two wildcard characters may be placed in the supplied patterns: the pound (#) character will match any number, and the asterisk (*) will match any text.

Our example has created two patterns to match. The initial pattern matches the supplied CONTENT_URI directly, and it is taken to reference the entire database table. The second pattern looks for an appended number to the path, which will be taken to reference just the record at that ID.

Access to the database is obtained through a reference given by the ShareDbHelper in onCreate(). The size of the database that is used should be considered when deciding whether this method will be appropriate for your application. Our database is quite small when it is created, but larger databases may take a long time to create, in which case the main thread should not be tied up while this operation is taking place; getWritableDatabase() may need to be wrapped in an AsyncTask and done in the background in these cases.

Now let's take a look at a sample activity accessing the data. As you can see in Figure 5-3, we will create a simple list that displays the results of a query against our provider's data.

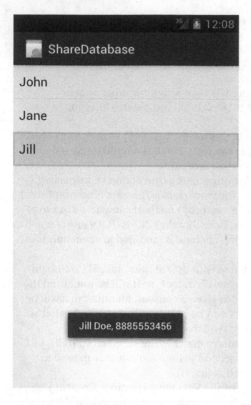

Figure 5-3. *Information from a* ContentProvider

Listings 5-28 and 5-29 show us the manifest and activity source to complete this example.

Listing 5-28. AndroidManifest.xml

```
<?xml version="1.0" encoding="utf-8"?>
<manifest xmlns:android="http://schemas.android.com/apk/res/android"
    package="com.examples.sharedb" android:versionCode="1" android:versionName="1.0">
    <uses-sdk android:minSdkVersion="4" />
    <application android:icon="@drawable/icon" android:label="@string/app_name">
      <activity android:name=".ShareActivity" android:label="@string/app_name">
        <intent-filter>
          <action android:name="android.intent.action.MAIN" />
          <category android:name="android.intent.category.LAUNCHER" />
        </intent-filter>
      </activity>
      <provider android:name=".FriendProvider"
          android:authorities="com.examples.sharedb.friendprovider">
      </provider>
    </application>
</manifest>
```

Listing 5-29. Activity Accessing the ContentProvider

```java
public class ShareActivity extends FragmentActivity implements
        LoaderManager.LoaderCallbacks<Cursor>, AdapterView.OnItemClickListener {
    private static final int LOADER_LIST = 100;
    SimpleCursorAdapter mAdapter;

    @Override
    public void onCreate(Bundle savedInstanceState) {
        super.onCreate(savedInstanceState);
        getSupportLoaderManager().initLoader(LOADER_LIST, null, this);

        mAdapter = new SimpleCursorAdapter(this,
                android.R.layout.simple_list_item_1, null,
                new String[]{FriendProvider.Columns.FIRST},
                new int[]{android.R.id.text1}, 0);

        ListView list = new ListView(this);
        list.setOnItemClickListener(this);
        list.setAdapter(mAdapter);

        setContentView(list);
    }

    @Override
    public void onItemClick(AdapterView<?> parent, View v, int position, long id) {
        Cursor c = mAdapter.getCursor();
        c.moveToPosition(position);

        Uri uri = Uri.withAppendedPath(FriendProvider.CONTENT_URI, c.getString(0));
        String[] projection = new String[]{FriendProvider.Columns.FIRST,
                FriendProvider.Columns.LAST,
                FriendProvider.Columns.PHONE};
        //Get the full record
        Cursor cursor = getContentResolver().query(uri, projection, null, null, null);
        cursor.moveToFirst();

        String message = String.format("%s %s, %s", cursor.getString(0),
                cursor.getString(1), cursor.getString(2));
        Toast.makeText(this, message, Toast.LENGTH_SHORT).show();
        cursor.close();
    }

    @Override
    public Loader<Cursor> onCreateLoader(int id, Bundle args) {
        String[] projection = new String[]{FriendProvider.Columns._ID,
                FriendProvider.Columns.FIRST};
        return new CursorLoader(this, FriendProvider.CONTENT_URI,
                projection, null, null, null);
    }
```

```
    @Override
    public void onLoadFinished(Loader<Cursor> loader, Cursor data) {
        mAdapter.swapCursor(data);
    }

    @Override
    public void onLoaderReset(Loader<Cursor> loader) {
        mAdapter.swapCursor(null);
    }
}
```

■ **Important**   This example requires the Support Library to provide access to the `Loader` pattern in Android 1.6 and above. If you are targeting Android 3.0+ in your application, you may replace `FragmentActivity` with `Activity`, and `getSupportLoaderManager()` with `getLoaderManager()`.

This example queries the `FriendsProvider` for all its records and places them into a list, displaying only the first-name column. In order for the `Cursor` to adapt properly into a list, our projection must include the ID column, even though it is not displayed.

If the user taps any of the items in the list, another query is made of the provider using a `Uri` constructed with the record ID appended to the end, forcing the provider to return only that one record. In addition, an expanded projection is provided to get all the column data about this friend.

The returned data is placed into a `Toast` and raised for the user to see. Individual fields from the cursor are accessed by their *column index*, corresponding to the index in the projection passed to the query. The `Cursor.getColumnIndex()` method may also be used to query the cursor for the index associated with a given column name.

A `Cursor` should always be closed when it is no longer needed, as we do with the `Cursor` created after a user click. The only exceptions to this are `Cursor` instances created and managed by the `Loader`.

5-10. Sharing Your SharedPreferences

Problem

You would like your application to provide the settings values it has stored in `SharedPreferences` to other applications of the system and even to allow those applications to modify those settings if they have permission to do so.

Solution

(API Level 1)

Create a `ContentProvider` to interface your application's `SharedPreferences` with the rest of the system. The settings data will be delivered using a `MatrixCursor`, which is an implementation that can be used for data that does not reside in a database. The `ContentProvider` will be protected by separate permissions to read/write the data within so that only permitted applications will have access.

How It Works

To properly demonstrate the permissions aspect of this recipe, we need to create two separate applications: one that actually contains our preference data and one that wants to read and modify it through the ContentProvider interface. This is because Android does not enforce permissions on anything operating within the same application. Let's start with the provider, shown in Listing 5-30.

Listing 5-30. ContentProvider for Application Settings

```
public class SettingsProvider extends ContentProvider {

    public static final Uri CONTENT_URI =
        Uri.parse("content://com.examples.sharepreferences.settingsprovider/settings");

    public static class Columns {
        public static final String _ID = Settings.NameValueTable._ID;
        public static final String NAME = Settings.NameValueTable.NAME;
        public static final String VALUE = Settings.NameValueTable.VALUE;
    }

    private static final String NAME_SELECTION = Columns.NAME + " = ?";

    private SharedPreferences mPreferences;

    @Override
    public int delete(Uri uri, String selection, String[] selectionArgs) {
        throw new UnsupportedOperationException(
                "This ContentProvider does not support removing Preferences");
    }

    @Override
    public String getType(Uri uri) {
        return null;
    }

    @Override
    public Uri insert(Uri uri, ContentValues values) {
        throw new UnsupportedOperationException(
                "This ContentProvider does not support adding new Preferences");
    }

    @Override
    public boolean onCreate() {
        mPreferences = PreferenceManager.getDefaultSharedPreferences(getContext());
        return true;
    }

    @Override
    public Cursor query(Uri uri, String[] projection, String selection,
            String[] selectionArgs, String sortOrder) {
        MatrixCursor cursor = new MatrixCursor(projection);
        Map<String, ?> preferences = mPreferences.getAll();
        Set<String> preferenceKeys = preferences.keySet();
```

413

```java
        if(TextUtils.isEmpty(selection)) {
            //Get all items
            for(String key : preferenceKeys) {
                //Insert only the columns they requested
                MatrixCursor.RowBuilder builder = cursor.newRow();
                for(String column : projection) {
                    if(column.equals(Columns._ID)) {
                        //Generate a unique id
                        builder.add(key.hashCode());
                    }
                    if(column.equals(Columns.NAME)) {
                        builder.add(key);
                    }
                    if(column.equals(Columns.VALUE)) {
                        builder.add(preferences.get(key));
                    }
                }
            }
        } else if (selection.equals(NAME_SELECTION)) {
            //Parse the key value and check if it exists
            String key = selectionArgs == null ? "" : selectionArgs[0];
            if(preferences.containsKey(key)) {
                //Get the requested item
                MatrixCursor.RowBuilder builder = cursor.newRow();
                for(String column : projection) {
                    if(column.equals(Columns._ID)) {
                        //Generate a unique id
                        builder.add(key.hashCode());
                    }
                    if(column.equals(Columns.NAME)) {
                        builder.add(key);
                    }
                    if(column.equals(Columns.VALUE)) {
                        builder.add(preferences.get(key));
                    }
                }
            }
        }
    }

    return cursor;
}

@Override
public int update(Uri uri, ContentValues values, String selection,
        String[] selectionArgs) {
    //Check if the key exists, and update its value
    String key = values.getAsString(Columns.NAME);
    if (mPreferences.contains(key)) {
        Object value = values.get(Columns.VALUE);
        SharedPreferences.Editor editor = mPreferences.edit();
```

```
            if (value instanceof Boolean) {
                editor.putBoolean(key, (Boolean)value);
            } else if (value instanceof Number) {
                editor.putFloat(key, ((Number)value).floatValue());
            } else if (value instanceof String) {
                editor.putString(key, (String)value);
            } else {
                //Invalid value, do not update
              return 0;
            }
            editor.commit();
            //Notify any observers
            getContext().getContentResolver().notifyChange(CONTENT_URI, null);
            return 1;
        }
        //Key not in preferences
        return 0;
    }
}
```

Upon creation of this ContentProvider, we obtain a reference to the application's default SharedPreferences rather than opening up a database connection as in the previous example. We support only two methods in this provider—query() and update()—and throw exceptions for the rest. This allows read/write access to the preference values without allowing any ability to add or remove new preference types.

Inside the query() method, we check the selection string to determine whether we should return all preference values or just the requested value. Three fields are defined for each preference: _id, name, and value. The value of _id may not be related to the preference itself, but if the client of this provider wants to display the results in a list by using CursorAdapter, this field will need to exist and have a unique value for each record, so we generate one. Notice that we obtain the preference value as an Object to insert in the cursor; we want to minimize the amount of knowledge the provider should have about the types of data it contains.

The cursor implementation used in this provider is a MatrixCursor, which is a cursor designed to be built around data not held inside a database. The example iterates through the list of columns requested (the projection) and builds each row according to these columns it contains. Each row is created by calling MatrixCursor.newRow(), which also returns a Builder instance that will be used to add the column data. Care should always be taken to match the order of the column data that is added to the order of the requested projection. They should always match.

The implementation of update() inspects only the incoming ContentValues for the preference it needs to update. Because this is enough to describe the exact item we need, we don't implement any further logic using the selection arguments. If the name value of the preference already exists, the value for it is updated and saved. Unfortunately, there is no method to simply insert an Object back into SharedPreferences, so you must inspect it based on the valid types that ContentValues can return and call the appropriate setter method to match. Finally, we call notifyObservers() so any registered ContentObserver objects will be notified of the data change.

You may have noticed that there is no code in the ContentProvider to manage the read/write permissions we promised to implement! This is handled by Android for us: we just need to update the manifest appropriately. Have a look at Listing 5-31.

Listing 5-31. AndroidManifest.xml

```xml
<manifest xmlns:android="http://schemas.android.com/apk/res/android"
    package="com.examples.sharepreferences"
    android:versionCode="1"
    android:versionName="1.0" >

    <uses-sdk ... />

    <permission
        android:name="com.examples.sharepreferences.permission.READ_PREFERENCES"
        android:label="Read Application Settings"
        android:protectionLevel="normal" />
    <permission
        android:name="com.examples.sharepreferences.permission.WRITE_PREFERENCES"
        android:label="Write Application Settings"
        android:protectionLevel="dangerous" />

    <uses-permission
        android:name="com.examples.sharepreferences.permission.READ_PREFERENCES" />
    <uses-permission
        android:name="com.examples.sharepreferences.permission.WRITE_PREFERENCES" />

    <application ... >
        <activity android:name=".SettingsActivity" >
            <intent-filter>
                <action android:name="android.intent.action.MAIN" />
                <category android:name="android.intent.category.LAUNCHER" />
            </intent-filter>
            <intent-filter>
                <action android:name="com.examples.sharepreferences.ACTION_SETTINGS" />
                <category android:name="android.intent.category.DEFAULT" />
            </intent-filter>
        </activity>

        <provider
            android:name=".SettingsProvider"
            android:authorities="com.examples.sharepreferences.settingsprovider"
            android:readPermission=
                    "com.examples.sharepreferences.permission.READ_PREFERENCES"
            android:writePermission=
                    "com.examples.sharepreferences.permission.WRITE_PREFERENCES" >
        </provider>
    </application>

</manifest>
```

Here you can see two custom <permission> elements declared and attached to our <provider> declaration. This is the only code we need to add, and Android knows to enforce the read permissions for operations such as query(), and the write permission for insert(), update(), and delete(). We have also declared a custom <intent-filter> on the activity in this application, which will come in handy for any external applications that may want to launch the settings UI directly. Listings 5-32 through 5-34 define the rest of this example.

Listing 5-32. res/xml/preferences.xml

```xml
<?xml version="1.0" encoding="utf-8"?>
<PreferenceScreen xmlns:android="http://schemas.android.com/apk/res/android" >
    <CheckBoxPreference
        android:key="preferenceEnabled"
        android:title="Set Enabled"
        android:defaultValue="true"/>
    <EditTextPreference
        android:key="preferenceName"
        android:title="User Name"
        android:defaultValue="John Doe"/>
    <ListPreference
        android:key="preferenceSelection"
        android:title="Selection"
        android:entries="@array/selection_items"
        android:entryValues="@array/selection_items"
        android:defaultValue="Four"/>
</PreferenceScreen>
```

Listing 5-33. res/values/arrays.xml

```xml
<?xml version="1.0" encoding="utf-8"?>
<resources>
    <string-array name="selection_items">
        <item>One</item>
        <item>Two</item>
        <item>Three</item>
        <item>Four</item>
    </string-array>
</resources>
```

Listing 5-34. Preferences Activity

```java
//Note the package for this application
package com.examples.sharepreferences;

public class SettingsActivity extends PreferenceActivity {

    @Override
    protected void onCreate(Bundle savedInstanceState) {
        super.onCreate(savedInstanceState);
        //Load the preferences defaults on first run
        PreferenceManager.setDefaultValues(this, R.xml.preferences, false);

        addPreferencesFromResource(R.xml.preferences);
    }
}
```

The settings values for this example application are manageable directly via a simple
PreferenceActivity, whose data is defined in the preferences.xml file.

■ **Note**   PreferenceActivity was deprecated in Android 3.0 in favor of PreferenceFragment, but at the time of this book's publication, PreferenceFragment has not yet been added to the Support Library. Therefore, we use PreferenceActivity here to allow support for earlier versions of Android.

Usage Example

Next let's take a look at Listings 5-35 through 5-37, which define a second application that will attempt to access our preferences data by using this ContentProvider interface.

Listing 5-35. AndroidManifest.xml

```xml
<manifest xmlns:android="http://schemas.android.com/apk/res/android"
    package="com.examples.accesspreferences">

    <uses-sdk ... />

    <uses-permission
        android:name="com.examples.sharepreferences.permission.READ_PREFERENCES" />
    <uses-permission
        android:name="com.examples.sharepreferences.permission.WRITE_PREFERENCES" />

    <application ... >
        <activity android:name=".MainActivity" >
            <intent-filter>
                <action android:name="android.intent.action.MAIN" />
                <category android:name="android.intent.category.LAUNCHER" />
            </intent-filter>
        </activity>
    </application>

</manifest>
```

The key point here is that this application declares the use of both our custom permissions as <uses-permission> elements. This is what allows it to have access to the external provider. Without these, a request through ContentResolver would result in a SecurityException.

Listing 5-36. res/layout/main.xml

```xml
<RelativeLayout xmlns:android="http://schemas.android.com/apk/res/android"
    android:layout_width="match_parent"
    android:layout_height="match_parent" >
    <Button
        android:id="@+id/button_settings"
        android:layout_width="match_parent"
        android:layout_height="wrap_content"
        android:text="Show Settings"
        android:onClick="onSettingsClick" />
```

```xml
<CheckBox
    android:id="@+id/checkbox_enable"
    android:layout_width="wrap_content"
    android:layout_height="wrap_content"
    android:layout_below="@id/button_settings"
    android:text="Set Enable Setting"/>
<LinearLayout
    android:layout_width="wrap_content"
    android:layout_height="wrap_content"
    android:layout_centerInParent="true"
    android:orientation="vertical">
    <TextView
        android:id="@+id/value_enabled"
        android:layout_width="wrap_content"
        android:layout_height="wrap_content" />
    <TextView
        android:id="@+id/value_name"
        android:layout_width="wrap_content"
        android:layout_height="wrap_content" />
    <TextView
        android:id="@+id/value_selection"
        android:layout_width="wrap_content"
        android:layout_height="wrap_content" />
</LinearLayout>
</RelativeLayout>
```

Listing 5-37. Activity Interacting with the Provider

```java
//Note the package as this is a different application
package com.examples.accesspreferences;

public class MainActivity extends Activity implements OnCheckedChangeListener {

    public static final String SETTINGS_ACTION =
        "com.examples.sharepreferences.ACTION_SETTINGS";
    public static final Uri SETTINGS_CONTENT_URI =
        Uri.parse("content://com.examples.sharepreferences.settingsprovider/settings");
    public static class SettingsColumns {
        public static final String _ID = Settings.NameValueTable._ID;
        public static final String NAME = Settings.NameValueTable.NAME;
        public static final String VALUE = Settings.NameValueTable.VALUE;
    }

    TextView mEnabled, mName, mSelection;
    CheckBox mToggle;

    private ContentObserver mObserver = new ContentObserver(new Handler()) {
        public void onChange(boolean selfChange) {
            updatePreferences();
        }
    };
```

```java
@Override
public void onCreate(Bundle savedInstanceState) {
    super.onCreate(savedInstanceState);
    setContentView(R.layout.main);

    mEnabled = (TextView) findViewById(R.id.value_enabled);
    mName = (TextView) findViewById(R.id.value_name);
    mSelection = (TextView) findViewById(R.id.value_selection);
    mToggle = (CheckBox) findViewById(R.id.checkbox_enable);
    mToggle.setOnCheckedChangeListener(this);
}

@Override
protected void onResume() {
    super.onResume();
    //Get the latest provider data
    updatePreferences();
    //Register an observer for changes that will
    // happen while we are active
    getContentResolver().registerContentObserver(SETTINGS_CONTENT_URI,
            false, mObserver);
}

@Override
public void onCheckedChanged(CompoundButton buttonView, boolean isChecked) {
    ContentValues cv = new ContentValues(2);
    cv.put(SettingsColumns.NAME, "preferenceEnabled");
    cv.put(SettingsColumns.VALUE, isChecked);

    //Update the provider, which will trigger our observer
    getContentResolver().update(SETTINGS_CONTENT_URI, cv, null, null);
}

public void onSettingsClick(View v) {
    try {
        Intent intent = new Intent(SETTINGS_ACTION);
        startActivity(intent);
    } catch (ActivityNotFoundException e) {
        Toast.makeText(this,
                "You do not have the Android Recipes Settings App installed.",
                Toast.LENGTH_SHORT).show();
    }
}

private void updatePreferences() {
    Cursor c = getContentResolver().query(SETTINGS_CONTENT_URI,
            new String[] {SettingsColumns.NAME, SettingsColumns.VALUE},
            null, null, null);
    if (c == null) {
        return;
    }
```

```
            while (c.moveToNext()) {
                String key = c.getString(0);
                if ("preferenceEnabled".equals(key)) {
                    mEnabled.setText( String.format("Enabled Setting = %s",
                        c.getString(1)) );
                    mToggle.setChecked( Boolean.parseBoolean(c.getString(1)) );
                } else if ("preferenceName".equals(key)) {
                    mName.setText( String.format("User Name Setting = %s",
                        c.getString(1)) );
                } else if ("preferenceSelection".equals(key)) {
                    mSelection.setText( String.format("Selection Setting = %s",
                        c.getString(1)) );
                }
            }

            c.close();
        }
    }
```

Because this is a separate application, it may not have access to the constants defined in the first (unless you control both applications and use a library project or some other method), so we have redefined them here for this example. If you were producing an application with an external provider you would like other developers to use, it would be prudent to also provide a JAR library that contains the constants necessary to access the Uri and column data in the provider, similar to the API provided by ContactsContract and CalendarContract.

In this example, the activity queries the provider for the current values of the settings each time it returns to the foreground and displays them in a TextView. The results are returned in a Cursor with two values in each row: the preference name and its value. The activity also registers a ContentObserver so that if the values change while this activity is active, the displayed values can be updated as well. When the user changes the value of the CheckBox onscreen, this calls the provider's update() method, which will trigger this observer to update the display.

Finally, if desired, the user could launch the SettingsActivity from the external application directly by clicking the Show Settings button. This calls startActivity() with an Intent containing the custom action string for which SettingsActivity is set to filter.

5-11. Sharing Your Other Data

Problem

You would like your application to provide the files or other private data it maintains to applications on the device.

Solution

(API Level 3)

Create a ContentProvider to act as an external interface for your application's data. ContentProvider exposes an arbitrary set of data to external requests through a database-like interface of query(), insert(), update(), and delete(), though the implementation is free to design how the data passes to the actual model from these methods.

ContentProvider can be used to expose any type of application data, including the application's resources and assets, to external requests.

How It Works

Let's take a look at a ContentProvider implementation that exposes two data sources: an array of strings located in memory, and a series of image files stored in the application's assets directory. As before, we must declare our provider to the Android system by using a <provider> tag in the manifest. See Listings 5-38 and 5-39.

Listing 5-38. Manifest Declaration for ContentProvider

```
<?xml version="1.0" encoding="utf-8"?>
<manifest xmlns:android="http://schemas.android.com/apk/res/android" ...>
    <application ...>
      <provider android:name=".ImageProvider"
          android:authorities="com.examples.share.imageprovider">
      </provider>
    </application>
</manifest>
```

Listing 5-39. Custom ContentProvider Exposing Assets

```
public class ImageProvider extends ContentProvider {

    public static final Uri CONTENT_URI =
        Uri.parse("content://com.examples.share.imageprovider");

    public static final String COLUMN_NAME = "nameString";
    public static final String COLUMN_IMAGE = "imageUri";

    private String[] mNames;

    @Override
    public int delete(Uri uri, String selection, String[] selectionArgs) {
        throw new UnsupportedOperationException("This ContentProvider is read-only");
    }

    @Override
    public String getType(Uri uri) {
        return null;
    }

    @Override
    public Uri insert(Uri uri, ContentValues values) {
        throw new UnsupportedOperationException("This ContentProvider is read-only");
    }

    @Override
    public boolean onCreate() {
        mNames = new String[] {"John Doe", "Jane Doe", "Jill Doe"};
        return true;
    }
```

```
@Override
public Cursor query(Uri uri, String[] projection, String selection,
    String[] selectionArgs, String sortOrder) {
    MatrixCursor cursor = new MatrixCursor(projection);
    for(int i = 0; i < mNames.length; i++) {
        //Insert only the columns they requested
        MatrixCursor.RowBuilder builder = cursor.newRow();
        for(String column : projection) {
            if(column.equals("_id")) {
                //Use the array index as a unique id
                builder.add(i);
            }
            if(column.equals(COLUMN_NAME)) {
                builder.add(mNames[i]);
            }
            if(column.equals(COLUMN_IMAGE)) {
                builder.add(Uri.withAppendedPath(CONTENT_URI, String.valueOf(i)));
            }
        }
    }
    return cursor;
}

@Override
public int update(Uri uri, ContentValues values, String selection,
    String[] selectionArgs) {
    throw new UnsupportedOperationException("This ContentProvider is read-only");
}

@Override
public AssetFileDescriptor openAssetFile(Uri uri, String mode) throws
    FileNotFoundException {
    int requested = Integer.parseInt(uri.getLastPathSegment());
    AssetFileDescriptor afd;
    AssetManager manager = getContext().getAssets();
    //Return the appropriate asset for the requested item
    try {
        switch(requested) {
        case 0:
            afd = manager.openFd("logo1.png");
            break;
        case 1:
            afd = manager.openFd("logo2.png");
            break;
        case 2:
            afd = manager.openFd("logo3.png");
            break;
        default:
            afd = manager.openFd("logo1.png");
        }
        return afd;
```

```
        } catch (IOException e) {
            e.printStackTrace();
            return null;
        }
    }
}
```

As you may have guessed, the example exposes three logo image assets. The images we have chosen for this example are shown in Figure 5-4.

Figure 5-4. Examples of logo1.png (left), logo2.png (center), and logo3.png (right) stored in assets

Because we are exposing read-only content in the assets directory, there is no need to support the inherited methods insert(), update(), or delete(), so we have these methods simply throw an UnsupportedOperationException.

When the provider is created, the string array that holds people's names is created and onCreate() returns true; this signals to the system that the provider was created successfully. The provider exposes constants for its Uri and all readable column names. These values will be used by external applications to make requests for data.

This provider supports only a query for all the data within it. To support conditional queries for specific records or a subset of all the content, an application can process the values passed in to query() for selection and selectionArgs. In this example, any call to query() will build a cursor with all three elements contained within.

The cursor implementation used in this provider is a MatrixCursor, which is a cursor designed to be built around data that is not held inside a database. The example iterates through the list of columns requested (the projection) and builds each row according to these columns it contains. Each row is created by calling MatrixCursor.newRow(), which also returns a Builder instance that will be used to add the column data. Care should always be taken to match the order that the column data is added to the order of the requested projection. They should always match.

The value in the name column is the respective string in the local array, and the _id value, which Android requires to utilize the returned cursor with most ListAdapters, is simply returned as the array index. The information presented in the image column for each row is actually a content Uri representing the image file for each row, created with the provider's content Uri as the base, with the array index appended to it.

When an external application actually goes to retrieve this content, through ContentResolver. openInputStream(), a call will be made to openAssetFile(), which has been overridden to return an AssetFileDescriptor pointing to one of the image files in the assets directory. This implementation determines which image file to return by deconstructing the content Uri once again and retrieving the appended index value from the end.

Usage Example

In Figure 5-5, we have an activity displaying a similar list as in the previous recipe. However, now we are also pulling asset data to display for each selection.

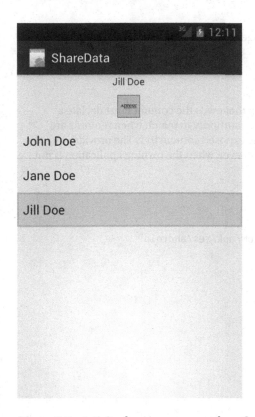

Figure 5-5. *Activity drawing resources from* `ContentProvider`

Let's take a look at how this provider should be implemented and accessed in the context of the Android application. See Listing 5-40.

Listing 5-40. `AndroidManifest.xml`

```xml
<?xml version="1.0" encoding="utf-8"?>
<manifest xmlns:android="http://schemas.android.com/apk/res/android"
    package="com.examples.share"
    android:versionCode="1"
    android:versionName="1.0">
    <uses-sdk android:minSdkVersion="3" />

    <application android:icon="@drawable/icon" android:label="@string/app_name">
        <activity android:name=".ShareActivity"
                android:label="@string/app_name">
```

```
            <intent-filter>
                <action android:name="android.intent.action.MAIN" />
                <category android:name="android.intent.category.LAUNCHER" />
            </intent-filter>
        </activity>
        <provider android:name=".ImageProvider"
          android:authorities="com.examples.share.imageprovider">
        </provider>
    </application>
</manifest>
```

To implement this provider, the manifest of the application that owns the content must declare a
<provider> tag pointing out the ContentProvider name and the authority to match when requests are
made. The authority value should match the base portion of the exposed content Uri. The provider must be
declared in the manifest so the system can instantiate and run it, even when the owning application is not
running. See Listings 5-41 and 5-42.

Listing 5-41. res/layout/main.xml

```
<?xml version="1.0" encoding="utf-8"?>
<LinearLayout xmlns:android="http://schemas.android.com/apk/res/android"
  android:orientation="vertical"
  android:layout_width="match_parent"
  android:layout_height="match_parent">
  <TextView
    android:id="@+id/name"
    android:layout_width="wrap_content"
    android:layout_height="20dip"
    android:layout_gravity="center_horizontal"
  />
  <ImageView
    android:id="@+id/image"
    android:layout_width="wrap_content"
    android:layout_height="50dip"
    android:layout_gravity="center_horizontal"
  />
  <ListView
    android:id="@+id/list"
    android:layout_width="match_parent"
    android:layout_height="match_parent"
  />
</LinearLayout>
```

Listing 5-42. Activity Reading from ImageProvider

```
public class ShareActivity extends FragmentActivity implements
        LoaderManager.LoaderCallbacks<Cursor>, AdapterView.OnItemClickListener {
    private static final int LOADER_LIST = 100;
    SimpleCursorAdapter mAdapter;
```

```
@Override
public void onCreate(Bundle savedInstanceState) {
    super.onCreate(savedInstanceState);
    getSupportLoaderManager().initLoader(LOADER_LIST, null, this);
    setContentView(R.layout.main);

    mAdapter = new SimpleCursorAdapter(this, android.R.layout.simple_list_item_1,
            null, new String[]{ImageProvider.COLUMN_NAME},
            new int[]{android.R.id.text1}, 0);

    ListView list = (ListView)findViewById(R.id.list);
    list.setOnItemClickListener(this);
    list.setAdapter(mAdapter);
}

@Override
public void onItemClick(AdapterView<?> parent, View v, int position, long id) {
    //Seek the cursor to the selection
    Cursor c = mAdapter.getCursor();
    c.moveToPosition(position);

    //Load the name column into the TextView
    TextView tv = (TextView)findViewById(R.id.name);
    tv.setText(c.getString(1));

    ImageView iv = (ImageView)findViewById(R.id.image);
    try {
        //Load the content from the image column into the ImageView
        InputStream in =
                getContentResolver().openInputStream(Uri.parse(c.getString(2)));
        Bitmap image = BitmapFactory.decodeStream(in);
        iv.setImageBitmap(image);
    } catch (FileNotFoundException e) {
        e.printStackTrace();
    }
}

@Override
public Loader<Cursor> onCreateLoader(int id, Bundle args) {
    String[] projection = new String[]{"_id",
            ImageProvider.COLUMN_NAME,
            ImageProvider.COLUMN_IMAGE};
    return new CursorLoader(this, ImageProvider.CONTENT_URI,
            projection, null, null, null);
}

@Override
public void onLoadFinished(Loader<Cursor> loader, Cursor data) {
    mAdapter.swapCursor(data);
}
```

```
    @Override
    public void onLoaderReset(Loader<Cursor> loader) {
        mAdapter.swapCursor(null);
    }
}
```

■ **Important**   This example requires the Support Library to provide access to the Loader pattern in Android 1.6 and above. If you are targeting Android 3.0+ in your application, you may replace FragmentActivity with Activity and getSupportLoaderManager() with getLoaderManager().

In this example, a managed cursor is obtained from the custom ContentProvider, referencing the exposed Uri and column names for the data. The data is then connected to a ListView through a SimpleCursorAdapter to display only the name value.

When the user taps any of the items in the list, the cursor is moved to that position and the respective name and image are displayed above. This is where the activity calls ContentResolver.openInputStream() to access the asset images through the Uri that was stored in the column field.

Figure 5-5 displays the result of running this application and selecting the last item in the list (Jill Doe).

Note that we have not closed the connection to the Cursor explicitly. Since the Loader created the Cursor, it is also the job of the Loader to manage its life cycle.

5-12. Integrating with System Documents

Problem

Your application creates or maintains content that you would like to expose to other applications via the system's document picker interface.

Solution

(API Level 19)

The DocumentsProvider is a specialized ContentProvider API that applications can use to expose their contents to the common documents picker interface in Android 4.4 and later. The advantage to using this framework is that it allows applications that manage access to storage services to expose the files and documents they own by using a common interface throughout the system. It also includes the ability for client applications to create and save new documents inside these applications (we will look more at the client side of this API in the next chapter).

A custom DocumentsProvider must identify all the files and directories it would like to expose by using a unique document ID string. This value does not need to match any specific format, but it must be unique and cannot change after it is reported to the system. The framework will persist these values for permissions purposes, so even across reboots the document IDs you provide (and later expect) must be consistent for any resource.

When subclassing DocumentsProvider, we will be implementing a different set of callbacks than the basic CRUD methods we used in the bare ContentProvider. The system's document picker interface will trigger the following methods on the provider as the user explores:

- queryRoots(): First called when the picker UI is launched to request basic information about the top-level "document" in your provider, as well as some basic metadata such as the name and icon to display. Most providers have only one root, but multiple roots can be returned if that better supports the provider's use case.

- queryChildDocuments(): Called when the provider is selected with the root's document ID in order to get a listing of the documents available under this root. If you return directory entries as elements underneath the root, the same method will be called again when one of those subdirectories is selected.

- queryDocument(): Called when a document is selected to obtain metadata about that specific instance. The data returned from this message should mirror what was returned from queryChildDocuments(), but for just the one element. This method is also called for each root to obtain additional metadata of the top-level directory in the provider.

- openDocument(): This is a request to open a FileDescriptor to the document so that the client application may read or write the document contents.

- openDocumentThumbnail(): If the metadata returned for a given document has the FLAG_SUPPORTS_THUMBNAIL flag set, this method is used to obtain a thumbnail to display in the picker UI for the document.

How It Works

We can modify our provider from the previous recipe to better integrate with the system's document picker UI, as seen in Figure 5-6.

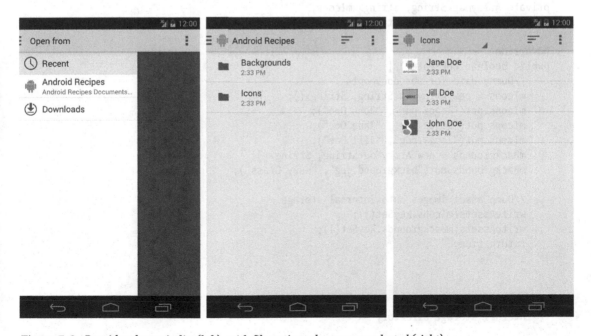

Figure 5-6. Provider shown in list (left), with file options shown once selected (right)

Achieving this takes a few modifications. Listing 5-43 shows our ImageProvider modified to subclass DocumentProvider instead.

Listing 5-43. ImageProvider as a DocumentsProvider

```java
public class ImageProvider extends DocumentsProvider {
    private static final String TAG = "ImageProvider";

    /* Cached recent selection */
    private static String sLastDocumentId;

    private static final String DOCID_ROOT = "root:";
    private static final String DOCID_ICONS_DIR = DOCID_ROOT + "icons:";
    private static final String DOCID_BGS_DIR = DOCID_ROOT + "backgrounds:";

    /* Default projection for a root when none supplied */
    private static final String[] DEFAULT_ROOT_PROJECTION = {
        Root.COLUMN_ROOT_ID, Root.COLUMN_MIME_TYPES,
        Root.COLUMN_FLAGS, Root.COLUMN_ICON, Root.COLUMN_TITLE,
        Root.COLUMN_SUMMARY, Root.COLUMN_DOCUMENT_ID,
        Root.COLUMN_AVAILABLE_BYTES
    };
    /* Default projection for documents when none supplied */
    private static final String[] DEFAULT_DOCUMENT_PROJECTION = {
        Document.COLUMN_DOCUMENT_ID, Document.COLUMN_MIME_TYPE,
        Document.COLUMN_DISPLAY_NAME, Document.COLUMN_LAST_MODIFIED,
        Document.COLUMN_FLAGS, Document.COLUMN_SIZE
    };

    private ArrayMap<String, String> mIcons;
    private ArrayMap<String, String> mBackgrounds;

    @Override
    public boolean onCreate() {
        //Dummy data for our documents
        mIcons = new ArrayMap<String, String>();
        mIcons.put("logo1.png", "John Doe");
        mIcons.put("logo2.png", "Jane Doe");
        mIcons.put("logo3.png", "Jill Doe");
        mBackgrounds = new ArrayMap<String, String>();
        mBackgrounds.put("background.jpg", "Wavy Grass");

        //Dump asset images onto internal storage
        writeAssets(mIcons.keySet());
        writeAssets(mBackgrounds.keySet());
        return true;
    }

    /*
     * Helper method to stream some dummy files out to the
     * internal storage directory
     */
```

```java
private void writeAssets(Set<String> filenames) {
    for(String name : filenames) {
        try {
            Log.d("ImageProvider", "Writing "+name+" to storage");
            InputStream in = getContext().getAssets().open(name);
            FileOutputStream out = getContext().openFileOutput(name, Context.MODE_
            PRIVATE);

            int size;
            byte[] buffer = new byte[1024];
            while ((size = in.read(buffer, 0, 1024)) >= 0) {
                out.write(buffer, 0, size);
            }
            out.flush();
            out.close();
        } catch (IOException e) {
            Log.w(TAG, e);
        }
    }
}

/* Helper methods to construct documentId from a file name */
private String getIconsDocumentId(String filename) {
    return DOCID_ICONS_DIR + filename;
}
private String getBackgroundsDocumentId(String filename) {
    return DOCID_BGS_DIR + filename;
}

/* Helper methods to determine document types */
private boolean isRoot(String documentId) {
    return DOCID_ROOT.equals(documentId);
}

private boolean isIconsDir(String documentId) {
    return DOCID_ICONS_DIR.equals(documentId);
}

private boolean isBackgroundsDir(String documentId) {
    return DOCID_BGS_DIR.equals(documentId);
}

private boolean isIconDocument(String documentId) {
    return documentId.startsWith(DOCID_ICONS_DIR);
}

private boolean isBackgroundsDocument(String documentId) {
    return documentId.startsWith(DOCID_BGS_DIR);
}
```

```
/*
 * Helper method to extract file name from a documentId.
 * Returns empty string for the "root" document.
 */
private String getFilename(String documentId) {
    int split = documentId.lastIndexOf(":");
    if (split < 0) {
        return "";
    }
    return documentId.substring(split+1);
}


/*
 * Called by the system to determine how many "providers" are
 * hosted here.  It is most common to return only one, via a
 * Cursor that has only one result row.
 */
@Override
public Cursor queryRoots(String[] projection) throws FileNotFoundException {
    if (projection == null) {
        projection = DEFAULT_ROOT_PROJECTION;
    }
    MatrixCursor result = new MatrixCursor(projection);
    //Add the single root for this provider
    MatrixCursor.RowBuilder builder = result.newRow();

    builder.add(Root.COLUMN_ROOT_ID, "root");
    builder.add(Root.COLUMN_TITLE, "Android Recipes");
    builder.add(Root.COLUMN_SUMMARY, "Android Recipes Documents Provider");
    builder.add(Root.COLUMN_ICON, R.drawable.ic_launcher);

    builder.add(Root.COLUMN_DOCUMENT_ID, DOCID_ROOT);

    builder.add(Root.COLUMN_FLAGS,
            //Results will only come from the local filesystem
            Root.FLAG_LOCAL_ONLY
            //We support showing recently selected items
            | Root.FLAG_SUPPORTS_RECENTS);
    builder.add(Root.COLUMN_MIME_TYPES, "image/*");
    builder.add(Root.COLUMN_AVAILABLE_BYTES, 0);

    return result;
}


/*
 * Called by the system to determine the child items for a given
 * parent.  Will be called for the root, and for each subdirectory
 * defined within.
 */
```

```
@Override
public Cursor queryChildDocuments(String parentDocumentId, String[] projection,
        String sortOrder) throws FileNotFoundException {
    if (projection == null) {
        projection = DEFAULT_DOCUMENT_PROJECTION;
    }
    MatrixCursor result = new MatrixCursor(projection);

    if (isIconsDir(parentDocumentId)) {
        //Add all files in the icons collection
        try {
            for(String key : mIcons.keySet()) {
                addImageRow(result, mIcons.get(key), getIconsDocumentId(key));
            }
        } catch (IOException e) {
            return null;
        }
    } else if (isBackgroundsDir(parentDocumentId)) {
        //Add all files in the backgrounds collection
        try {
            for(String key : mBackgrounds.keySet()) {
                addImageRow(result, mBackgrounds.get(key), getBackgroundsDocumentId(key));
            }
        } catch (IOException e) {
            return null;
        }
    } else if (isRoot(parentDocumentId)) {
        //Add the top-level directories
        addIconsRow(result);
        addBackgroundsRow(result);
    }

    return result;
}

/*
 * Return the same information provided via queryChildDocuments(), but
 * just for the single documentId requested.
 */
@Override
public Cursor queryDocument(String documentId, String[] projection)
        throws FileNotFoundException {
    if (projection == null) {
        projection = DEFAULT_DOCUMENT_PROJECTION;
    }

    MatrixCursor result = new MatrixCursor(projection);
```

```java
    try {
        String filename = getFilename(documentId);
        if (isRoot(documentId)) { //This is a query for root
            addRootRow(result);
        } else if (isIconsDir(documentId)) { //This is a query for icons
            addIconsRow(result);
        } else if (isBackgroundsDir(documentId)) { //This is a query for backgrounds
            addBackgroundsRow(result);
        } else if (isIconDocument(documentId)) {
            addImageRow(result, mIcons.get(filename),
                    getIconsDocumentId(filename));
        } else if (isBackgroundsDocument(documentId)) {
            addImageRow(result, mBackgrounds.get(filename),
                    getBackgroundsDocumentId(filename));
        }
    } catch (IOException e) {
        return null;
    }

    return result;
}

/*
 * Called to populate any recently used items from this
 * provider in the Recents picker UI.
 */
@Override
public Cursor queryRecentDocuments(String rootId, String[] projection)
        throws FileNotFoundException {
    if (projection == null) {
        projection = DEFAULT_DOCUMENT_PROJECTION;
    }

    MatrixCursor result = new MatrixCursor(projection);

    if (sLastDocumentId != null) {
        String filename = getFilename(sLastDocumentId);
        String recentTitle = "";
        if (isIconDocument(sLastDocumentId)) {
            recentTitle = mIcons.get(filename);
        } else if (isBackgroundsDocument(sLastDocumentId)) {
            recentTitle = mBackgrounds.get(filename);
        }

        try {
            addImageRow(result, recentTitle, sLastDocumentId);
        } catch (IOException e) {
            Log.w(TAG, e);
        }
    }
```

```
        Log.d(TAG, "Recents: "+result.getCount());
        //We'll return the last selected result to a recents query
        return result;
    }

    /*
     * Helper method to write the root into the supplied
     * Cursor
     */
    private void addRootRow(MatrixCursor cursor) {
        addDirRow(cursor, DOCID_ROOT, "Root");
    }

    private void addIconsRow(MatrixCursor cursor) {
        addDirRow(cursor, DOCID_ICONS_DIR, "Icons");
    }

    private void addBackgroundsRow(MatrixCursor cursor) {
        addDirRow(cursor, DOCID_BGS_DIR, "Backgrounds");
    }

    /*
     * Helper method to write a specific subdirectory into
     * the supplied Cursor
     */
    private void addDirRow(MatrixCursor cursor, String documentId, String name) {
        final MatrixCursor.RowBuilder row = cursor.newRow();

        row.add(Document.COLUMN_DOCUMENT_ID, documentId);
        row.add(Document.COLUMN_DISPLAY_NAME, name);
        row.add(Document.COLUMN_SIZE, 0);
        row.add(Document.COLUMN_MIME_TYPE, Document.MIME_TYPE_DIR);

        long installed;
        try {
            installed = getContext().getPackageManager()
                    .getPackageInfo(getContext().getPackageName(), 0)
                    .firstInstallTime;
        } catch (NameNotFoundException e) {
            installed = 0;
        }
        row.add(Document.COLUMN_LAST_MODIFIED, installed);
        row.add(Document.COLUMN_FLAGS, 0);
    }

    /*
     * Helper method to write a specific image file into
     * the supplied Cursor
     */
```

```
    private void addImageRow(MatrixCursor cursor, String title, String documentId)
            throws IOException {
        final MatrixCursor.RowBuilder row = cursor.newRow();

        String filename = getFilename(documentId);
        AssetFileDescriptor afd = getContext().getAssets().openFd(filename);

        row.add(Document.COLUMN_DOCUMENT_ID, documentId);
        row.add(Document.COLUMN_DISPLAY_NAME, title);
        row.add(Document.COLUMN_SIZE, afd.getLength());
        row.add(Document.COLUMN_MIME_TYPE, "image/*");

        long installed;
        try {
            installed = getContext().getPackageManager()
                    .getPackageInfo(getContext().getPackageName(), 0)
                    .firstInstallTime;
        } catch (NameNotFoundException e) {
            installed = 0;
        }
        row.add(Document.COLUMN_LAST_MODIFIED, installed);
        row.add(Document.COLUMN_FLAGS, Document.FLAG_SUPPORTS_THUMBNAIL);
    }


    /*
     * Return a reference to an image asset the framework will use
     * in the items list for any document with the FLAG_SUPPORTS_THUMBNAIL
     * flag enabled.  This method is safe to block while downloading content.
     */
    @Override
    public AssetFileDescriptor openDocumentThumbnail(String documentId, Point sizeHint,
            CancellationSignal signal) throws FileNotFoundException {
        //We will load the thumbnail from the version on storage
        String filename = getFilename(documentId);
        //Create a file reference to the image on internal storage
        final File file = new File(getContext().getFilesDir(), filename);
        //Return a file descriptor wrapping the file reference
        final ParcelFileDescriptor pfd =
                ParcelFileDescriptor.open(file, ParcelFileDescriptor.MODE_READ_ONLY);
        return new AssetFileDescriptor(pfd, 0, AssetFileDescriptor.UNKNOWN_LENGTH);
    }


    /*
     * Return a file descriptor to the document referenced by the supplied
     * documentId.  The client will use this descriptor to read the contents
     * directly.  This method is safe to block while downloading content.
     */
    @Override
    public ParcelFileDescriptor openDocument(String documentId, String mode,
            CancellationSignal signal) throws FileNotFoundException {
        //We will load the document itself from assets
```

```
    try {
        String filename = getFilename(documentId);
        //Create a file reference to the image on internal storage
        final File file = new File(getContext().getFilesDir(), filename);
        //Return a file descriptor wrapping the file reference
        final ParcelFileDescriptor pfd =
                ParcelFileDescriptor.open(file, ParcelFileDescriptor.MODE_READ_ONLY);

        //Save this as the last selected document
        sLastDocumentId = documentId;

        return pfd;
    } catch (IOException e) {
        Log.w(TAG, e);
        return null;
    }
    }
}
```

In this example, we show how to serve some image files used from internal storage. Our image data is static, and bundled in the assets directory of our APK for distribution. The files need to be moved to the appropriate storage volume, so when the provider is created, we read the image files out of assets and copy them to internal storage inside writeAssets(). Our provider will include two top-level directories, icons and backgrounds, each containing image files.

We have created a simple structure of converting file names into document IDs. In our case, root is the virtual top-level directory with our two subdirectories, and we create each ID as a pseudo-path to that file by using colon separators. The methods getIconsDocumentId(), getBackgroundsDocumentId(), and getFilename() are helpers to convert back and forth between our published ID and the actual image file name.

■ **Tip** Document IDs will be embedded in a content Uri by the framework, so if you are converting directory paths to IDs, you must use characters that are not otherwise considered a path separator by the Uri class.

Inside queryRoots(), we return a MatrixCursor that includes the basic metadata of the single provider root. Notice that the query methods of the provider should respect the column projection passed in, and return only the data requested. We are using an updated version of the add() method as well that takes the column name for each item. This version is convenient, as it monitors the projection passed into the MatrixCursor constructor, and silently ignores attempts to add columns not in the projection, thus eliminating the looping we did before to add elements.

The title, summary, and icon columns deal with the provider display in the picker UI. We have also defined the following:

- COLUMN_DOCUMENT_ID: Provides the ID we will be handed back later to reference this top-level root element

- COLUMN_MIME_TYPES: Reports the document types this root contains. We have image files, so we are using image/*.

In addition, `COLUMN_FLAGS` reports additional features the root item may support. The options are as follows:

- `FLAG_LOCAL_ONLY`: Results are on the device and don't require network requests.

- `FLAG_SUPPORTS_CREATE`: The root allows client applications to create a new document inside this provider. We will discuss how to do this on the client side in Chapter 6.

- `FLAG_SUPPORTS_RECENTS`: Tells the framework we can participate in the recent documents UI with results. This will result in calls to `queryRecentDocuments()` to obtain this metadata.

- `FLAG_SUPPORTS_SEARCH`: Similar to recents, tells the framework we can handle search queries via `querySearchDocuments()`

We have set the local and recents flags in our example. Once this method returns, the framework will call `queryDocument()` with the document ID of the root to get more information. Inside `addRootRow()` we populate the cursor with the necessary fields. For `COLUMN_MIME_TYPE`, we use the constant `MIME_TYPE_DIR` to indicate this element is a directory containing other documents. This same definition should be applied to any subdirectories in the hierarchy you create for the provider. Also, because all the files we are providing have existed since we installed the application, we provide the APK install date as the `COLUMN_LAST_MODIFIED` value; for a more dynamic filesystem, this could just be the modified date of the file on disk.

When the provider is selected by the user, we receive a call to `queryChildDocuments()` to list all the files in the root. For us, this includes adding a row to the cursor for each directory that will house images. The `addIconsRow()` and `addBackgroundsRow()` methods supply similar metadata as roots for each subdirectory. We will see `queryChildDocuments()` again for the subdirectories as well. When we see these IDs, it's time to add a row to the cursor for each logo image file we have in each bucket. The `addImageRow()` method constructs the appropriate column data with similar elements to the previous iterations.

We want to allow each image to be represented by a thumbnail image in the picker UI, so we set the `FLAG_SUPPORTS_THUMBNAIL` for `COLUMN_FLAGS` on each image row. This will trigger `openDocumentThumbnail()` for each element as they are displayed in the picker. In this method, we've shown how to open a `FileDescriptor` from internal storage and return it.

The `sizeHint` parameter should be used to ensure you don't return a thumbnail that is too large for display in the picker's list. Our images are all small to begin with, so we haven't checked this parameter here. It is safe, if necessary, to block and download content inside this method. For this case, a `CancellationSignal` is provided, which should be checked regularly in case the framework cancels the load before it is finished.

When a document is finally selected, `queryDocument()` will be called again with the ID of the logo image supplied. In this case, we must simply return the same results from `addImageRow()` for the single document requested. This will trigger a call to `openDocument()`, where we must return a valid `ParcelFileDescriptor` that the client can use to access the resource. Since our content is the same as our thumbnail, the same logic is used to return the result.

The definition for our provider in the manifest also looks a bit different from before. Since the provider will be queried directly by the framework, we must define some specific filters and permissions (see Listing 5-44).

Listing 5-44. `AndroidManifest.xml` DocumentsProvider Snippet

```
<provider
    android:name="com.androidrecipes.sharedocuments.ImageProvider"
    android:authorities="com.androidrecipes.sharedocuments.images"
    android:grantUriPermissions="true"
    android:exported="true"
    android:permission="android.permission.MANAGE_DOCUMENTS">
    <!-- Unique filter the system will use to find published providers -->
    <intent-filter>
        <action android:name="android.content.action.DOCUMENTS_PROVIDER" />
    </intent-filter>
</provider>
```

First, the provider must be exported so external applications can access it. This is usually the default behavior with a provider that has an `<intent-filter>` attached, but it's good to be explicit here. The filter must include the `DOCUMENTS_PROVIDER` action, which is how the framework will find installed providers it can access. Next, the provider must be protected by the `MANAGE_DOCUMENTS` permission. This is a system-level permission that only system applications can obtain, so this protects your provider from being exploited by other apps. Finally, the `grantUriPermissions` attribute should be enabled. This allows the framework to provide access permissions to client applications on a document-by-document basis, rather than giving each client access to the whole provider.

■ **Note**   This example application doesn't have a user interface to launch, but with the application installed, you can invoke the new provider by going to any system application that requires you to pick an image; the Contacts application is a good choice. When creating a new contact, you can add a photo, and selecting an existing image invokes the system picker UI.

Recent Documents

Remember in our example that we set the `FLAG_SUPPORTS_RECENTS` in the root metadata. We also provided an implementation of `queryRecentDocuments()` to react to these inquiries. There is no inherent limit to the number of recent documents any provider can return here, but you will want to pick something that is relevant and contextual to the user. Here, we return only the last selected logo image from our provider (something that we save on each open request in a static variable). The metadata here is the same as any other documents query, so the same `addImageRow()` method is invoked to populate the cursor.

With this in place, when we access the Recent section of our provider (as shown in Figure 5-7), we can see the last image selection made.

Figure 5-7. *Last select image shown in Recent UI*

Document Trees

(API Level 21)

If you would like to update your DocumentsProvider to support user selection of an entire directory, you need to provide some additional overrides. Listing 5-45 shows just the override excerpts that must be added to our ImageProvider.

Listing 5-45. Document Tree Support for ImageProvider

```
/*
 * Called by the system to determine how many "providers" are
 * hosted here.  It is most common to return only one, via a
 * Cursor that has only one result row.
 */
@Override
public Cursor queryRoots(String[] projection) throws FileNotFoundException {
    if (projection == null) {
        projection = DEFAULT_ROOT_PROJECTION;
    }

    MatrixCursor result = new MatrixCursor(projection);
    //Add the single root for this provider
    MatrixCursor.RowBuilder builder = result.newRow();
```

```
    builder.add(Root.COLUMN_ROOT_ID, "root");
    builder.add(Root.COLUMN_TITLE, "Android Recipes");
    builder.add(Root.COLUMN_SUMMARY, "Android Recipes Documents Provider");
    builder.add(Root.COLUMN_ICON, R.drawable.ic_launcher);

    builder.add(Root.COLUMN_DOCUMENT_ID, DOCID_ROOT);

    builder.add(Root.COLUMN_FLAGS,
            //Results will only come from the local filesystem
            Root.FLAG_LOCAL_ONLY
            //We support showing recently selected items
            | Root.FLAG_SUPPORTS_RECENTS
            //We support doc tree selection (API 21+)
            | Root.FLAG_SUPPORTS_IS_CHILD);
    builder.add(Root.COLUMN_MIME_TYPES, "image/*");
    builder.add(Root.COLUMN_AVAILABLE_BYTES, 0);

    return result;
}


/*
 * This method is required ONLY if you want to support document
 * tree selection (API 21+). Return whether a given document and
 * parent are related
 */
@Override
public boolean isChildDocument(String parentDocumentId, String documentId) {
    if (isRoot(parentDocumentId)) {
        //The subdirectories are children of root
        return isIconsDir(documentId)
                || isBackgroundsDir(documentId);
    }

    if (isIconsDir(parentDocumentId)) {
        //All icons are children of the icons directory
        return isIconDocument(documentId);
    }

    if (isBackgroundsDir(parentDocumentId)) {
        //All backgrounds are children of the backgrounds directory
        return isBackgroundsDocument(documentId);
    }

    //Otherwise, these ids don't know each other
    return false;
}
```

Our provider must implement the isChildDocument() method, allowing the framework to determine which document IDs have a parent/child relationships when queries are made. This method simply compares document IDs using our previous helper methods, returning true when the document ID we are handed is contained within the given parent directory.

Finally, we have to add Root.FLAG_SUPPORTS_IS_CHILD to the root definition to publish in the initial query that this provider supports requests for a document tree in addition to requests to a single document.

Figure 5-8 shows us the system-defined interface the user sees when a request is made to select a document tree from any external application.

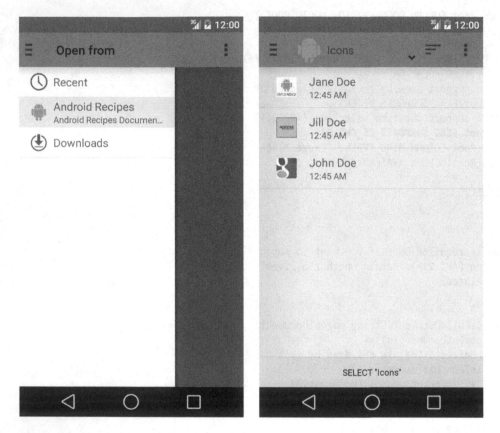

Figure 5-8. *Document tree selection interface*

Notice the variation in this selection with the SELECT "Icons" button at the bottom. Tapping this button will return a reference to the currently visible directory back to the calling application.

Summary

In this chapter, you investigated practical methods to persist data on Android devices. You learned how to quickly create a preferences screen as well as how to use preferences and a simple method for persisting basic data types. You saw how and where to place files, for reference as well as storage. You even learned how to share your persisted data with other applications. In Chapter 6, we will investigate how to leverage the operating system's services to do background operations and to communicate between applications.

■ ■ ■

Interacting with the System

The Android operating system provides a number of useful services that applications can leverage. Many of these services are designed to allow your application to function within the mobile system in ways beyond just interacting briefly with a user. Applications can schedule themselves for alarms, run background services, and send messages to each other—all of which allows an Android application to integrate to the fullest extent with the mobile device. In addition, Android provides a set of standard interfaces that are designed to expose all the data collected by its core applications to your software. Through these interfaces, any application may integrate with, add to, and improve upon the core functionality of the platform, thereby enhancing the experience for the user.

6-1. Notifying from the Background

Problem

Your application is running in the background, with no currently visible interface to the user, but must notify the user of an important event that has occurred.

Solution

(API Level 4)

Use `NotificationManagerCompat` to post a status bar notification. This class is part of the support library and provides a compatibility wrapper for the `NotificationManager` service that provides fallback on older versions.

Notifications provide an unobtrusive way of indicating that you want the user's attention. Perhaps new messages have arrived, an update is available, or a long-running job is complete; notifications are perfect for accomplishing these tasks.

How It Works

A notification can be posted to the `NotificationManager` from just about any system component, such as a `Service`, `BroadcastReceiver`, or `Activity`. In Listings 6-1 and 6-2, we will look at an activity that posts a series of different notification types when the user leaves the activity and goes to the home screen.

Listing 6-1. res/layout/activity_notification.xml

```xml
<?xml version="1.0" encoding="utf-8"?>
<LinearLayout xmlns:android="http://schemas.android.com/apk/res/android"
              android:orientation="vertical"
              android:layout_width="match_parent"
              android:layout_height="match_parent">
    <RadioGroup
        android:id="@+id/options_group"
        android:layout_width="match_parent"
        android:layout_height="0dp"
        android:layout_weight="1">

        <TextView
            android:layout_width="wrap_content"
            android:layout_height="wrap_content"
            android:textAppearance="?android:attr/textAppearanceLarge"
            android:text="Rich Styles"/>

        <RadioButton
            android:id="@+id/option_basic"
            android:layout_width="wrap_content"
            android:layout_height="wrap_content"
            android:text="Basic Notification"
            android:checked="true"/>

        <RadioButton
            android:id="@+id/option_bigtext"
            android:layout_width="wrap_content"
            android:layout_height="wrap_content"
            android:text="BigText Style"/>

        <RadioButton
            android:id="@+id/option_bigpicture"
            android:layout_width="wrap_content"
            android:layout_height="wrap_content"
            android:text="BigPicture Style"/>

        <RadioButton
            android:id="@+id/option_inbox"
            android:layout_width="wrap_content"
            android:layout_height="wrap_content"
            android:text="Inbox Style"/>

        <RadioButton
            android:id="@+id/option_reply"
            android:layout_width="wrap_content"
            android:layout_height="wrap_content"
            android:text="Notification with Reply"/>
```

```xml
    <RadioButton
        android:id="@+id/option_bundled"
        android:layout_width="wrap_content"
        android:layout_height="wrap_content"
        android:text="Bundled notification"/>

    <TextView
        android:layout_width="wrap_content"
        android:layout_height="wrap_content"
        android:layout_marginTop="8dp"
        android:textAppearance="?android:attr/textAppearanceLarge"
        android:text="Secured Styles"/>

    <RadioButton
        android:id="@+id/option_private"
        android:layout_width="wrap_content"
        android:layout_height="wrap_content"
        android:text="Public Version Lockscreen"/>

    <RadioButton
        android:id="@+id/option_secret"
        android:layout_width="wrap_content"
        android:layout_height="wrap_content"
        android:text="Secret Lockscreen"/>

    <RadioButton
        android:id="@+id/option_headsup"
        android:layout_width="wrap_content"
        android:layout_height="wrap_content"
        android:text="Heads-Up Notification"/>

</RadioGroup>

<Button
    android:layout_width="match_parent"
    android:layout_height="wrap_content"
    android:text="Post a Notification"
    android:onClick="onPostClick"/>
</LinearLayout>
```

Listing 6-2. Activity Firing a Notification

```java
public class NotificationActivity extends Activity {

    private static final String GROUP_KEY_MESSAGES = "messages";
    private RadioGroup mOptionsGroup;

    @Override
    public void onCreate(Bundle savedInstanceState) {
        super.onCreate(savedInstanceState);
        setContentView(R.layout.activity_notification);
```

445

```java
        mOptionsGroup = (RadioGroup) findViewById(R.id.options_group);

        if (Build.VERSION.SDK_INT >= Build.VERSION_CODES.N) {
            findViewById(R.id.option_reply).setVisibility(View.VISIBLE);
        } else {
            findViewById(R.id.option_reply).setVisibility(View.GONE);
        }
    }

    public void onPostClick(View v) {
        final int noteId = mOptionsGroup.getCheckedRadioButtonId();
        final Notification note;
        switch (noteId) {
            case R.id.option_basic:
            case R.id.option_bigtext:
            case R.id.option_bigpicture:
            case R.id.option_inbox:
                note = buildStyledNotification(noteId);
                break;
            case R.id.option_bundled:
                note = createBundledNotification();
                break;
            case R.id.option_reply:
                note = createDirectReplyNotification();
                break;
            case R.id.option_private:
            case R.id.option_secret:
            case R.id.option_headsup:
                note = buildSecuredNotification(noteId);
                break;
            default:
                throw new IllegalArgumentException("Unknown Type");
        }

        NotificationManagerCompat notificationManager = NotificationManagerCompat.from(this);
        notificationManager.notify(noteId, note);
    }

    private Notification buildStyledNotification(int type) {
        Intent launchIntent =
                new Intent(this, NotificationActivity.class);
        PendingIntent contentIntent =
                PendingIntent.getActivity(this, 0, launchIntent, 0);

        // Create notification with the time it was fired
        NotificationCompat.Builder builder = new NotificationCompat.Builder(
                NotificationActivity.this);

        builder.setSmallIcon(R.drawable.ic_launcher)
                .setTicker("Something Happened")
                .setWhen(System.currentTimeMillis())
```

```
                .setAutoCancel(true)
                .setDefaults(Notification.DEFAULT_SOUND)
                .setContentTitle("We're Finished!")
                .setContentText("Click Here!")
                .setContentIntent(contentIntent);

        switch (type) {
            case R.id.option_basic:
                //Return the simple notification
                return builder.build();
            case R.id.option_bigtext:
                //Include two actions
                builder.addAction(android.R.drawable.ic_menu_call,
                        "Call", contentIntent);
                builder.addAction(android.R.drawable.ic_menu_recent_history,
                        "History", contentIntent);
                //Use the BigTextStyle when expanded
                NotificationCompat.BigTextStyle textStyle =
                        new NotificationCompat.BigTextStyle(builder);
                textStyle.bigText("Here is some additional text to be displayed when the
                notification is "
                        + "in expanded mode.  I can fit so much more content into this giant
                        view!");

                return textStyle.build();
            case R.id.option_bigpicture:
                //Add one additional action
                builder.addAction(android.R.drawable.ic_menu_compass,
                        "View Location", contentIntent);
                //Use the BigPictureStyle when expanded
                NotificationCompat.BigPictureStyle pictureStyle =
                        new NotificationCompat.BigPictureStyle(builder);
                pictureStyle.bigPicture(BitmapFactory.decodeResource(getResources(),
                R.drawable.dog));

                return pictureStyle.build();
            case R.id.option_inbox:
                //Use the InboxStyle when expanded
                NotificationCompat.InboxStyle inboxStyle =
                        new NotificationCompat.InboxStyle(builder);
                inboxStyle.setSummaryText("4 New Tasks");
                inboxStyle.addLine("Make Dinner");
                inboxStyle.addLine("Call Mom");
                inboxStyle.addLine("Call Wife First");
                inboxStyle.addLine("Pick up Kids");

                return inboxStyle.build();
            default:
                throw new IllegalArgumentException("Unknown Type");
        }
    }
```

```
private Notification createDirectReplyNotification() {
    String replyLabel = getResources().getString(R.string.reply_label);
    RemoteInput remoteInput = new RemoteInput.Builder(KEY_TEXT_REPLY)
            .setLabel(replyLabel)
            .build();
    Intent intent = new Intent(this, ReplyReceiverService.class);
    PendingIntent replyPendingIntent = PendingIntent.getService(this, 0, intent,
            PendingIntent.FLAG_ONE_SHOT);
    NotificationCompat.Action action =
            new NotificationCompat.Action.Builder(R.drawable.ic_stat_name,
                    getString(R.string.label), replyPendingIntent)
                    .addRemoteInput(remoteInput)
                    .build();
    return new NotificationCompat.Builder(this)
            .setSmallIcon(R.drawable.ic_stat_name)
            .setContentTitle(getString(R.string.title))
            .setContentText(getString(R.string.content))
            .addAction(action)
            .build();
}

private Notification createBundledNotification() {
    NotificationManagerCompat notificationManager =
            NotificationManagerCompat.from(this);
    for (int i = 1; i <= 5; i++) {
        Notification notif = new NotificationCompat.Builder(this)
                .setContentTitle("New message from " + i)
                .setContentText("Message " + i)
                .setSmallIcon(R.drawable.ic_stat_name)
                .setGroup(GROUP_KEY_MESSAGES)
                .build();
        notificationManager.notify(i, notif);
    }

    return new NotificationCompat.Builder(this)
            .setContentTitle("5 new messages")
            .setSmallIcon(R.drawable.ic_stat_name)
            .setStyle(new NotificationCompat.InboxStyle()
                    .setBigContentTitle("5 new messages")
                    .setSummaryText("name@domain.com"))
            .setGroup(GROUP_KEY_MESSAGES)
            .setGroupSummary(true)
            .build();
}

@TargetApi(Build.VERSION_CODES.LOLLIPOP)
//These properties can be overridden by the user's notification settings
private Notification buildSecuredNotification(int type) {
    Intent launchIntent =
            new Intent(this, NotificationActivity.class);
    PendingIntent contentIntent =
            PendingIntent.getActivity(this, 0, launchIntent, 0);
```

```java
//Construct the base notification
NotificationCompat.Builder builder = new NotificationCompat.Builder(this)
        .setSmallIcon(R.drawable.ic_launcher)
        .setContentTitle("Account Balance Update")
        .setContentText("Your account balance is -$250.00")
        .setStyle(new NotificationCompat.BigTextStyle()
                .bigText("Your account balance is -$250.00; pay us please "
                        + "or we will be forced to take legal action!"))
        .setContentIntent(contentIntent);

switch (type) {
    case R.id.option_private:
        //Provide a unique version for secured lockscreens
        Notification publicNote = new NotificationCompat.Builder(this)
                .setSmallIcon(R.drawable.ic_launcher)
                .setContentTitle("Account Notification")
                .setContentText("An important message has arrived.")
                .setContentIntent(contentIntent)
                .build();

        return builder.setPublicVersion(publicNote)
                .build();
    case R.id.option_secret:
        //Hide the notification from a secured lockscreen completely
        return builder.setVisibility(Notification.VISIBILITY_SECRET)
                .build();
    case R.id.option_headsup:
        //Show a heads-up notification when posted
        return builder.setDefaults(Notification.DEFAULT_SOUND)
                .setPriority(Notification.PRIORITY_HIGH)
                .build();
    default:
        throw new IllegalArgumentException("Unknown Type");
    }
    }
}
```

A series of new notification elements are created using `Notification.Builder` when the user leaves the activity. We will discuss the expanded types shortly, and just focus on the basic type for now. An icon resource and title string may be provided, and these items will display in the status bar at the time the notification occurs. In addition, we pass a time value (in milliseconds) to display in the notification list as the event time. Here, we are setting that value to the time the notification fired, but it may take on a different meaning in your application.

■ **Important** We are using `NotificationCompat.Builder` in this example, which is part of the Support Library and allows us to call the new APIs going back to Android 1.6 without branching our code. If you are targeting only Android versions that natively support the notification features you need, you can replace `NotificationCompat.Builder` with `Notification.Builder` within the code.

Prior to creating the notification, we can fill it out with some other useful parameters, such as more detailed text to be displayed in the notifications list when the user pulls down the status bar.

One of the parameters passed to the builder is a PendingIntent that points back to our activity. This intent makes the notification interactive, allowing the user to tap it in the list and launch the activity.

■ **Note**   This intent will launch a new activity with each event. If you would rather an existing instance of the activity respond to the launch, if one exists in the stack, be sure to include intent flags and manifest parameters appropriately to accomplish this, such as Intent.FLAG_ACTIVITY_CLEAR_TOP and android:launchMode="singleTop".

To enhance the notification beyond the visual animation in the status bar, the notification defaults are modified to include that the system's default notification sound be played when the notification fires. Values such as Notification.DEFAULT_VIBRATION and Notification.DEFAULT_LIGHTS may also be added.

■ **Tip**   If you would like to customize the sound played with a notification, set the Notification.sound parameter to a Uri that references a file or ContentProvider to read from.

We finally add a series of flags to the notification for further customization. This example uses setAutoCancel() in the builder to enable Notification.FLAG_AUTO_CANCEL, which cancels or removes the notification from the list as soon as the user selects it. Without this flag, the notification remains in the list until it is manually dismissed or canceled programmatically by calling NotificationManager.cancel() or NotificationManager.cancelAll(). Another helpful flag to set with the builder is setOngoing(), which disables any user ability to remove the notification. It can be cancelled only programmatically. This is useful for notifying the user of background operations currently running, such as music playing or location tracking underway.

Additionally, here are some other useful flags to apply that do not have methods inside the builder. These flags can be set directly on the notification after it is constructed:

- FLAG_INSISTENT: Repeats the notification sounds until the user responds.

- FLAG_NO_CLEAR: Does not allow the notification to be cleared with the user's Clear Notifications button, but only through a call to cancel(). Once the notification is prepared, it is posted to the user with NotificationManager.notify(), which takes an ID parameter as well. Each notification type in your application should have a unique ID. The manager will allow only one notification with the same ID in the list at a time, and new instances with the same ID will take the place of those existing. In addition, the ID is required to cancel a specific notification manually.

When we run this example, an activity displays, allowing the user to select the notification type to post. Upon pressing the button, you can see the selected notification posted in the status bar, even if you leave the activity and it is no longer visible (see Figure 6-1).

Figure 6-1. *Notification that is occurring (left) and being displayed in the list (right)*

We will now dissect some of the richer notification features found in this example by the platform level in which they were introduced.

Expanded Notification Styles

(API Level 16)

Starting with Android 4.1, notifications have the capability to display additional rich information with interactivity directly in the notification view. These are known as *notification styles*. Any notification that is currently at the top of the window shade is expanded by default, and the user can expand any other notification with a two-finger gesture. Therefore, expanded views don't replace the traditional view; rather, they enhance the experience at certain times.

Three default styles (implementations of Notification.Style) are provided by the platform:

- BigTextStyle: Displays an extended amount of text, such as the full contents of a message or post

- BigPictureStyle: Displays a large, full-color image

- InboxStyle: Provides a list of items, similar to the inbox view from an application such as Gmail

You are not limited to using these, however. Notification.Style is an interface that your application can implement to display any custom expanded layout that may best fit your needs.

In addition to styles, Android 4.1 added inline actions for an expanded notification. This means that you can add multiple action items for the user to take directly from the window shade view rather than just the single callback intent when the user clicks the whole notification item. These items will show up on top of the expanded view, lined up at the bottom. Listing 6-3 shows the code from the previous example to add a BigTextStyle expanded notification collected together, and Figure 6-2 shows the result.

Listing 6-3. BigTextStyle Notification

```
//Create notification with the time it was fired
NotificationCompat.Builder builder =
        new NotificationCompat.Builder(NotificationActivity.this);

builder.setSmallIcon(R.drawable.icon)
      .setTicker("Something Happened")
      .setWhen(System.currentTimeMillis())
      .setAutoCancel(true)
      .setDefaults(Notification.DEFAULT_SOUND)
      .setContentTitle("We're Finished!")
      .setContentText("Click Here!")
      .setContentIntent(contentIntent);

//Add some custom actions
builder.addAction(android.R.id.drawable.ic_menu_call, "Call Back", contentIntent);
builder.addAction(android.R.id.drawable.ic_menu_recent_history,
        "Call History", contentIntent);

//Apply an expanded style
NotificationCompat.BigTextStyle expandedStyle =
        new NotificationCompat.BigTextStyle(builder);
expandedStyle.bigText("Here is some additional text to be displayed when"
    + " the notification is in expanded mode.   "
    + " I can fit so much more content into this giant view!");

Notification note = expandedStyle.build();
```

You can attach custom actions by using the addAction() method on the builder. You can see here how the actions that are added lay out with respect to the overall view. In this example, each action goes to the same place, but you can attach any PendingIntent to each action to make them travel to different places in your application.

Figure 6-2. `BigTextStyle` *in the window shade*

The only necessary modification to the previous example is that we wrap our existing `Builder` object in the `BigTextStyle` and apply any specific customizations there. In this case, the only additional piece of information is setting `bigText()` with the text to display in expanded mode. Then the notification is created from the `build()` method on the style, rather than the builder.

Let's take a look at `BigPictureStyle` in Listing 6-4 and Figure 6-3.

Listing 6-4. `BigPictureStyle` Notification

```
//Create notification with the time it was fired
NotificationCompat.Builder builder =
        new NotificationCompat.Builder(NotificationActivity.this);

builder.setSmallIcon(R.drawable.icon)
    .setTicker("Something Happened")
    .setWhen(System.currentTimeMillis())
    .setAutoCancel(true)
    .setDefaults(Notification.DEFAULT_SOUND)
    .setContentTitle("We're Finished!")
    .setContentText("Click Here!")
    .setContentIntent(contentIntent);
```

```
//Add some custom actions
builder.addAction(android.R.id.drawable.ic_menu_compass,
        "View Location", contentIntent);

//Apply an expanded style
NotificationCompat.BigPictureStyle expandedStyle =
        new NotificationCompat.BigPictureStyle(builder);
expandedStyle.bigPicture(
        BitmapFactory.decodeResource(getResources(), R.drawable.icon) );

Notification note = expandedStyle.build();
```

Figure 6-3. *BigPictureStyle in the window shade*

This code is almost identical to BigTextStyle, except that here we use the bigPicture() method to pass in the Bitmap that will be used as the full-color image. Finally, take a look at InboxStyle in Listing 6-5 and Figure 6-4.

Listing 6-5. InboxStyle Notification

```
//Create notification with the time it was fired
NotificationCompat.Builder builder =
        new NotificationCompat.Builder(NotificationActivity.this);
```

```
builder.setSmallIcon(R.drawable.icon)
        .setTicker("Something Happened")
        .setWhen(System.currentTimeMillis())
        .setAutoCancel(true)
        .setDefaults(Notification.DEFAULT_SOUND)
        .setContentTitle("We're Finished!")
        .setContentText("Click Here!")
        .setContentIntent(contentIntent);

//Apply an expanded style
NotificationCompat.InboxStyle expandedStyle =
        new NotificationCompat.InboxStyle(builder);
expandedStyle.setSummaryText("4 New Tasks");
expandedStyle.addLine("Make Dinner");
expandedStyle.addLine("Call Mom");
expandedStyle.addLine("Call Wife First");
expandedStyle.addLine("Pick up Kids");

Notification note = expandedStyle.build();
```

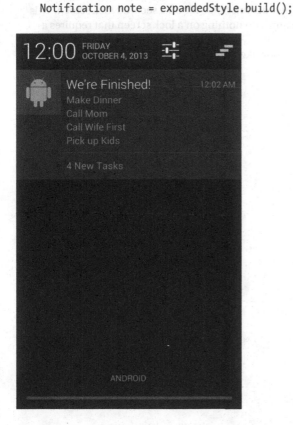

Figure 6-4. *InboxStyle in the window shade*

With Notification.InboxStyle, multiple items are added to the list by using the addLine() method. We also topped off the example with a summary line noting the number of items with setSummaryText(), a method that is available for use with all the previous styles as well.

455

As before, we've used the Support Library's NotificationCompat class, which allows us to call all these methods in an application running back to API Level 4. If your application is targeting Android 4.1 as the minimum platform, you can replace this with the native Notification.Builder.

One of the real powers of the Support Library is shown in this particular case. We are calling methods that are not available until API Level 16, but the Support Library takes care of version checking for us under the hood and simply ignores methods that a certain platform doesn't support; we don't have to branch our code to use new APIs.

As a result, when this same code is used on a device running Android 4.0 or earlier, the traditional notification will simply appear as if we hadn't taken advantage of the new features.

Notification Visibility and Privacy

(API Level 21)

As of Android 5.0, notifications are fully visible on the device lock screen without the need to pull down the status bar. This is true even if the device is secured with a passcode. To protect private information that may exist in a notification, you may supply additional parameters to define what one can see from the lock screen.

Notifications have a visibility setting that governs their default behavior on a secured lock screen. This means a lock screen with a passcode enabled. These features do nothing on a lock screen that requires a simple slide gesture to unlock.

Figure 6-5 illustrates what a default notification will look like on a secured lock screen, before we apply any custom visibility values.

Figure 6-5. *Default notification on secured lock screen*

There are three options for notification visibility:

- VISIBILITY_PRIVATE: A redacted version of the notification, containing only the application title and icon, will be visible until the device is unlocked. This is the default visibility setting.

    - In this case, a public version of the notification may be supplied to display until the device is unlocked.

- VISIBILITY_PUBLIC: The full notification will be visible, regardless of whether the device is locked or unlocked.

- VISIBILITY_SECRET: The notification is completely hidden from the lock screen. The user must unlock the device to see that it is even present.

■ **Caution**   The user can override all of these visibility controls in the device's notification settings. For example, if the user chooses to have all notifications publicly visible, even notifications you set as secret will appear on the lock screen.

Notifications support a priority setting in Android 4.1 and later. In Android 5.0, this allows us to surface a notification with higher priority (such as an incoming call) in a heads-up display mode. This mode will overlay the notification over any application content, without waiting for the user to pull down the status bar, forcing the user to react to it immediately. Notifications with their priority set to PRIORITY_HIGH or PRIORITY_MAX will be surfaced in heads-up mode when possible. Figure 6-6 shows an example of a heads-up notification.

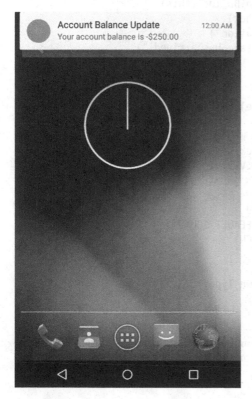

Figure 6-6. *Heads-up notification*

Listing 6-6 repeats the secured builder method from our example so we can examine these parts in greater detail.

Listing 6-6. Secured Notification Features

```
private Notification buildSecuredNotification(int type) {
    Intent launchIntent =
            new Intent(this, NotificationActivity.class);
    PendingIntent contentIntent =
            PendingIntent.getActivity(this, 0, launchIntent, 0);

    //Construct the base notification
    NotificationCompat.Builder builder = new NotificationCompat.Builder(this)
            .setSmallIcon(R.drawable.ic_launcher)
            .setContentTitle("Account Balance Update")
            .setContentText("Your account balance is -$250.00")
            .setStyle(new NotificationCompat.BigTextStyle()
                    .bigText("Your account balance is -$250.00; pay us please "
                            + "or we will be forced to take legal action!"))
            .setContentIntent(contentIntent);

    switch (type) {
        case R.id.option_private:
            //Provide a unique version for secured lock screens
            Notification publicNote = new Notification.Builder(this)
                    .setSmallIcon(R.drawable.ic_launcher)
                    .setContentTitle("Account Notification")
                    .setContentText("An important message has arrived.")
                    .setContentIntent(contentIntent)
                    .build();

            return builder.setPublicVersion(publicNote)
                    .build();
        case R.id.option_secret:
            //Hide the notification from a secured lock screen completely
            return builder.setVisibility(Notification.VISIBILITY_SECRET)
                    .build();
        case R.id.option_headsup:
            //Show a heads-up notification when posted
            return builder.setDefaults(Notification.DEFAULT_SOUND)
                .setPriority(Notification.PRIORITY_HIGH)
                .build();
        default:
            throw new IllegalArgumentException("Unknown Type");
    }
}
```

For this block of options, we have created a base notification that is meant to be an alert from the user's bank containing a current account balance. This is sensitive information that we should probably protect if the user secures the device.

The default behavior of the framework will hide the entire notification behind the redacted view we saw in Figure 6-5, but perhaps we can be a bit smarter about this. When the first user option is selected, we construct a second Notification instance and pass it to setPublicVersion(). This version has a more benign message that is safe to display until the device is unlocked. Figure 6-7 shows the public notification now displayed on the secured lock screen.

Figure 6-7. *Public version of private notification*

Notice in the previous option we did not modify the notification's visibility setting. This is because the value we need to provide this behavior, VISIBILITY_PRIVATE, is the default value. In the second user option, though, we want to hide the notification on the lock screen completely until the device is unlocked. In this case, we simply set the visibility of the notification to VISIBILITY_SECRET instead.

Finally, in cases where our notification is so important that the user should see it right away, we can elevate its priority to PRIORITY_HIGH. This will cause the notification to post immediately into the heads-up mode we saw in Figure 6-6.

■ **Reminder** On older platforms where these APIs are not supported, the framework will simply ignore the values set in this section.

NotificationListenerService

(API Level 18)

As of Android 4.3, a new service is available to applications that wish to monitor the status of all the notifications on the device. Applications can extend NotificationListenerService to receive updates whenever any application posts a new notification or when the user clears an existing notification. In addition, the application can programmatically cancel any specific notification, or clear all of them at once.

ENABLING NOTIFICATION ACCESS

Because this service provides your application global access to the active notifications list, permission must first be granted. However, in this case, your application cannot declare this as a standard permission it would like to obtain. Instead, the user must explicitly grant access from the Security section of the device's Settings application. There is a section for Notification Access, which will list all installed applications that have an exported NotificationListenerService for the user to enable or disable this feature.

Figure 6-8 shows what the Notification Access section of Settings looks like on a Nexus device, along with the prompt that a user will see after tapping your application item to enable access to this information.

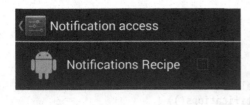

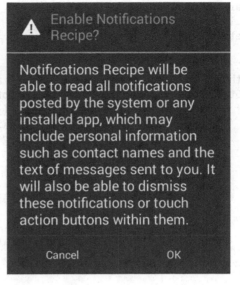

Figure 6-8. *Notification settings warning*

It is up to your application to guide the user to Settings to enable this service to receive events; the framework will not do it for you. You can take the user directly to the appropriate screen in Settings by firing an intent with the android.settings.ACTION_NOTIFICATION_LISTENER_SETTINGS action string to start the activity. As of Android 4.3, this string is not public in the SDK, so be aware that it may change in future versions.

Listing 6-7 shows a simple extension of NotificationListenerService.

Listing 6-7. NotificationListenerService Example

```
public class MonitorService extends NotificationListenerService {
    private static final String TAG = "RecipesMonitorService";

    @Override
    public void onNotificationPosted(StatusBarNotification sbn) {
        //Validate the notification came from this application
        if (!TextUtils.equals(sbn.getPackageName(), getPackageName())) {
            return;
        }

        Log.i(TAG, "Notification "+sbn.getId()+" Posted");
    }

    @Override
    public void onNotificationRemoved(StatusBarNotification sbn) {
        //Validate the notification came from this application
        if (!TextUtils.equals(sbn.getPackageName(), getPackageName())) {
            return;
        }
```

```
        //We are looking for the basic notification
        if (R.id.option_basic != sbn.getId()) {
            return;
        }

        //If the basic notification cancels, dismiss all of ours
        for (StatusBarNotification note : getActiveNotifications()) {
            if (TextUtils.equals(note.getPackageName(), getPackageName())) {
                if (Build.VERSION.SDK_INT < Build.VERSION_CODES.LOLLIPOP) {
                    cancelNotification(note.getPackageName(),
                            note.getTag(),
                            note.getId());
                } else {
                    cancelNotification(note.getKey());
                }
            }
        }
    }

}
```

There are two abstract methods you must implement: onNotificationPosted() and onNotificationRemoved(). These will be called by the framework when a new notification comes in or another is dismissed, respectively. The content passed in is a StatusBarNotification instance, which is just a basic wrapper around the original notification with some additional metadata (for example, the package name of the application that posted it and the ID or tag applied). The original notification is also still accessible as a parameter.

In this example, when a notification is added, we simply log the event if the notification came from our application. If a notification is removed, we check whether it was the basic style notification element and, if so, dismiss all the notifications posted from our application that are still active. The getActiveNotifications() method is helpful in obtaining everything currently visible to the user. We can verify which notifications came from us by comparing the package names of each one. When the package matches, we call cancelNotification() with the metadata from the notification element to remove it programmatically. You can also call cancelAllNotifications() to clear the entire window shade without any regard for where the active elements came from.

Listing 6-8 shows the AndroidManifest.xml snippet you will need to add.

Listing 6-8. NotificationListenerService Manifest Element

```
<service android:name=".MonitorService"
    android:permission="android.permission.BIND_NOTIFICATION_LISTENER_SERVICE">
    <intent-filter>
        <action android:name="android.service.notification.NotificationListenerService" />
    </intent-filter>
</service>
```

The two required elements here are the action string of the <intent-filter> and the declared permission. The framework will look for both of these when determining which NotificationListenerService elements it can bind to.

462

Bundled Notifications

(API Level 24)

As of Android 7.0, multiple notifications can be bundled together. This is especially useful when a message style application wants to display notifications indicating all unread messages.

Listing 6-9. Creating a Bundled Notification

```
private void createBundledNotification() {
    NotificationManagerCompat notificationManager =
            NotificationManagerCompat.from(this);
    for (int i = 1; i <= 5; i++) {
        Notification notif = new NotificationCompat.Builder(this)
                .setContentTitle("New message from " + i)
                .setContentText("Message " + i)
                .setSmallIcon(R.drawable.ic_stat_name)
                .setGroup(GROUP_KEY_MESSAGES)
                .build();
        notificationManager.notify(i, notif);
    }

    Notification summary = new NotificationCompat.Builder(this)
            .setContentTitle("5 new messages")
            .setSmallIcon(R.drawable.ic_stat_name)
            .setStyle(new NotificationCompat.InboxStyle()
                    .setBigContentTitle("5 new messages")
                    .setSummaryText("name@domain.com"))
            .setGroup(GROUP_KEY_MESSAGES)
            .setGroupSummary(true)
            .build();

    notificationManager.notify(6, summary);
}
```

The code in Listing 6-9 shows how to construct a bundled noticiation with five "new" messages and a summary. Note that all notifications have a unique id when calling `notificationManager.notify()`. The grouping of all the notifications into a bundle is done by calling `setGroup()` on the builder using the same key. A summary notification can be added by adding a final notification where you call `setGroupSummary(true)`. The result can be seen in Figure 6-9.

Figure 6-9. *Public version of private notification*

Direct Reply Notifications

(API Level 24)

Another new feature in Android 7.0 is Direct Reply Notifications. These are notifications where an action can trigger a text input inside the notification which is then sent using a PendingIntent. It allows a user to quickly reply to a message without the need to leave the current application. The code for how to create these notifications can be seen in Listing 6-10.

Listing 6-10. Creating a Direct Reply Notification

```
private Notification createDirectReplyNotification() {
    String replyLabel = getResources().getString(R.string.reply_label);
    RemoteInput remoteInput = new RemoteInput.Builder(KEY_TEXT_REPLY)
            .setLabel(replyLabel)
            .build();
    Intent intent = new Intent(this, ReplyReceiverService.class);
    PendingIntent replyPendingIntent = PendingIntent.getService(this, 0, intent,
            PendingIntent.FLAG_ONE_SHOT);
```

```
NotificationCompat.Action action =
        new NotificationCompat.Action.Builder(R.drawable.ic_stat_name,
                getString(R.string.label), replyPendingIntent)
                .addRemoteInput(remoteInput)
                .build();
    return new NotificationCompat.Builder(this)
            .setSmallIcon(R.drawable.ic_stat_name)
            .setContentTitle(getString(R.string.title))
            .setContentText(getString(R.string.content))
            .addAction(action)
            .build();
}
```

The key to creating a direct reply notification is to add an action with a remote input. This will present a text input field in the notification (see Figure 6-10) that can be extracted using the key provided to the RemoteInput. The result form the reply will be sent in the PendingIntent, in this case the service ReplyReceiverService (shown in Listing 6-11).

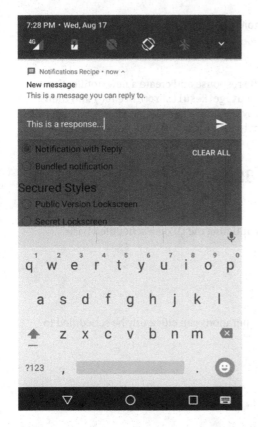

Figure 6-10. *Public version of private notification*

Listing 6-11. The Service Handling a Direct Reply

```
public class ReplyReceiverService extends IntentService {
    public static final String KEY_TEXT_REPLY = "key_text_reply";

    public ReplyReceiverService() {
        super("ReplyReceiverService");
    }

    @Override
    protected void onHandleIntent(Intent intent) {
        Bundle resultsFromIntent = RemoteInput.getResultsFromIntent(intent);
        String reply = resultsFromIntent.getString(KEY_TEXT_REPLY, null);
        Log.d("Reply", "Message: " + reply);
        Notification notification = new NotificationCompat.Builder(this)
                .setRemoteInputHistory(new CharSequence[]{reply})
                .setSmallIcon(R.drawable.ic_stat_name)
                .build();
        NotificationManagerCompat.from(this)
                .notify(R.id.option_reply, notification);
    }
}
```

In this example, our receiving service will simply extract the response and create a new notification. We start by extracting a Bundle from the Intent using RemoteInput.getResultsFromIntent() and then fetch the reply as a String. Finally, we confirm the user action by creating a new notification where we call setRemoteInputHistory() using the reply and finally calling notify() using the same notification id.

6-2. Creating Timed and Periodic Tasks

Problem

Your application needs to run an operation on a timer, such as updating the UI on a scheduled basis.

Solution

(API Level 1)

Use the timed operations provided by Handler. With Handler, operations can efficiently be scheduled to occur at a specific time or after a specified delay.

How It Works

Let's look at an example activity that displays the current time in a TextView. See Listing 6-12.

Listing 6-12. Activity Updated with a Handler

```java
public class TimingActivity extends Activity {

    TextView mClock;

    @Override
    public void onCreate(Bundle savedInstanceState) {
        super.onCreate(savedInstanceState);
        mClock = new TextView(this);
        setContentView(mClock);
    }

    private Handler mHandler = new Handler();
    private Runnable timerTask = new Runnable() {
        @Override
        public void run() {
            Calendar now = Calendar.getInstance();
            mClock.setText(String.format("%02d:%02d:%02d",
                    now.get(Calendar.HOUR),
                    now.get(Calendar.MINUTE),
                    now.get(Calendar.SECOND)) );
            //Schedule the next update in one second
            mHandler.postDelayed(timerTask,1000);
        }
    };

    @Override
    public void onResume() {
        super.onResume();
        mHandler.post(timerTask);
    }

    @Override
    public void onPause() {
        super.onPause();
        mHandler.removeCallbacks(timerTask);
    }
}
```

Here we've wrapped up the operation of reading the current time and updating the UI into a Runnable named timerTask, which will be triggered by the Handler that has also been created. When the activity becomes visible, the task is executed as soon as possible with a call to Handler.post(). After the TextView has been updated, the final operation of timerTask is to invoke the Handler to schedule another execution 1 second (1,000 milliseconds) from now by using Handler.postDelayed().

As long as the activity remains uninterrupted, this cycle will continue, with the UI being updated every second. As soon as the activity is paused (the user leaves or something else grabs his or her attention), Handler.removeCallbacks() removes all pending operations and ensures the task will not be called further until the activity becomes visible once more.

■ **Tip**   In this example, we are safe to update the UI because the Handler was created on the main thread. A Handler will always execute operations on the thread in which it was created, unless a Looper from another thread is passed explicitly to its constructor. We will see how this can be used for background queues in a later recipe, but it is also worth noting here that you can create a Handler from a background thread that posts to the main thread by passing it the result of Looper.getMainLooper(), which is a static reference to the Looper of the main UI thread.

6-3. Scheduling a Periodic Task

Problem

Your application needs to register to run a task periodically, such as checking a server for updates or reminding the user to do something.

Solution

(API Level 1)

Utilize the AlarmManager to manage and execute your task. AlarmManager is useful for scheduling future single or repeated operations that need to occur even if your application is not running. AlarmManager is handed a PendingIntent to fire whenever an alarm is scheduled. This intent can point to any system component, such as a BroadcastReceiver or Service, that can be executed when the alarm triggers.

AlarmManager supports a type parameter to govern the conditions of how the alarm is scheduled:

- ELAPSED_REALTIME: The alarm times are references to a value (in milliseconds) since the last device boot.

- ELAPSED_REALTIME_WAKEUP: The alarm times are referenced to time elapsed and will wake the device to trigger if it is asleep.

- RTC: The alarm times are referenced to UTC time.

- RTC_WAKEUP: The alarm times are referenced to UTC time and will wake the device to trigger if it is asleep.

■ **Note**   If you choose a wake-up alarm type, Android will wake the device from sleep but will not keep the device awake for you. You must obtain a WakeLock from PowerManager while doing your background work from a wake-up event. Otherwise, Android is likely to put the device back to sleep quickly, which will halt what you may be doing.

It should be noted that this method is best suited to operations that need to occur even when the application code may not be running. The AlarmManager requires too much overhead to be useful for simple timing operations that may be needed while an application is in use. These are better handled using the postAtTime() and postDelayed() methods of a Handler.

(API Level 21)

The JobScheduler system service in Android 5.0 and later is a more efficient solution for scheduling background work. One-shot or periodic tasks can be scheduled with the service for later execution. This method is preferred to straight alarms for many tasks because the framework will attempt to do what it can to batch operations together, minimizing the impact on device battery and network usage. This also means, however, that the default operation timing is inexact. If very strict timing requirements are necessary, alarms may be a better choice.

We can schedule tasks by constructing a unique JobInfo object for each task, which contains any extra metadata our application may need to accomplish the task. JobInfo also supports criteria for the conditions under which the task should execute. The JobInfo.Builder includes the following methods for applying the necessary criteria to your job request:

- setRequiredNetworkType(): Describes the network conditions that must exist for your job to run. For example, the system will not trigger a job with NETWORK_TYPE_ UNMETERED set unless the device is connected to Wi-Fi. The default indicates that no network access is necessary for this job.

- setRequiresCharging(): The device must be plugged into a charge for this job to run. This can be helpful for jobs that are infrequent and battery intensive.

- setRequiresDeviceIdle(): The device must be in idle mode for this job to run. This can be loosely correlated to saying the device must be inactive or asleep.

- setPersisted(): Controls whether the job should automatically be scheduled on a device reboot. The default is false, meaning the application would be responsible for scheduling a job manually on restart.

- setBackoffCriteria(): Controls how and when a failed job should be rescheduled to run again. This can be used to minimize unnecessary retries when a resource (such as network access) is temporarily unavailable.

- setPeriodic(): Indicates the job should be run regularly on the given interval until it is explicitly cancelled.

To execute the work, applications must provide a subclass of JobService that the framework can bind to. The framework will invoke this service when the scheduled time of the task occurs. Similar to AlarmManager, scheduled jobs will run even if the application process is not currently running at the time. One advantage to this approach is that the framework automatically handles obtaining wake locks for the scheduled jobs so work can continue even when the device is idle.

How It Works

Let's start with alarms and take a look at how AlarmManager can be used to trigger a service on a regular basis. See Listings 6-13 through 6-15.

Listing 6-13. Service to Be Triggered

```
public class AlarmService extends Service {

    @Override
    public int onStartCommand(Intent intent, int flags, int startId) {
        //Perform an interesting operation, we'll just display the current time
        Calendar now = Calendar.getInstance();
        DateFormat formatter = SimpleDateFormat.getTimeInstance();
        Toast.makeText(this, formatter.format(now.getTime()), Toast.LENGTH_SHORT).show();
```

```
        return START_NOT_STICKY;
    }

    @Override
    public IBinder onBind(Intent intent) {
        return null;
    }
}
```

Listing 6-14. res/layout/main.xml

```xml
<?xml version="1.0" encoding="utf-8"?>
<LinearLayout xmlns:android="http://schemas.android.com/apk/res/android"
    android:orientation="vertical"
    android:layout_width="match_parent"
    android:layout_height="match_parent">
    <Button
        android:id="@+id/start"
        android:layout_width="match_parent"
        android:layout_height="wrap_content"
        android:text="Start Periodic Task" />
    <Button
        android:id="@+id/stop"
        android:layout_width="match_parent"
        android:layout_height="wrap_content"
        android:text="Cancel Periodic Task" />
</LinearLayout>
```

Listing 6-15. Activity to Register/Unregister Alarms

```java
public class AlarmActivity extends Activity implements View.OnClickListener {

    private PendingIntent mAlarmIntent;

    @Override
    public void onCreate(Bundle savedInstanceState) {
        super.onCreate(savedInstanceState);
        setContentView(R.layout.main);
        //Attach the listener to both buttons
        findViewById(R.id.start).setOnClickListener(this);
        findViewById(R.id.stop).setOnClickListener(this);
        //Create the launch sender
        Intent launchIntent = new Intent(this, AlarmService.class);
        mAlarmIntent = PendingIntent.getService(this, 0, launchIntent, 0);
    }

    @Override
    public void onClick(View v) {
        AlarmManager manager = (AlarmManager)getSystemService(Context.ALARM_SERVICE);
        long interval = 5*1000; //5 seconds
```

```
    switch(v.getId()) {
    case R.id.start:
        Toast.makeText(this, "Scheduled", Toast.LENGTH_SHORT).show();
        manager.setRepeating(AlarmManager.ELAPSED_REALTIME,
                SystemClock.elapsedRealtime()+interval,
                interval,
                mAlarmIntent);
        break;
    case R.id.stop:
        Toast.makeText(this, "Canceled", Toast.LENGTH_SHORT).show();
        manager.cancel(mAlarmIntent);
        break;
    default:
        break;
    }
  }
}
```

In this example, we have provided a very basic service that will simply display the current time as a Toast every time it is triggered. That service must be registered in the application's manifest with a <service> tag. Otherwise, AlarmManager—which is external to your application—will not be aware of how to trigger it. The sample activity presents two buttons: one to begin firing regular alarms, and the other to cancel them.

The operation to trigger is referenced by a PendingIntent, which will be used to both set and cancel the alarms. We create an intent referencing the service directly, and then we wrap that intent inside a PendingIntent obtained with getService().

■ **Reminder**   PendingIntent has the creator methods getActivity() and getBroadcast() as well. Be sure to reference the correct application component you are triggering when creating this piece.

When the Start button is pressed, the activity registers a repeating alarm by using AlarmManager. setRepeating(). In addition to PendingIntent, this method takes some parameters to determine when to trigger the alarms. The first parameter defines the alarm type, in terms of the units of time to use and whether the alarm should occur when the device is in sleep mode. In the example, we chose ELAPSED_ REALTIME.

The remaining parameters (respectively) refer to the first time the alarm will trigger and the interval on which it should repeat. Because the chosen alarm type is ELAPSED_REALTIME, the start time must also be relative to elapsed time; SystemClock.elapsedRealtime() provides the current time in this format.

The alarm in the example is registered to trigger 5 seconds after the button is pressed, and then every 5 seconds after that. Every 5 seconds, a Toast will come onscreen with the current time value, even if the application is no longer running or in front of the user. When the user displays the activity and presses the Stop button, any pending alarms matching our PendingIntent are immediately canceled and will stop the flow of Toasts.

■ **Important**   Alarms do not persist through a device reboot. If a device is powered off and then back on, any previously registered alarms must be rescheduled.

A More Precise Example

What if we wanted to schedule an alarm to occur at a specific time? Perhaps exactly at 9:00 AM? Setting AlarmManager with some slightly different parameters could accomplish this. See Listing 6-16.

Listing 6-16. Precision Alarm

```
long firstTime;

//Get a Calendar (defaults to today)
//Set the time to 09:00:00
Calendar startTime = Calendar.getInstance();
startTime.set(Calendar.HOUR_OF_DAY, 9);
startTime.set(Calendar.MINUTE, 0);
startTime.set(Calendar.SECOND, 0);

//Get a Calendar at the current time
Calendar now = Calendar.getInstance();

if(now.before(startTime)) {
    //It's not 9AM yet, start today
    firstTime = startTime.getTimeInMillis();
} else {
    //Start 9AM tomorrow
    startTime.add(Calendar.DATE, 1);
    firstTime = startTime.getTimeInMillis();
}

//Set the alarm
if (Build.VERSION.SDK_INT < Build.VERSION_CODES.KITKAT) {
    manager.set(AlarmManager.RTC,
            nextStartTime(),
            mAlarmIntent);
} else {
    manager.setExact(AlarmManager.RTC,
            nextStartTime(),
            mAlarmIntent);
}
```

This example uses an alarm that is referenced to real time. A determination is made whether the next occurrence of 9:00 AM will be today or tomorrow, and that value is returned as the trigger time for the alarm. Starting in Android 4.4, the AlarmManager defaults all alarms to be inexact, meaning there is a small window within which they will trigger. Along with this new behavior, the setExact() API method was added to allow developers to declare that the following alarm cannot fall within an inexact window. Prior to 4.4, simply calling set() with the appropriate start time was sufficient.

■ **Tip**   After Android 4.4, repeating alarms cannot be scheduled for exact time intervals; they will always be interpreted using an inexact window. Alarms that must repeat at exactly the same time need to be rescheduled by the application after each trigger event.

Using Scheduled Jobs

(API Level 21)

Let's take a look at a similar example that takes advantage of JobScheduler instead. Listing 6-17 reveals a modified service to handle the work of showing the time as a job.

Listing 6-17. Worker as a JobService

```java
public class WorkerService extends JobService {
    private static final int MSG_JOB = 1;

    //Simple queue handler for executing the jobs that are scheduled
    private Handler mJobProcessor = new Handler(new Handler.Callback() {
        @Override
        public boolean handleMessage(Message msg) {
            JobParameters params = (JobParameters) msg.obj;
            Log.i("WorkerService", "Executing Job "+params.getJobId());
            //After completing our asynchronous work, we must trigger
            // jobFinished() to allow the next scheduled task to run.
            doWork();
            jobFinished(params, false);

            return true;
        }
    });

    @Override
    public boolean onStartJob(JobParameters jobParameters) {
        Log.d("WorkerService", "Start Job "+jobParameters.getJobId());
        //To simulate a long task, we delay execution by 7.5 seconds
        mJobProcessor.sendMessageDelayed(
                Message.obtain(mJobProcessor, MSG_JOB, jobParameters),
                7500
        );

        /*
         * Return false if the job was synchronously completed here,
         * true if you need to do more background work. In the latter
         * case, you must call jobFinished() to notify the system of
         * completion.
         */
        return true;
    }

    @Override
    public boolean onStopJob(JobParameters jobParameters) {
        Log.w("WorkerService", "Stop Job "+jobParameters.getJobId());
        //When a request to stop comes in, we have to cancel any pending jobs
        mJobProcessor.removeMessages(MSG_JOB);
```

```
        /*
         * Return true to have the job rescheduled, false to drop it
         */
        return false;
    }

    private void doWork() {
        //Perform an interesting operation, we'll just display the current time
        Calendar now = Calendar.getInstance();
        DateFormat formatter = SimpleDateFormat.getTimeInstance();
        Toast.makeText(this, formatter.format(now.getTime()), Toast.LENGTH_SHORT).show();
    }
}
```

Notice that we must provide this service as an implementation of a JobService. This provides the callbacks we need to interact with the JobScheduler. We have encapsulated the operation of showing the date into a doWork() method. To simulate a slightly more complex task, we delayed execution 7.5 seconds by posting it to a Handler as a Message.

The system will trigger a previously scheduled job via onStartJob(); this is the method you must use to begin your job task. The return value of onStartJob() tells the framework whether your job was simple enough to complete synchronously (that is, it's already done when the method returns) or whether an asynchronous task was started. If you return false in onStartJob(), the framework considers the task complete and you're done until the framework triggers a new job.

However, we return true to indicate our task will take a bit longer. This means we are responsible for notifying the framework when it does complete. JobScheduler will not trigger any more of the same job until the current job is complete.

After the requested delay, handleMessage() triggers to process our doWork() method. At this point, we have to call jobFinished() to indicate the task is finally complete. This method requires the original JobParameters object to identify the job, so we pass this along in the Message that is queued up. If something failed in our task, jobFinished() accepts a boolean parameter to tell the framework to reschedule the job according to the criteria set in the original JobInfo.

A JobService must also support cancellation of a pending job. If JobScheduler receives a cancel request while it is waiting on a job in progress, onStopJob() will be triggered on the service. The service is responsible for terminating the job as soon as this happens. In our example, we simply have to clear any pending tasks in the Handler queue so they do not fire.

■ **Tip**   If your task is synchronous, meaning you return false from onStartJob(), the framework assumes no work is pending so cancellation requests have no meaning and onStopJob() will never be called.

As you can see in Listing 6-18, we must define this service in the manifest. Additionally, since we are required to expose this service to the framework, Android requires that our service be protected by the BIND_JOB_SERVICE permission. This is a permission that only the Android framework can hold, so it protects our service from access by any other applications. Failing to supply this permission will result in an exception when attempting to schedule a job.

Listing 6-18. Partial AndroidManifest.xml

```xml
<manifest xmlns:android="http://schemas.android.com/apk/res/android" ...>
    <application ...>

        <service android:name=".WorkerService"
            android:permission="android.permission.BIND_JOB_SERVICE" />

    </application>
</manifest>
```

Now that our service is complete, we look to Listing 6-19 to wire our new service up to a similar activity that we can use to manage scheduling the work as a job.

Listing 6-19. Activity to Schedule a Background Job

```java
public class JobSchedulerActivity extends Activity implements View.OnClickListener {
    private static final int JOB_ID = 1;

    @Override
    protected void onCreate(Bundle savedInstanceState) {
        super.onCreate(savedInstanceState);
        setContentView(R.layout.main);

        //Attach the listener to both buttons
        findViewById(R.id.start).setOnClickListener(this);
        findViewById(R.id.stop).setOnClickListener(this);
    }

    @Override
    public void onClick(View view) {
        JobScheduler scheduler = (JobScheduler) getSystemService(JOB_SCHEDULER_SERVICE);
        long interval = 5*1000; //5 seconds

        JobInfo info = new JobInfo.Builder(JOB_ID,
                new ComponentName(getPackageName(), WorkerService.class.getName()))
                .setPeriodic(interval)
                .build();

        switch (view.getId()) {
            case R.id.start:
                //Android will return the same Job ID anytime the same info
                // is passed to schedule(), it will not duplicate jobs
                int result = scheduler.schedule(info);
                if (result <= 0) {
                    Toast.makeText(this, "Error Scheduling Job", Toast.LENGTH_SHORT).show();
                }
                break;
```

```
        case R.id.stop:
            //The Job ID must match what was passed to schedule, so keep it around
            scheduler.cancel(JOB_ID);
            break;
        default:
            break;
        }
    }
}
```

In this example, we represent the work to schedule as a JobInfo instance retrieved from a JobInfo. Builder. At a minimum, the info must contain the job ID and the name of the service that will execute the work. We also supply a periodic interval, telling the system to schedule this job every 5 seconds.

When the Start button is pressed, the info object is passed to JobScheduler.schedule() to begin triggering the periodic task. This will initiate the first job on our WorkerService approximately 5 seconds after this event. When we want to stop the periodic task, the Stop button triggers JobScheduler.cancel() with the matching job ID.

■ **Note**   The behavior you should observe in this example is that the time will be shown approximately every 12.5 seconds. This is because JobScheduler schedules the next periodic task *after* the previous one completes. Since we delay the task 7.5 seconds in our service before notifying completion, this extends the overall period.

6-4. Creating Sticky Operations

Problem

Your application needs to execute one or more background operations that will run to completion even if the user suspends the application.

Solution

(API Level 3)

Create an IntentService to handle the work. IntentService is a wrapper around Android's base service implementation, the key component to doing work in the background without interaction from the user. IntentService queues incoming work (expressed using intents), processing each request in turn, and then stops itself when the queue is empty.

IntentService also handles creation of the worker thread needed to do the work in the background, so it is not necessary to use AsyncTask or Java threads to ensure that the operation is properly in the background.

This recipe provides an example of using IntentService to create a central manager of background operations. In the example, the manager will be invoked externally with calls to Context.startService(). The manager will queue up all requests received, and process them individually with a call to onHandleIntent().

How It Works

Let's take a look at how to construct a simple IntentService implementation to handle a series of background operations. See Listing 6-20.

Listing 6-20. IntentService Handling Operations

```java
public class OperationsManager extends IntentService {

    public static final String ACTION_EVENT = "ACTION_EVENT";
    public static final String ACTION_WARNING = "ACTION_WARNING";
    public static final String ACTION_ERROR = "ACTION_ERROR";
    public static final String EXTRA_NAME = "eventName";

    private static final String LOGTAG = "EventLogger";

    private IntentFilter matcher;

    public OperationsManager() {
        super("OperationsManager");
        //Create the filter for matching incoming requests
        matcher = new IntentFilter();
        matcher.addAction(ACTION_EVENT);
        matcher.addAction(ACTION_WARNING);
        matcher.addAction(ACTION_ERROR);
    }

    @Override
    protected void onHandleIntent(Intent intent) {
        //Check for a valid request
        if(!matcher.matchAction(intent.getAction())) {
            Toast.makeText(this, "OperationsManager: Invalid Request",
                    Toast.LENGTH_SHORT).show();
            return;
        }

        //Handle each request directly in this method. Don't create more threads.
        if(TextUtils.equals(intent.getAction(), ACTION_EVENT)) {
            logEvent(intent.getStringExtra(EXTRA_NAME));
        }
        if(TextUtils.equals(intent.getAction(), ACTION_WARNING)) {
            logWarning(intent.getStringExtra(EXTRA_NAME));
        }
        if(TextUtils.equals(intent.getAction(), ACTION_ERROR)) {
            logError(intent.getStringExtra(EXTRA_NAME));
        }
    }
```

```java
    private void logEvent(String name) {
        try {
            //Simulate a long network operation by sleeping
            Thread.sleep(5000);
            Log.i(LOGTAG, name);
        } catch (InterruptedException e) {
            e.printStackTrace();
        }
    }

    private void logWarning(String name) {
        try {
            //Simulate a long network operation by sleeping
            Thread.sleep(5000);
            Log.w(LOGTAG, name);
        } catch (InterruptedException e) {
            e.printStackTrace();
        }
    }

    private void logError(String name) {
        try {
            //Simulate a long network operation by sleeping
            Thread.sleep(5000);
            Log.e(LOGTAG, name);
        } catch (InterruptedException e) {
            e.printStackTrace();
        }
    }
}
```

IntentService does not have a default constructor (one that takes no parameters), so a custom implementation must implement a constructor that calls through to super with a service name. This name is of little technical importance, as it is useful only for debugging; Android uses the name provided to name the worker thread that it creates.

All requests are processed by the service through the onHandleIntent() method. This method is called on the provided worker thread, so all work should be done directly here; no new threads or operations should be created. When onHandleIntent() returns, this is the signal to the IntentService to begin processing the next request in the queue.

This example provides three logging operations that can be requested using different action strings on the request intents. For demonstration purposes, each operation writes the provided message out to the device log by using a specific logging level (INFO, WARNING, or ERROR). Note that the message itself is passed as an extra of the request intent. Use the data and extra fields of each intent to hold any parameters for the operation, leaving the action field to define the operation type.

The service in the example maintains an IntentFilter, which is used for convenience to determine whether a valid request has been made. All of the valid actions are added to the filter when the service is created, allowing us to call IntentFilter.matchAction() on any incoming request to determine whether it includes an action we can process here.

Listings 6-21 and 6-22 reveal an example including an activity calling in to this service to perform work.

Listing 6-21. AndroidManifest.xml

```xml
<?xml version="1.0" encoding="utf-8"?>
<manifest xmlns:android="http://schemas.android.com/apk/res/android"
    package="com.examples.sticky">

    <application android:icon="@drawable/icon"
        android:label="@string/app_name">
        <activity android:name=".ReportActivity"
            android:label="@string/app_name">
            <intent-filter>
                <action android:name="android.intent.action.MAIN" />
                <category android:name="android.intent.category.LAUNCHER" />
            </intent-filter>
        </activity>

        <service android:name=".OperationsManager"></service>
    </application>
</manifest>
```

■ **Note**   Because IntentService is invoked as a *service*, it must be declared in the application manifest with a <service> tag as shown in Listing 6-21.

Listing 6-22. Activity Calling IntentService

```java
public class ReportActivity extends Activity {

    @Override
    public void onCreate(Bundle savedInstanceState) {
        super.onCreate(savedInstanceState);
        logEvent("CREATE");
    }

    @Override
    public void onStart() {
        super.onStart();
        logEvent("START");
    }

    @Override
    public void onResume() {
        super.onResume();
        logEvent("RESUME");
    }

    @Override
    public void onPause() {
        super.onPause();
        logWarning("PAUSE");
    }
```

```java
@Override
public void onStop() {
    super.onStop();
    logWarning("STOP");
}

@Override
public void onDestroy() {
    super.onDestroy();
    logWarning("DESTROY");
}

private void logEvent(String event) {
    Intent intent = new Intent(this, OperationsManager.class);
    intent.setAction(OperationsManager.ACTION_EVENT);
    intent.putExtra(OperationsManager.EXTRA_NAME, event);

    startService(intent);
}

private void logWarning(String event) {
    Intent intent = new Intent(this, OperationsManager.class);
    intent.setAction(OperationsManager.ACTION_WARNING);
    intent.putExtra(OperationsManager.EXTRA_NAME, event);

    startService(intent);
}
}
```

This activity isn't much to look at, as all the interesting events are sent out through the device log instead of to the user interface. Nevertheless, it helps illustrate the queue-processing behavior of the service we created in the previous example. As the activity becomes visible, it will call through all of its normal life-cycle methods, resulting in three requests made to the logging service. As each request is processed, a line will output to the log and the service will move on.

■ **Tip** These log statements are visible through the logcat tool provided with the SDK. The logcat output from a device or emulator is visible from within Android Studio or from the command line by typing adb logcat.

Notice also that when the service is finished with all three requests, a notification is logged out that the service has been stopped. IntentServices are kept around in memory only for as long as required to complete the job; this is a very useful feature for your services to have, making them good citizens of the system.

Pressing either the HOME or BACK buttons will cause more of the life-cycle methods to generate requests of the service, and the Pause/Stop/Destroy portion calls a separate operation in the service, causing their messages to be logged as warnings; simply setting the action string of the request intent to a different value controls this.

Notice that messages continue to be output to the log, even after the application is no longer visible (or even if another application is opened instead). This is the power of the Android service component at work. These operations are protected from the system until they are complete, regardless of user behavior.

A Possible Drawback

In each of the operation methods, a 5-second delay has been placed to simulate the time required for an actual request to be made of a remote API or some similar operation. When running this example, it also helps to illustrate that IntentService handles all requests sent to it in a serial fashion with a single worker thread. The example queues multiple requests in succession from each life-cycle method; however, the result will still be a log message every 5 seconds, because IntentService does not start a new request until the current one is complete (essentially, when onHandleIntent() returns).

If your application requires concurrency from sticky background tasks, you may need to create a more customized service implementation that uses a pool of threads to execute work. The beauty of Android being an open source project is that you can go directly to the source code for IntentService and use it as a starting point for such an implementation, minimizing the amount of time and custom code required.

6-5. Running Persistent Background Operations

Problem

Your application has a component that must be running in the background indefinitely, performing a particular operation or monitoring certain events to occur.

Solution

(API Level 1)

Build the component into a service. Services are designed as background components that an application may start and leave running for an indefinite amount of time. Services are also given elevated status above other background processes in terms of protection from being killed in low-memory conditions.

Services may be started and stopped explicitly for operations that do not require a direct connection to another component (like an activity). However, if the application must interact directly with the service, a binding interface is provided to pass data. In these instances, the service may be started and stopped implicitly by the system as is required to fulfill its requested bindings.

The key thing to remember with service implementations is to always be user friendly. An indefinite operation most likely should not be started unless the user explicitly requests it. The overall application should probably contain an interface or setting that allows the user to control enabling or disabling such a service.

How It Works

Listing 6-23 is an example of a persisted service that is used to track and log the user's location over a certain period.

Listing 6-23. Persistent Tracking Service

```
public class TrackerService extends Service implements LocationListener {

    private static final String LOGTAG = "TrackerService";

    private LocationManager manager;
    private ArrayList<Location> storedLocations;
```

```java
    private boolean isTracking = false;

    /* Service Setup Methods */
    @Override
    public void onCreate() {
        manager = (LocationManager)getSystemService(LOCATION_SERVICE);
        storedLocations = new ArrayList<Location>();
        Log.i(LOGTAG, "Tracking Service Running...");
    }

    @Override
    public void onDestroy() {
        manager.removeUpdates(this);
        Log.i(LOGTAG, "Tracking Service Stopped...");
    }

    public void startTracking() {
        if(!manager.isProviderEnabled(LocationManager.GPS_PROVIDER)) {
            return;
        }
        Toast.makeText(this, "Starting Tracker", Toast.LENGTH_SHORT).show();
        manager.requestLocationUpdates(LocationManager.GPS_PROVIDER, 30000, 0, this);

        isTracking = true;
    }

    public void stopTracking() {
        Toast.makeText(this, "Stopping Tracker", Toast.LENGTH_SHORT).show();
        manager.removeUpdates(this);
        isTracking = false;
    }

    public boolean isTracking() {
        return isTracking;
    }

    /* Service Access Methods */
    public class TrackerBinder extends Binder {
        TrackerService getService() {
            return TrackerService.this;
        }
    }

    private final IBinder binder = new TrackerBinder();


    @Override
    public IBinder onBind(Intent intent) {
        return binder;
    }
```

```java
    public int getLocationsCount() {
        return storedLocations.size();
    }

    public ArrayList<Location> getLocations() {
        return storedLocations;
    }

    /* LocationListener Methods */
    @Override
    public void onLocationChanged(Location location) {
        Log.i("TrackerService", "Adding new location");
        storedLocations.add(location);
    }

    @Override
    public void onProviderDisabled(String provider) { }

    @Override
    public void onProviderEnabled(String provider) { }

    @Override
    public void onStatusChanged(String provider, int status, Bundle extras) { }
}
```

This service monitors and tracks the updates it receives from the LocationManager. When the service is created, it prepares a blank list of Location items and waits to begin tracking. An external component, such as an activity, can call startTracking() and stopTracking() to enable and disable the flow of location updates to the service. In addition, methods are exposed to access the list of locations that the service has logged.

Because this service requires direct interaction from an activity or other component, a Binder interface is required. The Binder concept can get complex when a service has to communicate across process boundaries, but for instances like this, where everything is local to the same process, a very simple Binder is created with one method, getService(), to return the service instance itself to the caller. We'll look at this in more detail from the activity's perspective in a moment.

When tracking is enabled on the service, it registers for updates with LocationManager, and it stores every update received in its locations list. Notice that requestLocationUpdates() was called with a minimum time of 30 seconds. Because this service is expected to be running for a long time, it is prudent to space out the updates to give the GPS (and consequently the battery) a little rest.

Now let's take a look at a simple activity that allows the user access into this service. See Listings 6-24 through 6-26.

Listing 6-24. AndroidManifest.xml

```xml
<?xml version="1.0" encoding="utf-8"?>
<manifest xmlns:android="http://schemas.android.com/apk/res/android"
    package="com.examples.service">

    <application android:icon="@drawable/icon"
        android:label="@string/app_name">
        <activity android:name=".ServiceActivity"
```

```
        android:label="@string/app_name">
        <intent-filter>
            <action android:name="android.intent.action.MAIN" />
            <category android:name="android.intent.category.LAUNCHER" />
        </intent-filter>
    </activity>

    <service android:name=".TrackerService"></service>
</application>
<uses-permission android:name="android.permission.ACCESS_FINE_LOCATION"/>
</manifest>
```

■ **Reminder**   The service must be declared in the application manifest by using a `<service>` tag so Android knows how and where to call it. Also, for this example, the permission `android.permission.ACCESS_FINE_LOCATION` is required because we are working with the GPS.

Listing 6-25. `res/layout/main.xml`

```xml
<?xml version="1.0" encoding="utf-8"?>
<LinearLayout xmlns:android="http://schemas.android.com/apk/res/android"
    android:orientation="vertical"
    android:layout_width="match_parent"
    android:layout_height="match_parent">
    <Button
        android:id="@+id/enable"
        android:layout_width="match_parent"
        android:layout_height="wrap_content"
        android:text="Start Tracking" />
    <Button
        android:id="@+id/disable"
        android:layout_width="match_parent"
        android:layout_height="wrap_content"
        android:text="Stop Tracking" />
    <TextView
        android:id="@+id/status"
        android:layout_width="match_parent"
        android:layout_height="wrap_content" />
</LinearLayout>
```

Listing 6-26. Activity Interacting with Service

```java
public class ServiceActivity extends Activity implements View.OnClickListener {

    Button enableButton, disableButton;
    TextView statusView;

    TrackerService trackerService;
    Intent serviceIntent;

    @Override
    public void onCreate(Bundle savedInstanceState) {
        super.onCreate(savedInstanceState);
        setContentView(R.layout.main);
        enableButton = (Button)findViewById(R.id.enable);
        enableButton.setOnClickListener(this);
        disableButton = (Button)findViewById(R.id.disable);
        disableButton.setOnClickListener(this);
        statusView = (TextView)findViewById(R.id.status);

        serviceIntent = new Intent(this, TrackerService.class);
    }

    @Override
    public void onResume() {
        super.onResume();
        //Starting the service makes it stick, regardless of bindings
        startService(serviceIntent);
        //Bind to the service
        bindService(serviceIntent, serviceConnection, Context.BIND_AUTO_CREATE);
    }

    @Override
    public void onPause() {
        super.onPause();
        if(!trackerService.isTracking()) {
            //Stopping the service lets it die once unbound
            stopService(serviceIntent);
        }
        //Unbind from the service
        unbindService(serviceConnection);
    }

    @Override
    public void onClick(View v) {
        switch(v.getId()) {
        case R.id.enable:
            trackerService.startTracking();
            break;
        case R.id.disable:
            trackerService.stopTracking();
            break;
```

```
        default:
            break;
    }
    updateStatus();
}

private void updateStatus() {
    if(trackerService.isTracking()) {
        statusView.setText(
            String.format("Tracking enabled. %d locations
                logged.",trackerService.getLocationsCount()));
    } else {
        statusView.setText("Tracking not currently enabled.");
    }
}

private ServiceConnection serviceConnection = new ServiceConnection() {
    public void onServiceConnected(ComponentName className, IBinder service) {
        trackerService = ((TrackerService.TrackerBinder)service).getService();
        updateStatus();
    }

    public void onServiceDisconnected(ComponentName className) {
        trackerService = null;
    }
};
}
```

Figure 6-11 displays the basic activity with two buttons for the user to enable and disable location-tracking behavior, and a text display for the current service status.

Figure 6-11. *ServiceActivity layout*

While the activity is visible, it is bound to the TrackerService. This is done with the help of the ServiceConnection interface, which provides callback methods when the binding and unbinding operations are complete. With the service bound to the activity, you can now make direct calls on all the public methods exposed by the service.

However, bindings alone will not allow the service to run for the long term; accessing the service solely through its Binder interface causes it to be created and destroyed automatically along with the life cycle of this activity. In this case, we want the service to persist beyond when this activity is in memory. In order to accomplish this, the service is explicitly started via startService() before it is bound. There is no harm in sending start commands to a service that is already running, so we can safely do this in onResume() as well.

The service will now continue running in memory, even after the activity unbinds itself. In onPause(), the example always checks whether the user has activated tracking, and if not, it stops the service first. This allows the service to die if it is not required for tracking, which keeps the service from perpetually hanging out in memory if it has no real work to do.

Running this example and pressing the Start Tracking button will spin up the persisted service and the LocationManager. The user may leave the application at this point, and the service will remain running, all the while logging all incoming location updates from the GPS. Upon returning to this application, the user can see that the service is still running, and the current number of stored location points is displayed. Pressing Stop Tracking will end the process and allow the service to die as soon as the user leaves the activity once more.

6-6. Launching Other Applications

Problem

Your application requires a specific function that another application on the device is already programmed to do. Instead of overlapping functionality, you would like to launch the other application for the job instead.

Solution

(API Level 1)

Use an implicit intent to tell the system what you are looking to do, and determine whether any applications exist to meet the need. Most often, developers use intents in an explicit fashion to start another activity or service, like so:

```
Intent intent = new Intent(this, NewActivity.class);
startActivity(intent);
```

By declaring the specific component we want to launch, the intent is very explicit in its delivery. We also have the power to define an intent in terms of its action, category, data, and type to define a more implicit requirement of what task we want to accomplish.

External applications are always launched within the same Android task as your application when fired in this fashion, so once the operation is complete (or if the user backs out), the user is returned to your application. This keeps the experience seamless, allowing multiple applications to act as one from the user's perspective.

How It Works

When defining intents in this fashion, it can be unclear what information you must include, because there is no published standard and it is possible for two applications offering the same service (reading a PDF file, for example) to define slightly different filters to listen for incoming intents. You want to make sure to provide enough information for the system (or the user) to pick the best application to handle the required task.

The core piece of information to define on almost any implicit intent is the action: a string value that is passed either in the constructor or via `Intent.setAction()`. This value tells Android what you want to do, whether it is to view a piece of content, send a message, select a choice, and so on. From there, the fields provided are scenario specific, and often multiple combinations can arrive at the same result. Let's take a look at some useful examples.

Read a PDF File

Components to display PDF documents are not included in the core SDK, although almost every consumer Android device on the market today ships with a PDF reader application, and many more are available through Google Play. Because of this, it may not make sense to go through the trouble of embedding PDF display capabilities in your application.

Instead, Listing 6-27 illustrates how to find and launch another app to view the PDF.

Listing 6-27. Method to View PDF

```
private void viewPdf(Uri file) {
        Intent intent;
        intent = new Intent(Intent.ACTION_VIEW);
        intent.setDataAndType(file, "application/pdf");
        try {
            startActivity(intent);
        } catch (ActivityNotFoundException e) {
            //No application to view, ask to download one
            AlertDialog.Builder builder = new AlertDialog.Builder(this);
            builder.setTitle("No Application Found");
            builder.setMessage("We could not find an application to view PDFs."
                    +"  Would you like to download one from Android Market?");
            builder.setPositiveButton("Yes, Please",
                new DialogInterface.OnClickListener() {
                @Override
                public void onClick(DialogInterface dialog, int which) {
                    Intent marketIntent = new Intent(Intent.ACTION_VIEW);
                    marketIntent.setData(
                            Uri.parse("market://details?id=com.adobe.reader"));
                    startActivity(marketIntent);
                }
            });
            builder.setNegativeButton("No, Thanks", null);
            builder.create().show();
        }
    }
```

This example will open any local PDF file on the device (internal or external storage) by using the best application found. If no application is found on the device to view PDFs, a message will encourage the user to go to Google Play and download one.

The intent we create for this is constructed with the generic `Intent.ACTION_VIEW` action string, telling the system we want to view the data provided in the intent. The data file itself and its MIME type are also set to tell the system what kind of data we want to view.

■ **Tip** `Intent.setData()` and `Intent.setType()` clear each other's previous values when used. If you need to set both simultaneously, use `Intent.setDataAndType()`, as in the example.

If `startActivity()` fails with an `ActivityNotFoundException`, it means that no application is installed on the user's device that can view PDFs. We want users to have the full experience, so if this happens, a dialog box indicates the problem and asks whether the user would like to go to Market and get a reader. If the user presses Yes, another implicit intent will request that Google Play be opened directly to the application page for Adobe Reader, a free application the user may download to view PDF files. We'll discuss the `Uri` scheme used for this intent in the next recipe.

Notice that the example method takes a Uri parameter to the local file. Here is an example of how to retrieve a Uri for files located on internal storage:

```
String filename = NAME_OF_YOUR_FILE;
File internalFile = getFileStreamPath(filename);
Uri internal = Uri.fromFile(internalFile);
```

The method getFileStreamPath() is called from a Context, so if this code is not in an activity, you must have reference to a Context object to call on. Here's how to create a Uri for files located on external storage:

```
String filename = NAME_OF_YOUR_FILE;
File externalFile = new File(Environment.getExternalStorageDirectory(), filename);
Uri external = Uri.fromFile(externalFile);
```

This same example will work for any other document type as well by simply changing the MIME type attached to the intent.

Share with Friends

Another popular feature for developers to include in their applications is a method of sharing the application content with others, either through e-mail, text messaging, or prominent social networks. All Android devices include applications for e-mail and text messaging, and most users who wish to share via a social network (for example, Facebook or Twitter) also have those mobile applications on their devices.

As it turns out, this task can also be accomplished using an implicit intent because most of these applications respond to the Intent.ACTION_SEND action string in some way. Listing 6-28 is an example of allowing a user to post to any medium with a single intent request.

Listing 6-28. Sharing Intent

```
private void shareContent(String update) {
    Intent intent = new Intent(Intent.ACTION_SEND);
    intent.setType("text/plain");
    intent.putExtra(Intent.EXTRA_TEXT, update);
    startActivity(Intent.createChooser(intent, "Share..."));
}
```

Here, we tell the system that we have a piece of text that we would like to send, passed in as an extra. This is a very generic request, and we expect more than one application to be able to handle it. By default, Android will present the user with a list of applications that the user can select to open. In addition, some devices provide the user with a check box to set a selection as a default so the list is never shown again.

We would prefer to have a little more control over this process because we also expect multiple results every time. Therefore, instead of passing the intent directly to startActivity(), we first pass it through Intent.createChooser(), which allows us to customize the title and guarantee the selection list will always be displayed.

When the user selects a choice, that specific application will launch with the EXTRA_TEXT prepopulated into the message entry box, ready for sharing!

Use ShareActionProvider

(API Level 14)

Starting with Android 4.0, a new widget was introduced to assist applications in sharing content by using a common mechanism called ShareActionProvider. It is designed to be added to an item in the options menu to show up either on the action bar or in the overflow. It also has an added feature for the users in that, by default, it ranks the share options it provides by usage. Options that users click most frequently will always be at the top of the list.

Implementing ShareActionProvider in a menu is quite simple, and it requires only a few more lines of code than creating the share intent itself. Listing 6-29 shows how to attach the provider to a menu item.

Listing 6-29. res/menu/options.xml

```xml
<menu xmlns:android="http://schemas.android.com/apk/res/android">
    <item android:id="@+id/menu_share"
        android:showAsAction="ifRoom"
        android:title="Share"
        android:actionProviderClass="android.widget.ShareActionProvider"/>
</menu>
```

■ **Note**   If you do not define your Menu in XML, you can still attach the ShareActionProvider by calling setActionProvider() inside your Java code.

Listing 6-30 shows how to attach the share intent to the provider widget inside an activity.

Listing 6-30. Providing the Share Intent

```java
@Override
public boolean onCreateOptionsMenu(Menu menu) {
    //Inflate the menu
    getMenuInflater().inflate(R.menu.options, menu);

    //Find the item and set the share Intent
    MenuItem item = menu.findItem(R.id.menu_share);
    ShareActionProvider provider = (ShareActionProvider) item.getActionProvider();

    Intent intent = new Intent(Intent.ACTION_SEND);
    intent.setType("text/plain");
    intent.putExtra(Intent.EXTRA_TEXT, update);
    provider.setShareIntent(intent);

    return true;

}
```

And that's it! The provider handles all the user interaction, so your application doesn't even need to handle the user selection events for that MenuItem.

6-7. Launching System Applications

Problem

Your application requires a specific function that one of the system applications on the device is already programmed to do. Instead of overlapping functionality, you would like to launch the system application for the job instead.

Solution

(API Level 1)

Use an implicit intent to tell the system which application you are interested in. Each system application subscribes to a custom Uri scheme that can be inserted as data into an implicit intent to signify the specific application you need to launch.

External applications are always launched in the same task as your application when fired in this fashion, so once the task is complete (or if the user backs out), the user is returned to your application. This keeps the experience seamless, allowing multiple applications to act as one from the user's perspective.

How It Works

All of the following examples will construct intents that can be used to launch system applications in various states. Once constructed, you should launch these applications by passing the intent to startActivity().

Browser

The Browser application may be launched to display a web page or run a web search.

To display a web page, construct and launch the following intent:

```
Intent pageIntent = new Intent();
pageIntent.setAction(Intent.ACTION_VIEW);
pageIntent.setData(Uri.parse("http://WEB_ADDRESS_TO_VIEW"));

startActivity(pageIntent);
```

This replaces the Uri in the data field with the page you would like to view. To launch a web search inside the Browser, construct and launch the following intent:

```
String searchString = "Android Recipes";
Intent searchIntent = new Intent();
searchIntent.setAction(Intent.ACTION_WEB_SEARCH);
searchIntent.putExtra(SearchManager.QUERY, searchString);

startActivity(searchIntent);
```

This places the search query you want to execute as an extra in the Intent.

Phone Dialer

The Dialer application may be launched to place a call to a specific number by using the following intent:

```
Intent dialIntent = new Intent();
dialIntent.setAction(Intent.ACTION_DIAL);
dialIntent.setData(Uri.Parse("tel:8885551234"));

startActivity(dialIntent);
```

This replaces the phone number in the data Uri with the number to call.

■ **Note**   This action just brings up the Dialer; it does not place the call. Intent.ACTION_CALL can be used to place the call directly, although Google discourages using this in most cases. Using ACTION_CALL will also require that the android.permission.CALL_PHONE permission be declared in the manifest.

Maps

The Maps application on the device can be launched to display a location or to provide directions between two points. If you know the latitude and longitude of the location you want to map, then create the following intent:

```
Intent mapIntent = new Intent();
mapIntent.setAction(Intent.ACTION_VIEW);
mapIntent.setData(Uri.parse("geo:latitude,longitude"));

startActivity(mapIntent);
```

This replaces the coordinates for latitude and longitude of your location. For example, the Uri

```
"geo:37.422,-122.084
```

would map the location of Google's headquarters. If you know the address of the location to display, then create the following intent:

```
Intent mapIntent = new Intent();
mapIntent.setAction(Intent.ACTION_VIEW);
mapIntent.setData(Uri.parse("geo:0,0?q=ADDRESS"));

startActivity(mapIntent);
```

This inserts the address you would like to map. For example, the Uri

```
"geo:0,0?q=1600 Amphitheatre Parkway, Mountain View, CA 94043"
```

would map the address of Google's headquarters.

■ **Tip**   The Maps application will also accept a Uri that uses the + character to replace spaces in the Address query. If you are having trouble encoding a string with spaces in it, try ecndoing them using the URLEncoder class.

If you would like to display directions between two locations, create the following intent:

```
Intent mapIntent = new Intent();
mapIntent.setAction(Intent.ACTION_VIEW);
mapIntent.setData(Uri.parse("http://maps.google.com/maps?saddr=lat,lng&daddr=lat,lng"));

startActivity(mapIntent);
```

This inserts the locations for the start and end addresses.

You also can include only one of the parameters if you want to open the Maps application with one address being open-ended. For example, the Uri

```
"http://maps.google.com/maps?&daddr=37.422,-122.084"
```

would display the Maps application with the destination location prepopulated, but it would allow users to enter their own start address.

E-mail

Any e-mail application on the device can be launched into compose mode by using the following intent:

```
Intent mailIntent = new Intent();
mailIntent.setAction(Intent.ACTION_SEND);
mailIntent.setType("message/rfc822");
mailIntent.putExtra(Intent.EXTRA_EMAIL, new String[] {"recipient@gmail.com"});
mailIntent.putExtra(Intent.EXTRA_CC, new String[] {"carbon@gmail.com"});
mailIntent.putExtra(Intent.EXTRA_BCC, new String[] {"blind@gmail.com"});
mailIntent.putExtra(Intent.EXTRA_SUBJECT, "Email Subject");
mailIntent.putExtra(Intent.EXTRA_TEXT, "Body Text");
mailIntent.putExtra(Intent.EXTRA_STREAM, URI_TO_FILE);

startActivity(mailIntent);
```

In this scenario, the action and type fields are the only required pieces to bring up a blank e-mail message. All the remaining extras prepopulate specific fields of the e-mail message. Notice that EXTRA_EMAIL (which fills the To field), EXTRA_CC, and EXTRA_BCC are passed string arrays, even if there is only one recipient to be placed there. File attachments may also be specified in the intent by using EXTRA_STREAM. The value passed here should be a Uri pointing to the local file to be attached.

If you need to attach more than one file to an e-mail, the requirements change slightly to the following:

```
Intent mailIntent = new Intent();
mailIntent.setAction(Intent.ACTION_SEND_MULTIPLE);
mailIntent.setType("message/rfc822");
mailIntent.putExtra(Intent.EXTRA_EMAIL, new String[] {"recipient@gmail.com"});
mailIntent.putExtra(Intent.EXTRA_CC, new String[] {"carbon@gmail.com"});
mailIntent.putExtra(Intent.EXTRA_BCC, new String[] {"blind@gmail.com"});
```

```
mailIntent.putExtra(Intent.EXTRA_SUBJECT, "Email Subject");
mailIntent.putExtra(Intent.EXTRA_TEXT, "Body Text");

ArrayList<Uri> files = new ArrayList<Uri>();
files.add(URI_TO_FIRST_FILE);
files.add(URI_TO_SECOND_FILE);
//...Repeat add() as often as necessary to add all the files you need
mailIntent.putParcelableArrayListExtra(Intent.EXTRA_STREAM, files);

startActivity(mailIntent);
```

Notice that the intent's action string is now ACTION_SEND_MULTIPLE. All the primary fields remain the same as before, except for the data that gets added as the EXTRA_STREAM. This example creates a list of Uri elements pointing to the files you want to attach and adds them by using putParcelableArrayListExtra().

It is not uncommon for users to have multiple applications on their devices that can handle this content, so it is usually prudent to wrap either of these constructed intents with Intent.createChooser() before passing it on to startActivity().

SMS (Messages)

The Messages application can be launched into compose mode for a new SMS message by using the following Intent:

```
Intent smsIntent = new Intent();
smsIntent.setAction(Intent.ACTION_VIEW);
smsIntent.setType("vnd.android-dir/mms-sms");
smsIntent.putExtra("address", "8885551234");
smsIntent.putExtra("sms_body", "Body Text");

startActivity(smsIntent);
```

As with composing e-mail, you must set the action and type at a minimum to launch the application with a blank message. Including the address and sms_body extras allows the application to prepopulate the recipient (address) and body text (sms_body) of the message.

Neither of these keys has a constant defined in the Android framework, which means that they are subject to change in the future. However, as of this writing, the keys behave as expected on all versions of Android.

Contact Picker

An application may launch the default contact picker, enabling a selection from the user's Contacts database, by using the following intent:

```
static final int REQUEST_PICK = 100;

Intent pickIntent = new Intent();
pickIntent.setAction(Intent.ACTION_PICK);
pickIntent.setData(ContactsContract.Contacts.CONTENT_URI);

startActivityForResult(pickIntent, REQUEST_PICK);
```

This activity is also designed to return a Uri representing the selection the user made, so you will want to launch this by using startActivityForResult().

Google Play

Google Play can be launched from within an application to display a specific application's details page or to run a search for specific keywords. To launch a specific application's page, use the following intent:

```
Intent marketIntent = new Intent();
marketIntent.setAction(Intent.ACTION_VIEW);
marketIntent.setData(Uri.parse("market://details?id=PACKAGE_NAME_HERE"));

startActivity(marketIntent);
```

This inserts the unique package name (such as com.adobe.reader) of the application you want to display. If you would like to open Google Play with a search query, use this intent:

```
Intent marketIntent = new Intent();
marketIntent.setAction(Intent.ACTION_VIEW);
marketIntent.setData(Uri.parse("market://search?q=SEARCH_QUERY"));

startActivity(marketIntent);
```

This will insert the query string you would like to search on. The search query itself can take one of three main forms:

- q=<simple text string here>: In this case, the search will be a keyword-style search of the market.

- q=pname:<package name here>: In this case, the package names will be searched, and only exact matches will be returned.

- q=pub:<developer name here>: In this case, the developer name field will be searched, and only exact matches will be returned.

6-8. Letting Other Applications Launch Your Application

Problem

You've created an application that is absolutely the best at doing a specific task, and you would like to expose an interface for other applications on the device to be able to run your application.

Solution

(API Level 1)

Create an IntentFilter on the activity or service you would like to expose. Then publicly document the actions, data types, and extras that are required to access it properly. Recall that the action, category, and data/type of an intent can all be used as criteria to match requests to your application. Any additional required or optional parameters should be passed in as extras.

How It Works

Let's say you have created an application that includes an activity to play a video and will marquee the video's title at the top of the screen during playback. You want to allow other applications to play video using your application, so we need to define a useful intent structure for applications to pass in the required data and then create an `IntentFilter` on the activity in the application's manifest to match.

This hypothetical activity requires two pieces of data to do its job:

- The `Uri` of a video, either local or remote

- A string representing the video's title

If the application specializes in a certain type of video, we could define that a generic action (such as `ACTION_VIEW`) be used and filter more specifically on the data type of the video content we want to handle. Listing 6-31 is an example of how the activity would be defined in the manifest to filter intents in this manner.

Listing 6-31. `AndroidManifest.xml` `<activity>` Element with Data Type Filter

```
<activity android:name=".PlayerActivity">
    <intent-filter>
        <action android:name="android.intent.action.VIEW" />
        <category android:name="android.intent.category.DEFAULT" />
    <data android:mimeType="video/h264" />
    </intent-filter>
</activity>
```

This filter will match any intent with `Uri` data that is either explicitly declared as an H.264 video clip or is determined to be H.264 upon inspecting the `Uri` file. An external application would then be able to call on this activity to play a video by using the following lines of code:

```
Uri videoFile = A_URI_OF_VIDEO_CONTENT;
Intent playIntent = new Intent(Intent.ACTION_VIEW);
playIntent.setDataAndType(videoFile, "video/h264");
playIntent.putExtra(Intent.EXTRA_TITLE, "My Video");
startActivity(playIntent);
```

In some cases, it may be more useful for an external application to directly reference this player as the target, regardless of the type of video that application wants to pass in. In this case, we would create a unique custom action string for intents to implement. The filter attached to the activity in the manifest would then need to match only the custom action string. See Listing 6-32.

Listing 6-32. `AndroidManifest.xml` `<activity>` Element with Custom Action Filter

```
<activity android:name=".PlayerActivity">
    <intent-filter>
        <action android:name="com.examples.myplayer.PLAY" />
        <category android:name="android.intent.category.DEFAULT" />
    </intent-filter>
</activity>
```

An external application could call on this activity to play a video by using the following code:

```
Uri videoFile = A_URI_OF_VIDEO_CONTENT;
Intent playIntent = new Intent("com.examples.myplayer.PLAY");
playIntent.setData(videoFile);
playIntent.putExtra(Intent.EXTRA_TITLE, "My Video");
startActivity(playIntent);
```

Processing a Successful Launch

Regardless of how the intent is matched to the activity, once it is launched, we want to inspect the incoming intent for the two pieces of data the activity needs to complete its intended purpose. See Listing 6-33.

Listing 6-33. Activity Inspecting Intent

```
public class PlayerActivity extends Activity {

    public static final String ACTION_PLAY = "com.examples.myplayer.PLAY";

    @Override
    public void onCreate(Bundle savedInstanceState) {
        super.onCreate(savedInstanceState);
        setContentView(R.layout.main);

        //Inspect the Intent that launched us
        Intent incoming = getIntent();
        //Get the video URI from the data field
        Uri videoUri = incoming.getData();
        //Get the optional title extra, if it exists
        String title;
        if(incoming.hasExtra(Intent.EXTRA_TITLE)) {
            title = incoming.getStringExtra(Intent.EXTRA_TITLE);
        } else {
            title = "";
        }

        /* Begin playing the video and displaying the title */
    }

    /* Remainder of the Activity Code */

}
```

When the activity is launched, the calling intent can be retrieved with Activity.getIntent(). Because the Uri for the video content is passed in the data field of the intent, it is unpacked by calling Intent.getData(). The video's title is an optional value for calling intents, so we check the extras bundle to first see whether the caller decided to pass it in; if it exists, that value is unpacked from the intent as well.

Notice that the PlayerActivity in this example did define the custom action string as a constant, but it was not referenced in the sample intent we constructed to launch the activity. Since this call is coming from an external application, it does not have access to the shared public constants defined in this application.

For this reason, it is also a good idea to reuse the intent extra keys already in the SDK whenever possible, as opposed to defining new constants. In this example, we chose the standard Intent.EXTRA_TITLE to define the optional extra to be passed instead of creating a custom key for this value.

6-9. Interacting with Contacts

Problem

Your application needs to interact directly with the ContentProvider exposed by Android to the user's contacts to add, view, change, or remove information from the database.

Solution

(API Level 5)

Use the interface exposed by ContactsContract to access the data. ContactsContract is a vast ContentProvider API that attempts to aggregate the contact information stored in the system from multiple user accounts into a single data store. The result is a maze of Uris, tables, and columns, from which data may be accessed and modified.

The Contact structure is a hierarchy with three tiers: Contacts, RawContacts, and Data:

- A Contact conceptually represents a person, and it is an aggregation of all RawContacts believed by Android to represent that same person.

- RawContacts represents a collection of data stored in the device from a specific device account, such as the user's e-mail address book or Facebook account.

- Data elements are the specific pieces of information attached to RawContacts, such as an e-mail address, phone number, or postal address.

The complete API has too many combinations and options for us to cover them all here, so consult the SDK documentation for all possibilities. We will investigate how to construct the basic building blocks for performing queries and making changes to the Contacts data set.

How It Works

The Android Contacts API boils down to a complex database with multiple tables and joins. Therefore, the methods for accessing the data are no different from those used to access any other SQLite database from an application.

Listing/Viewing Contacts

Let's look at an example activity that lists all contact entries in the database and that displays more detail when an item is selected. See Listing 6-34.

■ **Important**   In order to display information from the Contacts API in your application, you will need to declare android.permission.READ_CONTACTS in the application manifest.

Listing 6-34. Activity Displaying Contacts

```
public class ContactsActivity extends FragmentActivity {

    private static final int ROOT_ID = 100;

    @Override
    protected void onCreate(Bundle savedInstanceState) {
        super.onCreate(savedInstanceState);
        FrameLayout rootView = new FrameLayout(this);
        rootView.setId(ROOT_ID);

        setContentView(rootView);

        //Create and add a new list fragment
        getSupportFragmentManager().beginTransaction()
            .add(ROOT_ID, ContactsFragment.newInstance())
            .commit();
    }

    public static class ContactsFragment extends ListFragment
            implements AdapterView.OnItemClickListener, LoaderManager.LoaderCallbacks<Cursor> {

        public static ContactsFragment newInstance() {
            return new ContactsFragment();
        }

        private SimpleCursorAdapter mAdapter;

        @Override
        public void onActivityCreated(Bundle savedInstanceState) {
            super.onActivityCreated(savedInstanceState);

            // Display all contacts in a ListView
            mAdapter = new SimpleCursorAdapter(getActivity(),
                    android.R.layout.simple_list_item_1, null,
                    new String[] { ContactsContract.Contacts.DISPLAY_NAME },
                    new int[] { android.R.id.text1 },
                    0);
            setListAdapter(mAdapter);
            // Listen for item selections
            getListView().setOnItemClickListener(this);

            getLoaderManager().initLoader(0, null, this);
        }
```

```java
@Override
public Loader<Cursor> onCreateLoader(int id, Bundle args) {
    // Return all contacts, ordered by name
    String[] projection = new String[] {
            ContactsContract.Contacts._ID,
            ContactsContract.Contacts.DISPLAY_NAME
    };

    return new CursorLoader(getActivity(),
            ContactsContract.Contacts.CONTENT_URI,
            projection, null, null,
            ContactsContract.Contacts.DISPLAY_NAME);
}

@Override
public void onLoadFinished(Loader<Cursor> loader, Cursor data) {
    mAdapter.swapCursor(data);
}

@Override
public void onLoaderReset(Loader<Cursor> loader) {
    mAdapter.swapCursor(null);
}

@Override
public void onItemClick(AdapterView<?> parent, View v,
        int position, long id) {
    final Cursor contacts = mAdapter.getCursor();
    if (contacts.moveToPosition(position)) {
        int selectedId = contacts.getInt(0); // _ID column
        // Gather email data from email table
        Cursor email = getActivity().getContentResolver()
                .query(ContactsContract.CommonDataKinds.Email.CONTENT_URI,
                        new String[] {ContactsContract.CommonDataKinds.Email.DATA},
                        ContactsContract.Data.CONTACT_ID
                            + " = " + selectedId,
                        null, null);
        // Gather phone data from phone table
        Cursor phone = getActivity().getContentResolver()
                .query(ContactsContract.CommonDataKinds.Phone.CONTENT_URI,
                        new String[] {ContactsContract.CommonDataKinds.Phone.NUMBER},
                        ContactsContract.Data.CONTACT_ID
                            + " = " + selectedId,
                        null, null);
        // Gather addresses from address table
        Cursor address = getActivity().getContentResolver()
                .query(ContactsContract.CommonDataKinds.StructuredPostal.CONTENT_URI,
                        new String[] {ContactsContract.CommonDataKinds
                            .StructuredPostal.FORMATTED_ADDRESS},
                        ContactsContract.Data.CONTACT_ID
                            + " = " + selectedId,
                        null, null);
```

501

```
                // Build the dialog message
                StringBuilder sb = new StringBuilder();
                sb.append(email.getCount() + " Emails\n");
                if (email.moveToFirst()) {
                    do {
                        sb.append("Email: " + email.getString(0));
                        sb.append('\n');
                    } while (email.moveToNext());
                    sb.append('\n');
                }
                sb.append(phone.getCount() + " Phone Numbers\n");
                if (phone.moveToFirst()) {
                    do {
                        sb.append("Phone: " + phone.getString(0));
                        sb.append('\n');
                    } while (phone.moveToNext());
                    sb.append('\n');
                }
                sb.append(address.getCount() + " Addresses\n");
                if (address.moveToFirst()) {
                    do {
                        sb.append("Address:\n"
                                    + address.getString(0));
                    } while (address.moveToNext());
                    sb.append('\n');
                }

                AlertDialog.Builder builder = new AlertDialog.Builder(getActivity());
                builder.setTitle(contacts.getString(1)); // Display name
                builder.setMessage(sb.toString());
                builder.setPositiveButton("OK", null);
                builder.create().show();

                // Finish temporary cursors
                email.close();
                phone.close();
                address.close();
            }
        }
    }
}
```

As you can see, referencing all the tables and columns in this API can result in very verbose code. All of the references to Uri elements, tables, and columns in this example are inner classes stemming off of ContactsContract. It is important to verify when interacting with the Contacts API that you are referencing the proper classes, as any Contacts classes not stemming from ContactsContract are deprecated and incompatible.

When the fragment containing the UI for the activity is created, we construct a simple query on the core Contacts table through a CursorLoader referencing Contacts.CONTENT_URI, requesting only the columns we need to wrap the cursor in a ListAdapter. The resulting cursor is displayed in a list on the user interface.

The example leverages the convenience behavior of ListFragment to provide a ListView as the content view so that we do not have to manage these components.

At this point, the user can scroll through all the contact entries on the device, and can tap one to get more information. When a list item is selected, the ID value of that particular contact is recorded and the application goes out to the other ContactsContract.Data tables to gather more-detailed information. Notice that the information for this single contact is spread across multiple tables (e-mails in an e-mail table, phone numbers in a phone table, and so on), requiring multiple queries to obtain.

Each CommonDataKinds table has a unique CONTENT_URI for the query to reference, as well as a unique set of column aliases for requesting the data. All of the rows in these data tables are linked to the specific contact through the Data.CONTACT_ID, so each cursor asks to return only rows where the values match.

With all the data collected for the selected contact, we iterate through the results to display in a dialog box to the user. Because the data in these tables is aggregated from multiple sources, it is not uncommon for all of these queries to return multiple results. With each cursor, we display the number of results, and then append each value included. When all the data is composed, the dialog box is created and shown to the user.

As a final step, all temporary and unmanaged cursors are closed as soon as they are no longer required.

Running the Application

The first thing that you may notice when running this application on a device that has any number of accounts set up is that the list seems insurmountably long, certainly much longer than what shows up when running the Contacts application bundled with the device. The Contacts API allows for the storage of grouped entries that may be hidden from the user and are used for internal purposes. Gmail often uses this to store incoming e-mail addresses for quick access, even if an address is not associated with a true contact.

In the next example, we will show how to filter this list, but for now marvel at the amount of data truly stored in the Contacts table.

Changing/Adding Contacts

Now let's look at an example activity that manipulates the data for a specific contact. See Listing 6-35.

■ **Important**   In order to interact with the Contacts API in your application, you must declare android. permission.READ_CONTACTS and android.permission.WRITE_CONTACTS in the application manifest.

Listing 6-35. Activity Writing to Contacts API

```java
public class ContactsEditActivity extends FragmentActivity {

    private static final String TEST_EMAIL = "tester@email.com";
    private static final int ROOT_ID = 100;

    @Override
    protected void onCreate(Bundle savedInstanceState) {
        super.onCreate(savedInstanceState);
        FrameLayout rootView = new FrameLayout(this);
        rootView.setId(ROOT_ID);

        setContentView(rootView);
```

```
        //Create and add a new list fragment
        getSupportFragmentManager().beginTransaction()
            .add(ROOT_ID, ContactsEditFragment.newInstance())
            .commit();
    }

    public static class ContactsEditFragment extends ListFragment implements
            AdapterView.OnItemClickListener,
            DialogInterface.OnClickListener,
            LoaderManager.LoaderCallbacks<Cursor> {

        public static ContactsEditFragment newInstance() {
            return new ContactsEditFragment();
        }

        private SimpleCursorAdapter mAdapter;
        private Cursor mEmail;
        private int selectedContactId;

        @Override
        public void onActivityCreated(Bundle savedInstanceState) {
            super.onActivityCreated(savedInstanceState);

            // Display all contacts in a ListView
            mAdapter = new SimpleCursorAdapter(getActivity(),
                    android.R.layout.simple_list_item_1, null,
                    new String[] { ContactsContract.Contacts.DISPLAY_NAME },
                    new int[] { android.R.id.text1 },
                    0);
            setListAdapter(mAdapter);
            // Listen for item selections
            getListView().setOnItemClickListener(this);

            getLoaderManager().initLoader(0, null, this);
        }

        @Override
        public Loader<Cursor> onCreateLoader(int id, Bundle args) {
            // Return all contacts, ordered by name
            String[] projection = new String[] { ContactsContract.Contacts._ID,
                    ContactsContract.Contacts.DISPLAY_NAME };
            //List only contacts visible to the user
            return new CursorLoader(getActivity(),
                    ContactsContract.Contacts.CONTENT_URI,
                    projection, ContactsContract.Contacts.IN_VISIBLE_GROUP+" = 1",
                    null,
                    ContactsContract.Contacts.DISPLAY_NAME);
        }
```

```java
@Override
public void onLoadFinished(Loader<Cursor> loader, Cursor data) {
    mAdapter.swapCursor(data);
}

@Override
public void onLoaderReset(Loader<Cursor> loader) {
    mAdapter.swapCursor(null);
}

@Override
public void onItemClick(AdapterView<?> parent, View v, int position, long id) {
    final Cursor contacts = mAdapter.getCursor();
    if (contacts.moveToPosition(position)) {
        selectedContactId = contacts.getInt(0); // _ID column
        // Gather email data from email table
        String[] projection = new String[] {
                ContactsContract.Data._ID,
                ContactsContract.CommonDataKinds.Email.DATA };
        mEmail = getActivity().getContentResolver().query(
                ContactsContract.CommonDataKinds.Email.CONTENT_URI,
                projection,
                ContactsContract.Data.CONTACT_ID + " = " + selectedContactId,
                null,
                null);

        AlertDialog.Builder builder = new AlertDialog.Builder(getActivity());
        builder.setTitle("Email Addresses");
        builder.setCursor(mEmail, this, ContactsContract.CommonDataKinds.Email.DATA);
        builder.setPositiveButton("Add", this);
        builder.setNegativeButton("Cancel", null);
        builder.create().show();
    }
}

@Override
public void onClick(DialogInterface dialog, int which) {
    //Data must be associated with a RAW contact, retrieve the first raw ID
    Cursor raw = getActivity().getContentResolver().query(
            ContactsContract.RawContacts.CONTENT_URI,
            new String[] { ContactsContract.Contacts._ID },
            ContactsContract.Data.CONTACT_ID + " = " + selectedContactId, null, null);
    if(!raw.moveToFirst()) {
        return;
    }

    int rawContactId = raw.getInt(0);
    ContentValues values = new ContentValues();
    switch(which) {
        case DialogInterface.BUTTON_POSITIVE:
            //User wants to add a new email
```

```
                    values.put(ContactsContract.CommonDataKinds.Email.RAW_CONTACT_ID,
                    rawContactId);
                    values.put(ContactsContract.Data.MIMETYPE, ContactsContract
                            .CommonDataKinds.Email.CONTENT_ITEM_TYPE);
                    values.put(ContactsContract.CommonDataKinds.Email.DATA, TEST_EMAIL);
                    values.put(ContactsContract.CommonDataKinds.Email.TYPE,
                            ContactsContract.CommonDataKinds.Email.TYPE_OTHER);
                    getActivity().getContentResolver()
                            .insert(ContactsContract.Data.CONTENT_URI, values);
                    break;
                default:
                    //User wants to edit selection
                    values.put(ContactsContract.CommonDataKinds.Email.DATA, TEST_EMAIL);
                    values.put(ContactsContract.CommonDataKinds.Email.TYPE,
                            ContactsContract.CommonDataKinds.Email.TYPE_OTHER);
                    getActivity().getContentResolver()
                            .update(ContactsContract.Data.CONTENT_URI, values,
                                    ContactsContract.Data._ID+" = "+mEmail.getInt(0), null);
                    break;
            }

            //Don't need the email cursor anymore
            mEmail.close();
        }
    }
}
```

In this example, we start out as before, performing a query for all entries in the Contacts database. This time, we provide a single selection criterion:

```
ContactsContract.Contacts.IN_VISIBLE_GROUP+" = 1"
```

The effect of this line is to limit the returned entries to only those that are visible to the user through the Contacts user interface. This will (drastically, in some cases) reduce the size of the list displayed in the activity and will make it more closely match the list displayed in the Contacts application.

When the user selects a contact from this list, a dialog box is displayed with a list of all the e-mail entries attached to that contact. If a specific address is selected from the list, that entry is edited; if the Add button is pressed, a new e-mail address entry is added. For the purposes of simplifying the example, we do not provide an interface to enter a new e-mail address. Instead, a constant value is inserted, either as a new record or as an update to the selected one.

Data elements, such as e-mail addresses, can be associated only with a RawContact. Therefore, when we want to add a new e-mail address, we must obtain the ID of one of the RawContacts represented by the higher-level contact that the user selected. For the purposes of the example, we aren't terribly interested in which one, so we retrieve the ID of the first RawContact that matches. This value is required only for doing an insert, because the update references the distinct row ID of the e-mail record already present in the table.

The Uri provided in CommonDataKinds that was used as an alias to read this data cannot be used to make updates and changes. Inserts and updates must be called directly on the ContactsContract.Data Uri. What this means (besides referencing a different Uri in the operation method) is that an extra piece of metadata, the MIMETYPE, must also be specified. Without setting the MIMETYPE field for inserted data, subsequent queries made may not recognize it as a contact's e-mail address.

Aggregating at Work

Because this example updates records by adding or editing e-mail addresses with the same value, it offers a unique opportunity to see Android's aggregation operations in real time. As you run this example application, you may notice that adding or editing contacts to give them the same e-mail address often triggers Android to start thinking that previously separate contacts are now the same people. Even in this sample application, as the managed query attached to the core Contacts table updates, notice that certain contacts will disappear as they become aggregated together.

■ **Note**   Contact aggregation behavior is not implemented fully on the Android emulator. To see this effect in full, you will need to run the code on a real device.

Maintaining a Reference

The Android Contacts API introduces one more concept that can be important, depending on the scope of the application. Because of this aggregation process that occurs, the distinct row ID that refers to a contact becomes quite volatile; a certain contact may receive a new _ID when it is aggregated together with another one.

If your application requires a longstanding reference to a specific contact, it is recommended that your application persist the ContactsContract.Contacts.LOOKUP_KEY instead of the row ID. When querying for a contact by using this key, a special Uri is also provided as the ContactsContract.Contacts.CONTENT_LOOKUP_URI. Using these values to query records over the long term will protect your application from getting confused by the automatic aggregation process.

6-10. Reading Device Media and Documents

Problem

Your application needs to import a user-selected document item (such as a text file, audio, video, or image) for display or playback.

Solution

(API Level 1)

Use an implicit intent targeted with Intent.ACTION_GET_CONTENT to bring up a picker interface from a specific application. Firing this intent with a matching content type for the media of interest (audio, video, or image are the most common) will present the user with a picker interface to select an item, and the intent result will include a content Uri pointing to the selection the user made.

(API Level 19)

Use an implicit intent targeted with Intent.ACTION_OPEN_DOCUMENT to bring up the system's document picker interface. This is a single common interface where all applications that support the requested content type will list the items the user may select. The content that populates this interface comes from applications that expose DocumentProvider for the requested type. These provider elements can come from the system or other applications. We will look at how to create one of your own later in this chapter.

■ **Tip**   ACTION_GET_CONTENT can still be used with API Level 19+, and it will launch the standard document picker into a compatibility mode that includes the newer integrated providers along with the options to pick a single application's picker interface.

How It Works

Let's take a look at this technique used in the context of an example activity. See Listings 6-36 and 6-37.

Listing 6-36. res/layout/main.xml

```xml
<?xml version="1.0" encoding="utf-8"?>
<LinearLayout xmlns:android="http://schemas.android.com/apk/res/android"
    android:orientation="vertical"
    android:layout_width="match_parent"
    android:layout_height="match_parent">
    <Button
        android:id="@+id/imageButton"
        android:layout_width="match_parent"
        android:layout_height="wrap_content"
        android:text="Images" />
    <Button
        android:id="@+id/videoButton"
        android:layout_width="match_parent"
        android:layout_height="wrap_content"
        android:text="Video" />
    <Button
        android:id="@+id/audioButton"
        android:layout_width="match_parent"
        android:layout_height="wrap_content"
        android:text="Audio" />
</LinearLayout>
```

Listing 6-37. Activity to Pick Media

```java
public class MediaActivity extends Activity implements View.OnClickListener {

    private static final int REQUEST_AUDIO = 1;
    private static final int REQUEST_VIDEO = 2;
    private static final int REQUEST_IMAGE = 3;


    @Override
    public void onCreate(Bundle savedInstanceState) {
        super.onCreate(savedInstanceState);
        setContentView(R.layout.main);

        Button images = (Button)findViewById(R.id.imageButton);
        images.setOnClickListener(this);
        Button videos = (Button)findViewById(R.id.videoButton);
```

```java
        videos.setOnClickListener(this);
        Button audio = (Button)findViewById(R.id.audioButton);
        audio.setOnClickListener(this);

    }

    @Override
    protected void onActivityResult(int requestCode, int resultCode, Intent data) {

        if(resultCode == Activity.RESULT_OK) {
            //Uri to user selection returned in the Intent
            Uri selectedContent = data.getData();

            if(requestCode == REQUEST_IMAGE) {
                //Pass an InputStream to BitmapFactory
            }
            if(requestCode == REQUEST_VIDEO) {
                //Pass the Uri or a FileDescriptor to MediaPlayer
            }
            if(requestCode == REQUEST_AUDIO) {
                //Pass the Uri or a FileDescriptor to MediaPlayer
            }
        }
    }

    @Override
    public void onClick(View v) {
        Intent intent = new Intent();
        //Use the proper Intent action
        if (Build.VERSION.SDK_INT >= Build.VERSION_CODES.KITKAT) {
            intent.setAction(Intent.ACTION_OPEN_DOCUMENT);
        } else {
            intent.setAction(Intent.ACTION_GET_CONTENT);
        }
        //Only return files to which we can open a stream
        intent.addCategory(Intent.CATEGORY_OPENABLE);

        //Set correct MIME type and launch
        switch(v.getId()) {
        case R.id.imageButton:
            intent.setType("image/*");
            startActivityForResult(intent, REQUEST_IMAGE);
            return;
        case R.id.videoButton:
            intent.setType("video/*");
            startActivityForResult(intent, REQUEST_VIDEO);
            return;
        case R.id.audioButton:
            intent.setType("audio/*");
            startActivityForResult(intent, REQUEST_AUDIO);
            return;
```

```
        default:
            return;
        }
    }
}
```

This example has three buttons for the user to press, each targeting a specific type of media. When the user presses any one of these buttons, an intent with the appropriate action for the platform level is fired to the system. On devices running 4.4 and later, this will display the system document picker. Previous devices will launch the proper picker activity from the application, showing a chooser if multiple applications can handle the content type. We have also included CATEGORY_OPENABLE to this intent, which indicates to the system that only items our application can open a stream to will be displayed in the picker.

If the user selects a valid item, a content Uri pointing to that item is returned in the result intent with a status of RESULT_OK. If the user cancels or otherwise backs out of the picker, the status will be RESULT_CANCELED and the intent's data field will be null.

With the Uri of the media received, the application is now free to play or display the content as deemed appropriate. Classes such as MediaPlayer and VideoView will take a Uri directly to play media content, while most others will take either an InputStream or a FileDescriptor reference. Both of these can be obtained from the Uri by using ContentResolver.openInputStream() and ContentResolver.openFileDescriptor(), respectively.

SELECTING ENTIRE DIRECTORIES

On API Level 21+, requests can be made for the user to select a directory entry using the Intent.OPEN_DOCUMENT_TREE action.

This will return a specialized Uri in the intent result that can be used to list the contents of a directory or create a new document in that location. The following snippet will take the result from a directory selection and list its contents.

```
protected void onActivityResult(int requestCode, int resultCode, Intent data) {
    if (data == null || data.getData() == null) return;
    final Uri result = data.getData();

    //Construct a Uri we can use to query the selected directory contents
    String subDocumentId = DocumentsContract.getTreeDocumentId(result);
    Uri subTree = DocumentsContract.buildChildDocumentsUriUsingTree(result, subDocumentId);

    //Query the directory and list its contents
    Cursor cursor = getContentResolver().query(subTree, null, null, null, null);
    if (cursor != null) {
        if (cursor.getCount() == 0) {
            //Directory is empty
        } else {
            StringBuilder sb = new StringBuilder();
            sb.append("Contents of Directory:\n");

            while (cursor.moveToNext()) {
                //Get the column containing the document name
```

```
                   int index = cursor.getColumnIndex(DocumentsContract.Document.COLUMN_
                   DISPLAY_NAME);
                   sb.append(cursor.getString(index));
                   sb.append("\n");
               }

               //Spit the file list out to logcat
               Log.d("DirectoryList", sb.toString());
           }

               cursor.close();
       } else {
               //There was an error reading the directory contents
       }
}
```

Using the `DocumentsContract` API, we can convert the user-selected directory `Uri` into one we can use to query the associated `DocumentsProvider` directly via `ContentResolver`. The resulting `Cursor` will contain all the metadata that provider has about each document in the selected directory.

6-11. Saving Device Media and Documents

Problem

Your application would like to create new documents or media and insert them into the device's global providers so that they are visible to all applications.

Solution

(API Level 1)

Utilize the `ContentProvider` interface exposed by `MediaStore` to perform inserts of media content. In addition to the media content itself, this interface allows you to insert metadata to tag each item, such as a title, description, or time created. The result of the `ContentProvider` insert operation is a `Uri` that the application may use as a destination for the new media.

(API Level 19)

On Android 4.4+ devices, we can also trigger an implicit intent targeted with `Intent.ACTION_CREATE_DOCUMENT` to save a new document in any of the device's registered `DocumentProvider` instances. This can be any type of document content, including (but not restricted to) media files. However, it is not meant to supersede `MediaStore`, which is still the best method for saving directly to the system's core `ContentProvider`. If you instead need to involve the user more directly in saving the content (including media), the document framework is a better path here.

How It Works

Let's take a look at an example of inserting an image or video clip into MediaStore. See Listings 6-38 and 6-39.

Listing 6-38. res/layout/save.xml

```xml
<?xml version="1.0" encoding="utf-8"?>
<LinearLayout xmlns:android="http://schemas.android.com/apk/res/android"
    android:layout_width="fill_parent"
    android:layout_height="fill_parent"
    android:orientation="vertical" >
    <Button
        android:id="@+id/imageButton"
        android:layout_width="fill_parent"
        android:layout_height="wrap_content"
        android:text="Images" />
    <Button
        android:id="@+id/videoButton"
        android:layout_width="fill_parent"
        android:layout_height="wrap_content"
        android:text="Video" />
    <Button
        android:id="@+id/textButton"
        android:layout_width="fill_parent"
        android:layout_height="wrap_content"
        android:text="Text Document" />

</LinearLayout>
```

Listing 6-39. Activity Saving Data in the MediaStore

```java
public class StoreActivity extends Activity implements View.OnClickListener {

    private static final int REQUEST_CAPTURE = 100;
    private static final int REQUEST_DOCUMENT = 101;

    @Override
    public void onCreate(Bundle savedInstanceState) {
        super.onCreate(savedInstanceState);
        setContentView(R.layout.save);


        Button images = (Button) findViewById(R.id.imageButton);
        images.setOnClickListener(this);
        Button videos = (Button) findViewById(R.id.videoButton);
        videos.setOnClickListener(this);

        //We can only create new documents above API Level 19
        Button text = (Button) findViewById(R.id.textButton);
        if (Build.VERSION.SDK_INT >= Build.VERSION_CODES.KITKAT) {
            text.setOnClickListener(this);
```

```java
    } else {
        text.setVisibility(View.GONE);
    }
}


@Override
protected void onActivityResult(int requestCode, int resultCode, Intent data) {
    if (requestCode == REQUEST_CAPTURE && resultCode == Activity.RESULT_OK) {
        Toast.makeText(this, "All Done!", Toast.LENGTH_SHORT).show();
    }
    if (requestCode == REQUEST_DOCUMENT && resultCode == Activity.RESULT_OK) {
        //Once the user has selected where to save the new document,
        // we can write the contents into it
        Uri document = data.getData();
        writeDocument(document);
    }
}

private void writeDocument(Uri document) {
    try {
        ParcelFileDescriptor pfd =
                getContentResolver().openFileDescriptor(document, "w");
        FileOutputStream out = new FileOutputStream(pfd.getFileDescriptor());
        //Construct some content for our file
        StringBuilder sb = new StringBuilder();
        sb.append("Android Recipes Log File:");
        sb.append("\n");
        sb.append("Last Written at: ");
        sb.append(DateFormat.getLongDateFormat(this).format(new Date()));

        out.write(sb.toString().getBytes());

        // Let the document provider know you're done by closing the stream.
        out.flush();
        out.close();
        // Close our file handle
        pfd.close();
    } catch (FileNotFoundException e) {
        Log.w("AndroidRecipes", e);
    } catch (IOException e) {
        Log.w("AndroidRecipes", e);
    }
}

@Override
public void onClick(View v) {
    ContentValues values;
    Intent intent;
    Uri storeLocation;
    final long nowMillis = System.currentTimeMillis();
```

```
        switch(v.getId()) {
        case R.id.imageButton:
            //Create any metadata for image
            values = new ContentValues(5);
            values.put(MediaStore.Images.ImageColumns.DATE_TAKEN, nowMillis);
            values.put(MediaStore.Images.ImageColumns.DATE_ADDED, nowMillis / 1000);
            values.put(MediaStore.Images.ImageColumns.DATE_MODIFIED, nowMillis / 1000);
            values.put(MediaStore.Images.ImageColumns.DISPLAY_NAME,
                    "Android Recipes Image Sample");
            values.put(MediaStore.Images.ImageColumns.TITLE,
                    "Android Recipes Image Sample");

            //Insert metadata and retrieve Uri location for file
            storeLocation = getContentResolver()
                    .insert(MediaStore.Images.Media.EXTERNAL_CONTENT_URI, values);
            //Start capture with new location as destination
            intent = new Intent(MediaStore.ACTION_IMAGE_CAPTURE);
            intent.putExtra(MediaStore.EXTRA_OUTPUT, storeLocation);
            startActivityForResult(intent, REQUEST_CAPTURE);
            return;
        case R.id.videoButton:
            //Create any metadata for video
            values = new ContentValues(7);
            values.put(MediaStore.Video.VideoColumns.DATE_TAKEN, nowMillis);
            values.put(MediaStore.Video.VideoColumns.DATE_ADDED, nowMillis / 1000);
            values.put(MediaStore.Video.VideoColumns.DATE_MODIFIED, nowMillis / 1000);
            values.put(MediaStore.Video.VideoColumns.DISPLAY_NAME, "Android Recipes Video
            Sample");
            values.put(MediaStore.Video.VideoColumns.TITLE, "Android Recipes Video Sample");
            values.put(MediaStore.Video.VideoColumns.ARTIST, "Yours Truly");
            values.put(MediaStore.Video.VideoColumns.DESCRIPTION,
                    "Sample Video Clip");


            //Insert metadata and retrieve Uri location for file
            storeLocation = getContentResolver()
                    .insert(MediaStore.Video.Media.EXTERNAL_CONTENT_URI, values);
            //Start capture with new location as destination
            intent = new Intent(MediaStore.ACTION_VIDEO_CAPTURE);
            intent.putExtra(MediaStore.EXTRA_OUTPUT, storeLocation);
            startActivityForResult(intent, REQUEST_CAPTURE);
            return;
        case R.id.textButton:
            //Create a new document
            intent = new Intent(Intent.ACTION_CREATE_DOCUMENT);
            intent.addCategory(Intent.CATEGORY_OPENABLE);

            //This is a text document
            intent.setType("text/plain");
            //Optional title to pre-set on document
```

```
        intent.putExtra(Intent.EXTRA_TITLE, "Android Recipes");
        startActivityForResult(intent, REQUEST_DOCUMENT);
    default:
        return;
    }
  }
}
```

■ **Note**　Because this example interacts with the Camera hardware, you should run it on a real device to get the full effect. Emulators will execute the code appropriately, but without real hardware the example will be less interesting.

In this example, when the user clicks the Image or Video button, metadata associated with the media is inserted into a ContentValues instance. Some of the more common metadata columns for both image and video are the following:

- TITLE: String value for the content title. Displayed in the Gallery applications as the content name

- DISPLAY_NAME: Name displayed in most selection interfaces such as the system document picker

- DATE_TAKEN: Integer value describing the date the media item was captured. Note this value is in milliseconds.

- DATE_ADDED: Integer value describing when the media was added to MediaStore. Note this value is in seconds, not milliseconds.

- DATE_MODIFIED: Integer value describing the last change to the media. This is used to sort items in the system document picker. Note this value is also in seconds.

The ContentValues are then inserted into the MediaStore by using the appropriate CONTENT_URI reference. Notice that the metadata is inserted before the media item itself is actually captured. The return value from a successful insert is a fully qualified Uri that the application may use as the destination for the media content.

In the previous example, we are using the simplified methods from Chapter 4, capturing audio and video by requesting that the system applications handle this process. Recall from Chapter 4 that both the audio and video capture intent can be passed with an extra, declaring the destination for the result. This is where we pass the Uri that was returned from the insert.

Upon a successful return from the capture activity, there is nothing more for the application to do. The external application has saved the captured image or video into the location referenced by our MediaStore insert. This data is now visible to all applications, including the system's Gallery application.

Creating Documents

Notice the third button, labeled Text Document, is visible and enabled only if we are running on a device with Android 4.4 or later. If the user clicks this button, we construct an intent request using ACTION_CREATE_ DOCUMENT to launch the system's document interface. However, in this case, the interface is launched, allowing the user to select where the new file should be saved (that is, in which provider application) and what its title should be. Along with this request, we set the MIME type to indicate the document type we want to create, which is plain text in our example. Finally, we can suggest a title by passing EXTRA_TITLE along with the intent, but the user is always given the right to change it later.

Once the user has selected where to save the new document, we are given a content Uri in onActivityResult() and we can open a stream and write our document's data to storage. The writeDocument() method of the example opens a FileDescriptor from the Uri and writes some basic text content into the new document. By closing the stream and descriptor, we signal to the owning provider that the document update is complete.

■ **Tip**   ACTION_CREATE_DOCUMENT is used to make a new document that you want to save. For editing an existing document in place, use ACTION_OPEN_DOCUMENT from the previous example to obtain a working Uri to an existing file. Keep in mind, however, that not all providers support writing. You will need to check the permissions of the Uri you are given before attempting to edit a document received in this way.

6-12. Reading Messaging Data

Problem

You need to query the ContentProvider of locally saved information on the device for sent and received SMS/MMS messages.

Solution

(API Level 19)

Use the contract interface exposed via the Telephony framework. The inner classes of Telephony define all the Uris and data columns used to read SMS messages, MMS messages, and additional metadata.

■ **Important**   You must request android.permission.READ_SMS in the manifest in order to gain read access to the Telephony provider.

The Telephony provider exposes an interface for the following blocks of data:

- Telephony.Sms: Contains the message content and recipient/delivery metadata for all SMS messages

- Telephony.Mms: Contains the message content and recipient/delivery metadata for all MMS messages

- Telephony.MmsSms: Contains the combined messages for SMS and MMS. Also includes custom Uris for requesting a list of conversations, drafts, and searching messages

- Telephony.Threads: Provides additional metadata about conversations, such as the message count and read status of the conversation thread

Text-based SMS messages are relatively straightforward, with their entire content housed within a few columns in the Telephony.Sms tables. Even if a message has multiple recipients, those are broken up into multiple messages with the same text content. MMS messages, however, are composed of multiple parts that are all stored separately in individual tables:

- Mms.Addr: Contains metadata about all the recipients involved in each MMS message. Each message can have a unique group of recipients.

- Mms.Part: Contains the contents of each piece included in the MMS message. The message text is stored as one part with any image, video, or other attachments stored as additional pieces. A MIME string designates the content type of each part.

Displaying a single SMS message can be done with a single query to the Telephony.Sms content Uri. Displaying a single MMS message, however, requires iterating through all of these subparts in Telephony. Mms to collect the data we need.

■ **Tip**   SMS/MMS data will be present only on a device that has telephony hardware, so you will likely want to add a <uses-feature android:name="android.hardware.telephony"/> declaration to the manifest to filter out devices that don't have the proper capabilities.

WRITING TO THE TELEPHONY PROVIDER

Writing message data and metadata into the Telephony provider has some special rules associated with it. While any application can request the WRITE_SMS permission (and have it granted), only the application selected by the user as the Default Messaging Application in Settings will be allowed to write data into the content provider.

Nondefault applications sending SMS messages by using the mechanisms we described in Chapter 3 will have their message contents written into the provider automatically by the framework, but the default application (as the sole application with provider access) will be responsible for writing its own content directly.

In order for a messaging application to be considered for selection as the default, the following criteria must exist in the application's manifest:

- A broadcast receiver registered for the android.provider.Telephony.SMS_DELIVER action to receive new SMS messages

- A broadcast receiver registered for the android.provider.Telephony.WAP_PUSH_ DELIVER action to receive new MMS messages

- An activity filtering for the android.intent.action.SENDTO action to send new SMS/ MMS messages

- A service filtering for the android.intent.action.RESPOND_VIA_MESSAGE action to send quick response messages to incoming callers

If you are writing a messaging application that must have write access to the provider, the same Uri and column structure defined in the Telephony contract that we discuss in this recipe can be used to insert(), update(), or delete() the provider contents as well.

How It Works

In this example, we will create a simple messaging application that reads conversation data from the Telephony provider and displays it in a list. Let's start with the code to query and parse the data coming from the provider. In Listing 6-40, we've created a custom AsyncTaskLoader implementation that allows us to query the provider on a background thread and return the result easily to the UI.

Listing 6-40. Loader for Conversation Data

```
public class ConversationLoader extends AsyncTaskLoader<List<MessageItem>> {

    public static final String[] PROJECTION = new String[] {
        //Determine if message is SMS or MMS
        MmsSms.TYPE_DISCRIMINATOR_COLUMN,
        //Base item ID
        BaseColumns._ID,
        //Conversation (thread) ID
        Conversations.THREAD_ID,
        //Date values
        Sms.DATE,
        Sms.DATE_SENT,
        // For SMS only
        Sms.ADDRESS,
        Sms.BODY,
        Sms.TYPE,
        // For MMS only
        Mms.SUBJECT,
        Mms.MESSAGE_BOX
    };

    //Thread ID of the conversation we are loading
    private long mThreadId;
    //This device's number
    private String mDeviceNumber;

    public ConversationLoader(Context context) {
        this(context, -1);
    }

    public ConversationLoader(Context context, long threadId) {
        super(context);
        mThreadId = threadId;
        //Obtain the phone number of this device, if available
        TelephonyManager manager =
                (TelephonyManager) context.getSystemService(Context.TELEPHONY_SERVICE);
        mDeviceNumber = manager.getLine1Number();
    }

    @Override
    protected void onStartLoading() {
        //Reload on every init request
        forceLoad();
    }
```

```
@Override
public List<MessageItem> loadInBackground() {
    Uri uri;
    String[] projection;
    if (mThreadId < 0) {
        //Load all conversations
        uri = MmsSms.CONTENT_CONVERSATIONS_URI;
        projection = null;
    } else {
        //Load just the requested thread
        uri = ContentUris.withAppendedId(MmsSms.CONTENT_CONVERSATIONS_URI, mThreadId);
        projection = PROJECTION;
    }

    Cursor cursor = getContext().getContentResolver().query(
            uri,
            projection,
            null,
            null,
            null);

    return MessageItem.parseMessages(getContext(), cursor, mDeviceNumber);
    }
}
```

AysncTaskLoader is fairly simple to customize. You just need to provide an implementation of loadInBackground() to do the interesting work, and include some logic in onStartLoading() to get the process running. In the framework, results are usually cached, and forceLoad() is called only if the content has changed, but for simplicity we are loading data from the provider on every request.

Our ConversationLoader will be used to obtain two message lists: a list of all conversations present, and a list of all the messages for a selected conversation (or thread). So when ConversationLoader is instantiated, the ID of the conversation thread is either passed in or ignored to determine the output results. We also obtain the phone number of our device from TelephonyManager for use later. This step is not integral to reading the provider, but will help us clean up the display later.

■ **Important**   When using TelephonyManager to get the device information, your application must also declare android.permission.READ_PHONE_STATE in the manifest.

In both request modes, we are making a query of the MmsSms.CONTENT_CONVERSATIONS_URI in the combined message table. This Uri is convenient for getting a conversation overview because it will return a list of all the known conversation threads by returning the latest message in each thread. This makes it easy to display the results directly to the user.

When listing all the conversations, we don't need to provide a customized projection, which will return all the columns. However, when looking at a specific thread, we pass in a specific column subset to inspect. This is mainly so we can obtain the MmsSms.TYPE_DISCRIMINATOR_COLUMN value, which tells us whether each message is SMS or MMS. This column is not available for the main conversations list, and it also isn't returned by default for a null projection.

SORTING COMBINED RESULTS

You likely will want to sort the results by date for these queries. A common implementation is to use the ordering clause in the provider query to sort the results returned. However, with a combined SMS/MMS query as we have used here, this is not straightforward. The DATE and DATE_SENT fields of SMS messages present their timestamps in elapsed milliseconds from epoch, while those same fields for MMS messages show timestamps in elapsed seconds from epoch.

The simplest method for sorting combined results is to normalize the timestamps when parsing out into a model (such as MessageItem), and then use the sorting features of Collections to sort the resulting object list.

After we have successfully queried the provider, we want to parse the contents into a common model object that we can easily display in a list. To do this, we pass the result Cursor to a factory method in a MessageItem class we've created, which you can see in Listing 6-41.

Listing 6-41. MessageItem Model and Parsing

```
public class MessageItem {
    /* Message Type Identifiers */
    private static final String TYPE_SMS = "sms";
    private static final String TYPE_MMS = "mms";

    static final String[] MMS_PROJECTION = new String[] {
        //Base item ID
        BaseColumns._ID,
        //MIME Type of the content for this part
        Mms.Part.CONTENT_TYPE,
        //Text content of a text/plain part
        Mms.Part.TEXT,
        //Path to binary content of a nontext part
        Mms.Part._DATA
    };

    /* Message Id */
    public long id;
    /* Thread (Conversation) Id */
    public long thread_id;
    /* Address string of message */
    public String address;
    /* Body string of message */
    public String body;
    /* Whether this message was sent or received on this device */
    public boolean incoming;
    /* MMS image attachment */
    public Uri attachment;
```

```java
/*
 * Construct a list of messages from the Cursor data
 * queried by the Loader
 */
public static List<MessageItem> parseMessages(Context context, Cursor cursor,
        String myNumber) {

    List<MessageItem> messages = new ArrayList<MessageItem>();
    if (!cursor.moveToFirst()) {
        return messages;
    }
    //Parse each message based on the type identifiers
    do {
        String type = getMessageType(cursor);
        if (TYPE_SMS.equals(type)) {
            MessageItem item = parseSmsMessage(cursor);
            messages.add(item);
        } else if (TYPE_MMS.equals(type)) {
            MessageItem item = parseMmsMessage(context, cursor, myNumber);
            messages.add(item);
        } else {
            Log.w("TelephonyProvider", "Unknown Message Type");
        }
    } while (cursor.moveToNext());
    cursor.close();

    return messages;
}

/*
 * Read message type, if present in Cursor; otherwise
 * infer it from the column values present in the Cursor
 */
private static String getMessageType(Cursor cursor) {
    int typeIndex = cursor.getColumnIndex(MmsSms.TYPE_DISCRIMINATOR_COLUMN);
    if (typeIndex < 0) {
        //Type column not in projection, use another discriminator
        String cType = cursor.getString(cursor.getColumnIndex(Mms.CONTENT_TYPE));
        //If a content type is present, this is an MMS message
        if (cType != null) {
            return TYPE_MMS;
        } else {
            return TYPE_SMS;
        }
    } else {
        return cursor.getString(typeIndex);
    }
}
```

```java
/*
 * Parse out a MessageItem with contents from an SMS message
 */
private static MessageItem parseSmsMessage(Cursor data) {
    MessageItem item = new MessageItem();
    item.id = data.getLong(data.getColumnIndexOrThrow(BaseColumns._ID));
    item.thread_id = data.getLong(data.getColumnIndexOrThrow(Conversations.THREAD_ID));

    item.address = data.getString(data.getColumnIndexOrThrow(Sms.ADDRESS));
    item.body = data.getString(data.getColumnIndexOrThrow(Sms.BODY));
    item.incoming = isIncomingMessage(data, true);
    return item;
}

/*
 * Parse out a MessageItem with contents from an MMS message
 */
private static MessageItem parseMmsMessage(Context context, Cursor data, String myNumber) {
    MessageItem item = new MessageItem();
    item.id = data.getLong(data.getColumnIndexOrThrow(BaseColumns._ID));
    item.thread_id = data.getLong(data.getColumnIndexOrThrow(Conversations.THREAD_ID));

    item.incoming = isIncomingMessage(data, false);

    long _id = data.getLong(data.getColumnIndexOrThrow(BaseColumns._ID));

    //Query the address information for this message
    Uri addressUri = Uri.withAppendedPath(Mms.CONTENT_URI, _id + "/addr");
    Cursor addr = context.getContentResolver().query(
            addressUri,
            null,
            null,
            null,
            null);
    HashSet<String> recipients = new HashSet<String>();
    while (addr.moveToNext()) {
        String address = addr.getString(addr.getColumnIndex(Mms.Addr.ADDRESS));
        //Don't add our own number to the displayed list
        if (myNumber == null || !address.contains(myNumber)) {
            recipients.add(address);
        }
    }
    item.address = TextUtils.join(", ", recipients);
    addr.close();

    //Query all the MMS parts associated with this message
    Uri messageUri = Uri.withAppendedPath(Mms.CONTENT_URI, _id + "/part");
    Cursor inner = context.getContentResolver().query(
            messageUri,
            MMS_PROJECTION,
            Mms.Part.MSG_ID + " = ?",
```

```
            new String[] {String.valueOf(data.getLong(data.getColumnIndex(Mms._ID)))},
            null);

    while(inner.moveToNext()) {
        String contentType = inner.getString(inner.getColumnIndex(Mms.Part.CONTENT_TYPE));
        if (contentType == null) {
            continue;
        } else if (contentType.matches("image/.*")) {
            //Find any part that is an image attachment
            long partId = inner.getLong(inner.getColumnIndex(BaseColumns._ID));
            item.attachment = Uri.withAppendedPath(Mms.CONTENT_URI, "part/" + partId);
        } else if (contentType.matches("text/.*")) {
            //Find any part that is text data
            item.body = inner.getString(inner.getColumnIndex(Mms.Part.TEXT));
        }
    }

    inner.close();
    return item;
}

/*
 * Validate if the message is incoming or outgoing by the
 * type/box information listed in the provider
 */
private static boolean isIncomingMessage(Cursor cursor, boolean isSms) {
    int boxId;
    if (isSms) {
        boxId = cursor.getInt(cursor.getColumnIndexOrThrow(Sms.TYPE));
        return (boxId == TextBasedSmsColumns.MESSAGE_TYPE_INBOX ||
                boxId == TextBasedSmsColumns.MESSAGE_TYPE_ALL) ?
                true : false;
    } else {
        boxId = cursor.getInt(cursor.getColumnIndexOrThrow(Mms.MESSAGE_BOX));
        return (boxId == Mms.MESSAGE_BOX_INBOX || boxId == Mms.MESSAGE_BOX_ALL) ?
                true : false;
    }
}
}
```

The MessageItem itself is a standard placeholder object for the message identifiers, name, text content, and image attachment (for MMS messages). Inside parseMessages(), we iterate through the Cursor data and construct a new MessageItem from each row. SMS and MMS are parsed differently, so we must first determine the message type. When the TYPE_DISCRIMINATOR_COLUMN is present, this is simple and we just check the value. In other cases, we can infer the type based on the column entries for each message.

Parsing an SMS message is straightforward, as we just need to read the ID, thread ID, address, body, and incoming status as columns directly from the main Cursor. Parsing an MMS message is slightly more involved because the message contents are segmented into parts. We can read the ID, thread ID, and incoming status from the main Cursor, but the address and content information need to be retrieved from additional tables.

First, we need to get the recipient information from the `Mms.Addr` table. MMS messages can be sent to multiple recipients, and each one is represented by a row in this table with a `MSG_ID` that matches the MMS message. We iterate through these elements and construct a comma-separated list of the results to attach to the `MessageItem`. Notice also that we are checking for our own number in this list to avoid having it added as well. Each message will also have an `Addr` entry for the local device number, and we don't want to display that in our UI each time, so we are filtering it out.

Next we need to parse out the message contents. These values are stored in the `Mms.Part` table, keyed by the `MSG_ID` again. MMS messages can have many types of content associated with them (contact data, videos, images, and so forth), but we are interested in displaying only the text or image data that may be present. As we iterate through the parts, we validate the MIME string of the content type to find any text or image components to add to our `MessageItem`. For image attachments, we simply store the Uri pointing to the content rather than decoding the image and saving it here.

■ **Note**   As of this writing, the SDK provides column constants for `Mms.Addr` and `Mms.Part`, but there is no exposed content Uri. This will likely change in the future, but for now we have to hard-code the paths off the base `Mms.CONTENT_URI` constant.

For both SMS and MMS messages, the status of whether the message is incoming or outgoing can be determined by looking at the message's box type. Messages that are marked in the Inbox or have no designation are considered incoming messages, while all other message box designations (Outbox, Sent, Drafts, and so forth) are considered outgoing.

Now that we have a parsed list of messages, let's take a look at Listings 6-42 and 6-43 to inspect the user interface implemented in this example.

Listing 6-42. Activity to Display SMS/MMS Messages

```
public class SmsActivity extends Activity
        implements OnItemClickListener, LoaderCallbacks<List<MessageItem>> {

    private MessagesAdapter mAdapter;

    @Override
    protected void onCreate(Bundle savedInstanceState) {
        super.onCreate(savedInstanceState);
        ListView list = new ListView(this);
        mAdapter = new MessagesAdapter(this);
        list.setAdapter(mAdapter);

        final Intent intent = getIntent();


        if (!intent.hasExtra("threadId")) {
            //Items are clickable if we are not showing a conversation
            list.setOnItemClickListener(this);
        }
        //Load the messages data
        getLoaderManager().initLoader(0, getIntent().getExtras(), this);

        setContentView(list);
    }
```

```java
    @Override
    public void onItemClick(AdapterView<?> parent, View view, int position, long id) {
        final MessageItem item = mAdapter.getItem(position);
        long threadId = item.thread_id;

        //Launch a new instance to show this conversation
        Intent intent = new Intent(this, SmsActivity.class);
        intent.putExtra("threadId", threadId);
        startActivity(intent);
    }

    @Override
    public Loader<List<MessageItem>> onCreateLoader(int id, Bundle args) {
        if (args != null && args.containsKey("threadId")) {
            return new ConversationLoader(this, args.getLong("threadId"));
        } else {
            return new ConversationLoader(this);
        }
    }

    @Override
    public void onLoadFinished(Loader<List<MessageItem>> loader, List<MessageItem> data) {
        mAdapter.clear();
        mAdapter.addAll(data);
        mAdapter.notifyDataSetChanged();
    }


    @Override
    public void onLoaderReset(Loader<List<MessageItem>> loader) {
        mAdapter.clear();
        mAdapter.notifyDataSetChanged();
    }

    private static class MessagesAdapter extends ArrayAdapter<MessageItem> {

        int cacheSize = 4 * 1024 * 1024; // 4MiB
        private LruCache<String, Bitmap> bitmapCache = new LruCache<String,
Bitmap>(cacheSize) {
            protected int sizeOf(String key, Bitmap value) {
                return value.getByteCount();
            }
        };

        public MessagesAdapter(Context context) {
            super(context, 0);
        }
```

```java
    @Override
    public View getView(int position, View convertView, ViewGroup parent) {
        if (convertView == null) {
            convertView = LayoutInflater.from(getContext())
                    .inflate(R.layout.message_item, parent, false);
        }

        MessageItem item = getItem(position);

        TextView text1 = (TextView) convertView.findViewById(R.id.text1);
        TextView text2 = (TextView) convertView.findViewById(R.id.text2);
        ImageView image = (ImageView) convertView.findViewById(R.id.image);

        text1.setText(item.address);
        text2.setText(item.body);
        //Set text style based on incoming/outgoing status
        Typeface tf = item.incoming ?
                Typeface.defaultFromStyle(Typeface.ITALIC) : Typeface.DEFAULT;
        text2.setTypeface(tf);
        image.setImageBitmap(getAttachment(item));

        return convertView;
    }

    private Bitmap getAttachment(MessageItem item) {
        if (item.attachment == null) return null;

        final Uri imageUri = item.attachment;
        //Pull image thumbnail from cache if we have it
        Bitmap cached = bitmapCache.get(imageUri.toString());
        if (cached != null) {
            return cached;
        }

        //Decode the asset from the provider if we don't have it in cache
        try {
            BitmapFactory.Options options = new BitmapFactory.Options();
            options.inJustDecodeBounds = true;
            int cellHeight = getContext().getResources()
                    .getDimensionPixelSize(R.dimen.message_height);
            InputStream is = getContext().getContentResolver().openInputStream(imageUri);
            BitmapFactory.decodeStream(is, null, options);

            options.inJustDecodeBounds = false;
            options.inSampleSize = options.outHeight / cellHeight;
            is = getContext().getContentResolver().openInputStream(imageUri);
            Bitmap bitmap = BitmapFactory.decodeStream(is, null, options);

            bitmapCache.put(imageUri.toString(), bitmap);
            return bitmap;
```

```
        } catch (Exception e) {
            return null;
        }
    }
  }
}
```

Listing 6-43. res/layout/message_item.xml

```xml
<?xml version="1.0" encoding="utf-8"?>
<RelativeLayout xmlns:android="http://schemas.android.com/apk/res/android"
    android:layout_width="match_parent"
    android:layout_height="wrap_content"
    android:minHeight="@dimen/message_height">
    <ImageView
        android:id="@+id/image"
        android:layout_width="@dimen/message_height"
        android:layout_height="@dimen/message_height"
        android:layout_alignParentRight="true"
        android:layout_centerVertical="true" />
    <TextView
        android:id="@+id/text1"
        android:layout_width="match_parent"
        android:layout_height="wrap_content"
        android:layout_toLeftOf="@id/image"
        android:layout_marginLeft="6dp"
        android:textStyle="bold" />
    <TextView
        android:id="@+id/text2"
        android:layout_width="match_parent"
        android:layout_height="wrap_content"
        android:layout_below="@id/text1"
        android:layout_toLeftOf="@id/image"
        android:layout_marginLeft="12dp" />

</RelativeLayout>
```

Our activity is used to display both types of message data. Upon creation, the activity calls initLoader() to construct a new ConversationLoader to query the provider. The arguments passed in are the extras received by the activity intent. When the application first launches, there are no incoming intent extras, so a ConversationLoader is constructed to load all conversation threads. Later, when the activity is launched with a specific thread ID, ConversationLoader will query all messages in that conversation.

Once the loading is complete, the data is presented in a ListView using our custom MessagesAdapter. This adapter inflates a custom item layout (from Listing 6-43) with two text rows and space for an image. The MessageItem address information is loaded into the top label, and the text content into the bottom label. If the message is MMS and an image attachment is present, we attempt to return the image via getAttachment() and insert it into the ImageView.

Loading these images from disk each time is expensive and a tad slow, so to improve scrolling performance in the list, we have added an LruCache to store recently loaded bitmaps in memory. The cache is set to 4MB in size, so as to not overinflate the application's heap over time. Additionally, each image is downsampled when returned from BitmapFactory (via BitmapFactory.Options.inSampleSize) to avoid loading an image that is larger than the space available in the list row and wasting memory.

527

We now have a basic messaging application that presents a read-only window into the SMS/MMS on our device. When launched, this application will list all the conversations by showing the latest message for each thread. When a conversation is tapped, a new activity will display, showing all the individual messages within that thread. Pressing the Back button will return to the main list so the user can select another conversation to view.

6-13. Interacting with the Calendar

Problem

Your application needs to interact directly with the ContentProvider exposed by the Android framework to add, view, change, or remove calendar events on the device.

Solution

(API Level 14)

Use the CalendarContract interface to read/write data to the system's ContentProvider for event data. CalendarContract exposes the API that is necessary to gain access to the device's calendars, events, attendees, and reminders. Much like ContactsContract, this interface defines mostly the data that is necessary to perform queries. The methods used will be the same as when working with any other system ContentProvider.

How It Works

Working with CalendarContract is very similar to working with ContactsContract; they both provide identifiers for the Uri and column values you will need to construct queries through the ContentResolver. Listing 6-44 illustrates an activity that obtains and displays a list of the calendars present on the device.

Listing 6-44. Activity Listing Calendars on the Device

```
public class CalendarListActivity extends ListActivity implements
        LoaderManager.LoaderCallbacks<Cursor>, AdapterView.OnItemClickListener {
    private static final int LOADER_LIST = 100;

    SimpleCursorAdapter mAdapter;

    @Override
    public void onCreate(Bundle savedInstanceState) {
        super.onCreate(savedInstanceState);
        getLoaderManager().initLoader(LOADER_LIST, null, this);

        // Display all calendars in a ListView
        mAdapter = new SimpleCursorAdapter(this,
                android.R.layout.simple_list_item_2, null,
                new String[] {
                        CalendarContract.Calendars.CALENDAR_DISPLAY_NAME,
                        CalendarContract.Calendars.ACCOUNT_NAME },
```

```
                    new int[] {
                            android.R.id.text1, android.R.id.text2 }, 0);
        setListAdapter(mAdapter);
        // Listen for item selections
        getListView().setOnItemClickListener(this);
    }

    @Override
    public void onItemClick(AdapterView<?> parent, View view, int position,
            long id) {
        Cursor c = mAdapter.getCursor();
        if (c != null && c.moveToPosition(position)) {
            Intent intent = new Intent(this, CalendarDetailActivity.class);
            // Pass the _ID and TITLE of the selected calendar to the next
            // Activity
            intent.putExtra(Intent.EXTRA_UID, c.getInt(0));
            intent.putExtra(Intent.EXTRA_TITLE, c.getString(1));
            startActivity(intent);
        }
    }

    @Override
    public Loader<Cursor> onCreateLoader(int id, Bundle args) {
        // Return all calendars, ordered by name
        String[] projection = new String[] { CalendarContract.Calendars._ID,
                CalendarContract.Calendars.CALENDAR_DISPLAY_NAME,
                CalendarContract.Calendars.ACCOUNT_NAME };

        return new CursorLoader(this, CalendarContract.Calendars.CONTENT_URI,
                projection, null, null,
                CalendarContract.Calendars.CALENDAR_DISPLAY_NAME);
    }

    @Override
    public void onLoadFinished(Loader<Cursor> loader, Cursor data) {
        mAdapter.swapCursor(data);
    }

    @Override
    public void onLoaderReset(Loader<Cursor> loader) {
        mAdapter.swapCursor(null);
    }
}
```

In contrast to our contacts example, here we use Android's Loader pattern to query the data and load the resulting Cursor into the list. This pattern provides a lot of benefit over managedCursor(), primarily in that all queries are automatically made on background threads to keep the UI responsive. The Loader pattern also has built-in reuse, so multiple clients wanting the same data can actually gain access to the same Loader through the LoaderManager.

With Loaders, our activity receives a series of callback methods when new data is available. Under the hood, CursorLoader also registers as a ContentObserver, so we will get a callback with a new Cursor when the underlying data set changes without even having to request a reload. But back to the calendar...

To obtain a list of the device calendars, we construct a query to the Calendars.CONTENT_URI with the column names we are interested in (here, the record ID, calendar name, and owning account name). When the query is complete, onLoadFinished() is called with a new Cursor pointing to the result data, which we then pass to our list adapter. When the user taps on a particular calendar item, a new activity is initialized to look at the specific events it contains. We will see this in more detail in the next section.

Viewing/Modifying Calendar Events

Listing 6-45 shows the contents of the second activity in this example that displays a list of all the events for the selected calendar.

Listing 6-45. Activity Listing and Modifying Calendar Events

```
public class CalendarDetailActivity extends ListActivity implements
        LoaderManager.LoaderCallbacks<Cursor>, AdapterView.OnItemClickListener,
        AdapterView.OnItemLongClickListener {
    private static final int LOADER_DETAIL = 101;

    SimpleCursorAdapter mAdapter;

    int mCalendarId;

    @Override
    protected void onCreate(Bundle savedInstanceState) {
        super.onCreate(savedInstanceState);

        mCalendarId = getIntent().getIntExtra(Intent.EXTRA_UID, -1);

        String title = getIntent().getStringExtra(Intent.EXTRA_TITLE);
        setTitle(title);

        getLoaderManager().initLoader(LOADER_DETAIL, null, this);

        // Display all events in a ListView
        mAdapter = new SimpleCursorAdapter(this,
                android.R.layout.simple_list_item_2, null,
                new String[] {
                        CalendarContract.Events.TITLE,
                        CalendarContract.Events.EVENT_LOCATION },
                new int[] {
                        android.R.id.text1, android.R.id.text2 }, 0);
        setListAdapter(mAdapter);
        // Listen for item selections
        getListView().setOnItemClickListener(this);
        getListView().setOnItemLongClickListener(this);
    }
```

```java
@Override
public boolean onCreateOptionsMenu(Menu menu) {
    menu.add("Add Event")
        .setIcon(android.R.drawable.ic_menu_add)
        .setShowAsAction(MenuItem.SHOW_AS_ACTION_ALWAYS);

    return true;
}

@Override
public boolean onOptionsItemSelected(MenuItem item) {
    showAddEventDialog();
    return true;
}

// Display a dialog to add a new event
private void showAddEventDialog() {
    final EditText nameText = new EditText(this);
    AlertDialog.Builder builder = new AlertDialog.Builder(this);
    builder.setTitle("New Event");
    builder.setView(nameText);
    builder.setNegativeButton("Cancel", null);
    builder.setPositiveButton("Add Event",
            new DialogInterface.OnClickListener() {
                @Override
                public void onClick(DialogInterface dialog, int which) {
                    addEvent(nameText.getText().toString());
                }
            });
    builder.show();
}

// Add an event to the calendar with the specified name
// and the current time as the start date
private void addEvent(String eventName) {
    long start = System.currentTimeMillis();
    // End 1 hour from now
    long end = start + (3600 * 1000);

    ContentValues cv = new ContentValues(5);
    cv.put(CalendarContract.Events.CALENDAR_ID, mCalendarId);
    cv.put(CalendarContract.Events.TITLE, eventName);
    cv.put(CalendarContract.Events.DESCRIPTION,
            "Event created by Android Recipes");
    cv.put(CalendarContract.Events.EVENT_TIMEZONE,
            Time.getCurrentTimezone());
    cv.put(CalendarContract.Events.DTSTART, start);
    cv.put(CalendarContract.Events.DTEND, end);

    getContentResolver().insert(CalendarContract.Events.CONTENT_URI, cv);
}
```

531

```java
        // Remove the selected event from the calendar
        private void deleteEvent(int eventId) {
            String selection = CalendarContract.Events._ID + " = ?";
            String[] selectionArgs = { String.valueOf(eventId) };
            getContentResolver().delete(CalendarContract.Events.CONTENT_URI,
                    selection, selectionArgs);
        }

        @Override
        public void onItemClick(AdapterView<?> parent, View view, int position,
                long id) {
            Cursor c = mAdapter.getCursor();
            if (c != null && c.moveToPosition(position)) {
                // Show a dialog with more detailed data about the event when
                // clicked
                SimpleDateFormat sdf = new SimpleDateFormat("yyyy-MM-dd HH:mm:ss");
                StringBuilder sb = new StringBuilder();

                sb.append("Location: "
                        + c.getString(
                                c.getColumnIndex(CalendarContract.Events.EVENT_LOCATION))
                        + "\n\n");
                int startDateIndex = c.getColumnIndex(CalendarContract.Events.DTSTART);
                Date startDate = c.isNull(startDateIndex) ? null
                        : new Date( Long.parseLong(c.getString(startDateIndex)) );
                if (startDate != null) {
                    sb.append("Starts At: " + sdf.format(startDate) + "\n\n");
                }
                int endDateIndex = c.getColumnIndex(CalendarContract.Events.DTEND);
                Date endDate = c.isNull(endDateIndex) ? null
                        : new Date( Long.parseLong(c.getString(endDateIndex)) );
                if (endDate != null) {
                    sb.append("Ends At: " + sdf.format(endDate) + "\n\n");
                }

                AlertDialog.Builder builder = new AlertDialog.Builder(this);
                builder.setTitle(
                        c.getString(c.getColumnIndex(CalendarContract.Events.TITLE)) );
                builder.setMessage(sb.toString());
                builder.setPositiveButton("OK", null);
                builder.show();
            }
        }

        @Override
        public boolean onItemLongClick(AdapterView<?> parent, View view,
                int position, long id) {
            Cursor c = mAdapter.getCursor();
            if (c != null && c.moveToPosition(position)) {
                // Allow the user to delete the event on a long-press
```

```java
        final int eventId = c.getInt(
                c.getColumnIndex(CalendarContract.Events._ID));
        String eventName = c.getString(
                c.getColumnIndex(CalendarContract.Events.TITLE));
        AlertDialog.Builder builder = new AlertDialog.Builder(this);
        builder.setTitle("Delete Event");
        builder.setMessage(String.format(
                "Are you sure you want to delete %s?",
                TextUtils.isEmpty(eventName) ? "this event" : eventName));
        builder.setNegativeButton("Cancel", null);
        builder.setPositiveButton("Delete Event",
                new DialogInterface.OnClickListener() {
                    @Override
                    public void onClick(DialogInterface dialog, int which) {
                        deleteEvent(eventId);
                    }
                });
        builder.show();
    }

    return true;
}

@Override
public Loader<Cursor> onCreateLoader(int id, Bundle args) {
    // Return all calendars, ordered by name
    String[] projection = new String[] { CalendarContract.Events._ID,
            CalendarContract.Events.TITLE, CalendarContract.Events.DTSTART,
            CalendarContract.Events.DTEND,
            CalendarContract.Events.EVENT_LOCATION };
    String selection = CalendarContract.Events.CALENDAR_ID + " = ?";
    String[] selectionArgs = { String.valueOf(mCalendarId) };


    return new CursorLoader(this, CalendarContract.Events.CONTENT_URI,
            projection, selection, selectionArgs,
            CalendarContract.Events.DTSTART + " DESC");
}

@Override
public void onLoadFinished(Loader<Cursor> loader, Cursor data) {
    mAdapter.swapCursor(data);
}

@Override
public void onLoaderReset(Loader<Cursor> loader) {
    mAdapter.swapCursor(null);
}
}
```

You can see that the code to query the list of events and display them is very similar; in this case, you query the Events.CONTENT_URI with the ID of the selected calendar as a selection parameter. After tapping an event, the user is presented with a simple dialog box with more details about the event itself. In addition, though, this activity includes a few more methods to create and delete events on this calendar.

To add a new event, an item is added to the options menu, which will show up in the overhead action bar if the device has one visible. When pressed, a dialog box appears, allowing the user to enter a name for this event. If the user elects to continue, a ContentValues object is created with the bare necessities required to create a new event. Because this event is nonrecurring, it must have both start and end times, as well as a valid time zone. We must also supply the ID of the calendar we are looking at so the event is properly attached. From there, the data is handed back to ContentResolver to be inserted into the Events table.

To delete an event, the user may long-press a particular item in the list and then confirm the deletion through a dialog box. In this case, all we need is the unique record ID of the selected event to pass in a selection string to ContentResolver.

Did you notice in both of these cases that we didn't write any code after the insert/delete to refresh the Cursor or the CursorAdapter? That's the power of the Loader pattern! Because the CursorLoader is observing the data set, when a change occurred, it automatically refreshed itself and handed a new Cursor to the adapter, which refreshes the display.

■ **Note**   Loaders were introduced in Android 3.0 (API Level 11), but they are also part of the Support Library. You can use them in your applications supporting all the way back to Android 1.6.

6-14. Logging Code Execution

Problem

You need to place log statements into your code for debugging or testing purposes, and they should be removed before shipping the code to production.

Solution

(API Level 1)

Leverage the BuildConfig.DEBUG flag to protect statements in the Log class so they print only on debug builds of the application. It can be extremely convenient to keep logging statements in your code for future testing and development, even after the application has shipped to your users. But if those statements are unchecked, you might risk printing private information to the console on a user's device. By creating a simple wrapper class around Log that monitors BuildConfig.DEBUG, you can leave log statements in place without fear of what they will show in the field.

How It Works

Listing 6-46 illustrates a simple wrapper class around the default Android Log functionality.

Listing 6-46. Logger Wrapper

```java
public class Logger {
    private static final String LOGTAG = "AndroidRecipes";

    private static String getLogString(String format, Object... args) {
        //Minor optimization, only call String.format if necessary
        if(args.length == 0) {
            return format;
        }

        return String.format(format, args);
    }

    /* The INFO, WARNING, ERROR log levels print always */

    public static void e(String format, Object... args) {
        Log.e(LOGTAG, getLogString(format, args));
    }

    public static void w(String format, Object... args) {
        Log.w(LOGTAG, getLogString(format, args));
    }

    public static void w(Throwable throwable) {
        Log.w(LOGTAG, throwable);
    }


    public static void i(String format, Object... args) {
        Log.i(LOGTAG, getLogString(format, args));
    }

    /* The DEBUG and VERBOSE log levels are protected by DEBUG flag */

    public static void d(String format, Object... args) {
        if(!BuildConfig.DEBUG) return;

        Log.d(LOGTAG, getLogString(format, args));
    }

    public static void v(String format, Object... args) {
        if(!BuildConfig.DEBUG) return;

        Log.v(LOGTAG, getLogString(format, args));
    }
}
```

This class provides a few simple optimizations around the framework's version to make logging a bit more civilized. First, it consolidates the log tag so your entire application prints under one consistent tag heading in logcat. Second, it takes input in the form of a format string so variables can be logged out cleanly without needing to break up the log string. The one additional optimization to this is that String.format() can be slow, so we want to call it only when there are actually parameters to format. Otherwise, we can just pass the raw string along directly.

Finally, it protects two of the five main log levels with the BuildConfig.DEBUG flag, so that log statements set to these levels print only in debug versions of the application. There are many cases where we want log statements to be output in the production application as well (such as error conditions), so it is prudent not to hide all the log levels behind the debug flag. Listing 6-47 quickly shows how this wrapper can take the place of traditional logging.

Listing 6-47. Activity Using Logger

```
public class LoggerActivity extends Activity {

    @Override
    public void onCreate(Bundle savedInstanceState) {
        super.onCreate(savedInstanceState);
        setContentView(R.layout.main);

        //This statement printed only in debug
        Logger.d("Activity Created");
    }

    @Override
    protected void onResume() {
        super.onResume();

        //This statement printed only in debug
        Logger.d("Activity Resume at %d", System.currentTimeMillis());
        //This statement always printed
        Logger.i("It is now %d", System.currentTimeMillis());
    }

    @Override
    protected void onPause() {
        super.onPause();

        //This statement printed only in debug
        Logger.d("Activity Pause at %d", System.currentTimeMillis());
        //This always printed
        Logger.w("No, don't leave!");
    }
}
```

6-15. Creating a Background Worker

Problem

You need to create a long-running background thread that sits waiting for work to execute and that can be terminated easily when it is no longer needed.

Solution

(API Level 1)

Let HandlerThread assist you in creating a background thread with a working Looper that can be attached to a Handler for processing work inside its MessageQueue. One of the most popular backgrounding methods in Android is AsyncTask, which is a fabulous class and should be used in your applications. However, it has some drawbacks that may make other implementations more efficient in certain cases. One of those drawbacks is that AsyncTask execution is one-shot and finite. If you want to do the same task repeatedly or indefinitely for the life cycle of a component such as an activity or service, AsyncTask can be a bit heavyweight. Often, you will need to create multiple instances to accomplish that goal.

The advantage of HandlerThread in cases like this is we can create one worker object to accept multiple tasks to handle in the background and it will process them serially through the built-in queue that Looper maintains.

How It Works

Listing 6-48 contains an extension of HandlerThread used to do some simple manipulation of image data. Because modifying images can take some time, we want to task this to a background operation to keep the application UI responsive.

Listing 6-48. Background Worker Thread

```
public class ImageProcessor extends HandlerThread implements Handler.Callback {
    public static final int MSG_SCALE = 100;
    public static final int MSG_CROP = 101;

    private Context mContext;
    private Handler mReceiver, mCallback;

    public ImageProcessor(Context context) {
        this(context, null);
    }

    public ImageProcessor(Context context, Handler callback) {
        super("AndroidRecipesWorker");
        mCallback = callback;
        mContext = context.getApplicationContext();
    }

    @Override
    protected void onLooperPrepared() {
        mReceiver = new Handler(getLooper(), this);
    }
```

```java
    @Override
    public boolean handleMessage(Message msg) {
        Bitmap source, result;
        //Retrieve arguments from the incoming message
        int scale = msg.arg1;
        switch (msg.what) {
        case MSG_SCALE:
            source = BitmapFactory.decodeResource(mContext.getResources(),
                    R.drawable.ic_launcher);
            //Create a new, scaled-up image
            result = Bitmap.createScaledBitmap(source,
                    source.getWidth() * scale, source.getHeight() * scale, true);
            break;
        case MSG_CROP:
            source = BitmapFactory.decodeResource(mContext.getResources(),
                    R.drawable.ic_launcher);
            int newWidth = source.getWidth() / scale;
            //Create a new, horizontally cropped image
            result = Bitmap.createBitmap(source,
                    (source.getWidth() - newWidth) / 2, 0,
                    newWidth, source.getHeight());
            break;
        default:
            throw new IllegalArgumentException("Unknown Worker Request");
        }

        // Return the image to the main thread
        if (mCallback != null) {
            mCallback.sendMessage(Message.obtain(null, 0, result));
        }
        return true;
    }

    //Add/Remove a callback handler
    public void setCallback(Handler callback) {
        mCallback = callback;
    }

    /* Methods to Queue Work */

    // Scale the icon to the specified value
    public void scaleIcon(int scale) {
        Message msg = Message.obtain(null, MSG_SCALE, scale, 0, null);
        mReceiver.sendMessage(msg);
    }

    //Crop the icon in the center and scale the result to the specified value
    public void cropIcon(int scale) {
        Message msg = Message.obtain(null, MSG_CROP, scale, 0, null);
        mReceiver.sendMessage(msg);
    }
}
```

The name HandlerThread may be a bit of a misnomer, as it does not actually contain a Handler that you can use to process input. Instead it is a thread designed to work externally with a Handler to create a background process. We have to still provide a customized implementation of Handler to execute the work we want done. In this example, our custom processor implements the Handler.Callback interface, which we pass into a new Handler owned by the thread. We do this simply to avoid the need to subclass Handler, which would have worked just as well. The receiver Handler is not created until the onLooperPrepared() callback because we need to have the Looper object that HandlerThread creates to send work to the background thread.

The external API we create to allow other objects to queue work all create a Message and send it to the receiver Handler to be processed in handleMessage(), which inspects the Message contents and creates the appropriate modified image. Any code that goes through handleMessage() is running on our background thread.

Once the work is complete, we need to have a second Handler attached to the main thread so we can send our results and modify the UI.

■ **Reminder**   Any code that touches UI elements *must* be called from the main thread *only*. This cannot be overstated.

This callback Handler receives a second Message containing the Bitmap result from the image code. This is one of the great features about using the Message interface to pass data between threads; each instance can take with it two integer arguments as well as any arbitrary Object so no additional code is necessary to pass in parameters or access your results. In our case, one integer is passed in as a parameter for the scale value of the transformation, and the Object field is used to return the image as a Bitmap. To see how this is used in practice, take a look at the sample application in Listings 6-49 and 6-50.

Listing 6-49. res/layout/main.xml

```xml
<LinearLayout xmlns:android="http://schemas.android.com/apk/res/android"
    android:layout_width="match_parent"
    android:layout_height="match_parent"
    android:orientation="vertical" >

    <Button
        android:layout_width="match_parent"
        android:layout_height="wrap_content"
        android:text="Scale Icon"
        android:onClick="onScaleClick" />
    <Button
        android:layout_width="match_parent"
        android:layout_height="wrap_content"
        android:text="Crop Icon"
        android:onClick="onCropClick" />

    <ImageView
        android:id="@+id/image_result"
        android:layout_width="match_parent"
        android:layout_height="match_parent"
        android:scaleType="center" />
</LinearLayout>
```

Listing 6-50. Activity Interacting with Worker

```java
public class WorkerActivity extends Activity implements Handler.Callback {

    private ImageProcessor mWorker;
    private Handler mResponseHandler;

    private ImageView mResultView;

    @Override
    public void onCreate(Bundle savedInstanceState) {
        super.onCreate(savedInstanceState);
        setContentView(R.layout.main);

        mResultView = (ImageView) findViewById(R.id.image_result);
        //Handler to map background callbacks to this Activity
        mResponseHandler = new Handler(this);
    }

    @Override
    protected void onResume() {
        super.onResume();
        //Start a new worker
        mWorker = new ImageProcessor(this, mResponseHandler);
        mWorker.start();
    }

    @Override
    protected void onPause() {
        super.onPause();
        //Terminate the worker
        mWorker.setCallback(null);
        mWorker.quit();
        mWorker = null;
    }

    /*
     * Callback method for background results.
     * This is called on the UI thread.
     */
    @Override
    public boolean handleMessage(Message msg) {
        Bitmap result = (Bitmap) msg.obj;
        mResultView.setImageBitmap(result);
        return true;
    }

    /* Action Methods to Post Background Work */

    public void onScaleClick(View v) {
        for(int i=1; i < 10; i++) {
```

```
            mWorker.scaleIcon(i);
        }
    }

    public void onCropClick(View v) {
        for(int i=1; i < 10; i++) {
            mWorker.cropIcon(i);
        }
    }
}
```

This sample makes use of our worker by creating a single running instance while the activity is in the foreground and passing image requests to it when the user clicks the buttons. To further illustrate the scale of this pattern, we queue up several requests with each button click. The activity also implements Handler. Callback and owns a simple Handler (which is running on the main thread) to receive result messages from the worker.

To start the processor, we just have to call start() on the HandlerThread, which sets up the Looper and Handler, and it begins waiting for input. Terminating it is just as simple; calling quit() stops the Looper and immediately drops any unprocessed messages. We also set the callback to null just so that any work that may be in process currently doesn't try to call the activity after this point.

Run this application and you can see how the background work doesn't slow the UI no matter how fast or how often the buttons are pressed. Each request just gets added to the queue and processed if possible before the user leaves the activity. The visible result is that each created image will be displayed below the buttons as that request finishes.

6-16. Customizing the Task Stack

Problem

Your application allows external applications to launch certain activities directly, and you need to implement the proper BACK vs. UP navigation patterns.

Solution

(API Level 4)

The NavUtils and TaskStackBuilder classes in the Support Library allow you to easily construct and launch the appropriate navigation stacks from within your application. The functionality of both these classes is actually native to the SDK in Android 4.1 and later, but for applications that need to target earlier platform versions as well, the Support Library implementation provides a compatible API that will still call the native methods whenever they are present.

BACK vs. UP

Android screen navigation provides for two specific user actions. The first is the action taken when the user presses the BACK button. The second is the action taken when the user presses the Home icon in the action bar, which is known as the *UP action*. For developers who are new to the platforms, the distinction can often be confusing, especially since in many cases both actions always perform the same function.

Conceptually, BACK should always navigate to the content screen that the user had been viewing prior to the current screen. The UP action, on the other hand, should navigate to the hierarchical parent screen of the current

541

screen. For most applications where the user drills down from the home screen to subsequent screens with more specific content, BACK and UP will go to the same place, and so their usefulness may be called into question.

Consider, though, an application with one or more activity elements that can be launched directly by another, external application. Say, for example, an activity is designed to view an image file. Or perhaps the application posts notification messages that allow the user to go directly to a lower-level activity when an event occurs. In these cases, the BACK action should take the user back to the application task he or she was using before jumping into your application. But the UP action provides a way to move back up your application's stack if the user decides to continue using this application rather than going back to the original task. In this instance, the entire stack of activity elements that your application normally has constructed to get to this point may not exist, and that is where TaskStackBuilder and some key attributes in your application's manifest can help.

How It Works

Let's define two applications to illustrate how this recipe works. First, look at Listing 6-51, which shows the <application> element of the manifest.

Listing 6-51. AndroidManifest.xml Application Tag

```
<application
    android:icon="@drawable/ic_launcher"
    android:label="TaskStack"
    android:theme="@style/AppTheme" >
    <activity
        android:name=".RootActivity"
        android:label="@string/title_activity_root" >
        <intent-filter>
            <action android:name="android.intent.action.MAIN" />
            <category android:name="android.intent.category.LAUNCHER" />
        </intent-filter>
    </activity>
    <activity android:name=".ItemsListActivity"
        android:parentActivityName=".RootActivity">
        <!-- Parent definition for the support library -->
        <meta-data android:name="android.support.PARENT_ACTIVITY"
            android:value=".RootActivity" />
    </activity>
    <activity android:name=".DetailsActivity"
        android:parentActivityName=".ItemsListActivity">
        <!-- Parent definition for the support library -->
        <meta-data android:name="android.support.PARENT_ACTIVITY"
            android:value=".ItemsListActivity" />
        <!-- Supply a filter to allow external launches -->
        <intent-filter>
            <action android:name="com.examples.taskstack.ACTION_NEW_ARRIVAL" />
            <category android:name="android.intent.category.DEFAULT" />
        </intent-filter>
    </activity>
</application>
```

The first step in defining ancestral navigation is to define the parent-child relationship hierarchy between each activity. In Android 4.1, the android:parentActivityName attribute was introduced to create this link. To support the same functionality in older platforms, the Support Library defines a <meta-data> value that can be attached to each activity to define the parent. Our example defines both attributes for each lower level activity to work with both the native API and the Support Library.

We have also defined a custom <intent-filter> on the DetailsActivity, which will allow an external application to launch this activity directly.

■ **Note**   If you are supporting only Android 4.1 and later with your application, you can stop here. All the remaining functionality to build the stack and navigate are built into Activity in these versions, and the default behavior happens without any extra code. In this case, you would need to implement only TaskStackBuilder if you want to somehow customize the task stack in certain situations.

With our hierarchy defined, we can create the code for each activity. See Listings 6-52 through 6-54.

Listing 6-52. Root Activity

```
public class RootActivity extends Activity implements View.OnClickListener {

    @Override
    public void onCreate(Bundle savedInstanceState) {
        super.onCreate(savedInstanceState);
        Button listButton = new Button(this);
        listButton.setText("Show Family Members");
        listButton.setOnClickListener(this);

        setContentView(listButton,
                new ViewGroup.LayoutParams(LayoutParams.MATCH_PARENT,
                        LayoutParams.WRAP_CONTENT));
    }

    @Override
    public void onClick(View v) {
        //Launch the next Activity
        Intent intent = new Intent(this, ItemsListActivity.class);
        startActivity(intent);
    }
}
```

Listing 6-53. Second-Level Activity

```
public class ItemsListActivity extends Activity implements OnItemClickListener {

    private static final String[] ITEMS = {"Mom", "Dad", "Sister", "Brother", "Cousin"};

    @Override
    protected void onCreate(Bundle savedInstanceState) {
        super.onCreate(savedInstanceState);
        //Enable ActionBar home button with up arrow
        getActionBar().setDisplayHomeAsUpEnabled(true);
        //Create and display a list of family members
        ListView list = new ListView(this);
```

```
        ArrayAdapter<String> adapter = new ArrayAdapter<String>(this,
                android.R.layout.simple_list_item_1, ITEMS);
        list.setAdapter(adapter);
        list.setOnItemClickListener(this);

        setContentView(list);
    }

    @Override
    public boolean onOptionsItemSelected(MenuItem item) {
        switch (item.getItemId()) {
        case android.R.id.home:
            //Create an intent for the parent Activity
            Intent upIntent = NavUtils.getParentActivityIntent(this);
            //Check if we need to create the entire stack
            if (NavUtils.shouldUpRecreateTask(this, upIntent)) {
                //This stack doesn't exist yet, so it must be synthesized
                TaskStackBuilder.create(this)
                        .addParentStack(this)
                        .startActivities();
            } else {
                //Stack exists, so just navigate up
                NavUtils.navigateUpFromSameTask(this);
            }
            return true;
        default:
            return super.onOptionsItemSelected(item);
        }
    }

    @Override
    public void onItemClick(AdapterView<?> parent, View v, int position, long id) {
        //Launch the final Activity, passing in the selected item name
        Intent intent = new Intent(this, DetailsActivity.class);
        intent.putExtra(Intent.EXTRA_TEXT, ITEMS[position]);
        startActivity(intent);
    }
}
```

Listing 6-54. Third-Level Activity

```
public class DetailsActivity extends Activity {
    //Custom Action String for external Activity launches
    public static final String ACTION_NEW_ARRIVAL =
            "com.examples.taskstack.ACTION_NEW_ARRIVAL";

    @Override
    protected void onCreate(Bundle savedInstanceState) {
        super.onCreate(savedInstanceState);
        //Enable ActionBar home button with up arrow
        getActionBar().setDisplayHomeAsUpEnabled(true);
```

```
        TextView text = new TextView(this);
        text.setGravity(Gravity.CENTER);
        String item = getIntent().getStringExtra(Intent.EXTRA_TEXT);
        text.setText(item);

        setContentView(text);
    }

    @Override
    public boolean onOptionsItemSelected(MenuItem item) {
        switch (item.getItemId()) {
        case android.R.id.home:
            //Create an intent for the parent Activity
            Intent upIntent = NavUtils.getParentActivityIntent(this);
            //Check if we need to create the entire stack
            if (NavUtils.shouldUpRecreateTask(this, upIntent)) {
                //This stack doesn't exist yet, so it must be synthesized
                TaskStackBuilder.create(this)
                    .addParentStack(this)
                    .startActivities();
            } else {
                //Stack exists, so just navigate up
                NavUtils.navigateUpFromSameTask(this);
            }
            return true;
        default:
            return super.onOptionsItemSelected(item);
        }
    }
}
```

This example application consists of three screens. The root screen just has a button to launch the next activity. The second activity contains a ListView with several options to select from. When any item in the list is selected, the third activity is launched, which displays the selection made in the center of the view. As you might expect, the user can use the BACK button to navigate back through this stack of screens. However, in this case, we have also enabled the UP action to provide the same navigation.

There is some common code in the two lower-level activities that enables the UP navigation. The first is a call to setDisplayHomeAsUpEnabled() on ActionBar. This enables the home icon in the bar to be clickable and also to display with the default back arrow that indicates an UP action is possible. Whenever this item is clicked by the user, onOptionsItemSelected() will trigger and the item's ID will be android.R.id.home, so we use this information to filter out when the user taps requests to navigate UP.

When navigating UP, we have to determine whether the activity stack we need already exists or we need to create it; the shouldUpRecreateTask() method does this for us. On platform versions prior to Android 4.1, it does this by checking whether the target intent has a valid action string that isn't Intent.ACTION_MAIN. On Android 4.1 and later, it decides this by checking the taskAffinity of the target intent against the rest of the application.

If the task stack does not exist, primarily because this activity was launched directly rather than being navigated to from within its own application, we must create it. TaskStackBuilder contains a host of methods to allow the stack to be created in any way that fits your application's needs. We are using the convenience method addParentStack(), which traverses all of the parentActivityName attributes (or PARENT_ACTIVITY on support platforms) and every intent necessary to re-create the path from this activity to the root. With the stack built, we just need to call startActivities() to have it build the stack and navigate to the next level up.

If the stack already exists, we can call on NavUtils to take us up one level with navigateUpFromSameTask(). This is really just a convenience method for navigateUpTo() that constructs the target intent by calling getParentActivityIntent() for us.

Now we have an application that is properly compliant with the BACK/UP navigation pattern, but how do we test it? Running this application as is will produce the same results for each BACK and UP action.

Let's construct a simple second application to launch our DetailsActivity to better illustrate the navigation pattern. See Listings 6-55 through 6-57.

Listing 6-55. AndroidManifest.xml

```xml
<manifest xmlns:android="http://schemas.android.com/apk/res/android"
    package="com.examples.taskstacklaunch"
    android:versionCode="1"
    android:versionName="1.0">

    <application android:label="TaskStackLaunch"
        android:icon="@drawable/ic_launcher"
        android:theme="@style/AppTheme">
        <activity
            android:name=".MainActivity">
            <intent-filter>
                <action android:name="android.intent.action.MAIN" />
                <category android:name="android.intent.category.LAUNCHER" />
            </intent-filter>
        </activity>
    </application>

</manifest>
```

Listing 6-56. res/layout/main.xml

```xml
<?xml version="1.0" encoding="utf-8"?>
<LinearLayout xmlns:android="http://schemas.android.com/apk/res/android"
    android:layout_width="match_parent"
    android:layout_height="match_parent"
    android:orientation="vertical" >
    <Button
        android:id="@+id/button_nephew"
        android:layout_width="match_parent"
        android:layout_height="wrap_content"
        android:text="Add a New Nephew" />
    <Button
        android:id="@+id/button_niece"
        android:layout_width="match_parent"
        android:layout_height="wrap_content"
        android:text="Add a New Niece" />
    <Button
        android:id="@+id/button_twins"
        android:layout_width="match_parent"
```

```
            android:layout_height="wrap_content"
            android:text="Add Twin Nieces!" />
</LinearLayout>
```

Listing 6-57. Activity Launching into the Task Stack

```java
public class MainActivity extends Activity implements View.OnClickListener {
    //Custom Action String for external Activity launches
    public static final String ACTION_NEW_ARRIVAL =
            "com.examples.taskstack.ACTION_NEW_ARRIVAL";

    @Override
    protected void onCreate(Bundle savedInstanceState) {
        super.onCreate(savedInstanceState);
        setContentView(R.layout.main);
        //Attach the button listeners
        findViewById(R.id.button_nephew).setOnClickListener(this);
        findViewById(R.id.button_niece).setOnClickListener(this);
        findViewById(R.id.button_twins).setOnClickListener(this);
    }

    @Override
    public void onClick(View v) {
        String newArrival;
        switch(v.getId()) {
        case R.id.button_nephew:
            newArrival = "Baby Nephew";
            break;
        case R.id.button_niece:
            newArrival = "Baby Niece";
            break;
        case R.id.button_twins:
            newArrival = "Twin Nieces!";
            break;
        default:
            return;
        }

        Intent intent = new Intent(ACTION_NEW_ARRIVAL);
        intent.putExtra(Intent.EXTRA_TEXT, newArrival);
        startActivity(intent);
    }
}
```

This application provides a few options for name values to pass in, and it then launches our previous application's DetailActivity directly. In this case, we see different behavior exhibited between BACK and UP. Pressing the BACK button will take the user back to the options selection screen, because that is the activity that launched it. But pressing the UP action button will launch the user into the original application's task stack, so it will go to the screen with the ListView of items instead. From this point forward, the user's task has changed, so BACK button actions will now also traverse the original stack, thus matching subsequent UP actions. Figure 6-12 illustrates this use case.

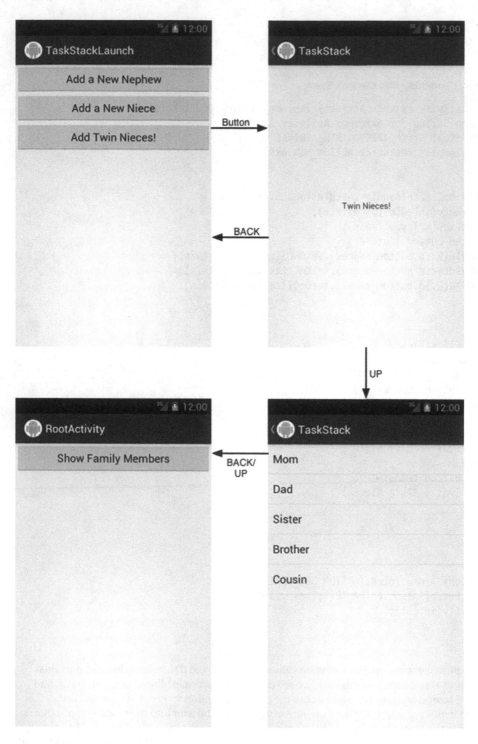

Figure 6-12. *BACK vs. UP navigation*

6-17. Implementing AppWidgets

Problem

Your application provides information that users need to quickly and consistently access. You want to add an interactive component of your application to the user's home screen.

Solution

(API Level 3)

Build an AppWidget that users can choose to install on the home screen as part of the application. AppWidgets are core functions that make Android stand apart from other mobile operating systems. The ability for users to customize their Home experience with quick access to applications they use most is a strong draw for many.

An AppWidget is a view element that is designed to run in the Launcher application's process but is controlled from your application's process. Because of this, special pieces of the framework that are designed to support remote process connections must be used. In particular, the view hierarchy of the widget must be provided wrapped in a RemoteViews object, which has methods to update view elements by ID without needing to gain direct access to them. RemoteViews supports only a subset of the layouts and widgets in the framework. The following list shows what RemoteViews supports currently:

- Layouts
  - FrameLayout
  - GridLayout
  - LinearLayout
  - RelativeLayout
- Widgets
  - AdapterViewFlipper
  - TextClock
  - Button
  - Chronometer
  - GridView
  - ImageButton
  - ImageView
  - ListView
  - ProgressBar
  - StackView
  - TextView
  - ViewFlipper

The view for your AppWidget must be composed of these objects only, or the view will not properly display.

Working in a remote process also means that most user interaction must be handled through PendingIntent instances, rather than traditional listener interfaces. The PendingIntent allows your application to freeze the intent action along with the Context that has permission to execute it; this is so the action can be freely handed off to another process and be run at the specified time as if it had come directly from the originating application Context.

Sizing

Android Launcher screens on handsets are typically made from a 4×4 grid of spaces in which you can fit your AppWidget. While tablets will have considerably greater space, this should be the design metric to keep in mind when determining the minimum height or width of your widget. Android 3.1 introduced the ability for a user to also resize an AppWidget after it had been placed, but prior to that, a widget's size was fixed to these values. Taken from the Android documentation, Table 6-1 defines a good rule of thumb to use in determining how many cells a given minimum size will occupy.

Table 6-1. Home Screen Grid Cell Sizes

Number of Cells	Available Space
1	40dp
2	110dp
3	180dp
4	250dp
n	$(70 \times n) - 30$

So, as an example, if your widget needed to be at least 200dp×48dp in size, it would require three columns and one row in order to display on the Launcher.

How It Works

Let's first take a look at constructing a simple AppWidget that can be updated from either the widget itself or the associated activity. This example constructs a random number generator (something I'm sure we all wish could be on our Launcher screen) that can be placed as an AppWidget. Let's start with the application's manifest in Listing 6-58.

Listing 6-58. AndroidManifest.xml

```
<application android:label="@string/app_name"
        android:icon="@drawable/ic_launcher">
        <!-- Simple AppWidget Components -->
        <activity android:name=".MainActivity">
            <intent-filter>
                <action android:name="android.intent.action.MAIN" />
                <category android:name="android.intent.category.LAUNCHER" />
            </intent-filter>
        </activity>
```

```
<receiver android:name=".SimpleAppWidget">
    <intent-filter>
        <action android:name="android.appwidget.action.APPWIDGET_UPDATE" />
    </intent-filter>
    <!-- This data required to configure the AppWidget -->
    <meta-data android:name="android.appwidget.provider"
        android:resource="@xml/simple_appwidget" />
</receiver>

<service android:name=".RandomService" />
</application>
```

The only required component here to produce the AppWidget is the `<receiver>` marked SimpleAppWidget. This element must point to a subclass of AppWidgetProvider, which, as you might expect, is a customized BroadcastReceiver. It must register in the manifest for the APPWIDGET_UPDATE broadcast action. There are several other broadcasts that it processes, but this is the only one that must be declared in the manifest. You must also attach a `<meta-data>` element that points to an `<appwidget-provider>`, which will eventually be inflated into AppWidgetProviderInfo. Let's have a look at that element now in Listing 6-59.

Listing 6-59. res/xml/simple_appwidget.xml

```
<?xml version="1.0" encoding="utf-8"?>
<appwidget-provider xmlns:android="http://schemas.android.com/apk/res/android"
    android:minWidth="180dp"
    android:minHeight="40dp"
    android:updatePeriodMillis="86400000"
    android:initialLayout="@layout/simple_widget_layout"/>
```

These attributes define the configuration for the AppWidget. Besides the size metrics, updatePeriodMillis defines the period on which Android should automatically call an update on this widget to refresh it. Be judicious with this value, and do not set it higher than you need to. In many cases, it is more efficient to have other services or observers notifying you of changes that require an AppWidget update. In fact, Android will not deliver updates to an AppWidget more frequently than 30 seconds. We have set our AppWidget to update only once per day. This example also defines an initialLayout attribute, which points to the layout that should be used for the AppWidget.

You can apply other useful attributes here as well:

- android:configure provides an activity that should be launched to configure the AppWidget before it is added to the Launcher.

- android:icon references a resource to be displayed at the widget icon on the system's selection UI.

- android:previewImage references a resource to display a full-size preview of the AppWidget in the system's selection UI (API Level 11).

- android:resizeMode defines how the widget should be resizable on platforms that support it: horizontally, vertically, or both (API Level 12).

Listings 6-60 and 6-61 reveal what the AppWidget layout looks like.

Listing 6-60. `res/layout/simple_widget_layout.xml`

```xml
<?xml version="1.0" encoding="utf-8"?>
<LinearLayout xmlns:android="http://schemas.android.com/apk/res/android"
    android:layout_width="match_parent"
    android:layout_height="match_parent"
    android:background="@drawable/widget_background"
    android:orientation="horizontal"
    android:padding="10dp" >
    <LinearLayout
        android:id="@+id/container"
        android:layout_width="0dp"
        android:layout_height="wrap_content"
        android:layout_weight="1"
        android:layout_gravity="center_vertical"
        android:orientation="vertical">
        <TextView
            android:id="@+id/text_title"
            android:layout_width="wrap_content"
            android:layout_height="wrap_content"
            android:layout_gravity="center_horizontal"
            android:textAppearance="?android:attr/textAppearanceMedium"
            android:text="Random Number" />
        <TextView
            android:id="@+id/text_number"
            android:layout_width="wrap_content"
            android:layout_height="wrap_content"
            android:layout_gravity="center_horizontal"
            android:textStyle="bold"
            android:textAppearance="?android:attr/textAppearanceLarge"/>
    </LinearLayout>

    <ImageButton
        android:id="@+id/button_refresh"
        android:layout_width="55dp"
        android:layout_height="55dp"
        android:layout_gravity="center_vertical"
        android:background="@null"
        android:src="@android:drawable/ic_menu_rotate" />

</LinearLayout>
```

Listing 6-61. `res/drawable/widget_background.xml`

```xml
<?xml version="1.0" encoding="utf-8"?>
<shape xmlns:android="http://schemas.android.com/apk/res/android"
    android:shape="rectangle">
    <corners
        android:radius="10dp" />
```

```
<solid
    android:color="#A333" />
<stroke
    android:width="2dp"
    android:color="#333" />
</shape>
```

It is always good practice with an AppWidget, especially in later platform versions where they can be resized, to define layouts that easily stretch and adapt to a changing container size. In this case, we have defined the background for the widget as a semitransparent rounded rectangle in XML, which could fill any size necessary. The children of the layout are also defined by using weight, so they will fill excess space. This layout is made of two TextView elements and an ImageButton. We have applied android:id attributes to all of these views because there will be no other way to access them once wrapped in a RemoteViews instance later. Listing 6-62 reveals our AppWidgetProvider mentioned earlier.

Listing 6-62. AppWidgetProvider Instance

```
public class SimpleAppWidget extends AppWidgetProvider {

    /*
     * This method is called to update the widgets created by this provider.
     * Normally, this will get called:
     * 1. Initially when the widget is created
     * 2. When the updatePeriodMillis defined in the AppWidgetProviderInfo expires
     * 3. Manually when updateAppWidget() is called on AppWidgetManager
     */
    @Override
    public void onUpdate(Context context, AppWidgetManager appWidgetManager,
            int[] appWidgetIds) {
        //Start the background service to update the widget
        context.startService(new Intent(context, RandomService.class));
    }
}
```

The only required method to implement here is onUpdate(), which will get called initially when the user selects the widget to be added and subsequently when either the framework or your application requests another update. In many cases, you can create the views and update your AppWidget directly inside this method. Because AppWidgetProvider is a BroadcastReceiver, it is not considered good practice to do long operations inside of it. If you must do intensive work to set up your AppWidget, you should start a service instead and perhaps a background thread as well to do the work, which is what we have done here.

For convenience, this method is passed an AppWidgetManager instance, which is necessary for updating the AppWidget if you do so from this method. It is also possible to have multiple AppWidgets loaded on a single Launcher screen. The array of IDs references each individual AppWidget so you can update them all at once. Let's have a look at that service in Listing 6-63.

Listing 6-63. AppWidget Service

```
public class RandomService extends Service {
    /* Broadcast Action When Updates Complete */
    public static final String ACTION_RANDOM_NUMBER =
            "com.examples.appwidget.ACTION_RANDOM_NUMBER";
```

```java
    /* Current Data Saved as a static value */
    private static int sRandomNumber;
    public static int getRandomNumber() {
        return sRandomNumber;
    }

    @Override
    public int onStartCommand(Intent intent, int flags, int startId) {
        //Update the random number data
        sRandomNumber = (int)(Math.random() * 100);

        //Create the AppWidget view
        RemoteViews views = new RemoteViews(getPackageName(),
                R.layout.simple_widget_layout);
        views.setTextViewText(R.id.text_number, String.valueOf(sRandomNumber));

        //Set an Intent for the refresh button to start this service again
        PendingIntent refreshIntent = PendingIntent.getService(this, 0,
                new Intent(this, RandomService.class), 0);
        views.setOnClickPendingIntent(R.id.button_refresh, refreshIntent);

        //Set an Intent so tapping the widget text will open the Activity
        PendingIntent appIntent = PendingIntent.getActivity(this, 0,
                new Intent(this, MainActivity.class), 0);
        views.setOnClickPendingIntent(R.id.container, appIntent);

        //Update the widget
        AppWidgetManager manager = AppWidgetManager.getInstance(this);
        ComponentName widget = new ComponentName(this, SimpleAppWidget.class);
        manager.updateAppWidget(widget, views);

        //Fire a broadcast to notify listeners
        Intent broadcast = new Intent(ACTION_RANDOM_NUMBER);
        sendBroadcast(broadcast);

        //This service should not continue to run
        stopSelf();
        return START_NOT_STICKY;
    }

    /*
     * We are not binding to this Service, so this method should
     * just return null.
     */
    @Override
    public IBinder onBind(Intent intent) {
        return null;
    }
}
```

This `RandomService` performs two operations when started. First, it regenerates and saves the random number data into a static field. Second, it constructs a new view for our `AppWidget`. In this way, we can use this service to refresh our `AppWidget` on demand. We must first create a `RemoteViews` instance, passing in our widget layout. We use `setTextViewText()` to update a `TextView` in the layout with the new number, and `setOnClickPendingIntent()` attaches click listeners. The first `PendingIntent` is attached to the Refresh button on the `AppWidget`, and the intent that it is set to fire will restart this same service. The second `PendingIntent` is attached to the main layout of the widget, allowing the user to click anywhere inside it, and it fires an intent to launch the application's main activity.

The final step with our `RemoteViews` initialized is to update the `AppWidget`. We do this by obtaining the `AppWidgetManager` instance and calling `updateAppWidget()`. We do not have the ID values for each `AppWidget` attached to the provider here, which is one method of updating them. Instead, we can pass a `ComponentName` that references our `AppWidgetProvider`, and this update will apply to all `AppWidgets` attached to that provider.

To finish up, we send a broadcast to any listeners that a new random number has been generated and we stop the service. At this point, we have all the code in place for our `AppWidget` to be live and working on a device. But let's add one more component and include an activity that interacts with the same data. See Listings 6-64 and 6-65.

Listing 6-64. `res/layout/main.xml`

```xml
<?xml version="1.0" encoding="utf-8"?>
<LinearLayout xmlns:android="http://schemas.android.com/apk/res/android"
    android:layout_width="match_parent"
    android:layout_height="match_parent"
    android:orientation="vertical" >
    <Button
        android:layout_width="match_parent"
        android:layout_height="wrap_content"
        android:text="Generate New Number"
        android:onClick="onRandomClick" />
    <TextView
        android:layout_width="wrap_content"
        android:layout_height="wrap_content"
        android:layout_gravity="center_horizontal"
        android:textAppearance="?android:attr/textAppearanceLarge"
        android:text="Current Random Number" />
    <TextView
        android:id="@+id/text_number"
        android:layout_width="wrap_content"
        android:layout_height="wrap_content"
        android:layout_gravity="center_horizontal"
        android:textSize="55dp"
        android:textStyle="bold" />

</LinearLayout>
```

Listing 6-65. Main Application Activity

```java
public class MainActivity extends Activity {

    private TextView mCurrentNumber;

    @Override
    protected void onCreate(Bundle savedInstanceState) {
        super.onCreate(savedInstanceState);
        setContentView(R.layout.main);

        mCurrentNumber = (TextView) findViewById(R.id.text_number);
    }

    @Override
    protected void onResume() {
        super.onResume();
        updateNumberView();
        //Register a receiver to receive updates when the service finishes
        IntentFilter filter = new IntentFilter(RandomService.ACTION_RANDOM_NUMBER);
        registerReceiver(mReceiver, filter);
    }

    @Override
    protected void onPause() {
        super.onPause();
        //Unregister our receiver
        unregisterReceiver(mReceiver);
    }

    public void onRandomClick(View v) {
        //Call the service to update the number data
        startService(new Intent(this, RandomService.class));
    }

    private void updateNumberView() {
        //Update the view with the latest number
        mCurrentNumber.setText(String.valueOf(RandomService.getRandomNumber()));
    }

    private BroadcastReceiver mReceiver = new BroadcastReceiver() {
        @Override
        public void onReceive(Context context, Intent intent) {
            //Update the view with the new number
            updateNumberView();
        }
    };
}
```

This activity displays the current value of the random number provided by our RandomService. It also responds to button clicks by starting the service to generate a new number. The nice side effect is that this will also update our AppWidget so the two will stay in sync. We also register a BroadcastReceiver to listen for the event when the service has finished generating new data, so that we can update the user interface here as well. Figure 6-13 shows the application activity, and the corresponding AppWidget added to the home screen.

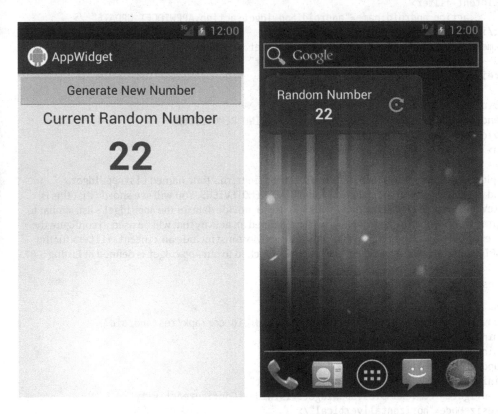

Figure 6-13. The Random Number Activity app (left) and AppWidget (right)

Collection-Based AppWidgets

(API Level 12)

Starting in Android 3.0, the things an AppWidget can display got a boost when collection views were added to the AppWidget framework. This allows applications to display information in a list, grid, or stack. In Android 3.1, AppWidgets also received the ability to be resized after being placed. Let's take a look at an example of an AppWidget that allows the user to see his or her media collection. Again, we'll start with the manifest in Listing 6-66.

Listing 6-66. AndroidManifest.xml

```xml
<application android:label="@string/app_name"
        android:icon="@drawable/ic_launcher">
    <!-- Collection AppWidget Components -->
    <activity android:name=".ListWidgetConfigureActivity">
        <intent-filter>
```

```xml
                <action android:name="android.appwidget.action.APPWIDGET_CONFIGURE"/>
            </intent-filter>
        </activity>

        <receiver android:name=".ListAppWidget">
            <intent-filter>
                <action android:name="android.appwidget.action.APPWIDGET_UPDATE" />
            </intent-filter>
            <meta-data android:name="android.appwidget.provider"
                android:resource="@xml/list_appwidget" />
        </receiver>

        <service android:name=".ListWidgetService"
            android:permission="android.permission.BIND_REMOTEVIEWS" />
        <service android:name=".MediaService" />
</application>
```

This example has a similar definition to the AppWidgetProvider, this time named ListAppWidget. We have defined a service with the special permission BIND_REMOTEVIEWS. You will see shortly that this is actually a RemoteViewsService, which the framework will use to provide data for the AppWidget's list, similar to how a ListAdapter works with ListView. Finally, we have defined an activity that will be used to configure the AppWidget before the user adds it. For this to take place, the activity must include an <intent-filter> for the APPWIDGET_CONFIGURE action. The AppWidgetProviderInfo attached to our AppWidget is defined in Listing 6-67.

Listing 6-67. res/xml/list_appwidget.xml

```xml
<?xml version="1.0" encoding="utf-8"?>
<appwidget-provider xmlns:android="http://schemas.android.com/apk/res/android"
    android:minWidth="110dp"
    android:minHeight="110dp"
    android:updatePeriodMillis="86400000"
    android:initialLayout="@layout/list_widget_layout"
    android:configure="com.examples.appwidget.ListWidgetConfigureActivity"
    android:resizeMode="horizontal|vertical"/>
```

In addition to the standard attributes we discussed in the previous example, we have added android:configure to point to our configuration activity, and android:resizeMode will enable this AppWidget to be resized in both directions. Listings 6-68 through 6-70 show the layouts we will use for both the AppWidget itself and for each row of the ListView.

Listing 6-68. res/layout/list_widget_layout.xml

```xml
<?xml version="1.0" encoding="utf-8"?>
<LinearLayout xmlns:android="http://schemas.android.com/apk/res/android"
    android:layout_width="match_parent"
    android:layout_height="match_parent"
    android:orientation="vertical"
    android:background="@drawable/list_widget_background">
    <TextView
        android:id="@+id/text_title"
        android:layout_width="match_parent"
        android:layout_height="45dp"
```

```
            android:gravity="center"
            android:textAppearance="?android:attr/textAppearanceMedium" />
    <FrameLayout
        android:layout_width="match_parent"
        android:layout_height="match_parent" >
        <ListView
            android:id="@+id/list"
            android:layout_width="match_parent"
            android:layout_height="match_parent" />
        <TextView
            android:id="@+id/list_empty"
            android:layout_width="wrap_content"
            android:layout_height="wrap_content"
            android:layout_gravity="center"
            android:text="No Items Available" />
    </FrameLayout>
</LinearLayout>
```

Listing 6-69. res/drawable/list_widget_background.xml

```
<?xml version="1.0" encoding="utf-8"?>
<shape xmlns:android="http://schemas.android.com/apk/res/android"
    android:shape="rectangle">
    <solid
        android:color="#A333" />
</shape>
```

Listing 6-70. res/layout/list_widget_item.xml

```
<?xml version="1.0" encoding="utf-8"?>
<LinearLayout xmlns:android="http://schemas.android.com/apk/res/android"
    android:id="@+id/list_widget_item"
    android:layout_width="match_parent"
    android:layout_height="?android:attr/listPreferredItemHeight"
    android:paddingLeft="10dp"
    android:gravity="center_vertical"
    android:orientation="vertical" >

    <TextView
        android:id="@+id/line1"
        android:layout_width="wrap_content"
        android:layout_height="wrap_content" />

    <TextView
        android:id="@+id/line2"
        android:layout_width="wrap_content"
        android:layout_height="wrap_content" />

</LinearLayout>
```

The layout of the AppWidget is a simple ListView with a TextView above it for a title. We have encapsulated the list into a FrameLayout so that we can also supply a sibling empty view as well.

■ **Tip**   Try as you might, you will be unsuccessful using most of the Android standard row layouts for ListView in an AppWidget, such as android.R.id.simple_list_item_1. This is because these elements typically contain views such as CheckedTextView that are not supported by RemoteViews. You will have to create your own layout for each row.

Before we look at the AppWidgetProvider for this example, let's first look at the configuration activity. This is the first thing the user will see after dropping the AppWidget onto the home screen, but before it is installed. The result from this activity will actually govern whether the AppWidgetProvider gets called at all! See Listings 6-71 and 6-72.

Listing 6-71. res/layout/configure.xml

```xml
<?xml version="1.0" encoding="utf-8"?>
<RelativeLayout xmlns:android="http://schemas.android.com/apk/res/android"
    android:layout_width="match_parent"
    android:layout_height="match_parent">
    <TextView
        android:id="@+id/text_title"
        android:layout_width="wrap_content"
        android:layout_height="wrap_content"
        android:textAppearance="?android:attr/textAppearanceLarge"
        android:text="Select Media Type:" />
    <RadioGroup
        android:id="@+id/group_mode"
        android:layout_width="wrap_content"
        android:layout_height="wrap_content"
        android:layout_below="@id/text_title"
        android:orientation="vertical">
        <RadioButton
            android:id="@+id/mode_image"
            android:layout_width="wrap_content"
            android:layout_height="wrap_content"
            android:text="Images"/>
        <RadioButton
            android:id="@+id/mode_video"
            android:layout_width="wrap_content"
            android:layout_height="wrap_content"
            android:text="Videos"/>
    </RadioGroup>

    <Button
        android:layout_width="match_parent"
        android:layout_height="wrap_content"
        android:layout_alignParentBottom="true"
        android:text="Add Widget"
        android:onClick="onAddClick" />

</RelativeLayout>
```

Listing 6-72. Configuration Activity

```java
public class ListWidgetConfigureActivity extends Activity {

    private int mAppWidgetId;
    private RadioGroup mModeGroup;

    @Override
    protected void onCreate(Bundle savedInstanceState) {
        super.onCreate(savedInstanceState);
        setContentView(R.layout.configure);

        mModeGroup = (RadioGroup) findViewById(R.id.group_mode);


        mAppWidgetId = getIntent()
                .getIntExtra(AppWidgetManager.EXTRA_APPWIDGET_ID,
                        AppWidgetManager.INVALID_APPWIDGET_ID);

        setResult(RESULT_CANCELED);
    }

    public void onAddClick(View v) {
        SharedPreferences.Editor prefs =
                getSharedPreferences(String.valueOf(mAppWidgetId), MODE_PRIVATE)
                        .edit();
        RemoteViews views = new RemoteViews(getPackageName(),
                R.layout.list_widget_layout);
        switch (mModeGroup.getCheckedRadioButtonId()) {
        case R.id.mode_image:
            prefs.putString(ListWidgetService.KEY_MODE,
                    ListWidgetService.MODE_IMAGE).commit();
            views.setTextViewText(R.id.text_title, "Image Collection");
            break;
        case R.id.mode_video:
            prefs.putString(ListWidgetService.KEY_MODE,
                    ListWidgetService.MODE_VIDEO).commit();
            views.setTextViewText(R.id.text_title, "Video Collection");
            break;
        default:
            Toast.makeText(this, "Please Select a Media Type.",
                    Toast.LENGTH_SHORT).show();
            return;
        }

        Intent intent = new Intent(this, ListWidgetService.class);
        intent.putExtra(AppWidgetManager.EXTRA_APPWIDGET_ID, mAppWidgetId);
        intent.setData(Uri.parse(intent.toUri(Intent.URI_INTENT_SCHEME)));

        //Attach the adapter to populate the data for the list in
        //the form of an Intent that points to our RemoveViewsService
        views.setRemoteAdapter(mAppWidgetId, R.id.list, intent);
```

```
        //Set the empty view for the list
        views.setEmptyView(R.id.list, R.id.list_empty);

        Intent viewIntent = new Intent(Intent.ACTION_VIEW);
        PendingIntent pendingIntent = PendingIntent.getActivity(this, 0, viewIntent, 0);
        views.setPendingIntentTemplate(R.id.list, pendingIntent);

        AppWidgetManager manager = AppWidgetManager.getInstance(this);
        manager.updateAppWidget(mAppWidgetId, views);

        Intent data = new Intent();
        data.putExtra(AppWidgetManager.EXTRA_APPWIDGET_ID, mAppWidgetId);
        setResult(RESULT_OK, data);
        finish();
    }
}
```

The layout for this activity provides a single RadioGroup to choose between images and videos, which will be the selected media type that the AppWidget displays in its list and on an Add button. By convention, when we enter the activity, we immediately set the result to RESULT_CANCELED. This is because if the user ever leaves this activity without going through the process of hitting Add, we don't want the AppWidget to show up on the screen. The framework checks the result of this activity to decide whether to add the AppWidget. We are also passed the ID of this AppWidget by the framework, which we save for later.

Once the user has made a selection and clicks Add, that selection is saved in a specific SharedPreferences instance named by the AppWidget's ID. We want to be able to allow the application to handle multiple widgets, and we want their configuration values to be separate, so we avoid using the default SharedPreferences to persist this data.

■ **Note** In Android 4.1, the ability to pass configuration data to the AppWidget as a Bundle of options was introduced. However, to keep compatibility with previous versions, we can use the SharedPreferences approach instead.

We also can begin to construct the RemoteViews for this AppWidget, setting the title based on the user's type selection. For a collection-based AppWidget, we must construct an intent that will launch an instance of RemoteViewsService to act as the adapter for the collection data, similar to a ListAdapter. This is attached to the RemoteViews with setRemoteAdapter(), which also takes the ID of the ListView we want the adapter to connect with. We also use setEmptyView() to attach the ID of our sibling TextView to display when the list is empty.

Each list item must have a PendingIntent attached to fire when the user clicks it. The framework is aware that you may need to supply specific information for every item, so it uses the pattern of a PendingIntent template that gets filled in by each item. Here we are creating the base intent for each item to fill in as a simple ACTION_VIEW, and attaching it via setPendingIntentTemplate(); the data and extras fields will be filled in later.

With all this in place, we call updateAppWidget() on the AppWidgetManager. In this case, we called a version of this method that takes a single ID rather than a ComponentName because we want to update only this specific AppWidget. We then set the result to RESULT_OK and finish, allowing the framework to add the AppWidget to the screen. Let's look briefly now at the AppWidgetProvider, which is shown in Listing 6-73.

Listing 6-73. List AppWidgetProvider

```java
public class ListAppWidget extends AppWidgetProvider {

    /*
     * This method is called to update the widgets created by this provider.
     * Because we supplied a configuration Activity, this method will not get called
     * for the initial adding of the widget, but will still be called:
     * 1. When the updatePeriodMillis defined in the AppWidgetProviderInfo expires
     */
    @Override
    public void onUpdate(Context context, AppWidgetManager appWidgetManager,
            int[] appWidgetIds) {
        //Update each widget created by this provider
        for (int i=0; i < appWidgetIds.length; i++) {
            Intent intent = new Intent(context, ListWidgetService.class);
            intent.putExtra(AppWidgetManager.EXTRA_APPWIDGET_ID, appWidgetIds[i]);
            intent.setData(Uri.parse(intent.toUri(Intent.URI_INTENT_SCHEME)));

            RemoteViews views = new RemoteViews(context.getPackageName(),
                    R.layout.list_widget_layout);
            //Set the title view based on the widget configuration
            SharedPreferences prefs =
                    context.getSharedPreferences(String.valueOf(appWidgetIds[i]),
                            Context.MODE_PRIVATE);
            String mode = prefs.getString(ListWidgetService.KEY_MODE,
                    ListWidgetService.MODE_IMAGE);
            if (ListWidgetService.MODE_VIDEO.equals(mode)) {
                views.setTextViewText(R.id.text_title, "Video Collection");
            } else {
                views.setTextViewText(R.id.text_title, "Image Collection");
            }

            //Attach the adapter to populate the data for the list in
            //the form of an Intent that points to our RemoveViewsService
            views.setRemoteAdapter(appWidgetIds[i], R.id.list, intent);

            //Set the empty view for the list
            views.setEmptyView(R.id.list, R.id.list_empty);

            //Set the template Intent for item clicks that each item will fill in
            Intent viewIntent = new Intent(Intent.ACTION_VIEW);
            PendingIntent pendingIntent = PendingIntent.getActivity(context, 0,
                    viewIntent, 0);
            views.setPendingIntentTemplate(R.id.list, pendingIntent);

            appWidgetManager.updateAppWidget(appWidgetIds[i], views);
        }
    }
```

```java
/*
 * Called when the first widget is added to the provider
 */
@Override
public void onEnabled(Context context) {
    //Start the service to monitor the MediaStore
    context.startService(new Intent(context, MediaService.class));
}

/*
 * Called when all widgets have been removed from this provider
 */
@Override
public void onDisabled(Context context) {
    //Stop the service that is monitoring the MediaStore
    context.stopService(new Intent(context, MediaService.class));
}

/*
 * Called when one or more widgets attached to this provider are removed
 */
@Override
public void onDeleted(Context context, int[] appWidgetIds) {
    //Remove the SharedPreferences we created for each widget removed
    for (int i=0; i < appWidgetIds.length; i++) {
        context.getSharedPreferences(String.valueOf(appWidgetIds[i]),
                Context.MODE_PRIVATE)
            .edit()
            .clear()
            .commit();
    }

}
}
```

The onUpdate() method of this provider is identical to the code found in the configuration activity, except that the provider is reading the current values of the user configuration settings rather than updating them. The code must be the same because we want to have the same AppWidget result from a subsequent update.

This provider also overrides onEnabled() and onDisabled(). These methods are called when the very first widget is added to the provider and after the very last widget is removed. The provider is using them to start and stop a long-running service that we will look at in more detail shortly, but its purpose is to monitor the MediaStore for changes so we can update our AppWidget. Finally, the onDeleted() callback is called for each AppWidget that gets removed. In our example, we use this to clear out the SharedPreferences we had created when the AppWidget was added.

Now look at Listing 6-74, which defines our RemoteViewsService for serving data to the AppWidget list.

Listing 6-74. RemoteViews Adapter

```java
public class ListWidgetService extends RemoteViewsService {

    public static final String KEY_MODE = "mode";
    public static final String MODE_IMAGE = "image";
    public static final String MODE_VIDEO = "video";

    @Override
    public RemoteViewsFactory onGetViewFactory(Intent intent) {
        return new ListRemoteViewsFactory(this, intent);
    }

    private class ListRemoteViewsFactory implements
            RemoteViewsService.RemoteViewsFactory {
        private Context mContext;
        private int mAppWidgetId;

        private Cursor mDataCursor;


        public ListRemoteViewsFactory(Context context, Intent intent) {
            mContext = context.getApplicationContext();
            mAppWidgetId = intent.getIntExtra(AppWidgetManager.EXTRA_APPWIDGET_ID,
                    AppWidgetManager.INVALID_APPWIDGET_ID);
        }

        @Override
        public void onCreate() {
            //Load preferences to get settings user set while adding the widget
            SharedPreferences prefs =
                    mContext.getSharedPreferences(String.valueOf(mAppWidgetId),
                            MODE_PRIVATE);
            //Get the user's config setting, defaulting to image mode
            String mode = prefs.getString(KEY_MODE, MODE_IMAGE);
            //Set the media type to query based on the user configuration setting
            if (MODE_VIDEO.equals(mode)) {
                //Query for video items in the MediaStore
                String[] projection = {MediaStore.Video.Media.TITLE,
                        MediaStore.Video.Media.DATE_TAKEN,
                        MediaStore.Video.Media.DATA};
                mDataCursor = MediaStore.Images.Media.query(getContentResolver(),
                        MediaStore.Video.Media.EXTERNAL_CONTENT_URI, projection);
            } else {
                //Query for image items in the MediaStore
                String[] projection = {MediaStore.Images.Media.TITLE,
                        MediaStore.Images.Media.DATE_TAKEN,
                        MediaStore.Images.Media.DATA};
                mDataCursor = MediaStore.Images.Media.query(getContentResolver(),
                        MediaStore.Images.Media.EXTERNAL_CONTENT_URI, projection);
            }
        }
```

```java
    /*
     * This method gets called after onCreate(), but also if an external call
     * to AppWidgetManager.notifyAppWidgetViewDataChanged() indicates that the
     * data for a widget should be refreshed.
     */
    @Override
    public void onDataSetChanged() {
        //Refresh the Cursor data
        mDataCursor.requery();
    }

    @Override
    public void onDestroy() {
        //Close the cursor when we no longer need it.
        mDataCursor.close();
        mDataCursor = null;
    }

    @Override
    public int getCount() {
        return mDataCursor.getCount();
    }

    /*
     * If your data comes from the network or otherwise may take a while to load,
     * you can return a loading view here.  This view will be shown while
     * getViewAt() is blocked until it returns
     */
    @Override
    public RemoteViews getLoadingView() {
        return null;
    }
    /*
     * Return a view for each item in the collection.  You can safely perform long
     * operations in this method.  The loading view will be displayed until this
     * method returns.
     */
    @Override
    public RemoteViews getViewAt(int position) {
        mDataCursor.moveToPosition(position);

        RemoteViews views = new RemoteViews(getPackageName(),
                R.layout.list_widget_item);
        views.setTextViewText(R.id.line1, mDataCursor.getString(0));
        views.setTextViewText(R.id.line2, DateFormat.format("MM/dd/yyyy",
                mDataCursor.getLong(1)));

        SharedPreferences prefs = mContext
            .getSharedPreferences(String.valueOf(mAppWidgetId), MODE_PRIVATE);
        String mode = prefs.getString(KEY_MODE, MODE_IMAGE);
        String type;
```

```
            if (MODE_VIDEO.equals(mode)) {
                type = "video/*";
            } else {
                type = "image/*";
            }

            Uri data = Uri.fromFile(new File(mDataCursor.getString(2)));

            Intent intent = new Intent();
            intent.setDataAndType(data, type);
            views.setOnClickFillInIntent(R.id.list_widget_item, intent);

            return views;
        }

        @Override
        public int getViewTypeCount() {
            return 1;
        }

        @Override
        public boolean hasStableIds() {
            return false;
        }

        @Override
        public long getItemId(int position) {
            return position;
        }
    }
}
```

The RemoteViewsFactory implementation that RemoteViewsService must return looks very much like a ListAdapter. Many of the methods such as getCount() and getViewTypeCount() perform the same functions as they do for local lists. When the RemoteViewsFactory is first created, we check the setting value the user had selected during configuration, and we then retrieve the appropriate Cursor from the system's MediaStore content provider to display either images or videos. When the factory is destroyed because it's no longer needed, that is our opportunity to close the Cursor. When an external stimulus tells AppWidgetManager that the data need to be refreshed, onDataSetChanged() will be called. To refresh our data, all we need to do is requery() the Cursor.

The getViewAt() method is where we obtain a view for each row in the list. This method is safe to call long-running operations in (such as network I/O); the framework will display whatever is returned from getLoadingView() instead until getViewAt() returns. In the example, we update the RemoteViews version of our row layout with the title and a text representation of the date for the given item. We must then fill in the PendingIntent template that was set in our original update. We set the file path of the image or video and the appropriate MIME type as the data field. Combined with ACTION_VIEW, this will open the file in the device's Gallery app (or any other application capable of handling the media) when the item is clicked.

You may notice in this example we didn't use explicit column names when retrieving the Cursor data. This is primarily because the projections between the two types have different names, so it is more efficient to access them by index. Finally, look at Listing 6-75, which reveals the background service that was started and stopped by the AppWidgetProvider.

567

Listing 6-75. Update Monitoring Service

```java
public class MediaService extends Service {

    private ContentObserver mMediaStoreObserver;

    @Override
    public void onCreate() {
        super.onCreate();
        //Create and register a new observer on the MediaStore when this service begins
        mMediaStoreObserver = new ContentObserver(new Handler()) {
            @Override
            public void onChange(boolean selfChange) {
                //Update all the widgets currently attached to our AppWidgetProvider
                AppWidgetManager manager =
                        AppWidgetManager.getInstance(MediaService.this);
                ComponentName provider = new ComponentName(MediaService.this,
                        ListAppWidget.class);
                int[] appWidgetIds = manager.getAppWidgetIds(provider);
                //This method triggers onDataSetChanged() in the RemoteViewsService
                manager.notifyAppWidgetViewDataChanged(appWidgetIds, R.id.list);
            }
        };
        //Register for Images and Video
        getContentResolver().registerContentObserver(
            MediaStore.Images.Media.EXTERNAL_CONTENT_URI, true, mMediaStoreObserver);
        getContentResolver().registerContentObserver(
            MediaStore.Video.Media.EXTERNAL_CONTENT_URI, true, mMediaStoreObserver);
    }

    @Override
    public void onDestroy() {
        super.onDestroy();
        //Unregister the observer when the Service stops
        getContentResolver().unregisterContentObserver(mMediaStoreObserver);
    }

    /*
     * We are not binding to this Service, so this method should
     * just return null.
     */
    @Override
    public IBinder onBind(Intent intent) {
        return null;
    }

}
```

The purpose of this service is to register a `ContentObserver` with the `MediaStore` while any `AppWidgets` are active. This way, when a photo or video is added or removed, we can update the list of our widget to reflect that. Whenever the `ContentObserver` triggers, we will call `notifyAppWidgetViewDataChanged()` on `AppWidgetManager` for every widget currently attached. This will trigger the `onDataSetChanged()` callback in the `RemoveViewsService` to refresh the lists. You can see the result of all this working together in Figures 6-14 and 6-15.

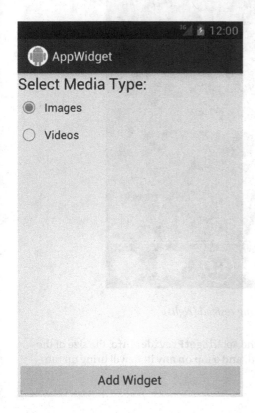

Figure 6-14. *Configuration activity prior to AppWidget being added*

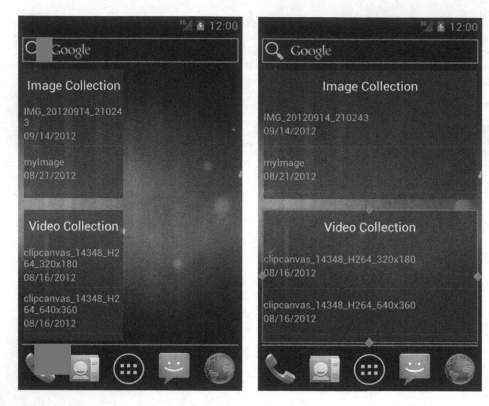

Figure 6-15. `AppWidget` *added for both types (left) and after being resized (right)*

You can see that by simply adding the resize attributes to the `AppWidgetProviderInfo`, the size of the `AppWidget` can be modified by the user. Each list can be scrolled, and a tap on any item will bring up the default viewing application to view the image or play the video.

6-18. Supporting Restricted Profiles

Problem

Your application targets an audience of various ages and abilities, and you need to provide the control to modify the app's behavior to suit each particular user.

Solution

(API Level 18)

`UserManager` provides some generic information about system-level features that may be unavailable to the user profile, via `getUserRestrictions()`, if that profile is set up to be restricted. Furthermore, applications can define custom feature sets that should be configurable in a restricted environment, and then obtain the current settings of the device from the `UserManager` by calling `getApplicationRestrictions()`.

Each application can define a set of RestrictionEntry elements that the system will present the device owner in user settings to configure the app for the restricted profile. Each element defines the type of setting (Boolean, single selection, or multiselection) and the data that should be visible in settings.

Android devices that support multiple user accounts provide the ability for the device owner (which is defined as the first account set up on the device) to create additional users or restricted profiles. Secondary users have their own applications, data spaces, and the same ability as the owner to administer the device, with the exception of managing other user accounts.

Restricted profiles were introduced in Android 4.3 as a way of providing restricted access to the applications and data that are part of the owner's account. These profiles do not have their own application space or associated data. Instead, they are a set of controls owners can place to restrict which of their own applications can be used and which features of those applications are accessible. The obvious use case for this is parental controls, but one could also use restricted profiles to put a device temporarily into a kiosk mode, for example.

■ **Tip** Multiple user accounts are not typically enabled in emulator images, and are usually supported on only tablet devices. These types of features are not common on handsets.

How It Works

To illustrate an application that takes advantage of restricted user environments, we've constructed a simple drawing application for children and young adults. We will use application-level restrictions to remove and modify certain application features. Listing 6-76 contains the layout of the user interface.

Listing 6-76. res/layout/activity_main.xml

```xml
<?xml version="1.0" encoding="utf-8"?>
<FrameLayout xmlns:android="http://schemas.android.com/apk/res/android"
    android:layout_width="match_parent"
    android:layout_height="match_parent" >

    <com.androidrecipes.restrictedprofiles.DrawingView
        android:id="@+id/drawing_surface"
        android:layout_width="match_parent"
        android:layout_height="match_parent"/>

    <Button
        android:id="@+id/button_purchase"
        android:layout_width="wrap_content"
        android:layout_height="wrap_content"
        android:layout_gravity="right"
        android:text="$$$$"
        android:onClick="onPurchaseClick"/>

    <SeekBar
        android:id="@+id/full_slider"
        android:layout_width="match_parent"
        android:layout_height="wrap_content"
        android:layout_gravity="bottom"
        android:max="45"/>
```

```
    <RadioGroup
        android:id="@+id/simple_selector"
        android:layout_width="match_parent"
        android:layout_height="wrap_content"
        android:layout_gravity="bottom"
        android:orientation="horizontal">
        <RadioButton
            android:id="@+id/option_small"
            android:layout_width="0dp"
            android:layout_height="wrap_content"
            android:layout_weight="1"
            android:textColor="#555"
            android:text="Small" />
        <RadioButton
            android:id="@+id/option_medium"
            android:layout_width="0dp"
            android:layout_height="wrap_content"
            android:layout_weight="1"
            android:textColor="#555"
            android:text="Medium" />
        <RadioButton
            android:id="@+id/option_large"
            android:layout_width="0dp"
            android:layout_height="wrap_content"
            android:layout_weight="1"
            android:textColor="#555"
            android:text="Big" />
        <RadioButton
            android:id="@+id/option_xlarge"
            android:layout_width="0dp"
            android:layout_height="wrap_content"
            android:layout_weight="1"
            android:textColor="#555"
            android:text="Really Big" />
    </RadioGroup>
</FrameLayout>
```

In this example, we have created a drawing surface on which the user can paint with a finger (which is a custom view we will see shortly), a button that allows the user to purchase upgraded content (in our case, better colors) from our fake store, and some UI at the bottom of the screen to adjust the line width of the drawings (a slider and a set of radio buttons). We will be using application restrictions to control the latter two features. See Listing 6-77 for the activity element.

Listing 6-77. Restricted Profiles Activity

```
public class MainActivity extends Activity implements
        OnSeekBarChangeListener, OnCheckedChangeListener {

    private Button mPurchaseButton;
    private DrawingView mDrawingView;
    private SeekBar mFullSlider;
    private RadioGroup mSimpleSelector;
```

```java
/* Profile Restriction Values */
private boolean mHasPurchases;
private int mMinAge;
/* Content Purchase Flags */
private boolean mHasCanvasColors = false;
private boolean mHasPaintColors = false;

@Override
protected void onCreate(Bundle savedInstanceState) {
    super.onCreate(savedInstanceState);
    setContentView(R.layout.activity_main);

    mPurchaseButton = (Button) findViewById(R.id.button_purchase);
    mDrawingView = (DrawingView) findViewById(R.id.drawing_surface);
    mFullSlider = (SeekBar) findViewById(R.id.full_slider);
    mSimpleSelector = (RadioGroup) findViewById(R.id.simple_selector);

    mFullSlider.setOnSeekBarChangeListener(this);
    mSimpleSelector.setOnCheckedChangeListener(this);

    if (Build.VERSION.SDK_INT >= Build.VERSION_CODES.JELLY_BEAN_MR2) {
        UserManager manager = (UserManager) getSystemService(USER_SERVICE);
        //Check for system-level restrictions
        Bundle restrictions = manager.getUserRestrictions();
        if (restrictions != null && !restrictions.isEmpty()) {
            showSystemRestrictionsDialog(restrictions);
        }
    }
}

@Override
protected void onStart() {
    super.onStart();
    /*
     * Restrictions may change while the app is in the background so we need
     * to check this each time we return
     */
    updateRestrictions();
    // Update UI based on restriction changes
    updateDisplay();
}

public void onPurchaseClick(View v) {
    AlertDialog.Builder builder =
            new AlertDialog.Builder(this);
    builder.setTitle("Content Upgrades")
            .setMessage(
                    "Tap any of the following items to add them.")
            .setPositiveButton("Canvas Colors $2.99",
                    mPurchaseListener)
            .setNeutralButton("Paint Colors $2.99",
```

```java
                        mPurchaseListener)
                .setNegativeButton("Both Items $4.99",
                        mPurchaseListener).show();
    }

    private DialogInterface.OnClickListener mPurchaseListener =
            new DialogInterface.OnClickListener() {
        @Override
        public void onClick(DialogInterface dialog, int which) {
            switch (which) {
                case DialogInterface.BUTTON_POSITIVE:
                    mHasCanvasColors = true;
                    break;
                case DialogInterface.BUTTON_NEUTRAL:
                    mHasPaintColors = true;
                    break;
                case DialogInterface.BUTTON_NEGATIVE:
                    mHasCanvasColors = true;
                    mHasPaintColors = true;
                    break;
            }
            Toast.makeText(getApplicationContext(), "Thank You For Your Purchase!",
                    Toast.LENGTH_SHORT).show();
            updateDisplay();
        }
    };

    private void showSystemRestrictionsDialog(Bundle restrictions) {
        StringBuilder message = new StringBuilder();
        for (String key : restrictions.keySet()) {
            //Make sure the value of the restriction is true
            if (restrictions.getBoolean(key)) {
                message.append(RestrictionsReceiver.getNameForRestriction(key));
                message.append("\n");
            }
        }

        AlertDialog.Builder builder = new AlertDialog.Builder(this);
        builder.setTitle("System Restrictions")
            .setMessage(message.toString())
            .setPositiveButton("OK", null)
            .show();
    }

    @Override
    public void onCheckedChanged(RadioGroup group, int checkedId) {
        float width;
        switch(checkedId) {
            default:
            case R.id.option_small:
                width = 4f;
                break;
```

```
        case R.id.option_medium:
            width = 12f;
            break;
        case R.id.option_large:
            width = 25f;
            break;
        case R.id.option_xlarge:
            width = 45f;
            break;
    }
    mDrawingView.setStrokeWidth(width);
}

@Override
public void onProgressChanged(SeekBar seekBar, int progress,
        boolean fromUser) {
    mDrawingView.setStrokeWidth(progress);
}

@Override
public void onStartTrackingTouch(SeekBar seekBar) { }

@Override
public void onStopTrackingTouch(SeekBar seekBar) { }

private void updateDisplay() {
    //Show/hide purchase button
    mPurchaseButton.setVisibility(
            mHasPurchases ? View.VISIBLE : View.GONE);

    //Update age-restricted content
    mFullSlider.setVisibility(View.GONE);
    mSimpleSelector.setVisibility(View.GONE);
    switch (mMinAge) {
        case 18:
            //Full-range slider
            mFullSlider.setVisibility(View.VISIBLE);
            mFullSlider.setProgress(4);
            break;
        case 10:
            //Four options
            mSimpleSelector.setVisibility(View.VISIBLE);
            findViewById(R.id.option_medium).setVisibility(View.VISIBLE);
            findViewById(R.id.option_xlarge).setVisibility(View.VISIBLE);
            mSimpleSelector.check(R.id.option_medium);
            break;
        case 5:
            //Big/small option
            mSimpleSelector.setVisibility(View.VISIBLE);
            findViewById(R.id.option_medium).setVisibility(View.GONE);
```

```
            findViewById(R.id.option_xlarge).setVisibility(View.GONE);
            mSimpleSelector.check(R.id.option_small);
            break;
        case 3:
        default:
            //No selection
            break;
    }

    //Update display with purchases
    mDrawingView.setPaintColor(mHasPaintColors ? Color.BLUE : Color.GRAY);
    mDrawingView.setCanvasColor(mHasCanvasColors ? Color.GREEN : Color.BLACK);
}

private void updateRestrictions() {
    // Check for restrictions
    if (Build.VERSION.SDK_INT >= Build.VERSION_CODES.JELLY_BEAN_MR2) {
        UserManager manager = (UserManager) getSystemService(USER_SERVICE);
        Bundle restrictions = manager
                .getApplicationRestrictions(getPackageName());
        if (restrictions != null) {
            // Read restriction settings
            mHasPurchases = restrictions.getBoolean(
                    RestrictionsReceiver.RESTRICTION_PURCHASE, true);
            try {
                mMinAge = Integer.parseInt(restrictions.getString(
                        RestrictionsReceiver.RESTRICTION_AGERANGE, "18"));
            } catch (NumberFormatException e) {
                mMinAge = 0;
            }
        } else {
            // We have no restrictions
            mHasPurchases = true;
            mMinAge = 18;
        }
    } else {
        // We are not on a system that supports restrictions
        mHasPurchases = true;
        mMinAge = 18;
    }
}
}
```

System Feature Restrictions

When the activity is created, after verifying that we are running on a device with API Level 18 or later, we determine whether any system-level restrictions exist, by using UserManager.getUserRestrictions(). This returns a Bundle that will be empty if there are no restrictions (that is, when running as the device owner or another full user). However, if restrictions do exist, we collect descriptions about them together and show a dialog box on the screen. A unique key and a Boolean value in the Bundle describe each restriction. For each possible key, if the value is true, that restriction applies; if the restriction does not apply, the value may be false or the key may not appear in the Bundle at all. Here is a list of the possible system restrictions:

- DISALLOW_CONFIG_BLUETOOTH: This profile cannot configure Bluetooth.

- DISALLOW_CONFIG_CREDENTIALS: This profile cannot configure system user credentials.

- DISALLOW_CONFIG_WIFI: This profile cannot modify the Wi-Fi access point configuration.

- DISALLOW_INSTALL_APPS: This profile cannot install new applications.

- DISALLOW_INSTALL_UNKNOWN_SOURCES: This profile cannot enable Unknown Sources in device settings for installing applications.

- DISALLOW_MODIFY_ACCOUNTS: This profile cannot add or remove device accounts.

- DISALLOW_REMOVE_USER: This profile cannot remove other users.

- DISALLOW_SHARE_LOCATION: This profile cannot toggle location-sharing settings.

- DISALLOW_UNINSTALL_APPS: This profile cannot uninstall applications.

- DISALLOW_USB_FILE_TRANSFER: This profile cannot transfer files over USB.

The descriptions we display are pulled from a helper utility inside RestrictionsReceiver, which is a BroadcastReceiver that we have defined in Listing 6-78.

Listing 6-78. Restrictions Receiver

```java
public class RestrictionsReceiver extends BroadcastReceiver {

    public static final String RESTRICTION_PURCHASE = "purchases";
    public static final String RESTRICTION_AGERANGE = "age_range";

    private static final String[] AGES = {"3+", "5+", "10+", "18+"};
    private static final String[] AGE_VALUES = {"3", "5", "10", "18"};

    @Override
    public void onReceive(Context context, Intent intent) {
        ArrayList<RestrictionEntry> restrictions = new ArrayList<RestrictionEntry>();

        RestrictionEntry purchase = new RestrictionEntry(RESTRICTION_PURCHASE, false);
        purchase.setTitle("Content Purchases");
        purchase.setDescription("Allow purchasing of content in the application.");
        restrictions.add(purchase);

        RestrictionEntry ages =
                new RestrictionEntry(RESTRICTION_AGERANGE, AGE_VALUES[0]);
        ages.setTitle("Age Level");
        ages.setDescription("Difficulty level for application content.");
        ages.setChoiceEntries(AGES);
        ages.setChoiceValues(AGE_VALUES);
        restrictions.add(ages);
```

```java
        Bundle result = new Bundle();
        result.putParcelableArrayList(Intent.EXTRA_RESTRICTIONS_LIST, restrictions);

        setResultExtras(result);
    }

    /*
     * Utility to get readable strings from restriction keys
     */
    public static String getNameForRestriction(String key) {
        if (UserManager.DISALLOW_CONFIG_BLUETOOTH.equals(key)) {
            return "Unable to configure Bluetooth";
        }
        if (UserManager.DISALLOW_CONFIG_CREDENTIALS.equals(key)) {
            return "Unable to configure user credentials";
        }
        if (UserManager.DISALLOW_CONFIG_WIFI.equals(key)) {
            return "Unable to configure Wifi";
        }
        if (UserManager.DISALLOW_INSTALL_APPS.equals(key)) {
            return "Unable to install applications";
        }
        if (UserManager.DISALLOW_INSTALL_UNKNOWN_SOURCES.equals(key)) {
            return "Unable to enable unknown sources";
        }
        if (UserManager.DISALLOW_MODIFY_ACCOUNTS.equals(key)) {
            return "Unable to modify accounts";
        }
        if (UserManager.DISALLOW_REMOVE_USER.equals(key)) {
            return "Unable to remove users";
        }
        if (UserManager.DISALLOW_SHARE_LOCATION.equals(key)) {
            return "Unable to toggle location sharing";
        }
        if (UserManager.DISALLOW_UNINSTALL_APPS.equals(key)) {
            return "Unable to uninstall applications";
        }
        if (UserManager.DISALLOW_USB_FILE_TRANSFER.equals(key)) {
            return "Unable to transfer files";
        }

        return "Unknown Restriction: "+key;
    }
}
```

Application-Specific Restrictions

Beyond hosting our description utility method, the primary purpose of RestrictionsReceiver is to define the set of custom restrictions we want to expose to the device owner explicitly for this application. When looking for restrictions that are exposed, the framework will send an ordered broadcast intent with the android.intent.action.GET_RESTRICTION_ENTRIES action string. It is then the responsibility of any receiver that filters this action to construct a list of `RestrictionEntry` elements and return that list in the result `Bundle`.

■ **Tip**   If your restriction settings are too complex to boil down to a handful of selectable items, or if you would simply prefer to better brand that experience, you may return an intent in the receiver's result `Bundle` with `EXTRA_RESTRICTIONS_INTENT` as the key. The intent should reference an activity you would like the device settings to launch in order to set up restrictions for the application. In this case, the key/value data for the restrictions should be returned via the activity's result.

We have defined two restriction settings we want to expose: one to allow the user to make purchases from within the application, and the other to modify the application experience based on the age level of the user. The first setting is created as a Boolean type with the default value of `false` (that is, this restriction's value is `false` by default), and the second is a single selection with options for ages from 3+ to 18+. Listing 6-79 shows the `<receiver>` snippet that must be in the manifest for this receiver to be published correctly.

Listing 6-79. Manifest Snippet for Restrictions Receiver

```
<receiver android:name=".RestrictionsReceiver">
    <intent-filter>
        <action android:name="android.intent.action.GET_RESTRICTION_ENTRIES"/>
    </intent-filter>
</receiver>
```

With this application installed, now these two settings will show up for the device owner to configure when setting up a restricted user profile.

In Listing 6-74, we see that when the activity starts up, the current set of application restrictions is checked by calling `UserManager.getApplicationRestrictions()` to get another `Bundle`. This `Bundle` contains the list of key/value pairs for the settings we defined in our receiver. We use the values in this `Bundle` to update the internal state of the activity, which controls how the user interface is displayed. If we have no restrictions (for example, we are the device owner), this method will return `null`.

Because this application is shared between the device owner and the restricted profile, we have to assume that these setting values can change while the activity is in the background, so for that reason these checks are done in `onStart()` rather than `onCreate()` or some other one-shot initialization routine.

The Purchases setting controls whether the Money button in the top corner is visible. If purchases are allowed, the user can tap this button and choose from our fake storefront to get a new line color, background color, or both to spice up their drawing.

The Age Level setting controls what the user can do to update the line width. For very young children, this setting will get in the way, so we keep a fixed line width and hide all the controls. As the children move up in age, we want to give them some options, so a set of radio buttons is provided with either two or four width selections. If the minimum age is set all the way up to 18+, then we replace this UI with a full slider element for the user to choose exactly the line width they want with single-pixel precision.

To finish off the example, Listing 6-80 reveals our custom finger-drawing view.

Listing 6-80. Finger-Drawing View

```java
public class DrawingView extends View {

    private Paint mFingerPaint;
    private Path mPath;

    public DrawingView(Context context) {
        super(context);
        init();
    }

    public DrawingView(Context context, AttributeSet attrs) {
        super(context, attrs);
        init();
    }

    public DrawingView(Context context, AttributeSet attrs,
            int defStyle) {
        super(context, attrs, defStyle);
        init();
    }

    private void init() {
        //Set up the paint brush
        mFingerPaint = new Paint(Paint.ANTI_ALIAS_FLAG);
        mFingerPaint.setStyle(Style.STROKE);
        mFingerPaint.setStrokeCap(Cap.ROUND);
        mFingerPaint.setStrokeJoin(Join.ROUND);
        //Default stroke width
        mFingerPaint.setStrokeWidth(8f);
    }

    public void setPaintColor(int color) {
        mFingerPaint.setColor(color);
    }

    public void setStrokeWidth(float width) {
        mFingerPaint.setStrokeWidth(width);
    }

    public void setCanvasColor(int color) {
        setBackgroundColor(color);
    }

    @Override
    public boolean onTouchEvent(MotionEvent event) {
        switch (event.getActionMasked()) {
            case MotionEvent.ACTION_DOWN:
                mPath = new Path();
```

```
                //Start at the touch down
                mPath.moveTo(event.getX(), event.getY());
                //Re-draw
                invalidate();
                break;
            case MotionEvent.ACTION_MOVE:
                //Add all touch points between events
                for (int i=0; i < event.getHistorySize(); i++) {
                    mPath.lineTo(event.getHistoricalX(i),
                            event.getHistoricalY(i) );
                }
                //Re-draw
                invalidate();
                break;
            default:
                break;
        }
        return true;
    }

    @Override
    protected void onDraw(Canvas canvas) {
        //Draw the background
        super.onDraw(canvas);
        //Draw the paint stroke
        if (mPath != null) {
            canvas.drawPath(mPath, mFingerPaint);
        }
    }
}
```

This is a basic View implementation that tracks all touch events and converts them into a Path to be drawn. On each new touch gesture, the old Path is discarded and the initial touch point is added to a new Path. On each subsequent move event, while the finger is dragging, the Path is updated with a line that follows the trail of touch events and the view is invalidated (which triggers onDraw() again). Since we are discarding the old contents on each new gesture, the view draws only the current stroke, and the existing contents will clear when the view is touched again.

Additionally, we have added external setters to update the stroke width and color parameters from the selections made in the UI. These values are simply modifications of the Paint that is used to draw the resulting line. Figure 6-16 shows the application running on the device owner's account, with all features running unrestricted.

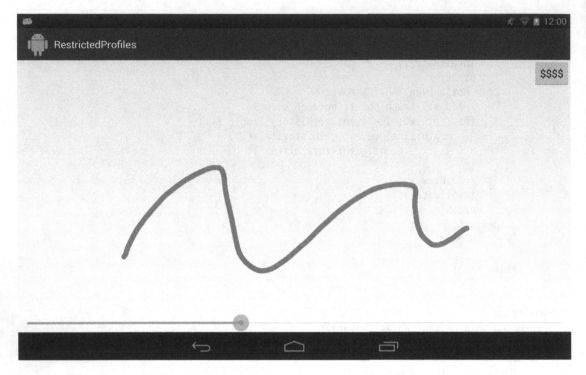

Figure 6-16. *Drawing app UI for unrestricted user*

If we create a restricted profile on this device, part of the configuration settings will be to enable our application for that profile, and then set the settings appropriately for the target user. See Figure 6-17 for an example of these settings from a Nexus 7 device.

Finally, with the restrictions set as shown in Figure 6-17, Figure 6-18 shows the same application running under the restricted profile.

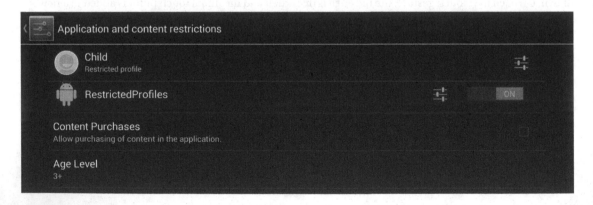

Figure 6-17. *Content settings for a restricted profile*

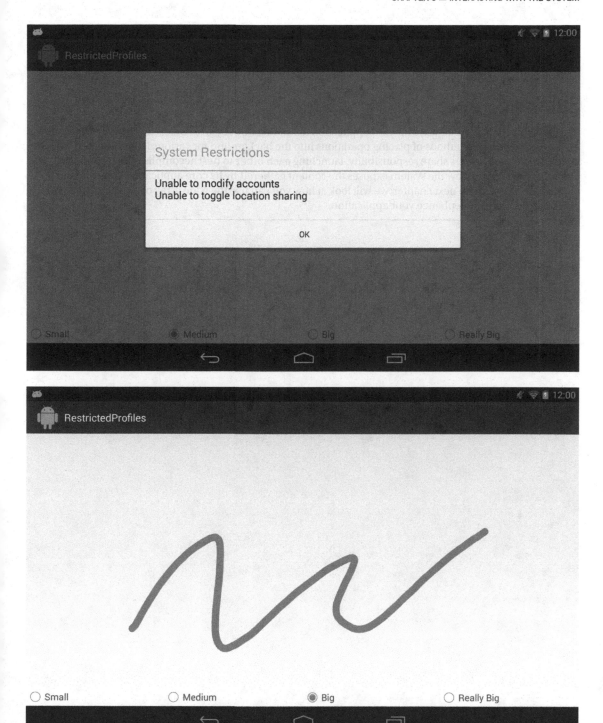

Figure 6-18. Dialog box showing system restrictions (top), application UI in restricted mode (bottom)

First we see the dialog box displayed with any system-level restrictions, followed by the main application UI. Notice in this case that the Purchase button is no longer visible and the stroke width control has been replaced with simpler choices.

Summary

In this chapter, you learned ways for your application to interact directly with the Android operating system. We discussed several methods of placing operations into the background for various lengths of time. You learned how applications share responsibility, launching each other to best accomplish the task at hand. Finally, we presented how the system exposes the content gathered by its core application suite for your application's use. In the next chapter, we will look at how you can use the wide array of publicly available Java libraries to further enhance your application.

CHAPTER 7

■ ■ ■

Graphics and Drawing

Android's UI toolkit is squarely focused on flexibility, and the ability to create content that flawlessly scales across all possible device types. We've already looked at how the view system helps developers adapt to this requirement. In this chapter, we will discuss additional techniques for enhancing your application's user interface using Android's extensible graphics object, the drawable. You will see how we can leverage drawables to make flexible and animated graphic elements that can be associated with any view. It's all about doing more work with fewer image resources in your application.

7-1. Creating Drawables as Backgrounds

Problem

Your application needs to create background images that can scale and fill any view space, and you don't want to waste time generating lots of image files.

Solution

(API Level 1)

Use Android's most powerful implementation of the XML resources system: creating shape drawables. When you are able to do so, creating these views as an XML resource makes sense because they are inherently scalable, and they will fit themselves to the bounds of the view when set as a background.

Shape Drawables are XML files with `<shape>` as the root element, which has a single attribute android:shape that can take the values rectangle, oval, line or ring. This elemnt can have one or several of the following child elements to further define the drawable;

- Corner: Defines rounded corners

- Gradient: Defines a gradient

- Padding: Adds a padding to the shape

- Solid: Defines a solid color filling the shape

- Stroke: Define the type, size and color of the stroke (outline) of the shape

Each of these elements has additional attributes that you can find in the official Android documentation. Android Studio will also provide a very convenient code completion when you edit these files by hand.

© Dave Smith and Erik Hellman 2016
D. Smith and E. Hellman, *Android Recipes*, DOI 10.1007/978-1-4842-2259-1_7

How It Works

Creating static background images for views can be tricky, given that the image must often be created in multiple sizes to display properly on all devices. This issue is compounded if it is expected that the size of the view may dynamically change based on its contents.

To avoid this problem, we create an XML file in res/drawable to describe a shape that we can apply as the android:background attribute of any view.

Gradient ListView Row

Our first example for this technique will be to create a gradient rectangle that is suitable to be applied as the background of individual rows inside a ListView. The XML for this shape is defined in Listing 7-1.

Listing 7-1. res/drawable/backgradient.xml

```
<?xml version="1.0" encoding="utf-8"?>
<shape xmlns:android="http://schemas.android.com/apk/res/android"
    android:shape="rectangle">
    <gradient
        android:startColor="#EFEFEF"
        android:endColor="#989898"
        android:type="linear"
        android:angle="270"
    />
</shape>
```

Here we chose a linear gradient between two shades of gray, moving from top to bottom. If we wanted to add a third color to the gradient, we would add an android:middleColor attribute to the <gradient> tag.

Now this drawable can be referenced by any view or layout used to create the custom items of your ListView. The drawable would be added as the background by including the attribute android:background="@drawable/backgradient" to the view's XML or by calling View.setBackgroundResource(R.drawable.backgradient) in Java code.

■ **Advanced tip**   The limit on colors in XML is three, but the constructor for GradientDrawable takes an int[] parameter for colors, and you may pass as many as you like.

When we apply this drawable as the background to rows in a ListView, the result will be similar to Figure 7-1.

Figure 7-1. *Gradient drawable as a row background*

Rounded View Group

Another popular use of XML drawables is to create a background for a layout that visually groups a handful of widgets together. For style, rounded corners and a thin border are often applied as well. This shape defined in XML would look like Listing 7-2.

Listing 7-2. res/drawable/roundback.xml

```xml
<?xml version="1.0" encoding="utf-8"?>
<shape xmlns:android="http://schemas.android.com/apk/res/android"
    android:shape="rectangle">
    <solid
        android:color="#FFF"
    />
    <corners
        android:radius="10dip"
    />
    <stroke
        android:width="5dip"
        android:color="#555"
    />
</shape>
```

587

In this case, we chose white for the fill color and dark gray for the border stroke. As mentioned in the previous example, this drawable can be referenced by any view or layout as the background by including the attribute `android:background="@drawable/roundback"` to the view's XML or by calling `View.setBackgroundResource(R.drawable.roundback)` in Java code.

When applied as the background to a view, the result is shown in Figure 7-2.

Figure 7-2. *Rounded rectangle with border as view background*

Drawable Patterns

The next category of drawables we are going to look at is patterns. Using XML, we can define some rules around which a smaller image should be stepped and repeated to make a pattern. This can be a great way to make full-screen background images that don't require a large `Bitmap` to be loaded into memory.

Applications can create a pattern by setting the `tileMode` attribute on a `<bitmap>` element to one of the following values:

- `Clamp`: The source bitmap will have the pixels along its edges replicated.

- `Repeat`: The source bitmap will be stepped and repeated in both directions.

- `Mirror`: The source bitmap will be stepped and repeated, alternating between normal and flipped images on each iteration and along each axis.

Figure 7-3 illustrates two small square images that will become the source for our patterns.

Figure 7-3. *Source bitmaps for patterns*

Listings 7-3 and 7-4 show examples of how to define an XML pattern as a background.

Listing 7-3. res/drawable/pattern_checker.xml

```
<?xml version="1.0" encoding="utf-8"?>
<bitmap xmlns:android="http://schemas.android.com/apk/res/android"
    android:src="@drawable/checkers"
    android:tileMode="repeat" />
```

Listing 7-4. res/drawable/pattern_stripes.xml

```
<?xml version="1.0" encoding="utf-8"?>
<bitmap xmlns:android="http://schemas.android.com/apk/res/android"
    android:src="@drawable/stripes"
    android:tileMode="mirror" />
```

■ **Tip**   Patterns can be made only with a `bitmap` that has intrinsic bounds, such as external images.

Figure 7-4 reveals the result of applying each of these patterns as view backgrounds.

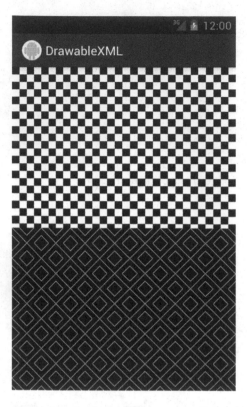

Figure 7-4. Background patterns

You can see that the checkerboard image is repeated unmodified, while the stripe pattern image is reflected both horizontally and vertically as it is repeated across the screen, creating the diamond effect you see in Figure 7-4.

Nine-Patch Images

The NinePatchDrawable is one of Android's greatest strengths when it comes to designing user interfaces that are flexible across devices. The nine-patch is a special image that is designed to stretch in only certain areas by designating sections of the image that are stretchable and areas that are not. In fact, the image type gets its name from the nine stretch zones that are created when an image is mapped (more on this in a moment).

Let's take a look at an example to better understand how this works. Figure 7-5 shows two images; the image on the left is the original, and the image on the right has been converted into a nine-patch.

Figure 7-5. Speech bubble source image, speech_background.png (left), and nine-patch conversion, speech_ background.9.png (right)

Notice the black markings on each side of the image on the right. A valid nine-patch image file is simply a PNG image in which the outer 1 pixel contains only either black or transparent pixels. The black pixels on each side define something about how the image will stretch and wrap the content inside:

- *Left side*: Black pixels here define areas where the image should stretch vertically. The pixels in these areas will be stepped and repeated to accomplish the stretch. The example image in Figure 7-5 has one of these areas.

- *Top side*: Black pixels here define areas where the image should stretch horizontally. The pixels in these areas will be stepped and repeated to accomplish the stretch. The example image in Figure 7-5 has two of these areas.

- *Right side*: Black pixels here define the vertical content area, which is the area where the view's content will display. In effect, it is defining the top and bottom padding values, but inherent to the background image.

- *Bottom side*: Black pixels here define the horizontal content area, which is the area where the view's content will display. In effect, it is defining the left and right padding values, but inherent to the background image. This must contain a single line of solid pixels defining the area.

This image was created using the draw9patch tool that is part of the Android SDK. To better visualize how these markings affect the resulting image, let's take a look at the image when loaded into this tool. See Figure 7-6.

Figure 7-6. Speech bubble inside draw9patch

You can now start to see where the nine-patch gets its name. The areas of the image that are not highlighted will not be stretched. The highlighted areas of each image will stretch in a single direction (either horizontal or vertical, based on their orientation), and the areas where the highlights intersect will stretch in both directions. In an image with the minimum of one stretchable zone in each direction, this would create nine individual mapped zones in the image: four corners that aren't modified, four middle areas that stretch once, and the single center section that stretches twice.

There isn't any special code required to create a NinePatchDrawable and use it as a background; the image file just needs to be named with the special .9.png extension so Android can package it correctly. Listing 7-5 shows how you might set this image as a background, and Figure 7-7 reveals what this image looks like when set as the background for a TextView.

Listing 7-5. res/layout/patch.xml

```xml
<?xml version="1.0" encoding="utf-8"?>
<RelativeLayout
    xmlns:android="http://schemas.android.com/apk/res/android"
    android:layout_width="match_parent"
    android:layout_height="match_parent" >
    <TextView
        android:layout_width="match_parent"
        android:layout_height="wrap_content"
        android:layout_centerVertical="true"
        android:gravity="center"
        android:text="This is a text speech bubble"
        android:background="@drawable/speech_background"/>
</RelativeLayout>
```

Figure 7-7. *Speech bubble as TextView background*

Note how the two 3-pixel-wide horizontal stretch zones evenly distributed the excess space between them, centering the origin point of the speech bubble. If you would like to create an offset between two stretch points, this can be done by varying their distance from the image center or by varying their size. If one zone is 3 pixels wide and the other is only 1 pixel wide, the wider zone will take up three times as much space when repeated.

7-2. Creating Custom State Drawables

Problem

You want to customize an element such as a Button or CheckBox that has multiple states (default, pressed, selected, and so on).

Solution

(API Level 1)

Create a StateListDrawable to apply to the element. Whether you have defined your drawable graphics yourself in XML or you are using images, Android provides the means via another XML element, the <selector>, to create a single reference to multiple images and the conditions under which they should be visible.

(API Level 21)

Use AnimatedStateListDrawable and StateListAnimator to provide animations along with the state transitions defined for the attached view. You can also make use of RippleDrawable at this API level to provide animated touch feedback on views as a growing ripple effect.

How It Works

Let's take a look at an example state-list drawable and then discuss its parts:

```xml
<?xml version="1.0" encoding="utf-8"?>
<selector
    xmlns:android="http://schemas.android.com/apk/res/android">
    <item android:state_enabled="false"
        android:drawable="@drawable/disabled" />
    <item android:state_pressed="true"
        android:drawable="@drawable/selected" />
    <item android:state_focused="true"
        android:drawable="@drawable/selected" />
    <!-- Default State -->
    <item android:drawable="@drawable/default" />
</selector>
```

■ **Note** The <selector> is order specific. Android will return the drawable of the first state it matches completely as it traverses the list. Bear this in mind when determining which state attributes to apply to each item.

Each item in the list identifies the state(s) that must be in effect for the referenced drawable to be the one chosen. Multiple state parameters can be added for one item if multiple state values need to be matched. Android will traverse the list and pick the first state that matches all criteria of the current view the drawable is attached to. For this reason, it is considered good practice to put your normal, or default, state at the bottom of the list with no criteria attached.

Here is a list of the most commonly useful state attributes. All of these are Boolean values:

- `state_enabled`: Value the view would return from `isEnabled()`

- `state_pressed`: View is pressed by the user on the touch screen

- `state_focused`: View has focus

- `state_selected`: View is selected by the user using keys or a D-pad

- `state_checked`: Value a checkable view would return from `isChecked()`

Now let's look at how to apply these state-list drawables to different views.

Button and Other Clickable Widgets

Widgets such as `Button` are designed to have their background drawable change when the view moves through the preceding states. As such, the `android:background` attribute in XML or the `View.setBackgroundDrawable()` method are the proper methods for attaching the state list. Listing 7-6 is an example with a file defined in `res/drawable/` called `background_button.xml`.

Listing 7-6. `res/drawable/background_button.xml`

```xml
<?xml version="1.0" encoding="utf-8"?>
<selector
    xmlns:android="http://schemas.android.com/apk/res/android">
    <item android:state_enabled="false"
        android:drawable="@drawable/button_disabled" />
    <item android:state_pressed="true"
        android:drawable="@drawable/button_selected" />
    <item android:state_focused="true"
        android:drawable="@drawable/button_selected" />
    <!-- Default State -->
    <item android:drawable="@drawable/button_default" />
</selector>
```

The three @drawable resources listed here are images in the project that the selector is meant to switch between. As we mentioned in the previous section, the last item will be returned as the default if no other items include matching states to the current view; therefore, we do not need to include a state to match on that item. Attaching this to a view defined in XML looks like the following:

```xml
<Button
    android:layout_width="wrap_content"
    android:layout_height="wrap_content"
    android:text="My Button"
    android:background="@drawable/background_button" />
```

CheckBox and Other Checkable Widgets

Many of the widgets that implement the Checkable interface, such as CheckBox and other subclasses of CompoundButton, have a slightly different mechanism for changing their state. In these cases, the background is not associated with the state, and customizing the drawable to represent the "checked" states is done through another attribute called the button. In XML, this is the android:button attribute, and in code the CompoundButton.setButtonDrawable() method should do the trick.

Listing 7-7 is an example with a file defined in res/drawable/ called background_checkable.xml. Again, the @drawable resources listed are meant to reference images in the project to be switched.

Listing 7-7. res/drawable/background_checkable.xml

```xml
<?xml version="1.0" encoding="utf-8"?>
<selector
    xmlns:android="http://schemas.android.com/apk/res/android">
    <item android:state_enabled="false"
        android:drawable="@drawable/check_disabled" />
    <!-- Due to top-down rules, pressed will always win over checked -->
    <item android:state_pressed="true"
        android:drawable="@drawable/check_pressed" />
    <item android:state_checked="true"
        android:drawable="@drawable/check_checked" />
    <!-- Default State -->
    <item android:drawable="@drawable/check_default" />
</selector>
```

And here they are attached to a CheckBox in XML:

```xml
<CheckBox
    android:layout_width="wrap_content"
    android:layout_height="wrap_content"
    android:button="@drawable/background_checkable" />
```

Animated State Transitions

(API Level 21)

Let's dress up our previous button example with some animated touch feedback. Listing 7-8 defines an updated background XML using a <ripple> element (which constructs a RippleDrawable).

Listing 7-8. res/drawable-v21/background_button.xml

```xml
<?xml version="1.0" encoding="utf-8"?>
<ripple xmlns:android="http://schemas.android.com/apk/res/android"
    android:color="#0CC">
    <!-- Default drawable to display -->
    <item android:drawable="@drawable/button_default"/>

    <!-- Clipping mask for the ripple to match default -->
    <item
        android:id="@android:id/mask"
        android:drawable="@drawable/button_default"/>
</ripple>
```

RippleDrawable takes multiple child drawables as layers and draws them all in order. We have included two layers in this example. The first is a static drawable that references the same default image as we had previously. This is what the user will see when the button is in the default state.

By default, RippleDrawable draws an animated circular ripple that emanates from the touch point when the containing view is pressed (this is also known as the ripple's hotspot). That circle is not clipped by the view's bounds (or any other bounds) unless a mask is provided. By adding the android:id/mask designation to the second <item> layer, we are telling the framework this drawable represents the bounds we would like to use to clip the ripple effect. The item itself is never drawn.

The color we wish to use for the ripple effect is applied using the android:color attribute on the root element. The framework will divide the given color into a slightly transparent version used to immediately highlight the view, and an opaque overlay that will animate. The animation rate is dependent on the touch feedback: quickly for a tap event, slowly for a long-press event.

Listing 7-9 adds an additional layer of feedback using a StateListAnimator. This animator will cause the button to shrink in size slightly when the button is pressed.

Listing 7-9. res/animator/button_press.xml

```xml
<?xml version="1.0" encoding="utf-8"?>
<selector xmlns:android="http://schemas.android.com/apk/res/android">
    <item android:state_enabled="true" android:state_pressed="true">
        <set android:ordering="together">
            <objectAnimator
                android:duration="@android:integer/config_shortAnimTime"
                android:propertyName="scaleX"
                android:valueTo="0.8"
                android:valueType="floatType" />
            <objectAnimator
                android:duration="@android:integer/config_shortAnimTime"
                android:propertyName="scaleY"
                android:valueTo="0.8"
                android:valueType="floatType" />
        </set>
    </item>
    <!-- Default State -->
    <item>
        <set android:ordering="together">
            <objectAnimator
                android:duration="@android:integer/config_shortAnimTime"
                android:propertyName="scaleX"
                android:valueTo="1.0"
                android:valueType="floatType" />
            <objectAnimator
                android:duration="@android:integer/config_shortAnimTime"
                android:propertyName="scaleY"
                android:valueTo="1.0"
                android:valueType="floatType" />
        </set>
    </item>
</selector>
```

This XML structure uses the same <selector> we've already used, but in the res/animator directory this represents a state-list collection of animator instances instead of drawables. In this case, each state is a pair of ObjectAnimator instances meant to scale the view in both major axes simultaneously. Applying this pair of state transitions to our button view now looks like this:

```
<Button
    android:layout_width="wrap_content"
    android:layout_height="wrap_content"
    android:text="My Button"
    android:background="@drawable/background_button"
    android:stateListAnimator="@animator/button_press" />
```

We can also spice up our check box with an animated transition. In Listing 7-10, we have updated the checkable drawable to an AnimatedStateListDrawable (via the <animated-selector> XML tag) that sequences a series of keyframe images as a transition between the default and checked states.

Listing 7-10. res/drawable-v21/background_checkable.xml

```
<?xml version="1.0" encoding="utf-8"?>
<animated-selector
    xmlns:android="http://schemas.android.com/apk/res/android">
    <item android:state_enabled="false"
        android:drawable="@drawable/check_disabled" />
    <item android:id="@+id/state_checked"
        android:state_checked="true"
        android:drawable="@drawable/check_checked" />
    <!-- Default State -->
    <item android:id="@+id/state_default"
        android:drawable="@drawable/check_default" />

    <!--
        These transitions support only AnimationDrawable, AnimatedVectorDrawable,
        or another Animatable as child elements.
    -->
    <transition android:fromId="@id/state_default" android:toId="@id/state_checked">
        <animation-list>
            <item android:duration="15" android:drawable="@drawable/check_default" />
            <item android:duration="15" android:drawable="@drawable/check_to_checked_01" />
            <item android:duration="15" android:drawable="@drawable/check_to_checked_02" />
            <item android:duration="15" android:drawable="@drawable/check_to_checked_03" />
            <item android:duration="15" android:drawable="@drawable/check_to_checked_04" />
            <item android:duration="15" android:drawable="@drawable/check_to_checked_05" />
            <item android:duration="15" android:drawable="@drawable/check_to_checked_06" />
            <item android:duration="15" android:drawable="@drawable/check_to_checked_07" />
            <item android:duration="15" android:drawable="@drawable/check_to_checked_08" />
            <item android:duration="15" android:drawable="@drawable/check_checked" />
        </animation-list>
    </transition>

</animated-selector>
```

The initial part of this file remains the same, with each item declaring the drawable that should be used to associate with each view state. Notice, however, that we've given two of these states unique IDs. This allows us to separately declare an animation that should be used as the visual transition between those two states. This animation must be wrapped in a <transition> element, and the following types are supported:

- AnimationDrawable (<animation-list> in XML): This is a keyframe animation that sequences between each of the elements it contains.

- AnimatedVectorDrawable (<animated-vector> in XML): A morphing animation applied to a vector path collection (discussed in more detail later in this chapter).

■ **Tip** When a <transition> is applied, the android:drawable attached to the <item> represents the *final* drawable to show after the animation is complete.

We have defined a single transition to move from the default state (via fromId) to the checked state (via toId) using the provided keyframes. By default, the framework will actually run this same transition in reverse when moving between the same states in the opposite direction, so we get another transition for free! However, if it is preferred to control different state transitions (like the reverse) using a different animation, you can define as many transitions within the XML as you like.

7-3. Applying Masks to Images

Problem

You need to apply one image or shape as a clipping mask to define the visible boundaries of a second image in your application.

Solution

(API Level 1)

Using 2D graphics and a PorterDuffXferMode, you can apply any arbitrary mask (in the form of another bitmap) to a bitmap image. The basic steps to this recipe are as follows:

1. Create a mutable Bitmap instance (blank), and a Canvas to draw into it.

2. Draw the mask pattern onto the Canvas first.

3. Apply a PorterDuffXferMode to the Paint.

4. Draw the source image on the Canvas using the transfer mode.

The key ingredient is the PorterDuffXferMode, which considers the current state of both the source and destination objects during a paint operation. The destination is the existing Canvas data, and the source is the graphic data being applied in the current operation.

There are many mode parameters that can be attached to this, which create varying effects on the result, but for masking we are interested in using the PorterDuff.Mode.SRC_IN mode. This mode will draw only at locations where the source and destination overlap, and the pixels drawn will be from the source; in other words, the source is clipped by the bounds of the destination.

The same effect can also be accomplished using the image as a BitmapShader to draw the content into another element. In this way, we are treating the image pixels as the "color" to be used to draw whatever shape or element we have that makes up the image mask. We will explore both options in this recipe.

How It Works

Rounded Corner Bitmap

One extremely common use of image masking is to apply rounded corners to a bitmap image before displaying it. For this example, Figure 7-8 is the original image we will be masking.

Figure 7-8. *Original source image*

To illustrate this, we have created a custom view that receives an image and draws it as a rounded rectangle to the provided Canvas with a BitmapShader. This view also manages the sizing math necessary to center the image inside the custom view.

Listings 7-11 and 7-12 show our custom view and its use inside an activity.

Listing 7-11. View Applying a Rounded Rectangle Mask to a Bitmap

```
public class RoundedCornerImageView extends View {

    private Bitmap mImage;
    private Paint mBitmapPaint;

    private RectF mBounds;
    private float mRadius = 25.0f;

    public RoundedCornerImageView(Context context) {
        super(context);
        init();
    }
```

```java
    public RoundedCornerImageView(Context context,
            AttributeSet attrs) {
        super(context, attrs);
        init();
    }

    public RoundedCornerImageView(Context context,
            AttributeSet attrs, int defStyle) {
        super(context, attrs, defStyle);
        init();
    }

    private void init() {
        //Create image paint
        mBitmapPaint = new Paint(Paint.ANTI_ALIAS_FLAG);
        //Create rect for drawing bounds
        mBounds = new RectF();
    }

    @Override
    protected void onMeasure(int widthMeasureSpec,
            int heightMeasureSpec) {
        int height, width;
        height = width = 0;

        //Requested size is the image content size
        int imageHeight, imageWidth;
        if (mImage == null) {
            imageHeight = imageWidth = 0;
        } else {
            imageHeight = mImage.getHeight();
            imageWidth = mImage.getWidth();
        }
        //Get the best measurement and set it on the view
        width = getMeasurement(widthMeasureSpec, imageWidth);
        height = getMeasurement(heightMeasureSpec, imageHeight);

        setMeasuredDimension(width, height);
    }

    /*
     * Helper method to measure width and height
     */
    private int getMeasurement(int measureSpec, int contentSize) {
        int specSize = MeasureSpec.getSize(measureSpec);
        switch (MeasureSpec.getMode(measureSpec)) {
            case MeasureSpec.AT_MOST:
                return Math.min(specSize, contentSize);
            case MeasureSpec.UNSPECIFIED:
                return contentSize;
```

```java
        case MeasureSpec.EXACTLY:
            return specSize;
        default:
            return 0;
    }
}


@Override
protected void onSizeChanged(int w, int h,
        int oldw, int oldh) {
    if (w != oldw || h != oldh) {
        //We want to center the image, so we offset our
        //values whenever the view changes size
        int imageWidth, imageHeight;
        if (mImage == null) {
            imageWidth = imageHeight = 0;
        } else {
            imageWidth = mImage.getWidth();
            imageHeight = mImage.getHeight();
        }
        int left = (w - imageWidth) / 2;
        int top = (h - imageHeight) / 2;
        //Set the bounds to offset the rounded rectangle
        mBounds.set(left, top, left+imageWidth,
                top+imageHeight);
        //Offset the shader to draw the Bitmap inside the rect
        // Without this, the bitmap will be at 0,0 in the view
        if (mBitmapPaint.getShader() != null) {
            Matrix m = new Matrix();
            m.setTranslate(left, top);
            mBitmapPaint.getShader().setLocalMatrix(m);
        }
    }
}


public void setImage(Bitmap bitmap) {
    if (mImage != bitmap) {
        mImage = bitmap;
        if (mImage != null) {
            BitmapShader shader = new BitmapShader(mImage,
                    TileMode.CLAMP, TileMode.CLAMP);
            mBitmapPaint.setShader(shader);
        } else {
            mBitmapPaint.setShader(null);
        }
        requestLayout();
    }
}
```

```
    @Override
    protected void onDraw(Canvas canvas) {
        //Let the view draw backgrounds, etc.
        super.onDraw(canvas);
        //Draw the image with the calculated values
        if (mBitmapPaint != null) {
            canvas.drawRoundRect(mBounds, mRadius, mRadius,
                    mBitmapPaint);
        }
    }
}
```

Listing 7-12. Activity Displaying RoundedCornerImageView

```
public class ShaderActivity extends Activity {

    @Override
    protected void onCreate(Bundle savedInstanceState) {
        super.onCreate(savedInstanceState);
        RoundedCornerImageView iv =
                new RoundedCornerImageView(this);
        Bitmap source = BitmapFactory.decodeResource(
                getResources(), R.drawable.dog);

        iv.setImage(source);
        setContentView(iv);
    }
}
```

Inside our custom view, when a new image is passed in via setImage(), we create a new BitmapShader to wrap the image pixels and set it on the paintbrush we will use to draw. Later, when the view is measured and laid out, we will get a call in onSizeChanged() when the view has a size; at this point, we measure the bounds the image needs to have to be centered inside the view. We must also offset the shader by using a Matrix. Otherwise, the rounded rectangle mask will draw in the center, but our image will still be in the top-left corner of the view.

Now, when the view is ready to draw, we can simply call drawRoundRect() on our Canvas with the bounds we calculated and the paintbrush configured earlier. This draws a rounded rectangle in the view, but uses the pixels from the bitmap to color, or shade, the shape. The result of these efforts is shown in Figure 7-9.

Figure 7-9. *Image with a rounded rectangle mask applied*

Arbitrary Mask Image

Let's look at an example that's a little more interesting. Here we take two images: the source image and an image representing the mask we want to apply (in this case, an upside-down triangle). See Figure 7-10.

Figure 7-10. *Original source image (left) and arbitrary mask image to apply (right)*

The chosen mask image does not have to conform to the style chosen here, with black pixels for the mask and transparent everywhere else. However, it is the best choice to guarantee that the system draws the mask exactly as you expect it to be.

We will first draw the triangle image on the Canvas, and this will serve as our mask for the image. Then, applying the PorterDuff.Mode.SRC_IN transform as we paint the source image into the same Canvas, the result will be the source image with rounded corners.

This is because the SRC_IN transfer mode tells the paint object to paint pixels only on the Canvas locations where the source and destination (the triangle we already drew) overlap, and the pixels that are drawn come from the source. Listing 7-13 is the simple activity code to mask the image and display it in a view.

Listing 7-13. Activity Applying an Arbitrary Mask to a Bitmap

```
public class MaskActivity extends Activity {

    @Override
    public void onCreate(Bundle savedInstanceState) {
        super.onCreate(savedInstanceState);
        ImageView iv = new ImageView(this);
        iv.setScaleType(ImageView.ScaleType.CENTER);

        //Create and load images (immutable, typically)
        Bitmap source = BitmapFactory.decodeResource(getResources(), R.drawable.dog);
        Bitmap mask = BitmapFactory.decodeResource(getResources(), R.drawable.triangle);

        //Create a *mutable* location, and a canvas to draw into it
        final Bitmap result =
                Bitmap.createBitmap(source.getWidth(), source.getHeight(), Config.
                ARGB_8888);
        Canvas canvas = new Canvas(result);
        Paint paint = new Paint(Paint.ANTI_ALIAS_FLAG);
        paint.setColor(Color.BLACK);

        canvas.drawBitmap(mask, 0, 0, paint);
        paint.setXfermode(new PorterDuffXfermode(Mode.SRC_IN));
        canvas.drawBitmap(source, 0, 0, paint);
        paint.setXfermode(null);

        iv.setImageBitmap(result);
        setContentView(iv);
    }
}
```

The result looks something like Figure 7-11.

Figure 7-11. *Image with a mask applied*

View Outlines

(API Level 21)

On devices running Android 5.0 and later, the framework supports dynamic shadows to indicate view elevation (via the elevation and translationZ properties). In order for this feature to work, the framework must understand the visual boundaries of your view. In simple cases, this can be handled internally, but if we apply an arbitrary mask, we must also indicate where the shadowing should occur with a matching ViewOutlineProvider. Listing 7-14 indicates a modified version of the image mask that also provides an appropriate outline for shadows.

Listing 7-14. Mask Activity with View Outline

```
public class MaskActivity extends Activity {

    @Override
    public void onCreate(Bundle savedInstanceState) {
        super.onCreate(savedInstanceState);
        ImageView iv = new ImageView(this);
        iv.setScaleType(ImageView.ScaleType.CENTER);
```

```
//Create and load images (immutable, typically)
Bitmap source = BitmapFactory.decodeResource(getResources(), R.drawable.dog);
Bitmap mask = BitmapFactory.decodeResource(getResources(), R.drawable.triangle);

//Create a *mutable* location, and a canvas to draw into it
final Bitmap result =
        Bitmap.createBitmap(source.getWidth(), source.getHeight(), Config.
        ARGB_8888);
Canvas canvas = new Canvas(result);
Paint paint = new Paint(Paint.ANTI_ALIAS_FLAG);
paint.setColor(Color.BLACK);

canvas.drawBitmap(mask, 0, 0, paint);
paint.setXfermode(new PorterDuffXfermode(Mode.SRC_IN));
canvas.drawBitmap(source, 0, 0, paint);
paint.setXfermode(null);

iv.setImageBitmap(result);
if (Build.VERSION.SDK_INT >= Build.VERSION_CODES.LOLLIPOP) {
    //Elevate the view to make a visible shadow
    iv.setElevation(32f);
    //Draw an outline that matches the mask to provide the proper shadow
    iv.setOutlineProvider(new ViewOutlineProvider() {
        @Override
        public void getOutline(View view, Outline outline) {
            int x = (view.getWidth() - result.getWidth()) / 2;
            int y = (view.getHeight() - result.getHeight()) / 2;

            Path path = new Path();
            path.moveTo(x, y);
            path.lineTo(x+result.getWidth(), y);
            path.lineTo(x+result.getWidth()/2, y+result.getHeight());
            path.lineTo(x, y);
            path.close();

            outline.setConvexPath(path);
        }
    });
}
setContentView(iv);
    }
}
```

The ViewOutlineProvider has one required method, getOutline(). This method is called any time the outline needs to be updated because of a size or configuration change. For efficiency, we are passed an Outline instance within which to fill the appropriate shape. Since our triangle is an irregular outline shape, we must construct a Path that represents the same triangle and apply it using setConvexPath().

Notice we have also set a static elevation value in the new example. This is so the shadowing effects can be seen and verified, as in Figure 7-12.

Figure 7-12. Image mask with outline shadow

If the outline is simple enough, Android can also use it as a clipping mask for the view. To indicate that a view should use its outline as a clipping mask, simply call setClipToOutline(true). Listing 7-15 uses this tactic to clip our image with a circular mask.

■ **Note**   Android currently supports clipping with only rectangular, circular, and rounded rectangle outlines. The triangle outline we just made, for example, cannot be used as a clip.

Listing 7-15. Activity Applying Circular Outline Clip to a View

```java
public class OutlineActivity extends Activity {

    @Override
    protected void onCreate(Bundle savedInstanceState) {
        super.onCreate(savedInstanceState);
        ImageView iv = new ImageView(this);
        iv.setScaleType(ImageView.ScaleType.CENTER);

        //Elevate the view to make a visible shadow
        iv.setElevation(32f);

        iv.setImageResource(R.drawable.dog);

        //Tell the view to use its outline as a clipping mask
        iv.setClipToOutline(true);

        //Provide the circular view outline for clipping and shadows
        iv.setOutlineProvider(new ViewOutlineProvider() {
            @Override
            public void getOutline(View view, Outline outline) {
                ImageView iv = (ImageView) view;
                int radius = iv.getDrawable().getIntrinsicHeight() / 2;
                int centerX = (view.getRight() - view.getLeft()) / 2;
                int centerY = (view.getBottom() - view.getTop()) / 2;

                outline.setOval(centerX - radius,
                        centerY - radius,
                        centerX + radius,
                        centerY + radius);
            }
        });

        setContentView(iv);
    }
}
```

This outline is much more straightforward, producing a centered circle mask surrounding the centered image, as we can see in Figure 7-13.

Figure 7-13. Image with clipping outline

7-4. Drawing over View Content

Problem

You want to display content on top of what is currently visible, but without inserting or otherwise modifying the existing view hierarchy.

Solution

(API Level 1)

Place your content into a PopupWindow, which is a new temporary window in which you can place views that will be displayed on top of the current activity window. PopupWindow can be shown anywhere onscreen, either by providing an explicit location or by providing an existing view that the PopupWindow should be anchored to.

(API Level 18)

You may also use the newer ViewOverlay to draw content on top of your views. ViewOverlay allows you to add any number of Drawable objects to a private layer managed by the parent view. Those objects will be drawn on top of the corresponding view as long as their bounds are within the bounds of the parent.

How It Works

In order to draw content on top of our view hierarchy, we first need to create the content to display. Listing 7-16 constructs a simple group of views that will be the content of our PopupWindow.

Listing 7-16. res/layout/popup.xml

```xml
<?xml version="1.0" encoding="utf-8"?>
<LinearLayout
    xmlns:android="http://schemas.android.com/apk/res/android"
    android:layout_width="wrap_content"
    android:layout_height="wrap_content"
    android:orientation="vertical">
    <TextView
        android:layout_width="wrap_content"
        android:layout_height="wrap_content"
        android:layout_gravity="center_horizontal"
        android:text="This is a PopupWindow" />
    <EditText
        android:layout_width="250dp"
        android:layout_height="wrap_content"
        android:layout_gravity="center_horizontal" />
    <Button
        android:layout_width="wrap_content"
        android:layout_height="wrap_content"
        android:layout_gravity="center_horizontal"
        android:text="Close" />
</LinearLayout>
```

When we display this content in a pop-up anchored to a view, by default the PopupWindow will display just below the view, left-aligned. However, if there is not enough space below the view to display the PopupWindow, it will be displayed above the anchor view instead. To make the pop-up visually distinct in both cases, we can provide a custom background drawable that switches on the android:state_above_anchor attribute. Listing 7-17 and Figure 7-14 illustrate the custom drawables we will be using for this example.

Listing 7-17. res/drawable/popup_background.xml

```xml
<?xml version="1.0" encoding="utf-8"?>
<selector
    xmlns:android="http://schemas.android.com/apk/res/android" >
    <item android:state_above_anchor="true"
        android:drawable="@drawable/speech_background_top" />
    <!-- Default State -->
    <item
        android:drawable="@drawable/speech_background_bottom" />
</selector>
```

Figure 7-14. *Background nine-patch drawables*

You may recognize these background images from the speech bubble nine-patch example in Recipe 7-1. We've slightly modified the stretch zones so that the extension point is always on the same side.

Listings 7-18 and 7-19 illustrate an example activity and layout that construct and display a PopupWindow in response to a button click. In this example, the PopupWindow will be shown anchored to the button that was clicked.

Listing 7-18. res/layout/activity_main.xml

```xml
<?xml version="1.0" encoding="utf-8"?>
<FrameLayout
    xmlns:android="http://schemas.android.com/apk/res/android"
    android:layout_width="match_parent"
    android:layout_height="match_parent">
    <Button
        android:id="@+id/button"
        android:layout_width="match_parent"
        android:layout_height="wrap_content"
        android:text="Show PopupWindow"
        android:onClick="onShowWindowClick" />
    <Button
        android:layout_width="match_parent"
        android:layout_height="wrap_content"
        android:layout_gravity="bottom"
        android:text="Show PopupWindow"
        android:onClick="onShowWindowClick" />
</FrameLayout>
```

Listing 7-19. Activity Displaying a PopupWindow

```java
public class MainActivity extends Activity
        implements View.OnTouchListener {
    private PopupWindow mOverlay;

    @Override
    protected void onCreate(Bundle savedInstanceState) {
        super.onCreate(savedInstanceState);
        setContentView(R.layout.activity_main);
```

```
        //Inflate the popup content layout; we do not have access
        // to the parent view yet, so we pass null as the
        // container view parameter.
        View popupContent =
                getLayoutInflater().inflate(R.layout.popup, null);

        mOverlay = new PopupWindow();
        //Popup should wrap content view
        mOverlay.setWindowLayoutMode(
                WindowManager.LayoutParams.WRAP_CONTENT,
                WindowManager.LayoutParams.WRAP_CONTENT);
        //Set content and background
        mOverlay.setContentView(popupContent);
        mOverlay.setBackgroundDrawable(getResources()
                .getDrawable(R.drawable.popup_background));

        //Default behavior is not to allow any elements in
        // the PopupWindow to be interactive, but to enable
        // touch events to be delivered directly to the
        // PopupWindow. All outside touches will be delivered
        // to the main (Activity) window.
        mOverlay.setTouchInterceptor(this);

        //Call setFocusable() to enable elements in the
        // PopupWindow to take focus, which will also enable
        // the behavior of dismissing the PopupWindow on any
        // outside touch.
        mOverlay.setFocusable(true);

        //Call setOutsideTouchable() if you want to enable
        // outside touches to auto-dismiss the PopupWindow
        // but don't want elements inside the PopupWindow to
        // take focus
        mOverlay.setOutsideTouchable(true);
    }

    @Override
    protected void onPause() {
        super.onPause();
        //PopupWindow is like Dialog, it will leak
        // if left visible while the Activity finishes.
        mOverlay.dismiss();
    }

    @Override
    public boolean onTouch(View v, MotionEvent event) {
        //Handle direct touch events passed to the PopupWindow
        return true;
    }

    public void onShowWindowClick(View v) {
        if (mOverlay.isShowing()) {
```

```
            //Dismiss the pop-up
            mOverlay.dismiss();
        } else {
            //Show the PopupWindow anchored to the button we
            // pressed. It will be displayed below the button
            // if there's room, otherwise above.
            mOverlay.showAsDropDown(v);
        }
    }
}
```

In this example, we create a simple layout with two buttons, both set to trigger the same action. When either button is clicked, the PopupWindow will be displayed anchored to that view by using the showAsDropDown() method.

■ **Reminder** A PopupWindow can also be shown at a specific location by using its showAtLocation() method instead. Similar to showAsDropDown(), this method takes a View parameter, but it is used only to get window information.

The results of this example, when the button is pressed, can be seen in Figure 7-15.

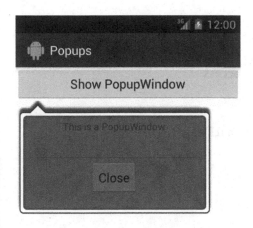

Figure 7-15. *Activity with PopupWindow shown*

When the activity is first created, the PopupWindow is initialized and the layout mode is set to WRAP_CONTENT. We must do this in code, even though it was defined in our layout XML, because the layout parameters in the XML are erased during manual inflation with a null parent view container. We then supply the content view and custom background we created. We will discuss the other flags set on the overlay shortly.

For now, if you were to try to run this application as is, you might notice that the PopupWindow doesn't display when the bottom button is tapped. This is because of the WRAP_CONTENT layout mode we set. Remember that if no space is available below the anchor view, the pop-up should display above it. However, that is determined by how big the pop-up is vs. how much space is left in the main window. If we don't give the window a defined size, it will measure to whatever space remains and try to scrunch the content inside. In order to fix this, we are going to add a dimens.xml file to the project and modify onCreate() for our activity, as in Listings 7-20 and 7-21.

Listing 7-20. res/values/dimens.xml

```
<?xml version="1.0" encoding="utf-8"?>
<resources>
    <dimen name="popupWidth">350dp</dimen>
    <dimen name="popupHeight">250dp</dimen>
</resources>
```

Listing 7-21. Modified onCreate() for Fixed Size

```
@Override
protected void onCreate(Bundle savedInstanceState) {
    super.onCreate(savedInstanceState);
    setContentView(R.layout.activity_main);

    //Inflate the popup content layout; we do not have access
    // to the parent view yet, so we pass null as the
    // container view parameter.
    View popupContent =
            getLayoutInflater().inflate(R.layout.popup, null);

    mOverlay = new PopupWindow();
    //Popup should wrap content view
    mOverlay.setWindowLayoutMode(
            WindowManager.LayoutParams.WRAP_CONTENT,
            WindowManager.LayoutParams.WRAP_CONTENT);
    mOverlay.setWidth(getResources()
            .getDimensionPixelSize(R.dimen.popupWidth));
    mOverlay.setHeight(getResources()
            .getDimensionPixelSize(R.dimen.popupHeight));
    //Set content and background
    mOverlay.setContentView(popupContent);
    mOverlay.setBackgroundDrawable(getResources()
            .getDrawable(R.drawable.popup_background));

    //Default behavior is not to allow any elements in
    // the PopupWindow to be interactive, but to enable
    // touch events to be delivered directly to the
    // PopupWindow. All outside touches will be delivered
```

```
        // to the main (Activity) window.
        mOverlay.setTouchInterceptor(this);

        //Call setFocusable() to enable elements in the
        // PopupWindow to take focus, which will also enable
        // the behavior of dismissing the PopupWindow on any
        // outside touch.
        mOverlay.setFocusable(true);

        //Call setOutsideTouchable() if you want to enable
        // outside touches to auto-dismiss the PopupWindow
        // but don't want elements inside the PopupWindow to
        // take focus
        mOverlay.setOutsideTouchable(true);
}
```

Now our overlay window has a defined size, which we've pulled from a dimension resource to preserve pixel density independence across devices. When we run the example and click the buttons, we can see the PopupWindow display below the top button and above the bottom button, as shown in Figure 7-16.

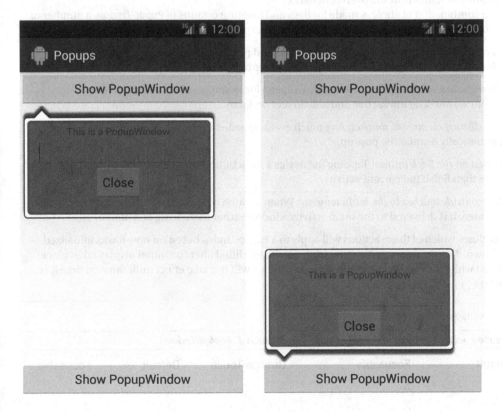

Figure 7-16. *Activity with PopupWindow anchored to each button*

Working with PopupWindow Behavior

PopupWindow has a number of useful flags we can set to govern its behavior and interaction points. By default, the pop-up is touchable, meaning it can receive direct touch events. In order to act on those events, we call setTouchInterceptor()to provide an OnTouchListener as the destination for those touch events.

By default, the pop-up is *not* focusable, which means views inside it cannot receive focus (as an EditText or a Button can). We have these widgets in our content view, so we have set the focusable flag to true to enable the user to interact with these elements. The final flag is setOutsideTouchable(), which we have also enabled. By default, this value is false, but we can set it to true to send touch events outside the pop-up content area to the PopupWindow rather than the main window underneath. Doing so enables the PopupWindow to dismiss itself on any outside touch events. It is most common to use this flag when you do not want to enable focus on the pop-up, but still want the dismiss behavior it provides.

There are a handful of constructors available to create a new PopupWindow. We used the basic version without any parameters, but a few versions also take a Context parameter. When passing a Context to the constructor, the framework creates a PopupWindow that has a default system background included, whereas the version we used does not. We did not need the system background because we supplied our own custom drawable. It is interesting to note that when either case occurs (either the framework or the application supplies a background for the pop-up), the content view you give to PopupWindow is actually wrapped in another private ViewGroup to manage that background instance. This is important because that extra container also slightly modifies how the overlay behaves.

Based on the combination of choices made for flags and creation options of PopupWindow, a number of user interaction behaviors will change. The behaviors we will explore are as follows:

- ***Receive touch events*: Events will be received and processed in the** OnTouchListener, **supplied via** setTouchInterceptor()**.**

- *Allow inside view interaction*: Focusable widgets (for example, a Button) inside the content view will be interactive and able to receive focus.

- *Auto-dismiss on outside touches*: Any touch event outside the content view area will automatically dismiss the pop-up.

- *Dismiss on the Back button*: Tapping the device's Back button will dismiss the pop-up rather than finish the current activity.

- *Allow outside touches to the main window*: When a touch occurs outside the content view area, it is delivered to the main activity window rather than being consumed.

Table 7-1 outlines which of these actions will apply to a PopupWindow based on how it was initialized prior to being shown. These values are not static; they can be modified after the initial display takes place. If a flag is modified while the PopupWindow is visible, the change will not take effect until the next time it is shown or its update() method is called.

Table 7-1. *PopupWindow Behaviors*

	Created with Context or Background			Standard PopupWindow	
Action	Default	Focusable	Outside Touch	Default	Focusable
1	X	X	X		
2		X			X
3		X	X		
4		X			
5	X		X	X	

In addition to what we've already discussed, you can see from this information that if your content overlay needs to process touch events, you will need to ensure that a Context or background image is supplied.

Animating the PopupWindow

After playing with the previous example, you may have noticed that the PopupWindow has a default animation associated with it when it is shown or dismissed. This can be customized or removed by passing a new resource via setAnimationStyle(). This method takes a resource ID referencing a style that defines a pair of animations, one for the window entrance and another for the window exit. Listing 7-22 illustrates the style resource we need to create in order to customize the PopupWindow animation.

Listing 7-22. res/values/styles.xml

```xml
<resources>
    <!-- Define this element below any existing themes -->
    <style name="PopupAnimation">
        <item name="android:windowEnterAnimation">
            @android:anim/slide_in_left</item>
        <item name="android:windowExitAnimation">
            @android:anim/slide_out_right</item>
    </style>
</resources>
```

■ **Tip** It is not necessary to define your own animation styles to customize the transition. There are a host of styles defined within android.R.style that the framework uses to transition other standard window types such as dialog boxes or toasts. To use these animations, just pass the associated ID such as android.R.style.Animation_Dialog or android.R.style.Animation_Toast.

Each of these items can be a reference to animations you define in XML or animations already available in the framework. Here, we have chosen to reference the slide-in and slide-out animations already present in the framework. In Listing 7-23, we then modify our example activity's onCreate() to apply our custom animations. For brevity, we have also removed the configuration flags.

Listing 7-23. Activity onCreate() Showing PopupWindow with Custom Animation

```java
@Override
protected void onCreate(Bundle savedInstanceState) {
    super.onCreate(savedInstanceState);
    setContentView(R.layout.activity_main);

    //Inflate the popup content layout; we do not have access
    // to the parent view yet, so we pass null as the
    // container view parameter.
    View popupContent =
            getLayoutInflater().inflate(R.layout.popup, null);
```

```
    mOverlay = new PopupWindow();
    //Popup should wrap content view
    mOverlay.setWindowLayoutMode(
            WindowManager.LayoutParams.WRAP_CONTENT,
            WindowManager.LayoutParams.WRAP_CONTENT);
    mOverlay.setWidth(getResources()
            .getDimensionPixelSize(R.dimen.popupWidth));
    mOverlay.setHeight(getResources()
            .getDimensionPixelSize(R.dimen.popupHeight));
    //Set content and background
    mOverlay.setContentView(popupContent);
    mOverlay.setBackgroundDrawable(getResources()
            .getDrawable(R.drawable.popup_background));

    //Set a custom animation enter/exit pair, or 0 to
    // disable animations. You can also use animation
    // styles defined in the platform, such as
    // android.R.style.Animation_Toast
    mOverlay.setAnimationStyle(R.style.PopupAnimation);

    //Default behavior is not to allow any elements in
    // the PopupWindow to be interactive, but to enable
    // touch events to be delivered directly to the
    // PopupWindow. All outside touches will be delivered
    // to the main (Activity) window.
    mOverlay.setTouchInterceptor(this);
}
```

■ **Tip** You can also remove the animation completely by calling setAnimationStyle(0), or reset the default animation with setAnimationStyle(-1).

Now when we run the application again, the custom slide animations are used to transition the PopupWindow on and off screen.

Using ViewOverlay

(API Level 18)

Another simple way to draw content over your views is to use the more recent ViewOverlay implementation. ViewOverlay, and its cousin ViewGroupOverlay, allows you to add any number of drawable objects to be drawn on top of the view. Applications cannot create a ViewOverlay directly, and instead obtain a ViewOverlay by calling getOverlay() on any view in the hierarchy. Views are constrained to drawing within their bounds, so any content in an overlay whose location extends outside the hosting view's bounds will be clipped.

To illustrate this capability, we have created a simple application that draws markup content on top of the main view in an activity. The view we are drawing on is purposefully generic to point out that any View subclass (whether it displays text, HTML, an image, or some custom content) can work with an overlay. The application will place either an arrow flag or a resizable box over the interactive view at the location the user touches. The flag can be moved or the box resized as long as the user holds a finger down and drags. Once the touch is released, the marker is permanent on the view until it is tapped a second time, which will remove the marker completely.

First, let's have a look at the resources used via Listing 7-24 and Figure 7-17.

Listing 7-24. `res/drawable/box.xml`

```xml
<?xml version="1.0" encoding="utf-8"?>
<shape xmlns:android="http://schemas.android.com/apk/res/android"
    android:shape="rectangle">
    <solid
        android:color="@android:color/transparent"/>
    <stroke
        android:width="3dp"
        android:color="#F00" />
</shape>
```

Figure 7-17. `res/drawable/flag_arrow.png`

Listing 7-25 shows the layout used for the main activity. We have created a main view containing some text (@+id/textview) that we will be drawing on, and a selector at the bottom to determine which type of marker to place.

Listing 7-25. `res/layout/activity_main.xml`

```xml
<LinearLayout
    xmlns:android="http://schemas.android.com/apk/res/android"
    android:layout_width="match_parent"
    android:layout_height="match_parent"
    android:orientation="vertical" >

    <TextView
        android:id="@+id/textview"
        android:layout_width="match_parent"
        android:layout_height="0dp"
        android:layout_weight="1"
        android:gravity="center"
        android:text="Android Recipes" />

    <RadioGroup
        android:id="@+id/container_options"
        android:layout_width="match_parent"
        android:layout_height="wrap_content"
        android:orientation="horizontal"
        android:background="#CCC">
        <RadioButton
            android:id="@+id/option_box"
            android:layout_width="0dp"
            android:layout_height="wrap_content"
            android:layout_weight="1"
            android:text="Box" />
```

619

```
            <RadioButton
                android:id="@+id/option_arrow"
                android:layout_width="0dp"
                android:layout_height="wrap_content"
                android:layout_weight="1"
                android:text="Arrow" />
        </RadioGroup>

</LinearLayout>
```

Finally, we have the activity in Listing 7-26. This activity finds the main view and sets an OnTouchListener to monitor the touch events going through that view. This causes the onTouch() method to be called for each touch event, which we then use to determine whether the user has touched, dragged, or released a finger on the main view.

Listing 7-26. Activity with Interactive ViewOverlay

```
public class MainActivity extends Activity implements View.OnTouchListener {

    private RadioGroup mOptions;

    private ArrayList<Drawable> mMarkers;
    private Drawable mTrackingMarker;
    private Point mTrackingPoint;

    @Override
    protected void onCreate(Bundle savedInstanceState) {
        super.onCreate(savedInstanceState);
        setContentView(R.layout.activity_main);

        //Receive touch events for the view we want to draw on
        findViewById(R.id.textview).setOnTouchListener(this);

        mOptions =
            (RadioGroup)findViewById(R.id.container_options);

        mMarkers = new ArrayList<Drawable>();
    }

    /*
     * Touch events from the view we are monitoring
     * will be delivered here.
     */
    @Override
    public boolean onTouch(View v, MotionEvent event) {
        switch (mOptions.getCheckedRadioButtonId()) {
            case R.id.option_box:
                handleEvent(R.id.option_box, v, event);
                break;
            case R.id.option_arrow:
                handleEvent(R.id.option_arrow, v, event);
                break;
```

```java
            default:
                return false;
    }
    return true;
}

/*
 * Process touch events when user has selected to draw a box
 */
private void handleEvent(int optionId, View v,
        MotionEvent event) {
    int x = (int) event.getX();
    int y = (int) event.getY();
    switch (event.getAction()) {
        case MotionEvent.ACTION_DOWN:
            Drawable current = markerAt(x, y);
            if (current == null) {
                //Add a new marker on a new touch
                switch(optionId) {
                    case R.id.option_box:
                        mTrackingMarker = addBox(v, x, y);
                        mTrackingPoint = new Point(x, y);
                        break;
                    case R.id.option_arrow:
                        mTrackingMarker = addFlag(v, x, y);
                        break;
                }
            } else {
                //Remove the existing marker
                removeMarker(v, current);
            }
            break;
        case MotionEvent.ACTION_MOVE:
            //Update the current marker as we move
            if (mTrackingMarker != null) {
                switch(optionId) {
                    case R.id.option_box:
                        resizeBox(v, mTrackingMarker,
                                mTrackingPoint, x, y);
                        break;
                    case R.id.option_arrow:
                        offsetFlag(v, mTrackingMarker,
                                x, y);
                        break;
                }

            }
            break;
```

```
            case MotionEvent.ACTION_UP:
            case MotionEvent.ACTION_CANCEL:
                //Clear state when gesture is over
                mTrackingMarker = null;
                mTrackingPoint = null;
                break;
        }
    }

    /*
     * Add a new resizable box at the given coordinate
     */
    private Drawable addBox(View v, int x, int y) {
        Drawable box = getResources().getDrawable(R.drawable.box);

        //Start with a zero size box at the touch point
        Rect bounds = new Rect(x, y, x, y);
        box.setBounds(bounds);

        //Add to the ViewOverlay
        mMarkers.add(box);
        v.getOverlay().add(box);

        return box;
    }

    /*
     * Update an existing box to resize based on the given
     * coordinate.
     */
    private void resizeBox(View v, Drawable target,
            Point trackingPoint, int x, int y) {
        Rect bounds = new Rect(target.getBounds());
        //If the new touch point is to the left of the tracking
        // point, grow left. Otherwise, grow to the right
        if (x < trackingPoint.x) {
            bounds.left = x;
        } else {
            bounds.right = x;
        }

        //If the new touch point is above the tracking point,
        // grow up. Otherwise, grow down
        if (y < trackingPoint.y) {
            bounds.top = y;
        } else {
            bounds.bottom = y;
        }
```

```java
        //Update drawable bounds and redraw
        target.setBounds(bounds);
        v.invalidate();
    }

    /*
     * Add a new flag marker at the given coordinate
     */
    private Drawable addFlag(View v, int x, int y) {
        //Make a new marker drawable
        Drawable marker =
            getResources().getDrawable(R.drawable.flag_arrow);

        //Create bounds to match image size
        Rect bounds = new Rect(0, 0,
                marker.getIntrinsicWidth(),
                marker.getIntrinsicHeight());
        //Center marker bottom around coordinate
        bounds.offset(x - (bounds.width() /2),
                y - bounds.height());
        marker.setBounds(bounds);
        //Add to the overlay
        mMarkers.add(marker);
        v.getOverlay().add(marker);

        return marker;
    }

    /*
     * Update the position of an existing flag marker
     */
    private void offsetFlag(View v, Drawable marker,
            int x, int y) {
        Rect bounds = new Rect(marker.getBounds());
        //Move drawable bounds to align with the new coordinate
        bounds.offset(x - bounds.left - (bounds.width() / 2),
                y - bounds.top - bounds.height());
        //Update and redraw
        marker.setBounds(bounds);
        v.invalidate();
    }

    /*
     * Remove the requested marker item
     */
    private void removeMarker(View v, Drawable marker) {
        mMarkers.remove(marker);
        v.getOverlay().remove(marker);
    }
```

```
    /*
     * Find the first marker that contains the requested
     * coordinate, if one exists.
     */
    private Drawable markerAt(int x, int y) {
        //Return the first marker found containing the given point
        for (Drawable marker : mMarkers) {
            if (marker.getBounds().contains(x, y)) {
                return marker;
            }
        }

        return null;
    }
}
```

Inside onTouch(), the selection from the RadioGroup is checked to determine the marker type. For the initial ACTION_DOWN, we call either addBox() or addFlag() to create a new Drawable, set its size and location with setBounds(), and apply it to the main view's ViewOverlay. To add the marker to the overlay, we simply call add(). Since ViewOverlay doesn't provide any good method of tracking the items added, we also maintain a list of our own, which will be useful in finding a marker based on touch later.

As the finger moves around in ACTION_MOVE, we either update the location of the flag, or resize the box to fit between the initial touch point and our current touch location. In both cases, this is accomplished by again updating the bounds Rect of the Drawable. Once the finger is released, we clear the tracking state, and the marker is now in its permanent home.

■ **Note** Drawable elements get their size and location from the bounds Rect. Bitmap content that comes from an image resource such as a PNG has an intrinsic height and width that we can use to generate the size portion of the bounds, but content taken from XML has no intrinsic size and must be explicitly set. Regardless, especially when used in a ViewOverlay, bounds are used to place the content at the right location, so it is key to remember to call setBounds() at least once for each element you add.

If a new touch comes down at the location of an existing marker (checked using the markerAt() helper method), we simply delete the marker by removing it from the ViewOverlay. Figure 7-18 shows the initial layout on the left, with some markers added to the overlay on the right.

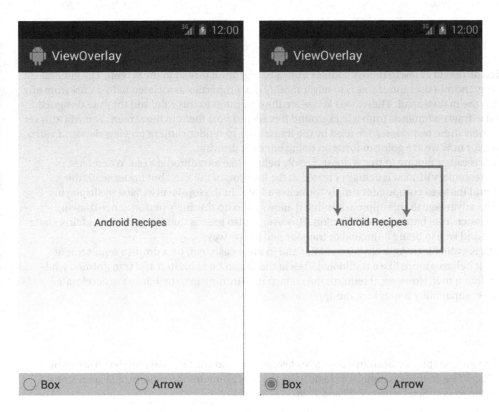

Figure 7-18. Activity with drawable content inside the ViewOverlay

---

■ **Caution** Calling getOverlay() on a ViewGroup will return a ViewGroupOverlay instead, which has additional add() and remove() methods to work with a view instead of a drawable. Beware that this does not work the same way as described in this section. This cannot be used to add a new view on top of the existing hierarchy; it can be used only to elevate an existing view already inside that container to the overlay. It also has the consequence of removing that view from its container when added to the overlay, which will modify the layout of the ViewGroup. If you want to place views on top of the main window, use the PopupWindow technique described earlier in this section.

7-5. High-Performance Drawing

Problem

Your application needs to render a complex scene or animation to the screen, often from a background thread.

Solution

(API Level 1)

Use SurfaceView or TextureView to render content from a background thread to the screen. The general rule in developing Android user interfaces is to never modify any properties associated with a View from any thread other than the main thread. These two classes are the exception to this rule, and they are designed specifically to take draw commands from a background thread and post them to the screen. You will also see in later chapters how these two classes are used by the framework to render camera preview data and video output. However, for now we are going to focus on doing our own drawing.

SurfaceView is rather unique in that it doesn't really behave like a traditional View. When one is instantiated, a secondary Window is actually created at the location of the View but underneath the current Window, and the View component simply "punches a hole" in the top-level Window by displaying transparently. The advantage to this approach is that it allows us to do this high-performance drawing without any assistance from hardware acceleration. However, it also means that SurfaceView is fairly static and does not respond well to being animated or transformed in any way.

TextureView is available in Android 4.0 and later and in most cases can be a drop-in replacement for SurfaceView. It behaves more like a traditional View in that it can be animated and transformed while content is being drawn to it. However, it requires the context it is running in to be hardware accelerated, which may cause compatibility issues in some applications.

How It Works

Let's take a look at an example application where a background thread continuously renders a series of objects to a SurfaceView. In this example, we create a display that animates the motion of several icons continuously on the screen. See Listings 7-27 and 7-28.

Listing 7-27. res/layout/main.xml

```
<FrameLayout
    xmlns:android="http://schemas.android.com/apk/res/android"
    android:layout_width="match_parent"
    android:layout_height="match_parent"
    android:orientation="vertical" >
    <Button
        android:id="@+id/button_erase"
        android:layout_width="match_parent"
        android:layout_height="wrap_content"
        android:text="Erase" />
    <SurfaceView
        android:id="@+id/surface"
        android:layout_width="300dp"
        android:layout_height="300dp"
        android:layout_gravity="center" />

</FrameLayout>
```

Listing 7-28. Surface Drawing Activity

```java
public class SurfaceActivity extends Activity implements
        View.OnClickListener, View.OnTouchListener, SurfaceHolder.Callback {

    private SurfaceView mSurface;
    private DrawingThread mThread;

    @Override
    public void onCreate(Bundle savedInstanceState) {
        super.onCreate(savedInstanceState);
        setContentView(R.layout.main);
        //Attach listener to button
        findViewById(R.id.button_erase).setOnClickListener(this);

        //Set up the surface with a touch listener and callback
        mSurface = (SurfaceView) findViewById(R.id.surface);
        mSurface.setOnTouchListener(this);
        mSurface.getHolder().addCallback(this);
    }

    @Override
    public void onClick(View v) {
        mThread.clearItems();
    }

    public boolean onTouch(View v, MotionEvent event) {
        if (event.getAction() == MotionEvent.ACTION_DOWN) {
            mThread.addItem((int) event.getX(), (int) event.getY());
        }
        return true;
    }

    @Override
    public void surfaceCreated(SurfaceHolder holder) {
        mThread = new DrawingThread(holder,
                BitmapFactory.decodeResource(getResources(), R.drawable.ic_launcher));
        mThread.start();
    }

    @Override
    public void surfaceChanged(SurfaceHolder holder, int format, int width,
            int height) {
        mThread.updateSize(width, height);
    }

    @Override
    public void surfaceDestroyed(SurfaceHolder holder) {
        mThread.quit();
        mThread = null;
    }
```

627

```java
private static class DrawingThread extends HandlerThread implements Handler.Callback {
    private static final int MSG_ADD = 100;
    private static final int MSG_MOVE = 101;
    private static final int MSG_CLEAR = 102;

    private int mDrawingWidth, mDrawingHeight;
    private boolean mRunning = false;

    private SurfaceHolder mDrawingSurface;
    private Paint mPaint;
    private Handler mReceiver;
    private Bitmap mIcon;
    private ArrayList<DrawingItem> mLocations;

    private class DrawingItem {
        //Current location marker
        int x, y;
        //Direction markers for motion
        boolean horizontal, vertical;

        public DrawingItem(int x, int y, boolean horizontal, boolean vertical) {
            this.x = x;
            this.y = y;
            this.horizontal = horizontal;
            this.vertical = vertical;
        }
    }

    public DrawingThread(SurfaceHolder holder, Bitmap icon) {
        super("DrawingThread");
        mDrawingSurface = holder;
        mLocations = new ArrayList<DrawingItem>();
        mPaint = new Paint(Paint.ANTI_ALIAS_FLAG);
        mIcon = icon;
    }

    @Override
    protected void onLooperPrepared() {
        mReceiver = new Handler(getLooper(), this);
        //Start the rendering
        mRunning = true;
        mReceiver.sendEmptyMessage(MSG_MOVE);
    }

    @Override
    public boolean quit() {
        // Clear all messages before dying
        mRunning = false;
        mReceiver.removeCallbacksAndMessages(null);

        return super.quit();
    }
```

```java
@Override
public boolean handleMessage(Message msg) {
    switch (msg.what) {
    case MSG_ADD:
        //Create a new item at the touch location, with a randomized start direction
        DrawingItem newItem = new DrawingItem(msg.arg1, msg.arg2,
                Math.round(Math.random()) == 0,
                Math.round(Math.random()) == 0);
        mLocations.add(newItem);
        break;
    case MSG_CLEAR:
        //Remove all objects
        mLocations.clear();
        break;
    case MSG_MOVE:
        if (!mRunning) return true;

        //Render a frame
        Canvas c = mDrawingSurface.lockCanvas();
        if (c == null) {
            break;
        }
        //Clear canvas first
        c.drawColor(Color.BLACK);
        //Draw each item
        for (DrawingItem item : mLocations) {
            //Update location
            item.x += (item.horizontal ? 5 : -5);
            if (item.x >= (mDrawingWidth - mIcon.getWidth()) ) item.horizontal =
            false;
            if (item.x <= 0) item.horizontal = true;
            item.y += (item.vertical ? 5 : -5);
            if (item.y >= (mDrawingHeight - mIcon.getHeight()) ) item.vertical =
            false;
            if (item.y <= 0) item.vertical = true;

            c.drawBitmap(mIcon, item.x, item.y, mPaint);
        }
        mDrawingSurface.unlockCanvasAndPost(c);
        break;
    }

    //Post the next frame
    if (mRunning) {
        mReceiver.sendEmptyMessage(MSG_MOVE);
    }
    return true;
}
```

```
        public void updateSize(int width, int height) {
            mDrawingWidth = width;
            mDrawingHeight = height;
        }

        public void addItem(int x, int y) {
            //Pass the location into the Handler using Message arguments
            Message msg = Message.obtain(mReceiver, MSG_ADD, x, y);
            mReceiver.sendMessage(msg);
        }

        public void clearItems() {
            mReceiver.sendEmptyMessage(MSG_CLEAR);
        }
    }
}
```

This example constructs a simple background DrawingThread to render and draw content to a SurfaceView. This thread is a subclass of HandlerThread, which is a convenient framework helper for generating background workers that process incoming messages. We talked in more detail about this pattern in Chapter 6, but for now suffice it to say that our background thread operates by responding to messages sent to the Handler it owns inside handleMessage(). SurfaceView is really two components: a Surface underneath the Window and a transparent View in the hierarchy. To draw, we really need access to the underlying Surface, which is wrapped in a SurfaceHolder.

The construction of the Surface doesn't actually happen until the view gets attached to the current window, so we can't just grab it right away. Instead, SurfaceHolder has a callback interface when the Surface is created, destroyed, or changed so that we can use it to manage the life cycle of the components that depend on it (in this case, the DrawingThread). Here we wait for surfaceCreated() to construct a new DrawingThread and start rendering, and in surfaceDestroyed() we need to stop rendering to the Surface as it is no longer valid. The final callback, surfaceChanged(), is the only place where the dimensions of the Surface are supplied, so we make sure to update our drawing code with those values whenever they are available.

We have defined three commands for the thread to react to: add, clear, and move. The add method will be triggered when the user taps on the SurfaceView by adding a drawing item to the display list with its initial location set to the location of the touch. The clear method will remove all items from the display list, which is triggered when the button is pressed.

Inside the move method, the thread renders each frame to the SurfaceView. Every drawing operation should be prefaced with lockCanvas(), which provides a Canvas to apply drawing calls. Then the thread iterates through each item in its display list, updates it to a new position, and draws an icon to the Canvas at that location. It also checks whether any item has hit a boundary of the Surface, so it can reverse direction in those cases. We must preface each frame with drawColor() to clear the previous frame's contents. Without this, as the icons move, you would see a trail behind them of the icon's previous locations. In some applications, this may be desirable (such as a painting application where each event should be added to the others), but not for our example. After all the drawing calls are made, the application must call unlockCanvasAndPost() to render the data to the screen.

By continuously posting MSG_MOVE to itself, the DrawingThread runs through this process indefinitely until the thread is quit by the application. An advantage to doing this processing via HandlerThread is that the operations can be cancelled at any time with quit() and the thread can die cleanly, rather than trying to interrupt the thread execution.

You can see the results of this application running in Figure 7-19. The user can tap on the black box an indefinite number of times and watch the number of flying icons stack up. Because the drawing code uses only one bitmap for all the icons, the number of items the view can support is very high without running into any memory concerns.

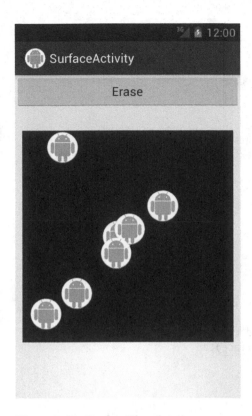

Figure 7-19. *SurfaceView drawing scene*

TextureView

(API Level 14)

If your application is targeting Android 4.0 and later, you can also use TextureView, which has a few additional properties that may make it ideal for your application; the most useful is that it can be transformed. Have a look at Listings 7-29 and 7-30, where we have modified the previous example to use TextureView.

Listing 7-29. res/layout/texture.xml

```
<FrameLayout
    xmlns:android="http://schemas.android.com/apk/res/android"
    android:layout_width="match_parent"
    android:layout_height="match_parent">
    <Button
        android:id="@+id/button_transform"
        android:layout_width="match_parent"
        android:layout_height="wrap_content"
        android:text="Rotate" />
    <TextureView
        android:id="@+id/surface"
        android:layout_width="300dp"
```

```
            android:layout_height="300dp"
            android:layout_gravity="center" />

</FrameLayout>
```

Listing 7-30. Texture Drawing Activity

```java
@TargetApi(Build.VERSION_CODES.ICE_CREAM_SANDWICH)
public class TextureActivity extends Activity implements
        View.OnClickListener, View.OnTouchListener, TextureView.SurfaceTextureListener {

    private TextureView mSurface;
    private DrawingThread mThread;

    @Override
    public void onCreate(Bundle savedInstanceState) {
        super.onCreate(savedInstanceState);
        setContentView(R.layout.texture);
        //Attach listener to button
        findViewById(R.id.button_transform).setOnClickListener(this);

        //Set up the surface with a touch listener and callback
        mSurface = (TextureView) findViewById(R.id.surface);
        mSurface.setOnTouchListener(this);
        mSurface.setSurfaceTextureListener(this);
    }

    @Override
    public void onClick(View v) {
        //Rotate the entire drawing view
        mSurface.animate()
                .rotation(mSurface.getRotation() < 180.f ? 180.f : 0.f);
    }

    public boolean onTouch(View v, MotionEvent event) {
        if (event.getAction() == MotionEvent.ACTION_DOWN) {
            mThread.addItem((int) event.getX(), (int) event.getY());
        }
        return true;
    }

    @Override
    public void onSurfaceTextureAvailable(SurfaceTexture surface, int width,
            int height) {
        mThread = new DrawingThread(new Surface(surface),
                BitmapFactory.decodeResource(getResources(), R.drawable.ic_launcher));
        mThread.updateSize(width, height);
        mThread.start();
    }
```

```java
@Override
public void onSurfaceTextureSizeChanged(SurfaceTexture surface, int width,
        int height) {
    mThread.updateSize(width, height);
}

@Override
public void onSurfaceTextureUpdated(SurfaceTexture surface) { }

@Override
public boolean onSurfaceTextureDestroyed(SurfaceTexture surface) {
    mThread.quit();
    mThread = null;

    //Return true to allow the framework to release the surface
    return true;
}

private static class DrawingThread extends HandlerThread implements Handler.Callback {
    private static final int MSG_ADD = 100;
    private static final int MSG_MOVE = 101;
    private static final int MSG_CLEAR = 102;

    private int mDrawingWidth, mDrawingHeight;
    private boolean mRunning = false;

    private Surface mDrawingSurface;
    private Rect mSurfaceRect;
    private Paint mPaint;

    private Handler mReceiver;
    private Bitmap mIcon;
    private ArrayList<DrawingItem> mLocations;

    private class DrawingItem {
        //Current location marker
        int x, y;
        //Direction markers for motion
        boolean horizontal, vertical;

        public DrawingItem(int x, int y, boolean horizontal, boolean vertical) {
            this.x = x;
            this.y = y;
            this.horizontal = horizontal;
            this.vertical = vertical;
        }
    }
```

```java
    public DrawingThread(Surface surface, Bitmap icon) {
        super("DrawingThread");
        mDrawingSurface = surface;
        mSurfaceRect = new Rect();
        mLocations = new ArrayList<DrawingItem>();
        mPaint = new Paint(Paint.ANTI_ALIAS_FLAG);
        mIcon = icon;
    }

    @Override
    protected void onLooperPrepared() {
        mReceiver = new Handler(getLooper(), this);
        //Start the rendering
        mRunning = true;
        mReceiver.sendEmptyMessage(MSG_MOVE);
    }

    @Override
    public boolean quit() {
        // Clear all messages before dying
        mRunning = false;
        mReceiver.removeCallbacksAndMessages(null);

        return super.quit();
    }

    @Override
    public boolean handleMessage(Message msg) {
        switch (msg.what) {
        case MSG_ADD:
            //Create a new item at the touch location, with a randomized start direction
            DrawingItem newItem = new DrawingItem(msg.arg1, msg.arg2,
                    Math.round(Math.random()) == 0,
                    Math.round(Math.random()) == 0);
            mLocations.add(newItem);
            break;
        case MSG_CLEAR:
            //Remove all objects
            mLocations.clear();
            break;
        case MSG_MOVE:
            //Do nothing if we are canceled
            if (!mRunning) return true;

            //Render a frame
            try {
                Canvas c = mDrawingSurface.lockCanvas(mSurfaceRect);

                //Clear canvas first
                c.drawColor(Color.BLACK);
                //Draw each item
```

```java
            for (DrawingItem item : mLocations) {
                //Update location
                item.x += (item.horizontal ? 3 : -3);
                if (item.x >= (mDrawingWidth - mIcon.getWidth()) )
                    item.horizontal = false;
                if (item.x <= 0)
                    item.horizontal = true;

                item.y += (item.vertical ? 3 : -3);
                if (item.y >= (mDrawingHeight - mIcon.getHeight()) )
                    item.vertical = false;
                if (item.y <= 0)
                    item.vertical = true;

                c.drawBitmap(mIcon, item.x, item.y, mPaint);
            }

            mDrawingSurface.unlockCanvasAndPost(c);
        } catch (Exception e) {
            e.printStackTrace();
        }
        break;
    }
    //Post the next frame
    if (mRunning) {
        mReceiver.sendEmptyMessage(MSG_MOVE);
    }

    return true;
}

public void updateSize(int width, int height) {
    mDrawingWidth = width;
    mDrawingHeight = height;
    mSurfaceRect.set(0, 0, mDrawingWidth, mDrawingHeight);
}

public void addItem(int x, int y) {
    //Pass the location into the Handler using Message arguments
    Message msg = Message.obtain(mReceiver, MSG_ADD, x, y);
    mReceiver.sendMessage(msg);
}

public void clearItems() {
    mReceiver.sendEmptyMessage(MSG_CLEAR);
}
    }
}
```

635

In this modified example, our layout has a TextureView instance. Similar to SurfaceView, the underlying surface to draw on is not created until the view is attached to the Window, so we must rely on a callback before accessing it. For TextureView, this callback is a SurfaceTextureListener. For the most part, the functionality mirrors SurfaceHolder.Callback with onSurfaceTextureAvailable(), onSurfaceTextureChanged(), and onSurfaceTextureDestroyed(). However, there is one additional callback method we aren't currently using in this example called onSurfaceTextureUpdated(). This method will be called anytime the SurfaceTexture renders a new frame.

The drawing surface that TextureView provides is slightly different, in that there is no SurfaceHolder wrapping it to access. Instead, we can access a SurfaceTexture instance, which we can wrap in a new Surface to do our drawing. This, in turn, requires one small modification of our DrawingThread. SurfaceHolder has a convenience version of lockCanvas() that takes no parameters and marks the entire Surface as dirty. When working with Surface directly, this method does not exist, so we need to pass a Rect into lockCanvas() that tells it which section of the Surface to return as a Canvas for new rendering. Because we still want this to be the entire surface, we maintain the size of the Rect in updateSize(), which will get called by the listener whenever the surface changes.

To showcase the ability to transform the SurfaceTexture live while it is rendering, we have replaced the Erase button with a Rotate button. Clicking this button will cause the TextureView to do a half-circle rotation animation each time. Clicking the button while the current animation is running will cancel it and start a new rotation from the current point, so if you click the button rapidly, you can get the view to rotate into some pretty odd angles. The entire time the SurfaceTexture will continue to animate without skipping a beat. You can see in Figure 7-20 the application with the TextureView rotated upside-down.

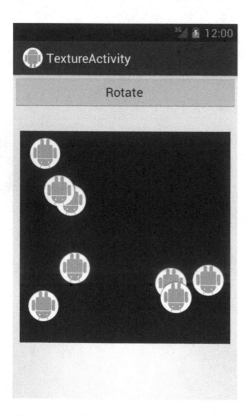

Figure 7-20. *TextureView drawing scene*

7-6. Custom Drawables

Problem

You would like to create a reusable Drawable class and need to do custom drawing using a Canvas.

Solution

(API Level 1)

The Drawable class in Android can be extended into a custom implementation where you have full control of the drawing operations. This is sometimes more preferable than using a custom View, as it is more lightweight and less complicated to implement.

How It Works

There are two classes you can extend when implementing your own custom drawable, Drawable or DrawableContainer. The latter one provides more features, while the first one is more simple. In this example we will extend Drawable, as we only intend to show how a custom Drawable can be used in Android applications. The code for this class can be seen in Listing 7-31.

Listing 7-31. MyCustomDrawable

```java
public class MyCustomDrawable extends Drawable {
    private final Paint mPaint;

    public MyCustomDrawable() {
        // Default values for our Paint object
        mPaint = new Paint();
        mPaint.setColor(Color.BLACK);
        mPaint.setStyle(Paint.Style.STROKE);
        mPaint.setStrokeWidth(4);
        mPaint.setAntiAlias(true);
        mPaint.setShadowLayer(4, 4, 4, Color.GRAY);
    }

    @Override
    public void inflate(@NonNull Resources r, @NonNull XmlPullParser parser,
                        @NonNull AttributeSet attrs, Resources.Theme theme)
            throws XmlPullParserException, IOException {
        super.inflate(r, parser, attrs, theme);
        TypedArray typedArray = null;
        try {
            typedArray = r.obtainAttributes(attrs, new int[]{android.R.attr.color});
            int color = typedArray.getColor(0, Color.BLACK);
            mPaint.setColor(color);
        } finally {
            if (typedArray != null) {
                typedArray.recycle();
            }
        }
    }
```

637

```java
    @Override
    public void draw(@NonNull Canvas canvas) {
        float width = canvas.getWidth();
        float height = canvas.getHeight();
        float radius = (width > height ? height * 0.4f : width * 0.4f);
        canvas.drawCircle(width / 2f, height / 2f, radius, mPaint);
    }

    @Override
    public void setAlpha(int alpha) {
        mPaint.setAlpha(alpha);
    }

    @Override
    public void setColorFilter(ColorFilter colorFilter) {
        mPaint.setColorFilter(colorFilter);
    }

    @Override
    public int getOpacity() {
        return PixelFormat.TRANSLUCENT;
    }
}
```

In the preceding code, we are simply drawing a circle with a radius that is 40% of the width or height, whichever is smallest. Note that our custom drawable doesn't have any other dependencies than the Canvas it receives in the draw() method. This makes the custom drawables easier to work with than custom views. The size of the drawable is determined by calling getWidth() and getHeight() form the Canvas when it is time to draw. There is no need to calculate the size yourself.

The other methods are optional, but in this case we have delegated setAlpha() and setColorFilter() to the Paint object we use for drawing. The default for the Paint object is set in the constructor of the Drawable.

One change that came in API Level 24 is the support for referencing custom drawables in XML. The way to do so is to place an XML file in the folder named drawable-24 of your resources. The content of this XML file is shown in Listing 7-32.

Listing 7-32. XML file for custom drawable on API Level 24 and later

```xml
<?xml version="1.0" encoding="utf-8"?>
<drawable xmlns:android="http://schemas.android.com/apk/res/android"
        class="com.androidrecipes.customdrawables.MyCustomDrawable"
        android:color="#0000FF"/>
```

It is possible to specify additional XML attributes, and accessing them is similar to how a custom view would access XML attributes or styling information. In this case we only support the android:color attribute, as shown in Listing 7-31.

By using the drawable XML tag and having the class attribute contain the full class name of the custom drawable, we can now point to this from other XML files such as layout files or state drawables. An example of this can be seen in Listing 7-33.

Listing 7-33. XML layout with an ImageView using a custom drawable

```
<ImageView
    android:id="@+id/image"
    android:layout_width="72dp"
    android:layout_height="72dp"
    android:src="@drawable/my_drawable"
    android:layout_centerInParent="true"/>
```

7-7. Tinting Drawable Elements

Problem

You would like to avoid duplicating common assets that vary only by color by dynamically coloring a baseline asset at runtime.

Solution

(API Level 1)

Use a color filter to apply a color mask to any Drawable instance. Drawable color filters are typically fully opaque, but the framework also supports partial blending via PorterDuff.XferMode. This method can be executed only from Java code.

(API Level 21)

Use the native tint functionality available on any Drawable instance via android:tint in XML or setTint() from Java code. In this case, blending can be applied via android:tintMode or setTintMode(); either of which takes a Porter-Duff constant to represent the transfer mode.

How It Works

In this example, we will take the four images found in Figure 7-21 and dynamically apply colors to them to produce the output in Figure 7-22.

Figure 7-21. *Base icons before tinting (placed in res/drawable)*

Figure 7-22. *Activity with tinted drawables*

■ **Note**   For a Porter-Duff color blend to apply correctly, areas of the icons that should not be modified need to be fully transparent, not solid white. The remaining pixels don't need to be black, but they must be fully opaque.

Listing 7-34 shows us the simple layout used to place these images into the activity.

Listing 7-34. res/layout/activity_filter.xml

```xml
<?xml version="1.0" encoding="utf-8"?>
<LinearLayout xmlns:android="http://schemas.android.com/apk/res/android"
    android:layout_width="match_parent"
    android:layout_height="match_parent"
    android:orientation="horizontal"
    android:padding="8dp">

    <ImageView
        android:id="@+id/icon_marker"
        android:layout_width="0dp"
        android:layout_height="wrap_content"
```

```
        android:layout_weight="1"
        android:src="@drawable/ic_marker"/>

    <ImageView
        android:id="@+id/icon_gear"
        android:layout_width="0dp"
        android:layout_height="wrap_content"
        android:layout_weight="1"
        android:src="@drawable/ic_gear"/>

    <ImageView
        android:id="@+id/icon_check"
        android:layout_width="0dp"
        android:layout_height="wrap_content"
        android:layout_weight="1"
        android:src="@drawable/ic_check"/>

    <ImageView
        android:id="@+id/icon_heart"
        android:layout_width="0dp"
        android:layout_height="wrap_content"
        android:layout_weight="1"
        android:src="@drawable/ic_heart"/>
</LinearLayout>
```

The one thing to notice from this layout is that we are not applying any special filters here. For this first technique, colors cannot be applied from XML. Listing 7-35 shows us an activity with the code to tint the icons.

Listing 7-35. Color Filter Activity

```java
public class ColorFilterActivity extends ActionBarActivity {

    @Override
    protected void onCreate(Bundle savedInstanceState) {
        super.onCreate(savedInstanceState);
        setContentView(R.layout.activity_filter);

        applyIconFilters();
    }

    private void applyIconFilters() {

        ImageView iconView = (ImageView) findViewById(R.id.icon_marker);
        //Draw icon solid purple
        iconView.getDrawable().setColorFilter(0xFFAA00AA, PorterDuff.Mode.SRC_ATOP);

        iconView = (ImageView) findViewById(R.id.icon_gear);
        //Draw icon solid green
        iconView.getDrawable().setColorFilter(0xFF00AA00, PorterDuff.Mode.SRC_ATOP);

        iconView = (ImageView) findViewById(R.id.icon_check);
        //Draw icon solid blue
        iconView.getDrawable().setColorFilter(0xFF0000AA, PorterDuff.Mode.SRC_ATOP);
```

```
        iconView = (ImageView) findViewById(R.id.icon_heart);
        //Draw icon solid red
        iconView.getDrawable().setColorFilter(0xFFAA0000, PorterDuff.Mode.SRC_ATOP);
    }
}
```

Using the setColorFilter() method, any Drawable can be drawn with a tint. The simplest version of this method (which we have used here) accepts the ARGB color value and a PorterDuff.Mode for pixel transfer and blending. Our choice of SRC_ATOP ensures that the chosen color will be drawn fully and the original image pixel ignored.

■ **Tip**   If your base image has variations (for example, a gradient) that you would like to show through, pick a filter color that is partially transparent and/or try a different PorterDuff.Mode value, such as MULTIPLY.

There is another version of setColorFilter() that accepts a ColorFilter instance for more complex overlays. The LightingColorFilter, for example, is designed to simulate a light source effect.

A NOTE ABOUT CONSTANT STATE

If you find yourself repeating the same image resource multiple times within the same activity (in a list, for example), and attempt to set multiple tint values, you may find that all the drawables will show only the last color you have set. This is because of something called *shared constant state*. It's a fancy way of saying that every drawable created from the same resource shares a common state object because they are, for the most part, assumed to be immutable objects, and this saves memory resources.

However, it has a side effect that changing a property on one drawable's state affects all the others as well. To avoid this problem, anytime you make a change that affects the state of a single drawable, you should first call its mutate() method. This makes a copy of the state object before making the change. The method can be called inline with your modifier of choice, such as the following:

```
iconView.getDrawable().mutate().setColorFilter(...)
```

This will ensure that the color change you make doesn't affect the other drawables created from the same resource.

As a final note, drawables can generally be mutated only once, so it's not a good habit to use this as a copy or clone mechanism. Unique instances should still be retrieved from resources, and simply mutated before they are changed.

Native Tinting

(API Level 21)

Starting in Android 5.0, this same effect can be applied to drawables from XML by using the android:tint attribute, or in code via setTint(). Underneath your code, the framework is using the same technique you just saw, although slightly more efficiently since the framework can now share states that have a common tint. Listings 7-36 through 7-39 redefine our icon assets as tinted drawables.

Listing 7-36. res/drawable/tinted_marker.xml

```xml
<?xml version="1.0" encoding="utf-8"?>
<bitmap xmlns:android="http://schemas.android.com/apk/res/android"
    android:src="@drawable/ic_marker"
    android:tint="#FFAA00AA" />
```

Listing 7-37. res/drawable/tinted_gear.xml

```xml
<?xml version="1.0" encoding="utf-8"?>
<bitmap xmlns:android="http://schemas.android.com/apk/res/android"
    android:src="@drawable/ic_gear"
    android:tint="#FF00AA00" />
```

Listing 7-38. res/drawable/tinted_check.xml

```xml
<?xml version="1.0" encoding="utf-8"?>
<bitmap xmlns:android="http://schemas.android.com/apk/res/android"
    android:src="@drawable/ic_check"
    android:tint="#FF0000AA" />
```

Listing 7-39. res/drawable/tinted_heart.xml

```xml
<?xml version="1.0" encoding="utf-8"?>
<bitmap xmlns:android="http://schemas.android.com/apk/res/android"
    android:src="@drawable/ic_heart"
    android:tint="#FFAA0000" />
```

Now when we insert these drawables into the activity layout, there is no further colorization work to do. See Listings 7-40 and 7-41.

Listing 7-40. res/layout/activity_tinted.xml

```xml
<?xml version="1.0" encoding="utf-8"?>
<LinearLayout xmlns:android="http://schemas.android.com/apk/res/android"
    android:orientation="horizontal"
    android:layout_width="match_parent"
    android:layout_height="match_parent"
    android:padding="8dp">
    <ImageView
        android:id="@+id/icon_marker"
        android:layout_width="0dp"
        android:layout_height="wrap_content"
        android:layout_weight="1"
        android:src="@drawable/tinted_marker" />
    <ImageView
        android:id="@+id/icon_gear"
        android:layout_width="0dp"
        android:layout_height="wrap_content"
        android:layout_weight="1"
        android:src="@drawable/tinted_gear"/>
```

```
<ImageView
    android:id="@+id/icon_check"
    android:layout_width="0dp"
    android:layout_height="wrap_content"
    android:layout_weight="1"
    android:src="@drawable/tinted_check"/>
<ImageView
    android:id="@+id/icon_heart"
    android:layout_width="0dp"
    android:layout_height="wrap_content"
    android:layout_weight="1"
    android:src="@drawable/tinted_heart"/>
</LinearLayout>
```

Listing 7-41. Simple Activity for Tinted Drawables

```
public class TintActivity extends ActionBarActivity {

    @Override
    protected void onCreate(Bundle savedInstanceState) {
        super.onCreate(savedInstanceState);
        setContentView(R.layout.activity_tinted);
    }
}
```

The tinted images replace the originals inside the layout XML, and the Java code previously used to apply filters is no longer there.

■ **Tip**   You can still play with transfer modes in the native tint API. Using the `android:tintMode` attribute, a Porter-Duff constant will pair with the tint color. Omitting the attribute is the same as applying `android:tintMode="src_in"`.

7-8. Using Scalable Vector Assets

Problem

You would like to reduce the number of resource files your application includes by using scalable vector assets instead of static images. You also want this to work on API Levels below 21, which lacks native support for vector-based images.

Solution

(API Level 9)

Construct a `VectorDrawableCompat` from your image asset's path data. Android does not natively support reading common vector file formats, such as SVG (primarily due to lacking CSS support), but it does support the same path data syntax. This means that with some minor conversion, you can create a single XML vector asset that is fully scalable across all screen densities.

Vector images used to be only available on API Level 21 and later, but thanks to the latest additions to the support libraries, it is now available with limited support from API Level 9 and with some support for animations from API Level 11. Full support is still only available form API Level 21 and later.

■ **Note**   For more information on SVG path data syntax, refer to the W3C reference: http://www.w3.org/TR/ SVG11/paths.html.

Android also supports animated path manipulations using AnimatedVectorDrawableCompat, but this is only available from API Level 11 and later. This class provides a holder for mapping ObjectAnimator instances to target paths within a VectorDrawableCompat.

How It Works

In this example, we are going to take the SVG image shown in Figure 7-23, and convert it into something we can display as a VectorDrawable.

Figure 7-23. *SVG image exported from Adobe Illustrator*

SVG files are really just XML content, and Listing 7-42 shows the raw file data.

Listing 7-42. assets/example.svg

```
<?xml version="1.0" encoding="utf-8"?>
<!DOCTYPE svg PUBLIC "-//W3C//DTD SVG 1.1//EN" "http://www.w3.org/Graphics/SVG/1.1/DTD/
svg11.dtd">
<svg version="1.1" id="Layer_2" xmlns="http://www.w3.org/2000/svg" xmlns:xlink="http://www.
w3.org/1999/xlink" x="0px" y="0px"
        width="163px" height="154px" viewBox="0 0 163 154" style="enable-background:new 0 0
163 154;" xml:space="preserve">

<style type="text/css">
        .st0{fill:#3355CC;stroke:#000000;stroke-width:0.25;stroke-miterlimit:10;}
</style>
```

```
<circle class="st0" cx="81.5" cy="77" r="14.7"/>
<path class="st0" d="M81.5,3c-11.2,0-19.2,9.1-19.2,20.3
        c0,8.3,6.7,15.4,13,18.6c-0.9-1.3-1.4-2.8-1.4-4.4c0-4.2,3.4-7.6,7.6-7.6
        c4.2,0,7.6,3.4,7.6,7.6c0,1.8-0.6,3.5-1.7,4.8c6.8-2.9,13.3-10.3,13.3-19
        C100.7,12.1,92.7,3,81.5,3z"/>
<path class="st0" d="M29.2,24.7c-7.9,7.9-7.1,20,0.8,28
        c5.9,5.9,15.7,6.2,22.3,4c-1.5-0.3-3-1-4.2-2.1c-3-3-3-7.8,0-10.8
        c3-3,7.8-3,10.8,0c1.3,1.3,2,2.9,2.2,4.6c2.7-6.9,2.1-16.7-4-22.8
        C49.2,17.5,37.1,16.7,29.2,24.7z"/>
<path class="st0" d="M7.5,77c0,11.2,9.1,19.2,20.3,19.2
        c8.3,0,15.4-6.7,18.6-13c-1.3,0.9-2.8,1.4-4.4,1.4c-4.2,0-7.6-3.4-7.6-7.6
        c0-4.2,3.4-7.6,7.6-7.6c1.8,0,3.5,0.6,4.8,1.7c-2.9-6.8-10.3-13.3-19-13.3
        C16.6,57.8,7.5,65.8,7.5,77z"/>
<path class="st0" d="M29.2,129.3c7.9,7.9,20,7.1,28-0.8
        c5.9-5.9,6.2-15.7,4-22.3c-0.3,1.5-1,3-2.1,4.2c-3,3-7.8,3-10.8,0
        c-3-3-3-7.8,0-10.8c1.3-1.3,2.9-2,4.6-2.2c-6.9-2.7-16.7-2.1-22.8,4
        C22,109.3,21.2,121.4,29.2,129.3z"/>
<path class="st0" d="M81.5,151c11.2,0,19.2-9.1,19.2-20.3
        c0-8.3-6.7-15.4-13-18.6c0.9,1.3,1.4,2.8,1.4,4.4c0,4.2-3.4,7.6-7.6,7.6
        c-4.2,0-7.6-3.4-7.6-7.6c0-1.8,0.6-3.5,1.7-4.8c-6.8,2.9-13.3,10.3-13.3,19
        C62.3,141.9,70.3,151,81.5,151z"/>
<path class="st0" d="M133.8,129.3c7.9-7.9,7.1-20-0.8-28
        c-5.9-5.9-15.7-6.2-22.3-4c1.5,0.3,3,1,4.2,2.1c3,3,3,7.8,0,10.8
        s-7.8,3-10.8,0c-1.3-1.3-2-2.9-2.2-4.6c-2.7,6.9-2.1,16.7,4,22.8
        C113.8,136.5,125.9,137.3,133.8,129.3z"/>
<path class="st0" d="M155.5,77c0-11.2-9.1-19.2-20.3-19.2
        c-8.3,0-15.4,6.7-18.6,13c1.3-0.9,2.8-1.4,4.4-1.4c4.2,0,7.6,3.4,7.6,7.6
        c0,4.2-3.4,7.6-7.6,7.6c-1.8,0-3.5-0.6-4.8-1.7c2.9,6.8,10.3,13.3,19,13.3
        C146.4,96.2,155.5,88.2,155.5,77z"/>
<path class="st0" d="M133.8,24.7c-7.9-7.9-20-7.1-28,0.8
        c-5.9,5.9-6.2,15.7-4,22.3c0.3-1.5,1-3,2.1-4.2c3-3,7.8-3,10.8,0
        c3,3,3,7.8,0,10.8c-1.3,1.3-2.9,2-4.6,2.2c6.9,2.7,16.7,2.1,22.8-4
        C141,44.7,141.8,32.6,133.8,24.7z"/>
</g>
</svg>
```

That may look like a lot of mess, especially if you aren't familiar with SVG path syntax. The good news is that almost all of it can be copied into an XML resource unchanged. Every <path> element in the SVG will have a corresponding element inside VectorDrawable. Android vectors don't support SVG's specialized types, such as <circle>, so we will have to manually construct that as a new path. Android also doesn't support CSS styling, so the class attribute used to set the stroke/fill colors on each path will have to be translated into Android attributes. Have a look at Listing 7-43 for the converted vector image.

Listing 7-43. res/drawable/svg_converted.xml

```xml
<?xml version="1.0" encoding="utf-8"?>
<vector xmlns:android="http://schemas.android.com/apk/res/android"
    android:width="163dp"
    android:height="154dp"
    android:viewportWidth="163"
    android:viewportHeight="154">
```

```
<!-- This was the circle element from the SVG file -->
<path
    android:fillColor="#3355CC"
    android:pathData="M66.8,77 a14.7,14.7 0 0,1 29.4,0 a14.7,14.7 0 0,1 -29.4,0z"/>

<!-- The remaining paths are copied over verbatim -->
<path
    android:fillColor="#3355CC"
    android:pathData="M81.5,3c-11.2,0-19.2,9.1-19.2,20.3
            c0,8.3,6.7,15.4,13,18.6c-0.9-1.3-1.4-2.8-1.4-4.4c0-4.2,3.4-7.6,7.6-7.6
            c4.2,0,7.6,3.4,7.6,7.6c0,1.8-0.6,3.5-1.7,4.8c6.8-2.9,13.3-10.3,13.3-19
            C100.7,12.1,92.7,3,81.5,3z"/>
<path
    android:fillColor="#3355CC"
    android:pathData="M29.2,24.7c-7.9,7.9-7.1,20,0.8,28
            c5.9,5.9,15.7,6.2,22.3,4c-1.5-0.3-3-1-4.2-2.1c-3-3-3-7.8,0-10.8
            c3-3,7.8-3,10.8,0c1.3,1.3,2,2.9,2.2,4.6c2.7-6.9,2.1-16.7-4-22.8
            C49.2,17.5,37.1,16.7,29.2,24.7z"/>
<path
    android:fillColor="#3355CC"
    android:pathData="M7.5,77c0,11.2,9.1,19.2,20.3,19.2
            c8.3,0,15.4-6.7,18.6-13c-1.3,0.9-2.8,1.4-4.4,1.4c-4.2,0-7.6-3.4-7.6-7.6
            c0-4.2,3.4-7.6,7.6-7.6c1.8,0,3.5,0.6,4.8,1.7c-2.9-6.8-10.3-13.3-19-13.3
            C16.6,57.8,7.5,65.8,7.5,77z"/>
<path
    android:fillColor="#3355CC"
    android:pathData="M29.2,129.3c7.9,7.9,20,7.1,28-0.8
            c5.9-5.9,6.2-15.7,4-22.3c-0.3,1.5-1,3-2.1,4.2c-3,3-7.8,3-10.8,0
            c-3-3-3-7.8,0-10.8c1.3-1.3,2.9-2,4.6-2.2c-6.9-2.7-16.7-2.1-22.8,4
            C22,109.3,21.2,121.4,29.2,129.3z"/>
<path
    android:fillColor="#3355CC"
    android:pathData="M81.5,151c11.2,0,19.2-9.1,19.2-20.3
            c0-8.3-6.7-15.4-13-18.6c0.9,1.3,1.4,2.8,1.4,4.4c0,4.2-3.4,7.6-7.6,7.6
            c-4.2,0-7.6-3.4-7.6-7.6c0-1.8,0.6-3.5,1.7-4.8c-6.8,2.9-13.3,10.3-13.3,19
            C62.3,141.9,70.3,151,81.5,151z"/>
<path
    android:fillColor="#3355CC"
    android:pathData="M133.8,129.3c7.9-7.9,7.1-20-0.8-28
            c-5.9-5.9-15.7-6.2-22.3-4c1.5,0.3,3,1,4.2,2.1c3,3,3,7.8,0,10.8
            s-7.8,3-10.8,0c-1.3-1.3-2-2.9-2.2-4.6c-2.7,6.9-2.1,16.7,4,22.8
            C113.8,136.5,125.9,137.3,133.8,129.3z"/>
<path
    android:fillColor="#3355CC"
    android:pathData="M155.5,77c0-11.2-9.1-19.2-20.3-19.2
            c-8.3,0-15.4,6.7-18.6,13c1.3-0.9,2.8-1.4,4.4-1.4c4.2,0,7.6,3.4,7.6,7.6
            c0,4.2-3.4,7.6-7.6,7.6c-1.8,0-3.5-0.6-4.8-1.7c2.9,6.8,10.3,13.3,19,13.3
            C146.4,96.2,155.5,88.2,155.5,77z"/>
```

```
<path
    android:fillColor="#3355CC"
    android:pathData="M133.8,24.7c-7.9-7.9-20-7.1-28,0.8
        c-5.9,5.9-6.2,15.7-4,22.3c0.3-1.5,1-3,2.1-4.2c3-3,7.8-3,10.8,0
        c3,3,3,7.8,0,10.8c-1.3,1.3-2.9,2-4.6,2.2c6.9,2.7,16.7,2.1,22.8-4
        C141,44.7,141.8,32.6,133.8,24.7z"/>
</vector>
```

The root element for a VectorDrawable XML definition is <vector>. The width, height, and viewbox attributes from the original <svg> element have been moved here as android:width, android:height, android:viewportWidth, and android:viewportHeight to define the natural size of the image.

The only CSS style parameter that matters here is fill color, which has been added as an android:fillColor attribute on each path. Finally, all the path data is moved from the SVG d attribute to android:pathData. The original <circle> element has been replaced by an equivalent <path>, since that is the only vector type that Android supports.

SVG PATH SYNTAX PRIMER

We did have to make one conversion by hand in the SVG example for the <circle>, so let's dissect the conversion to get a better understanding for SVG path syntax. In the original SVG file, we had the following element:

```
<circle class="st0" cx="81.5" cy="77" r="14.7"/>
```

The following path in the Android vector replaced the circle:

```
android:pathData="M66.8,77 a14.7,14.7 0 0,1 29.4,0 a14.7,14.7 0 0,1 -29.4,0z"
```

The path is a series of drawing commands strung together. Each letter character signifies the beginning of a new command, so we could look at the path like this instead:

```
M66.8,77
a14.7,14.7 0 0,1 29.4,0
a14.7,14.7 0 0,1 -29.4,0
z
```

The path contains three distinct commands:

- M: *Moveto* moves the pen to a specific point, noted by the trailing numbers separated as x,y. Capital letters are an absolute position; lowercase indicates a distance relative to the current pen location.

- a: *Arc* draws an arc from the current pen location to the specified point using the specified radius.

- z: Closes the path. Not required, but will draw a line from the current position to the start position if they are not the same.

The initial circle defines a center point (cx,cy) at (81.5,77), with a radius of 14.7. The new path begins on the left of the circle (less one radius) at the same vertical point, so we begin with a move to (66.8,77). It then draws an arc with the same radius to a new point 29.4 units to the right at the same vertical location; this draws the top half of the circle. The same arc is repeated again, moving back left 29.4 units to draw the bottom half of the circle. The numbers in the middle of both arcs (0 0,1) are flags to indicate that the arc should not be prerotated, and that the arc should sweep in the clockwise direction both times. Finally the path is closed to form a solid circle.

Vector Animation

In this example, we will morph an X shape into a checkmark using path animations. Both elements are defined as vector paths using SVG syntax. Listing 7-44 defines the paths as string resources. This type of animation is only supported on API Level 21 and later.

Listing 7-44. res/values/strings.xml

```
<resources>
    <string name="path_cross">M24,0 l 0,48 M0,24 l 48,0</string>
    <string name="path_check">M9,36 l 20,0 M27,36 l 0,-36</string>
</resources>
```

These paths introduce a new command, called *lineto* with a lowercase *l*. This command simply draws a line from the current position to the relative distance defined after the letter. The "cross" path, for example, draws two straight lines: one vertical from 24,0 to 24,48, and another horizontal from 0,24 to 48,24. Similarly, the "check" path draws two diagonal lines to form its shape. These paths have been abstracted to a resource because they will need to be referenced from multiple places in this example.

Listing 7-45 defines the VectorDrawable to form the initial X shape.

Listing 7-45. res/drawable/vector_cross.xml

```
<?xml version="1.0" encoding="utf-8"?>
<vector xmlns:android="http://schemas.android.com/apk/res/android"
    android:height="64dp"
    android:width="64dp"
    android:viewportHeight="48"
    android:viewportWidth="48">
    <group
        android:name="rotateContainer"
        android:pivotX="24.0"
        android:pivotY="24.0"
        android:rotation="45.0">
        <path
            android:name="cross"
            android:strokeColor="#A00"
            android:strokeWidth="4"
            android:pathData="@string/path_cross" />
    </group>
</vector>
```

This image uses the "cross" path, and then rotates it 45 degrees so it looks like an X rather than a cross. Path elements themselves cannot be transformed via translation, rotation, or scale. Instead, they must be wrapped in a <group>, which does support these transformations for all paths it contains. Each element is also given a name, which we will use to reference the individual components shortly.

As it stands, this could be placed into a view and drawn as a static image. To animate it, however, we need to wrap this vector in an AnimatedVectorDrawable to pair it with animation objects. See Listing 7-46.

Listing 7-46. res/drawable/animated_check.xml

```
<?xml version="1.0" encoding="utf-8"?>
<animated-vector xmlns:android="http://schemas.android.com/apk/res/android"
    android:drawable="@drawable/vector_cross">

    <target
        android:name="cross"
        android:animation="@animator/check_animation"/>

    <target
        android:name="rotateContainer"
        android:animation="@animator/rotate_check_animation" />
</animated-vector>
```

The AnimatedVectorDrawable maps animation objects to targets inside the supplied vector (passed as the android:drawable). The XML references each target element, whether path or group, by its name and matches it with the animation we would like to apply. Listings 7-47 and 7-48 show the animation definitions.

Listing 7-47. res/animator/check_animation.xml

```
<?xml version="1.0" encoding="utf-8"?>
<set xmlns:android="http://schemas.android.com/apk/res/android"
    android:ordering="sequentially">

    <!-- Forward path animation -->
    <objectAnimator
        android:duration="@android:integer/config_longAnimTime"
        android:propertyName="pathData"
        android:valueFrom="@string/path_cross"
        android:valueTo="@string/path_check"
        android:valueType="pathType" />

    <!-- Reverse path animation -->
    <objectAnimator
        android:duration="1000"
        android:propertyName="pathData"
        android:valueFrom="@string/path_check"
        android:valueTo="@string/path_cross"
        android:valueType="pathType"
        android:startOffset="@android:integer/config_longAnimTime"/>
</set>
```

Listing 7-48. res/animator/rotate_check_animation.xml

```xml
<?xml version="1.0" encoding="utf-8"?>
<set xmlns:android="http://schemas.android.com/apk/res/android"
    android:ordering="sequentially">

    <objectAnimator
        android:duration="@android:integer/config_longAnimTime"
        android:propertyName="rotation"
        android:valueFrom="45"
        android:valueTo="405"/>
    <objectAnimator
        android:duration="1000"
        android:propertyName="rotation"
        android:valueFrom="405"
        android:valueTo="45"
        android:startOffset="@android:integer/config_longAnimTime"/>
</set>
```

The animation set applied to the target path contains two pathData animators. This allows us to morph the path from one command set to another; in this case from the cross to the check, and then back again. This is possible as long as the two paths have the same number of data points—in other words, the same commands in the same order with the same number of parameters.

The animators applied to the container group simply rotate the entire image one full circle to give the animation slightly more visual appeal while the path morph is going on. Both animations are reversed after a pause with a much longer duration to easily see exactly how the framework transforms each path.

■ **Note** AnimatedVectorDrawableCompat does not provide access from code to its animators. This means you cannot attach a listener or internally restart the animation separate from the drawable it is attached to.

To complete the example, we have Listings 7-49 and 7-50 to provide an activity and layout into which we can place these new drawables.

Listing 7-49. res/layout/activity_vector.xml

```xml
<LinearLayout xmlns:android="http://schemas.android.com/apk/res/android"
              xmlns:tools="http://schemas.android.com/tools"
              xmlns:app="http://schemas.android.com/apk/res-auto"
              android:orientation="vertical"
              android:layout_width="match_parent"
              android:layout_height="match_parent"
              tools:context=".VectorActivity">

    <ImageView
        android:id="@+id/image_static"
        android:layout_width="match_parent"
        android:layout_height="0dp"
        android:layout_weight="2"/>
```

```
    <ImageView
        android:id="@+id/image_icon"
        android:layout_width="48dp"
        android:layout_height="48dp"
        android:layout_weight="1"
        android:layout_gravity="center_horizontal"
        app:srcCompat="@drawable/ic_tag_faces_black_24dp"/>

    <ImageView
        android:id="@+id/image_animated"
        android:layout_width="match_parent"
        android:layout_height="0dp"
        android:layout_weight="1"
        android:scaleType="center"/>

    <Button
        android:id="@+id/animate_button"
        android:layout_width="match_parent"
        android:layout_height="wrap_content"
        android:text="Morph Drawable"
        android:onClick="onMorphClick"/>
</LinearLayout>
```

Listing 7-50. Activity Displaying Vector Drawables

```java
public class VectorActivity extends AppCompatActivity {

    private AnimatedVectorDrawableCompat mAnimatedDrawable;

    @Override
    protected void onCreate(Bundle savedInstanceState) {
        super.onCreate(savedInstanceState);
        setContentView(R.layout.activity_vector);

        //Set the converted SVG vector as a static image
        ImageView imageView = (ImageView) findViewById(R.id.image_static);
        VectorDrawableCompat vectorDrawableCompat
                = VectorDrawableCompat.create(getResources(), R.drawable.svg_converted,
                getTheme());
        imageView.setImageDrawable(vectorDrawableCompat);

        if (Build.VERSION.SDK_INT >= Build.VERSION_CODES.HONEYCOMB) {
            //Create the vector path morph animation
            imageView = (ImageView) findViewById(R.id.image_animated);

            mAnimatedDrawable = AnimatedVectorDrawableCompat.create(this, R.drawable.
            animated_check);
            imageView.setImageDrawable(mAnimatedDrawable);
            findViewById(R.id.animate_button).setEnabled(true);
        } else {
            findViewById(R.id.animate_button).setEnabled(false);
        }
    }
```

```
public void onMorphClick(View v) {
    mAnimatedDrawable.start();
}
}
```

The layout contains three ImageView instances and a Button. Our converted SVG image is placed statically into the top view using the method imageView.setImageDrawable(). The second ImageView has the vector drawable set using the attribute app:srcCompat, which is what you must use if you want to set vetor drawables in XML and have it supported below API Level 21. The animated item is placed in the third ImageView in the bottom. Whenever the user presses the button, our path morphing animation will run. The path morphing animation only works from API Level 21 and later. For earlier versions we can only support simple animations. You can see the results in Figure 7-24.

Figure 7-24. *Activity containing vector images*

Summary

In this chapter, we've explored ways to use drawables as a flexible background, to communicate state changes, and as a scalable vector path. We looked at image-processing techniques such as image masking. Finally, you saw some more advanced methods of direct drawing using overlays, surfaces, and textures. In the final chapter, we will explore some high-performance techniques for heavy processing of code in your applications using native (C/C++) code and RenderScript.

CHAPTER 8

■ ■ ■

Working with Android NDK and RenderScript

Developers predominantly write Android applications in Java. However, in some situations, it's desirable (or even necessary) to express at least part of the code in another language (notably C or C++). This may come from a need to access resources only available in native code (such as kernel drivers), or to obtain better performance from critical sections of code. Google addresses these situations by providing the Android Native Development Kit (NDK) and RenderScript.

Android NDK

The Android NDK complements the Android SDK by providing a toolset to use C/C++ for implementing parts of your app in native code. The NDK provides headers and libraries for building native activities, handling user input, using hardware sensors, and more. The NDK is commonly used in the following scenarios:

- Improving the performance of CPU-bound code for doing heavy processing or computation. RenderScript (addressed later in this chapter) also offers solutions for this.

- Accessing system resources not directly exposed through the runtime APIs. This might include specific device drivers or kernel resources.

- Increasing cross-platform portability that comes with a C/C++ development environment. Many game development engines/frameworks utilize the NDK for this reason.

Native code is platform specific, so the Android NDK must cross-compile your code for every device architecture where your application will be deployed. The latest Android NDK (r10b as of this writing) supports the following device architectures: armv5, armv7, x86, arm64-v8a, x86_64, and mips64. These are also known as the *application binary interface*, or ABI, of the device.

© Dave Smith and Erik Hellman 2016
D. Smith and E. Hellman, *Android Recipes*, DOI 10.1007/978-1-4842-2259-1_8

BUILDING NDK CODE

Starting with version 2.2 of the Android Gradle build tools, the default method for building native code in your project is through the CMake system. This system is a topic too large to cover in this book, but it is basically a system for generating native build scripts. This means that through the CMake build script, called CMakeLists.txt, an actual makefile will be generated during the build step and the NDK build tools executed.

The CMakeLists.txt file consists of a number of API calls to the CMake API. Following are the most important of these API calls, explained in order to make your C/C++ code build with the Android Gradle build tools.

- cmake_minimum_required(VERSION 3.4.1): This call sets the version of CMake to be used for this build. Currently, this should be 3.4.1 for Android.

- add_library(libname SHARED path/to/file.c): The add_library call is used to add code that will be compiled by the build tools. It has at least three parameters; the name of the library (libname), the type of build (SHARED or STATIC), and one or multiple pats to a source file (path/to/file.c). In most cases you want to use SHARED for your own code, while using STATIC for external libraries you want to include.

- include_directories(${ANDROID_NDK}/path/to/headers): For header files that belong to additional external libraries that are not on the default NDK path, you need to call include_directories() with the correct paths.

- find_library(lib-name lib): Several libraries are automatically included in the NDK build path, so you won't need to use add_library() or include_directories() for those, but should use find_library() instead. These are listed under Libraries -> Stable API on the Android NDK documentation site (see https://developer.android. com/ndk/reference/index.html). The two parameters for this call are the name used by CMake (lib-name) and the library name as defined by the NDK (lib).

- target_link_libraries(shared_lib_name other_lib ${lib-name}): The final CMake call is to target_link_libraries(), which tells CMake how to construct the final shared library that will be included in your APK. The first parameter is the same as the one you gave for the library for your own native code, and the rest of the parameters are either names from the other add_library() calls or the variables defined by the calls you did with find_library().

In order to link your CMake project to your Gradle project, you need to modify your build.gradle file to recognize the external build tool. This can most easily be done by right-clicking on the module where your CMakeLists.txt is placed, selecting "Link C++ Project with Gradle" and selecting the CMakeLists.txt to use. This will result in the following added to the android section of the build.gradle for your module.

```
externalNativeBuild {
    cmake {
        path 'CMakeLists.txt'
    }
}
```

Make sure the CMakeLists.txt is placed in the same folder as the build.gradle file or relative paths won't work properly.

The Android NDK will generate shared library files for each supported ABI that the final build tools can package into the final APK. Generally, an application includes all these binaries into the same APK to simplify distribution. However, if the native code in an application gets too large, this might put the APK file over the size limits of your chosen distributor. Google Play, for example, has a 100MB APK limit at the writing of this book.

To reduce APK size, many developers will split their build into multiple APK files, one for each supported ABI. Prominent app stores, such as Google Play, also support uploading multiple APKs and will handle distributing the appropriate binary to the appropriate device for you.

Using the Gradle build system, the split can be managed by providing a unique product flavor for each ABI:

```
productFlavors {
    x86 {
        ndk {
            abiFilter "x86"
        }
    }
    arm {
        ndk {
            abiFilter "armeabi-v7a"
        }
    }
    arm {
        ndk {
            abiFilter "armeabi-v8a"
        }
    }
    mips {
        ndk {
            abiFilter "mips"
        }
    }
}
```

Then exporting a unique APK for each ABI is as simple as building and exporting another product flavor.

8-1. Adding Native Bits with JNI

Problem

You have a small amount of native code that you want to execute within the larger context of a Java application project.

Solution

Android supports the use of the Java Native Interface (JNI) APIs to bridge between your Java code and native execution. With JNI, native shared libraries can be dynamically loaded into the runtime to provide implementations of specific methods declared on the application's Java classes.

To add JNI to a project, you must accomplish the following steps:

1. Declare the methods that will be implemented in C/C++ in your Java class with the native keyword.

2. Write and compile your native code into a shared library (.so file) that can be dynamically loaded using the Android NDK.

3. Notify the runtime to load your native code by using calls to System. loadLibrary() prior to invoking any native methods.

Following is a sample Java snippet to illustrate this implementation:

```
package com.androidrecipes.app;
public class NativeWrapper {

    //Declare any methods with a C/C++ implementation as native
    public static native void nativeMethod();

    static {
        //Tell the runtime to load your shared library, in this case "libnative_wrapper.so"
        System.loadLibrary("native_wrapper");
    }
}
```

In order for this to work, the application runtime must have a way of binding the native method code to the invocations coming from Java. The JNI APIs provide two distinct mechanisms for mapping native methods to Java:

- Define your native method names by using the default JNI specification of class-name mangling. In the previous example, the native method name would be Java_com_androidrecipes_app_NativeWrapper_nativeMethod().

  - There is a JDK command-line tool, javah, which will generate these for you.

- Use an explicit method table to map Java methods to native method signatures. In this case, the method names in your native code can be anything you choose, but the entire thing must be coded by hand (that is, no tools to generate the boilerplate code).

We will explore how to implement both of these options in the upcoming example.

■ **Note**   Android's *libc* implementation (known as *bionic*) is not binary compatible with other common implementations such as *glibc* or *uClibc*. If you are porting native code from other platforms, you must recompile it with the NDK to produce binaries that are appropriate for the Android runtime.

How It Works

In this example, we are using an API unique to the NDK called *cpufeatures*. This library allows us to examine the CPU architecture information of the device, as well as determine support for certain instruction sets (such as NEON or SSE3). We want to expose this information to our activity code, written in Java, so we will need to implement some JNI code to bind the two.

■ **Note**   The available NDK APIs are documented in the Programmer's Guide that can be found in the docs/ directory of the NDK installation. The section "Stable APIs" lists each of the features, and the minimum platform required, if applicable.

First, we must start with a Java class that we can use as the starting point for our JNI bindings (see Listing 8-1). Whenever we want to invoke our native code from Java, it will be done through this class.

Listing 8-1. Java Class with Native Methods Defined

```
package com.androidrecipes.ndkjni;

public class NativeLib {
    /**
     * Return the number of available cores on the device
     */
    public static native int getCpuCount();

    public static native String getCpuFamily();

    static {
        System.loadLibrary("features");
    }
}
```

Notice that each method we intend to implement in C/C++ is declared with the `native` keyword. This tells the runtime it should find this method in a native shared library somewhere. Second, we have to notify the runtime of which shared library contains our code. In this case, we are telling the runtime to look for a file named `libfeatures.so` (to be built later) in our application's directory path.

Now we must create the native implementation of these two declared methods. Listings 8-2 and 8-3 show the native header file and implementation file that describe these methods by using their JNI signatures.

Listing 8-2. src/main/jni/NativeLib.h

```c
#include <jni.h>
/* Header for class com_androidrecipes_ndkjni_NativeLib */

#ifndef _Included_com_androidrecipes_ndkjni_NativeLib
#define _Included_com_androidrecipes_ndkjni_NativeLib
#ifdef __cplusplus
extern "C" {
#endif
/*
 * Class:     com_androidrecipes_ndkjni_NativeLib
 * Method:    getCpuCount
 * Signature: ()I
 */
JNIEXPORT jint JNICALL Java_com_androidrecipes_ndkjni_NativeLib_getCpuCount
  (JNIEnv *, jclass);

/*
 * Class:     com_androidrecipes_ndkjni_NativeLib
 * Method:    getCpuFamily
 * Signature: ()Ljava/lang/String;
 */
JNIEXPORT jstring JNICALL Java_com_androidrecipes_ndkjni_NativeLib_getCpuFamily
  (JNIEnv *, jclass);

#ifdef __cplusplus
}
#endif
#endif
```

Listing 8-3. src/main/jni/NativeLib.c

```c
#include "NativeLib.h"

#include <android/log.h>
#include <cpu-features.h>

JNIEXPORT jint JNICALL Java_com_androidrecipes_ndkjni_NativeLib_getCpuCount
  (JNIEnv *env, jclass clazz)
{
    return android_getCpuCount();
}

JNIEXPORT jstring JNICALL Java_com_androidrecipes_ndkjni_NativeLib_getCpuFamily
  (JNIEnv *env, jclass clazz)
{
    AndroidCpuFamily family = android_getCpuFamily();
    switch (family)
    {
        case ANDROID_CPU_FAMILY_ARM:
            return (*env)->NewStringUTF(env, "ARM (32-bit)");
```

```
    case ANDROID_CPU_FAMILY_X86:
        return (*env)->NewStringUTF(env, "x86 (32-bit)");
    case ANDROID_CPU_FAMILY_MIPS:
        return (*env)->NewStringUTF(env, "MIPS (32-bit)");
    case ANDROID_CPU_FAMILY_ARM64:
        return (*env)->NewStringUTF(env, "ARM (64-bit)");
    case ANDROID_CPU_FAMILY_X86_64:
        return (*env)->NewStringUTF(env, "x86 (64-bit)");
    case ANDROID_CPU_FAMILY_MIPS64:
        return (*env)->NewStringUTF(env, "MIPS (64-bit)");
    case ANDROID_CPU_FAMILY_UNKNOWN:
    default:
        return (*env)->NewStringUTF(env, "Vaporware");
    }
}
```

USING JAVAH

If you would prefer not to craft the native signatures yourself, one option is to use `javah` to do the work. This is a command-line tool provided by the JDK that will inspect a given Java class for native methods, and produce a header that includes each method signature inside. To have `javah` generate the header for our example, execute the following commands:

```
$ cd <project_directory>/src/main
$ javah -jni -classpath <project_bin_directory> -d jni com.androidrecipes.ndkjni.NativeLib
```

We deconstruct this command into its parts to get a better idea of what happens:

- `-jni`: Tell the tool to generate a header file for our Java class.

- `-classpath <project_bin_directory>`: Reference the directory in your project where the compiled Java class output sits. ADT/Eclipse uses `bin/classes`, and Android Studio uses `build/intermediates/classes/<build_type>`.

- `-d jni`: Place the output in the `jni/` directory (that is, `src/main/jni`).

- `com.androidrecipes.ndkjni.NativeLib`: The fully qualified class name of the Java class to inspect.

This will produce a `com_androidrecipes_ndkjni_NativeLib.h` file with the same content seen in Listing 8-2. The file name is not important, and it can be renamed to something easier to manage.

Notice the long method names used to uniquely identify each method inside the shared library. Any typographical error in these method names will cause an `UnsatisfiedLinkError` at runtime because the JNI APIs wouldn't be able to find the appropriate native implementation. Each method name is prefixed with Java, followed by the package name, Java class name, and finally Java method name.

Each native method will also have matching parameters for each parameter the Java method declared, with two additional items. The `JNIEnv` pointer is a reference to the JNI API functions that can be invoked from the native code. The `jclass` is a reference to the owning Java class this method is attached to. This is present because our Java methods were defined as `static`. If they were instance methods in Java, this second parameter would be a jobject instead, and would reference the owning object instance of the method call. Finally, the return values of the methods have been converted (int -> jint and String -> jstring) to JNI-friendly types.

Speaking of JNI APIs, you must also include the jni.h header file in your implementation. In our example, and for anyone using javah, this will be done for you in the generated header. This allows your native code to access the features provided for bridging between Java and native code.

■ **Note** JNI programming is too large a topic to cover in this book. If you want to become more familiar with programming using JNI, reference the Oracle JNI documentation: http://docs.oracle.com/javase/7/docs/technotes/guides/jni/.

The android_getCpuCount() and android_getCpuFamily() functions are defined by cpufeatures, which we have access to by including cpu-features.h in our code. Our JNI methods are just wrappers around these functions to pipe the results back into Java. The CPU count will return the number of cores the device has available as an integer. This value can be directly returned, as a jint is just a simple type of integer.

When returning the CPU family, this value is an enum that we must convert to a human-friendly string. String values in C are quite different from Java; the former is a null-terminated character array, while the latter is a full object with additional metadata besides just the characters. Because of this, we cannot simply return a string literal from C to Java. We have to call the NewStringUTF() transformation function provided by JNIEnv to allocate a new Java string object (jstring) from the character data.

To build the native code, we have to construct a CMakeLists.txt placed in the same folder as the build.gradle makefile; this can be found in Listings 8-4.

Listing 8-4. CMakeLists.txt

```
cmake_minimum_required(VERSION 3.4.1)

add_library(features SHARED src/main/c/NativeLib.c )

include_directories(${ANDROID_NDK}/sources/android/cpufeatures )

add_library(cpufeatures STATIC
            ${ANDROID_NDK}/sources/android/cpufeatures/cpu-features.c )

find_library(log-lib log )

target_link_libraries(features cpufeatures ${log-lib} )
```

The CMakeLists.txt here tells the build tools that we want to include the NativeLib.c file in the shared library named features. We also build a static version of the cpufeatures library and include the native logging library. Finally, we tell CMake to link all of these together to form the final .so file for our application.

With a working native library in place, we turn to Listings 8-5 and 8-6 to show us a simple activity that displays this information for the current device in a view.

Listing 8-5. `res/layout/activity_main.xml`

```xml
<?xml version="1.0" encoding="utf-8"?>
<FrameLayout xmlns:android="http://schemas.android.com/apk/res/android"
    android:layout_width="match_parent"
    android:layout_height="match_parent">

    <TextView
        android:id="@+id/text_info"
        android:layout_width="wrap_content"
        android:layout_height="wrap_content"
        android:layout_gravity="center"/>
</FrameLayout>
```

Listing 8-6. Activity Invoking JNI Library

```java
public class MainActivity extends Activity {

    private TextView mInfoText;

    @Override
    protected void onCreate(Bundle savedInstanceState) {
        super.onCreate(savedInstanceState);
        setContentView(R.layout.activity_main);

        mInfoText = (TextView) findViewById(R.id.text_info);

        getInfo();
    }

    private void getInfo() {
        String text = String.format("%s CPU with %d core(s)",
                NativeLib.getCpuFamily(),
                NativeLib.getCpuCount() );
        mInfoText.setText(text);
    }
}
```

In our application code, we simply need to call our native methods as if they were any other Java method. The Android runtime will do the work of invoking our native code and returning to Java once the execution is complete. Run this example on your device and you will see a text string defining your processor architecture and number of available cores!

Native Method Tables

As an alternate implementation to class-name mangling, we can use explicit method tables to create references to native methods that are easier to read and maintain. In this case, as you can see in Listing 8-7, we are going to leverage the `JNI_OnLoad` callback. This is invoked when the library is loaded, and gives us a good initialization point for our method mappings.

663

Listing 8-7. src/main/jni/NativeLibAlternate.c

```c
//JNI APIs, was included by our custom header before
#include <jni.h>

#include <android/log.h>
#include <cpu-features.h>

static jint native_getCpuCount(JNIEnv *env, jclass clazz)
{
    return android_getCpuCount();
}

static jstring native_getCpuFamily(JNIEnv *env, jclass clazz)
{
    AndroidCpuFamily family = android_getCpuFamily();
    switch (family)
    {
        case ANDROID_CPU_FAMILY_ARM:
            return (*env)->NewStringUTF(env, "ARM (32-bit)");
        case ANDROID_CPU_FAMILY_X86:
            return (*env)->NewStringUTF(env, "x86 (32-bit)");
        case ANDROID_CPU_FAMILY_MIPS:
            return (*env)->NewStringUTF(env, "MIPS (32-bit)");
        case ANDROID_CPU_FAMILY_ARM64:
            return (*env)->NewStringUTF(env, "ARM (64-bit)");
        case ANDROID_CPU_FAMILY_X86_64:
            return (*env)->NewStringUTF(env, "x86 (64-bit)");
        case ANDROID_CPU_FAMILY_MIPS64:
            return (*env)->NewStringUTF(env, "MIPS (64-bit)");
        case ANDROID_CPU_FAMILY_UNKNOWN:
        default:
            return (*env)->NewStringUTF(env, "Vaporware");
    }
}

//Construct a table mapping Java method signatures to native function pointers
static JNINativeMethod method_table[] = {
    { "getCpuCount", "()I", (void *) native_getCpuCount },
    { "getCpuFamily", "()Ljava/lang/String;", (void *) native_getCpuFamily }
};

//Use the OnLoad initializer to register the method table with the runtime
jint JNI_OnLoad(JavaVM* vm, void* reserved) {
    JNIEnv* env;
    if ((*vm)->GetEnv(vm, (void**)&env, JNI_VERSION_1_6) != JNI_OK) {
        return JNI_ERR;
    } else {
        jclass clazz = (*env)->FindClass(env,
                "com/androidrecipes/ndkjni/NativeLib");
```

```
        if (clazz) {
            jint ret = (*env)->RegisterNatives(env, clazz, method_table,
                    sizeof(method_table) / sizeof(method_table[0]));
            if (ret == 0) {
                return JNI_VERSION_1_6;
            }
        }
    }
    return JNI_ERR;
    }
}
```

The gist of the boilerplate code in JNI_OnLoad is to find a reference to the Java class we created (using reflection) and attach a method table to it using the RegisterNatives function from the JNI environment. This method takes an array of JNINativeMethod structures, each containing the following (in order):

- Method name of the method on the Java class, as a string

- Method signature of the method on the Java class. This is a string that defines the parameters and return types the Java method takes, to uniquely identify an overloaded method version.

- A function pointer to the native function we created to handle the invocation

---

■ **Note**   For more information on how to construct JNI method signature strings, reference the Oracle JNI documentation: http://docs.oracle.com/javase/7/docs/technotes/guides/jni/spec/types.html.

Notice that the native method parameters must still remain the same (they are still required to have the proper parameters list, including the environment and class pointer). However, now we can name the methods whatever we like because the method table is responsible for doing the mapping. As before, typos in your method table will cause an UnsatisfiedLinkError. However, unlike before, this will cause the code to fail when the runtime class loader loads the NativeLib Java class into memory. This gives us the benefit of failing slightly faster than waiting until a method is actually invoked.

8-2. Building a Purely Native Activity

Problem

Your application UI requires tighter integration with native code, and it would be simpler to build the entire activity element with the NDK.

Solution

Use a NativeActivity implementation in your application. The NDK provides an import library, titled android_native_app_glue, which provides bindings between the activity APIs and a native implementation. This library provides life-cycle callbacks and handlers for processing input events, such as touch or sensor input.

While your application does technically still have a Java-based activity running, NativeActivity takes care of all the JNI binding and life-cycle forwarding so your code can be pure C/C++ for that activity's behavior, allowing you to take a deeper approach to integrating NDK APIs.

In addition to life-cycle callbacks, android_native_app_glue provides event handlers for dealing with input events. Touch events, key events, and sensor (for example, accelerometer) events can all be processed from a queue directly in the native code. This process is slightly more complex than Java, because the native code is also responsible for polling and dequeueing events as they come in for processing; this results in a bit more boilerplate code than we would have with Java.

How It Works

In this example, we will construct an activity in native code that responds to touch events by rendering a different color to the screen in OpenGL. As the user's finger drags around the view, the color will change based on the latest touch position. Even with such a simple goal, we will see how much more code is required to accomplish this goal when we leave the Java framework behind.

■ **Note**   OpenGL programming topics are outside the scope of this book, and aren't the focus of this example. The OpenGL used in this example came directly from the Android NDK Sample for OpenGL.

This project will not contain any Java source code, for an activity or otherwise. Instead, NativeActivity supports metadata in the application's manifest to define the shared library that should be loaded by the framework and "glued" into the activity life cycle. Listing 8-8 highlights the pieces we need to have in the AndroidManifest.xml file.

Listing 8-8. AndroidManifest.xml

```xml
<manifest xmlns:android="http://schemas.android.com/apk/res/android"
    package="com.androidrecipes.nativeactivity"
    android:versionCode="1"
    android:versionName="1.0" >

    <application
        android:hasCode="false"
        ... >
        <activity
            android:name="android.app.NativeActivity"
            android:configChanges="orientation"
            android:label="@string/app_name" >
            <!-- Where to find NativeActivity implementation -->
            <meta-data
                android:name="android.app.lib_name"
                android:value="native-activity" />

            <intent-filter>
                <action android:name="android.intent.action.MAIN" />
                <category android:name="android.intent.category.LAUNCHER" />
            </intent-filter>
        </activity>
    </application>

</manifest>
```

The key elements in this manifest are the following:

- Our activity element must be an `android.app.NativeActivity`.
  - We can also subclass this and use a custom implementation, but the root must be a `NativeActivity`.
- A `<meta-data>` element should exist with the name `android.app.lib_name` and a value representing the shared library name.
  - This library name is the same as the name passed to `System.loadLibrary()` in the previous example. It should match a file named `lib<name>.so` in your APK.
  - In our case, the contract is that our code will be in `libnative-activity.so`.
- Optional: If you do not provide any additional Java code in your application, you can set `android:hasCode` to `false` in the `<application>` element.
  - This is simply a startup optimization if your app has no Java code to offer. You cannot set this attribute if your package has any Java classes at all!The bulk of our interesting code, then, will be found in the native implementation that we eventually build into that shared library. Let's have a look at that code in Listing 8-9.

Listing 8-9. `src/main/jni/activity.c`

```c
#include <EGL/egl.h>
#include <GLES/gl.h>

#include <android/log.h>
#include <android/window.h>
#include <android_native_app_glue.h>

#define LOGI(...) ((void)__android_log_print(ANDROID_LOG_INFO, "AndroidRecipes", __VA_
ARGS__))
#define LOGD(...) ((void)__android_log_print(ANDROID_LOG_DEBUG, "AndroidRecipes", __VA_
ARGS__))
#define LOGW(...) ((void)__android_log_print(ANDROID_LOG_WARN, "AndroidRecipes", __VA_
ARGS__))

//Data structure to hold that last known touch location
struct touch_state
{
    int32_t x;
    int32_t y;
};

//Data structure to hold the global state of the activity
struct driver
{
    struct android_app* app;
    struct touch_state state;
```

```
    EGLDisplay display;
    EGLSurface surface;
    EGLContext context;
    int32_t width;
    int32_t height;
};

/**
 * Helper function to render the next color frame in OpenGL
 */
static void render_frame(struct driver* driver)
{
    if (driver->display == NULL) {
        // No display.
        return;
    }

    float red = (float)driver->state.x / driver->width;
    float green = (float)driver->state.y / driver->height;
    float blue = 1 - (float)driver->state.x / driver->width;
    //Render the new color based on touch position
    glClearColor(red, green, blue, 1.0f);
    //Tell OpenGL to refresh the color buffer
    glClear(GL_COLOR_BUFFER_BIT);
    //Place the new frame onto the display buffer
    eglSwapBuffers(driver->display, driver->surface);
}

/**
 * Initialize an EGL context for the current display.
 */
static int engine_init_display(struct driver* driver) {
    // initialize OpenGL ES and EGL

    /*
     * Here specify the attributes of the desired configuration.
     * Below, we select an EGLConfig with at least 8 bits per color
     * component compatible with on-screen windows
     */
    const EGLint attribs[] = {
            EGL_SURFACE_TYPE, EGL_WINDOW_BIT,
            EGL_BLUE_SIZE, 8,
            EGL_GREEN_SIZE, 8,
            EGL_RED_SIZE, 8,
            EGL_NONE
    };
    EGLint w, h, dummy, format;
    EGLint numConfigs;
    EGLConfig config;
    EGLSurface surface;
    EGLContext context;
```

```c
    EGLDisplay display = eglGetDisplay(EGL_DEFAULT_DISPLAY);

    eglInitialize(display, 0, 0);

    /* Here, the application chooses the configuration it desires. In this
     * sample, we have a very simplified selection process, where we pick
     * the first EGLConfig that matches our criteria */
    eglChooseConfig(display, attribs, &config, 1, &numConfigs);

    /* EGL_NATIVE_VISUAL_ID is an attribute of the EGLConfig that is
     * guaranteed to be accepted by ANativeWindow_setBuffersGeometry().
     * As soon as we picked a EGLConfig, we can safely reconfigure the
     * ANativeWindow buffers to match, using EGL_NATIVE_VISUAL_ID. */
    eglGetConfigAttrib(display, config, EGL_NATIVE_VISUAL_ID, &format);

    ANativeWindow_setBuffersGeometry(driver->app->window, 0, 0, format);

    surface = eglCreateWindowSurface(display, config, driver->app->window, NULL);
    context = eglCreateContext(display, config, NULL, NULL);

    if (eglMakeCurrent(display, surface, surface, context) == EGL_FALSE) {
        LOGW("Unable to eglMakeCurrent");
        return -1;
    }

    eglQuerySurface(display, surface, EGL_WIDTH, &w);
    eglQuerySurface(display, surface, EGL_HEIGHT, &h);

    driver->display = display;
    driver->context = context;
    driver->surface = surface;
    driver->width = w;
    driver->height = h;

    // Initialize GL state.
    glHint(GL_PERSPECTIVE_CORRECTION_HINT, GL_FASTEST);
    glEnable(GL_CULL_FACE);
    glShadeModel(GL_SMOOTH);
    glDisable(GL_DEPTH_TEST);

    return 0;
}

/**
 * Tear down the EGL context currently associated with the display.
 */
static void engine_term_display(struct driver* driver) {
    if (driver->display != EGL_NO_DISPLAY) {
        eglMakeCurrent(driver->display, EGL_NO_SURFACE, EGL_NO_SURFACE, EGL_NO_CONTEXT);
```

```c
        if (driver->context != EGL_NO_CONTEXT) {
            eglDestroyContext(driver->display, driver->context);
        }
        if (driver->surface != EGL_NO_SURFACE) {
            eglDestroySurface(driver->display, driver->surface);
        }
        eglTerminate(driver->display);
    }

    driver->display = EGL_NO_DISPLAY;
    driver->context = EGL_NO_CONTEXT;
    driver->surface = EGL_NO_SURFACE;
}


/*
 * This event handler will receive lifecycle events for
 * the enclosing Activity instance.
 */
static void handle_cmd(struct android_app* app, int32_t cmd)
{
    struct driver* driver = (struct driver*)app->userData;
    switch (cmd)
    {
        case APP_CMD_SAVE_STATE:
            LOGI("Save state");
            // The system has asked us to save our current state.  Do so.
            driver->app->savedState = malloc(sizeof(struct touch_state));
            *((struct touch_state*)driver->app->savedState) = driver->state;
            driver->app->savedStateSize = sizeof(struct touch_state);
            break;

        case APP_CMD_INIT_WINDOW:
            LOGI("Init window");
            // The window is being shown, get it ready.
            if (driver->app->window != NULL) {
                engine_init_display(driver);
                render_frame(driver);
            }
            break;

        case APP_CMD_TERM_WINDOW:
            LOGI("Terminate window");
            // The window is being hidden or closed, clean it up.
            engine_term_display(driver);
            break;

        case APP_CMD_PAUSE:
            LOGI("Pausing");
            break;
```

```
        case APP_CMD_RESUME:
            LOGI("Resuming");
            break;

        case APP_CMD_STOP:
            LOGI("Stopping");
            break;

        case APP_CMD_DESTROY:
            LOGI("Destroying");
            break;

        case APP_CMD_LOST_FOCUS:
            LOGI("Lost focus");
            break;

        case APP_CMD_GAINED_FOCUS:
            LOGI("Gained focus");
            break;
    }
}

/*
 * This event handler will be triggered to process input
 * events received by the polling loop in main.
 */
static int32_t handle_input(struct android_app* app, AInputEvent* event)
{
    struct driver* driver = (struct driver*)app->userData;
    //Save the latest touch event for use in rendering
    if (AInputEvent_getType(event) == AINPUT_EVENT_TYPE_MOTION)
    {
        driver->state.x = AMotionEvent_getX(event, 0);
        driver->state.y = AMotionEvent_getY(event, 0);
        return 1;
    }
    else if (AInputEvent_getType(event) == AINPUT_EVENT_TYPE_KEY)
    {
        LOGI("Received key event: %d", AKeyEvent_getKeyCode(event));
        if (AKeyEvent_getKeyCode(event) == AKEYCODE_BACK)
        {
            //Finish the Activity
            if (AKeyEvent_getAction(event) == AKEY_EVENT_ACTION_UP)
            {
                ANativeActivity_finish(app->activity);
            }
        }
        return 1;
    }
    return 0;
}
```

```
/*
 * This is the main entry point for the native code. This
 * code is called on a separate thread, created by the
 * native_app_glue APIs.
 */
void android_main(struct android_app* state)
{
    struct driver driver;

    app_dummy(); // prevent glue from being stripped

    memset(&driver, 0, sizeof(driver));
    //Hold a reference to our state driver in the app struct
    state->userData = &driver;
    //Define app event handlers
    state->onAppCmd = &handle_cmd;
    state->onInputEvent = &handle_input;

    driver.app = state;

    if (state->savedState != NULL) {
        // We are starting with a previous saved state; restore from it.
        driver.state = *(struct touch_state*)state->savedState;
    }

    while(1)
    {
        int ident;
        int fdesc;
        int events;
        struct android_poll_source* source;

        //Infinite loop to poll for incoming events in the message queue
        while ((ident = ALooper_pollAll(0, &fdesc, &events, (void**)&source)) >= 0)
        {
            //Each event will be processed in the handler function we attached
            if (source)
                source->process(state, source);

            //This will be set when the activity is being destroyed
            if (state->destroyRequested)
                return;
        }

        //On each loop, render the next frame...
        // OpenGL throttles this so the main loop will effectively
        // run at the framebuffer update rate (16.7ms in most cases)
        render_frame(&driver);
    }
}
```

With the native activity APIs, the android_main() function is the entry point into your code. This function is called during the onCreate() phase of the activity, and it is *created on a separate thread*. This means that whatever happens inside this method is not synchronized with the rest of the life-cycle events in the activity.

Your code should keep this method active unless the activity should be destroyed. In our example, as is typical, we are using this method to infinitely loop, processing queued input events and rendering display frames. We will look at each of these in more detail shortly.

Upon initialization, we are handed an android_app data structure. This structure will contain any saved state if this activity creation is part of a configuration change (that is, rotation), and provides hooks for us to attach callback functions for additional events.

The onAppCmd function pointer should reference a callback where life-cycle events can be triggered, such as pause, resume, save instance state, and so forth. We have attached the handle_cmd() function to receive these callback events. Callbacks to this function will happen on the **application's main thread**.

The OpenGL setup and teardown for this example is done in the engine_init_display() and engine_term_display() functions. These methods are invoked when the life cycle tells us that the activity window has been created (APP_CMD_INIT_WINDOW) or terminated (APP_CMD_TERM_WINDOW).

We also make use of APP_CMD_SAVE_STATE, which is called during configuration change events (just as we would see onSaveInstanceState in Java). In our case, we use this event to persist the current touch state so we can reconstruct the same color after rotation. This value will be available to the new activity in android_main() via the android_app data structure.

The onInputEvent callback will be responsible for handling any processed events the main loop pulls from the queue. This callback will fire each time the main loop dequeues an event from an input source with ALoop_pollAll() and calls process() on that source. We have defined handle_input() to manage these events. All event types that the framework delivers will be dropped here, so we have to first distinguish which events are touch events (that is, AINPUT_EVENT_TYPE_MOTION). For each event received, we simply save the x/y value into the global state.

On each iteration through the main loop, render_frame() will be called, which will read the latest x/y touch position and compute a color value. That color is rendered to the display using the OpenGL command glClearColor(); the frame is actually displayed when eglSwapBuffers() is called.

■ **Tip**   The framework throttles buffer swap calls at the update rate of the GPU (usually 60fps), so eglSwapBuffers() will block until a new buffer is available after a frame is fully rendered. This effectively means that eglSwapBuffers() clocks our loop at 60fps without any additional timing.

Building our native code with the NDK requires CMakeLists.txt file to define the build modules. We can see it for this project in Listings 8-10.

Listing 8-10. CMakeLists.txt

```
cmake_minimum_required(VERSION 3.4.1)

add_library(native-activity SHARED src/main/c/activity.c )

include_directories(${ANDROID_NDK}/sources/android/native_app_glue )

add_library(native_app_glue  STATIC
            ${ANDROID_NDK}/sources/android/native_app_glue/android_native_app_glue.c )

find_library(log-lib log )
```

```
find_library(android android )

find_library(egl-lib EGL )

find_library(gles-lib GLESv1_CM )

target_link_libraries(native-activity native_app_glue
                      ${log-lib} ${android} ${egl-lib} ${gles-lib} )
```

The CMakeLists.txt file tells the NDK to compile our single activity.c file into a module named native-activity (that is, a file named libnative-activity.so). Notice how this name matches the name we supplied to the manifest earlier. The makefile also defines the imports required to access the native_app_glue API provided by the NDK.

With working native libraries built into the project, you can now run the example and watch the colors change as you drag your finger across the screen—all without a single line of Java code!

RenderScript

Google released RenderScript to take high-performance computation algorithms on Android to the next level. As device hardware capabilities advance, increased computing power on both the CPU and GPU (and even special-purpose processors) open up new possibilities in the types of processing we can do on-device as opposed to offloading heavy work to a server. Multicore programming also drives up the complexity of your code's threading model and architecture.

RenderScript consists of three main components:

- A C99-based scripting language that focuses on breaking algorithms into individual "kernels" that can be easily parallelized

- Complier engine to reflect script kernels into Java classes that allow developers to invoke their scripts directly from Java without use of the NDK

- Runtime engine with a manufacturer-supplied driver that allows OEMs to report what hardware capabilities their device has (primarily, number of available cores) to process data

RenderScript *kernels* are functions invoked across a large input data set, known as an *allocation*. The RenderScript engine invokes a given kernel over every item in an input allocation to produce a result in a second output allocation. As an example, if a kernel is designed to process image data, the input allocation would be the original image bitmap to process, and the output allocation would contain the processed image bitmap data. The following is an example of what a kernel function looks like:

```
#pragma version(1)
#pragma rs java_package_name(com.example.renderscript)

float multiplier;

void root(const uchar4 *in_element, uchar4 *out_element, uint32_t x, uint32_t y)
{
    //Process "in" and set the result in "out"
}
```

Each time this function is invoked, the in_element parameter points to the current element inside the input allocation. The x and y parameters indicate the position the current element has within the allocation data set. The job of the kernel function is to set the appropriate value of out_element, which represents the corresponding element in the output allocation, based on the algorithm you want to apply before returning. The types of these parameters will depend on the type of allocation you expect; the uchar4 is a vector type commonly used for an allocation of ARGB pixel data.

A script file can have only one kernel function, but you may add additional setup functions or global fields that need to be set before the kernel is invoked. The RenderScript compiler will reflect any functions or global fields added to the script into Java methods (the fields will be reflected into setter methods). For example, the multiplier field in this script will become set_multiplier() in the reflected Java class. You can use these to supply parameters to your script or do additional setup before the kernel is invoked.

Using the RenderScript Support Package

RenderScript has been a public API only since Android 3.0 (API Level 11), but you may have noticed that the Android team at Google is fond of backporting their frameworks to allow developers to use them on older devices. The RenderScript support package allows applications to use its features on devices going back to Android 2.2 (FroYo).

To accomplish this, the build tools include a set of precompiled NDK libraries into your application's APK to install onto devices that don't natively support all the RenderScript features available in the support package.

■ **Note** Currently the RenderScript support package includes NDK libraries for only ARMv7, ARMv8, x86, x86_64, and MIPS. There is no support for ARMv5 devices.

Using the RenderScript support package is a slightly different process than simply copying in additional Java libraries or resources at compile time. The build tools include hooks to copy the appropriate libraries after the build into the APK without needing to place them in your application source tree. To inform the build tools that this step needs to take place, we must add the following lines to the defaultConfig of our build.gradle file:

```
defaultConfig {

    targetSdkVersion 18
    renderscriptTargetApi 18
    renderscriptSupportMode true
}
```

The minimum target is API 18, and 18.1.0 is the minimum supported build tools version. Keep in mind that this doesn't mean the application must have its minimum SDK set to Android 4.3; but it does mean your application should have its target SDK set to at least that level.

With these parameters in place, the build tools will handle all the rest of the work for you. The only additional required step is to use the classes from the android.support.v8.renderscript package in your app rather than the native versions.

■ **Important**   You must import android.support.v8.renderscript.* instead of the android. renderscript package in your Java code!

The remaining sections in this chapter that deal with RenderScript are structured to make use of the RenderScript support package. However, in most cases you only need to change the import statements included to move exclusively to the native versions instead.

8-3. Filtering Images with RenderScript

Problem

Your application needs a simple way to apply common filters to images.

Solution

RenderScript has a large collection of *script intrinsics*, or premade and encapsulated RenderScript kernels designed to do common tasks. You can use these intrinsics to do computation with RenderScript without even the need to write the script code! With each new Android release, new intrinsics are added, creating a library of useful functions to draw from. In this recipe, we are going to examine three of the most common intrinsics:

- ScriptInstrinsicBlur: Applies a Gaussian blur to each element in the input allocation. The radius of the blur is configurable on the script.

- ScriptIntrinsicColorMatrix: Applies a color matrix filter to each element in the input allocation. Similar to the ColorFilter applied to a Drawable. It has an additional convenience method for setting grayscale.

- ScriptIntrinsicConvolve3x3: Applies a 3×3 convolve matrix to each element in the input allocation. This matrix is commonly used to create photo filter effects such as sharpen, emboss, and edge detect.

How It Works

Let's explore an example application that uses RenderScript to apply filters to an image resource. As we can see in Figure 8-1, this application will consist of a grid with six images. Each instance will have a different image filter applied.

Figure 8-1. RenderScript image filters (top to bottom, left to right): None, Grayscale, Edge Detect, Blur, Sharpen, Emboss)

In Listing 8-11, we find the layout for our activity that will construct this simple grid.

Listing 8-11. res/layout/activity_main.xml

```xml
<?xml version="1.0" encoding="utf-8"?>
<TableLayout xmlns:android="http://schemas.android.com/apk/res/android"
    android:layout_width="match_parent"
    android:layout_height="match_parent"
    android:stretchColumns="*">
    <TableRow>
        <ImageView
            android:id="@+id/image_normal"
            android:layout_weight="1"
            android:layout_margin="5dp"
            android:scaleType="fitCenter" />
        <ImageView
            android:id="@+id/image_blurred"
            android:layout_weight="1"
            android:layout_margin="5dp"
            android:scaleType="fitCenter" />
    </TableRow>
```

```
    <TableRow>
        <ImageView
            android:id="@+id/image_greyscale"
            android:layout_weight="1"
            android:layout_margin="5dp"
            android:scaleType="fitCenter" />
        <ImageView
            android:id="@+id/image_sharpen"
            android:layout_weight="1"
            android:layout_margin="5dp"
            android:scaleType="fitCenter" />
    </TableRow>

    <TableRow>
        <ImageView
            android:id="@+id/image_edge"
            android:layout_weight="1"
            android:layout_margin="5dp"
            android:scaleType="fitCenter" />
        <ImageView
            android:id="@+id/image_emboss"
            android:layout_weight="1"
            android:layout_margin="5dp"
            android:scaleType="fitCenter" />
    </TableRow>

</TableLayout>
```

Each cell in this grid will be filled in with the same image, but with a different filter applied to it. In the first cell, we will display the base image without any filtering. The next two cells will be filtered using `ScriptInstrinsicBlur` and `ScriptIntrinsicColorMatrix`. The remaining cells will be filtered using various matrices and a `ScriptIntrinsicConvolve3x3`. In Listing 8-12, we find the activity code.

Listing 8-12. Image Filter Activity

```
import android.support.v8.renderscript.*;

public class MainActivity extends Activity {

    private enum ConvolutionFilter {
        SHARPEN, LIGHTEN, DARKEN, EDGE_DETECT, EMBOSS
    };

    @Override
    protected void onCreate(Bundle savedInstanceState) {
        super.onCreate(savedInstanceState);
        setContentView(R.layout.activity_main);
        //Create the source data, and a destination for the filtered results
        Bitmap inBitmap = BitmapFactory.decodeResource(getResources(), R.drawable.dog);
        Bitmap outBitmap = inBitmap.copy(inBitmap.getConfig(), true);
        //Show the normal image
        setImageInView(outBitmap.copy(outBitmap.getConfig(), false), R.id.image_normal);
```

```java
        //Create the RenderScript context
        final RenderScript rs = RenderScript.create(this);
        //Create allocations for input and output data
        final Allocation input = Allocation.createFromBitmap(rs, inBitmap,
                Allocation.MipmapControl.MIPMAP_NONE,
                Allocation.USAGE_SCRIPT);
        final Allocation output = Allocation.createTyped(rs, input.getType());

        //Run blur script
        final ScriptIntrinsicBlur script = ScriptIntrinsicBlur
                .create(rs, Element.U8_4(rs));
        script.setRadius(4f);
        script.setInput(input);
        script.forEach(output);
        output.copyTo(outBitmap);
        setImageInView(outBitmap.copy(outBitmap.getConfig(), false), R.id.image_blurred);

        //Run grayscale script
        final ScriptIntrinsicColorMatrix scriptColor = ScriptIntrinsicColorMatrix
                .create(rs, Element.U8_4(rs));
        scriptColor.setGreyscale();
        scriptColor.forEach(input, output);
        output.copyTo(outBitmap);
        setImageInView(outBitmap.copy(outBitmap.getConfig(), false), R.id.image_greyscale);

        //Run sharpen script
        ScriptIntrinsicConvolve3x3 scriptC = ScriptIntrinsicConvolve3x3
                .create(rs, Element.U8_4(rs));
        scriptC.setCoefficients(getCoefficients(ConvolutionFilter.SHARPEN));
        scriptC.setInput(input);
        scriptC.forEach(output);
        output.copyTo(outBitmap);
        setImageInView(outBitmap.copy(outBitmap.getConfig(), false), R.id.image_sharpen);

        //Run edge detect script
        scriptC = ScriptIntrinsicConvolve3x3.create(rs, Element.U8_4(rs));
        scriptC.setCoefficients(getCoefficients(ConvolutionFilter.EDGE_DETECT));
        scriptC.setInput(input);
        scriptC.forEach(output);
        output.copyTo(outBitmap);
        setImageInView(outBitmap.copy(outBitmap.getConfig(), false), R.id.image_edge);

        //Run emboss script
        scriptC = ScriptIntrinsicConvolve3x3.create(rs, Element.U8_4(rs));
        scriptC.setCoefficients(getCoefficients(ConvolutionFilter.EMBOSS));
        scriptC.setInput(input);
        scriptC.forEach(output);
        output.copyTo(outBitmap);
        setImageInView(outBitmap.copy(outBitmap.getConfig(), false), R.id.image_emboss);

        //Tear down the RenderScript context
        rs.destroy();
    }
```

```java
    private void setImageInView(Bitmap bm, int viewId) {
        ImageView normalImage = (ImageView) findViewById(viewId);
        normalImage.setImageBitmap(bm);
    }

    /*
     * Helper to obtain matrix coefficients for each type of
     * convolution image filter.
     */
    private float[] getCoefficients(ConvolutionFilter filter) {
        switch (filter) {
            case SHARPEN:
                return new float[] {
                        0f, -1f, 0f,
                        -1f, 5f, -1f,
                        0f, -1f, 0f
                };
            case LIGHTEN:
                return new float[] {
                        0f, 0f, 0f,
                        0f, 1.5f, 0f,
                        0f, 0f, 0f
                };
            case DARKEN:
                return new float[] {
                        0f, 0f, 0f,
                        0f, 0.5f, 0f,
                        0f, 0f, 0f
                };
            case EDGE_DETECT:
                return new float[] {
                        0f, 1f, 0f,
                        1f, -4f, 1f,
                        0f, 1f, 0f
                };
            case EMBOSS:
                return new float[] {
                        -2f, -1f, 0f,
                        -1f, 1f, 1f,
                        0f, 1f, 2f
                };
            default:
                return null;
        }
    }
}
```

Before we can filter the images, we must initialize a RenderScript context with RenderScript.create(). We must also create two Allocation instances, one for the input data and one for the output result. These are the buffers that each RenderScript kernel will act on. There are convenience functions to create an Allocation from many common data structures in the framework, and in this case we have elected to make one directly from our input image Bitmap.

You can see that each script follows a similar pattern. We must first create the script we want to run, initializing it with the data size to be used for the Allocation. We chose Element.U8_4() because our bitmap has ARGB pixel data, so each element (that is, pixel) is 4 unsigned bytes in size. We then must set up any parameters the script needs, and execute it by calling forEach(). Once the script execution is complete, we copy the results from the output Allocation into a new Bitmap to display in the ImageView.

For our blur filter, the radius is the only configurable parameter. The intrinsic accepts a radius value between 0 and 25. We use the color matrix filter to make a grayscale filter for our image by calling setGreyscale() during its setup. If we were to provide a distinct matrix, it would be passed using setColorMatrix() instead.

■ **Tip**   ScriptIntrinsicColorMatrix is also equipped to do color conversions between YUV and RGB color spaces.

Finally, we apply the remaining filters by obtaining a coefficients matrix for the given filter and passing them to the script via setCoefficients(). The 3×3 matrices for these filters are well known and easily obtainable on the Web. The values in the matrix define, as the script moves over each pixel in the allocation, how the value of the output pixel should be multiplied based on the current value of the input pixel and its neighbors. The value in the center of the matrix represents the current pixel, and the surrounding values represent the neighboring pixels.

For example, the darken filter decreases the value of the current pixel by half (0.5 multiplier), but otherwise the surrounding pixels do not affect the result. The sharpen filter magnifies the initial value five times, and then subtracts the value from the pixels above, below, and on each side to achieve the effect.

■ **Tip**   When playing around with convolution matrices, the sum of all the matrix values should equal 1 to preserve the original brightness of the image. If the sum is larger, the image will be brighter, and if the sum is smaller, the image will be darker. The edge detect filter in the example has a net sum of 0, which is why that image is very dark.

8-4. Manipulating Images with RenderScript

Problem

Your application needs to take advantage of the RenderScript power and performance, but a script intrinsic hasn't been written to accomplish the proper task.

Solution

We can construct our own script kernel implementation that the build tools will compile and reflect into Java classes, which we will be able to invoke in the same manner as the intrinsics found in the previous example.

How It Works

In this example, we are going to build a RenderScript kernel to apply a watery ripple effect to an image, as you can see in Figure 8-2.

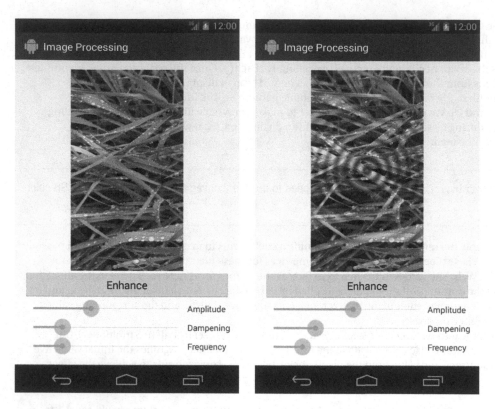

Figure 8-2. *Image-processing example with unfiltered (left) image and ripple applied (right)*

The user will be able to control how the ripple effect looks by using three sliders for the ripple amplitude, dampening, and frequency. Tapping the Enhance button will trigger RenderScript to apply the filter with the selected parameters. Have a look at Listing 8-13 for the kernel implementation.

Listing 8-13. src/main/rs/ripple.rs

```
#pragma version(1)
#pragma rs java_package_name(com.androidrecipes.imageprocessing)

float centerX;
float centerY;
float minRadius;

//Amplitude control of the wave peaks
float scalar;
//Wave Dampener, larger values damp out the ripples sooner
float damper;
//Sine frequency, larger values show more ripples
float frequency;
```

```
void root(const uchar4* v_in, uchar4* v_out, const void* usrData,
        uint32_t x, uint32_t y)
{
    //Compute distance from the center
    float dx = x - centerX;
    float dy = y - centerY;
    float radius = sqrt(dx*dx + dy*dy);

    if (radius < minRadius)
    {
        //Use the original pixel
        *v_out = *v_in;
    }
    else
    {
        float4 f4 = rsUnpackColor8888(*v_in);
        float shiftedRadius = radius - minRadius;

        //Determine sine function multiplier based on distance
        float multiplier = (scalar * exp(-shiftedRadius * damper)
                * -sin(shiftedRadius * frequency)) + 1;

        //Lighten or darken pixel, within min/max range defined
        float3 transformed = f4.rgb * multiplier;
        *v_out = rsPackColorTo8888(transformed);
    }
}
```

The root() function is the main kernel, which will execute over each pixel in the image bitmap (our input allocation). The ripple effect will be applied by determining how far away the input pixel is from the center point, and calculating whether it should be lightened or darkened based on a decaying sine wave function. This function causes the ripples to die away as we get farther from the center point. We have also defined damper, scalar, and frequency factors that can be set externally to control how the ripple output looks. The script also supports controlling the center point of the ripple, and how far out from the center the ripples should begin.

■ **Note**   The decaying sine wave function is $y = e-ktsin(\omega t).$, where t represents the distance from center.

We use a function provided by RenderScript, rsUnpackColor8888(), to convert the input pixel into an ARGB float vector so we can easily do math with other floats. Types like float4 and float3 are vector types defined by RenderScript, meaning they represent a group of floats. These types generally also include special accessor functions to get access to specific portions of the data. For example, we use float4.rgb in this example to return a smaller vector of just the RGB pixel data, masking out the alpha channel.

The sine wave function provides us with a multiplier between 0f and 2f, which we can apply to the pixel to modify its brightness to get slightly closer to either black or white. With a vector type, the multiplication is applied as a dot product, so each color value is multiplied by the same factor. Before placing the modified pixel into the output allocation, we must pack it back into the appropriate format using rsPackColorTo8888().

■ **Tip**   If your algorithm requires analyzing neighboring data in the allocation, you can set the input allocation as a script global as well. This allows you to read any item in the allocation you wish, via rs_ GetElementAt_*type*(), to do your computations.

The build tools will compile this script, and a new Java class will be generated in the project, ScriptC_ ripple. This class will give us access to all the globals we need to set, and a new method, forEach_root(), to invoke the kernel processing. Listings 8-14 and 8-15 show us how we can build this into an activity.

Listing 8-14. src/main/res/layout/activity_main.xml

```
<?xml version="1.0" encoding="utf-8"?>
<LinearLayout xmlns:android="http://schemas.android.com/apk/res/android"
    android:orientation="vertical"
    android:layout_width="match_parent"
    android:layout_height="match_parent"
    android:padding="16dp">
    <ImageView
        android:id="@+id/image"
        android:layout_width="match_parent"
        android:layout_height="0dp"
        android:layout_weight="1"
        android:scaleType="centerInside"/>
    <GridLayout
        android:layout_width="match_parent"
        android:layout_height="wrap_content">
        <Button
            android:id="@+id/button_enhance"
            android:layout_width="match_parent"
            android:layout_height="wrap_content"
            android:layout_columnSpan="2"
            android:text="Enhance"/>
        <TextView
            android:layout_width="wrap_content"
            android:layout_height="wrap_content"
            android:layout_row="1"
            android:layout_column="1"
            android:layout_gravity="center_vertical"
            android:text="Amplitude"/>
        <SeekBar
            android:id="@+id/control_amplitude"
            android:layout_width="wrap_content"
            android:layout_height="wrap_content"
            android:layout_row="1"
            android:layout_column="0"
            android:layout_gravity="fill_horizontal"/>
        <TextView
            android:layout_width="wrap_content"
            android:layout_height="wrap_content"
            android:layout_row="2"
```

```
            android:layout_column="1"
            android:layout_gravity="center_vertical"
            android:text="Dampening"/>
        <SeekBar
            android:id="@+id/control_dampening"
            android:layout_width="wrap_content"
            android:layout_height="wrap_content"
            android:layout_row="2"
            android:layout_column="0"
            android:layout_gravity="fill_horizontal"/>
        <TextView
            android:layout_width="wrap_content"
            android:layout_height="wrap_content"
            android:layout_row="3"
            android:layout_column="1"
            android:layout_gravity="center_vertical"
            android:text="Frequency"/>
        <SeekBar
            android:id="@+id/control_frequency"
            android:layout_width="wrap_content"
            android:layout_height="wrap_content"
            android:layout_row="3"
            android:layout_column="0"
            android:layout_gravity="fill_horizontal"/>
    </GridLayout>
</LinearLayout>
```

Listing 8-15. Image-Processing Activity

```java
public class MainActivity extends Activity implements
        View.OnClickListener {

    private ImageView mImage;
    private SeekBar mAmplitude, mDampening, mFrequency;

    @Override
    public void onCreate(Bundle savedInstanceState) {
        super.onCreate(savedInstanceState);
        setContentView(R.layout.activity_main);
        mImage = (ImageView) findViewById(R.id.image);
        mAmplitude = (SeekBar) findViewById(R.id.control_amplitude);
        mDampening = (SeekBar) findViewById(R.id.control_dampening);
        mFrequency = (SeekBar) findViewById(R.id.control_frequency);

        /*
         * Settings Ranges:
         * A = 0.01 - 1.0
         * D = 0.0001 - 0.01
         * F = 0.01 - 0.5
         */
```

```
        mAmplitude.setProgress(40);
        mDampening.setProgress(20);

        mFrequency.setProgress(10);
        mFrequency.setMax(50);

        mImage.setImageResource(R.drawable.background);

        findViewById(R.id.button_enhance).setOnClickListener(this);
    }

    @Override
    public void onClick(View v) {
        drawRipples(mImage, R.drawable.background);
    }

    private void drawRipples(ImageView iv, int imID) {
        Bitmap bmIn = BitmapFactory.decodeResource(
                getResources(), imID);
        Bitmap bmOut = Bitmap.createBitmap(bmIn.getWidth(),
                bmIn.getHeight(), bmIn.getConfig());

        //Initialize the RenderScript context
        RenderScript rs = RenderScript.create(this);
        //Create data allocations
        Allocation allocIn = Allocation.createFromBitmap(rs, bmIn,
                Allocation.MipmapControl.MIPMAP_NONE,
                Allocation.USAGE_SCRIPT);
        Allocation allocOut = Allocation.createTyped(rs,
                allocIn.getType());
        //Obtain script instance and initial parameters
        ScriptC_ripple script = new ScriptC_ripple(rs,
                getResources(), R.raw.ripple);

        //Set up ripple control values
        script.set_centerX(bmIn.getWidth() / 2);
        script.set_centerY(bmIn.getHeight() / 2);
        script.set_minRadius(0f);
        //Grab user controls from the UI
        float amplitude = Math.max(0.01f, mAmplitude.getProgress() / 100f);
        script.set_scalar(amplitude);
        float dampening = Math.max(0.0001f, mDampening.getProgress() / 10000f);
        script.set_damper(dampening);
        float frequency = Math.max(0.01f, mFrequency.getProgress() / 100f);
        script.set_frequency(frequency);

        //Run the script
        script.forEach_root(allocIn, allocOut);
```

```
        allocOut.copyTo(bmOut);
        iv.setImageBitmap(bmOut);
        //Tear down the RenderScript context
        rs.destroy();
    }

}
```

Here we've constructed a basic activity interface that includes a view to display the current image and three sliders for the user to control the amplitude, dampening, and frequency of our ripples filter. Inside the onClick() handler we initialize a RenderScript context and create two allocations for our script. The input allocation is constructed from our initial bitmap, and the output allocation is a blank set that we will later convert back to an image. We've also created a blank (and mutable) bitmap into which we will copy the output data.

Finally, we allocate a new ScriptC_ripple instance, to begin setting up the filter. All the parameters we defined as script globals conveniently have setter methods on ScriptC_ripple. The center point is configured to the middle of the image, and the sine wave control parameters are pulled from the sliders in the user interface. With all the setup complete, we invoke forEach_root() to iterate over the image allocation, applying the ripple filter.

▪ **Tip** The RenderScript compiler generates the ScriptC Java code form the script files automatically. If you cannot see these classes in the Java, you may need to quickly rebuild or resync the project to get the RenderScript compiler to run again.

Now we have to get the data back from the output allocation and into something we can use. We copy the contents into our blank mutable bitmap using Allocation.copyTo() and display the result by placing it back into the ImageView. Once a script's execution is complete, it is also good to tear down the RenderScript context so resources can be reclaimed.

Play around with the settings to see how they change the result. You might also think about adding a user control for the center point and inner radius!

8-5. Faking Translucent Overlays with Blur

Problem

You want to provide the illusion that one view is overlaying another with a partially transparent frosted or blurred effect.

Solution

We can call on ScriptIntrinsicBlur once again, along with some custom View and Drawable code to create a blurred copy of a background image, and apply that copy to provide the visual appearance of a partially transparent overlay. Rendering a live blurred overlay in real time is computationally expensive, and the performance of the application will suffer. So instead, we are going to achieve the same effect by computing a blurred image of our background content ahead of time and using drawing tricks to implement the same effect while still keeping our application responsive.

How It Works

In this example, we have a ListView shown on top of a full-color background image. The ListView is equipped with a custom header view that offsets the list content such that the first item sits most of the way down the screen when scrolled to the top. As the list scrolls up, we will demonstrate two techniques for creating a blurred overlay: the first will gradually fade the image from clear to blurred, and the second will slide the blurred overlay up along with the list until it is fully covered.

To visualize where we are headed with this, have a look at Figures 8-3 and 8-4.

Figure 8-3. *Fading blur example: initially clear (left) and partially blurred as we scroll (right)*

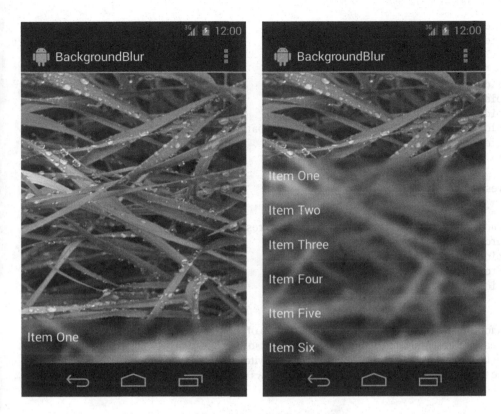

Figure 8-4. *Sliding blur example: blurred overlay follows the list*

You can see in the fading blur example that the background initially starts completely clear. As the list content scrolls up, the blur becomes more visible and is uniform to the entire view. In the sliding blur example, the blurred overlay always follows the list item content; as more of the list items are shown, the blur takes up more of the view. Let's start by looking at the resources in this application. See Listings 8-16 and 8-17.

Listing 8-16. `res/layout/activity_blur.xml`

```xml
<?xml version="1.0" encoding="utf-8"?>
<FrameLayout xmlns:android="http://schemas.android.com/apk/res/android"
    android:layout_width="match_parent"
    android:layout_height="match_parent">
    <!-- Background Views for each blur type -->
    <com.androidrecipes.backgroundblur.BackgroundOverlayView
        android:id="@+id/background_slide"
        android:layout_width="match_parent"
        android:layout_height="match_parent"
        android:scaleType="centerCrop" />
    <ImageView
        android:id="@+id/background_fade"
        android:layout_width="match_parent"
        android:layout_height="match_parent"
```

```
        android:scaleType="centerCrop"
        android:visibility="gone" />

    <ListView
        android:id="@+id/list"
        android:layout_width="match_parent"
        android:layout_height="match_parent"
        android:cacheColorHint="@android:color/transparent"
        android:scrollbars="none"/>
</FrameLayout>
```

Listing 8-17. `res/menu/blur.xml`

```xml
<?xml version="1.0" encoding="utf-8"?>
<menu xmlns:android="http://schemas.android.com/apk/res/android" >
    <item android:id="@+id/menu_slide"
        android:title="Sliding Blur" />
    <item android:id="@+id/menu_fade"
        android:title="Fading Blur" />
</menu>
```

The layout for the application is simply a `ListView` on top of some image content. We have two views behind the list, each representing one of the two types of blur; so only one of these will be visible at any point in time. In this case, we are using the options menu to switch between the two modes, so we have also created a simple two-option `<menu>` element. Listing 8-18 shows our activity, where the RenderScript code will live.

Listing 8-18. Blurred Overlay Activity

```java
public class BlurActivity extends Activity implements
        AbsListView.OnScrollListener,
        AdapterView.OnItemClickListener {

    private static final String[] ITEMS = {
            "Item One", "Item Two", "Item Three", "Item Four", "Item Five",
            "Item Six", "Item Seven", "Item Eight", "Item Nine", "Item Ten",
            "Item Eleven", "Item Twelve", "Item Thirteen", "Item Fourteen", "Item Fifteen"};

    private BackgroundOverlayView mSlideBackground;
    private ImageView mFadeBackground;
    private ListView mListView;
    private View mHeader;

    @Override
    protected void onCreate(Bundle savedInstanceState) {
        super.onCreate(savedInstanceState);
        setContentView(R.layout.activity_blur);

        mSlideBackground = (BackgroundOverlayView) findViewById(R.id.background_slide);
        mFadeBackground = (ImageView) findViewById(R.id.background_fade);
        mListView = (ListView) findViewById(R.id.list);
```

```java
        //Apply a clear header view to shift the start position of the list elements down
        mHeader = new HeaderView(this);
        mListView.addHeaderView(mHeader, null, false);
        mListView.setAdapter(new ArrayAdapter<String>(this,
                android.R.layout.simple_list_item_1, ITEMS));

        mListView.setOnScrollListener(this);
        mListView.setOnItemClickListener(this);

        initializeImage();
    }

    @Override
    public boolean onCreateOptionsMenu(Menu menu) {
        getMenuInflater().inflate(R.menu.blur, menu);
        return true;
    }

    @Override
    public boolean onOptionsItemSelected(MenuItem item) {
        //Based on the selection, show the appropriate background view
        switch(item.getItemId()) {
            case R.id.menu_slide:
                mSlideBackground.setVisibility(View.VISIBLE);
                mFadeBackground.setVisibility(View.GONE);
                return true;
            case R.id.menu_fade:
                mSlideBackground.setVisibility(View.GONE);
                mFadeBackground.setVisibility(View.VISIBLE);
                return true;
            default:
                return super.onOptionsItemSelected(item);
        }
    }

    /*
     * The heart of our transparency tricks.  We obtain a normal copy
     * and a pre-blurred copy of the background image.
     */
    private void initializeImage() {
        Bitmap inBitmap = BitmapFactory.decodeResource(getResources(), R.drawable.
background);
        Bitmap outBitmap = inBitmap.copy(inBitmap.getConfig(), true);

        //Create the RenderScript context
        final RenderScript rs = RenderScript.create(this);
        //Create allocations for input and output data
        final Allocation input = Allocation.createFromBitmap(rs, inBitmap,
                Allocation.MipmapControl.MIPMAP_NONE,
                Allocation.USAGE_SCRIPT);
        final Allocation output = Allocation.createTyped(rs, input.getType());
```

691

```
        //Run a blur at the maximum supported radius (25f)
        final ScriptIntrinsicBlur script = ScriptIntrinsicBlur.create(rs, Element.U8_4(rs));
        script.setRadius(25f);
        script.setInput(input);
        script.forEach(output);
        output.copyTo(outBitmap);

        //Tear down the RenderScript context
        rs.destroy();

        //Apply the two copies to our custom drawable for fading
        OverlayFadeDrawable drawable = new OverlayFadeDrawable(
                new BitmapDrawable(getResources(), inBitmap),
                new BitmapDrawable(getResources(), outBitmap));
        mFadeBackground.setImageDrawable(drawable);

        //Apply the two copies to our custom ImageView for sliding
        mSlideBackground.setImagePair(inBitmap, outBitmap);
    }

    @Override
    public void onItemClick(AdapterView<?> parent, View v, int position, long id) {
        //On a click event, animated scroll the list back to the top
        mListView.smoothScrollToPosition(0);
    }

    @Override
    public void onScroll(AbsListView view, int firstVisibleItem,
            int visibleItemCount, int totalItemCount) {
        //Make sure views have been measured first
        if (mHeader.getHeight() <= 0) return;

        //Adjust sliding effect clip point based on scroll position
        int topOffset;
        if (firstVisibleItem == 0) {
            //Header is still visible
            topOffset = mHeader.getTop() + mHeader.getHeight();
        } else {
            //Header has been detached, at this point we should be all the way up
            topOffset = 0;
        }
        mSlideBackground.setOverlayOffset(topOffset);

        //Adjust fading effect based on scroll position
        // Blur completely once 85% of the header is scrolled off
        float percent = Math.abs(mHeader.getTop()) / (mHeader.getHeight() * 0.85f);
        int level = Math.min((int)(percent * 10000), 10000);
        mFadeBackground.setImageLevel(level);
    }
```

```
    @Override
    public void onScrollStateChanged(AbsListView view,
            int scrollState) { }
}
```

When the activity is created, we apply a very simple list adapter with some static data elements inside. We also apply a custom HeaderView as the header to our list; we see this implementation in Listing 8-19, and this is what shifts the list items down in the initial view of Figures 8-3 and 8-4.

Listing 8-19. Clear List Header View

```
public class HeaderView extends View {

    public HeaderView(Context context) {
        super(context);
    }

    public HeaderView(Context context, AttributeSet attrs) {
        super(context, attrs);
    }

    public HeaderView(Context context, AttributeSet attrs, int defStyle) {
        super(context, attrs, defStyle);
    }

    /*
     * Measure this view's height to always be 85% of the
     * measured height from the parent view (ListView)
     */
    @Override
    protected void onMeasure(int widthMeasureSpec, int heightMeasureSpec) {
        View parent = (View) getParent();
        int parentHeight = parent.getMeasuredHeight();

        int height = Math.round(parentHeight * 0.85f);
        int width = MeasureSpec.getSize(widthMeasureSpec);

        setMeasuredDimension(width, height);
    }
}
```

There isn't much to this; it is simply a view designed to measure out its height to be 85 percent of the height of its parent (which in our case is always the ListView). This allows us to use HeaderView as a measured spacer, even though it contains no real content. This approach is more flexible to device screen differences than hard-coding a fixed view height.

Back in Listing 8-22, inside initializeImage(), we use the ScriptIntrinsicBlur function to create a blurred copy of our background image. As we discussed in the previous recipes on image filters, the blur radius determines the level of distortion, and can be a value greater than 0 and up to 25.

When RenderScript has completed the blur, we take the image pair (initial and blurred) and send them two places. The first is to a custom OverlayFadeDrawable instance, which we will use for our fade example. The second is a BackgroundOverlayView, which we will use for our slide example. We will take a look at these items shortly.

The activity is responsible for monitoring list scrolling and reporting those changes to the background views. The activity is registered as the OnScrollListener for the ListView, so as the view scrolls, the onScroll() method is called regularly. Inside this method, we calculate the offset position based on the header view, and feed that data into the two background views. Finally, the activity is also set to receive click events on individual list items. When this occurs, the list is scrolled back to the top with an animation.

To see how we draw the blur transitions, let's first have a look at the Drawable in Listing 8-20.

Listing 8-20. Overlay Fade Drawable

```java
public class OverlayFadeDrawable extends LayerDrawable {
    /*
     * Implementation of a Drawable container to hold our normal
     * and blurred images as layers
     */
    public OverlayFadeDrawable(Drawable base, Drawable overlay) {
        super(new Drawable[] {base, overlay});
    }

    /*
     * Force a redraw when the level value is externally changed
     */
    @Override
    protected boolean onLevelChange(int level) {
        invalidateSelf();
        return true;
    }

    @Override
    public void draw(Canvas canvas) {
        final Drawable base = getDrawable(0);
        final Drawable overlay = getDrawable(1);
        //Get the level as a percentage of the maximum value
        final float percent = getLevel() / 10000f;
        int setAlpha = Math.round(percent * 0xFF);

        //Optimize for end-cases to avoid overdraw
        if (setAlpha == 255) {
            overlay.draw(canvas);
            return;
        }
        if (setAlpha == 0) {
            base.draw(canvas);
            return;
        }

        //Draw composite if in-between
        base.draw(canvas);

        overlay.setAlpha(setAlpha);
        overlay.draw(canvas);
        overlay.setAlpha(0xFF);
    }
}
```

You may recall from Chapter 7 that a Drawable is just an abstraction of something to be displayed. We have chosen to extend the LayerDrawable in the framework, which is a container of *N* elements that are drawn in order as layers by default. We won't be leveraging the default drawing behavior, but using LayerDrawable as our base allows the framework to handle some of the other complex logic of invalidating each layer for us.

To update the state, we use the item's level parameter. Recall that this Drawable was set on an ImageView, and when the scroll position changed, we called setImageLevel() to update the background. That level is passed directly into this instance, and with each call to draw(), the level is inspected to determine how to blend the two images. We explicitly optimize for the two cases where the alpha is at 0 percent or 100 percent to minimize pixel overdraw (once either element is fully opaque, drawing the other is a waste). However, if the value is in the middle, we will draw the initial image first, with the partially visible blurred copy drawn on top. Now let's have a look at the drawing tricks for the sliding blur in Listing 8-21.

Listing 8-21. Background Overlay View

```java
public class BackgroundOverlayView extends ImageView {

    private Paint mPaint;
    private Bitmap mOverlayImage;
    private int mClipOffset;

    /*
     * Customization of ImageView to allow us to draw a
     * composite of two images, but still leverage all
     * the image-scaling features of the framework.
     */
    public BackgroundOverlayView(Context context) {
        super(context);
        init();
    }

    public BackgroundOverlayView(Context context, AttributeSet attrs) {
        super(context, attrs);
        init();
    }

    public BackgroundOverlayView(Context context, AttributeSet attrs, int defStyle) {
        super(context, attrs, defStyle);
        init();
    }

    private void init() {
        mPaint = new Paint(Paint.ANTI_ALIAS_FLAG);
    }

    /*
     * Set the normal and blurred image copies in our view
     */
    public void setImagePair(Bitmap base, Bitmap overlay) {
        mOverlayImage = overlay;
```

```
        /* Apply the normal image to the base ImageView, which
         * will allow it to apply our ScaleType for us and provide
         * a Matrix we can use to draw both images scaled accordingly
         * later on. This will also invalidate the view to trigger
         * a new draw.
         */
        setImageBitmap(base);
    }

    /*
     * Adjust the vertical point where the normal and blurred
     * copy should switch.
     */
    public void setOverlayOffset(int overlayOffset) {
        mClipOffset = overlayOffset;
        invalidate();
    }

    @Override
    protected void onDraw(Canvas canvas) {
        //Draw base image first, clipped to the top section
        // We clip the base image to avoid unnecessary overdraw in
        // the bottom section of the view.
        canvas.save();
        canvas.clipRect(getLeft(), getTop(), getRight(), mClipOffset);
        super.onDraw(canvas);
        canvas.restore();

        //Obtain the matrix used to scale the base image, and apply it
        // to the blurred overlay image so the two match up
        final Matrix matrix = getImageMatrix();
        canvas.save();
        canvas.clipRect(getLeft(), mClipOffset, getRight(), getBottom());
        canvas.drawBitmap(mOverlayImage, matrix, mPaint);
        canvas.restore();
    }
}
```

This is an extension of ImageView that does some custom drawing. We are using ImageView because it contains a lot of image-scaling logic that we want to leverage. In our layout, we set the scaleType parameter to centerCrop so the view could take care of scaling and placing our background nicely. Notice when the activity sets the images on this view, the base image is passed directly to the base implementation as the main image. We do this for two reasons: primarily so the framework can do the image-scaling math, but also so we can easily draw the base image by just calling through to super.onDraw() later on.

With each scroll position change, the offset is passed into this view via setOverlayOffset(), which also invalidates the view, forcing a new draw pass. In the drawing portion of the view, we utilize that offset marker to create two clipping masks for the Canvas. The main purpose of this is to draw only the portion of the blurred overlay that we want to show to match the list position. However, we can use the same offset to clip off the base image drawing as well. This is again to eliminate pixel overdraw in our view, which will make the app perform much more smoothly. Even though the effect is that we are drawing a semitransparent overlay, we never actually draw any pixel in this view more than once.

As a final reminder of what we've created, Figure 8-5 shows the application with the list scrolled completely up and the blur overlay covering the complete view.

Figure 8-5. *Blur overlay shown completely*

Summary

With the Android NDK, developers can add just the right amount of native C/C++ code to their applications to complement the Java SDK. Whether that is a handful of functions using JNI, or an entire activity class, the NDK offers the power necessary to make great applications even better. With RenderScript, developers can unlock the true computing power of the mobile device without wasting time dealing with the multicore and multithreaded synchronization issues. This opens up opportunities for image processing and other algorithmic computation to be done on the device, instead of offloaded to a remote server.

Index

Get the eBook for only $4.99!

Why limit yourself?

Now you can take the weightless companion with you wherever you go and access your content on your PC, phone, tablet, or reader.

Since you've purchased this print book, we are happy to offer you the eBook for just $4.99.

Convenient and fully searchable, the PDF version enables you to easily find and copy code—or perform examples by quickly toggling between instructions and applications.

To learn more, go to http://www.apress.com/us/shop/companion or contact support@apress.com.

Printed in the United States
By Bookmasters